FOOD AND EVOLUTION

Toward a Theory of Human Food Habits

AND EVOLUTION

Toward a Theory of Human Food Habits

EDITED BY MARVIN HARRIS
AND ERIC B. ROSS

TEMPLE UNIVERSITY PRESS
Philadelphia

Temple University Press, Philadelphia 19122
Copyright © 1987 by Temple University. All rights reserved
Published 1987
Printed in the United States of America

The paper used in this publication meets the minimum requirements of
American National Standard for Information Sciences—Permanence of
Paper for Printed Library Materials, ANSI Z39.48-1984

Library of Congress Cataloging-in-Publication Data
Food and evolution.
    Includes bibliographies and indexes.
    1. Food habits.   2. Human evolution.   3. Nutrition—Social
aspects.   4. Man, Primitive—Food.   I. Harris, Marvin, 1927–
II. Ross, Eric B.   [DNLM: 1. Food Habits.   GT 2860 F686]
GN407.F65   1986   306   86-5773
ISBN 0-87722-435-8 (alk. paper)

ACKNOWLEDGMENTS

Although now substantially revised, the initial drafts of the papers in this volume were presented at the 94th Symposium of the Wenner-Gren Foundation for Anthropological Research at Cedar Key, Florida, October 23–30, 1983. On behalf of all the participants, the editors wish to thank the foundation and its staff for their support and advice. We were especially aware of our debts to Lita Osmundsen, the foundation's director of research.

The editors are also deeply grateful to the staff of Temple University Press, especially to Jane Cullen, Jennifer French, and Jane Barry for their heroic production and copyediting feats.

CONTENTS

Introduction   1

Part I. Theoretical Overview

  1. An Overview of Trends in Dietary Variation from   7
     Hunter-Gatherer to Modern Capitalist Societies
                              ERIC B. ROSS

  2. Foodways: Historical Overview and Theoretical   57
     Prolegomenon   MARVIN HARRIS

Part II. Bioevolutionary Antecedents and Constraints

  3. Primate Diets and Gut Morphology: Implications for   93
     Hominid Evolution   KATHARINE MILTON

  4. Omnivorous Primate Diets and Human   117
     Overconsumption of Meat
                       WILLIAM J. HAMILTON III

  5. Fava Bean Consumption: A Case for the Co-   133
     Evolution of Genes and Culture
                          SOLOMON H. KATZ

Part III. Nutritional and Biopsychological Constraints

  6. Problems and Pitfalls in the Assessment of Human   163
     Nutritional Status   P. L. PELLETT

  7. Psychobiological Perspectives on Food Preferences   181
     and Avoidances   PAUL ROZIN

  8. The Preference for Animal Protein and Fat: A   207
     Cross-Cultural Survey   H. LEON ABRAMS, JR.

9. Biocultural Consequences of Animals Versus Plants   225
as Sources of Fats, Proteins, and Other Nutrients
LESLIE SUE LIEBERMAN

Part IV. Pre-State Foodways: Past and Present

10. The Significance of Long-Term Changes in Human   261
Diet and Food Economy   MARK N. COHEN

11. Life in the "Garden of Eden": Causes and   285
Consequences of the Adoption of Marine Diets by
Human Societies   DAVID R. YESNER

12. The Analysis of Hunter-Gatherer Diets: Stalking an   311
Optimal Foraging Model
BRUCE WINTERHALDER

13. How Much Food Do Foragers Need?   341
KRISTEN HAWKES

14. Aboriginal Subsistence in a Tropical Rain Forest   357
Environment: Food Procurement, Cannibalism, and
Population Regulation in Northeastern Australia
DAVID R. HARRIS

15. Ecological and Structural Influences on the   387
Proportions of Wild Foods in the Diets of Two
Machiguenga Communities   ALLEN JOHNSON
and MICHAEL BAKSH

16. Limiting Factors in Amazonian Ecology   407
KENNETH R. GOOD

Part V. The Political Economy and the Political Ecology of
Contemporary Foodways

17. Loaves and Fishes in Bangladesh   427
SHIRLEY LINDENBAUM

18. Animal Protein Consumption and the Sacred Cow   445
Complex in India   K. N. NAIR

19. The Effects of Colonialism and Neocolonialism on the   455
    Gastronomic Patterns of the Third World
                      RICHARD W. FRANKE

20. Stability and Change in Highland Andean Dietary   481
    Patterns   BENJAMIN S. ORLOVE

21. Social Class and Diet in Contemporary Mexico   517
                         GRETEL H. PELTO

22. From Costa Rican Pasture to North American   541
    Hamburger   MARC EDELMAN

Part VI. Discussion and Conclusions

23. The Evolution of Human Subsistence   565
                      ANNA ROOSEVELT

24. Biocultural Aspects of Food Choice   579
                   GEORGE ARMELAGOS

Afterword   595

About the Contributors   601
Glossary   607
Name Index   613
Subject Index   625

INTRODUCTION

THIS BOOK RESULTS FROM AN INTERDISCIPLINARY EFFORT TO AD-vance our understanding of why human beings in differing times and places eat what they do. It begins, at the most fundamental level, with the collective view of the editors and other contributors that knowledge and comprehension of human foodways, and the web of practices and beliefs associated with them, must depend upon our seeking general principles and recurrent processes beneath the immediate appearance of a worldwide confusion of seemingly capricious preferences, avoidances, and aversions.

Once this decision is made, however, a complex set of explanatory strategies and options still remains to be explored and integrated, since the knowledge we have of human food customs and practices derives from data collection that has traditionally been dispersed among varied specialties and theoretical strategies. We cannot claim that all the relevant disciplines or all the salient levels of analysis and perspective are represented in the chapters that follow, nor do we presume that this work encompasses an adequate representation of those that are. But we hope at least to have helped to broaden the general scope of inquiry beyond the horizons of any single viewpoint, while still maintaining what we emphatically regard as a commitment to a nomothetic approach.

The disciplinary perspectives of the contributors to this volume range over primatology (Hamilton, Milton), nutrition (Pellett, Lieberman), biological anthropology (Armelagos, Katz), archaeology (Yesner, Cohen, Roosevelt, D. Harris), psychology (Rozin), and agricultural economics (Nair). Although cultural anthropologists predominate numerically, they too offer a great diversity of insight and information based on their varying professional interests and, in particular, their wide spectrum of regional specializations: Bangladesh (Lindenbaum), Amazonia (Johnson and Baksh, Good, Ross), Paraguay (Hawkes), Canadian sub-arctic (Winterhalder), Southeast Asia and Africa (Franke), Mexico (Pelto), Costa Rica (Edelman), Peru (Orlove), and Europe (Ross).

In attempting to integrate the diversity of disciplinary viewpoints that these scholars represent, the editors chose an evolutionary framework as the only suitably broad yet coherent and unifying one available to us. In its biological dimensions, at least, it seemed self-evident that the core of human dietary practice, all subsequent embellishment aside, must be regarded in terms of the

1

emergence of the hominidae and the co-evolution of human diet and our physical potential for cultural behavior. It seems likely, for example, that hunting for vertebrates, increased meat consumption, and expanded tool use were implicated in the evolutionary processes that led to the expansion and reorganization of the australopithecine brain and to the development of Homo's unique capacities for consciousness and semantic universality. There is, at least, little doubt that, throughout most of the Pleistocene, the evolution of biological repertoires and the evolution of behavioral repertoires were closely intertwined—and that diet is one domain where the intersection was particularly noteworthy.

With the appearance of *Homo sapiens,* if not earlier, however, a progressively greater independence—or lag—between biological and cultural selection reduced the rate and incidence of gene-culture co-evolution. Radically different modes of production, accompanied by massive changes in food habits, emerged in the later phases of human prehistory and throughout subsequent history without any discernible evidence of related changes in gene frequencies. Increasingly, behavior associated with the procurement, distribution, and consumption of food came, like the rest of human behavior, to be propagated through learning rather than genetic replication. And although selection based on consequences for reproductive success continued to operate, it was increasingly supplemented, if not displaced, by selection based on the more immediate consequences for the satisfaction of biopsychological needs and drives. Though the feedback between these two levels of selection became increasingly indirect and delayed, the biological level still cannot be excluded from our attempt to understand general as well as particular aspects of the evolution of foodways. Indeed, in a small number of cases such as that of fava bean (see Chapter 5) and milk consumption, specific preferences and avoidances continue to be associated with genetic polymorphisms found with varying frequencies among different populations.

In evolutionary perspective, however, most of the great changes in human diet can be more readily associated with shifts in modes of production that are not in turn linked to such genetic variations. The transition from upper paleolithic to neolithic modes of production, for example, generally involved a shift from narrow reliance on animal foods to broad-spectrum regimens in which the consumption of domesticated tubers and grains gained ascendancy over meat and other animal foods (pastoral modes of production, of course, followed a divergent trajectory). The next great general evolutionary changes in foodways may be associated with the rise of archaic agro-managerial states whose dense, socially stratified populations were dependent on one or two staple grains and which maintained distinctive consumption patterns for elites and commoners. The further evolution of imperial state systems with massive potentials for trade and great capacities for modifying their habitats through public works doubtless increased such class or caste distinctions in dietary practice and gave rise to new rural/urban and core/periphery distinctions. These effects of political-economic evolution and of ever more formidable political-ecological integration finally attained global proportions with the emergence of the capitalist world system, leading in our own times to a return to highly carnivorous diets for privileged regions and classes at the cost of impoverished diets and often de facto vegetarianism in dependent and underdeveloped areas.

The contributions to this volume have been arranged with these broad evolutionary considerations in mind. Following the editors' theoretical overviews, Parts II and III deal with the biological, nutritional, and psychological factors that reflect species-specific and/or population-specific consequences of human genetic repertoires. Part IV deals with food patterns associated with pre-state sociocultural systems as revealed through both archaeological and ethnographic researches. And Part V concerns itself with foodways in contemporary state-level societies, with emphasis upon the consequences of underdevelopment and participation in the capitalist world system.

Needless to say, it is impossible for any single volume to provide a thoroughly comprehensive treatment of so complex a subject as the evolution of human food habits or to reach any definitive theoretical outcome. What we have hoped to do, however, is to provide a guide and a framework for much needed future investigation, and an incentive for others to join in that necessarily collaborative enterprise.

M. H. and E. B. R.

PART I

Theoretical Overview

THE TWO ESSAYS THAT FOLLOW SHARE AN EXPLICIT MATE-rialist strategy and are addressed specifically to the question of the general determinants of food preferences and avoidances. They range over a variety of pre-state and state-level foodways, highlighting food practices that have generally been regarded as beyond the pale of nomothetic approaches or whose cost-benefit significance is in dispute. The epistemological basis for distinguishing idealist from materialist approaches to foodways rests on the separation of data obtained through emic operations from those obtained through etic operations. Emic foodways data result from eliciting operations in which the participants' sense of what people eat or ought to eat, and the symbolic significance of food preferences and avoidances, dominate data collection. On the other hand, etic foodways data do not necessarily require eliciting operations and are reported in a data language whose units and categories are imposed by the observers (e.g., calories, proteins, costs and benefits).

Beyond the separation of emics from etics, materialist approaches to foodways start with the assumption that puzzling dietary habits are the outcome of determinative processes in which biopsychological, technological, economic, demographic, and environmental factors predominate. These infrastructural processes account for the evolution of distinctive forms of structures and superstructures. Once such structures (e.g., domestic and political organization) and superstructures (e.g., religious and symbolic systems, philosophies, aesthetic standards) are in place, they of course exert an influence over all aspects of social life, including foodways. Religious food taboos, for example, have a distinctive role to play in the maintenance of food habits. But recognition that structural and superstructural features react back upon infrastructure does not lessen the distinction between materialist and idealist approaches or justify taking refuge in an eclecticism that is incapable of weighing one causal component against another or of stating the conditions under which now infrastructure, now superstructure, achieves dominance. The restraints imposed by infrastructure upon structure and superstructure remain dominant in the determinative processes that lead to continuity or change in food-

5

ways: foodways that acquire adverse etic cost-benefit balances will tend to be se-
lected against; foodways that have favorable etic cost-benefit balances will tend to
be selected for. Participants' emic valuations of foodways arise from infrastruc-
ture. Major changes in infrastructure cause major changes in foodways and their
emic valuations. Changes in emic valuations change major foodways, but only
when such changes are favored by infrastructural conditions.

As both essays stress, the balance of etic costs and benefits that provides the
cultural and biopsychological selection pressures for and against particular food-
ways often differs markedly according to age- and sex-related status roles and
social strata. Hierarchies based on sex, class, ethnicity, and other distinctions are
usually associated with favorable cost/benefits for some status roles but unfavora-
ble cost/benefits for others.

Where such conditions prevail, the study of foodways must form part of the
study of political economy and political ecology. As in contemporary state societies
and their neocolonial dependencies, what people eat is often what they are allowed
to eat or obliged to eat as a consequence of their subordination to the material
priorities of ruling classes and corporate elites.

6

1

ERIC B. ROSS

An Overview of Trends in Dietary Variation from Hunter-Gatherer to Modern Capitalist Societies

THE STUDY OF VARIATION AND CHANGE IN HUMAN DIETS—especially in that most enigmatic dimension of dietary custom, food preferences and avoidances—is important in several respects. In a general way, it compels us to confront and challenge the possibilities and limits of cultural explanation (see Ross 1980), while, more specifically, it enables us to begin to seek (and hopefully to formulate) generalizable and predictive principles in a domain of culture where we are routinely led to believe that such principles are unlikely to apply. For it is precisely in the matter of dietary customs that the concept of culture has been most consistently invoked to suggest that, at the heart of what seems the most material and practical of human affairs, there lies an ineluctable core of arbitrary, fortuitous, or irrational thought. The seemingly inexhaustible variety and range of human dietary patterns thus has been taken to represent quintessential evidence of the inexorable power of the human mind, through the device of culture, to transcend the constraints of material and historical circumstances.

The implications of such arguments are not merely academic, for they suggest that where such circumstances coincide with impoverished diets, the power to alter and improve them must be ultimately as arbitrary and fortuitous as the forces that originally induced them. What basis does such a view provide for people to devise a program to change and improve their lives? If, as some have suggested (see Sahlins 1976:171), contemporary cultural patterns are, in the end, the arbitrary or random variants of mysterious structures in the human mind, then change too must be arbitrary, and the avenues by which certain definite desired ends might be achieved are beyond effective reach.

Our attempt here to explore the forces and circumstances that appear to shape the diverse patterns of human diet is, in contrast, inherently an effort to explain how human behavior in general diversifies in intelligible, if not predictable, ways. But, ultimately, it must take into account a more practical end: we do not study human dietary customs merely because they are interesting, but because at the end of the day they help to define the quality of life of real people. Variation in what people eat reflects substantive variation in status and power and characterizes societies that are internally stratified into rich and poor, sick and healthy, developed and underdeveloped, overfed and under-nourished. An anthropology that, by one methodological device or another, reduces such features of any social system to arbitrary reflections of the human mind only entraps itself in a self-indulgent relativism that precludes all like-lihood of raising a coherent critical voice.

It is a necessary requisite of the perspective I advocate that diet be viewed within a historically formulated understanding of any given social system, as an evolutionary product of environmental conditions and of the basic forces, es-pecially the social institutions and social relations, that effectively determine their use. In this paper, a preliminary effort has been undertaken to suggest some of the implications of such an approach.

Hunters, Horticulturalists, and Dietary Preferences

Much recent attention in the field of human diet has been given to the lifestyles of pre-industrial populations. Ross (1978a) marked one of the first attempts to redirect such work away from an almost exclusively symbolic approach to one that envisaged diet as part of a larger adaptational process. At much the same time, others were beginning to apply concepts of animal ecology—in particular, optimal foraging theory (see Winterhalder and Smith 1981)—to extant popula-tions of human hunters.

To date, however, the blessings of such applications have been decidedly mixed. One reason, at least, has been that the populations studied have not been economic isolates. As a specific kind of cost-benefit model, foraging theo-ry is most successful where energy is the principal behavioral constraint. But no living human societies are immune to the additional constraints imposed by other human beings, which range from the relatively benign to the invasive. And few if any hunting populations are ever as isolated as those who study them may like to believe.

An additional problem is perhaps more distinctively theoretical. One of the enduring issues involved in dietary custom—and one of decided relevance to the general question of dietary variation—is that of taboos (see Harris 1977,

1979; Ross 1978a). Yet optimal foraging theory has yielded little insight into such matters—indeed, may be considered to have confounded them—and the reasons why suggest some formidable limitations that I will briefly suggest here.

In neotropical regions such as Amazonia, several factors have been concurrently implicated in the avoidance of certain game animals (Ross 1978a). First, there is the biomorphological character of the animals themselves: comparative evidence suggests that larger game animals—such as the tapir—are extremely vulnerable to predation, much as their even larger paleolithic antecedents were to prehistoric hunters. Second, there is the question of alternative resources: where aquatic resources exist, if they are productive, they tend to be more efficient and stable sources of food than game animals and to claim a greater share of labor time. Third, much depends on the degree of sedentism of the human population, since this has a profound effect on the distribution and density of game. The interaction of these factors can be expressed by the following principle: access to productive aquatic resources inclines to an increase in sedentarism, since such resources are relatively immobile; increased sedentarism will usually mean greater development of horticulture (Carneiro 1968), while a more sedentary, horticultural lifestyle will differentially diminish access to the spectrum of available game animals. Thus, small ones, which reproduce rapidly or are commensal in nature, tend to be found near settlements, regardless of continued hunting, while larger animals such as tapir and deer require treks into ever deeper forest. If aquatic resources are lucrative enough, such animals will rarely be hunted and may eventually be regarded as inedible; indeed, if aquatic resources are unusually plentiful—for example, estuarine or lacustrine—even some smaller animals may not be targeted as a source of food. Thus, Wilbert has observed of the Warao of the Orinoco delta "that some of the nutritionally most valuable game animals, especially tapir, and here and there also deer and paca, are traditionally tabooed" (1972:68–69), while Basso has noted that the Kalapalo, who inhabit the rich river and lake network of the Upper Xingu, "regard virtually all land animals . . . as disgusting and refuse to eat them" (1973:14, 16; Carneiro 1970; Murphy and Quain 1955:29).

In contrast, where the aquatic resources that so enhance the opportunities for sedentary life are not present, hunting tends to remain necessarily the paramount subsistence activity, insofar as the intake of proteins and fats is concerned. An example is provided by the Aché of eastern Paraguay, who still spend a considerable portion of their year as hunters. At such times there is no horticultural activity, and fishing is relatively insignificant "because the streams that flow through [their] territory are poorly supplied with fish" (Clastres 1972:155). Thus, in contrast to the riverine Kalapalo, the Aché seem to exclude virtually no potential animal food from their diet (Hill and Hawkes 1983).

In between these two extremes lies a continuum of degrees of exclusion, determined by various mixes of hunting and fishing productivity, which in turn depend on such variables as settlement size, type of horticulture, exposure to trade, and warfare.

It is reasonable to suppose that hunters such as the Aché will regard the tapir as edible, if our delineation of the determinants of preferences and avoidances is more or less an accurate one. Indeed, as Hawkes and Hill have recently commented, "Several tapir were shot during the study period, and we recorded 10 man hours spent in pursuit of them without success. If one tapir were to have been killed during this period it would have been the number one ranked item in the optimal diet" (ibid.). But, in fact, in their account of the "optimal" Aché diet, tapir does not appear. As they explain, "The resource rankings of this model say nothing about the quantitative importance of a resource to optimal foragers. High ranked items may be so rarely encountered that they contribute only a very small proportion of the diet" (ibid.).[1]

In the case of tapir, they seem to have made so little contribution to the Aché diet—indeed, none at all during the research period—that they were not even included in the model's rankings of what Aché preferences ought to have been. Initially this may seem vaguely to express the remarkably ambiguous role that the tapir occupies as the largest, yet one of the most elusive, game animals. But the optimal foraging model, at least in this instance, contains a notable irony, for Hill and Hawkes tell us that the tapir would have been the highest-ranked animal had it made any contribution to the diet at all. This suggests, as we have already seen, that the model is much less interested in the dynamics of hunting tapir in general than in the productivity of one successfully hunted tapir, however rare an occurrence that might be. The question is whether native preferences would arise out of the former or the latter. The anthropologists' "optimal" diet model at least suggests that the model's preference is based upon the latter. But this creates a significant dilemma, for although the model would then view the tapir as the optimal prey, ethnographic observation indicates that, as among so many other neotropical groups, it is the white-lipped peccary that is the primary target of Aché hunting (Hill and Hawkes 1983). This contradiction compels us to affirm that our primary aim is to comprehend the forces that shape ethnographically recorded preferences and real dietary consequences—not to displace them with a model that contains its own peculiar and often compelling logic.

Thus, optimal foraging tells us little if anything about why the tapir is frequently excluded from the diet among many hunter-horticulturalists. The reason for this is simple: as we have previously suggested, the tapir's sensitivity to human predation renders it progressively more scarce the more sedentary a community of hunters becomes. But by the admission of its own advocates, optimal foraging theory disregards the question of an animal's abundance or scarcity (Winterhalder 1981:93–94). On these terms, the tapir, once admitted to the model, would never fall out of the diet—a conclusion clearly contradicted by evidence.

It can only be said that this may not matter too much when considering exclusively hunting peoples, who, being mobile, can minimize the scarcity of such animals by following them without being compelled to confine themselves to a convenient distance from a stable home-base. But, certainly, once there is any measure of sedentarism to consider, the contradictions of the model begin to diminish its credibility. Indeed, paradoxically, what began as a putatively materialist model ends by emulating the more abstract, symbolic models it presumably sought to displace in its lack of due consideration for the dynamic environment in which cultural behavior operates. That cautionary lesson is not to be restricted to pre-industrial populations.

Calories, Hunting, and Dietary Breadth

One of the great differences between the diets of hunting peoples and those of hunting-horticultural populations hinges on their respective sources of calories. Among the former, the harvest of game, fish, wild plants, and insects not only embodies human energy investment but also constitutes the sole source of calories in the diet—excepting whatever flows in through non-traditional channels. For that reason, foraging societies may be more readily analyzed with energy-based models. On the other hand, where horticulture is also a constituent of the economy, it not only induces a greater degree of sedentarism, but also provides more secure sources of calories. As this occurred, for example, during the Neolithic, the role of energy as a limiting factor in human activity gave way to other factors such as fats and proteins (Gross 1975; Reidhead 1980). The difference may readily be seen in a comparison of the Aché and the Achuara Jívaro of Peru: among the former, hunting supplies an estimated 80 percent of dietary calories (Hawkes, Hill, and O'Connell 1982:385), whereas among the horticultural Achuara 74 percent are derived from manioc and plantains (Ross 1976; 1978a:4). This in turn has profound implications for dietary strategies, for it means that where Aché hunting patterns must reconcile energy inputs and outputs fairly efficiently, Achuara hunting is effectively subsidized by horticulture and can be undertaken at an energetic loss if that proves necessary to bring in adequate supplies of other essential nutrients.

On the other hand, because among strictly foraging populations hunting is also a source of calories, such groups frequently manifest an apparently excessive intake of meat. This has been a source of some confusion. Hawkes, Hill, and O'Connell (1982:385), for example, have observed that the rather large meat harvest of the Aché is "quite surprising in view of recent generalizations

11

about lowland South America and low-latitude hunters in general." In fact, such surprise derives from an essential misunderstanding: the generalizations to which they refer were concerned largely with hunter-horticultural populations (Gross 1975; Ross 1978a). That noted, the scale of Aché hunting returns corresponds to what we know of other foraging peoples, among whom calories are in general the principal limiting nutrient and for whom meat is often the major source of energy (see Speth and Spielmann 1983 for a discussion of some of the implications of this for nutrition and subsistence strategies). For the same reason, foragers often are disposed to favor animal species that are particularly rich in fat—whether it is beaver among the Amerindians of the Canadian boreal forest (Berkes and Farkas 1978:161; Winterhalder 1981) or tapir and coleoptera larvae among the Aché (Clastres 1972). As a result, it has perhaps not been uncommon for foraging populations, in a diverse assortment of biomes, to have a "surprisingly" high protein intake—in order to amass sufficient calories. Thus, to take them once more as an example, the Aché average 150 grams of protein per capita per day during their hunting treks (Hawkes, Hill, and O'Connell 1982:385). On the other hand, high game harvest may not necessarily guarantee caloric sufficiency, and there is little doubt that boreal forest hunters were under considerable energy stress (Berkes and Farkas 1978:162; Winterhalder 1981:67–68)—a situation that undoubtedly facilitated their growing dependence upon purchased food during the post-contact period (Feit 1982). But we may be at least entitled to speculate that it is almost intrinsic to the energy-limited economy of foragers that they should tend to over-predate. If so, this may help to explain the severe game depletions of the Pleistocene, which paved the way for more diversified and sedentary lifestyles during the Neolithic.

The increasingly sophisticated interpretation of the archaeological record suggests that the transition to the Neolithic was accompanied by a fairly general decline in dietary quality, evidenced in stature and decreased longevity (see Chapter 10; Buikstra 1983). There seems certainly to have been a decline in the availability of quality protein, previously provided by hunting, and an increase in the consumption of starchy plant foods. It may well have been during this period that sedentary groups first evidenced the meat craving that is reported among so many hunting-horticultural peoples today. It has been suggested that such a craving—a preference for meat as the exemplary food—embodies a form of cultural motivation, since hunting is often a problematical and unrewarding task. But there may also be a physiological component. Judith and Richard Wurtman (1983) have described, for example, the quite different effects on brain chemistry of diets high in protein or carbohydrates. Whereas a diet with a high protein-to-carbohydrate ratio leads to a lowering of brain serotonin levels and elevates the desire for carbohydrates, one lower in protein and higher in carbohydrates—the general pattern for most horticultural populations since the Neolithic—increases serotonin levels and induces a "craving" for protein.

It is interesting to consider that, to some degree at least, the excess consumption of meat that characterizes many contemporary industrial populations may have its roots in the revolutionary transformation of the human consumption patterns that the rise of horticulture initiated. Most horticultural populations, subsisting on diets relatively high in carbohydrates, may have an elevated desire for protein-rich foods, but there are, as we have noted, practical limits to the satisfaction of such ends as long as protein is largely derived from wild animals. With the development and eventual expansion of animal domestication, however, new opportunities opened up, and in comparatively recent times, in advanced industrial nations, this has meant that although consumption of calories has remained high, the desire for increased protein intake has been able to be met. This, on the other hand, as we will see in a later section, has been achieved only through far-reaching social and economic developments that have involved an unprecedented level of integration of diverse local cultural systems, and has meant an intensification of economic, social, and political stratification, locally, nationally, and on a global scale.

Hunting, Taboos, and the Market Economy

We have observed that among foraging populations, the level of intake of protein may, in fact, be an artifact of the quest for calories. By the same token, the contribution of various animals to the diet may be in part a function of their utility beyond consumption as food: for example, where they provide skins for clothing, as with deer among the pre-contact Archaic Indians of Michigan (Keene 1981:186). This, once more, suggests that it would be erroneous to regard the motives underlying all elements in the diet as entirely circumscribed by dietary considerations.

This is, perhaps, even more the case among post-contact hunters and hunter-horticulturalists, whose dietary preferences (and even avoidances) are frequently as much affected by outside influences and pressures as by cultural traditions. These exogenous factors are often disregarded when diet is considered, since an overwhelmingly "cultural" perspective on food customs tends to impel researchers to look inward, toward indigenous ideological templates. But, as Leacock has aptly noted, "in most instances, [even] peoples with a gatherer-hunter heritage have not lived solely as gatherer-hunters for a long time" (1982:160). (For example, although the Yanoama Indians of the Venezuelan rain forest have been widely regarded as a relatively unacculturated population, their staple crop is the plantain—a European introduction.) Thus, the

Aché have been presented in various essays as if they personified an authentic paleolithic lifestyle (e.g., Hawkes, Hill, and O'Connell 1982). But, in fact, it is practically impossible (if, obviously, theoretically practicable) to comprehend the dynamics of Aché foraging without taking into account that the group under study spends around half the year in a Catholic mission, where, in between hunting treks, its members are "under the supervision of the mission staff. . . . they grow manioc, sugarcane, corn, and sweet potatoes, and they keep a few pigs, goats, chickens, and burros," as well as being provided with "additional resources in the form of milk, sugar, rice, flour, noodles, and salt" (Hawkes, Hill, and O'Connell 1982:381–82). It is difficult to believe that this has not had a serious effect on foraging strategies. If nothing else, it must have reduced the frequency of hunting over the course of a year, with the probable result that pressure on game has slackened (but see Chapter 13).

Like the Aché, most pre-industrial peoples have, over the last few centuries, been incorporated in varying measure into an ever expanding market economy, a process that has influenced their customary behaviors—including diet—in ways that we are only slowly beginning to appreciate (Leacock 1981:39–62; Tanner 1979). One serious way has been through pressure to exploit resources for the production of non-food commodities. Thus, in Canada, though beaver was already exploited before the arrival of Europeans, increasing involvement by Indians such as the Cree in the fur trade seems to have increased the role of the beaver as a food source (Feit 1982:380; Tanner 1979:60–61; Winterhalder 1981:87). This, however, had at times the additional effect of nearly decimating the species (Feit 1982:390; Tanner 1979:61), thus affecting diet in the opposite direction.

In Amazonia today, there are few Amerindians who do not participate to some degree in such commercial activities as selling or bartering skins and timber. In Peru and parts of Ecuador, for example, jaguar and peccary skins in large numbers find their way to the entrepôt city of Iquitos, from which point they proceed to the United States and Europe (Ross 1983). At present, for a group such as the Achuara, peccaries constitute over half of the total fresh weight of all game harvested; and although there is no doubt of their traditional significance as a source of food (Ross 1979), their central importance in recent decades as a source of valuable credit with local river traders undoubtedly induces hunters to kill more of them than nutritional requirements alone might warrant. To that extent, if protein intake among the Achuara is higher than is strictly necessary in dietary terms (Ross 1978a), it would be wrong to draw the inference that this is evidence of the abundance of tropical forest game (a conclusion recently drawn by Chagnon and Hames 1979). It may only reflect commercial pressures.

Such outside influence has worked in a diversity of ways, as the Achuara case suggests. The Achuara today tend to regard such animals as tapir, deer, and capybara as inedible (Ross 1978a). But, as with other pre-industrial populations, it is impossible to regard Amazon human ecology apart from the historical processes of the last centuries as the Amazon was drawn into the net of a global capitalist economy (Ross 1978b). There is, for example, some reason to believe that in the late nineteenth century Achuara communities were considerably larger than they are today and that they hunted and ate deer and tapir (Izaguirre 1925:175–78; Steward and Metraux 1948:619, 623). An increase in commercial contacts by the turn of the century seems to have altered subsistence patterns, however. First, guns were acquired. Although they may have been adopted as an instrument of warfare—which was endemic among the Achuara and other Jívaroan groups—they tended in general to displace traditional weapons. The acquisition of such shotguns in turn encouraged a more dispersed pattern of smaller settlements (a trend reinforced by new epidemic diseases) and a decline in communal hunting, a change that tended to discourage the pursuit of larger animals. Furthermore, since the use of guns depended upon access to ammunition through the rather unreliable agency of river traders, the ascendancy of such hunting instruments tended to be accompanied by an increasing measure of discrimination in targets, which, at least in the Achuara case, seems to have intensified the trend toward reliance on small animals and fish (Ross 1978a).

The Achuara are certainly not unique in this regard. Although there may be some debate about whether traditional or new technology is more effective for neotropical hunters (see Hames 1979; Ross 1978a; 1979; Yost and Kelley 1983), it seems fairly clear that the effort required to afford and/or secure ammunition for their guns has introduced a level of risk into Amerindian hunting that in many instances has led to a significant contraction in the scope of hunting activities and, hence, in the range of contributions that hunting makes to the diet. Thus, Goldman has written of the riverine Cubeo of the Colombian Amazon:

> Hunting may have been more prominent in the past, when only native weapons, spears and blowguns using curare-tipped darts were fashionable. Today the Indians hunt with muzzle-loading shot-guns that only a few possess because of the expense and trouble. A hunter is not disposed to take risks with his small store of shot, powder and percussion caps. (1963:57; see also Jackson 1983:46)

In some cases the introduction of new technology reinforced a pre-existent seasonal scheduling. Thus, in many riverine areas of the Amazon it is commonly the case that a marked seasonality in water levels dramatically affects game and fish densities. In the high-water periods, for example, aquatic resources decline severely; fish, in particular, become very scarce, and among some communities—as Stocks (1983:246) reports for the Cocamilla of the

Huallaga floodplain in eastern Peru—"there is a relative and consciously perceived strain on subsistence." Among the Shipibo on the Ucayali River, flood waters cover as much as 90 percent of their catchment zone. This may restrict fishing, but at the same time it tends to concentrate the animal population in a fairly confined land surface along the natural river levees (Behrens 1981:194–95). It is during this season, then, that "the Shipibo increasingly invest in shotgun shells and try their luck hunting. Less affluent Indians buy powder and shot to operate their ancient muzzle-loaders" (Hoffmann 1964:265). At this time of year, moreover, hunters "exploit otherwise rarely eaten game such as armadillo, coatimundi, majas [paca], and tapir" (Behrens 1981:195)—a reminder that edibility, and preferences and avoidances, are essentially processual.

If guns reinforced a pre-existent hunting strategy as in this instance, they were also able to curtail certain traditional targets. Sometimes this was because of an initial increase in the kill-rate or an intensification of the rate of game dispersal, which reduced the long-term yield of some species in a given region. But, in other cases, some animals were simply less efficiently harvested with guns. Thus, at the turn of the century, Up de Graff observed that in Jívaro country

> the big monkeys are the hardest game to bring down with shot-gun or rifle. I have shot them to pieces with a Winchester, until their entrails actually fell to the ground, before they have fallen. Even when dead, very frequently they remain suspended by the tail, and the tree has to be climbed before they can be recovered. But the poisoned dart from a blow-gun . . . kills them within two minutes. (1923:213)

Curare, being a muscle-relaxant, loosened the dying animal's hold on the branches, allowing it to drop to the ground to be readily claimed by a hunter.

In some cases the introduction of guns seems, in this way, to have effected a transformation in the concept of the comestibility of such animals. Thus, as Hill and Hawkes (1983:185) write of capuchin monkeys: "The Aché consider these monkeys as game (the Aché have hunted only with bows until very recently), whereas neighboring Guarani-speaking Indians, Paraguayans and Brazilian peasants, who all hunt with shotguns, do not consider these monkeys as prey (or even as edible in some cases)."

A particularly interesting example of how ecological conditions have affected concepts of edibility, and how resource use and dietary custom have both been altered under outside, commercial influence, is provided by the Miskito Indians of Nicaragua's eastern coast (the ethnographic present is the pre-Sandinista period). They have access to "a wide range of biotopes," which, being unrestricted by hostile neighbors—in contrast to the situation in so many parts of Amazonia—they have been able to exploit quite successfully. But living immediately by coastal waters that include "the largest sea turtle feeding grounds in the Western hemisphere" (Nietschmann 1972b:71), their use of terrestrial game resources has tended to be very selective—much as we would be led to expect from our earlier discussion (see Chapter 11; Chisholm, Nelson, and Schwarcz 1983)—in terms of both species hunted and hunting frequency. The Miskito, in fact, derive about 82 percent of their total annual harvest of meat from aquatic resources, with most hunting occurring during the months of highest rainfall when turtling declines (compare the riverine Shipibo, who derive about 76 percent of annual animal flesh from fish and similarly intensify hunting when fishing becomes seasonally restricted).

That hunting is relatively unimportant through most of the year and that "more than 65 percent of the active adult men concentrate their meat-getting activities only on turtling" (Nietschmann 1972a:59) are two factors that undoubtedly have contributed to the continuing productivity of hunting zones. As most game animals have not been subjected to persistent predation, the Miskito have been enabled to hunt in a highly selective fashion, which has meant that the more elusive and problematical targets have tended to be disregarded. Predictably enough, the tapir was traditionally regarded as inedible (Loveland 1976:81).

Increasingly involved in commercial exchange, which has meant catching turtles for the sale of their meat and shell (employed in the manufacture of combs, jewelry, etc.), and in need of cash to maintain their economy, which has become dependent on non-traditional techniques of turtling and fishing, the Miskito hunters have, however, been compelled to change their strategy. Commercial motives have become intertwined with purely dietary considerations. As Nietschmann has observed: "Miskito hunters and fishermen are focusing on animals with a high market potential in the village. . . . populations of green turtles, white-lipped peccary, and white-tailed deer are receiving additional pressure from human populations because of their taste preference and marketable potential" (1972a:60, 63). As a result, in "response to the decline of other meat sources" (Nietschmann 1973:112), particularly green turtles, the tapir has reentered the Miskito diet.

Protein Restriction and the Differential Costs of Dietary Pressure

The transition to horticulture led, in many regions, to new problems of resource availability, not least with regard to high-quality protein. This point has been widely noted in the recent anthropological literature (e.g., Speth and Scott 1984). In considerations of the varied human responses to this particular problem, most attention has been fixed on subsistence strategies; by comparison, little regard has been paid to social responses that often had as much effect on dietary outcome in actual consumption by real individuals. Clearly this is not a matter that is easily assessed from the archaeological record, except in terms of certain material sequelae that express states of nutrition-related health. In this regard there is evidence that the development of horticulture, although it may have led to an increase in birthrate, actually was responsible for a rise in child mortality—perhaps due to lower consumption of quality protein and a rise in diseases associated with greater sedentarism (Hassan 1975:44). There is also reason to suspect that women suffered a reversal in quality of life. More children would, for example, have entailed greater labor costs for women (Ember 1983:296), which—along with more frequent pregnancies—would have meant increased physical stress, particularly as observations from recent and contemporary horticultural societies suggest that men rarely share more than a fraction of the energetic costs of child rearing, though they may disproportionately benefit from the economic advantages of more offspring.

Such studies also indicate that women bear a greater amount of the burden of diminished consumption. Indeed, this suggests an important possibility in regard to the rise of horticulture itself. A major force behind increased efforts to domesticate plants and animals was the depletion of wild game during the late Paleolithic (Butzer 1971; Hayden 1984; Martin 1985). As this occurred, the likelihood is that the equality of distribution that typically characterizes foraging populations (Leacock 1981; Lee 1982) gave way before an attempt by men to monopolize animal flesh. (This has been observed in recent times by Lindenbaum among the Fore of highland New Guinea, where it induced women to adopt the practice of supplementing their own diet with the flesh of their deceased relatives [1979:24].) If women were thus disproportionately stressed as wild resources were depleted, there is reason to suppose that they were also more likely to take the initiative in a variety of ways in intensifying production: that is, in engaging in and developing precisely those subsistence activities that, in aggregate, we describe as the rise of horticulture.

Nonetheless, in most of the pre-industrial horticultural societies that we know about today, there is dietary stress, and it is rare that this is suffered equitably through some unitary, group accommodation; summaries of average per capita intake disguise the fact that work effort, intake, or both are apportioned among the population according to such criteria as age and gender, with adult men being the typically favored group. (This generalization can probably be extended to most industrialized societies as well.)

Undoubtedly the withholding of food in varying degrees from certain categories of individuals, such as neonates, must be regarded as a kind of attenuated infanticide—one that seems to have a long-standing role in human and, indeed, in hominid and pre-hominid history. The tendency to restrict the diet of adult females is more ambiguous in intent and more complex in its ramifications, especially when it applies to those who are pregnant or lactating. Yet it is relatively common to find taboos or some kind of dietary restrictions—frequently regarding the consumption of protein-rich foods—that are invoked precisely during these periods. If implemented with any consistency, such customs would in many instances jeopardize the mother's health or her capacity to bear healthy offspring. Thus, Sharma (1955) has associated the "greatly restricted diet" of many Burmese mothers with a high rate of infantile beriberi. On the other hand, such prohibitions often exist where resources are problematical, in which case the outcome of a new pregnancy or the survival of a new infant must be weighed against the well-being of older children and of the mother herself (see Chapter 2). To consider the latter for the moment: there is widespread evidence of an association between reduced diet in pregnancy and smaller infants; although this may put the neonate at risk, it also tends to reduce the risk of childbirth (Shorter 1982:165)—no inconsequential consideration in pre-industrial societies.

Gender variation in diets has probably had a long history, if we may judge by research among non-human primates and human hunter-gatherers. Harding, for example, in 1,032 hours of observations of free-ranging olive baboons at Gilgil, Kenya, recorded 47 incidents of these baboons killing and eating small animals. Although such activities played a very small role in their total subsistence, consumption was largely restricted to adult males and generally seemed to reflect male statuses within the troop (1973, 1974).

Among chimpanzees studied by Teleki and others at Gombe National Park, although actual killing was virtually monopolized by adult males (Teleki 1975:149–50, 154), there was elaborate and extensive sharing, which, although it seems to have been associated with adult male status far less than among Gilgil baboons, was certainly structured along gender lines. As Teleki observes, "As pursuit is undertaken almost exclusively by adult males, who in turn become the owners of large portions, females (and to a lesser extent subadults) become highly dependent upon mature males for this particular item" (1975:153). Since the overall predation rate is relatively low and thus the nutritional significance of such food is small, there is reason to view such meat consumption patterns as an instrument of social relations (Wrangham 1977).

Among humans too, food distribution is embedded in the prevailing pattern of social relationships, both reflecting and helping to reinforce status and power. Even if hunting-gathering societies have tended, in the main, to be fairly egalitarian, the likelihood is that a sexual division of labor has necessarily entailed certain dietary divergences along gender lines. How early on such a division of labor evolved—or even precisely why it did—is too complicated an issue to discuss here, and it is, at any rate, a largely speculative question. (For example, one recent explanation of why females do not hunt is derived from contemporary evidence of amenorrhea among Western women runners; it suggests that because "the human manner of hunting involves outrunning prey with endurance," it would be adaptive for females not to hunt, as participation in such activities would have impaired their fertility [Graham 1975:811]. However likely this argument may be, it remains hypothetical, though it is probably the case that the sexual division of labor, which largely defines hunting as a male activity, is based on some such biosocial factor involving fertility.) For the present, we can only note that, with the evolution of a pattern of labor in which males monopolized the hunt, the likelihood arose of dietary differences between men and women—if only because the former were likely to consume a certain percentage of their catch while away from home, just as women were apt to do while gathering or, later on, while engaged in horticultural tasks. Thus, Jellife and co-workers observe of the Hadza, a foraging group in northern Tanganyika, that "the diet of the two sexes differs greatly as much of the food is eaten as soon as it is obtained—the men eating on the spot small animals or carrion" (Jelliffe et al. 1962:909). A similar situation is reported among the pastoralist Karimojong of eastern Africa:

> Among the Karimojong during the dry season, young men tending the camp herds (at some distance from the home settlement) may subsist wholly on animal products, while the children and older adults at the settlement will rely on only plant foods and some milk. During the wet season, more animal foods will be available to those who remain at the settlement, and camp herdsmen will have greater access to cultivated plant foods. Hence at any given time males are likely to be consuming more protein-rich animal foods than are females. (Little and Morren 1976: 59–60)

Among many hunting-horticultural societies, perhaps because pressure on game resources is greater than among foragers, the distribution of meat within communities tends to reflect status to a considerable degree: that of men over women and that among men. Thus, among the Achuara, when families apportion out cuts of meat among their relations, it is likely that nothing will be given to the family of a man who is absent from the village. Among the Yanoama of the southern Venezuelan rain-forest, Good (Chapter 16) reports that meat in most cases is distributed to men, who in turn allocate portions to the women and children. Larger portions tend to go to the more important men, while lower-status men may receive none, especially in the larger villages where game is more sparse and demand is greater. Because male status is associated with hunting ability, moreover, the families of low-ranking men suffer doubly as far as meat consumption is concerned. This, in turn, may have decided demographic consequences. First, it imposes a special risk to women, who evidence a relatively high mortality during their reproductive years (Neel 1977:163), probably because nutritional stress renders them more vulnerable than men to disease (Chagnon 1974:160). Second, it affects the rate of infanticide, since, when food is scarce, women will be more likely to regard a neonate as competing with themselves and their older children. (Thus, headmen, with greater access to resources, tend to have offspring with a sex ratio indicating a significantly lower rate of female infanticide than is found for other males [Chagnon 1979].)

Whether gender-oriented food restrictions or prohibitions in other societies have similar consequences is difficult to ascertain; few studies have made any systematic effort to assess either the degree to which such beliefs are actually translated into practice or their effects. It is nonetheless notable that they are frequently meant to be applied to women of child-bearing age and they almost universally encompass nutritionally important protein sources (Bolton 1972; Katona-Apte 1975; Ogbeide 1974; Trant 1954; Wellin 1955). In some cases, at least, this may have the effect of diverting such foods, which are often scarce, to adult males in the event that they become available (Trant 1954)—a diversion that is commonly justified by the argument that the male workload is greater, even though the woman may be pregnant and working.

The effect if such dietary limitations are, in fact, enforced is that "women may be in a constant state of protein drain," as Ogbeide has argued for Mid-West state in Nigeria (1974:215), or, perhaps, suffering from anemia (Maher 1981:81). The same effect would follow, however, where prohibitions are not necessarily explicit, but where social relations within the family are conditioned by the family's ties to the wider society, in which male status is regarded as more privileged. In India, "as one moves up in the scale of income or expenditure classes, the consumption of animal protein also increases significantly" (Chapter 18). There, because women tend to work for less than men or are unwaged and thus control little income, they have less status within the household and are presumed to have less claim to consume such food (or to need it less). Thus, within the low-income rural Indian household, one finds a continuum of dietary privilege, with the woman generally situated at the bottom. According to Katona-Apte:

> At meals, the wife feeds her husband first, then the children, boys before girls; only then does she eat. Often she eats separately with her daughters. If available, the major portions of such nourishing foods as meat, fish, egg, or milk, and sweets, are served to the males, because it is believed that they need it for strength or growth, and often not much is left over for the females. It is not unusual to find households where the women are vegetarians, but the males are not. Vegetarianism among females may be rationalized on religious grounds, thus leaving more (or all) of the high protein foods for the males. (1975:45)

A similar situation is reported from Berber-speaking communities in Morocco, where

> men eat before women and children and consider prized food items such as meat to be their prerogative. Women and children learn to refuse meat, and on formal occasions, to eat what the men leave. . . . If they are guests [women] will often swear that they have eaten already, and if they are not, that they are not hungry. One woman used to assure her fellow diners that she preferred bones to meat. Men, on the other hand, are supposed to be exempt from facing scarcity, which is shared out among women and children. (Maher 1981:80–81)

In this case the results have been noted: high mortality among children and malnutrition among adult females (ibid.:81).

As I have noted, the origins of such dietary divergence may lie deep in human prehistory, but such degrees of subordination of women's diet to the prerogatives of male consumption seem to have emerged largely with the evolution of ranked societies, as a woman's status came to depend on that of her husband or other male kin. For example, "Bemba women dispense food as a family service that redounds to the husband's stature. . . . Among the Mae Enga, women's labor furnishes produce that is consumed by the pigs which are distributed in political negotiations by men" (Leacock 1981:159).

This trend reaches its height in class societies, particularly in the case of modern industrial capitalism, with the "structural separation of the public economy of capitalism and the private economy of the home" (Davis 1981:229)— the contrast between paid and unpaid work—with women disproportionately relegated to the latter, to producing children, facilitating the reproduction of the labor force (in the case of the working class),[2] and generally supporting the position of the men on whom their own livelihoods depend.[3] As Rowbotham has commented, if the woman "wants to 'improve' herself, she has in fact to 'improve' the situation of her husband. She has to translate her ambition into his person" (1983:21).

Where resources were scarce, this inevitably meant that in order to fortify the man's role in the public domain, premium food would be diverted to him, or to children capable of bringing in income. Thus, in the Manchester slums early in this century,

> dining precedence in the homes of the poor had its roots in household economics: A mother needed to exercise strict control over who got which foods and in what quantity. Father ate his fill first, to 'keep his strength up,' though naturally the cost of protein limited his intake of meats. He dined in single state or perhaps with his wife. Wage-earning youth might take the next sitting, while the younger end watched, anxious that any tidbit should not have disappeared before their turn came. (Roberts 1971:84)

There was usually little meat in the diet of the English working class during the 19th century and well into the present one (Drummond and Wilbraham

1958:329–30; Oliver 1895), but what little there was, was likely to be consigned to the working husband. According to Jessie Dawson, a pioneer women's health worker in the Edwardian era, this was very likely to remain true even if the wife was herself working; she concluded that "working mothers sacrificed themselves for their husbands and their children while they themselves lived in 'semi-starvation'" (quoted in Rudd 1982:xvii–xviii; Oliver 1895).

Similar situations recur so often in differing cultures that it must be concluded that even without explicit prohibitions on the diets of women, significant dietary differences between men and women have existed routinely, though it is perhaps only in the situations of dire poverty created by industrial capitalism that the disparity has reduced the nutritional situation of women to a precarious level. It is difficult to know how much more difference pregnancy- and lactation-related taboos could make, especially when one bears in mind that in pre-industrial populations, being pregnant or breast-feeding was probably woman's general condition during her child-bearing years, so that such taboos, in fact, described not an occasional constraint on intake, but a more or less continual state. What they characterize, then, is no less than what I have been describing: a general tendency since very early times for males to capture a greater share of high-protein foods. What I have suggested, moreover, is that the impetus for this has not been entirely dietary (though it certainly has had significant nutritional consequences) and that the way in which such esteemed foods are channeled also tends to reflect and reinforce social relations and status hierarchies. Regardless of actual practice, even the beliefs about their proper usage may play such a role.

Ecology, Economy, and Domesticated Animals in Europe

In looking, in an earlier section, at taboos in the Neotropics, I tried to demonstrate that the valuation of certain animals as food varied according to various material factors that affected the costs involved in obtaining them, relative to alternative resources. In general, despite the many obvious differences between societies that depend on hunting and those that depend on animal domestication, much the same argument applies to the latter. Indeed, in most instances there was probably little discontinuity between hunting and early domestication. (For example, the distinction between wild pigs that were hunted and pigs that were "domesticated" but allowed to forage most of the time in the forest, where they interbred with "wild" pigs, was not so very great.) Which species rose to prominence as domesticated animals in one region or another thus depended very often on circumstances not altogether dissimilar to the ones that made them favored hunting targets. One of the most important factors in this respect has always been the dietary habits of such animals themselves, a biomorphological characteristic that constrains their use (Jewell 1969); even in contemporary capitalist economies, this remains an important determinant of what animals are raised where.

Thus, in Europe, the distribution of such animals as pigs, cattle, and sheep has long depended upon their different feeding habits and needs—and upon the climatic conditions that favored them. Cattle and sheep, being ruminants, have been most prominent where there has been grassland, whereas swine have tended to be more important where concentrated natural feeds such as nuts, rather than bulky roughages, have been available. This basis for their distribution, in space and through time, has considerable temporal depth. From the earliest periods of animal domestication, Western Europe's extensive cover of broad-leafed deciduous forests, was chiefly occupied by swine that foraged on wild acorns and beechnuts. The distribution of cattle and sheep on the other hand, was largely determined by the absence of forest and a consequent limitation upon pig raising; it depended as well, however, upon adequate feed, which meant that, to the north, it was limited by the supply of winter fodder and, in the more arid, drought-prone, southern regions of Europe, by the difficulties of summer grazing (Pounds 1973:291). Thus, cattle tended to be most numerous in areas of northwestern Europe where the climate favored extensive natural pasture, whereas sheep, which were more hardy, assumed importance in the dry zones around the Mediterranean (ibid.:291–92).

If one bears in mind that several millennia of human activity have profoundly transformed the European landscape, so that extensive forests where pigs roamed have given way to pasture where cattle or sheep graze or have been cleared for human occupation, while, in turn, new crops have often created new conditions in which to raise swine (see Ross 1983), it is particularly noteworthy to what extent European animal domestication remains regionalized by climatic and environmental factors. Thus, as far as ruminants are concerned, cattle predominate in Europe's central latitudes, and beef consumption is low in the cold Scandinavian countries and arid southern regions such as Greece, Spain, and Portugal, where sheep far outstrip cattle (United Nations 1981:118–22, 130–32). The role of pigs is no longer defined by deciduous forest—although in some parts, such as southwestern Spain, this old association remains intact (Parsons 1962)—but by the availability of other concentrated feeds, whether crops such as maize or potatoes or waste-products of human activities. As a result, unlike grazing, but rather like milk-producing, the rearing of swine is closely identified with areas of comparatively high human density where intensive rather than extensive forms of land use are required, where farm units have evolved into small enterprises with a premium on efficiency. Thus, the highest rates of pork and bacon consumption are found in Northern and Central Europe, areas that have some of the highest population densities in the world: countries such as Germany, Austria, Belgium, and Luxembourg (United Nations 1981:118–22, 130–32).

If it was forest that originally helped to make swine so important in the early European diet, it was the eventual contraction of European forests that caused pork to decline in dietary significance. Even in the Neolithic, when the process of deforestation began, the archaeological record indicates a notable adverse effect on the prevalence of swine (Clark 1947). The general decline of the importance of pork, however, occurred over numerous centuries during which anthropogenic grassland gradually took over from oak and beech, in the wake of land clearing for agriculture and other human industries, such as building and smelting, which required timber. Thus, pigs were still of great importance well into the Middle Ages, although this often depended upon special edicts to protect acorn-producing districts, where foraging was at times a crown privilege (Steven and Carlisle 1959). The erosion of forest, however, accelerated around the 13th century, a period characterized by a dramatic rise in population and agricultural expansion (Duby 1972, 1974; White 1964). By the fifteenth and sixteenth centuries, the distribution of pigs had been reduced largely to urban zones. There they could still thrive in the refuse in city streets, whose garbage they transformed into flesh that had become such a luxury that the rich often incorporated it into dowry payments (Forster and Ranum 1979).

The decline of forest was, inevitably, not uniform. As I have already noted, there are areas in Spain where oak forests still survive—albeit through active human efforts—and continue to sustain enormous numbers of swine and to guarantee pork a special place in the diet (Parsons 1962:214–15). By the same token, certain regions were especially vulnerable to human activity and were deforested earlier and more rapidly than the rest of Western Europe. One such area was highland Scotland.

The case of Scotland is enlightening, not just because it illustrates the relationship between change in dietary custom and the kind of environmental transformations that I have been discussing, but because it also provides an excellent opportunity, in the context of a complex sociopolitical system, to examine how "taboos" seem to emerge and wane in changing material circumstances—much as we saw in our earlier consideration of neotropical societies.

Deforestation in the Scottish Highlands was particularly rapid, as a rugged landscape and harsh weather had limited the spread of deciduous vegetation, encouraging instead the development of a hardier pine forest that was much less favorable to foraging hogs. Archaeological evidence testifies to the fact that swine once did inhabit these upland regions (Clutton-Brock 1976; Ritchie 1920), and we know that even into the 12th century Scottish highland lairds and various monkish orders raised herds of swine and ate pork (MacKenzie 1935:57). The practice does not seem to have survived the process of forest erosion, however.

Agriculture, perhaps the principal factor behind deforestation, was largely confined by rain, wind, and cold to the same restricted glens and valleys where oak and beech found a limited haven. The expansion of agriculture was thus necessarily at the expense of pigs. Nor could it offer much to substitute for mast. Given the unusually harsh climate and generally poor soil conditions (Grant 1961; Handley 1953; Watson 1964), agricultural harvests were precarious and unreliable and rarely produced enough for human consumption, let alone surplus for animals. Cattle, at least, could be grazed on upland pasture and moorland, which cover more than 65 percent of the surface area of the Highlands. Few might survive the long, arduous winters (Handley 1953:69–71; Lea 1977), but at least those that did not had not taken food out of human mouths, while those that did could be restored in the spring to provide milk and cheese or sold to pay rent and enable people to buy oats with which to supplement their diet of dairy products (Grant 1961; Keltie 1875; Smout 1969). On the other hand, with the demise of deciduous forest, the pig had become "the farm animal least able to live off the country" (Darling 1955:326), and evidence suggests that although their numbers declined, those that remained acquired a powerful reputation for a rapacious omnivory that threatened everything from crops to untended infants (O'Dell 1939; Sinclair 1796:227). Such behavior prompted the levying of fines against the owners of destructive pigs and eventually led numbers of highland lairds to order their tenants "not to raise swine" (O'Dell and Walton 1962:93). It was, perhaps, out of such policies that the idea evolved of a Highland "taboo."

The ecological costs of swine rearing were thus compounded by financial ones, with the result that by 1650 at least, Highlanders—who by 1578 were described by Bishop Leslie as taking "lytle plesure" in swine flesh (quoted in MacKenzie 1935:58)—rarely raised hogs any longer and were said to regard the consumption of pork with such disdain that some observers could only attribute it to a deep-seated religious prejudice or taboo (Findlater 1802; Robertson 1799:326; Smith 1798; Salaman 1949:348; Smout 1969:132). An English song, "The Brewer," published in London in 1731 but written some 70 to 100 years earlier, made reference to "The Jewish Scots that scorn to eat / The flesh of swine" (quoted in MacKenzie 1935:43–44).

Most attempts to ascribe the Highland disaffection for pigs to religious taboo rest upon a notably arcane logic: for example, Donald MacKenzie's argument that since, among Celtic peoples, the rare group that disliked pork were the Galatians (a fact he attributes to their conversion to the ancient cult of Attis, who was slain by a boar), the Highland Scots must be descended from Galatian migrants (1935:66–68). Yet, as I have suggested, the explanation was actually far more mundane—and never that difficult to see. Indeed, in the 1730s, an English officer named Burt had written: "I own I never saw any swine among the mountains, and there is good reason for it; those people have no offal wherewith to feed them; and were they to give them other food, one single sow would devour all the provisions of a family" (Quoted in MacKenzie 1935:45). He went on, moreover, to describe the relative superficiality of the ideological aspect of the Highland "prejudice" against pork:

> It is here a general notion that where the chief declares against pork, his followers affect to show the same dislike; but of this affectation I happened once to see an example. One of the chiefs who brought hither with him a gentleman of his own clan dined with several of us at a public house where the chief refused to eat pork, and the laird did the same; but some days afterwards the latter being invited to our mess and under no restraint, he ate it with as good an appetite as any of us. (Quoted in MacKenzie 1935:45)

The Rise and Fall of Vegetarianism in Western Europe

Except perhaps that the decline of swine went further than elsewhere in Western Europe during this period, largely because the demise of forest was greater and more rapid and agricultural potential was in general so much less, the diminishing role of pork in the Scottish Highlands conformed to a general process of dietary transformation. But pork was not the only animal flesh to depart from the European diet as demographic growth proceeded. Indeed, by the 12th century, while pork still retained a notable position in the diet, ruminants were already being affected by increasing pressure on the land from agricultural developments. As Pounds (1973:290) has observed:

> Meat and milk products formed only a very small part of the human diet in most parts of Europe, and with the exception of the pig, animals primarily served other ends than the provision of food. The ox was used mainly as a draught animal, and the paucity of references to the dairy cow, or vacca, suggests how unimportant was cow's milk in most areas. The sheep was bred more for its wool than for its food value, though ewe's milk, and the cheese made from it, were locally important.

In the following centuries, the dietary picture worsened, with pork of course declining in importance, so that in areas such as England, by the 14th century, "the staple diet of the peasantry was the famous English 'white meats' (milk, cheese, eggs and poultry)" (Crawford and Broadley 1938:206). By the 16th century, increasing emphasis upon cereal production was seriously displacing animal husbandry throughout much of Europe, while, because cereal prices were still rising, according to Braudel: "There was no money for buying extras. Meat consumption diminished in the long run until about 1850" (1967:130). By the 17th century, the emerging similarities to the dietary economy of China were quite remarkable. In China, for example, cattle were conserved for agricultural labor, and Chinese pharmacologists admonished that eating beef was unhealthy (Schafer 1977:99). Well into the present century, what beef was consumed was usually the flesh of dead farm animals (and, even then, the meat was typically sold in an urban market). In Western Europe, where cattle raising persisted, they were kept, as centuries earlier, largely as a source of rural power. There were usually enough milch cows that milk remained an important part of the diet, but what beef was eaten "often came from sick or half-dead beasts who could no longer function as work animals" (Blum 1978:186). As in China, many physicians espoused the view that it was healthier to eat meat in moderation (which, of course, in the circumstances was probably true). With the build-up in merchant fleets, fish came to play a much more important part in the diet, and the number of meatless days in the Catholic calendar grew until, by the middle of the 17th century, they accounted for about one-half of the days in the year in England and France (Braudel 1967:146; Wilson 1973:31).

Up until the beginning of the 19th century, Western Europe was largely a non-meat-eating region as far as most of its inhabitants were concerned. Indeed, for the working class, meat remained scarce through most of the last century, with bread, potatoes, and tea the dietary staples (Drummond and Wilbraham 1958:329–30; Oddy 1970). Yet the ecological circumstances, at least, that had brought about such a deterioration in the diet were by the late 18th century beginning to be overcome by political and economic events, particularly the opening up of new lands by colonial activities.

First, from newly settled regions in the Americas had come new cultigens such as maize and potatoes, which laid the basis for a new intensification of mixed agriculture. The potato in particular opened up formerly marginal lands and supplemented grain harvests—a contribution of critical importance in areas such as Scotland and Switzerland, where climatic conditions made cereal production so problematical. As Netting has written of the latter country, where potato cultivation spread during the first decade of the 19th century:

> The growing of potatoes permitted the use of a wider range of land, including high-altitude, steep, and fallow plots, for food production; potatoes required little or no new investment for cultivating and processing tools; they achieved higher caloric yields per unit of land with perhaps less labor expenditure; they were more dependable than grain in the alpine zone; and they filled a nutritional need. (1981:164)

Throughout Europe, moreover, the tuber provided the possibility of a surplus that could be invested in animals such as pigs, initiating a veritable renaissance in swine rearing. The potato, for example, made its appearance in Scotland around the middle of the 18th century (MacKay 1955:37), and its impact on the putative religious dread of pigs was dramatic. As Robert Henderson, a Scottish farmer, wrote in 1811: "About the year 1760, one would scarce have seen twenty swine in a parish throughout Dumfriesshire; but about 1770, they began to appear more plentiful, and every farmer then kept one or two." Within a few more years, a flourishing trade in cured hams had arisen, and the county of Dumfries was sending six times as many hams to London as Yorkshire was (1811:10–12). By the end of the century, James Robertson was able to write:

> Not many years ago, the Highlanders in general had a disgust of this kind of food, without being able to give any reason for it; but their dislike to pork has greatly worn off; in so much that in a short time this loathing of swine's flesh will be accounted a singularity even among the Highlanders. (1799:32)

England and the Political Economy of Meat

Nevertheless, it was not primarily the introduction of new cultigens that revolutionized meat production in Europe, particularly in England. The salient development was, rather, colonialist expansion, which appropriated the comestible resources as well as other raw materials of new territories abroad. (China, by contrast, having never become the same kind of mercantile expansionist state, remained largely dependent on its own food base and thus never diverged from the more or less vegetarian diet imposed by its demographic pressure for agricultural intensification.)

Beginning as early as the 17th century, England had begun to achieve hegemony, by military, political, and financial means, over the pasturelands of her Celtic neighbors in Scotland and Ireland. Indeed, climate and rugged terrain were not the only constraints on agriculture that faced Highland Scots by this period, for, just as the English were conquering Jacobite forces and dismantling the feudal structure of the Scottish clans, so was the English market insidiously eroding the traditional subsistence economy. At first this entailed a demand for cattle; but by the second half of the 18th century, industrialization of the English textile industry was calling for new reserves of raw wool, so that flocks of sheep began to displace both Highland cattle and the people who had subsisted predominantly on the dairy products that they supplied (Ross 1983:104–5). The Highlanders themselves were forced to leave for the lowlands or the coasts, while the wool went to the mills of Yorkshire and Scottish mutton ended up in the butcher shops and markets of London.

By the same period, Ireland—which had been drawn into the orbit of England's control since the 12th century—was producing beef and pork for the use and profit of English settlers. Even more important at this date was the fact that Ireland, whose land was now largely in the hands of English colonists and crown grantees, had become a vital component in the operation of England's Caribbean colonies, to which it supplied large quantities of barrelled beef and pork (O'Donovan 1940:49). As observed in *The Interest of England in the Preservation of Ireland,* published in 1689: "The islands and plantations of America are in a manner wholly sustained by the vast quantities of beef, pork, butter and other provisions of the product of Ireland" (quoted in O'Donovan 1940:73).

By the second half of the next century, however, the bulk of Irish livestock, meat, and dairy products had begun to shift in increasing quantities to England, largely as a result of the rise of the factory system, which drew English labor out of the countryside and put great pressure on domestic food supplies in the new manufacturing districts. There were, as a result, shortages and rising prices, which industrialists were eager to moderate for several reasons. First, they were becoming a major focus for working-class discontent and protest by the end of the 18th century (Morton 1979) and thus threatened social and economic stability. Second, increasing rivalry with other developing industrial nations in Europe compelled English factory owners to sell at competitive prices, which required holding down wages—a process that, in turn, was seen to depend to some degree on the cost of basic foods. It was these economic imperatives, as much as anything else, that lay behind England's impulse to procure Scottish and Irish meat (Stamp 1975:240) and, in the end, to base her own industrial growth on the relegation of these peripheral regions to an ancillary role as pastoralist food reserve. By 1850 much of the meat in London's markets was "imported" from England's Celtic fringe. In that year, for example, Henry Mayhew wrote of Newgate, which he called "the greatest meat market in the world," that "one-fourth of the beef and mutton consigned to [it], is from Scotland. . . . Aberdeen is the place from which the largest supply of beef is obtained; the greatest quantity of mutton is sent from Edinburgh and Leith." Of pork, he noted, "The great supply . . . is from Ireland; from Belfast, Derry, Drogheda, Dublin, Waterford, Cork, and Limerick; and from Inverness and Invergordon in Scotland" (1850:204–5).

The effect on Scotland and Ireland was enduring. Even today the Highlands, which embrace almost half the land area of Scotland, contain only 5 percent of the country's population, and there are 10 times as many sheep as people (Grant 1961; Grieve 1972); Ireland—though three-quarters free of English political rule—remains a "cattle-farm" for its island neighbor. A sign in a typical butcher's window in England testifies to the persistent heritage of the ecological division of labor upon which modern English industrial society was based when it advertises: "Scotch beef, English lamb, Devon pork, Irish bacon."

In the 18th century, the impact of English colonialism on Ireland was particularly devastating—especially in terms of the diet of the peasantry whose labor produced the commodities that found their way into English stomachs. Up until the mid-17th century, the rural diet continued to consist largely of milk, cheese, grains, and some pork from swine that foraged in local forests (Lucas 1960). This pattern was disrupted by the desire of English landlords to reduce subsistence acreage and increase the land area allocated for production for export. At this date, no one can say whether it was landlord or peasant who most clearly recognized the value of the potato as an acre-economizing crop—whether landlords encouraged tenants to cultivate it in order to squeeze more people onto less land, or peasants intensified their use of this new crop as they came to recognize that it could compensate them for the reduced acreage onto which they were forced—but one way or the other, as the years went by, the more Ireland's economy was subordinated to the English market, the narrower the rural diet grew and the greater the role of the potato in it until, by the early 1800s, it was practically the sole food of the Irish peasantry (Dutton 1824:352; Salaman 1943). (By contrast, in Switzerland, which remained economically autonomous, the consequences of adopting the potato were more unambiguously beneficial [Netting 1981:159–69].) The result, in turn, was that their subsistence base grew increasingly vulnerable to any disruption of the potato harvest. Thus, in 1846, when a hitherto unknown blight destroyed most of the potato crop, a terrible famine devastated the rural population, causing widespread death by starvation and disease and emigration on an unprecedented scale.

What was most interesting was that in the midst of this crisis, the export of Irish grain and livestock not only continued but intensified. Indeed, far from inducing any modification in English colonial rule, the Great Famine of the 1840s actually provided England with an incredible opportunity, while the peasantry was virtually prostrate, to intensify pre-famine trends in land clearance and cattle rearing. The result was that between 1851 and 1910, land in pasturage (including grass, meadow, and clover) rose steadily from 10.7 to 13.1 million acres (O'Donovan 1940). Just from the period 1846–49 to 1870–74, the number of Irish cattle exported to England climbed from almost 202,000 to about 558,000 (ibid.:213–14). By 1880 it could be written:

> Agriculture of most other kinds has been steadily dwindling down; 519,307 acres out of a total tillage area of 5,500,000 had gone out of cultivation in ten years. The wheat culture was ruined. . . . The breadth of land even under oats had declined by 320,000 acres. . . . 50.2 percent of the entire surface of the country and two-thirds of its wealth, were devoted to the raising of cattle. (Dublin Mansion House Relief Committee 1881:2)

By the 1890s, about 65 percent of Ireland's total meat production went to England, where it constituted on average about 30 percent of what English officialdom described as the "domestic" supply. Yet during the first half of the century, as an ever greater proportion of the English population, swelled by a great demographic explosion, had been drawn into industrial production, the English demand for food had already reached levels for which the food reserves of Scotland and Ireland proved increasingly inadequate. By mid-century it was already apparent that England's diet in general depended upon foods imported from an ever more diverse array of places. Thus, by 1856 George Dodd was writing in his book, *The Food of London:*

> Let the query be, whence does London obtain its butchers' meat? We find that live stock is brought to the metropolis by all the great turnpike roads, by seven railways, and by steamers. . . . We find that these animals arrive from almost every part of England, from the Lowlands and the Highlands of Scotland, from Wales and from Ireland, from Denmark and from Holland. . . . [There are also] bacon and salt meat from Ireland; hams from Yorkshire and Germany and Spain; game from all the sporting counties of the north; rabbits from the southern counties and from Ostend; poultry from half the counties in England; eggs from Ireland and France. . . . If the daily bread of the metropolis be the subject of inquiry, we must travel yet farther to trace the sources of supply; to the southern Russians around Odessa and Taganrog (unless war interrupt), the Moldavians around Galatz, the Prussians around Danzig, the Americans in the Mississippi States, to say nothing of nations nearer home, or of our own farmers. (1856:102)

Thus, the dietary resources of England were increasingly extra-territorial, dependent not primarily upon local subsistence but on commercial and political relations with other regions around the globe. I have already alluded to the domestic political pressures that were implicated in this process—the calculated recognition that too great a rise in food prices, especially of meat and bread, would fuel social discontents and class tensions—but it is important to note as well that as England's role as an imperialist power became more and more the basis of its food supply, so political realities shifted to a wider stage, one on which it was necessary to maintain a constant protective guard over the mercantile agents of its emergent world economy.

Nor should it be forgotten that foodstuffs from around the world were also a lucrative field for investment, and that the range of edible commodities that flowed into England (as, to a lesser extent, into other Western European markets) was less the result of a desire to vary the national resource base for its own sake (though in that diversity lay a certain political security) than a reflection of the profitable diversification of England's investment of finance capital.

Having begun much earlier in the Celtic regions, in time this process had extended into the continental arena—where it was a powerful motive force behind the hegemonic struggles among the varied European powers—and by the late 19th century had reached as far as Australasia and the Americas. In the course of the 19th century, for example, much of Latin America had come under the sway of English commercial interests, primarily in the field of textiles. By 1880 English entrepreneurs virtually controlled the guano trade and the transportation network of Peru and nitrate production in Chile, while the face value of British capital investments in Latin America as a whole had reached more than £179 million (Rippy 1959:25–26). In the following decades, English capital was directed increasingly into the field of meat exports.

Argentina is a case in point. In the 1870s, with its vast grasslands, it was one of the potentially most productive and lucrative regions for meat production in the Americas. But like similar frontier zones at this time, before the advent of modern transport and refrigeration facilities, its ranges were largely devoted to sheep rearing, since wool was a far less perishable commodity. Cattle served primarily to provide meat for the Argentine consumer, while tallow and hides were generally shipped abroad. But an estimated 45 percent of sheep and 20 percent of cattle herds were already owned by English, Scottish, and Irish colonists who had good reason to regard Europe as their ultimate market (Hanson 1938:7–10).

It was the development of refrigeration that enabled Argentine beef (and, equally, that of North America during the same period [Ross 1980:202]) to be developed for export. But the impetus behind the export of beef was at least twofold: first, there was the English market, which was a significant factor underlying many innovations in food preservation during this period (Hanson 1938:18); and, second, there was English capital, which was the pivotal element in developing the requisite infrastructure to sustain an export economy in such regions. Thus,

> in the River Plate region livestock improved by the continued heavy import of British blooded animals, moved on British-owned railroads to British-equipped and financed plants, from which the finished product was shipped on British steamships to England, for a long time the only import market. (Hanson 1938:18)

Perhaps nothing demonstrates so clearly the closely interwoven development of English diet, food importation, and modern English industrial capitalism in the late 19th century as the fact that one of the wealthiest families in Britain today—the Vesteys—made its original fortune, as Liverpool merchants, by dominating the Argentine meat market and going on to establish Dewhurst, Ltd., the largest chain of butcher shops in the country (New York Times 1980).

To the north of Argentina, Uruguay too was transformed into a supplier to the English diet, but in an altogether different way. By the 1880s over a million and a half cattle were slaughtered annually. Beef was mainly consumed domestically, but one-third of these animals were killed only for tallow and hides, which were exported. Nearly 150,000 of them, however, ended up at the English factory at Fray Bentos on the Uruguay River, where they were rendered into "Liebig Extract of Meat"—every 110 pounds of which represented the distillation of 15 cattle (Consulate-General of Uruguay 1883:48–57). This extract, spread on bread by the English working class, became one of their chief sources of protein in the late 19th century.

The English Working-Class Diet and the Nutritional Costs of Empire

As we saw in our discussion of pre-industrial foraging and non-stratified horticultural societies, inequalities in diet emerged as a consequence of a sexual division of labor. But, in general, these were limited by the need for material reciprocity between men and women, as well as by structural constraints upon the potential for monopolization of resources. With stratified social systems, on the other hand, and especially with the evolution of class-structured systems, access to strategic resources was defined by differential power and expressed by monopolies over land or the forces of production. In Norman England in the 13th century, for example, this was clearly demonstrated by the legal concept of the "royal forest," a domain which covered about one-quarter of the surface of England and was considered quite distinct from land that the monarch held in his or her own right. In such areas habitation and all economic activities—such as foraging swine—were a source of crown revenue (Young 1979:5–6, 57).

It was, in fact, the conflict between king and barons over this monopoly that led to the Magna Carta; but it was not until about 1400 that the prerogative of the crown was actually transformed into the more general privilege of the ruling class of which the monarch was the paramount figure. In 1390 a statute

> ordained that no artificer, laborer, or other layman with lands or tenements valued at less than forty shillings a year nor any priest or clerk with a preferment not worth ten pounds a year should hunt deer, hares, conies, or any other "gentlemen's game" on penalty of one year in prison. The English game laws from that time marked a change from the medieval pattern and formed an alliance of king and landed gentry to protect their privileges from the lower classes. (Young 1979:169)

In such circumstances, many of the poor could obtain sufficient food only by poaching. But the assault upon class privilege that this entailed was countered by draconian laws that regarded poaching as a criminal offense—not because it jeopardized the diet of the rich in any substantive way, but because it threatened the social order, of which dietary differences were but a reflection.

In the 18th century, the relationship between diet and rank was best exemplified by the uses of venison, which, distributed as a gift or apportioned among dinner guests, was probably more of a mechanism for bestowing or repaying social or political favors than it was ever a source of nutrition among the well-to-do (Thompson 1977:158–59). In the Scottish Highlands, social access to venison became even more well established. During the second half of the 19th century, where lands from which the indigenous peasantry had been brutally cleared to make room for cattle and sheep were now apportioned among great estates (whose ownership then and now provides an excellent cross-section of the British ruling class), deer parks—eventually amounting to three million acres or 15 percent of the land area of Scotland (McEwen 1981:9; Ross 1983:105)—were created to provide outdoor sport for the Scottish and English aristocracy. They too, in due course, were forced to cope with poaching by those few Highlanders who remained.

It was in the 18th century, however, that the extent to which the parameters of diet were, in fact, also markers of class differentials in power was made most clear. In 1723 the so-called Black Act defined the criminality of poaching in the most extreme terms imaginable. According to Thompson:

> The main group of offences was that of hunting, wounding or stealing red or fallow deer, and the poaching of hares, conies or fish. These were made capital if the persons offending were armed and disguised, and, in the case of deer, if the offences were committed in any of the king's forests, whether the offenders were armed or disguised or not. (1977:22)

By the 19th century, with the majority of the working class now ensconced in urban districts, laws safeguarding the privileges of the landed gentry were less important than those protecting the factory owners. Thus, the political upheaval generated by the Corn Laws, which had sought to subsidize the gentry through price supports for their grain, had brought a recognition that as industry captured the leading role in the economy, it was more important to moderate the price of bread and create a more secure environment for the growth of manufacturing.

But the stratification of the English diet, far from abating, intensified under the new industrial regime. The contrast in breakfast provides a useful illustration. The morning meal of the gentry frequently assumed prodigious proportions during this period. As one authority observed in 1887:

> In a country house, which contains, probably, a sprinkling of good and bad appetites and digestions, breakfasts should consist of a variety to suit all tastes, viz: fish, poultry, or game, if in season; sausages, and one meat of some sort, such as mutton cutlets, or filets of beef; omelettes, and eggs served in a variety of ways; bread of both kinds, white and brown, and fancy bread of as many kinds as can conveniently be served; two or three kinds of jam, orange marmalade, and fruits when in season; and on the side table, cold meats such as ham, tongue, cold game, or game pie,

galantines, and in winter a round of spiced beef. (Quoted in Read and Manjón 1981:27–28)

In contrast, the breakfast of the working class usually consisted of little more than bread and butter and tea (Oliver 1895), and certainly provided few resources with which to titillate fastidious appetites.[4]

Nor was their general dietary picture much better. Through most of the 19th century (and well into the 20th), it included a narrow and precarious range of foods, with bread and potatoes the dietary staples and intake of milk, meat, and fat rather low and problematical (McCabe 1974; Oddy 1970). Well-sweetened tea also came to play an increasingly important role—to such an extent that even today many working people in England refer to their evening meal, whatever it consists of, as "tea"—but, significantly, it depended more than any other item of the diet on England's colonial position. By 1880 the United Kingdom as a whole was importing over 45.5 million pounds of tea just from India (House of Commons 1871, 1888), where tea export on such a scale necessarily reduced subsistence agriculture still further in a country where colonial commerce had already so threatened food production that famines had become a recurrent threat (Bhatia 1967:31; Dutt 1940:132).

There is no doubt that as new supplies of more substantial food were secured from abroad, certain sectors of the population benefited, including skilled workers. But the English population was also on the rise, and what meat, for example, was imported does not seem to have been sufficient to preclude often severe rises in prices (McCabe 1974:138–39), which effectively deprived many working-class families of access to such food. Thus, as Drummond and Wilbraham (1958) argue in *The Englishman's Food,* the opening of the twentieth century saw malnutrition more rife in England than it had been since the great dearths of medieval and Tudor times. The impoverished quality of the diet of the working class was reflected, in turn, in infant mortality rates in the major urban areas that were on a par with those found in many Third World countries today (Ross and Harris, in press) and in such levels of physical decline that, at the time of the Boer War (1899–1902), the army's rejection of recruits—who came largely from the manufacturing districts—was running at 40 percent nationally and as high as 60 percent in some areas (Howe 1972:181).

Once we have surveyed the general process of English mercantile expansion into meat-producing regions around the world, the question naturally arises: how was such meat distributed if the majority of the population seems to have consumed so little? The obvious point to be made is that the middle and upper classes claimed a disproportionate share; often what the working class was able to afford was some meat by-product, such as Liebig's extract, or a cut of meat that was "meat" in name only. (That distinction between the quality of cuts that are not merely purchased by, but even marketed to, different income strata is still a fixture of distribution in our own time. Thus, in Hampstead, one of the most affluent parts of London, it is easy to find quality filets of beef; in Hackney, perhaps the poorest borough in the city, cuts that contain less meat than fat and gristle and are "as lacking in nutritional value as in aesthetic appeal, make up at least half the window displays" of most butcher shops along the principal shopping route [Harrison 1983:27].) Such differences in diet as a whole, not just in meat, were translated into the class disparities in mortality, longevity, stature, and so on which were still conspicuous well into the 20th century—and which today are noticeable in differences in infant birth weights; 50 percent of a sample of Hackney babies were below 3,000 grams at birth, compared with 17 percent in Hampstead (Phillips 1984:10).

I noted earlier that even within working-class families, there were important contrasts in diet, so that most meat apparently was reserved for adult males, with wives skimping themselves on their behalf and children being underfed until it was time for them to go out to work, at which point they were often "fattened up" (Rudd 1982:xvii).

But perhaps more important than anything else in depriving the poor of cheaper and adequate supplies of meat was the demand placed on this commodity by the army and navy, which were entrusted with the immediate responsibility for safeguarding the interests of the English ruling class and its industrial and merchant sectors overseas. Suffering unemployment and a poor diet at home, the English worker often had to risk his life overseas in the military service, in defense of a system that otherwise consigned him to misery, in order to be employed and fed. For it seems that whatever the merits of military cooking, in quantity at least it was so far superior to the civilian diet—officially it included a pound of bread and three-fourths of a pound of meat per day through most of the 19th century (Skelley 1977:63; Smurthwaite 1980:42)—that "military authorities frequently observed that the health of recruits improved even on basic army meals" (ibid.:68).

It is difficult to delineate with any precision the level of demand represented by the armed services, but it seems to have been prodigious, especially in time of war—and the British army and navy were fighting somewhere in the world every year of Queen Victoria's lengthy reign (Farwell 1972:1). Thus, during the Crimean War (1854–55), the English government frequently contracted with pork suppliers in Cork for a million pounds at a time—not a surprising quantity when just one ship, the *Duke of Wellington,* a giant steamer, was provisioned at the start of service with 20 tons each of salt beef and salt pork (Dodd 1856:279). Records of the British War Office's Commissariat Department provide a bit more detail, indicating that between 1813 and 1835, the department contracted for 69.6 million pounds of Irish salted beef and 77.9 million pounds of Irish salted pork (House of Commons 1836:514). Many Irish were able to eat meat produced by their own country only by joining the army of the country that had colonized theirs, and, of course, in so doing, helped England to establish and maintain colonies elsewhere.

Thus, it was not just the case that England's global commercial interests drew upon foreign resources in order to subsidize its domestic economic expansion. It was, in fact, a far more complex system than that, for, in provisioning the armed forces, its foreign trade also made the empire a self-sustaining system, with the resources from one region helping to sustain the process of acquisition or protection of markets and colonies elsewhere. When, for example, England was sending its troop ships to South Africa during the so-called Zulu War—a conflict that ended not only with the destruction of the Zulu state but with British ascendancy over the Boer Transvaal Republic (Morton 1979:485)—it was able to call upon large quantities of provisions from the United States, Canada, and Australia. According to army records, the ships sailing between February 22, 1879, and June 6, 1879, transported over 1.3 million pounds of tinned beef alone, most of it from these countries (House of Commons 1878–79:266–67).

There is no doubt, then, that the English economy was importing meat at a considerable rate; but far less of it apparently was finding its way into the domestic economy than is commonly assumed. Much of it—and it may never be possible to say what proportion—appears to have been destined to fuel the military apparatus of the English empire. What seems clear, however, is that although this considerably enhanced the economic welfare of the ruling class, its implications for the working class were far more ambiguous. While there is little doubt that the patriotic sideshows that accompanied imperial wars and conquests did much to diminish class division at home, there is no particular reason to believe that they contributed to any significant material enhancement of urban, industrial life in terms of the shelter, employment, or diet of working people.

The Economy of Feast and Famine

While England was creating its international division of labor, the United States, with its extensive forests and vast grasslands, much of them later transformed into great grain-producing regions, was largely self-sufficient. Indeed, for a long time in the late 19th century it supplied considerable quantities of meat—salted, tinned, and refrigerated—and grain and flour to England. (In 1885 these exports included 288 million pounds of bacon, 20.5 million pounds of salted beef, 94.2 million pounds of ham, and 85.4 million pounds of fresh meat [JRASE 1887:xxiv]; between 1875 and 1889, over 90 percent of the fresh beef imported into Britain was from the United States [Hanson 1938:70].)

I have described elsewhere (Ross 1980) the various interweaving strands of the process by which the United States, evolving into an industrial capitalist nation-state, was itself impelled to explore food resources beyond its immediate territory. For all the great transformations that this entailed, however, it is important, in light of earlier discussion, to note the extent to which the respective roles of cattle and pigs continue to depend on relatively persistent ecological conditions. Thus, with swine today largely supported by grain, the distribution and intensity of hog rearing is ultimately governed by the soil and climatic factors that affect grain production. In contrast, although beef cattle must be fattened for market in feed-lots, forages constitute over 70 percent of beef cattle feed, agriculture having largely reached—if not exceeded—the limits of its effective distribution (Thomas and Hopkins 1983:13), and range and pasture still accounting for one-third of the land in the continental United States (Fowler 1961:30; Hodgson 1976:627–29). The question of whether grain is eventually employed to feed cattle or swine is itself in large measure a function of the size of the corn surplus and of various other factors—for example, the cost of fertilizer—that affect corn prices. This, in turn, means that the price of corn is a cardinal factor in determining the relative supply and, hence, the price of pork and beef, which in turn is one of the major proximate determinants of consumption patterns (Ross 1980).

Nonetheless, given the persisting importance of climatic, edaphic, and other environmental factors, it would be fatuous to suggest that the ecological conditions involved in patterns of diet in the United States have not been closely interwoven with the character of the economy that deploys them—an economy, moreover, that, like that of England, is not restricted to its own territorial limits. The reasons for this are far too complicated to detail in the present paper. But it must be remembered that the U.S. economy was never autonomous, that it originated as a constituent in an Atlantic mercantile economy (North 1966), and that, as a result, the development of its indigenous resources was conditioned from the start, not just by the character of those resources, but by external economic and political forces as well. These have remained a potent influence ever since and, indeed, have intensified as the world capitalist system has become more integrated over the last century through advances in transport and communication (Ross 1980).

What I wish to emphasize here, however, is how the rise of U.S. monopoly capitalism introduced powerful new factors in the determination of the American diet. With the increasing centralization of the U.S. food industry, a process that dates back to the late 19th century, there came about an increasing amalgamation of political and economic power. (The most visible manifestations of this are the career trajectories of individuals who have moved back and forth between governmental offices and corporation boardrooms and the figures from major corporations who dominate important national and foreign policy-making committees [Domhoff 1970:111–55]. An excellent example was former secretary of agriculture Earl Butz, who had previously been a director of Ralston-Purina, Stokely-Van Camp, and other companies (Finger et al. 1974:153). One result has been that the political and military leverage of the state has been deployed to enlarge corporate markets and to expand their sources of raw materials, not necessarily because those resources are unavailable domestically, but because it may be more profitable to acquire or process them abroad. If that means that such products—whether food or manufactures—can be marketed in the United States more cheaply and more widely than home-produced varieties, it is profit rather than patriotism that has priority. (By the same token, consumers are more apt to buy cheaper products, regardless of their point of origin.)

Indeed, one of the most important consequences of the increasing intensification of capitalist production in regard to food has been precisely that "modern agriculture has become, first and foremost, the production of profits and only incidentally the production of agricultural products" (Greenfield Popular Union n.d.). We have already noted this shift in its embryonic form among pre-industrial peoples drawn into capitalist relations, who have come to hunt certain animals at least as much to sell their skins as to consume their flesh. This trend has obviously advanced much further under modern industrial capitalism, where few people participate directly in actual food production and must depend instead on the profit-seeking strategies of surrogate food-producers. These, moreover, have evolved into enormous corporations controlling vast resources whose distribution transcends any specific national or cultural boundaries and whose use is dictated by many imperatives other than that of maximizing food output. As an example of how this has affected consumer options: up until the late 19th century, pigs tended to predominate over cattle in the United States because they were more efficient meat-producing animals. It was especially important, when farming was largely in the hands of modestly capitalized holdings, that 70 to 75 percent of a pig was edible, compared with 50 to 55 percent of a steer (Thompson and Kilbourn 1941:80). The giant meat-processing companies that arose in the 1880s, however, were able to circumvent some of the risks that plagued small farmers, such as fluctuations in the price of grain, by getting into the feed-grain business. They were also, perhaps more significantly, in a position to invest considerable capital in developing profitable uses for former waste products of slaughtering. As these uses—fertilizers, pharmaceuticals, soap, shoe manufacturing—became increasingly lucrative, indeed as they became "the gold mine of the [packing] industry" (Clemen 1923:347), the fact that less of a steer was actually edible than a pig made the former animal potentially more profitable (Ross 1980). This, in turn, played a major role in shifting the base of mass-produced meat from pork to beef.

The dietary implications of corporate management of food resources went dramatically further, however, as the evolution of industrial capitalism shattered any vestigial boundaries between food production and other sectors of economic life and relegated food to the status of commodity rather than that of nutrient (a transformation that is often painfully obvious when one studies the ingredients of "food" sold in a modern supermarket). Today, as a result of the great acceleration of capital concentration, even such former giants of the U.S. food industry as Armour and Swift have become subsidiaries of even more powerful and more widely diversified holding companies, themselves usually embedded in a complex network of interlocking directorships of companies embracing a diverse array of economic specialties (Ross 1980). Through such financial interconnections, the activities of corporations involved in food production are necessarily circumscribed by numerous countervailing pressures that require food to be weighed in the accounts against alternative strategies for enhancing corporate profits, ranging from oil-drilling to launching telecommunications satellites. Thus, at the end of the day, when a company such as Dow Chemical produces lettuce or Greyhound (which owns Swift), meat, food producing must be regarded essentially as financially opportunistic. As such, it is inherently vulnerable to displacement at some point by more cost-effective rivals for capital investment. Whether agriculture or the quality of diet is the worse for having temporarily benefited company shareholders is not on evidence an overriding consideration, least of all for the relatively small number of great banks that maintain ultimate controlling interest in such companies and therefore effectively guide the destiny of the U.S. diet (Ross 1980:211). Under such conditions, it is certainly impossible to argue that the economy is organized in such a way as to optimize food production.

The implications of this situation are far-reaching. On the one hand, it has been instrumental in dramatically reducing by many millions of acres the amount of land under cultivation in the United States (Greenfield Popular Union n.d.:291). On the other, it has transformed the quality of subsistence in many underdeveloped countries where U.S.-based multinationals have extended their activities because land and labor are cheaper and more readily controlled and where they may take practical advantage of and, indeed, shape the geopolitical strategies of the U.S. government. The classic illustrations of this process are the so-called banana republics of Central America; but today U.S. agribusiness companies range over the globe—from R. J. Reynolds–Del Monte in Mexico to Libby in Kenya (though the latter is now owned by Nestlé, a Swiss conglomerate).

Nonetheless, Latin America has always represented a special domain where U.S. economic interests have been particularly domineering and where more than three-fourths of U.S. agribusiness subsidiaries in the Third World currently operate (Burbach and Flynn 1980:108). Even where U.S. companies are

41

not directly involved, it is still often the policy of U.S. aid programs, or loan programs that the United States dominates, to develop local or regional resources in a direction that has the advantage of North American business at heart (U.S. Congress 1984:96–97). As a result, between 1964 and 1973, 87 percent of government credit in Guatemala ended up financing production for export (Burbach and Flynn 1980:104). Similarly, as a consequence of the use of investment capital from the U.S.-dominated Inter-American Development Bank, Costa Rica was encouraged to increase the cattle raising, with the result that between 1962 and 1972, beef rose as a proportion of major exports from 2.9 to 10.0 percent (DeWitt 1977:134–35; see Chapter 22). Costa Rica has not been alone: during the 1960s and 1970s, beef production increased significantly in most Central American countries, disturbing vast areas of forest and displacing subsistence crops; rising beef exports were accompanied by declining domestic meat consumption in those countries (Myers 1981). In the end, Central American beef exports have amounted to only 1 percent of total U.S. beef consumption, mostly in the fast-food sector, but their impact has been far greater, if only in political terms, when one considers that "it is believed that . . . [such imports] have done more to stem inflation [in the United States] . . . than any other single government initiative" (ibid.:5)—much as food imports did in 19th-century England.

But unlike England's imports at that time, these imports only add to a general excess of protein and fat consumption. One must be clear: there remain sectors of the U.S. population that are undernourished. But to whatever degree cheap beef from Central America facilitates meat consumption by the many who already eat enough, it only contributes to a pattern of consumption that is, on average, in excess of nutritional requirements (Page and Friend 1978:195; and see Chapter 9), especially among males (Rizek and Jackson 1982:148). The ultimate explanation for this level of consumption remains obscure, though I have made tentative suggestions earlier in this paper. For the moment, however, what is more important is the manner in which the U.S. diet is now entangled with geopolitical issues that concern the quality of diet in other countries. Much as English colonialism harvested Irish pork and beef and reduced the Irish themselves to a virtually vegetarian diet, so adding unnecessary fats and protein to the average U.S. diet means depriving others of critical nutritional needs.[5] Even before they began to devote grain-producing land to cattle grazing, the countries of Central America were already suffering from an insufficiency of calories and quality protein, relying on a mixed diet of corn, beans, and rice to provide essential amino acids and energy (Frisancho, Garn, and Ascoli 1970:1225). As the proportions of these elements in the traditional diet have been threatened by changes in land use and declining cultivation (May and McLellan 1972:211), the biological value of the diet as a whole also has been endangered and the risk of protein-energy malnutrition, already present, elevated (Araya, et al., 1981). Moreover, as these countries have sought to compensate for lost subsistence production by importing staples, food prices have tended to rise, compounding the problem of securing an adequate diet among the poor and further increasing the peril of malnutrition (Burbach and Flynn 1980:103–5).

Conclusions

Understanding how the circumstances emerged that created this situation has, on the face of it, taken us far from earlier discussions of diet among foraging populations. But, as I stated at the onset, I intended to explore variation and differentiation in human diet with the aim of confronting the web of social realities in which diet is embedded. That intention hopefully has given an evolutionary continuity to the paper and shed light on some of the persisting forces that, for better or worse, have shaped dietary behavior at the succession of levels of societal development. For one of the more interesting observations to be drawn from the preceding discussion is that at no time in the knowable human past or present has diet been a clear-cut question of nutritional intake. It has always been complicated by a social dimension, and the social relations through which the material questions of diet must be regarded have grown increasingly variegated and influential over time. The result is that although the bio-morphological or genetic constraints underlying human consumption in the broadest sense have not significantly altered, the factors interposed between them and the ultimate dietary configuration of any given human population have multiplied considerably and assumed a pre-eminent role.

Even the recent or contemporary foraging or hunting-horticultural populations that contribute to attempts to reconstruct the early human economy (and, indeed, most of the living non-human primates whose "natural" behavior helps us to model early hominid behavior patterns) live within the orbit of the nation-state and the influence of market economies, and so cannot be viewed as purely "culturally" determined economies—if such entities ever existed. It is interesting, then, that those who maintain that dietary customs emanate from within a discretely defined cultural domain do not restrict their arguments to the more isolated populations, but effectively concede that the matter of cultural determination is, like language, either universal or nothing, that even the inhabitants of the contemporary industrial state must eat what they think. This argument can only achieve, at best, a superficial credibility, and does so only through its resistance to historical analysis and an implicit insistence on the relative historical impermeability of culture. I have sought to demonstrate by example how impoverished this would leave the examination of dietary custom.

43

Another expression of a purely cultural analysis to which I have called attention is the deemphasizing of intra-population variation. One of the dangers of cultural explanation has always been its inclination to summarize human customs in a way that exaggerates the ideological, if not the behavioral, unity of social groups, rather than calling attention to the contradictions and stresses that constitute the essential dynamic of historical process. In doing so, it not only subverts our understanding of history but indeed seems to repudiate it and thus diminishes our comprehension of both the conditions that underlie the need for social and political change and the forces that must be harnessed to realize it. As I noted earlier, one of the reasons for studying human diet is precisely that it can give us an insight into the quality of human life and, in so doing, afford an opportunity to test and question facile judgments about progress and equality. To that extent, at least, it may contribute to a better and more thoughtful understanding of the course toward necessary and productive change. In that respect, anthropology has so much to offer that it would be disheartening if it did not meet the challenge.

Notes

1. Winterhalder, commenting on this particular problem, suggests that over a long enough period of research, the model of dietary breadth will reach identity with "the resources actually captured and consumed" (1981:68). But, this is, at best, an unfalsifiable assumption—after all, one can always claim that the period of research should be just a little longer.

2. Of course, in Western capitalist countries since the industrial revolution, the employment of women outside the home has not been insignificant, but there has tended to be a very high degree of occupational segregation by sex, characterized by notable pay differentials. Moreover, even when women have worked outside the home, they have still tended to assume the major burden of domestic labor as well (Oakley 1981:163–86).

3. This is true even for most women of the upper class, where, as in the instance of the contemporary United States, class power is "based upon large corporate wealth that is looked after by male members of the intermarrying families that are its basis" (Domhoff 1970:56).

4. Variety remains a significant distinction between the diets of the rich and the poor. A recent survey of eating patterns of pregnant women in Hampstead and Hackney, respectively a well-to-do and very poor part of London, indicates that whereas the more affluent are eating as many as 32 different foods per day (often in salads), the poor consume about 12 or 13 (Phillips 1984:10). The general lack of variety that came to characterize working-class consumption in the last century probably was one of the reasons for their affection for the new sauces and relishes (whose very lists of ingredients described the vastness of the Empire) that added a necessary piquancy to an otherwise bland and stodgy diet.

5. It should be noted, of course, that it is not only U.S. companies that have this effect in Latin America. As Burbach and Flynn comment, "Land that once produced blackbeans in Brazil is now being used to grow the soybeans that are turned into animal feed to fatten cattle for the Japanese market" (1980:105).

References Cited

Araya, Hector, et al.
    1981   Nutritive Value of Basic Foods and Common Dishes of Guatamala Rural Populations. *Ecology of Food and Nutrition* 11:171–76.

Basso, E.
    1973   *The Kalapalo Indians of Central Brazil.* New York: Holt, Rinehart and Winston.

Behrens, C.
    1981   Time Allocation and Meat Procurement Among the Shipibo Indians of Eastern Peru. *Human Ecology* 9:189–220.

Berkes, F., and C. Farkas
    1978   Eastern James Bay Cree Indians: Changing Patterns of Wild Food Use and Nutrition. *Ecology of Food and Nutrition* 7:155–72.

Bhatia, B.
    1967   *Famines in India: A Study of Some Aspects of the Economic History of India (1860–1965).* London: Asia Publishing House.

Blum, J.
    1978   *The End of the Old Order in Rural Europe.* Princeton: Princeton University Press.

Bolton, J.
    1972   Food Taboos Among the Orang Asli in West Malaysia: A Potential Nutritional Hazard. *American Journal of Clinical Nutrition.* 25:789–99.

Braudel, F.
    1967   *Capitalism and Material Life, 1400–1800.* New York: Harper and Row.

Buikstra, J.
    1983   Maize: Prehistoric Choice—Contemporary Controversy; or, Maize Misunderstood. Paper read at the Wenner-Gren Foundation Symposium 94, 23–30 October, Cedar Key, Florida.

Burbach, R., and P. Flynn
    1980   *Agribusiness in the Americas.* New York: Monthly Review Press.

Butzer, K.
    1971   *Environment and Archaeology: An Ecological Approach to Prehistory.* Chicago: Aldine.

Carneiro, R.
    1970   The Transition from Hunting to Horticulture in the Amazon Basin. *Proceedings of the Eighth International Congress of Anthropological and Ethnological Sciences,* pp. 244–48. Tokyo: Science Council of Japan.
    1968   Slash and Burn Cultivation among the Kuikuru and Its Implications for

Cultural Development in the Amazon Basin. In *Man in Adaptation: The Cultural Present,* Y. Cohen, ed., pp. 132–45. Chicago: Aldine.

Chagnon, N.
1974   *Studying the Yanomamo.* New York: Holt, Rinehart and Winston.
1979   Mate Competition, Favoring Close Kin and Village Fissioning Among the Yanomamo Indians. In *Evolutionary Biology and Human Social Behavior: An Anthropological Perspective,* N. Chagnon and W. Irons, eds., pp. 86–132. North Scituate, Mass.: Duxbury Press.

Chagnon, N., and R. Hames
1979   Protein Deficiency and Tribal Warfare in Amazonia: New Data. *Science* 203:910–13.

Clark, G.
1947   Sheep and Swine in the Husbandry of Prehistoric Europe. *Antiquity* 21:122–36.

Clastres, P.
1972   The Guayaki. In *Hunters and Gatherers Today,* M. Bicchieri, ed., pp. 138–74. New York: Holt, Rinehart and Winston.

Clemen, R.
1923   *The American Livestock and Meat Industry.* New York: Ronola Press.

Clutton-Brock, J.
1976   The Animal Resources. In *The Archaeology of Anglo-Saxon England,* D. Wilson, ed., pp. 373–92. London: Methuen.

Consulate-General of Uruguay
1983   *The Republic of Uruguay.* London: Edward Stanford.

Crawford, W., and H. Broadley
1938   *The People's Food.* London: William Heinemann.

Darling, F.
1955   *West Highland Survey: An Essay in Human Ecology.* Oxford: Oxford University Press.

Davis, A.
1981   *Women, Race and Class.* London: Women's Press.

DeWitt, R.
1977   *The Inter-American Development Bank and Political Influence with Special Reference to Costa Rica.* New York: Praeger.

Dodd, G.
1856   *The Food of London.* London: Longman, Brown, Green, and Longmans.

Domhoff, G. W.
1970   *The Higher Circles.* New York: Vintage.

Drummond, J., and A. Wilbraham
1958   *The Englishman's Food: A History of Five Centuries of English Diet.* London: Jonathan Cape.

Dublin Mansion House Relief Committee
1881   *The Irish Crisis of 1879–80.* Dublin: Browne and Nolan.

Duby, G.
1972   Medieval Agriculture 900–1500. In *The Fontana Economic History of Europe: The Middle Ages,* C. Cipolla, ed., pp. 175–200. London: Fontana.

1974 *The Early Growth of the European Economy.* Ithaca: Cornell University Press.

Dutt, R.
1940 *India Today.* London: Victor Gollancz.
Dutton, H.
1824 *A Statistical and Agricultural Survey of the County of Galway.* Dublin: Dublin University Press.

Ember, C.
1983 The Relative Decline in Women's Contribution to Agriculture with Intensification. *American Antrhopologist* 85:285–304.

Farwell, B.
1972 *Queen Victoria's Little Wars.* New York: Harper and Row.

Feit, H.
1982 The Future of Hunters Within Nation-States: Anthropology and the James Bay Cree. In *Politics and History in Band Societies,* E. Leacock and R. Lee, eds., pp. 373–411.

Findlater, C.
1802 *General View of the Agriculture of the County of Peebles.* Edinburgh: Archibald Constable.

Finger, B., et al.
1974 Agribusiness Gets the Dollar. *Southern Exposure* 2:150–57.
Forster, R., and O. Ranum
1979 Introduction. In *Food and Drink in History,* R. Forster and O. Ranum, eds., pp. vii–xiii. Baltimore: Johns Hopkins Press.

Fowler, S.
1961 *The Marketing of Livestock and Meat.* Danville: Interstate Printers.
Frisancho, R.; S. Garn; and W. Ascoli
1970 Unequal Influence of Low Dietary Intakes on Skeletal Maturation During Childhood and Adolescence. *American Journal of Clinical Nutrition* 23:1220–27.

Goldman I.
1963 *The Cubeo: Indians of the Northwest Amazon.* Urbana: University of Illinois Press.

Graham, S.
1975 Running and Menstrual Dysfunction: Recent Medical Discoveries Provide New Insights into the Human Division of Labor by Sex. *American Anthropologist* 87:878–82.

Grant, I.
1961 *Highland Folk Ways.* London: Routledge and Kegan Paul.
Greenfield Popular Union
n.d. *At the Crossroads: Agriculture and Agricultural Labor in the Connecticut River Valley.* Turner's Falls, Mass.: Greenfield Popular Union.

Grieve, R.
1972 Problems and Objectives in the Highlands and Islands. In *The Remoter Rural Areas of Britain,* J. Ashton and W. Long, eds., pp. 130–45. Edinburgh: Oliver and Boyd.

Gross, D.
  1975   Protein Capture and Cultural Development in the Amazon. *American Anthropologist* 77:526–49.
Hames, R.
  1979   A Comparison of the Efficiencies of the Shotgun and the Bow in Neotropical Forest Hunting. *Human Ecology* 7:219–52.
Handley, J.
  1953   *Scottish Farming in the Eighteenth Century.* London: Faber and Faber.
Hanson, S.
  1938   *Argentine Meat and the British Market.* Stanford: Stanford University Press.
Harding, R.
  1973   Predation by a Troop of Olive Baboons (*Papio anubis*). *American Journal of Physical Anthropology* 38:587–92.
  1974   The Predatory Baboon. *Expedition* 16:30–39.
Harris, M.
  1977   *Cannibals and Kings: The Origins of Cultures.* New York: Random House.
  1979   *Cultural Materialism: The Struggle for a Science of Culture.* New York: Random House.
Harrison, P.
  1983   *Inside the Inner City.* Harmondsworth: Penguin.
Hassan, F.
  1975   Determination of the Size, Density and Growth Rate of Hunting-Gathering Populations. In *Population, Ecology and Social Evolution,* S. Polgar, ed., pp. 27–52. The Hague: Mouton.
Hawkes, K.; K. Hill; and J. O'Connell
  1982   Why Hunters Gather: Optimal Foraging and the Aché of Eastern Paraguay. *American Ethnologist* 9:379–98.
Hayden, B.
  1984   Resources, Rivalry and Reproduction: The Influence of Basic Resource Characteristics on Reproductive Behavior. In *Culture and Reproduction,* W. Handwerker, ed., pp. 5–21. Boulder: Westview Press.
Henderson, R.
  1811   *A Treatise on the Breeding of Swine, and Curing of Bacon; with Hints on Agricultural Subjects.* Leith: Archibald Allardice.
Hill, K., and K. Hawkes
  1983   Neotropical Hunting Among the Aché of Eastern Paraguay. In *Adaptive Responses of Native Amazonians,* R. Hames and W. Vickers, eds., pp. 139–88. New York: Academic Press.
Hodgson, H.
  1976   Forages, Ruminant Livestock and Food. *BioScience* 26:625–30.
Hoffmann, H.
  1964   Money, Ecology and Acculturation Among the Shipibo of Peru. In *Explorations in Cultural Anthropology,* W. Goodenough, ed., pp. 259–76. New York: McGraw-Hill.

House of Commons
    1836   *Accounts and Papers: Estimates; Army; Navy; Ordnance.* London: Her Majesty's Stationery Office.
    1871   *Accounts and Papers 50: East India.* London: HMSO.
    1878–   *Accounts and Papers: Army Estimates: Army; Militia and Volunteers.*
    79   London: Her Majesty's Stationery Office.
    1888   *Accounts and Papers: 77.* London: HMSO.
Howe, M.
    1972   *Man, Environment and Disease in Britain.* New York: Barnes and Noble.
Izaguirre, B.
    1925   *Historia de las Misiones Franciscanas y Narración de los Progresos de la Geografía en el Oriente del Perú.* Vol. 9. Lima: Imprenta Medalla.
Jackson, J.
    1983   *The Fish People: Linguistic Exogamy and Tukanoan Identity in Northwest Amazonia.* Cambridge: Cambridge University Press.
Jelliffe, D., et al.
    1962   The Children of Hadza Hunters. *Journal of Pediatrics* 60:907–13.
Jewell, P.
    1969   Wild Animals and Their Potential for New Domestication. In *The Domestication and Exploitation of Plants and Animals,* P. Ucko and G. Dimbledy, eds., pp. 101–9. Chicago: Aldine-Atherton.
Journal of the Royal Agricultural Society of England (*JRASE*)
    1887   Statistics Affecting British Agricultural Interests. *JRASE,* 2d ser., 23: i–xxviii.
Katona-Apte, J.
    1975   The Relevance of Nourishment to the Reproductive Cycle of the Female in India. In *Being Female: Reproduction, Power and Change,* D. Raphael, ed., pp. 43–53. The Hague: Mouton.
Keene, A.
    1981   Optimal Foraging in a Nonmarginal Environment: A Model of Prehistoric Subsistence Strategies in Michigan. In *Hunter-Gatherer Foraging Strategies: Ethnographic and Archaeological Analyses,* B. Winterhalder and E. A. Smith, eds., pp. 171–93. Chicago: University of Chicago Press.
Keltie, J.
    1875   *A History of the Scottish Highlands.* Edinburgh: A. Fullarton and Co.
Lea, K.
    1977   *A Geography of Scotland.* Newton Abbot: David and Charles.
Leacock, E.
    1981   *Myths of Male Dominance: Collected Articles on Women Cross-Culturally.* New York: Monthly Review Press.
    1982   Relations of Production in Band Society. In *Politics and History in Band Societies,* E. Leacock and R. Lee, eds., pp. 159–70. Cambridge: Cambridge University Press.
Lee, R.
    1982   Politics, Sexual and Non-Sexual, in an Egalitarian Society. In *Politics and*

History in Band Societies, E. Leacock and R. Lee, eds., pp. 37–59. Cambridge: Cambridge University Press.

Lindenbaum, S.
1979   *Kuru Sorcery: Disease and Danger in the New Guinea Highlands.* Palo Alto: Mayfield.

Little, M., and G. Morren
1976   *Ecology, Energetics and Human Variability.* Dubuque: William C. Brown.

Loveland, F.
1976   Tapirs and Manatees: Cosmological Categories and Social Process Among Rama Indians of Eastern Nicaragua. In *Frontier Adaptations in Lower Central America,* M. Helms and F. Loveland, eds., pp. 67–82. Philadelphia: Institute for the Study of Human Issues.

Lucas, A. T.
1960   Irish Food Before the Potato. *Gwerin* 3(2):8–43.

McCabe, A.
1974   The Standard of Living on Merseyside, 1850–1875. In *Victorian Lancashire,* S. Bell, ed., pp. 127–49. Newton Abbot: David and Charles.

McEwen, J.
1981   *Who Owns Scotland.* Edinburgh: Polygon.

MacKay, F.
1955   *MacNeill of Carskey: His Estate Journal, 1703–1743.* Edinburgh: M. MacDonald.

MacKenzie, D.
1935   *Scottish Folklore and Folk-Life: Studies in Race, Culture and Tradition.* Glasgow: Blackie and Son.

Maher, V.
1981   Work, Consumption, and Authority Within the Household. In *Of Marriage and the Market: Women's Subordination in International Perspective,* K. Young et al., eds., pp. 69–87. London: CSE Books.

Martin, Paul
1985   Prehistoric Overkill: The Global Model. In *Quaternary Extinctions: A Prehistoric Revolution,* P. Martin and R. Klein, eds., pp. 354–403. Tucson: The University of Arizona Press.

May, J., and D. McLellan
1972   *The Ecology of Malnutrition in Mexico and Central America.* New York: Hafner Publishing.

Mayhew, H.
1850   *The Morning Chronicle Survey of Labour and the Poor.* London.

Morton, A. L.
1979   *A People's History of England.* London: Lawrence and Wishart.

Murphy, R., and B. Quain
1955   *The Trumai Indians of Central Brazil.* Monographs of the American Ethnological Society, 24. Locust Valley, New York: J. J. Augustin.

Myers, N.
1981   The Hamburger Connection: How Central America's Forests Become North America's Hamburgers. *Ambio* 10:3–8.

Neel, J.
1977   Health and Disease in Unacculturated Amerindian Populations. In *Health and Disease in Tribal Societies,* K. Elliot and J. Whelan, eds. Amsterdam: Elsevier.

Netting, R.
1981   *Balancing on an Alp: Ecological Change and Continuity in a Swiss Mountain Community.* Cambridge: Cambridge University Press.

Nietschmann, B.
1972a   Hunting and Fishing Focus Among the Miskito Indians, Eastern Nicaragua. *Human Ecology* 1:41–67.
1972b   Hunting and Fishing Productivity of the Miskito Indians, Eastern Nicaragua. *Actas y Memorias de XXXIX Congreso Internacional de Americanistas,* vol. 4, pp. 69–88. Lima: Instituto de Estudios Peruanos.
1973   *Between Land and Water.* New York: Seminar Press.

North, D.
1966   *The Economic Growth of the United States.* New York: W. W. Norton.

Oakley, A.
1981   *Subject Women.* London: Fontana.

Oddy, D.
1970   Working-Class Diets in Late Nineteenth-Century Britain. *Economic History Review* 23:314–23.

O'Dell, A.
1939   *The Historical Geography of the Shetland Islands.* Lerwick: T. and J. Manson.

O'Dell, A., and K. Walton
1962   *The Highlands and Islands of Scotland.* London: Thomas Nelson and Sons.

O'Donovan, J.
1940   *The Economic History of Livestock in Ireland.* Dublin: Cork University Press.

Ogbeide, O.
1974   Nutritional Hazards of Food Taboos and Preferences in Mid-West Nigeria. *American Journal of Clinical Nutrition* 27:213–16.

Oliver, T.
1895   The Diet of Toil. *Lancet,* June 29, pp. 1629–635.

Page, L., and B. Friend
1978   The Changing United States Diet. *BioScience* 28:192–97.

Parsons, J.
1962   The Acorn-Hog Economy of the Oak Woodlands of Southwestern Spain. *Geographical Review* 52(1961):211–35.

Phillips, A.
1984   The Cost of Eating for Two. *Guardian,* June 10.

Pounds, N.
1973   *An Historical Geography of Europe, 450 B.C.–A.D. 1330.* Cambridge: Cambridge University Press.

51

Read, J., and M. Manjón
  1981   *The Great British Breakfast.* London: Michael Joseph.
Reidhead, V.
  1980   The Economics of Subsistence Change. In *Modeling of Prehistoric Subsistence Economies,* T. K. Earle and A. L. Christensen, eds., pp. 141–86. New York: Academic Press.
Rippy, J.
  1959   *British Investments in Latin America, 1822–1949.* Minneapolis: University of Minnesota Press.
Ritchie, J.
  1920   *The Influence of Man on Animal Life in Scotland: A Study in Faunal Evolution.* Cambridge: Cambridge University Press.
Rizek, R., and E. Jackson
  1982   Current Food Consumption Practices and Nutritional Sources in the American Diet. In *American Products in Human Nutrition,* D. Beitz and R. Hansen, eds., pp. 121–62. New York: Academic Press.
Roberts, R.
  1971   *Salford: The Classic Slum.* Harmondsworth: Penguin.
Robertson, J.
  1799   *General View of the Agriculture in the County of Perth.* Perth: Board of Agriculture.
Ross, E.
  1976   *The Achuara Jívaro: Cultural Adaptation in the Upper Amazon.* Ann Arbor: University Microfilms.
  1978a   Food Taboos, Diet and Hunting Strategy: The Adaptation to Animals in Amazon Cultural Ecology. *Current Antrhopology* 19:1–36.
  1978b   The Evolution of the Amazon Peasantry. *Journal of Latin American Studies* 10:193–218.
  1979   Reply to Lizot. *Current Anthropology* 20:151–55.
  1980   Patterns of Diet and Forces of Production: An Economic and Ecological History of the Ascendancy of Beef in the United States Diet. In *Beyond the Myths of Culture: Essays in Cultural Materialism,* E. Ross, ed., pp. 181–225. New York: Academic Press.
  1983   The Riddle of the Scottish Pig. *BioScience* 33:99–106.
Ross, E., and M. Harris
  In press *Death, Sex, and Fertility: Population Regulation in Pre-Industrial and Developing Societies.* New York: Columbia University Press.
Rowbotham, S.
  1983   *Dreams and Dilemmas: Collected Writings.* London: Virago Press.
Rudd, J.
  1982   Introduction to *Her People,* by K. Dayus. London: Virago Press.
Sahlins, M.
  1976   *Culture and Practical Reason.* Chicago: University of Chicago Press.
Salaman, R.
  1943   *The Influence of the Potato on the Course of Irish History.* Dublin: Richview Press.

1949   *The History and Social Influence of the Potato.* Cambridge: Cambridge University Press.

Schafer, E.
    1977   T'ang. In *Food in Chinese Culture: Anthropological and Historical Perspectives,* K. Chang, ed., pp. 85–140. New Haven: Yale University Press.

Sharma, D.
    1955   Mother, Child and Nutrition. *Journal of Tropical Pediatrics* 1:47–53.

Shorter, E.
    1982   *A History of Women's Bodies.* Harmondsworth: Penguin.

Sinclair, J.
    1796   *The Statistical Account of Scotland, Drawn up from the Observations of the Ministers of the Different Parishes.* Edinburgh: William Creech.

Skelley, A.
    1977   *The Victorian Army at Home.* London: Croom Helm.

Smith, J.
    1798   *General View of the Agriculture of the County of Argyll.* Edinburgh: Mundell and Son.

Smout, T.
    1969   *A History of the Scottish People, 1560–1830.* London: Collins.

Smurthwaite, D.
    1980   A recipe for Discontent: The Victorian Soldier's Cuisine. In *Report, 1979–80,* 41–54. London: National Army Museum.

Speth, J., and S. Scott
    1984   The Role of Large Mammals in Late Prehistoric Horticultural Adaptations: The View from Southeastern New Mexico. Manuscript.

Speth, J., and K. Spielmann
    1983   Energy Source, Protein Metabolism, and Hunter-Gatherer Subsistence Strategies. *Journal of Anthropological Archaeology* 2:1–31.

Stamp, D.
    1975   *Chisholm's Handbook of Commercial Geography.* 19th edition. London: Longman.

Steven, H., and A. Carlisle
    1959   *The Native Pinewoods of Scotland.* Edinburgh: Oliver and Boyd.

Steward, J. H., and A. Metraux
    1948   Tribes of the Peruvian and Ecuadorian Montaña. In *Handbook of South American Indians,* vol. 3, J. H. Steward, ed., pp. 535–656. Washington, D.C.: Smithsonian Institution.

Stocks, A.
    1983   Cocamilla Fishing: Patch Modification and Environmental Buffering in the Amazon *Varzea.* In *Adaptive Responses of Native Amazonians,* R. Hames and W. Vickers, eds., pp. 239–67. New York: Academic Press.

Tanner, A.
    1979   *Bringing Home Animals: Religious Ideology and Mode of Production of the Mistassini Cree Hunters.* Canada: Memorial University of Newfoundland.

Teleki, G.
　　1975　　Primate Subsistence Patterns: Collector-Predators and Gatherer-Hunters. *Journal of Human Evolution* 4:125–84.
Thomas, G., and L. Hopkins
　　1983　　The Ecologic Aspects of Animal Protein Production. *Nutrition Today,* July–August, pp. 9–29.
Thompson, E.
　　1977　　*Whigs and Hunters: The Origin of the Black Act.* Harmondsworth: Penguin.
Thompson, R., and G. Kilbourn
　　1941　　The Meat Packing Industry. In *The Development of American Industries: Their Economic Significance,* J. Glover and W. Cornell, eds., pp. 63–83. New York: Prentice-Hall.
Trant, H.
　　1954　　Food Taboos in East Africa. *Lancet* 2:703–5.
United Nations, Department of International Economic and Social Affairs
　　1981　　*1979/80 Statistical Yearbook.* New York: UN.
United States Congress, Office of Technology Assessment
　　1984　　*Technologies to Sustain Tropical Forest Resources.* Washington, D.C.: U.S. Government Printing Office.
Up de Graff, F. W.
　　1923　　*Head Hunters of the Amazon: Seven Years of Exploration and Adventures.* Garden City, New York: Garden City Publishing.
Watson, J.
　　1964　　Foreword. In *The Third Statistical Account of Scotland: The County of Peebles and the County of Selkirk,* J. Bulloch and J. Urquhart, eds., pp. 7–8. Glasgow: Collins.
Wellin, E.
　　1955　　Maternal and Infant Feeding Practices in a Peruvian Village. *Journal of the American Dietetic Association* 31:889–94.
White, L.
　　1964　　*Medieval Technology and Social Change.* New York: Oxford University Press.
Wilbert, J.
　　1972　　*Survivors of Eldorado: Four Indian Cultures of South America.* New York: Praeger.
Wilson, C.
　　1973　　*Food and Drink in Britain.* London: Constable.
Winterhalder, B.
　　1981　　Foraging Strategies in the Boreal Forest: An Analysis of Cree Hunting and Gathering. In *Hunter-Gatherer Foraging Strategies: Ethnographic and Archaeological Analysis,* B. Winterhalder and E. A. Smith, eds., pp. 66–98. Chicago: University of Chicago Press.
Winterhalder, B., and E. A. Smith (eds.)
　　1981　　*Hunter-Gatherer Foraging Strategies: Ethnographic and Archaeological Analyses.* Chicago: University of Chicago Press.

Wrangham, R.
    1977   Feeding Behaviour of Chimpanzees in Gombe National Park, Tanzania. In *Primate Ecology,* T. Clutton-Brock, ed., pp. 503–38. London: Academic Press.
Wurtman, J., and R. Wurtman
    1983   Studies on the Appetite for Carbohydrates in Rats and Humans. *Journal of Psychiatric Research* 17:213–21.
Yost, J., and P. Kelley
    1983   Shotguns, Blowguns, and Spears: The Analysis of Technological Efficiency. In *Adaptive Responses of Native Amazonians,* R. Hames and W. Vickers, eds., pp. 189–224. New York: Academic Press.
Young, C.
    1979   *The Royal Forests of Medieval England.* Leicester: Leicester University Press.

2

MARVIN HARRIS

Foodways: Historical Overview and Theoretical Prolegomenon

THE RECENT HISTORY OF ANTHROPOLOGICAL APPROACHES TO food preferences and aversions is necessarily a history of divergent research strategies. Idealist approaches have emphasized the discovery and appreciation of foodways in which emic, mental, and superstructural factors appear dominant. Materialist approaches have sought to relate foodways to biopsychological, etic, and behavioral variables. Eclectic approaches have sought a middle ground, acknowledging the general influence of material variables but allowing for a number—or even a majority—of exceptions.

Cultural Idealist Approaches

In general, cultural idealists explain variations in food preferences and aversions as a consequence of "culture" (by which they mean the learned emic and mental components of social life). This strategy has resulted in three kinds of explanatory propositions: (1) food customs are said to be the consequence of idiographic-historical continuities that regress to an unknown beginning; (2) they are the consequence of arbitrary "taste," chance, or whim; (3) they are the functional symbolic or behavioral correlates or expressions of given systems of values and beliefs. To the extent that none of these varieties of propositions invoke selection principles that can account for specific observed variations in food customs (as well as uniformities) or for the occurrence of the constraining values and beliefs, they constitute a very weak form of scientific statement or none at all.

Materialist Strategies

Cultural materialist strategies are based on the assumption that biopsychological, environmental, demographic, technological, and political-economic factors exert a powerful influence on the foods that can be produced and consumed by any given human population. However difficult to measure, there are nutritional needs that must be satisfied and psycho-chemical limits of taste and toxic tolerances that must be observed. Moreover, we know from the study of prehistory, history, and ethnography that human diets have undergone a profound series of changes correlated with shifts in basic modes of production. During the later portions of the Paleolithic in both hemispheres, for example, meat appears to have been a focus of much productive effort; in the transitional phases antecedent to agriculture, a broader spectrum of foods was exploited; with the development of intensive agriculture, the essential amino acids were supplied primarily through a combination of grains and legumes; finally, the spread of industrial agriculture has led fo a renewed focus on animal foods. We also know from the study of prehistory, history, and ethnography that divergences in these broad patterns are often correlated with particular local conditions of climate, soil, fauna, and flora. The convergent and divergent trajectories of human foodways therefore invite nomothetic explanations to no lesser degree than other aspects of culture or the evolution of the earth and its bioforms.

These preliminary generalizations may appear obvious and hence uninteresting, but they are the beginning, not the end, of the materialist thrust. It is reasonable to expect that more complex and interesting generalizations concerning similarities and differences in food patterns should be discoverable. To operate on the assumption that they are not discoverable in any given instance of a preference or aversion seems justified only as a paradigm of last resort— that is, one to be invoked only after the formulation, testing, and rejection of plausible nomothetic alternatives.

Idealist Approaches: Food As Thought

Starting with Lévi-Strauss's (1963:89) observation that "natural species are chosen not because they are 'good to eat' but because they are 'good to think,'" it has become intellectually fashionable to give research priority to the meaning of food and to its mental, ideological, and symbolic functions. Foodways in this idealist tradition convey messages whose decipherment depends on knowing little or nothing about biochemical, nutritional, economic, or other

58

material aspects of comestibles. To the extent that food preferences or aversions can be explained, their explanation "must be sought not in the nature of the food items" but rather in the system of signs, the fundamental semantic structures of a "people's underlying thought pattern" (Soler 1979:129). The proposition that food is good for thought before it is good to eat has many ardent supporters: "Food has little to do with nourishment. We do not eat what we eat because it is convenient or because it is good for us or because it is practical or because it tastes good" (Welsch 1981:369).

For Lévi-Strauss food is a kind of language whose attributes are "good to think" because they unconsciously express fundamental themes in the human psyche. Like languages, cuisines convey messages through a small number of universal binary contrasts, namely, raw/rotten, raw/cooked, cooked/rotten. For "structural" analysis, these can be joined to form a "culinary triangle" in terms of which the "structure" of every culture's foodways can be specified (Lévi-Strauss 1965). On the basis of a food's proximity to the raw, cooked, or rotten corner of the triangle, one can discern something about its social meaning. Roasted foods, for example, because of their direct contact with fire, are farthest away from rotten foods. Therefore, roasts are served to honored guests rather than boiled meat. The latter is closer to the rotten vertex, since water intercedes between the food and the flame. No empirical support has been found for the universal or even singular presence of Lévi-Strauss's culinary triangle (Goody 1982:215–20). But if such a universal "structure" existed, its significance for understanding preferences, aversions, and foodways in general would be minimal, since nowhere does Lévi-Strauss pose the question of why the behavioral expressions of cooking, roasting, and boiling involve particular meats, vegetables, beverages, and so on in different societies.

Food as Meaning: Mary Douglas

For Douglas, as for Lévi-Strauss, the main task of anthropologists interested in foodways is the decipherment of the cryptic messages they contain. To explain the ancient Israelite swine taboo, one does not need to study the natural history, archaeology, ecology, and economy of swine production, nor the nutritive role and value of pork. All the important properties of swine reside in the mental images of ancient Israelite culture as revealed in the Pentateuch. Douglas's explanation rests on three such properties: (1) swine were taxonomically anomalous and hence unclean because even though they have cloven hoofs, they do not chew the cud like "proper ungulates"; (2) swine, occasional consumers of carrion, were seen as carnivores, animals whose consumption was inappropriate for God's people; (3) the taboo on pork was a marker and intensifier of national identity, separating the Israelites from their neighbors (Douglas 1966, 1972). It is obvious that Douglas's inferences about Israelite mental life are essentially untestable. (How can we know what the priests of Leviticus really were thinking about beyond what is preserved in the Bible?) Moreover, even if the decoding operations are correct, there is no nomothetic output. The question of why the Israelites got it into their heads that "proper ungulates" must be cud-chewers is never broached. Given that in many cultures the pig is venerated rather than abominated, the taxonomic scheme of Leviticus is more likely to be a consequence of an aversion to swine than a cause of it. This observation applies as well to the rejection of carnivorous animals. An idiographic approach to this aversion seems wholly unjustified, since there are scores of other cultures that avoid carnivores. Indeed, Hayden (1981:398) notes that "one of the more remarkable features of hunter/gatherer subsistence is the uniformly low priority of carnivores and raptors as a human food resource." Finally, as far as Israelite social identity is concerned, pig avoidance was not an unambiguous symbol. Enemies such as the Babylonians and Phoenicians also had a swine taboo; among the Egyptians there were Osirian cults that abominated pigs (Darby, Ghalioungui, and Grivetti 1977:195); nor is it likely that pork was consumed in significant quantities by the Israelites' pastoral neighbors.

More recently Douglas (1984) has turned to deciphering patterns of food ensembles—meals and dishes. Expectations concerning what is a meal and when various kinds of meals ought to take place are cross-culturally variable. Douglas has studied the emic abstract and ideological dimensions of this subject, concentrating on the ideal patterning of main dishes and subordinate dishes, everyday meals and extraordinary meals, as expressions of social values (e.g., hospitality, ethnic solidarity, ritual) entirely independently of economic or nutritional-dietary factors.

The scientific value of relentlessly dematerializing food and cooking remains obscure. According to Douglas (1984:22), this approach has "special strengths" for cultural analysis "wherever we are interested in measures of behavior that are independent of income or wealth." But why would anyone propose to study foodways in stratified societies independently of income and wealth?

In challenging approaches that give priority to the semantic and symbolic aspects of foodways, materialists do not seek to deny the fact that food conveys meaning as well as nourishment. Rather, the issue is the extent to which the selection of foods to convey meaning is an autonomous process that can be understood apart from the processes that are responsible for selecting foods for nourishment; or, in more extreme forms of idealism, whether the selection of foods to convey meaning actually dominates the selection of foods for nourishment. Materialists find formulations of either genre especially unacceptable if they rule out infrastructural or political-economic causation without exploring any of the potentially relevant variables. Sahlins (1976:171), for example, has proposed that the preference for beef in the United States expresses a culturally arbitrary designation of cattle as a symbol of wealth and virility that dominates the allocation of agricultural resources and capital. As Ross (1980) has shown, this is a completely upside-down version of how beef achieved its gastronomic pre-eminence in the United States. Contrary to Sahlin's proposal that the preference for beef extends back to Indo-European ancestors, the etic preference for beef over pork in the United States is of rather recent origin. The designation of beef as a symbol of wealth, generosity, and virility did not generate the ecological, technological, demographic, and political ascendancy of the beef industry; it was the ascendancy of the industry as a result of those processes that has bestowed upon beef its special symbolic pre-eminence. It is not the magic of arbitrary symbols that restricts the composition of hamburgers to beef and only beef (and beef fat), but the beef industry's political clout in Congress and the Department of Agriculture (Harris 1986:125). Similarly one-sided and premature idealist conclusions characterize much of the treatment of South American tropical forest animal foodways, but space does not permit more than a passing reference (Kensinger and Kracke 1981; cf. Ross 1978; 1980).

Materialists accept the fact that some aspects of foodways express arbitrary, aesthetic, symbolic, and ritual preferences, but in view of the evidence of the constraining effects of biology, ecology, economy, and politics on foodway (see below), extreme skepticism is warranted whenever it is alleged that arbitrary aesthetic, symbolic, and ritual aspects of culture have shaped major food complexes.

The principal objection to such idealist explanations of foodways is that they tend to shut off scientifically productive inquiry. Nothing is more facile and intellectually sterile than to attribute a foodway to "culture" in the guise of a given set of ideologically determined "tastes" or values. Thus, it is scientifically inadmissible to attribute beef rejection in India to the Hindu religion without enquiring why the Hindu religion is different from Islam, Judaism, and Christianity in this regard (e.g., Simons 1982:209). Ditto for attributing Aztec state cannibalism to Aztec religion (Montellano 1978) without inquiring why cannibalism is not found in other major state religions. The acceptability of "religion" as an answer to why people behave in certain ways rather than others may reveal a deep-seated cultural commitment on the part of Western social scientists not to press the issue of material causality against the grain of revealed and unexaminable religious truths. To materialists it is no more acceptable to explain foodways in terms of religious precepts than it is to explain human origins in terms of creationism.

Eclecticism

While appearing to stand midway between the idealist and materialist positions (or in both at once), eclecticism actually strongly biases the interpretation of particular foodways in favor of idiographic and idealist explanations. The reason for this is that the discovery of an absence of nomothetic and material causation requires less effort than the discovery of its presence. The likelihood of explaining a particular foodway of nomothetic-materialist terms is directly related to the degree to which researchers are committed to such an explanation. This does not mean that researchers fudge their data or deliberately overlook negative evidence in order to fulfill their paradigmatic expectations. Rather, it means that the limited intellectual and material investment that anthropological and other foodways researchers are willing or able to make in a particular case rules out the possibility of an even-handed exploration of idealist and materialist options. The recent history of anthropological studies of foodways demonstrates that the manifestations of paradigmatic commitments are always more sharply contrastive in practice than in principle. For example, under eclectic auspices, mid-century anthropologists amassed a corpus of food avoidances and preferences designed to prove the futility of materialist principles. These cases were uncritically incorporated as pedagogical centerpieces in graduate education and continue to serve as a model for eclectic analysis, as we shall see in subsequent sections.

Irrational and Harmful Foodways

Cases demonstrating the ability of arbitrary and irrational cultural beliefs to create anti-economic, thoroughly useless, and harmful foodways have a special significance in the history of anthropological theory and continue to merit attention. At issue is whether foodways that are entirely useless or unambiguously harmful to material well-being occur in great numbers all over the world. Materialists of course admit that not all aspects of foodways functionally enhance human health and well-being. But that a large proportion of foodways would be materially useless and harmful—without material advantage to some group if not to all groups—clashes with the basic principles of cultural selection in materialist paradigms.

Robert Lowie was a prolific collector of anti-economic and harmful foodways during the first half of this century. Lowie had a reputation for hard-nosed empiricism, but on surprisingly slight evidence he repeatedly flaunted examples of what he called the "capricious irrationality" of preferences and aversions involving domestic animals or their products.

Pigs: "Throughout Melanesia the pig greatly affects social prestige without noticeably adding to mass subsistence" (Lowie 1942:541). "It is most important that while swine appear as domestic animals in prehistoric Egypt, not one practical purpose for keeping them has ever come to light" (1938:304).

Cattle as a source of meat: "A Shilluk keeps hundreds of cattle, yet slaughters them so rarely that he is obliged to maintain his hunting techniques for an adequate supply of meat. . . Oxen normally serve no purpose at all" (1960:242). "The Zulu and other Bantu tribes of South Africa . . . hardly ever slaughter their animals except on festive occasions" (1966 [orig. 1917]:82). "But these Negroes, who . . . eschew a beef diet, expend enormous effort on massaging the humps of their beasts and twisting their horns into grotesque shapes" (1960:242).

Cattle as a source of milk: "On the other hand we have the even more astonishing fact that Eastern Asiatics, such as the Chinese, Japanese, Koreans, and Indo-Chinese, have an inveterate aversion to the use of milk" (1966 [orig. 1917]:82). "There are African tribes that churn butter only to smear it as a cosmetic on their bodies" (1938:307).

Sheep and goats: "The Lango . . . will milk neither sheep nor goats. . . . People from sheer acquisitiveness will accumulate vast herds that cannot be economically exploited. . . . The Pangwe keep sheep and goats not to eat them . . . but mainly for the pure pleasure of possession" (1938:307).

Horses: "We expend thousands for breeding race horses but have never taken up the milking of mares" (1938:306–7).

Pigeons: "The Bambala take good care of their pigeons . . . yet 'they serve no utilitarian purpose'" (1938:304).

Chickens: "In Burma and in its vicinity—the probable ancient center of chicken-raising—poultry are not primarily kept for utilitarian purposes, and the eggs are hardly, if ever, consumed. What the natives mainly want is to use the thigh bones of the cock for divination" (1938:303–4).

Dingoes: "The Australian kept his dog, the dingo, without training it to catch game or render any service whatsoever" (1938:305).

Materialist Refutations

These extravagant claims set the stage for ecological and materialist approaches to foodways at the end of the 1950s. It is important to remember that Lowie's rejection of utilitarian components was absolute and that this invited refutations that merely sought to demonstrate some degree of functional utility in order to justify the materialist strategy. Ultimately, of course, the success of materialist approaches to foodways requires not merely that there be benefits rooted in infrastructure and political economy, but that these outweigh the costs. In order to advance to this more difficult and problematic assessment, however, there had to be a phase of research in which it was sufficient merely to show that the irrationalist claims were false as stated.

The Melanesian pig problem was one of the first to be scrutinized and reinterpreted (Vayda, Leeds, and Smith 1961). Mass ritual slaughters of pigs were seen as both a provider of animal fats and proteins and a systematic regulator of warfare and environmental depletions (Rappaport 1967, 1984; cf. Luzbetak 1954). Criticism has been directed at the strength and effectiveness of the homeostatic functions attributed to the peace-slaughter-warfare cycle (McArthur 1977), but no one would wish to return to Lowie's view that pigs are raised in Melanesia "without noticeably adding to mass subsistence." As Morren (1977) points out, through inter-group rivalries and exchange, the Maring ritual cycle promotes increased meat production in a region conspicuously deficient in animal protein (Hornabrook 1977:55). Although there is waste, not everyone bears its burden equally, giving rise to political power based on the leverage of pig distributions and exchanges.

Another focus of reinterpretation was the East African cattle complex (Deshler 1965; Schneider 1957). It was established that, contra Lowie: (1) the restriction of beef eating to ritual occasions did not necessarily mean that meat would be available in larger quantities without the ritual restrictions; (2) concentration on milk rather than meat or blood might be energetically advantageous; and (3) maintenance of large numbers of poorly fed animals can be a form of "banking" against drought and other disasters. As for Lowie's total-loss dingo: (1) dingoes are sometimes (not never) used in the hunt; (2) more often, semi-feral individuals are followed and deprived of their prey; (3) the symbiosis between dingo and hunter is enhanced by keeping them as pets and letting them loose to breed; and (4) dingoes are eaten as emergency food (Harris 1986:186–89; Meggitt 1965).

Although Lowie did not mention the sacred cattle of India, the prohibition on the slaughter and consumption of beef among Hindus is a classic example of an allegedly useless and harmful foodway that on closer scrutiny turned out to have many utilities and benefits (Harris 1966; Vaidyanathan et al. 1982). Lowie's assertions about the costliness of the Chinese aversion to milk and the irrational aversion to mare's milk in the United States were also challenged (Harris 1968:366–70; 1985:88–108). It goes without saying, of course, that Lowie had no inkling that the digestibility of cow's milk is linked to population-genetic differences in lactase production among adults (see below). Although the explanation of Chinese milk aversion involves more than lactose malabsorbtion (Harris 1977:149–51; 1986:130–53), past ignorance of this factor shows why premature "irrationalist" conclusions must be rejected.

Finally, the low level of Lowie's resistance to inaccurate data can be seen in his assertion that there was "not one practical purpose for keeping swine" in ancient Egypt. Swine were in fact eaten in dynastic times by followers of Seth, and their services were in demand for seeding and manuring crops" (Darby et al. 1977:171–99).

Massa White Sorghum Taboo

Anthropologists continue to make a special point of identifying what appear to be irrational and uneconomic foodways, often throwing facts and logic to the wind in order to do so. One recent example worth considering at some length is Igor de Garine's (1980) claim that the Massa of the Cameroon reject a variety of sorghum that would double or triple their output, solely because they wish to remain culturally distinct from their neighbors. Garine is opposed to studies in which "the material aspects of food and nutrition are dealt with excellently but no observations are made on the underlying [*sic*] symbolic systems." He is also opposed to studies where although "food themes are analyzed at length through traditional mythology, nothing is available about food economy and daily intake" (ibid.:40).

Garine's approach, like Lowie's, is an avowedly eclectic one that seeks to combine both points of view: "Before attempting to seek correlations, it is necessary to establish the facts and describe food and nutrition in a given society from as many angles as possible, and not merely give priority to some aspect of reality whether it be mythology or biomass" (1980:41). According to Garine (1979:81), the Massa, Tupuri, and Mussey live close together within the "same natural milieu," have the same technologies, know about each other's cultures, intermarry frequently, and share a common origin. Yet their foodways are distinct. Garine attributes these differences to ideological factors: "They all hold more or less the same cards but they play them differently according to motivations which are mainly of cultural origin" (1980:53).

Nothing is plainer in Garine's own accounts, however, than that the groups do *not* hold the same etic, behavioral, ecological, economic, or political cards. The Massa hold the areas closest to the river bank, which historically offered the best opportunities for cattle pasture and fishing; the Tupuri live along smaller streams and wetlands suitable for intensive agriculture but not for fishing; the Mussey have access neither to large rivers nor to wetlands. These contrastive ecological-economic arrangements did not result from cultural whim but from a process of migration and political-military confrontation over access

65

to the most favorable habitats: "The bloodiest fights between neighboring groups have been over access to permanent water supplies, dry-season pastures, and the fertile soils that surround them" (Garine 1978:44). Arriving first, the Massa "occupied the best alluvial soils close to permanent water" (Garine 1980:49); the Tupuri were next, and the Massey last. All three groups, however, are politically subordinate ot the Fulani and to the state governments of either Chad or Cameroon, which have instituted various schemes for hydro-agricultural development and compulsory cotton planting and rice cultivation.

According to Garine, southern Massa formerly refused to plant "late white pricked sorghum" (*S. dura*), which is planted by their neighbors, the Tupuri. "He who dared plant white sorghum would die before the ripening of the crop" (Garine 1980:67). Yet late white pricked sorghum is a higher-yielding variety than the red sorghum (*S. caudatum*) that is the traditional cereal staple of the Massa. Garine insists that although the southern Massa possessed the hydromorphic soils required by *S. dura,* they refused for "a long time" to cultivate it; had they done so, it would have "doubled the yield and considerably attenuated the harshness of the hungry season" (Garine 1979:83). The reason for this irrational behavior was that by acting "non-adaptively" from a biological point of view they were able to affirm their identity as "Massa" against the pressure of their white-sorghum-eating neighbors, the Tupuri.

Given the fact that the Massa traditionally emphasized cattle raising and fishing rather than agriculture, one would like to know how the substitution of late white for early red sorghum would have affected the seasonal rhythms of the Massa subsistence pattern as compared with the subsistence patterns of the Tupuri. However, even on the evidence presented, Garine succeeds in demonstrating not the arbitrariness of cultural selection, but just the opposite. We are told that the techniques for planting late white sorghum derive from the Fulani overlords of the Massa, Tupuri, and Mussey. As a result of population increase, compulsory planting of cash crops such as peanuts, cotton, and rice, poisoning of fish stocks with pesticide run-off, and the development of a cash economy, all three groups have had to change their traditional mode of subsistence. All three have taken over the planting of white sorghum: "Today pricked white sorghum has spread to most of the groups where adequate soil is available. Conversely, traditional red sorghum appears as backward, heavy to digest and dirty" (Garine 1980:67). What this case illustrates is not "arbitraire culturelle"—Garine's term—but selection against an aversion that significantly impeded the optimization of resource use under altered infrastructural and political-economic conditions. This is not to deny that food taboos are used by ethnic groups to intensify their social identity, but to predict that such markers will be selected against if they result in punitive economic deprivations (see below).

Pregnancy and Post-Partum Avoidances

Some of the most notorious cases of allegedly irrational and harmful foodways are associated with pregnancy and post-partum food aversions. Numerous instances of foodway interdictions seem to be aimed at lowering rather than raising the nutritional status of pregnant and lactating women. Protein needs increase during pregnancy, "yet repeatedly we have found taboos, superstitions, and prohibitions that serve to eliminate or reduce potential sources of protein from the diet of the menstruating, pregnant, or lactating woman" (Wood 1979:154). Despite the widespread concurrence by anthropologists that such practices often endanger the health of mother and neonates, there are few if any reliable studies that support this veiwpoint. It cannot be doubted that some pregnancy and lactation aversions reduce the consumption of nutritious foods. But this does not necessarily mean that the diet is impaired: it might even be improved if alternative foods are available or if preferred foods are added. Moreover, aversions associated with nutritionally impaired diets are not necesarily the cause of the impairment; that is, removal of the aversion may not lead to any improvement if there are prior material restraints on the availability of the interdicted items.

In a study based on interviews with 1,200 women in Tamil Nadu, Ferro-Luzzi (1980a) identified over a hundred food avoidances of menstruation, pregnancy, and lactation. The information was collected by asking the women if they avoided the items on a prepared list. No attempt was made to check the correspondence between emic responses and etic observations, nor was there any comparison of the etic diet of women before they became pregnant with their diets after they became pregnant or after they gave birth. Thus, it is impossible on the basis of Ferro-Luzzi's data to say anything definitive about the effect of the taboos on nutrition and health.

Nonetheless, if we suppose some kind of positive correlation between the emic aversions and etic performance, Ferro-Luzzi's data suggest, contrary to her own convictions, that the taboos per se result in very few, if any, critical nutritional deprivations. For example, out of 1,067 women who were customarily non-vegetarian (who at meat, fish, or eggs), only 13 percent said that fish should be avoided during pregnancy (Ferro-Luzzi 1980:101–2). Some 97.5 percent of women in all categories approved of the consumption of milk and milk products during pregnancy; of the few who rejected milk products, none rejected milk. Although the total list of avoided fruits was large, the only fruits commonly said to be spurned were papayas and pineapples, neither of which is widely cultivated in Tamil Nadu. The only seed with a high consensus for avoidance was sesame, scarcely a crippling loss, given its expense and the availability of numerous substitutes. The most commonly to-be-avoided grain was *Setari italica,* described as a "poor man's millet which most people prefer not to eat anyway." The most to-be-avoided pulse was borregram (*Dolichos biflorus*), again a rarely grown and unesteemed item. Finally, it should be emphasized that "restrictions on other cereals and pulses were extremely rare" (ibid.: 107), thereby ensuring the *possibility* of maintaining an adequate diet, regardless of the elicited pregnancy aversions. ("Possibility" is emphasized because dietary regimens in India are for most people, including pregnant women, at best marginal. But the question here is whether food aversions create or exacerbate this situation.)

Turning to the post-partum and lactation periods, we find a more comprehensive set of proscriptions. Yet there still is no indication that faithful compliance with the list of items to be avoided would necessarily result in the lowering of nutritional standards. Even if the nursing mother actually drops the consumption of a dozen or more foods that she consumed prior to pregnancy, everything depends on how much she can consume of the optional foods that remain open for her. For the first "few days" only liquid foods must be eaten (Ferro-Luzzi 1980c:109), but these liquids include milk, rice water, soups, and coffee (with sugar). Although "the majority of women avoided [read "said they avoided"] non-vegetarian food for at least a week" (ibid.:110), only 6 percent of non-vegetarians said that they became pure vegetarians for one month or more (ibid.:109). Within "a few days" bread, legumes, vegetables, and rice can be added to the liquid diet. Hence, despite the restricted list of edibles, continuity of the basic diet of rice and legumes supplemented by milk, milk products, meat, and fish is provided for. In addition, the possitility remains that special concessions in terms of the quantity or quality of permitted foods may compensate for the interdicted items (see below). Some special foods may be added, but these possibilities were not investigated (Ferro-Luzzi 1977).

Emics and Etics of Post-Partum Taboos

The all-important question concerning apparently harmful pregnancy and post-partum foodways is their effect on the daily etic consumption of nutrients. This effect cannot be measured merely by collecting all the items that women say they should not or must not eat. It can only be measured by comparing what a sample of women consumed during their "normal" state with what they consumed during their pregnancy or post-partum. Moreover, it must be kept in mind that late pregnancy and lactation are often associated with shifts in other activities as well as changes in diet (e.g., relief from arduous labor, protective and inactive "lying in"). These changes should also be considered in assessing the nutritional adequacy of pregnancy and post-partum foodways.

Some information relevant to the emic/etic versions of lactation-period taboos is available from Wilson's (1980) study of Ru Mada, a fishing village on the East Coast of Malaysia. As in Tamil Nadu, the woman of Ru Mada can collectively produce a long list of items to be avoided post-partum: sour and "cold foods," all fruits except bananas and durain, all vegetables, all fried foods, several species of fish, curry, gravy, and sauces. These prohibitions are to be observed for 40 days, during which the mother's activity is restricted and she must spend much of her time on a bed raised above a warming fire. Wilson constructed a hypothetical one-day lying-in diet from interviews with 50 women and then observed the actual lying-in diet of two lactating women (one of the 9th and the other on the 20th day of confinement). Here is how the two versions compare:

Emic Diet	*Etic Diet*
Rice (bowls)	Rice (bowls and rice cakes)
Fish (small, lean, none fried)	Fish (roast, salt, *fried,* stewed, *curried*)
European bread roll	European bread roll
Egg	Egg
Banana	
Coffee	Coffee
Plain biscuit	Plain biscuit
Black pepper	
Tumeric	Tumeric
Yeast (on rice or in water)	
Sugar (in coffee)	Sugar (in coffee, tea, and cakes)
	Tea
	Coconut (grated)
	Soy sauce
	Chilis
	Margarine
	Milo chocolate drink (fortified)
	Condensed milk
	Curry (in fish)

Note first that the etic diet contains eight items not mentioned in the emic diet. This is a remarkable rate of discrepancy, since only two women were observed for one day each. Second, there are three explicitly interdicted items (italicized) on the etic list (*fried* fish, *soy sauce, curry*), again an extraordinary rate in relation to the number of observations. Finally, it is clear that the addition of four prestige foods—European bread rolls, margarine, condensed milk, and Milo—represents a systematic attempt to supplement rather than deplete the lactating mother's diet.

Having compared this diet with the recommended diet allowance (RDA) for lactating Malaysian women, Wilson concludes that the etic nutrient intake was "low" and "inimical to the woman's health" (1980:73). This may be true, although it should be noted that both women were less active during their confinement, spending about two to five hours a day lying on their warming beds and giving up strenuous activities such as chopping wood that they had engaged in even during late pregnancy. No one would wish to argue that the lying-in diet was optimal. But Wilson presents no evidence that it was inferior to the diet of non-pregnant and non-lactating women *as a consequence of the food aversions.* In fact, one of the women gained 9.3 kg during her pregnancy, about 25 percent of which was probably depot fat (Thompson and Hytten 1977:18). Her postpartum diet was actually the same in proteins (58.9 gm per day) as her etic pregnancy diet and slightly higher in calories (2,039 per day) and calcium. It seems likely, therefore, that her lactation diet was somewhat privileged (see Rajalakshmi and Ramakrishnan 1980) in comparison with the daily intake of non-pregnant and non-lactating women, even though it did not come up to the recommended level. Hence, it is not possible to attribute the failure of Ru Mada mothers to reach the Malaysian RDA for lactating women (even if the RDA is correct for lying-in, inactive lactating women) to the influence of the lying-in food aversions. Many factors other than food taboos may be responsible for the failure to reach the RDA, such as Ru Mada's productive capacity, per capita income, the conflicting demands on family budgets for the support of other members, especially male fishermen, and the costs and benefits of rearing additional children. Indeed, it should be stressed that there may be systemic advantages in not making an all-out effort to divert resources to each lactating woman at every birth (Harris 1985). In any event there is no evidence that the mere removal of the food taboos would result in the provision of the extra nutrients recommended for lactating women.

The Significance of Allegedly Irrational and Harmful Foodways

The refutation of cases of irrational and harmful foodways (and of irrational and harmful cultural beliefs in general) has important practical implications. If malnutrition and undernutrition are largely the result of misguided beliefs, then the indicated remedy is an educational effort aimed at introducing more salutary ideas about nutrition. If, on the other hand, the causes of malnutrition and undernutrition lie in the infrastructural and political-economic nexus, then nutrition education may serve more as a sop to conscience and a source of employment than as a contribution to improved diet (DeWalt and Pelto 1977:82). DeWalt and Pelto's study of Nopalcingo, a Mexican community in the state of Mexico, suggests that knowledge of modern food values is not sufficient to implement household dietary improvements: "The problem, then, is not education or unwise allocation of resources but financial means. . . . increasing the resources that families have to work with is likely to have a dramatic effect on nutritional adequacy" (ibid.:91–92).

To repeat, materialist strategies do not deny that a significant number of foodways may in fact be harmful. Some of these may owe their existence to mistaken notions about the relationship between diet and health. But these mistaken notions are not necessarily the result of irrational cultural premises. For example, infants and small children with diarrhea are often placed on liquid diets with reduced protein intake. Research indicates that this practice is life-threatening (N. Scrimshaw 1981:229). If we set aside the possibility that the standard folk remedy for infant diarrhea is another form of indirect infanticide whose population-regulating effects are advantageous for juveniles and adults (S. Scrimshaw 1981; 1983), the fact remains that it is scarcely an irrational or capricious cultural phenomenon. Western-trained physicians and health workers have until recently recommended similar diets (ibid.:230), and it has only recently been demonstrated that solid proteinacious foods are indicated for diarrhetic infants and children.

Given the fallibility of Western experts, especially those operating in the fields of health, nutrition, and economic development, anthropologists have an obligation to remain highly skeptical about blanket condemnations of exotic foodways as useless or harmful. It is tempting, for example, to dismiss widespread notions about "hot" and "cold" foods as superstitions, but this dismissal would not be based on any corpus of sustained research. The little research that has been done actually suggests that in India foods classified as "hot" not only impart subjective feelings of bodily warmth and burning sensations in the eyes and urinary tract, but result in elevated levels of urinary sulfur excretion and nitrogen retention (Lindenbaum 1977:145). It is only since 1965 (Cuatrecasas et al. 1965; Bayless and Rosenzweig 1966) that Western physicians and health experts have come to the realization that the rejection of cows' milk in adulthood is not an irrational cultural "taste prejudice" of backward peoples, but a physiologically justified aversion based on the genetically determined enzymatic activity normal to most of humankind.

Given the recently acquired knowledge about rapid fall-off with age of lactase production among most human populations, the complete withdrawal of animal milk from children suffering from diarrhea (one of the symptoms of lactase deficiency) in India (Lindenbaum 1977:146) cannot be dismissed as an altogether harmful practice without further research.

Toward a Theory of Foodways: Emics and Etics

We are now in a position to generalize some of the critical issues which must be dealt with in the development of a comprehensive theory of food preferences and avoidances under materialist auspices. To begin with, due attention must be paid to the possibility of differences between etic and emic versions of foodways. For example, it is generally supposed that families in the United States eat definite meals together. Videotape studies of etic behavior shows that in some U.S. urban domiciles parents may eat not at a table but on their bed or watching television, while children eat in the living room or grab snacks in the kitchen (DeHavenon 1977). Similarly, Harrison (1975) has shown that U.S. households tend to give grossly unreliable estimates of their beer consumption. An important issue in the sacred cow controversy is the discrepancy between the etic rate of bovicide as revealed by lopsided sex ratios and the ideology that insists that unwanted cattle are kept alive (Vaidyanathan, Nair, and Harris 1982).

The fact that a rule exists for avoiding a particular species does not mean that the rule is uniformly obeyed. Many interdicted foods are actually consumed surreptitiously: rat-eating castes in India, for example, deny that they do so in order to escape the onus of pollution. Old people in the United States deny that they eat pet food. Jews and Moslems consume pork in restaurants out of sight of family and friends.

Conformity to a foodway may depend on circumstances not explicit in the rule. Many interdicted species, such as eagles, buzzards, snakes, and dogs, are consumed during hungry seasons, droughts, and other emergencies. If these species are scarce and if they are poor sources of energy and other nutritional benefits, it would be their regular consumption rather than their interdiction that would weigh against materialist strategies.

Foodways and Status Privileges

Within-group adherence to foodway aversions and preferences may be a specific function of status position. This means that benefits and costs may be distributed unevenly among age cohorts, between males and females, and during the phases of the life cycle (e.g., pregnancy, lactation, marriage, and widowhood). No materialist principles predict that everyone benefits or suffers equally from foodways (or other cultural beliefs and practices). Proscription of a food for one status group may be the precondition, under a given set of infrastructural and political-economic arrangements, for its consumption by others. In highland New Guinea and throughout South Asia, men protect their access to scarce choice animal foods by interdicting consumption by women (Lindenbaum 1977; 1979:133–37). Among the Amazon Tapirapé only senior adult males consume deer meat. Wagley (1977:67) sees this and other Tapirapé animal taboos as "decidedly dysfunctional." Yet the deer meat taboo is not clearly dysfunctional from the point of view of the senior males. Moreover, the question of how much deer meat there would be for anybody if everyone consumed it equally remains unanswered. Recent quantitative studies of Amazonian aboriginal subsistence point up the extreme vulnerability of tropical mammalian species to depletions (Baksh 1982; Good 1982 and Chapter 16; Harris 1984; Paolisso and Sackett 1982; Sponsel 1983). Many preferences and avoidances associated with gender hierarchies are best regarded as forms of rationing (Gross and Underwood 1971; Harris 1985; Maher 1981; Miller 1981).

Membership in various types of egalitarian and stratified groups may bestow differential rights and obligations with respect to foodways. Apparently arbitrary specialists often reflect a systemic division of labor, an apportionment of risks, and an equal or unequal distribution of nutritional benefits. The oft-noted specialized preferences and aversions of sibs and lineages, and especially of castes and ethnic groups, suggest an underlying allocation of environmental and economic niches. So-called totemic taboos may reduce the number of people competing for eponymous game animals and plants.

India is especially well-endowed with segmentary specialties based on an apparently irrational interdiction of certain species of animals and crops (Sopher 1980:196). In Kerala, for example, there are Hindu castes of low rank that specialize in the production and consumption of fish. This may protect them from competition from higher-ranking castes for whom fish and fishing are proscribed (Klausen 1968). Similarly, the defilement that animal slaughter and beef consumption confer on Hindus is the precondition for the economic success of Moslem butchers. In turn, the avoidance of pork by Hindus and Moslems confers a monopoly on pig raising by Christians and untouchables. Similar ethnic and caste niches characterize much of African social structure and are clearly evident, though not discussed, in Garine's account of the Massa, Tupuri, and Mussey.

None of this should be taken to mean that segmentary foodways necessarily moderate exploitative relationships in stratified societies. On the contrary, the balance sheet of sumptuary privileges, as in the case of the restriction of alcoholic beverages to the nobilities of Polynesia and Inca Peru, may be entirely lopsided. In general, ruling classes enjoy access to foodways that are taboo to commoners or that are too expensive for commoners to enjoy. Vegetarianism has entirely different dietary implications for upper-caste Hindus who can afford to consume copious quantities of milk and milk products and for lower-caste Hindus (see Chapter 18). Similarly, upper-class Moslems may have ready access to alcohol or other drugs while enjoying the social and economic benefits that flow from sobriety among the masses.

Use and Non-Use for Optimization

There are no materialist principles that lead to the prediction that all edible plants and animals will be used. A considerable amount of non-use is essential for optimization-selection models. Such models assume that some edible species are more useful than others; therefore, some potentially useful species will be neglected in order to optimize the cost/benefits of production and the maintenance of nutritional standards. The fact, for example, that the !Kung recognize 105 edible plant species but derive 75 percent of their plant food calories from only 14 of them (Lee 1979:159) conforms to optimization models. Similarly, the fact that the !Kung consume only 80 out of 262 animal species (ibid.:226) suggests optimization, not waste. Obviously the place to begin to understand the list of frequently used, as opposed to seldom or never used, species is the measurement of their abundance, their seasonality, the time and energy costs of "harvesting" them, and their nutritional value (ibid.:168). "Tastiness," a criterion mentioned by Lee, is also a viable index of behavioral cost/benefits, provided that the standards of taste derive from biopsychologically determined preferences and aversions (possibly the preference for sweet foods over bitter ones, for example—see below). If "taste" simply means emic preference or avoidance, however, we are obviously back in the quagmire of cultural arbitrariness that is the first resort for idealists but the last for materialists.

Optimal foraging models predict that plant and animal species whose exploitation lowers the average calorie cost/benefit ratio of foraging activities will not be gathered or hunted (Hames and Vickers 1982; Hawkes, Hill, and O'Connell 1982; Winterhalder and Smith 1981; and see Chapter 13). Energetic efficiency can be maximized by concentrating on species that rank high on the optimal diet list. Alternative dietary currencies should also be considered in calculating efficiency ratios—protein, fat, fiber, vitamins, minerals, and so on. These have yet to be incorporated into mathematical models, but their effects on aversions and preferences can scarcely be ignored. The quest for fats and proteins, for example, frequently takes precedence over the quest for calories, even though hunting is a much more calorie-expensive activity (Good 1982; Gross 1982; Lee 1979:262; Speth 1983).

From a slightly different angle, it is clear that the broader the range of exploited dietary resources, the greater the opportunity for problems of scheduling to occur (Flannery 1968). The need to prioritize subsistence efforts can result in the neglect of relatively abundant species. The Nootka, for example, ignored runs of pilchard fish because there were other, more important seasonal economic tasks to be performed (Hayden 1981:398). Notions of conflicting priorities, scheduling, and maximization underlie the argument that economic and ecological cost/benefits are responsible for tabooing the flesh of such specialized domestic animals as the pig, horse, camel, dog, and cat (Harris 1986). Ross's (1978) explanation of why hunting activity in some parts of aboriginal Amazonia focuses on small accessible animals such as monkeys and birds to the neglect of larger, more furtive semi-aquatic species such as tapir, capybara, and deer is also predicated on the need to prioritize effort as well as on the cost/benefits per species. Optimization principles also provide a likely solution to the widely noted avoidance of raptors and carnivores. These creatures not only tend to be solitary, hard to find, and dangerous when found, but they are notably deficient in fat, which is much sought after by hunter-gatherers and village horticulturalists.

Optimization "currencies" cannot be restricted to nutritional costs/benefits, since many edible plants and animals have non-nutritive uses. The costs of avoiding the consumption of domesticated species such as cats, dogs, horses, and cattle may be systemically overridden by their multiple, non-nutritive, specialized, technological functions: cats for mousing, dogs for lookouts, herding, hunting, and scavenging; horses for riding, traction, milking; cattle for traction, milking, manuring. In other words, under conditions related to the entire infrastructural and political-economic conjunction, an animal species may be too valuable alive for it to be raised and slaughtered for food. Carroll (n.d.) has found, for example, that North American Indian groups who had access to large game animals such as buffalo or deer seldom reared dogs for food consumption but exploited them instead for their contribution to the hunt. The widespread prohibition on the slaughter of human beings for food is founded on the benefit side on the fact that in state societies, at least, people are exceedingly more useful alive than dead; and on the cost side on the fact that people are the most expensive and dangerous of all species in either their domesticated or their "wild" form (i.e., as strangers and aliens).

Optimization principles further lead to the prediction that among hunter/gatherers, the larger the percentage of potentially edible species in a given habitat that are actively exploited, the lower the overall efficiency of food production is likely to be. This follows not only from optimal foraging theory but also from the principles of ecological food chains. Band and village peoples whose diets stretch all the way from earthworms, seed, acorns, and clay to shellfish, snails, and cormorants are likely to be nutritionally vulnerable. They would be much better off energetically eating closer to the top of the chain rather than at the bottom—sea mammals and fish rather than molluscs; ungulates rather than seeds; suidae rather than acorns. As an index of "hard times" (Cohen 1977), extreme breadth of diet seems to have relevance to the development of prehistoric "broad-spectrum revolutions" (Flannery 1968 and see Chapter 10), which set the stage for the shift to agriculture in the Old and New Worlds. According to Binford (1983:212), the phenomenon should be called a "broad-spectrum depression," not a "revolution":

> As hunters and gatherers were packed in a region, they were forced to move down the animal body-size chain, to exploit a wider variety of species, to make use of increasing numbers of smaller and smaller food packages, to compensate for the more specialized (and no longer viable) strategies they employed as spatially unfettered hunters.

The extent to which this same principle can be applied to agricultural and state-level societies remains unexplored. It seems applicable in the case of the Aztecs (Harris 1978; 1986:225–34), but the effect may be masked in other states by the characteristic flourishing of *haute cuisine*, which leaves no edible unturned in its search for ever more exotic concoctions (Goody 1982). Closely packed peasant populations theoretically ought to be receptive to a wide variety of food options and to be relatively free of general taboos (as distinguished from status and life cycle taboos). The generalization seems to hold for the Chinese peasantry, who are notorious for making "judicious use of every kind of edible vegetable and insect as well as offal" (quoted in Chang 1977:13). India, with its proliferation of caste and ethnic taboos, seems to be the glaring exception. Yet, in a sense, the Indian peasantry and lower classes are also notable for their willingness to eat almost anything that their habitat and technology can provide. The broad spectrum is there from insects to carrion, but the various parts of the spectrum have been allocated to different segments of the population. As far as diversity of daily fare is concerned, China is (or was until recently) probably as restricted as India. It is reported that coolies in 19th-century North China ate "sweet potatoes three times a day, every day, all through the year with small amounts of salted turnip, bean curd, and pickled beans" (Spence 1977:267). A more favorable view of the diet of a majority of northern Chinese characterizes it as "monotonous" (Hsu and Hsu 1977:315).

In advanced industrial societies, per capita income is higher and hence daily menus are more diversified. But, paradoxically, among lower- and middle-class post-peasants, the spectrum of exploited foods may be narrower than among densely populated agro-managerial societies. The United States, with its rejection of mutton, goat, donkey, horse, dog, and insects, is a conspicuous example. A plausible explanation for gastronomic provinciality lies in the availability of energetically more efficient and abundant species such as cattle, swine, and poultry (Harris 1986). The absence of famines may also be relevant. The collective foodways experience of the Chinese, for example, has been dominated by prolonged periods of malnutrition and famine during which insects were luxuries and daily fare consisted of ground leaves, sawdust, thistles, cotton seeds, peanut shells, and ground pumice (Spence 1977:261). As long as daily U.S. foodways provide abundant, reliable, and relatively cheap alternative sources of animal fats and proteins, the list of rejected animals does not constitute a challenge to optimization principles, especially in view of the important non-food functions fulfilled by domesticated species. Similar considerations seem relevant to the rejection or neglect of certain parts of animals: head, hoofs, spleen, entrails, and so on, which have alternative commercial utilities. Very little of the carcasses of cattle or swine is actually wasted by modern meat-packing industries.

Short-Term versus Long-Term Optimizations

An important qualification of optimization theories of foodways must be made in relation to collective wisdom embodied in rituals and symbols that obstruct the use of species vulnerable to depletion and extinction. If a human group has witnessed the depletion of a species or the degrading of a habitat, it is entirely plausible that an appropriate ambivalent or negative attitude would survive the passage of several generations and persist even after the endangered species or habitat had been restored to exploitable levels. If these attitudes and their corresponding practices result in a dampening of exploitation rates, they will tend to be propagated even if short-run cost/benefits favor more intensive use.

The suggestion that some tropical forest hunting taboos are the forerunners of modern environmental conservation movements (McDonald 1977; Ross 1978), therefore, does not pose an unrealistic systemic "tracking" problem for pre-industrial peoples. If one assumes that there are always etic violations and modification of taboos, the net result of restricting use will be dampening of production and the maintenance of sustainable "harvests" as opposed to periodic or permanent crashes.

The ritual restrictions on East African cattle slaughter appear to operate with a similar logic: by confining slaughter to ritual occasions, they dampen the tendency to intensify slaughter and consumption beyond sustainable yields. Similarly, the taboo on the slaughter of cattle and the consumption of beef in India does not prevent slaughter and consumption by Moslems, Christians, and outcasts, but the dampening effect of the restrictions ensures a steady supply of cheap beef in India's urban markets as well as cheap traction animals for the countryside.

Toward a Theory of Food Taboos

Many if not most food aversions have a secular quality to them in the sense that consumption of the interdicted item is said to bring misfortune or ill-health through some emically ordinary process. The term "taboo" might usefully be reserved for aversions of a more sacred sort—namely, those which are backed up by elaborated religious notions of obedience to the will of a deity. A recurrent criticism of optimization models holds that if aversions are initiated by adverse cost/benefits, then there is no need for the elaboration of religious proscriptions. Self-interest should be sufficient to maintain the aversive behavior, and if there is any need for an emic rule at all, it would be more effective to couch it in terms of utility rather than sanctity.

The need and occasion for sacred interdictions, however, may arise from several circumstances. First of all, there is the problem of ambiguity and ambivalence. The very notion that both costs and benefits must be taken into account suggests that the utility or non-utility of an item is a matter of degree and that there will normally be arguments both for and against eating it. In this light, one can understand why the pig, so highly productive in river bank and forest settings, would recurrently become the focus of intensely ambivalent feelings and hence of taboos in a semi-arid habitat. Similarly, eggs, which are a frequent focus of taboos, present the difficult problem of whether it is better to eat the egg now or the chicken later. Snakes, some being poisonous, others not, also invite sacred interdictions.

Taboos are culturally selected for their ability to overcome the ambiguity and ambivalence generated by the complex systemic interrelationships in which foodways are embedded. The voice of God dispels doubts. If a taboo is associated with higher levels of collective material well-being, it will be maintained. If not, the taboo will be withdrawn or reversed. Given the scientific community's doubts and confusions about the relationships among diet, health, and development, it is easy to understand why foodways have been such a prolific source of taboos. Doubts and ambiguities and, hence, taboos are especially likely to arise when the systemic cost/benefits of an item shift from favorable to adverse as a consequence of ecological and infrastructural changes (Harris 1979:192–95, 248–53).

A slightly different scenario envisages the elaboration of taboos as a means of resolving more overt conflicting interests and segmentary differences with respect to the exploitation of resources. Caste and ethnic foodway specialties in India are made more stable by their elaboration in Hindu theology. This does not mean, of course, that taboos benefit every segment equally (Sopher 1980:196).

Finally, there is no reason to suppose that all foodway taboos are selected for their contribution to the favorable resolution of ambiguous cost/benefits. As the proscriptions in Leviticus demonstrate, some foodway taboos may be elaborated precisely because the abominated items possess no significant utility or are altogether unavailable in a people's habitat. The theological justifications for such taboos may have no specific relationship to infrastructural or political-economic nomothetic processes and may best be examined under other paradigmatic auspices. As previously indicated, the taboos that pose a puzzle for cultural materialist principles are those that result in a significant deterioration of cost/benefits to all segments of a society. This principle in no way leads to the denial of non-infrastructural or political-economic cost-benefit functions for foodway taboos as icons in theology or in the intensification of social identity. What is predicted is that religions that persist in tabooing systemically valuable and irreplaceable foods will be selected against.

Biopsychological Determinants

It is clear that any thoroughgoing optimization model implies that there are biopsychological needs and drives that foodways satisfy with varying degrees of efficiency. Economizing of costs implies at the very least a genetically determined propensity to conserve energy. More specific biogenetic factors shape the need for essential nutrients and undoubtedly endow human beings with certain food preferences and aversions at birth. The problem of identifying and measuring these genetically determined constraints on foodways, however, is surrounded by all of the classic difficulties of nature/nurture distinctions. Despite a vast amount of research, RDAs remain "prudent" estimates subject to wide individual and population differences of both biological and cultural origin (see Chapters 6 and 9).

Research aimed at determining the relative strength of the biological and cultural contributions to the origin and maintenance of specific aversions and preferences is urgently needed as a foundation for materialist explanations of both constant and variable foodways. There is some evidence, for example, that the widespread preference for animal fats and proteins displayed by the majority of known societies has a genetic component (Abrams 1979, 1980; Hamilton and Busse 1978; see also Chapters 4 and 8). Meat is known to stimulate distinctive behavioral responses in other primates. Chimpanzees, for example, are omnivores who invest considerable effort to get a small caloric reward in the pursuit of prey species—principally juvenile monkeys and galagos. While hunting, distributing, and consuming meat, chimpanzees display distinctive social behavior, such as a higher than normal amount of requests, excitement, sharing, and social control (Goodall 1979; Teleki 1981:331). The special importance of meat in the establishment of social responses strongly suggests that meat has special nutritional significance for chimpanzees and that their meat-eating behavior expresses an instinctive recognition of that significance, elaborated and modified by social traditions and individual experience. Conjointly, predation against and consumption of vertebrate animals may in itself be locked into a genetically programmed set of responses that impart a special psychosocial significance to meat. In this connection, it should be noted that chimpanzees ignore carrion and that only actively hunted or freshly killed vertebrates elicit intense social behavior (Teleki 1981:328–29; but see Hasegawa et al. 1983). It cannot be mere coincidence that meat and other animal products also play a special role in the foodways of most human populations, particularly as a focus of exchange, redistribution, and social cohesion (Good 1982; Harris 1986:19–46), but this does not necessarily mean that genetic coding accounts for all or any of the cross-species similarities. In the human case, the preferential status accorded meat (especially fatty meat) and animal foods may simply reflect purely traditional cultural codings that favor meat and animal products as cost-efficient packages of calories and essential nutrients. The favored status of meat and meat products could be propagated and preserved by reinforcement in the form of the extra health, vigor, and body size conferred by high levels of meat consumption, without any genetic program for meat preference.

The case for certain genetically controlled innate human taste preferences rests on firmer ground. Neonates prior to any feeding experience exhibit distinct facial responses to sweet and bitter substances: a marked relaxation of the face versus open-mouthed grimacing with a flat, protruded tongue. Similarly distinctive facial reactions to sweet and bitter are found in other mammalian species and among culturally differentiated human adults, and can reasonably be interpreted as brain-stem-controlled communicators of preference and aversion (Steiner 1979:251–52). Presumably the innate preference for sweet-tasting substances is a bioevolutionary adaptation based on the fact that sweetness is characteristic of high-energy substances and hence is a predictor of nutritive value (Rozin 1982:228). Similarly, the innate aversion to bitter substances suggests a bioevolutionary adaptation that protects against the ingestion of harmful and poisonous substances. However, even in these instances, cultural programming can override innate tendencies, as can be seen in the early morning coffee taken without sugar or cream and the "black drink" (*Ilex vomitoria*) ingested daily by southeast Woodlands and Amazonian Amerindian groups for its narcotic and emetic effects (Hudson 1979).

A limited number of foodways may best be understood as examples of recent (i.e., post-Pleistocene) gene-culture co-evolution. Among Europeans, and possibly other populations, the ability of adults to produce lactase, the enzyme necessary for digesting lactose, appears to have evolved during the spread of an early neolithic dairying complex. Because of the clothing they wore and their cloudy days, long nights, and long winters, early neolithic peoples of Europe were prone to vitamin D deficiency. Vitamin D is essential for the absorption of calcium and the prevention of rickets and osteomalacia. Lactase promotes the absorption of calcium and hence can play a role in compensating for vitamin D–deficient diets, resulting in the selection of the gene for lactase sufficiency in adulthood (Simoons 1982:215). This scenario explains why Europeans have a preference for, and Chinese an aversion to, fresh liquid milk. But it does not explain why the Chinese have never taken up dairying. Aside from the beneficial effect on calcium absorption, the nutritional benefits of milk and milk products do not depend on the ability to drink fresh fluid milk. In cheese and fermented products, bacteria do the work of lactase and break lactose down into simple sugars. By exploiting such products, India, despite a rate of lactose malabsorption similar to that of China, has become a major dairying center. The explanation for the Chinese aversion to milk must return therefore to considerations of the geographical, ecological, and political-economic features that have molded basic Chinese subsistence patterns in contrast to those of other Eurasian states (Harris 1986:130–53).

Culture-gene co-evolution also seems to be involved in shaping a preference for fava beans (*Vicia faba*) in certain regions of Europe, Africa, and Asia. Why fava beans are eaten at all is a puzzle, since it is well known that ingestion of the beans produces a potentially fatal hemolytic shock in some members of fava-eating populations. Those at risk carry the gene for glucose-6-phosphate dehydrogenase (G6PD) deficiency. As many as 5 to 30 percent of the affected populations carry the gene. A possible explanation is that there are strong oxidant chemicals present in fava that increase resistance to malaria, both in normals and in female heterozygote carriers of G6PD. The benefits of this resistance outweigh the costs and thereby maintain the cultural preference for planting and consuming the beans as well as contributing to the preservation of a balanced genetic polymorphism (Katz 1979; 1982:176–78; and see Chapter 5).

A final complication of the study of foodway selection arises from the ingestion of harmful substances such as caffeine, nicotine, alcohol, cocaine, and other psychoactive chemicals. The biopsychology of these narcotics and stimulants obviously operates in conformity with optimizations that can override and cancel normal nutritional and energetic cost/benefits. Their presence or absence and their degree of use is clearly subject to cultural mediation, but the possibility of genetic population differences in the appeal and effect of various psychoactive substances should not be ruled out.

Many additional gene-brain-body-nature-culture interactions relevant to foodways undoubtedly remain to be discovered. There is new evidence, for example, of direct linkages between dietary amino acids such as tryptophan and tyrosine and the synthesis of neurotransmitters such as serotonin, dopamine, and norepinephrine with consequent alteration of motor activity, mood, problem-solving abilities, sleep patterns, and sensitivity to pain (Kolata 1983).

The mix of factors responsible for the distribution of preferences for salt and spices such as chili and malabar pepper, thyme, marjoram, oregano, and tarragon promises to be equally complex. Reported effects of chili (Rozin and Schiller 1980) and malabar pepper include increased salivation, flavor enhancement, sense of satiety, and reduced flatulence from diets heavy in beans and pulses. Spicing as a form of food preservation alternative to salting should not be excluded, especially in view of the health hazards associated with too much dietary salt. Thyme, marjoram, oregano, and tarragon contain aromatic deoxidants whose chemical composition is similar to the industrial preservatives BHA and BHT. Salt preferences may vary with the amount of meat and other dietary sources of sodium (cf. Denton 1983). Very little work has been done on the possibility that genetic polymorphisms and direct behavior-modifying effects may also be involved in all of the above-mentioned preferences.

The Political Economy of Foodways

Control over the production and consumption of food has been a source of power and wealth from prehistoric times to the present. Since the onset of European mercantile and capitalist expansion in the 15th century, rapid changes in world foodways have resulted from the struggle for political hegemony and the search for profit. To tell the story of the transfer of animal and plant domesticants to and from the Eastern and Western hemispheres is to tell the recent history of the globe (Mintz 1979; Ross n.d.; Wolf 1983). The effects, both beneficial and harmful, are impossible to summarize. But one trend in particular—namely, the increasing role of profit in the development of mass preferences and aversions—should be noted. Increasingly the solution to the puzzle of why certain foodways develop and persist must be found in a combination of biopsychological, infrastructural, political-economic, and profitability factors. The use of tobacco, for example, is in part attributable to an innate vulnerability to nicotine addiction, in part to the toleration of governments that allow or even encourage the nicotine habit to develop while supressing the use of other addictive drugs, and in part to the huge profits made by tobacco companies, which in turn finance scientifically designed advertising campaigns and other promotional activities. A similar set of factors must be considered in explaining the popularity of coffee, tea, chocolate, alcohol, and "soft" drinks. All of these beverages exploit innate vulnerabilities to sugar and/or addictive and/or psychoactive substances, principally caffeine and alcohol; they are protected and subsidized by governments; they are a source of profit for national and multinational corporations; and they are relentlessly promoted and advertised.

The vulnerability of modern industrial populations to foodways that lead to obesity and cardiovascular disorders also arises from a similar set of causes (Turner 1981). For the first time in history or prehistory, many nations no longer confront hungry seasons or periodic famine. Even the poorer classes have access to quantities of starches, sugars, and fats sufficient to make them obese at their required levels of daily activity and calorie expenditure. With this phenomenon has come the realization that the "on" switches of human appetite are far more sensitive than the "off" switches. The reason for this asymmetry is that throughout the past three million years, natural selection has favored individuals who eat to store fat whenever there is an opportunity to do so. Individuals who did not eat to store fat were at a disadvantage during hungry seasons and famines. Because of the relatively few opportunities for people in hunter-gatherer societies to sustain weight gains over long periods, very little selection has occurred against those whose eating to store fat results in health-threatening obesity. This defect in the human genome may eventually be overcome by scientific and political-economic interventions aimed at controlling weight gain, but in the meantime the weak biological shut-off system is a standing invitation to the food industry to manipulate aversions and preferences regardless of health-damaging consequences.

References Cited

Abrams, L.
    1979   The Relevance of Paleolithic Diet in Determining Contemporary Nutritional Needs. *Journal of Applied Nutrition* 31:43–59.
    1980   Vegetarianism: An Anthropological/Nutritional Evaluation. *Journal of Applied Nutrition* 32:53–87.

Baksh, M.
    1982   The Impact of Increased Fish and Game Scarcity on Machiguenga Subsistence Behavior. Paper read at the annual meeting of the American Anthropological Association, Washington, D.C.

Bayless, T. M., and N. Rosensweig
    1966   A Racial Difference in the Incidence of Lactase Deficiency. *Journal of the American Medical Association* 197:968–72.

Binford, L.
    1983   *In Pursuit of the Past.* New York: Thames and Hudson.

Carroll, M.
    n.d.   Why We Don't Eat Dogs—Usually. Manuscript.

Chang, K. C.
  1977   Introduction. In *Food in Chinese Culture: Anthropological and Historical Perspectives*, K. C. Chang, ed., pp. 3–21. New Haven: Yale University Press.
Cohen, M. N.
  1977   *The Food Crisis in Prehistory.* New Haven: Yale University Press.
Cuatrecasas, P.; D. H. Lockwood; and J. Caldwell
  1965   Lactase Deficiency in the Adult. *Lancet* 1:14–18.
Darby, W.; P. Ghalioungui; and L. Grivetti
  1977   *Food: The Gift of Osiris.* 2 vols. New York: Academic Press.
DeHavenon, A. L.
  1977   Rank Ordered Behavior in Four Urban Families: A Comparative Video-Analysis of Patterns of Superordination in Two Black and White Families. Ph.D. dissertation, Columbia University.
Denton, D.
  1983   *The Hunger for Salt: An Anthropological, Physiological and Medical Analysis.* New York: Springer-Verlag.
Deshler, W. W.
  1965   Native Cattle Keeping in Eastern Africa. In *Man, Culture, and Animals*, Anthony Leeds and A. P. Vayda, eds., pp. 153–68. Washington, D.C.: American Association for the Advancement of Science.
DeWalt, K., and G. Pelto
  1977   Food Use and Household Ecology in a Modernizing Mexican Community. In *Nutrition and Anthropology in Action*, T. Fitzgerald, ed., pp. 74–93. Amsterdam: Van Gorcum.
Douglas, M.
  1966   *Purity and Danger: An Analysis of Concepts of Pollution and Taboo.* New York: Praeger.
  1972   Deciphering a Meal. *Daedalus* 101:61–82.
  1984   Standard Social Usages of Food. In *Food and the Social Order: Studies of Food and Festivities in Three American Communities*, Mary Douglas, ed., pp. 1–39. New York: Russell Sage Foundation.
Ferro-Luzzi, G. E.
  1977   Remarks on D. P. McDonald's "Food Taboos." *Anthropos* 73:593–94.
  1980a   Food Avoidances at Puberty and Menstruation in Tamiland. In *Food, Ecology, and Culture: Readings in the Anthropology of Dietary Practices*, J. Robson, ed., pp. 93–100. New York: Gordon and Breach.
  1980b   Food Avoidance in Pregnant Women in Tamiland. In *Food, Ecology, and Culture: Readings in the Anthropology of Dietary Practices*, J. Robson, ed., pp. 101–8. New York: Gordon and Breach.
  1980c   Food Avoidances During the Puerperium and Lactation in Tamiland. In *Food, Ecology, and Culture: Readings in the Anthropology of Dietary Practices*, J. Robson, ed., pp. 109–17. New York: Gordon and Breach.
Flannery, K.
  1968   Archaeological Systems Theory and Early MesoAmerica. In *An-

thropological Archaeology in the Americas, B. Meggars, ed., pp. 67–87. Washington, D.C.: Anthropological Society of Washington.

Garine, I. de
1978   Population, Production, and Culture in the Plains Societies of Northern Cameroon and Chad: The Anthropologist in Development Projects. *Current Anthropology* 19:42–65.
1979   Culture et Nutrition. *Communications* 31:70–90.
1980   Approaches to the Study of Food and Prestige in Savannah Tribes: Massa and Mussey of Northern Cameroon and Chad. *Social Science Information* 19:39–78.

Good, K.
1982   Limiting Factors in Amazonian Ecology. Paper read at the annual meeting of the American Anthropological Association, Washington, D.C.

Goodall, J.
1979   Life and Death at Gambi. *National Geographic* 155:592–620.

Goody, J.
1982   *Cooking, Cuisine, and Class: A Study of Comparative Sociology.* New York: Cambridge University Press.

Gross, D.
1982   Village Movement in Relation to Resources in Amazonia. In *Adaptive Responses of Native Amazonians,* R. Hames and W. Vickers, eds., pp. 429–49. New York: Academic Press.

Gross, D., and B. Underwood
1971   Technological Change and Caloric Costs: Sisal Agriculture in Northeastern Brazil. *American Anthropologist* 73:725–40.

Hames, R., and W. Vickers
1982   Optimal Diet Breadth Theory as a Model to Explain Variability in Amazonian Hunting. *American Ethnologist* 9:358–78.

Hamilton, W. J., and C. D. Busse
1978   Primate Carnivory and Its Significance to Human Diets. *BioScience* 28:761–66.

Harris, M.
1966   The Cultural Ecology of India's Sacred Cattle. *Current Anthropology* 7:51–66.
1968   *The Rise of Anthropological Theory.* New York: T. Y. Crowell.
1977   *Cannibals and Kings: The Origins of Cultures.* New York: Random House.
1978   Cannibals and Kings: An Exchange. *New York Review of Books,* June 25, pp. 51–52.
1979   *Cultural Materialism: The Struggle for a Science of Culture.* New York: Random House.
1984   Animal Capture and Yanomamo Warfare: Retrospect and New Evidence. *Journal of Anthropological Research* 40:183–201.
1985   Desperate Choices: Gender Hierarchies and the Diet of Pregnant and

Lactating Women. Paper read at the annual meeting of the American Anthropological Association, Washington, D.C.

1986   *Good to Eat: Riddles of Food and Culture.* New York: Simon and Schuster.

Harrison, G.
1975   Sociocultural Correlates of Food Utilization and Waste in a Sample of Urban Households. Ph.D. dissertation, University of Arizona.

Hasegawa, T., et al.
1983   New Evidence on Scavenging Behavior in Wild Chimpanzees. *Current Anthropology* 24:231–32.

Hawkes, K.; K. Hill; and J. F. O'Connell
1982   Why Hunters Gather: Optimal Foraging and the Aché of Eastern Paraguay. *American Ethnologist* 9:379–98.

Hayden, B.
1981   Subsistence and Ecological Adaptations of Modern Hunter-Gatherers. In *Omnivorous Primates: Gathering and Hunting in Human Evolution,* R. S. O. Harding and G. Teleki, eds., pp. 334–422. New York: Columbia University Press.

Hornabrook, R.
1977   Human Ecology and Biomedical Research: A Critical Review of the International Biological Programme in New Guinea. In *Subsistence and Survival: Rural Ecology in the Pacific,* T. P. Bayliss-Smith and R. G. Feacham, eds., pp. 23–61. New York: Academic Press.

Hsu, V. Y. H., and F. L. K. Hsu
1977   Modern China: North. In *Food in Chinese Culture.* K. C. Chang ed., pp. 295–331, New Haven: Yale University Press.

Hudson, C. (ed.)
1979   *The Black Drink: A Native American Tea.* Athens: University of Georgia.

Katz, S.
1979   Une Exemple d'Evolution Bioculturelle: La Feve. *Communication* 31:53–69.

1982   Food, Behavior and Biocultural Evolution. In *The Psychology of Human Food Selection,* L. M. Barker, ed., pp. 171–88. Westport, Conn.: AVI.

Kensinger, K. M., and W. B. Kracke (eds.)
1981   *Food Taboos in Lowland South America.* Working Papers on South American Indians, Bennington, Vt.: Bennington College.

Klausen, A. M.
1968   *Kerala Fishermen.* Oslo: Scandinavian University Books.

Kolata, G.
1983   Food Affects Human Behavior. *Science* 218:1209–10.

Lee, R.
1979   *The !Kung San: Men, Women, and Work in a Foraging Society.* New York: Cambridge University Press.

Lévi-Strauss, C.
1963   *Totemism.* Boston: Beacon Press.

1965   Le Triangle Colinaire. *L'Arc* 26:19–29.

Lindenbaum, S.
1977   The "Last Course": Nutrition and Anthropology in Asia. In *Nutrition and Anthropology in Action*, T. Fitzgerald, ed., pp. 141–55. Amsterdam: Van Gorcum.
1979   *Kuru Sorcery: Disease and Danger in the New Guinea Highlands*. Palo Alto: Mayfield.

Lowie, R.
1938   Subsistence. In *General Anthropology*, Franz Boas, ed., pp. 282–326. New York: D. C. Heath.
1942   The Transitions of Civilizations in Primitive Society. *American Journal of Sociology* 47:527–43.
1960   *Lowie's Selected Papers in Anthropology*, C. DuBois, ed. Berkeley: University of California Press.
1966   *Culture and Ethnology*. New York: Basic Books [orig. 1917].

Luzbetak, L.
1954   The Socio-Religious Significance of a New Guinea Pig Festival. *Anthropological Quarterly* 2:59–80, 102–28.

McArthur, M.
1977   Nutritional Research in Melanesia: A Second Look at the Tsembaga. In *Subsistence and Survival: Rural Ecology in the Pacific*, T. P. Bayliss-Smith and R. G. Feacham, eds., pp. 91–128. New York: Academic Press.

McDonald, D. P.
1977   Food Taboos: A Primitive Environmental Protection Agency. *Anthropos* 72:734–38.

Maher, V.
1981   Work, Consumption, and Authority Within the Household. In *Of Marriage and the Market: Women's Subordination in International Perspective*, K. Young et al., eds., pp. 69–87. London: CSE Books.

Meggitt, M.
1965   The Association Between Australian Aborigines and Dingoes. In *Man, Culture, and Animals*, A. Leeds and A. Vayda, eds., pp. 7–26. Washington, D.C.: American Association for the Advancement of Science.

Miller, B.
1981   *The Endangered Sex*. Ithaca: Cornell University Press.

Mintz, S.
1979   Time, Sugar and Sweetness. *Marxist Perspectives* 9:56–73.

Montellano, O. de
1978   Aztec Cannibalism: An Ecological Necessity? *Science* 200:611–17.

Morren, G.
1977   From Hunting to Herding: Pigs and the Control of Energy in Montane New Guinea. In *Subsistence and Survival: Rural Ecology in the Pacific*, T. P. Bayliss-Smith and R. G. Feacham, eds., pp. 273–315. New York: Academic Press.

Paolisso, M., and R. Sackett
    1982   Hunting Productivity Among the Yukpa Indians of Venezuela. Paper read at the annual meeting of the American Anthropological Association, Washington, D.C.
Rajalakshmi, S., and C. V. Ramakrishnan
    1980   The Nutritional Scene in Jambudweepam (Asia). Paper read at the meeting on the Anthropology of Food and Nutrition, Bad Homburg, October 13–15, under the auspices of Maison des Sciences de l'Homme and Werner-Reimers-Stiftung.
Rappaport, R.
    1967   *Pigs for the Ancestors.* New Haven: Yale University Press.
    1984   *Pigs for the Ancestors.* 2d ed. New Haven: Yale University Press.
Ross, E.
    1978   Food Taboos, Diet, and Hunting Strategy: The Adaptation to Animals in Amazon Cultural Ecology. *Current Anthropology* 19:1–36.
    1980   Patterns of Diet and Forces of Production: An Economic and Ecological History of the Ascendancy of Beef in the United States Diet. In *Beyond the Myths of Culture: Essays in Cultural Materialism,* Eric Ross, ed., pp. 181–225. New York: Academic Press.
    1983   "The Political Ecology of the Irish Famine." Manuscript.
Rozin, P.
    1982   Human Food Selection: The Interaction of Biology, Culture, and Individual Experience. In *The Psychobiology of Human Food Selection,* L. M. Barker, ed., pp. 225–54. Westport, Conn.: AVI.
Rozin, P., and D. Schiller
    1980   The Nature and Acquisition of a Preference for Chili Pepper by Humans. *Motivation and Emotion* 4:77–101.
Sahlins, M.
    1976   *Culture and Practical Reason.* Chicago: University of Chicago Press.
Schneider, H.
    1957   The Subsistence Cattle Among the Pakot and in East Africa. *American Anthropologist* 59:278–300.
Scrimshaw, N.
    1981   Significance of the Interactions of Nutrition and Infection in Children. In *Textbook of Pediatric Nutrition,* Robert Suskind, ed., pp. 229–40. New York: Raven Press.
Scrimshaw, S.
    1981   Infant Mortality and Behavior in the Regulation of Family Size. In *Fertility Decline in the Less Developed Countries,* Nick Eberstadt, ed., pp. 195–318. New York: Praeger.
    1983   Infanticide as Deliberate Fertility Regulation. In *Determinants of Fertility in Developing Countries: Fertility Regulation and Institutional Influences,* R. Lee and R. Bulatoo, eds., pp. 245–66. Washington, D.C.: National Academy of Science Press.
Simoons, F.
    1982   Geography and Genetics as Factors in the Psychobiology of Human

Food Selection. In *The Psychobiology of Human Food Selection,* L. M. Barker, ed., pp. 205–24. Westport, Conn.: AVI.

Soler, J.
1979   The Semiotics of Food in the Bible. In *Food and Drink in History,* R. Foster and O. Ranum, eds., pp. 126–38. Baltimore: Penguin.

Sopher, D. E.
1980   Indian Civilization and the Tropical Savanna Environment. In *Human Ecology in Savanna Environments,* D. Harris, ed., pp. 185–207. New York: Academic Press.

Spence, J.
1977   Chi'Ing. In *Food in Chinese Culture: Anthropological and Historical Perspectives,* K. C. Chang, ed., pp. 261–94. New Haven: Yale University Press.

Speth, J.
1983   *Bison Kills and Bone Counts.* Chicago: University of Chicago Press.

Sponsel, L.
1983   Yanomama Warfare, Protein Capture, and Cultural Ecology: A Critical Analysis of the Arguments of the Opponents. *Interciencia* 8:204–10.

Steiner, J.
1979   Oral and Facial Innate Motor Response to Gustatory and Some Olfactory Stimuli. In *Preference Behavior and Chemoreception,* J. Kroeze, ed., pp. 247–62. London: Information Retrieval.

Teleki, G.
1981   The Omnivorous Diet and Eclectic Feeding Habits of Chimpanzees in Gombe National Park, Tanzania. In *Omnivorous Primates: Gathering and Hunting in Human Evolution,* R. S. O. Harding and G. Teleki, eds., pp. 303–43. New York: Columbia University Press.

Thompson, A., and F. Hytten
1977   Physiological Basis of Nutritional Needs During Pregnancy and Lactation. In *Nutritional Impacts on Women Throughout Life,* K. Moghisi and T. Evans, eds., pp. 10–22. New York: Harper and Row.

Turner, M. R. (ed.)
1981   *Preventive Nutrition and Society.* New York: Academic Press.

Vaidyanathan, A.; K. N. Nair; and M. Harris
1982   Bovine Sex and Species Ratios in India. *Current Anthropology* 23:365–83.

Vayda, A.; A. Leeds; and D. Smith
1961   The Place of Pigs in Melanesian Subsistence. In *Proceedings of the 1961 Annual Spring Meeting of the American Ethnological Society,* pp. 69–77. Seattle: University of Washington Press.

Wagley, C.
1977   *Welcome of Tears.* New York: Oxford University Press.

Welsch, R.
1981   An Interdependence of Foodways and Architecture: A Foodways Contrast on the American Plains. In *Food in Perspective: Proceedings of the Third International Conference on Ethnological Food Research, Cardiff,*

Wales, 1977, Alexander Fenton and Trefor Owen, eds., pp. 263–376. Edinburgh: John Donald.

Wilson, C.
    1980   Food Taboos of Childbirth: The Malay Example. In *Food, Ecology, and Culture: Readings in the Anthropology of Dietary Practices,* J. Robson, ed., pp. 67–74. New York: Gordon and Breach.

Winterhalder, B., and E. A. Smith (eds.)
    1981   *Hunter-Gatherer Foraging Strategies: Ethnographic and Archaeological Analyses.* Chicago: University of Chicago Press.

Wolf, E.
    1983   *Europe and the People Without History.* Berkeley: University of California Press.

Wood, C.
    1979   *Human Sickness and Health: A Biocultural View.* Palo Alto: Mayfield.

PART II

Bioevolutionary Antecedents and Constraints

LIKE MOST PRIMATES, HUMANS ARE OMNIVORES IN THE NAR-row sense of consuming both plants and animals. This omnivorous capability is undoubtedly a phylogenetic characteristic—a part of "human nature." Yet om-nivory is a rather vague dietary concept. Non-human primates display consider-able species-specific variation in the ratio of plants to animals in the diet. Primate foodways also differ in the ratio of particular kinds of plants or plant parts (e.g., roots, leaves, fruits, seeds) and in the kinds of animal materials consumed (e.g., insects, vertebrates). The question arises, therefore, as to whether human beings have a phylogenetic "legacy" that leads us to prefer animal over plant foods (or vice versa) or to prefer certain kinds of plants over others and certain kinds of animal materials over others. The essays that follow address this question.

The logical first place to look for an answer is in the human gut. To the extent that human foodways are a phylogenetic legacy, one would expect them to be asso-ciated with phylogenetically distinct morphological and physiological features. As Milton shows in Chapter 3, human gut morphology and physiology are poorly designed for processing large quantities of bulky, fibrous plant material. This does not necessarily mean that the human digestive tract has been selected for an ability to digest large amounts of animal flesh. Indeed, Hamilton's essay (Chapter 4) explicitly denies this possibility, citing the dangers posed by the overconsumption of meat in contemporary societies. Hamilton's data on chacama baboons suggest instead that primate preferences for animal foods (mostly insects) are oppor-tunistic and can largely be accounted for by the more favorable energy input/out ratio associated with meat (a theme that is explored in greater detail in Part IV).

While Milton and Hamilton are concerned with pan-human phylogenetic con-straints on human foodways, the possibility that intra-specific genetic poly-morphisms account for variations in foodways associated with particular popula-

tions must also be kept in mind. This possibility is addressed in Katz's study of the role of fava beans in circum-Mediterranean foodways (Chapter 5). Like the better-known case of selection for adult lactase sufficiency and milk consumption as a buffer against calcium-deficiency diseases, the ability to consume fava beans also appears to have been selected for the biochemical protection the beans provide against malaria. Although Katz's gene-culture co-evolution model possesses considerable cogency with respect to a number of important food preferences and aversions, and is especially welcome as the explanation of apparently irrational foodways that cannot be explained culturologically, it seems unlikely that the vast majority of human intra-specific food preferences and avoidances can be traced to such one-to-one culture-gene associations.

KATHARINE MILTON

Primate Diets and Gut Morphology:
Implications for Hominid Evolution

THERE IS CURRENTLY STRONG INTEREST IN DEVELOPING A BET-
ter understanding of the probable food habits and dietary niche of early humans
(Isaac 1978; Peters and O'Brian 1981; Stahl 1984). Without such information,
we are handicapped in our ability to interpret the significance of many features
of human morphology and to construct viable models of early human ecology
(Isaac 1978; Sussman 1978). Further, it is increasingly obvious that many of the
major health problems faced today by more modern technological societies
stem from factors related to diet. This strongly suggests that the average diet
in such societies is not entirely suitable for human nutritional needs (Burkitt,
Walker, and Painter, 1972; Trowell 1978; Truswell 1977). In this paper, I review information about dietary choice in primates, paying particular attention to
members of the Hominoidea. I then examine features of the human gut, comparing it with the guts of other mammals, both primates and non-primates, to
distinguish any features that appear to set humans apart. I conclude by speculating on the probable diet of early humans, using the behavior of extant
pongids as a partial foundation for my speculations.

Omnivory

Humans are generally viewed as omnivores (Fischler 1981; Harding 1981). By
definition, an omnivore is any animal that takes food from more than one
trophic level. Most mammals are in fact omnivorous (Landry 1970; Morris and
Rogers 1983a, 1983b), including such diverse forms as pigs, tayras, dogs, pan-
das, bears, primates, skunks, some bats, and dozens of rodents. Though all
omnivorous mammals appear to have basically similar nutritional requirements,
different species satisfy these needs in different ways, using a tremendous

93

range and variety of foods. Describing a given species as omnivorous, therefore, does little to clarify what foods it may depend on, or how its digestive
capabilities may differ from those of other omnivores, or why it may show
decided preferences for some food types over others.

Both pure herbivores, such as bovids, and pure carnivores, such as felids,
show highly characteristic metabolic specializations to the peculiar end products of their respective and specialized diets (Morris and Rogers 1983b). In
bovids, microbial fermentation results in little glucose being absorbed from the
gut. Ruminant metabolism is adapted toward the use of acetate rather than
glucose for fatty acid synthesis and a constant high rate of gluconeogenesis
(Morris and Rogers 1982; Van Soest 1982). Further, because bovids typically
obtain all essential amino acids and most vitamins from gut flora, they do not
have to choose foods to meet these needs. Similarly, pure carnivores, with
strict adherence to a diet of animal tissue, absorb little glucose as a result of
digestive processes and show a pattern of carbohydrate metabolism differing
from that of omnivores (Morris and Rogers 1982). Pure carnivores have lost
the ability to synthesize certain proteins (enzymes) that appear to be of no
advantage to them because of their highly specialized diets. Adult cats, for
example, require a dietary source of argenine, an amino acid typically synthesized by adult omnivores in sufficient amounts to meet maintenance requirements (Morris and Rogers 1982, 1983a, 1983b). In general, the pure carnivore
appears intolerant of diets adequate for the adult omnivore (ibid.).

Humans are not ruminants; nor do they possess the suite of specialized
metabolic adaptations to diet that distinguishes the pure carnivore. Thus, in
terms of metabolic adaptations to diet, humans fall in with other omnivorous
mammals. To clarify more precisely what type of omnivory may have characterized ancestral hominids, it is useful to examine certain broad characteristics
of the primate diet, paying special attention to hominoids.

The Primate Diet

The adaptive radiation and eventual dominance of angiosperms during the Cre-
taceous opened up a variety of new dietary opportunities (Regal 1977). Potential foods included not only insects that pollinated angiosperm flowers but also
the pollen, nectar, fruits, seeds, and foliage of the angiosperms themselves.
The primate line is believed to have differentiated by the Middle Paleocene,
arising from some type of terrestrial insectivorous stock (Eisenberg 1981).

If present-day primates are any indication, early primates appear to have
taken strong advantage of arboreal plant foods. All extant primates take food

from the first trophic level, but not all primates take food from the second, at least not intentionally. A very few prosimians (e.g., *Galago demidovii*) take the bulk (wet weight) of their diet from animal matter (Charles-Dominique 1977), but the overwhelming majority of primates take the bulk (wet weight) of the diet from plants, eating only small amounts of animal matter (Gaulin and Konner 1977; Harding 1981; Hladik 1977). This indicates that the adaptive radiation of primates, particularly the anthropoids, occurred by virtue of their ability to penetrate the as yet unfilled arboreal plant food niche and radiate to the point where they came to dominate a strong subset of the available arboreal dietary resources.

In the tropical forest, almost all potential plant food comes from dicotyledonous species using the C_3 carbon pathway. In sharp contrast, many potential plant foods in the savannas come from monocotyledonous species using the C_4 carbon pathway. I do not know whether these differences in plant food types are reflected to any degree in the digestive physiology of primates. Certainly, if extant primates are any indication, the primate gut was initially adapted for both the nutritive and the defensive components of dicotyledonous C_3 rather than monocotyledonous C_4 plant foods. Recent experimental work on human fiber digestion shows that human microflora are very sensitive to different fiber sources. As a group, humans are very efficient at degrading the relatively unlignified hemicelluloses and cellulose of dicot vegetable fibers such as cabbage or carrots but are less efficient on monocot cereal fibers such as wheat bran or monocot plant fibers such as alfalfa, with a high cellulose to hemicellulose ratio and considerable lignification (Van Soest et al. 1983). Though most extant primates eat primarily dicotyledonous plant species, a few species (e.g., *Papio* spp., *Theropithecus gelada*) eat quantities of grass blades and presumably are able to degrade the dietary fiber of grasses with some degree of efficiency. The current dependence of most large human populations on quantities of monocotyledonous plant foods, particularly cereal grains, is a notable departure from the traditional plant foods consumed by the majority of primates, both in the past and today. Monocot cereal grains also tend to be high in phytate, which, because of its high anionic character, is ideal for forming complexes with mineral elements, particularly transitional elements such as zinc, iron, and manganese (Lloyd, McDonald, and Crompton 1978). Any primate turning to phytate-rich plant foods as a major dietary staple may require other special foods in the diet to avoid potential mineral deficiencies due to complexing of phytates with essential minerals. Animal foods, for example, are a good source of zinc, which could help to augment losses due to binding of this element in cereal foods by phytates.

In choosing foods, small primates, because of the increase in the ratio of metabolic requirements to gut capacity (Demment and Van Soest 1985), tend to select rapidly digestible plant foods with little bulk, such as sugary fruit or gum (Gaulin and Konner 1977; Hladik 1977). These high-quality plant foods are supplemented to a greater or lesser extent by animal matter, typically insects. Larger-bodied primates generally include some foliage in the diet, eating leaves and buds as well as fruits, seeds, gum, flowers, and cambium. When eating foliage, most primates focus their attention on young rather than mature leaves in spite of the fact that mature leaves are far more abundant. Younger leaves generally show a higher protein-to-fiber ratio than mature leaves and tend to be less lignified, thus offering greater nutritive returns to the feeder (Milton 1979). Some larger-bodied primates routinely seek out foods from the second trophic level, particularly insects, but occasionally vertebrates (e.g., *Cebus* spp., *Papio* spp., *Pan troglodytes*), whereas others rarely appear to ingest animal matter intentionally (e.g., *Alouatta* spp.).

A wealth of available data indicates that primates, particularly anthropoids, typically include a number of different plant parts and plant species in the daily diet. Over an annual cycle, for example, howler monkeys (*Alouatta palliata*) living in lowland tropical forest on Barro Colorado Island, Republic of Panama, take foods from more than 109 plant species (Milton 1980). Further, on any given day, howlers may take foods from 10 to 20 or more different plant species. Two other primate species sympatric with howlers in this same forest, the black-handed spider monkey (*Ateles geoffroyi*) and the capuchin monkey (*Cebus capucinus*), also take foods from well over a hundred plant species per annum, using 10 or more plant species per day (Hladik and Hladik 1969; Oppenheimer 1968; Milton, unpublished data). Arboreal and semi-arboreal animals of some other orders do not appear to include as many plant species in the diet either per annum or per day. For example, the Barro Colorado forest has also been the site of detailed study of the dietary ecology of the red-tailed tree squirrel (*Sciurus granatensis*), two-toed sloth (*Choloepus hoffmanni*), three-toed sloth (*Bradypus variegatus*), and coati (*Nasua narica*) (Glanz et al. 1982; Montgomery and Sunquist 1978; Russell 1979). These species range from purely herbivorous (the two sloth species) to omnivorous (squirrel and coati); in no case do individuals of any of these species even begin to approach the dietary diversity reported for the monkey species in this forest. The large number of plant species eaten by most primate species is an interesting and perhaps unique characteristic of the primate diet (but see Sussman 1978 for a contrasting view).

Conversely, scant data suggest that primate species routinely including animal prey in the diet tend to show strong prey specificity within particular habitats (see, e.g., the work of Charles-Dominique [1977] on the Gabon lorisids). The broad plant food niche of primates and the apparently more narrow and specialized animal food niche are an aspect of primate food choice that warrants further study and quantification.

The Hominoid Diet

An examination of the food choices of hylobatids and pongids shows that all species conform to the general primate trend just described in that they eat considerable plant material, supplementing it with some animal matter, typically eaten in small or even trace amounts. Mountain gorillas are almost exclusively herbivorous (Fossey and Harcourt 1977; Goodall 1977), followed by orangutans (Rodman 1977, 1984) and siamangs (Chivers 1977; Gittins and Raemaekers 1980), both of which eat notable amounts of leaves, shoots, stems, and/or bark as well as fruit and some insect matter (Table 3.1). Gibbons and chimpanzees focus very strongly on fruit in the diet, eating some foliage and from 4 percent to 13 percent animal matter (Gittins and Raemakers 1980; Rodman 1984; Wrangham 1977). The diet of the pygmy chimpanzee is not as yet well documented, but it appears to feed partially on fruit and partially on fibrous vegetable matter, particularly that of ground cover species, supplemented by some animal matter (Kano 1983).

As a dietary category, ripe fruit tends to be relatively high in soluble carbohydrates but low in protein, whereas leaves tend to be relatively high in protein but low in soluble carbohydrates (Milton 1979, 1981). Primate species routinely including large quantities of foliage in the diet each day would not be expected to take foods from the second trophic level unless such foods were required for some essential trace nutrient such as vitamin B_{12}.

The Primate Digestive Tract

The above data show that primates are omnivores of a particular type in that the great majority show a clear focus on plant foods, eating only modest amounts of animal matter. Generally, however, when we think of plant-eating animals, primates do not come to mind; rather, we think of cows, sheep, horses, koalas, kangaroos, and the like. All of these highly herbivorous forms routinely eat the phytosynthetic tissues of plants as their staple item of diet, and all show digestive tracts that are amazingly specialized in form when compared with those of most primates. As an order, primates show a digestive tract that, in its general form, is not greatly modified from the primitive mammalian pattern (Mitchell 1905). In many respects the anthropoid gut is simpler in form than that of prosimians, and it has been suggested that their respective gut forms may have been independently derived from the primitive mammalian pattern (Mitchell 1905). The relatively unspecialized form of the normative primate gut supports the view that, as an order, primates, particularly the

TABLE 3.1. Food Choices of Hominoids (Percentage of Feeding Time)[a]

Species	Fruit	Leaves, Shoots, and Stems	Other Plant Foods	Animal Matter	Source
Gorilla gorilla beringei (mountain gorilla)	2	86	2 flowers 7 wood 3 roots	Negligible— "grubs"	a
Pongo pygmaeus (orangutan)	53 (often unripe)	25	15 bark	<1 insects	b
Pan troglodytes (common chimpanzee)	63 (ripe) 68	20 28	— gum	3 insects 4 insects, eggs, fledglings[b]	b c
Pan paniscus (pygmy chimpanzee)	—	—	—	termites(?)	d
Hylobates syndactylus (siamang)	36	43	6 flowers	15	e
Hylobates lar (lar gibbon)	50	29	7 flowers	13	e
Hylobates agilis (agile gibbon)	58	39	3 flowers	1	e
Homo sapiens (modern hunter-gatherers, excluding highest latitudes)	Plant foods, ≥60			ca. 30–40	f

SOURCES: *a*, Fossey and Harcourt (1977); *b*, Rodman (1984); *c*, Hladik (1977); *d*, Kano (1983); *e*, Gittins and Raemaekers (1980); *f*, Lee (1968).

[a]Values should not necessarily sum to 100 percent as different sources may not present data on all food types eaten by their study subjects.

[b]Chimpanzees were also observed to hunt mammals at Gombe site (Teleki 1981).

anthropoids, have traditionally focused on very high-quality plant foods that are not extensively fibrous or lignified and supplemented them with some second-trophic-level foods. Primates deviating from this pattern of gut morphology appear to represent special radiations that have turned heavily to foliage as a dietary staple (i.e., Colobinae, Indriidae).

It should be noted that within lineages the ancestral pattern tends to dominate gut form (Mitchell 1905). Gut form, therefore, cannot in itself be used to predict diet. For example, a well-developed cecum is generally associated with diets high in plant fiber. All extant prosimians have a cecum, in most cases capacious, but have not been noted to eat any great amount of plant fiber. In many cases the prosimian cecum appears to function as a fermentation chamber for plant exudates and/or chitin of insect exoskeletons (Clemans 1980; Sheine 1979). Conversely, if one examines animals from other orders, the hippopotamus and the giant panda are both strongly herbivorous, and both lack a cecum (Hill and Rewell 1948; P. J. Van Soest, pers. comm.). The bear, a decided omnivore, has a gut as simple in form as that of the mink, a strong carnivore (Hill and Rewell 1948). A sacculated stomach and the strong development of both the cecum *and* colon are generally good predictors of diets high in plant fiber. But the absence of such features does not mean that a given species is

TABLE 3.2. Relative Gut Volume Proportions for Some Hominoid Species (Percentage of Total Volume)

Species	Stomach	Small Intestine	Cecum	Colon	Source of Raw Data
Gorilla gorilla (gorilla)	25	14	7	53	a
Pongo pygmaeus (orangutan)	17	28	3	54	a
Pan troglodytes (chimpanzee)	20	23	5	52	a
Hylobates syndactylus (siamang)	24	25	1	49	a
Hylobates pileatus (pillated gibbon)	24	29	2	45	a
Homo sapiens (human)	17	67	n.a.	17	b
Homo sapiens	24	56	1	19	c
Homo sapiens	10	63	3	23	d

SOURCES: *a*, Chivers and Hladik (1979); *b*, Maynard and Loosli (1969); *c*, D. J. Chivers, pers. comm.; *d*, R. W. Sussman, pers. comm. All calculations of relative volumes by the author.

NOTE: These figures are not scaled with respect to inter-specific differences in body size and as such should only be used inter-specifically as an indication of the *pattern* of gut proportions of the different species. As data are often taken from immature specimens or single specimens, all of these data, perhaps excluding those for *Homo sapiens*, should be regarded as rough estimates.

not strongly herbivorous, nor does it mean that a given species is strongly carnivorous. Staple items of diet or even trophic levels may alter within members of a particular family or genus, but, very broadly, phylogeny appears to dominate function in terms of gut form (Mitchell 1905). This is not to imply that all members of a particular lineage share the same gut scale or proportions, for such is most emphatically not the case. Within lineages, many features of the gut can show modification, particularly in the volume or length of particular sections (see Table 3.2). Work on a number of bird and mammal species likewise shows that within species, between individuals, and perhaps even in the same individual, the nature of the diet can affect gut scale and proportions (Gentle and Savory 1975; Gross, Wang, and Wunder, in press; Koong et al. 1982; Miller 1975; Moss 1972; Murray, Tulloch, and Winter 1977). There are also presumed to be a number of more subtle differences within lineages and intra-specifically in terms of morphological and physiological features of the gut such as mucosa thickness, villi length, and the like (Hill 1949; Hladik 1967; Karasov and Diamond 1983; Sonntag 1924).

The Hominoid Digestive Tract

In keeping with the above observation, all members of the Hominoidea show the same basic gut pattern. Hominoids have a simple acid stomach, a small cecum terminating in a true appendix, and a well-sacculated colon. The hominoid appendix represents a shared trait of this superfamily not found in other extant primates. The night monkey (*Aotus* spp.) is reported to show some development of an appendix, though not to the same extent as hominoids (Hill and Rewell 1948). The hominoid appendix appears to represent the culmination of a strong trend in primates for lymphoid tissue to collect in the cecal apex (Berry 1900; Hill and Rewell 1948). In hominoids, this lymphoid tissue has migrated from the cecal apex into a discrete structure. The functions of the hominoid appendix are not known, but it is clearly an active, functioning organ (Hill and Rewell 1948). In humans, the appendix secretes an alkaline fluid containing amylase, eripsin, and mucin. Davenport (1971) suggests that the human appendix is an especially lively site of antibody production. In rabbits, the appendix has been found to serve immunological functions, producing antibodies against certain protein antigens (Draper and Sussdorf 1965; Hanaoka, Nomoto, and Waksman 1970; Konda and Harris 1966). Other species with an appendix are the capybara (*Hydrochoerus hydrochaeris*) and the wombat (*Lasiorhinus latifrons*). The rabbit, capybara, and wombat, like all hominoids, are strongly herbivorous.

Though the basic form of the hominoid gut is similar throughout the superfamily, there are notable differences between humans and other hominoids when relative gut proportions are compared (Table 3.2). Humans concentrate by far the greatest gut volume in the small intestine ($\geq$56 percent), whereas gibbons and orangutans show the greatest gut volume in the colon. In addition, the size of the human gut relative to body mass is small in comparison with most other anthropoids (R. D. Martin, pers. comm.). A variety of animal studies indicate that increases in energy requirements without a decrease in dietary quality will increase the size of the small intestine and decrease the colon (Cripps and Williams 1975; Fell, Smith, and Campbell 1963; Gross, Wang, and Wunder, in press). Certainly the present-day gut proportions of humans in modern technological societies indicate utilization of nutritionally dense, energetically concentrated foods. At the present time, however, it is difficult to evaluate the implications of differences in gut proportions between humans and other hominoids. As noted, many animal species are able to respond rapidly to changes in dietary quality in terms of modification of gut proportions. The size of the present-day human small intestine could be an ancient or a relatively recent trait. Indeed, it is not known whether all modern human populations show such gut proportions. On average, for example, individuals in Western societies are estimated to take in no more than 10 grams of fiber per day, whereas members of some rural African populations may take in more than 170. A difference of this magnitude, in view of the gut plasticity demonstrated for animals of some other orders, suggests that there may be some differences in gut proportions between extant human populations. Of interest would be data on the gut proportions of human populations on different dietary substrates as well as data on the plasticity of the hominoid gut in terms of its responses to changes in diet.

Burkitt, Walker, and Painter (1972), in observing defecation patterns of rural Ugandans eating unrefined, fibrous diets, commented that they showed transit times two to five times as rapid as those of British navy personnel eating refined Western diets and produced some four to five times more fecal matter. A number of other studies of human fiber digestion likewise show that increasing the fiber level of the diet (which generally implies lowered dietary quality) significantly decreases mean transit time (e.g., Wrick et al. 1983). A similar response was found in chimpanzees fed trial diets of different fiber levels (Milton and Demment, in prep.). Extrapolating to the natural environment, this pattern of digestive kinetics indicates that when dietary quality in the natural environment declines, both humans and chimps respond by increasing intake, which results in a more rapid turnover rate of ingesta. This kinetic response could help to ensure that individuals of both species continue to supply energy and nutrients to body tissue at an optimal rate in spite of some fluctuations in the availability of higher-quality foods in the natural environment.

The relatively small size of the human colon appears to represent the de-

rived rather than ancestral condition of Hominoidea. The colon of human neonates is more similar to that of pongids than is the case for mature individuals
(Hill 1949). Humans show regression of the colon as they mature, whereas
pongids show elongation, particularly of the left colon. Hill (1949) points out
that in the arrangement of the colon, as in many other features of anatomy,
pongids appear to have a gerontomorphic status as compared with humans.
The marked sacculation of the human colon can also be viewed as a possible
retention feature.

When compared with those of most other mammals, the relative proportions
of the human gut are unusual (my calculations, using data from Chivers and
Hladik 1980 and Hladik 1967). Pure carnivores, such as felids, or more omnivorous carnivora, such as canids, do not have gut proportions similar to humans'. Rather, more carnivorous animals tend to show considerable volume in
the stomach or in the stomach *and* small intestine. For example, 70 percent of
the gut volume of the adult cat occurs in the stomach, whereas for dogs this
figure is 62 percent. Highly herbivorous forms also differ from humans. Ruminants tend to show the greatest volume in the region of the stomach, whereas
non-ruminant herbivores such as equines show tremendous volume in the
cecum and colon. Swine, often regarded as good omnivore analogues for humans, in fact differ considerably. Some swine have a specialized area in the
stomach near the pyloric region that is totally lacking in humans; further, swine
are characterized by a large cecum relative to that of humans and a tremendous
proportion of gut volume in the lower tract (Ehle et al. 1982; Stanogias and
Pearce 1985a, 1985b). Work by Ehle et al. (1982) suggests that pigs may also
have a somewhat different pattern of lower-gut turnover than humans as a
result of cecal pulsing.

When the relative proportions of the human gut are compared with those of
other primates, it is still difficult to find a good match. Most anthropoids show
notable volume in the cecum and/or colon or have a highly specialized stomach
(e.g., Colobinae). Prosimians show gut proportions somewhat similar to those
of humans in that the small intestine tends to dominate the gut. However, like
some carnivora, some prosimians show greater relative volume in the stomach
than is the case for humans; further, most prosimians have a notable cecum
that in some cases is highly specialized (Clemens 1980).

One primate whose gut proportions are strikingly similar to those of humans
is the New World capuchin monkey (*Cebus* spp.). Like humans, capuchins concentrate most gut volume in the small intestine. The ratio of gut mass to body
mass in capuchins is also small in comparison with other non-human anthropoids (R. D. Martin, pers. comm.). Capuchin monkeys eat a high-quality
diet made up of unusually rich wild foods, both sugary fruits and protein- and
oil-rich seeds. Capuchins also routinely devote 40 to 50 percent of their daily
foraging time to seeking out second-trophic-level foods, including soft-bodied

102

grubs, cicadas, and small vertebrates (Oppenheimer 1968; Parker and Gibson 1977; Terborgh 1983; Milton, unpublished data).

Scant data on one specimen of *Papio papio* suggest that this species may be somewhat similar to humans in relative gut proportions (Chivers and Hladik 1980; Hladik 1969). Here too there appears to be an emphasis on the volume of the small intestine relative to other sections of the gut. Savanna baboons, like capuchin monkeys, are unusually selective feeders who specialize in high-quality foods. Baboons at times may devote almost all of their daylight hours to painstakingly seeking out small, nutritious food items such as corms, acacia gum, grass seeds, flowers, fruits, and animal matter, including copious quantities of insects when these are available (DeVore and Hall 1965; Hamilton, Buskirk, and Buskirk 1978). Baboons also feed opportunistically on small vertebrates, particularly immature animals (DeVore and Hall 1965; Harding 1973; Strum 1981).

Capuchin monkeys and savanna baboons are also unusual primates in that both use the hand to a considerable degree both to find and to prepare food items for consumption (Beck 1975; Parker and Gibson 1977). Capuchins are noted for their manual dexterity. They routinely use the hand to crack hard-shelled fruits, to unroll dead leaves in search of insect prey, and to pry among palm fronds for insects and small vertebrates (Parker and Gibson 1977). Baboons rely heavily on the hand when feeding, particularly to remove dirt from food items, to peel, husk, and open food items, and to grasp live prey. M. W. Demment (pers. comm.) points out that an adult male baboon (*Papio cynocephalus*) may pick up as many as 3,000 individual food items in a single day of feeding, each weighing no more than one-tenth of a gram dry weight. Thus, savanna baboons are heavily committed to the use of the hand in feeding. The frequent modification of a dietary item before ingestion in effect buffers the teeth and digestive tract of these species from the physical effects of many items in their diet. The similarity in relative gut proportions of humans, capuchin monkeys, and perhaps savanna baboons is not derived from a close common ancestor. Rather, it appears to represent similar adaptive trends in gut morphology in response to diets made up of unusually high-quality dietary items that are capable of being digested and absorbed primarily in the small intestine.

Food Choices of Early Humans

As discussed above, the comparative anatomy of the hominoid digestive tract indicates that modern human gut proportions and scale represent the derived rather than the ancestral condition for the superfamily Hominoidea. There can be little doubt that the ancestral line giving rise to this superfamily and ultimately to hominids was markedly herbivorous. Kliks (1978) has presented evidence from analyses of human coprolites to document the fact that until quite recently, many human populations took in an impressive amount of plant fiber in the diet, estimated from rehydration at perhaps some 130 grams of fiber per day. In addition, human coprolites also contain undigested residues of animal tissue, including such materials as bones, teeth, hair, feathers, keratinized skin, fish scales, and insect cuticle that at times contribute more than 10 percent of the total weight of undigested residues (Kliks 1978). Without more data on the comparative gut proportions of modern human populations and the degree of short-term gut plasticity characteristic of humans and apes, it is difficult to state whether the gut proportions and scale of modern humans as reported in this paper in fact characterized early humans. However, my prediction is that all extant humans will be found to have a gastrointestinal tract dominated by the small intestine, though considerable variation may be recorded for the size of the colon region.

Examination of the diets and activity patterns of extant pongids, in combination with evidence from the hominid fossil record, suggests that early humans focused feeding on energy-rich, high-quality foods. With an adult body weight of 93 kilograms (female) to 160 kilograms (male), gorillas are by far the largest anthropoids (Clutton-Brock and Harvey 1977). Gorillas typically feed on quantities of leafy material, a dietary category that is low in soluble carbohydrates. On such a diet, large body size confers decided energetic and nutritional advantages. In mammalian herbivores and omnivores, relative gut capacity and body mass show a linear relationship, whereas maintenance metabolism and body mass show an exponential relationship (Demment and Van Soest 1985; Parra 1978). In effect, a larger herbivore has proportionately more room in the gut and can exploit foods with a lower protein/fiber ratio than its smaller-sized counterparts (Demment and Van Soest 1985; Janis 1976; Nuzum 1985; Parra 1978). The large body size of the gorilla facilitates exploitation of a fibrous dietary matrix, but on such a diet energy appears to be in short supply. Gorillas are relatively inactive for terrestrial anthropoids and also show low levels of social interaction. This suggests that energy may be limited, so that behaviors that conserve energy are favored.

Similarly, orangutans, though often described as fruit-eaters, in fact concentrate much of their feeding on unripe fruit, leaves, and bark (Rodman 1977). Like gorillas, orangutans tend toward a fibrous dietary substrate that is often presumed to be low in soluble carbohydrates, and, again like gorillas, they are relatively immobile. Ninety percent of their travel takes place at a slow pace through the trees; the average day range is only some 300 meters (Rodman 1977). Further, orangutans are relatively unsocial and are one of the few anthropoid species not associating in any type of relatively permanent social group.

In contrast to gorillas and orangutans, chimpanzees focus their feeding primarily on high-quality foods. The keystone of the chimpanzee diet is ripe fruit, and individuals are very active, often traveling three to four kilometers a day in search of sufficient ripe fruit to meet nutritional requirements. Over 70 percent of chimpanzee travel takes place on the ground. Chimps use smaller, more dispersed food sources than orangutans and show longer median interpatch distances between food sources in ≥10-minute feeding bouts (Rodman 1984). They supplement their basic ripe fruit diet with young leaves of unusually high quality (Hladik 1977) as well as insect and mammal prey. Male chimpanzees have been observed to hunt monkeys and pigs, and meat resulting from communal kills may be shared. (However, it should be noted that no more than 6 percent of the total annual diet of chimpanzees is estimated to come from second-trophic-level foods; see Table 3.1.) Chimpanzees are also extremely social and have a rich repertoire of facial gestures and calls. When feeding, chimpanzees make use of stones to crack hard-shelled fruits (Boesch and Boesch 1981) and use twigs and grasses to harvest termites (McGrew 1974). Thus, like capuchin monkeys and savanna baboons, chimpanzees rely on the hand for many fine-level manipulations with respect to food preparation, and in their case tools may also be employed (see e.g., Parker and Gibson 1977).

In summary, these comparative data on the dietary foci and behaviors of extant pongids strongly suggest that in the hominoid line, a focus on lower-quality, more fibrous plant foods leads to selection for a larger-bodied and relatively inactive and unsocial primate. In pongids, there is a clear pattern toward increasing the relative size of the hindgut and increasing the fiber content of the diet with increasing body size (Milton and Demment, in prep.).

Early humans are believed to have evolved in a savanna-mosaic setting. High-quality foods, both plant and animal, are more patchily distributed in both space and time in a savanna environment than in tropical forests (Milton 1981; Milton and May 1976; D. Olson, pers. comm.). This implies that early hominids in such a setting may have had both large day ranges and large home ranges if they concentrated on higher-quality, more digestible foods. In the hominid line, bipedalism is a more energetically efficient terrestrial locomotor mode than quadrupedalism (Rodman and McHenry 1980). Rodman and McHenry (1980) have hypothesized that selective pressures related to increased travel efficiency between widely dispersed food sources in a savanna setting may underlie in the adaptation of bipedalism in the hominid line.

One way to lower foraging costs when moving from the tropical forest into a savanna-mosaic setting is simply to lower dietary quality. The "robust" australopithecines may have opted for this type of dietary strategy. Their relatively large post-canine teeth and massive skull bones suggest that they fed on tough, fibrous, and/or hard plant foods (Grine 1981). M. Demment (pers. comm.) suggests that dietary competition between the digestively specialized ungulates and the robust australopithecines may have contributed to the eventual extinction of the robust forms. However, another way to lower foraging costs when moving into a patchy savanna environment is to continue to specialize in high-quality foods and to cover increased foraging costs both by improving food-search efficiency and by eating even higher-quality foods (Milton 1980, 1981). This may have been the dietary strategy of the "gracile" australopithecines. Ultimately, however, an adaptive peak should be reached, such that no further improvement on this basic foraging strategy can occur, because there are a finite number of ways to locate a finite number of high-quality dietary items efficiently in the savanna.

All australopithecines, both robust and gracile, are characterized by thick molar enamel and large cheek teeth. Australopithecines show somewhat more cranial expansion than extant pongids, but the difference is slight (Holloway 1973; Leutenegger 1973). In contrast, members of the genus *Homo* show thinner molar enamel, a dramatic reduction in cheek tooth size, and considerable cranial expansion (Grine 1981; McHenry 1982; S. Ambrose, pers. comm.). In combination, these dental and cranial features, as well as an increase in body size, apparently with no loss of mobility or sociality, strongly imply that early members of the genus *Homo* made a dramatic breakthrough with respect to diet—a breakthrough that enabled them to circumvent the nutritional constraints imposed on body size increases in the apes. It would appear that early humans were able in some manner to greatly improve their intake and uptake of energy, apparently without any decrease in dietary quality.

Such a dietary breakthrough had to go beyond improved food search efficiency or simple utilization of available high-quality foods, for I think that the gracile australopithecines were probably already at the apex of possibilities in this respect. There had to be some type of novel innovation—either technological or social or both—that altered the dietary potential of proto-humans (see, e.g., Lancaster 1968, 1975). A technological innovation could somehow make a low-quality but available and abundant food into a high-quality food. A social innovation, such as cooperative hunting and food sharing, could make formerly inaccessible or restricted high-quality food accessible and relatively dependable. An innovation such as language could help to coordinate foraging activities and thereby greatly enhance foraging efficiency (see, e.g., Lancaster 1968, 1975). I cannot state what this innovation was, but perhaps it was both technological and social, for certainly we see the strong development of both trends in human evolution. I can, however, speculate on possible selective pressures.

For most of its evolutionary history, the ancestral line leading to hominoids presumably lived in a forested environment. Plant foods are presumed to have composed the bulk of the diet, complemented perhaps by a modest amount of second-trophic-level food (Kliks 1978; Milton 1981, 1984). Data from extant hunter-gatherer societies suggest that this basic pattern of primate omnivory may also have been practiced by most hunter-gatherer groups living in tropical areas (Lee 1968). It is only in temperate to Arctic latitudes that second-trophic-level foods are noted at times to compose the bulk of the diet (Lee 1968). Early hominids and humans are believed to have evolved in the tropics. If this assumption is correct, it is doubtful, by analogy with both the diets of extant primates and what is known of the diets of extant tropical hunter-gatherer societies, that animal protein in itself composed the bulk of the early human diet (Hayden 1981; Speth and Spielmann 1983). Indeed, research suggests that for most modern humans large quantities of animal protein may actually be detrimental to both normal growth and good health (Edozien and Switzer 1978; Nelson 1975). Human populations such as the Arctic Eskimo, whose diet is composed primarily of animal matter, show special adaptations for energy and nitrogen metabolism, and it is speculated that some of their dietary adaptations may be under some degree of genetic control (Draper 1977). Further, Arctic Eskimos do not eat a diet of pure animal protein but rather eat a mixture of animal protein and animal fat. Animal protein seems most appropriate in the human diet when it is eaten in combination with notable amounts of either fat or carbohydrates and used primarily to meet demands for amino acids and nitrogen (Edozien and Switzer 1978; Maynard and Loosli 1969; Nelson 1975). It seems unlikely that animal protein has ever served as the principal item of diet for the majority of tropical-living human populations.

Given the patchy nature of higher-quality foods in a savanna environment, however, I would suggest that both animal protein and animal fat may have been important dietary resources for early humans. Though relatively few non-human primate species live in the savannas, those that do frequently include animal matter in the diet, at times in considerable amounts (Hamilton, Buskirk, and Buskirk 1978). This suggests that in a savanna environment, animal matter may be somewhat more available for larger-bodied primates than it is in a tropical forest. If early humans were able to depend on protein-rich animal foods to fulfill their daily amino acid requirements, this would buffer the digestive tract from selective pressures related to the need to efficiently process large quantities of proteinacious plant matter—typically leaves. A larger body mass could perhaps be supported with less gut mass, as is suggested to be the case for some carnivores as well as capuchin monkeys and modern humans (Chivers and Hladik 1979; R. D. Martin, pers. comm.). Routinely using some animal matter in the diet would make proportionately more room available in the gut to process carbohydrate-rich plant foods, the traditional energy source for the great majority of primate species.

Plant foods differ in many important respects from animal foods, placing the plant-eating animal under somewhat different selective pressures than carnivores with respect to features of foraging success (Milton 1984; Westoby 1974). Plant foods are sessile and tend to be buffered from consumption by internal, chemical characteristics such as low nutrient content, high cell wall matter, or secondary compounds. In contrast, animal prey is typically highly mobile and protected from predation by external defenses such as speed, spines, teeth, or claws (Milton 1984). If early humans devoted some foraging effort each day to the procurement of second- as well as first-trophic-level foods, their foraging strategy, necessarily focused for most of their past evolutionary history on the efficient exploitation of sessile plant foods, must have undergone some rather radical modifications. The pressures to become efficient at procuring foods from two rather than one trophic level may have set in motion a new suite of behaviors (see, e.g., Strum 1981), leading eventually to what we recognize as the *Homo* grade of development. Like some other researchers (e.g., Isaac 1978; Lancaster 1968, 1975), I see a division of labor with respect to food procurement in combination with food sharing as a pivotal adaptation in human evolution. Indeed, I think that the implications of this type of dietary innovation have not been fully appreciated, for, in effect, a division of labor and food sharing provide a means whereby individuals of a given species can efficiently utilize foods from two trophic levels simultaneously—a foraging strategy that appears to be truly unique among mammals.

Acknowledgments

Portions of this paper were presented at the 1984 Gordon Conference on Evolution of the Human Diet in the session titled "Comparative Studies of Modern Feeding Systems." As the paper that I presented at the Wenner-Gren–sponsored Food Preferences and Aversions Conference was already committed to another volume, I am pleased to be able to publish this material in its stead. I thank David Chivers and Robert Sussman for generously sharing with me their original data on the gut proportions of modern humans. Conversations with Peter Van Soest and Montague Demment contributed greatly to many ideas in this paper.

References Cited

Beck, B.
  1975   Baboons, Chimpanzees and Tools. *Journal of Human Evolution* 3:509–16.
Berry, R. J. A.
  1900   The True Caecal Apex or the Vermiform Appendix: Its Minute and Comparative Anatomy. *Journal of Anatomy and Physiology* 35:83–100.
Boesch, C., and H. Boesch
  1981   Sex Differences in the Use of Natural Hammers by Wild Chimpanzees: A Preliminary Report. *Journal of Human Evolution* 10:585–93.

Burkitt, D. P.; A. R. P. Walker; and N. S. Painter
  1972   Effect of Dietary Fiber on Stools and Transit Times and Its Role in the Causation of Disease. *Lancet* 2:1408–11.

Charles-Dominique, P.
  1977   *Ecology and Behavior of Nocturnal Primates.* New York: Columbia University Press.

Chivers, D. J.
  1977   The Feeding Behaviour of Siamang (*Symphalangus syndactylus*). In *Primate Ecology,* T. H. Clutton-Brock, ed., pp. 355–413. London: Academic Press.

Chivers, D. J., and C. M. Hladik
  1980   Morphology of the Gastrointestinal Tract in Primates: Comparisons with Other Mammals in Relation to Diet. *Journal of Morphology* 166:337–86.

Clemens, E. T.
  1980   The Digestive Tract: Insectivore, Prosimian and Advanced Primate. In *Comparative Physiology: Primitive Mammals,* K. Schmidt-Nielson, L. Bolis, and C. R. Taylor, eds., pp. 90–99. Cambridge: Cambridge University Press.

Clutton-Brock, T. H., and P. H. Harvey
  1977   Species Differences in Feeding and Ranging Behaviour in Primates. In *Primate Ecology,* T. H. Clutton-Brock, ed., pp. 557–84. Cambridge: Cambridge University Press.

Cripps, A. W., and V. J. Williams
  1975   The Effects of Pregnancy and Lactation on Food Intake, Gastrointestinal Anatomy and the Absorptive Capacity of the Small Intestine in the Albino Rat. *British Journal of Nutrition* 33:17–32.

Davenport, H. W.
  1971   *Physiology of the Digestive Tract.* 3d ed. Chicago: Year Book Medical Publishers.

Demment, M. W., and P. J. Van Soest
  1985   A Nutritional Explanation for Body-Size Patterns of Ruminant and Non-Ruminant Herbivores. *American Naturalist* 125:641–72.

DeVore, I., and K. R. L. Hall
  1965   Baboon Ecology. In *Primate Behavior,* I. DeVore, ed., pp. 20–52. New York: Holt, Rinehart and Winston.

Draper, H. H.
  1977   The Aboriginal Eskimo Diet in Modern Perspective. *American Anthropologist* 79:309–16.

Draper, L. R., and D. H. Sussdorf
  1965   Roles of the Liver and Appendix in the Serum Hemolysin in Rabbits. *Journal of Immunology* 95:306–13.

Edozien, J. C., and B. R. Switzer
  1978   Influence of Diet on Growth in the Rat. *Journal of Nutrition* 108:282–90.

Ehle, F. R.; J. L. Jeraci; J. B. Robertson; and P. J. Van Soest
  1982   The Influence of Dietary Fiber on Digestibility, Rate of Passage and
          Gastrointestinal Fermentation in Pigs. *Journal of Animal Science*
          55:1071–80.

Eisenberg, J. F.
  1981   *The Mammalian Radiations.* Chicago: University of Chicago Press.

Fell, B. F.; K. A. Smith; and R. M. Campbell
  1963   Hypertrophic and Hyperplastic Changes in the Alimentary Canal of the
          Lactating Rat. *Journal of Pathology and Bacteriology* 85:179–88.

Fischler, C.
  1981   Food Preferences, Nutritional Wisdom and Sociocultural Evolution. In
          Food, Nutrition and Evolution, D. N. Walcher and N. Kretchmer, eds.,
          pp. 59–68. New York: Masson.

Fossey, D., and A. H. Harcourt
  1977   Feeding Ecology of Free-Ranging Mountain Gorilla (*Gorilla gorilla
          beringei*). In *Primate Ecology,* T. H. Clutton-Brock, ed., pp. 415–47.
          London: Academic Press.

Gaulin, S. J. C., and M. Konner
  1977   On the Natural Diet of Primates, Including Humans. In *Nutrition and the
          Brain,* vol. 1, R. J. Wurtman and J. J. Wurtman, eds., pp. 1–86. New
          York: Raven Press.

Gentle, M. J., and C. J. Savory
  1975   The Effects of Dietary Dilution on the Intestinal Anatomy of the Ja-
          panese Quail (*Coturnix coturnix japonica*). *Research in Veterinary Science*
          19:284–87.

Gittins, S. P., and J. J. Raemaekers
  1980   Siamang, Lar and Agile Gibbon. In *Malayan Forest Primates,* D. J.
          Chivers, ed., pp. 63–106. New York: Plenum Press.

Glanz, W. E., et al.
  1982   Seasonal Food Use and Demographic Trends in *Sciurus granatensis.* In
          The Ecology of a Tropical Forest, E. G. Leigh, A. S. Rand, and D. M.
          Windsor, eds., pp. 239–52. Washington, D.C.: Smithsonian Press.

Goodall, A. G.
  1977   Feeding Behaviour of a Mountain Gorilla Group (*Gorilla gorilla beringei*)
          in the Tshibinda-Kahuzi Region (Zaire). In *Primate Ecology,* T. H. Clut-
          ton-Brock, ed., pp. 450–79. London: Academic Press.

Grine, F. E.
  1981   Trophic Differences Between "Gracile" and "Robust" Austra-
          lopithecines: A Scanning Electron Microscope Analysis of Occlusal
          Events. *South African Journal of Science* 77:203–30.

Gross, J.; Z. Wang; and B. A. Wunder
  In press Adaptations to Food Quality and Energy Needs: Changes in Gut Mor-
          phology and Capacity of *Microtus ochrogaster. Journal of Mammalogy.*

Hamilton, W. J.; R. E. Buskirk; and W. H. Buskirk
  1978   Omnivory and Utilization of Food Resources by Chacma Baboons, *Papio
          ursinus. American Naturalist* 112:911–24.

110

Hanaoka, M.; K. Nomoto; and B. H. Waksman
    1980   Appendix and M-Antibody Formation I: Immune Response and Tolerance to Bovine Globulin in Irradiated, Appendix-Shielded Rabbits. *Journal of Immunology* 104:616–25.

Harding, R. S. O.
    1973   Predation by a Troop of Olive Baboons (*Papio anubis*). *American Journal of Physical Anthropology* 38:587–92.
    1981   An Order of Omnivores: Nonhuman Primate Diets in the Wild. In *Omnivorous Primates: Gathering and Hunting in Human Evolution,* R. S. O. Harding and G. Teleki, eds., pp. 191–214. New York: Columbia University Press.

Hayden, B.
    1981   Subsistence and Ecological Adaptations of Modern Hunter/Gatherers. In *Omnivorous Primates: Gathering and Hunting in Human Evolution,* R. O. Harding and G. Teleki, eds., pp. 344–421. New York: Columbia University Press.

Hill, W. C. O.
    1949   Some Points in the Enteric Anatomy of the Great Apes. *Proceedings of the Zoological Society of London* 119:19–32.

Hill, W. C. O., and R. E. Rewell
    1948   The Caecum of Primates: Its Appendages, Mesenteries and Blood Supply. *Transactions of the Zoological Society of London* 26:199–257.

Hladik, A., and C. M. Hladik
    1969   Rapports Trophiques Entre Vegetation et Primates dans la Foret de Barro Colorado (Panama). *Terre et Vie* 23:25–117.

Hladik, C. M.
    1967   Surface Relative du Tractus Digestif de Quelques. Primates: Morphologie des Villosites Intestinales et Correlations Avec le Regime Alimentaire. *Mammalia* 31:120–47.
    1977   Adaptive Strategies of Primates in Relation to Leaf-Eating. In *The Ecology of Arboreal Folivores,* G. G. Montgomery, ed., pp. 373–96. Washington, D.C.: Smithsonian Press.

Holloway, R. L.
    1973   Endocranial Volumes of Early African Hominids and the Role of the Brain in Human Mosaic Evolution. *Human Evolution* 2:449–59.

Isaac, G.
    1978   Food Sharing and Human Evolution: Archaeological Evidence from the Plio-Pleistocene of East Africa. *Journal of Anthropological Research* 34:311–25.

Janis, C.
    1976   The Evolutionary Strategy of the Equidae and the Origins of Rumen and Cecal Digestion. *Evolution* 30:757–74.

Kano, T.
    1983   An Ecological Study of the Pygmy Chimpanzee (*Pan paniscus*) of Yalosidi, Republic of Zaire. *International Journal of Primatology* 4:1–32.

Karasov, W. H., and J. M. Diamond
    1983   Adaptive Regulation of Sugar and Amino Acid Transport by Vertebrate Intestine. *American Journal of Physiology* 245 (*Gastrointestinal Liver Physiology* 8):G443–62.

Kliks, M.
    1978   Paleodietetics: A Review of the Role of Dietary Fiber in Preagricultural Human Diets. In *Topics in Dietary Fiber Research,* G. A. Spiller and R. J. Amen, eds., pp. 181–202. New York: Plenum Press.

Konda, S., and T. N. Harris
    1966   Effect of Appendectomy and of Thymectomy, with X-irradiation, on the Production of Antibodies in Two Protein Antigens in Young Rabbits. *Journal of Immunology* 97:805–14.

Koong, L. J., et al.
    1982   Effects of Plane of Nutrition on Organ Size and Fasting Heat Production in Pigs. *Journal of Nutrition* 113:1626–31.

Lancaster, J. B.
    1968   Primate Communication Systems and the Emergence of Human Language. In *Primates: Studies in Adaptation and Variability,* P. C. Jay, ed., pp. 439–57. New York: Holt, Rinehart and Winston.
    1975   *Primate Behavior and the Emergence of Human Culture.* New York: Holt, Rinehart and Winston.

Landry, S. O.
    1970   *The Rodentia as Omnivores. Quarterly Review of Biology* 45:351–72.

Lee, R. B.
    1968   What Hunters Do for a Living; or, How to Make Out on Scarce Resources. In *Man the Hunter,* R. B. Lee and I. DeVore, eds., pp. 30–48. Chicago: Aldine Press.

Leutenegger, W.
    1973   Encephalization in Australopithecines: A New Estimate. *Folia Primatolica* 19:9–17.

Lloyd, L. E.; B. E. McDonald; and E. W. Crompton
    1978   *Fundamentals of Nutrition.* 2d ed. San Francisco: W. H. Freeman.

McGrew, W. C.
    1974   Tool Use in Wild Chimpanzees in Feeding Upon Driver Ants. *Journal of Human Evolution* 3:501–8.

McHenry, H. M.
    1982   The Pattern of Human Evolution: Studies on Bipedalism, Mastication and Encephalization. *Annual Review of Anthropology* 11:151–73.

Maynard, L. A., and J. K. Loosli
    1969   *Animal Nutrition.* New York: McGraw-Hill.

Miller, M. R.
    1975   Gut Morphology of Mallards in Relation to Dietary Quality. *Journal of Wildlife Management* 39:168–73.

Milton, K.
    1979   Factors Influencing Leaf-Choice by Howler Monkeys: A Test of Some Hypotheses of Food Selection by Generalist Herbivores. *American Naturalist* 114:362–78.

1980   *The Foraging Strategy of Howler Monkeys: A Study in Primate Econom-ics.* New York: Columbia University Press.

1981   Distribution Patterns of Tropical Plant Foods as an Evolutionary Stim-ulus to Mental Development in Primates. *American Anthropologist* 83:534–48.

1984   The Role of Food Processing Factors in Primate Food Choice. In *Adap-tations for Foraging in Nonhuman Primates,* P. Rodman and J. Cant, eds., pp. 249–79. New York: Columbia University Press.

Milton, K., and M. W. Demment

In prep. Digestive Kinetics and Assimilation Efficiencies of Chimpanzees (*Pan troglodytes*): A Model for Human Fiber Digestion.

Milton, K., and M. L. May

1976   Body Weight, Home Range and Diet in Primates. *Nature* 259:459–62.

Mitchell, P. C.

1905   On the Intestinal Tract of Mammals. *Transactions of the Zoological Soci-ety of London* 17:437–536.

Montgomery, G. G., and M. E. Sunquist

1978   Habitat Selection and Use by Two-Toed and Three-Toed Sloths. In *The Ecology of Arboreal Folivores,* G. G. Montgomery, ed. pp. 329–60. Washington, D.C.: Smithsonian Press.

Morris, J. G., and Q. Rogers

1982   Metabolic Basis for Some of the Nutritional Peculiarities of the Cat. *Journal of Small Animal Practice* 23:599–613.

1983a   Nutritionally Related Metabolic Adaptations of Carnivores and Rumi-nants. In *Plant, Animal and Microbial Adaptations to Terrestrial En-vironment,* N. S. Margaris, M. Arianoutsou-Faraggitaki, and R. J. Re-iter, eds., pp. 165–80. New York: Plenum.

1983b   Nutritional Implications of Some Metabolic Anomalies of the Cat. In *American Animal Hospital Association 50th Annual Meeting Proceed-ings,* pp. 325–31. San Antonio: AAHA.

Moss, R.

1972   Effects of Captivity on Gut Lengths in Red Grouse. *Journal of Wildlife Management* 36:99–104.

Murray, D. M.; N. M. Tulloch; and W. H. Winter

1977   The Effect of Three Different Growth Rates on Some Offal Components of Cattle. *Journal of Agricultural Science* (Cambridge) 89:119–28.

Nelson, R. A.

1975   Implications of Excessive Protein. In *Proceedings Western Hemisphere Nutrition Congress IV,* P. L. White and N. Selvy, eds., pp. 71–76. Ac-ton, Mass.: Publishing Sciences Group.

Nuzum, C. T.

1985   Morphological Correlations. *Science* 229:428.

Oppenheimer, J. R.

1968   Behavior and Ecology of the White-Faced Monkey (*Cebus capucinus*) on Barro Colorado Island. Ph.D. dissertation, University of Illinois, Ur-bana.

Parker, S. T., and K. R. Gibson
    1977   Object Manipulation, Tool Use and Sensorimotor Intelligence as Feeding Adaptations in Cebus Monkeys and Great Apes. *Journal of Human Evolution* 6:623–41.

Parra, R.
    1978   Comparison of Foregut and Hindgut Fermentation in Herbivores. In *The Ecology of Arboreal Folivores*, G. G. Montomgery, ed., pp. 205–30. Washington, D.C.: Smithsonian Press.

Peters, C. R., and E. M. O'Brian
    1981   The Early Hominid Plant Food Niche: Insights from an Analysis of Plant Exploitation by *Homo, Pan* and *Papio* in Eastern and Southern Africa. *Current Anthropology* 22:127–40.

Regal, P. J.
    1977   Ecology and Evolution of Flowering Plant Dominance. *Science* 196:622–29.

Rodman, P. S.
    1977   Feeding Behaviour of Orang-utans of the Kutai Nature Reserve, East Kalimantan. In *Primate Ecology*, T. H. Clutton-Brock, ed., pp. 384–414. London: Academic Press.
    1984   Foraging and Social Systems of Orang-utans and Chimpanzees. In *Adaptations for Foraging in Nonhuman Primates*, P. S. Rodman and J. Cant, eds., pp. 134–60. New York: Columbia University Press.

Rodman, Peter S., and H. M. McHenry
    1980   Bioenergetics and the Origins of Hominid Bipedalism. *American Journal of Physical Anthropology* 52:103–6.

Russell, J. K.
    1979   Reciprocity in the Social Behavior of Coatis (*Nasua narica*). Ph.D. dissertation, University of North Carolina, Chapel Hill.

Sheine, W. S.
    1979   Digestibility of Cellulose in Prosimian Primates. *American Journal of Physical Anthropology* 50:480–81.

Sonntag, C. F.
    1924   *The Morphology and Evolution of the Apes and Man.* London: John Bale Sons and Danielsson.

Speth, J. D., and K. A. Spielmann
    1983   Energy Source, Protein Metabolism, and Hunter-Gatherer Subsistence Strategies. *Journal of Anthropological Archaeology* 2:1–31.

Stahl, A.
    1984   Hominid Diet Before Fire. *Current Anthroplogy* 25:151–68.

Stanogias, G., and G. R. Pearce
    1985a   The Digestion of Fiber by Pigs 1: The Effects of Amount and Type of Fibre on Apparent Digestibility, Nitrogen Balance and Rate of Passage. *British Journal of Nutrition* 53:513–30.
    1985b   The Digestion of Fibre by Pigs 2: Volatile Fatty Acid Concentrations in Large Intestine Digesta. *British Journal of Nutrition* 53:531–36.

Strum, S.
    1981   Processes and Products of Change: Baboon Predatory Behavior at

Gilgil, Kenya. In *Omnivorous Primates: Gathering and Hunting in Human Evolution,* R. S. O. Harding and G. Teleki, eds., pp. 255–302. New York: Columbia University Press.

Sussman, R. W.
1978 Foraging Patterns of Nonhuman Primates and the Nature of Food Preferences in Man. *Federation Proceedings, Anthropology and the Assessment of Nutritional Status* 37:55–60.

Teleki, G.
1981 The Omnivorous Diet and Eclectic Feeding Habits of Chimpanzees in Gombe National Park, Tanzania. In *Omnivorous Primates: Gathering and Hunting in Human Evolution,* R. S. O. Harding and G. Teleki, eds., pp. 303–43. New York: Columbia University Press.

Terborgh, J.
1983 *Five New World Primates: A Study in Comparative Ecology.* Princeton: Princeton University Press.

Trowell, H.
1978 The Development of the Concept of Dietary Fiber in Human Nutrition. *American Journal of Clinical Nutrition* 31:S3–S11.

Truswell, A. S.
1977 Diet and Nutrition of Hunter-Gatherers. In *Health and Disease in Tribal Societies,* pp. 213–26. Aba Foundation Symposium no. 49 (new series). New York: Elsevier.

Van Soest, P. J.
1982 *Nutritional Ecology of the Ruminant.* Corvallis, Oreg.: O & B Books.

Van Soest, P. J., et al.
1982 Comparative Fermentation of Fibre in Man and Other Animals. Paper read at the International Symposium on Dietary Fiber, Palmerston, North, New Zealand.

Van Soest, P. J., et al.
1983 Some in vitro and in vivo Properties of Dietary Fiber from Noncereal Sources. ACS Symposium Series, no. 214, Unconventional Sources of Dietary Fibre, I. Furda, ed., pp. 135–141. Washington, D.C.: American Chemical Society.

Westoby, M.
1974 An Analysis of Diet Selection by Large Generalist Herbivores. *American Naturalist* 108:290–304.

Wrick, K. L.; J. B. Robertson; P. J. Van Soest; B. A. Lewis; J. M. Rivers; D. A. Roe; and L. R. Hackler
1983 The Influence of Dietary Fiber Source on Human Intestinal Transit and Stool Output. *Journal of Nutrition* 113:1464–79.

Wrangham, R. W.
1977 Feeding Behaviour of Chimpanzees in Gombe National Park, Tanzania. In *Primate Ecology,* T. H. Clutton-Brock, ed., pp. 504–38. London: Academic Press.

WILLIAM J. HAMILTON III

Omnivorous Primate Diets and Human Overconsumption of Meat

EVOLUTIONARY ANALYSIS OF CONTEMPORARY HUMAN DIETARY preferences is an aggregate science, consisting of several distinct approaches. These include: (1) analysis of early hominid diets; (2) the study of the diets of non-human primate species and possible regulating principles underlying them; and (3) theories concerned with patterns of foraging by animal species in general.

What is the relationship of our dietary past to present human dietary predilections? Here I briefly evaluate some evidence concerning early hominid diets and the diets of certain contemporary ground-dwelling primates. The dietary habits of contemporary primates may help qualify our interpretation of evidence about past and present hominid diets.

Legacy Hypotheses

Some explanations of contemporary human behavior are based upon early hominid or pre-hominid traits, thus implying adaptive inertia—that is, biological evolution less rapid than environmental change. Such hypotheses suggest that some traits are not adaptive under current conditions and are legacies from earlier evolution. Inertia or legacy explanations for behavior may be more relevant to humans than to other animal species because of the rapidity with which humans have changed their own environments. (But changes in patterns of human behavior may also be more rapid than biological evolution if cultural change is involved, a possibility considered later in this paper.) Inertia explanations have been offered to explain various human characteristics. For example,

Orians (1980) and Balling and Falk (1982) suggest that the contemporary habitat and overall environment of human choice, expressed today by lawn and garden styles, resembles the early African savanna landscape inhabited by our prehistoric ancestors. These authors speak of a generalizable human preference based upon an adaptive response to that environment. Conceding that humans like what they are familiar with and what is advertised or preferred by neighbors, they contend nevertheless that there is an innate preference for a short-cropped, grassy landscape, and that this preference emerged in prehistoric African savannas.

The proponents of such legacy arguments do not reject the influence of evolutionary and/or cultural responses to changed environmental and social conditions. Rather, they insist that some part of the evolutionary past, near or remote, remains incorporated into the human behavioral repertoire. Eibl-Eibesfeldt (1979) and many others (e.g., Alexander 1971; Bigelow 1969) use the same sort of argument when they suggest that humans once lived in small bands, and that patterns of social support, including the expression of group hostility, originated in such groups. These patterns, they conclude, linger today in our behavioral repertoire even though such behavior may sometimes be disadvantageous to contemporary individuals and to entire populations.

I am using a similar argument when I suggest that overconsumption of meat and sugar by some contemporary human populations may be based *in part* upon the dietary predilections of our omnivorous ancestors. Since some contemporary individuals and entire human populations eat no meat at all, a legacy argument cannot be a global explanation for current attitudes toward particular foods. Some of the differences between populations and individuals are related to cultural phenomena, a topic discussed below.

Analysis of adaptive inertia, the expression in contemporary populations of traits adaptive to ancestral conditions, is not easily made. The amount of evolutionary baggage we carry may be quite different for various behavior patterns, depending upon the rigor of natural selection upon them through time and upon their malleability. Thus, without specific knowledge of the genetic and cultural bases for contemporary behavioral predispositions, it may be difficult to evaluate the extent to which a behavior pattern has wholly or in part been determined by our prehistoric past. Evolutionary scenario-spinners can suggest hypotheses far more easily than empiricists can test them. Reconstruction of behavioral prehistory and application of findings to contemporary societies cannot be as rigorous a science as one would like. In many senses it is an imperfect skill involving inferred comparisons of past and present populations. In the case of humans, the evidence comes from physical and cultural anthropology, comparative animal behavior, and, indeed, any relevant source. For past hominid populations, only indirect and fragmentary evidence remains, and it is inevitably subject to conflicting explanations and to revision as new paradigms and information emerge.

Genetic Lags in Human Dietary Adaptation

Foods available to contemporary human populations are, to a large degree, the result of relatively recently developed food sources. Information about the genetic basis of human abilities to digest various foods, insofar as it exists, suggests considerable variability. Some inter-population genetic variation in human digestive capacities reflects historic differences in the availability of various kinds of foods. For example, Simoons (1981) shows that celiac or wheat-eating disease (dietary intolerance of wheat flour) occurs with increasing frequency in populations more recently exposed to wheat as a dietary staple. On a smaller geographic scale, McNicholl and co-workers (1981) make the same point. In the familiar example of lactose, high incidence of tolerance is correlated with a history of pastoral lifestyles (Kretchmer 1972; Simoons 1970). Population differences in tolerance of alcohol and other dietary novelties suggest that human capacities to utilize new foods and withstand drugs without ill effect have evolved during recent millennia. By comparison, there are abiding constraints that have not responded to cultural changes in dietary need and availability. The inability of humans and other primates to synthesize vitamin C is one example. In spite of the enormous amount of disease and death caused by vitamin C deficiency, or scurvy (Kretchmer 1981), humans, unlike many other mammalian species, remain unable to synthesize this vitamin. Humans, it would seem, have a limited ability to adjust to new dietary opportunities they have either chanced upon or created. During recent millennia and centuries, the cross-cultural spread of new foods into various human populations has resulted in diet-related health problems.

What time scale are we considering when we explain contemporary dietary behavior in terms of our evolutionary legacies? The answer depends upon largely unmeasured rates of change, cultural or genetic. Does our failure to make optimal use of particular dietary items reflect our genetic history as tree shrews, australopithecines, or *Homo erectus,* or does it reflect an even more recent past? Since not all traits are subject to the same degree of selective pressure or are equally responsive to selection, any generalization about the significance of behavioral legacies needs to take into account everything we know about the sequence of previous events. For animal matter consumption—and for human diets in general—the available record leaves us with ambiguous evidence (Isaac and Crader 1981).

Cultural Change

Culture is an elusive process, extraordinarily difficult to analyze, since biological theories of cultural evolution are a novelty and are inadequately tested and refined. At one end of the spectrum is the suggestion that classical natural selection bears a close relationship to cultural processes (e.g., Durham 1976; Lumsden and Wilson 1981). It follows from this position that a search for the adaptive significance of culturally determined phenomena will be successful. If this were so, the analytical problem would be greatly simplified because we could eventually identify the relationship between contemporary nutritive practices and attitudes and inclusive fitness. But if, as is more likely the case, cultural selection follows different rules and is partially or wholly divorced from recent natural selection, the evaluation of hypotheses relating diet to past and present evolutionary adaptation will be more difficult. What I see as an untenable position is the conclusion, tacit or explicit, that culture is an entirely human phenomenon and that it can be studied without considering evolutionary influences. Here I adopt an intermediate position: although the capacity for culture has evolved, specific cultural practices have not, at least not in a classical Darwinian sense. If, as Boyd and Richerson (1982, 1983) suggest, what we have inherited is a set of cultural learning rules, then inheritance and culture may lead to practices that are not necessarily in the best interests of the individuals and populations practicing them. In this sense legacy arguments remain relevant. If the rules governing our practice and inheritance of culture evolved in an environment quite different from contemporary conditions, it is possible that cultural practices were once more closely tuned to inclusive fitness maximization. Thus, contrary to one prevailing opinion—that culture is a process allowing for rapid matching of behavior to benefit or optimization—it is also possible to conclude that culture impedes rapid evolutionary change, particularly when the environment is changing as rapidly as are contemporary human diets. Perhaps at a slower pace of environmental change, culture could more closely match practice to inclusive fitness than it has in recent millennia. This view of culture, correct or not, reconciles human culture with natural selection.

The capacity for culture has evolved in those few species—notably early humans—who encountered the most variable environments. Humans are at the extreme end of the spectrum of species in terms of the amount of environmental change they are subject to. The degree to which human behavior is determined by their social milieu is exceptional when they are compared with other animal species, and, as noted above, there is no reason to assume that specific expressions of culture are adaptive. In fact, there is extensive evidence suggesting that this is not the case—for example, the observation that diet-related diseases multiplied with the development of agriculture. In what is now Illinois, pre-agricultural people showed levels of tooth wear not evident after maize agriculture emerged; however, a higher level of dental caries characterizes the later populations (Cook and Buikstra 1973).

In the case of human social structure, a distinction has been made between ecologically and culturally imposed monogamy (Alexander et al. 1979). The same distinction can be applied to human diets. Food choices based upon environmental constraints may be distinguished from those which are cultural phenomena. Thus, many of the dietary peculiarities of various contemporary human populations can be considered to be culturally imposed. It follows that culture is a potential extra-evolutionary cause of maladaptive dietary practices. Nevertheless, I reject the suggestion that biological evolution is irrelevant once we conclude that a particular dietary practice is culturally determined.

Primate Omnivory and Contemporary Human Diets

The extrapolation from omnivorous primate to man requires accepting some untested and possibly untestable assumptions. If we assume that human ancestors possessed in general form the dietary predilections of contemporary omnivorous primates, it follows that with improved hunting and other procurement abilities, the proportion of animal matter in human diets could and probably did increase. The quantity of animal matter and products in the diets of some contemporary people can then be understood in terms of a nearly unlimited availability of animal matter superimposed upon food category preferences acquired in the past. According to this hypothesis, some humans are led by inherited biases to choose a diet that our ancestors sought but could not have obtained for any protracted interval. This does not mean that the search was not profitable to ancestral hominids, and I will show below how it may be advantageous to primates, which, nevertheless, incorporate animal matter into their diets at a rate that makes it, on the average, only a minor part of their diet.

This is another argument for changed environmental conditions and a genetic system that has lagged in its tracking of environmental change. Since there is considerable evidence suggesting evolutionary adaptation in human digestive abilities, what is the case for the inertia argument? I would argue that we must consider each human dietary change and adaptation to it as a separate case. In some cases a simple enzyme difference determines human digestive capability. Other adjustments are not so simple, perhaps requiring complex changes in behavior not readily made in evolutionary time. Perhaps the most compelling evidence in favor of the inertia argument is that we suffer ill effects from some foods that nevertheless figure prominently in our diet. One such case is meat, as epidemiological evidence clearly shows. Some individuals and populations *are* overconsuming meat and fat to the detriment of their health, and the inertia argument offers one explanation for this biologically anomalous situation. This is a strong argument against the suggestion that nutritional wisdom (summarized by Fischler 1981) effectively guides all of the quantitative and qualitative details of human diets. However, some caution is necessary relative to this

121

conclusion because the diseases associated with meat overconsumption have their greatest impact upon post-reproductive individuals. Is meat overconsumption really reducing inclusive fitness?

Sugar overconsumption can be explained in the same way. Fruits are the next choice after animal matter for omnivorous primates. But ripe and sweet fruit is only seasonally available, and much fruit is eaten by baboons and other primates when it has not reached sugar maturity. This is not necessarily by choice, but baboons are not orchardists. They must compete with one another, as well as with bats, pigeons, and a host of other animals, for the fruits of their forests. Sour fruit is better than none at all. For baboons and many other omnivorous creatures, a competitive world precludes dependence upon the fruit equivalent of sugared cereals and candy. But given the occasional choice, many primates consume quantities of ripe and sweet fruit and will linger in a tree loaded with ripe fruit for prolonged intervals.

Primate Omnivory

Omnivory, as used here, refers to the propensity to consume and process three broad classes of food: leafy material, fruits and seeds, and animal matter. By this definition humans are omnivores, although not all human individuals choose this full range of food types. Omnivory represents a vast dietary difference from carnivory, frugivory, and folivory. Although lions sometimes eat grass, and folivorous and frugivorous mammals may ingest some animal matter, the bulk of their diet is largely limited to one class of foods. For the omnivores, there are fluctuations, often seasonal, in the proportions of these classes of foods in the diet.

Like human diets, the diets of free-ranging primate populations differ widely. Highly folivorous primate diets are less relevant to our understanding of human diets than are those of the omnivores. Omnivorous primates choose categories of food broadly overlapping those accepted by contemporary humans. Intra- and inter-specific differences in the diets of omnivorous primates may be due to (1) heritable differences, (2) conditions of seasonal availability, (3) socially induced limitations upon food availability, and (4), in a limited number of cases, culturally learned and transmitted methods for processing foods.

Because of my field research experience with chacma baboons, *Papio ursinus,* I focus initially on the dietary characteristics of populations of this species and on the bases of individual and population differences in diet. I then discuss observations of animal matter consumption by this species, its social and ecological correlates, and the relevance of animal matter consumption by omnivorous primates to meat overconsumption by some contemporary human populations.

Dietary habits of savanna baboons are considered here as one model for the ecological determinants of early human food consumption. However, it is doubtful that any contemporary human integrated into a social group could survive for long on a baboon's diet. Some of the items require longer processing times than humans might be able to afford. Others are highly distasteful or toxic. So I am not suggesting that baboons are precise primate counterparts to either contemporary or prehistoric humans. But, like some other omnivorous primates, especially the ground-dwelling macaques, langurs, and chimpanzees, they are probably the best primate models, and perhaps the best animal models, for humans and their dietary choices. Principles determining the dietary intake of savanna baboons may provide insights into the origins and consequences of omnivory in primates, including humans.

Folivorous primates excepted, there is an inverse correlation between the amount of animal matter in primate diets and body size (Hamilton and Busse 1978). The basis for this correlation is also discussed by Kay and Hylander (1978) and Kay (1984). These authors conclude that it would be impossible for a large primate to satisfy its total energy requirements on an insect diet. Larger primates, even though they may prefer animal matter to other kinds of food, consume vegetation and fruits and seeds as the bulk of their diet during most seasons (Hamilton, Buskirk, and Buskirk 1978). There is a simple explanation for the unfulfilled carnivorous appetites of the larger primates. They are incapable of capturing adults of prey species as large as or larger than themselves. Moreover, when they do catch small mammals or birds, their largest prey, high-ranking individuals may monopolize access to thse items (Hamilton and Busse 1982). Occasionally insect outbreaks make animal matter plentiful and easily available. When this happens the proportion of dietary animal matter soars (Hamilton, Buskirk, and Buskirk 1978). Evidence provided in Table 4.1 shows that one large primate, the chacma baboon, weighing up to 30 kilograms or more, occasionally subsists largely upon animal matter, sometimes for protracted intervals, if this resource is sufficiently abundant and available. A similar dietary response to animal matter abundance is seen in many contemporary human populations. But in the usual day-to-day search for food, insects and larger animals are captured infrequently by baboons and other omnivorous primates, and in most cases a large primate does not have an advantage over a smaller one in catching an individual insect. This applies both within and between species. Insects are usually seized one at a time, processed if necessary (for example, by eliminating the gut contents of large caterpillars), and then consumed. The outbreak quantified in the last column of Table 4.1 involved a single species of coccid scale insect. These insects and their shells were

TABLE 4.1. Chacma Baboon Food Preferences in Percentages of Time Spent Eating Foods in Each Class

| | No Insect Outbreak | Insect Outbreak | |
| | | | |
Choices	Five Troops	Troop A	Troop H
Animal matter (including insects)	0.7%	2.3%	72.1%
Fruits and seeds	77.3%	84.2%	20.3%
Vegetation	21.8%	13.1%	7.3%
Euphorics	0.2%	0.4%	0.2%
Soil	T	T	0.1%

SOURCE: Hamilton, Buskirk, and Buskirk (1978).
NOTES: Percentages of time five chacma baboon troops in Namibia and Botswana spent eating foods in broad classes were averaged over a one-year period. The second and third columns compare intake by two Botswana troops of the same population over a two-month interval when scale insects were abundantly available to one troop (H). The animal matter category consists largely of insects. T = trace.

scraped in groups from leaves by the baboons. They have a soft chitinous exoskeleton and are swallowed whole. Presumably their ingestion would not leave identifiable microwear striations on baboon teeth (see below).

Hamilton and Busse (1978) extrapolated these and other observations of chacma baboon foraging to other omnivorous primates, including humans. The rationale for doing so is that other omnivores also attempt to maximize the rate of caloric intake, and, *when readily available,* animal matter is the most energy-rich food. This reasoning assumes that the primary basis for choice within the range of acceptable dietary items is energy maximization. If animal matter provides the greatest net energy yield per unit foraging time, it will be the chosen category of food. Food selection by animals in general may be based upon optimization of net energy gain, within the range of acceptable items (Pulliam 1974; Pyke, Pulliam, and Charnov 1977; Schoener 1971), most nutrient needs being incidentally met in the process.

Surely omnivores have dietary needs not completely satisfied by animal products. What, then, is the optimal proportion of animal matter in the diet, and what factors influence this proportion? Since no omnivorous primate subsists even for a day solely on animal matter, there may never be a conflict between animal matter consumption and nutritional adequacy. Nor is there any evidence to suggest that consumption of various classes of dietary constituents by free-ranging primates has any adverse effects, although this generalization may be made more from ignorance than from quantified measurement. On the other hand, there *is* evidence that secondary compounds may reduce the digestibility of certain plants (e.g., McKay et al. 1978). Optimization of energy gain needs to be evaluated relative to the costs of ingestion of deleterious foods, and other foraging costs.

Table 4.1 summarizes the bulk percentage of various dietary categories consumed by five chacma baboon troops representing two populations. These data show that items other than animal matter make up the bulk of the annual diet. But these data alone say little or nothing about preference. Often there are no fruits and seeds, and only traces of animal matter, readily available to these animals. As the environment changes throughout the year and between years, preferences can be identified only by observing choices when *alternatives* are present. Two major factors determine these choices: the availability of alternative kinds of food, and the amount of effort required to process a food type and obtain its desirable or usable portion. Additional evidence comes from the daily intake pattern for food classes. Often, available animal matter and fruits are eaten in the first hours of the day. Individuals may then become less selective throughout the day. We (Hamilton, Buskirk, and Buskirk 1978) frequently observed adult male chacma baboons eating handfuls of the relatively unpalatable silicaceous leaves of *Salvadora persica* late in the day, but never in the first half of the daily cycle.

Based upon our observation of chacma baboons in the presence of food alternatives, a clear order of preferences can be determined:

1. Least preferred: leafy material, including grasses
2. More preferred: rhizomes, fresh grass seeds, fruits, and flowers
3. Most preferred: animal matter, including, but not limited to, insects

Derivation of this order is based upon the observation that grasses and their choice basal parts are almost completely ignored when *fresh* acacia seeds (which are soft and do not need to be cracked) and fruits of various sorts are abundant. When occasional insect outbreaks occur, the troops head for these concentrations in the morning and spend most of the day eating them, bypassing the usual seeds and fruits (Hamilton, Buskirk, and Buskirk 1978). At the same time, neighboring troops that do not have the host plants of the erupting insect populations in their home ranges were consuming other, non-animal foods.

Normally insects become available in small, localized patches. In November 1982 caterpillar larvae were locally infesting the foliage of the euphorbiaceous tree, *Croton megalobotrys*. For over ten days these sites of insect infestation were the first target of the foraging baboons. After an hour or two of foraging in the infested areas, capture rates declined, and the troop moved off to forage on the bases of fresh grass stalks. During the following days they spent their mornings digging in shallow duff, manually ripping open cocoons and eating

125

pupae one by one. This, too, was a morning activity, followed by consumption of herbaceous material for the rest of the day. No fruits were available at the time.

Sometimes heavy insect outbreaks are distant from roost locations. In the case of the coccid insect outbreak described in Table 4.1, morning movement to this resource took the troop to the most remote part of its home range. Hence, encounter rates and accessibility cannot account for the morning choice of insects in this case. Optimum foraging models based upon random movement through home ranges are thus not applicable.

Our focal chacma baboon troops achieved their lowest success in insect matter consumption for termites, solitary grasshoppers, and ants. Consumption of these insects is an individual and facultative activity, and although there is intense competition for these sometimes highly localized resources, they provide a relatively small part of individual baboon diets.

Tooth Micro-wear Patterns

Considerable recent attention has been given to the micro-wear patterns of australopithecine and other mammalian teeth in an attempt to establish correlations with diets. On the basis of tooth micro-wear patterns, Walker (1981) concludes that the robust australopithecines were neither grazers nor browsers and that they did not eat husked (hard) seeds. He therefore dismisses Jolly's (1970) australopithecine seed-eating hypothesis and Szalay's (1975) suggestion that the heavy enamel of australopithecine teeth is an adaptation to bone-crushing or -crunching, since both seed-cracking and bone-crunching produce micro-wear characteristics not found on australopithecine teeth. His further conclusion, that australopithecines were frugivores, is based upon his observation that the tooth micro-wear patterns of 20 East African specimens cannot be distinguished from those of drills, chimpanzees, and orangutans, which he assumes to be frugivores. Walker (1981) further assumes that the seeds of fruits eaten by australopithecines were not processed, as this also would have produced distinctive microwear patterns.

There is much to say about the emerging evidence from this promising avenue of research, and what studies of contemporary primates and their diets may contribute. I know of no measurements of baboon tooth micro-wear, yet much of my subsequent discussion of primate diets focuses upon them. Baboons do process fruits without, in most cases, attempting to crush their seeds. Fleshy portions of stone fruits are usually removed by manual or oral manipulation; less frequently, the seeds are passed. The only persistent crushing I have observed is of dry acacia seeds. Nevertheless, these seeds figure prominently in most savanna and hamadryas baboon diets. Insect chitin, which also produces distinctive tooth micro-wear patterns, would not cause much tooth abrasion in baboons, since most baboon insect-foraging is for caterpillars, soft insects, pupae of various sorts, and soft-bodied termites. Although I observed one population of baboons feeding almost exclusively on large adult grasshoppers (*Schistocerca*) for over two months, other troops may for years eat only a few grasshoppers and almost no other hard-bodied, chitinous insects.

Thus, opportunism, selection, and processing of food items by omnivorous primates may limit the degree of certainty about what can be concluded from tooth micro-wear patterns. Analysis of tooth micro-wear seems to be a valuable method for excluding certain kinds of food processing, but because of the several ways that some omnivores can process particular food items, micro-wear studies may have limited utility in determining the kinds of food that are actually eaten. Even in the case of grass, which produces distinctive striations on teeth (Baker, Jones, and Wardrop 1959), tooth micro-wear evidence may not identify the extent to which it is eaten. Baboons usually process grasses so that only soft basal parts are eaten. In the case of vertebrate consumption, baboons are meticulous, rejecting bones and pelts while stripping off and consuming soft flesh. It may be useful not to know what baboon tooth wear patterns are for the moment, so that the evidence of tooth micro-wear can be tested without the risk of post hoc reasoning. Presumably tooth micro-wear patterns are generated by persistent, as opposed to casual, use of particular dietary items. For baboons I would predict some evidence for the consumption of grass, and little else. Striations from grass consumption may be more pronounced for some savanna baboon populations than for others, since there are significant differences between populations in the amount of grass in the diet. Other kinds of plant foods, including certain fibrous fruits, may also influence baboon tooth wear patterns. I would predict individual population, age, and sex differences in baboon tooth micro-wear patterns, with more variation than has been observed for mammals with more stereotyped diets.

Our current knowledge of baboon and other omnivorous primate diets suggests that there may also be considerable population variation in australopithecine tooth micro-wear patterns, if australopithecines were omnivores too. Thus, Walker's (1981) identification of possible australopithecine diets may need to be enlarged to include a much more diverse diet.

Hunter-Gatherers as Models

Most populations of human hunter-gatherers were exterminated by the spread of other cultures before their diets were well studied. Analysis of the diets of extant hunter-gatherers, while interesting, is in part compromised by changes in their densities compared with aboriginal conditions, and by culturally induced changes in diet. Interpretations are further complicated by omnipresent exchange systems between tribes, often involving food. The hunter-gatherer populations that lived on the richer soils of the planet were replaced long ago by agriculturalists. Since rich soils support rich vegetation, and a potentially greater biomass of non-human animal species, it follows that pre-agricultural humans probably lived at their greatest densities in these areas. Now the only relatively undisturbed hunter-gatherers live in arid regions or other areas not well suited to agriculture and pastoralism. Studies of the diets of hunter-gatherers now living on marginal lands probably provide poor and incomplete information about the diet of the vast majority of early humans. An ecologist might insist upon the following characteristics before considering a population appropriate for the evolutionary analysis of diet:

1. Mean density determined by evolutionarily relevant parameters—not by human disturbance other than that of the subject population in the case of hunter-gatherers

2. Dietary items that are the same as or equivalent to those which shaped the dietary habits of the species

3. Social groupings that have approximately the character and size of evolving populations (i.e., they are not modified by the provision of human agricultural products or freed by human interference from density-regulating processes by predators)

These are not difficult requirements to fulfill for many small animals, or even for some larger species living in areas remote from human activities. They are also relatively easily met by dietary specialist species. Problems arise in the data base and its interpretation for those omnivores whose diets broadly overlap those of humans and who live in the vicinity of human populations. It is not only humans whose diets have been modified by agriculture and other forms of human-induced change. Baboons in particular—at least the majority of populations that live near human habitation—also accept the easy calorie.

In the case of extant hunter-gatherers, the intrusion of trade has changed the availability of food via the introduction of new items. Improvisations such as spears, bows and arrows, gill nets, guns, and dogs have also modified the hunting process. A cultural anthropologist would be fortunate indeed to find a population of hunter-gatherers uninfluenced by any of these extra-cultural artifacts and conditions.

Another serious interpretive dilemma concerns density. Ecologists assume that over a short period of perhaps a few millennia or a few centuries, the density of local animal populations fluctuates around some relatively constant mean. This has many implications for determinations of a "natural" diet. Over a few years one can, with some luck, witness some years of extreme weather and expect conditions for the study population to approximate the evolutionarily relevant diet and conditions stated in the foregoing list.

Schaller and Lowther (1969) attempted to determine the ability of early hominids to make a living scavenging on the East African plains. To do so, they strolled across the Serengeti plains, looking for partially eaten and abandoned mammal carcasses, helpless gazelle fawns, and other easily captured prey. Although I admire the direct approach they took to the problem, I am unconvinced by their conclusions. The experience of two men scavenging in a vast park not otherwise hunted by humans does not satisfy conditions 1 and 3 of the list. If hunting success were density-dependent, Schaller and Lowther's (1969) Serengeti experience might have been quite different. Persistent scavenge hunting (Hamilton 1973) by larger groups of hominids over long intervals might not have been as successful. Prey availability is limited not only by prey abundance but also by prey wariness, which increases with hunting pressure. A more appropriate but impractical experiment would be to introduce social groups to an area and to measure their foraging success over a period of years, observing the eventual equilibrium between human density and prey- and carrion-procurement success.

Optimality Models

Optimality models for foraging predict the outcome of an animal's choosing foods that provide an adequate diet at the least cost and risk. Optimality models emphasize the time and energy costs of handling (processing) food, the risks entailed in doing so, and the need to obtain a balanced diet. Under the basic assumption that evolution has produced maximally efficient design (Krebs and Davies 1981), the foraging behavior of an organism or population closely matches changed environments. Thus, "legacy" behaviors discussed earlier are outcomes not predicted by optimality models, since they are dietary preferences that have not kept pace with environmental changes. This does not mean that if we accept a particular legacy argument we must reject the applicability of optimality theory to human dietary choices. It suggests only that there may be cases where non-optimality can be identified, perhaps because of the rapidity of environmental change. For contemporary humans in particular, a simple optimality model for choice of food seems unlikely to be applicable, since culture has probably not closely tracked natural selection. It is possible to argue that humans evolved dietary preferences that, in the past, optimized the quality and quantity of their diet, and that the contemporary mismatch of diet to nutritive needs is based upon prehistoric evolutionary events.

Conclusions

Until there is a more unified and widely accepted set of hypotheses concerning what culture is and how it influences human dietary habits, an evolutionary theory of human food choices will not be possible. The position taken in this paper is that culture adapted early hominids to the environment more precisely than it now does for most contemporary human populations. This suggests that human culture has produced evolved characteristics that today lead some contemporary populations, indirectly or directly, to adopt diets not suited to optimum health.

If a degree of fixation of choice for broad categories of food items is the basis of some human food preferences, it may be possible to find primate or animal species that have evolved similar fixations. Certain living omnivorous primate species may be well suited to analyses relating food availability to the extent to which it is eaten. If the assumptions stated in this paper are valid, studies of the diets of omnivorous primates can tell us much about why many contemporary humans eat the foods they do, regardless of whether they are the best available diets to sustain optimum health.

References Cited

Alexander, R. D.
>   1971   The Search for an Evolutionary Philosophy of Man. *Proceedings of the Royal Society of Victoria,* 84:99–119.

Alexander, R. D.; J. L. Hoagland; R. D. Howard; K. M. Noonan; and P. W. Sherman
>   1979   Sexual Dimorphisms and Breeding Systems in Pinnipeds, Ungulates, Primates, and Humans. In *Evolutionary Biology and Human Social Behavior,* N. A. Chagnon and W. Irons, eds., pp. 402–35. North Scituate: Duxbury.

Baker, G.; L. H. P. Jones; and I. D. Wardrop
>   1959   Causes of Wear on Sheep's Teeth. *Nature* 184:1583–85.

Balling, J. D., and J. H. Falk
>   1982   Development of Visual Preference for Natural Environments. *Environment and Behavior* 14:5–28.

Bigelow, R.
>   1969   *The Dawn Warriors.* Boston: Little, Brown.

Boyd, R., and P. J. Richerson
>   1982   Cultural Transmission and the Evolution of Cooperative Behavior. *Human Ecology* 10:325–51.

>   1985   *Culture and the Evolutionary Process.* Chicago: University of Chicago Press.

Cook, D. C., and J. E. Buikstra

    1973   Circular Caries: A New Tool in Nutritional Assessment in the Past. Paper read at the annual meeting of the American Association of Physical Anthropologists, Dallas.

Durham, W. H.

    1978   Toward a Coevolutionary View of Human Biology and Culture. In *The Sociobiology Debate,* A. Caplan, ed., pp. 428–48. New York: Harper and Row.

Eibl-Eibesfeldt, I.

    1979   *The Biology of Peace and War.* New York: Viking.

Fischler, C.

    1981   Food Preferences, Nutritional Wisdom and Sociocultural Evolution. In *Food, Nutrition and Evolution,* D. N. Walcher and N. Kretchmer, eds., pp. 59–68. New York: Masson.

Hamilton, W. J.

    1973   *Life's Color Code.* New York: McGraw-Hill.

Hamilton, W. J.; R. E. Buskirk; and W. H. Buskirk

    1978   Omnivory and Utilization of Food Resources by Chacma Baboons, *Papio ursinus. American Naturalist* 112:911–24.

Hamilton, W. J., and C. D. Busse

    1978   Primate Carnivory and Its Significance to Human Diets. *Bioscience* 28:761–66.

    1982   Social Dominance and Predatory Behavior of Chacma Baboons. *Journal of Human Evolution* 11:567–73.

Isaac, D. L., and D. C. Crader

    1981   To What Extent Were Early Hominids Carnivorous? An Archaeological Perspective. In *Omnivorous Primates,* R. S. O. Harding and G. Teleki, eds., pp. 37–103. New York: Columbia University Press.

Jolly, C. J.

    1970   The Seed-Eaters: A New Model of Human Differentiation Based on a Baboon Analogy. *Man* 5:5–26.

Kay, R. F.

    1984   On the Use of Anatomical Features to Infer Foraging Behavior in Extinct Primates. In *Adaptation for Foraging in Nonhuman Primates,* J. G. H. Cant and P. S. Rodman, eds., pp. 21–53. New York: Columbia University Press.

Kay, R. F., and W. L. Hylander

    1978   The Dental Structure of Mammalian Folivores with Special Reference to Primates and Phalangeroidea (Marsupialia). In *The Ecology of Arboreal Folivores,* G. G. Montgomery, ed., pp. 173–196. Washington, D.C.: Smithsonian Press.

Krebs, J. R., and N. B. Davies

    1981   *An Introduction to Behavioral Ecology.* Sunderland, Mass.: Sinauer Associates.

131

Kretchmer, N.
    1972   Lactose and Lactase. *Scientific American* 227:71–78.
    1981   Food: A Selection Agent in Evolution. In *Food, Nutrition and Evolution,* D. N. Walcher and N. Kretchmer, eds., pp. 37–48. New York: Masson.

Lumsden, C. J., and E. O. Wilson
    1981   *Genes, Mind and Culture: The Coevolutionary Process.* Cambridge: Harvard University Press.

McKay, D.; P. G. Watterman; C. N. Mbi; J. S. Cartlan; and T. T. Strutsaker
    1978   Phenolic Content of Vegetation in Two African Rain Forests: Ecological Implication. *Science* 202:61–64.

McNicholl, B., et al.
    1981   History, Genetics and Natural History of Celiac Disease–Gluten Enteropathy. In *Food, Nutrition and Evolution,* D. N. Walcher and N. Kretchmer, eds., pp. 169–77. New York: Masson.

Orians, G. H.
    1980   Habitat Selection: General Theory and Applications to Human Behavior. In *The Evolution of Human Social Behavior,* J. S. Lockard, ed., pp. 49–66. New York: Elsevier.

Pulliam, R. H.
    1974   On the Theory of Optimal Diets. *American Naturalist* 108:59–74.

Pyke, G. H.; H. R. Pulliam; and E. L. Charnov
    1977   Optimal Foraging: A Selective Review of Theory and Tests. *Quarterly Review of Biology* 52:137–54.

Schaller, G. W., and G. R. Lowther
    1969   The Relevance of Carnivore Behavior to the Study of Early Hominids. *Southwestern Journal of Anthropology* 25:307–41.

Schoener, T. W.
    1971   Theory of Feeding Strategies. *Annual Review of Ecology and Systematics.* 2:369–404.

Simoons, F. J.
    1970   Primary Adult Lactose Intolerance and the Milk-Drinking Habit: A Problem in Biological and Cultural Interrelations, II: A Cultural-Historical Hypothesis. *American Journal of Digestive Diseases* 15:695–710.
    1981   Celiac Disease as a Geographic Problem. In *Food, Nutrition and Evolution,* D. N. Walcher and N. Kretchmer, eds., pp. 179–99. New York: Masson.

Szalay, F. S.
    1975   Hunting-Scavenging Protohominids: A Model of Hominid Origins. *Man* (n.s.) 10:420–29.

Walker, A.
    1981   Diet and Teeth. *Philosophy Transactions of the Royal Society of London* B 292:57–64.

5

SOLOMON H. KATZ

Fava Bean Consumption: A Case for the Co-Evolution of Genes and Culture

OVER THE LAST 15 YEARS MY COLLEAGUES AND I HAVE BEEN investigating the interface between human nutritional needs and the traditional cultural food practices that satisfy the nutrient needs of the individual and the population as a whole (Katz and Foulks 1970). For example, we have studied the interrelations between human biology and culture in the traditional preparation and processing of maize into specific foods by American native populations (Katz, Hediger, and Valleroy 1974). In this work we have developed evidence that the traditional cultural practices encompassing the preparation and processing of maize significantly enhance its nutritional quality. Maize was the major food supporting the growth of Meso-American civilization. Alkali treatment almost certainly facilitated the intensification of maize agriculture, which in turn led to substantial modifications in the organization and structure of Meso-American society. These social modifications ultimately had effects on the demography and the ecology of Meso-American populations and hence influenced their genetic composition. Thus, over many centuries there was an indirect link between the cultural processes underlying the development of this technology and biological adaptability and evolution within these societies (Katz, Hediger, Valleroy 1975).

Although maize preparation practices offer considerable insight into the evolution of cultural practices linked to the supply of essential nutrients, their direct effects on the genetic composition of the population, and hence its biological evolution, have not been amenable to further quantitative analyses. In order to take this biocultural evolutionary approach further, we have been attempting to develop models and hypotheses about how food practices influence specific genetic characteristics. Accordingly, this paper considers and extends our work (Katz 1973, 1979; Katz and Schall 1979) on the cultural factors underlying fava bean consumption and the genetics of favism (a severe hemolytic anemia) in the circum-Mediterranean region. Since the genetic condition underlying favism is already documented, the test case presented in this paper allows for the development of more comprehensive heuristic models that use various human foods to evaluate quantitatively the co-evolutionary interactions between biologically based genetic adaptations and traditional cultural practices.

The consumption of fava beans has been associated with some of the strongest dietary aversions and prescriptions in recorded history. In fact, it is reasonable to hypothesize that there is a direct biocultural evolutionary connection between the traditional aversion to fava bean consumption and its effects on genetically susceptible individuals. To explore and develop this hypothesis, this paper will briefly review some of the salient aspects of biocultural evolutionary theory and then examine fava bean consumption as a test case of some of the important biocultural, ecological, and evolutionary problems confronting the conceptualization of food preferences and aversions.

Food and Biocultural Evolution

The heuristic biocultural evolutionary approach holds that in every human population there is a time-dependent dynamic equilibrium among ecological, sociocultural, human biological, and demographic variables (see Figure 5.1). The

FIGURE 5.1a. The Ecosystems Approach

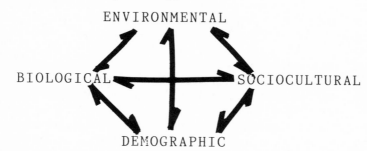

NOTE: This figure shows the interactions among the following: 1) the biological dimension, which consists of the genetic and phenotypic characteristics of the population; 2) the sociocultural dimension, which consists of the cultural history and the current knowledge or information that is resident in the minds of its members and is accessible to the population as a whole (and includes its material products); 3) the environmental, which includes the non-cultural aspects of the ecosystem in which the population resides; and 4) the demographic dimension, which includes the structure, size, and composition of the population. The interactions are to indicate a dynamic equilibrium where all of the variables are continuously interacting over time and the information content of the system can be continuously changing.

mechanisms of evolution that change the gene pool of a population can also be conceptualized as shifting the genetic "information" pool of the population. Cultural traditions, practices, and knowledge form a "cultural information pool," which complements and supplements the "biological information pool," and these processes of interaction form a dynamic equilibrium over time in any particular ecosystem. This conceptualization of biocultural evolution assists in the testing of hypotheses about the mechanisms of storage, change, and transmission within the biological and sociocultural information pools and particularly about the interactions between the two pools over a wide range of time intervals (Katz and Schall 1979; see also Katz 1973).

FIGURE 5.1b. Information and Biocultural Evolution

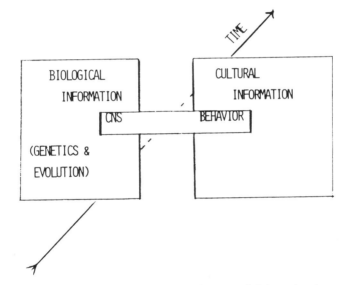

NOTE: The mechanisms underlying the evolution of the genetic information changes are understood relatively well, and the mechanisms by which the human central nervous system receives, processes, creates, stores, and sends its information are being successfully investigated. Likewise, there is increasing systematic understanding about the analogous ways in which the sociocultural system develops, changes, stores, transforms, and communicates (i.e., evolves) its information, particularly in response to the needs of the biological system. However, to systematically integrate the knowledge we have concerning evolution of these three interacting systems (i.e., genetic, neurobiological and behavioral, and sociocultural) represents one of the greatest challenges to anthropology. This paper seeks to explore this problem in presenting an integrated approach to the consumption of fava beans, which represents a particularly rich source of data and hypotheses relevant to this topic.

In the context of this broad biocultural evolutionary model, there are some obvious constraints upon the evolution of implicit and explicit knowledge about foods and their consumption within a society. Understanding the full significance and origins of this knowledge could significantly help in our understanding of some aversive food behaviors. Among other factors, we know that there is a biological component accounting for the "fit" between the food consumed and biological needs and processes. These needs can be divided into various categories of nutritional value (such as protein efficiency and related ratios, caloric content, trace elements, vitamins, and so forth). Obviously this fit between food and nutritional value becomes more significant as the food ascends a scale of importance as a source of sustenance within a particular population.

The ecological component is a crucial variable associated with the environmental constraints upon the relative abundance of the food and the ease with which it can be gathered or hunted in the wild state, cultivated, or domesticated. Climatic variables such as rainfall, altitude, sunlight, and temperature, together with soil conditions, all help to establish a possible range of variation. Another component consists of the pharmacological properties of the food. Many edible plants contain highly active toxins, psychoactive drugs, and a wide variety of other compounds whose influence can mimic or even replace the full range of artificially synthesized drugs. Clearly, the special effects of psychoactive drugs synthesized or extracted from plants (e.g., alcohol and coca) must be taken into consideration—for example, their addictive properties. Related to the pharmacological variable is a genetic component, which can limit the fit between populations of consumers and the metabolism and digestibility of the foods they eat. Often the natural constituents of foods contain a factor or factors that may be specifically compatible or incompatible with the genetic constitutions of individuals within the population (Katz 1979).

These biological factors play roles of varying importance in the development and evolution of cultural "knowledge" concerning the processing of food from the raw to a "cooked" state. This leads to several questions about the fit between biological and cultural factors. (1) How close is the fit between the knowledge that accumulates in traditional societies over time and present scientific evidence about optimal patterns of preparation and consumption? For example, to what degree are culturally prescribed food combinations during the same meal or time period nutritionally advantageous? (2) What are the principles by which societies acquire, maintain, and distribute this knowledge of foods over time and space? (3) To what degree is this knowledge about foods linked to other practices within society, and to what extent does it provide an adaptive basis for integrating other aspects of traditional practices, beliefs, myths, and symbols? (4) What are the conditions that favor experimental or nonadaptive uses of foods, whether traditional or nontraditional? (5) What is the nutritional significance of various processing traditions such as heating,

136

fermentation (with yeasts, molds, bacteria, etc.), sprouting, peeling, drying, mashing, spicing, and the combinations with other foods and chemicals that are associated with the transformation of raw produce into foods? (6) What governs the degree of explicit (as opposed to implicit) knowledge a society accrues about specific foods or food in general? (7) What role do food aversions play in this evolutionary process?

Not only could answers to these and other questions provide the basis for more cogent theoretical developments on the relationship between food and biocultural evolution; they could also have an immediate impact upon our specific understanding of such contemporary human food behaviors as aversions and consumption generally. More theoretically, this kind of conceptualization of the evolutionary feedback relations between and among the elements of the human food chain for any particular population can provide useful heuristic models for the understanding of human ecology. One such conceptualization of the important variables and their relations is presented in Figure 5.2 (see Katz 1982). As our knowledge about any particular food source increases, we can use this kind of heuristic model as a potential resource for formulating addi-

FIGURE 5.2. The Human Food Chain

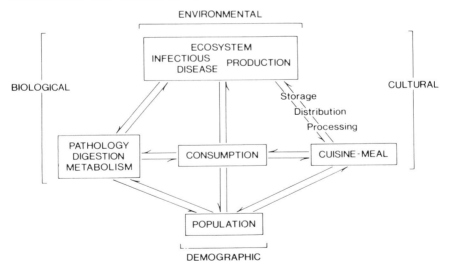

NOTE: This chain presents a more complex model based on a more detailed development of Figure 5.1a. The dimensions are designed to show some of the relations among the important variables in the human food chain. The environmental, the sociocultural, and the biological are all developed more completely to show the continuity of relationships throughout the chain.

tional questions. The aim of the remainder of this paper is to exemplify the utility of this approach for examining the interface between biological evolution and adaptation and the cultural beliefs and practices that shape human food behaviors, using fava beans as an example of a most unusual, important, and often deadly food resource.

The Distribution of Favism

Fava bean consumption provides a particularly interesting test case, since it involves a genetically mediated sensitivity that has been clearly associated in modern times with a potent food aversion in some populations. In the circum-Mediterranean region, individuals with a sex-linked genetic deficiency of the red blood cell (RBC) enzyme, glucose-6-phosphate dehydrogenase (G6PD) deficiency or Gd$^-$, are highly sensitive to RBC hemolysis after consumption of fava beans (*Vicia faba*) (Bottini et al. 1970; Katz and Schall 1986; Livingstone 1967, 1973; Motulsky 1965). Usually within several hours, but occasionally up to nine days, after consuming fava beans, hemizygous deficient males and homozygous deficient females can suffer a severe hemolytic anemia (Livingstone 1973; Mager, Razin, and Hershko 1969; Mager, Chevion, and Glaser 1980; Sartori 1971). In approximately 1 in 12 cases in modern times, this anemia can result in death (Belsey 1973; Bottini 1973; Huheey and Martin 1975; Livingstone 1964), and before modern medical treatment was instituted over the last few decades, the mortality rate was probably even greater.

Worldwide Distribution of G6PD Deficiency

Although favism occurs principally in the circum-Mediterranean region (Motulsky 1965), Gd$^-$ is found throughout the tropical regions of the world (Bottini et al. 1970; Katz 1982; Katz and Schall 1986), throughout Europe, northern and equatorial Africa, the southern Caspian region, the entire Middle East, India and southeast Asia, southern China (Canton), Indonesia, and New Guinea. Since hemizygous males all have the full potential for developing anemia upon exposure to various foods, drugs, and viruses, it can be accurately stated that G6PD deficiency is the most common known genetic disorder in the world (Katz, Adair, and Schall; Katz and Schall 1977; Katz et al. 1978; Kirkman 1968; Motulsky 1965).

Livingstone and a number of other investigators have hypothesized on the basis of its semi-tropical and tropical distribution that G6PD deficiency is associated with resistance to malaria (Bienzle et al. 1972; Livingstone 1967, 1973; Luzzato, Usanga, and Reddy 1969; Siniscalco et al. 1961; Siniscalco et al.

1966). However, it is important to point out that there are at least as many variants of the enzyme as there are of hemoglobin; hemoglobin variants number well over a hundred (L. Luzzato, pers. comm.; see also Belsey 1973).[1] The most common variants are GdB^-, found in the circum-Mediterranean area, which has the least enzymatic activity (0–7 percent), probably accounting for its victims' particular sensitivity to fava bean consumption; GdA^-, found in tropical African populations, with moderate activity (8–20 percent); and Gd Canton$^-$, found first in China, also with moderate activity. Elsewhere I have hypothesized that forms other than GdB^- interact with naturally occurring dietary oxidants in their particular ecosystem (Katz and Schall, 1986).

Favism and Malaria

The occurrence of GdB^- gene in those populations that regularly consume fava beans is quite high, with frequencies between 5 and 30 percent regularly reported in the literature (Livingstone 1967, 1973; Luzzato, Usango, and Reddy 1969; Motulsky 1965; Siniscalco et al. 1966). With this high an occurrence of a serious illness, it is highly likely that extensive biocultural adaptations have taken place over the thousands of years since this gene first evolved in the circum-Mediterranean region. My colleagues and I initially hyopthesized that regardless of the nutritional value and agricultural productivity of fava beans, the mortality rate from favism would be high enough that other crops would have evolved to take their place. Since, however, their consumption has continued essentially unabated, we reasoned that extensive knowledge would evolve about the sensitivity of susceptible individuals in order to minimize the beans' effects (Katz 1979, 1982; Katz, Adair, and Schall 1975; Katz and Schall 1977, 1979, 1986; Katz et al. 1978). Nevertheless, the evidence that favism is still a major disease throughout the region suggests that this evolved knowledge or "cultural information" was not sufficient to overcome the harmful effects of continued consumption (Katz 1979).

In a further attempt to resolve this evolutionary paradox, we generated another hypothesis that examines the benefits of the continued consumption of fava beans, particularly in view of the presence of seasonal malaria in most of the region. We were impressed by the fact that highly effective anti-malarial drugs such as primaquine also produce a hemolytic anemia in GdB^- (Mediterranean type deficient) individuals. Hence, we reasoned that the mechanism of action of these drugs might be correlated with the effects of fava beans (Huheey and Martin 1975; Katz, Adair, and Schall 1975). In other words, antimalarial drugs that are potent oxidants may stress the GdB^- RBCs in the same way that fava beans do. Moreover, if this was the case, it was also possible that this response by GdB^- cells accounted for the mechanism by which

FIGURE 5.3. Geographic Distribution of Fava Bean Consumption, Malaria, and G6PD Deficiency

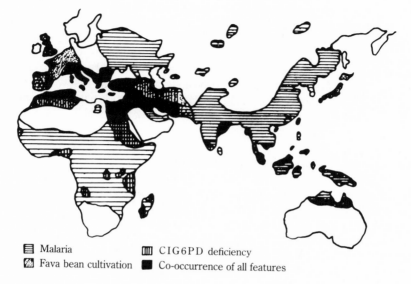

目 Malaria   ⊞ CIG6PD deficiency
🮖 Fava bean cultivation   ■ Co-occurrence of all features

GdB⁻ cells maintained their resistance to malaria. The latter hypothesis suggested furthermore that fava beans could have anti-malarial properties for individuals not susceptible to their serious hemolytic effects. In terms of biocultural evolution, this hypothesis suggests that a balance exists between the selective advantages of the GdB⁻ gene in areas with high malaria and the advantages of culturally encouraged consumption of fava beans for GdB (normal) individuals in the same areas (see Figure 5.3).

We have not yet carried out a definitive field test of the in vitro malarial resistance of RBCs taken from individuals with normal and abnormal genotypes before and after the consumption of fava beans in circum-Mediterranean populations. There is, nevertheless, considerable evidence already available that supports the hyopthesis that fava beans have anti-malarial properties. These data are presented under a series of biochemical and pharmacological, epidemiological, nutritional and agricultural, population genetic, and cultural headings.

Biochemical and Pharmacological Factors

Recently developed biochemical and pharmacological evidence on the mechanism by which an RBC is resistant to malaria suggests that the intra-erythrocytic stage of the malarial parasite life cycle is particularly dependent on erythrocytic nicotinamide-adenine dinucleotide phosphate (NADPH) as a source for maintaining high levels of reduced glutathione (GSH) (Crosby 1956; Eaton and Eckman 1977; Eaton et al. 1976; Eckman and Eaton 1977; Etkin and Eaton 1975; Friedman 1978; Sartori 1971). GSH is probably utilized for maintaining the protein synthesis necessary for this phase of the parasitic life cycle (Kosower and Kosower 1970, 1974). As protein synthesis and other intra-parasitic metabolic activities continue, they produce an abundance of hydrogen peroxide, which passes out from the parasite into the RBC. There the hydrogen peroxide is reduced to water and oxygen by a peroxidase enzyme, which requires erythrocytic stores of GSH to function (Liebowitz and Cohen 1968). In the case of the GdB$^-$ RBC, the enzyme G6PD has only 1 to 10 percent of its normal activity (Eaton et al. 1976). This is critical, since the G6PD enzyme is the source of the glucose-6 phosphate metabolism necessary for NADPH formation, which is used in turn for the parasite metabolism. This condition results in a considerable decrease of available NADPH for the production of both RBCs and parasitic GSH. Without sufficient GSH to reduce the rapid build-up of hydrogen peroxide (H_2O_2) in the RBC (Liebowitz and Cohen 1968), there is a rapid increase in methemoglobin, Heinz body formation, and subsequent oxidant damage from free radicals upon the membrane of the RBC (Friedman 1978). Several investigators (e.g., Eaton et al. 1976; Friedman 1978; Sartori 1971) have postulated that the added oxidant stress provided by a malarial parasite in a G6PD-deficient erythrocyte is sufficient to result in a rapid build-up of oxidant-induced damage to the RBC membrane, so that it either prematurely ruptures or is sequestered by the spleen. (It is possible that the increased sequestration by the spleen and/or premature rupture of the infected RBCs leads to increased anti-body formation against the early forms of the parasite. This would increase host resistance to the earlier stages of parasitic infection and might provide an efficient mechanism for increased immune resistance to malarial infection; however, this hypothesis has yet to be confirmed.) The net effect is a 2- to 80-fold decrease in the level of malarial infection in individuals with G6PD deficiency (Luzzato, Usanga, and Reddy 1969).

Fava beans have a number of strong oxidant pyrimidines (vicine, divicine, isouramil) (Beutler 1970; Chevion and Novak 1983; Jamalian, Aylward, and Hudson 1977; Kosower and Kosower 1967; Lin 1963; Lin and Ling 1962a, 1962b, 1962c). In addition, they contain other, related compounds, as well as high quantities of L-DOPA (Kosower and Kosower 1967), which can be converted either in cooking or in metabolism by tyrosinase to the active oxidant L-DOPAquinone (Beutler 1970). Fava beans could, therefore, provide a series of strong oxidant stresses on the GdB$^-$ RBC. Experiments in our laboratories (Katz and Schall 1977, 1979) and in others (Walker and Bowman 1960) lead to the conclusion that fava beans dramatically decrease GSH levels and, like anti-malarial drugs, produce sufficient oxidant stress to hemolyse the GdB$^-$

FIGURE 5.4. Effects of Fava Beans and Malarial Parasitism on the Oxidant
Sensitivity of the Red Blood Cell

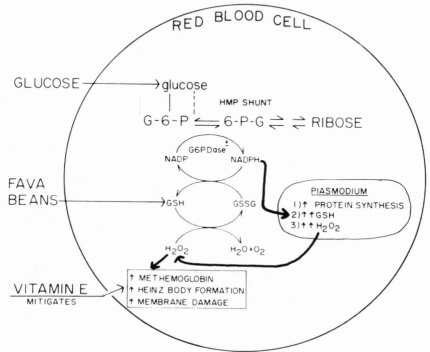

NOTE: This figure appeared in S. H. Katz and J. Schall, Favism and Malaria: A Model of
Nutrition and Biocultural Evolution. In N. Etkin, ed., *Plants Used in Indigenous Medicine and
Diet: Biobehavioral Approaches.* New York: Redgrave Press, 1986. © 1986 by Redgrave
Publishing Company. Reproduced here courtesy of Redgrave Press.

RBC. These findings interrelating glucose metabolism, fava bean effects, vitamin E, the significance of malarial factors, and oxidant stress in the RBC are summarized in Figure 5.4. Furthermore, it is likely that the same oxidant stress occurs in normal, G6PD-sufficient cells, except that the stress is not great enough to allow permanent damage from hydrogen peroxide. However, we hypothesize that the combination of oxidant stress provided by consumption of fava beans and infection by the malarial plasmodium is sufficient to interrupt the normal development of the parasite.

I presented this concept at the Center for Tropical Diseases in Jerusalem. Subsequent research (Golenser et al. 1983) was designed to determine in vitro the susceptibility of G6PD-deficient and normal erythrocytes incubated with and without isouramil, one of the principle pyrimidine oxidants of fava beans. The addition of isouramil decreased malarial parasite growth rates in G6PD-deficient cells, but not in normal cells. In parasitized erythrocytes, the addition of isouramil had direct anti-malarial effects in both normal and GDPD-deficient cells during the trophozioite and schizont parasite stages (Golenser et al. 1983). This evidence helps to confirm our hypothesis at the biochemical level.

Furthermore, I propose that the anti-malarial effect of fava beans is sufficient to create the kind of equilibrium necessary to maintain a balanced presence of the genetic mechanism (GdB$^-$) and a pattern of fava bean consumption in which both factors promote resistance to malarial infections. Additional evidence supporting this hypothesis is the fact that high-level depletion of vitamin E, which normally protects the RBC from the damaging effects of hydrogen peroxide, can result in protection against hemolysis in GdB$^-$ individuals (Spielberg et al., 1979). Alternatively, animal studies by Eaton and Eckman (1977) and human studies by Friedman (1978) concluded that vitamin E deficiency allows for a more rapid accumulation of damage to normal cells infected by malarial parasites and a lowering of overall infection rates by intercepting the plasmodial life cycle, presumably in much the same as was in the G6PD-deficient cell. Hence, it is likely that the consumption of fava beans lowers the GSH of GdB+ individuals sufficiently to have a net positive protective effect on their resistance to malaria.

Epidemiological Data

We reasoned that if fava beans had some kind of anti-malarial effect on male hemizygous normals and female homo- and heterozygous individuals, then the fava bean should be widely distributed in association with the occurrence of the GdB$^-$ genotype and malaria. The evidence on the distribution of all three variables shows a remarkable concurrence among them, suggesting the likelihood of a significant interaction. Moreover, the available data on the seasonality of malaria and fava bean consumption in Egypt, Iran, Greece, and Italy (Belsey 1973; Katz, Adair, and Schall 1975) indicate a high degree of overlap between the peak season of consumption and the peak occurrence of the malarial vector (see Figure 5.5 and Katz and Schall 1979). Although these epidemiological data could reflect merely the coincidence between the climatic

FIGURE 5.5. Seasonal Variation in Malarial Vectors, Fava Bean Harvest, and Fava Consumption

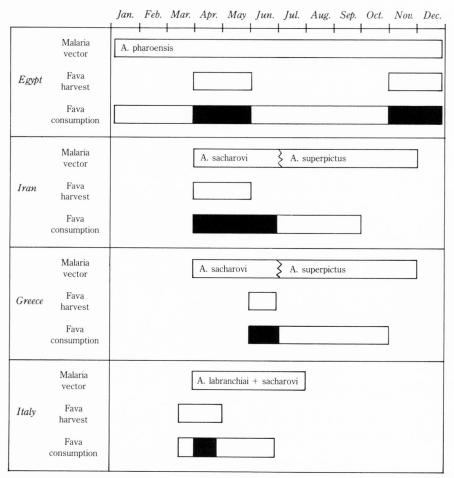

NOTE: The shaded areas refer to peak consumption periods for fava beans. The ragged lines separating the species of mosquito indicate overlapping seasonal life cycles for these vectors.

TABLE 5.1. Comparative Nutritional Values for
Mediterranean Region Legumes

Legumes	% Protein (dry weight)	Protein Efficiency Ratio[a] (cooked legumes)
Chick peas	17.8	2.05 ± 0.10
Lentils	24.0	1.14 ± 0.14
Kidney beans	22.5	1.51 ± 0.22
Fava beans	23.5	1.17 ± 0.17

[a]Grams protein consumed, divided by grams of weight gain, in rats.
NOTE: Adapted from FAO Reports on the nutritional contents for
legumes (Food and Agricultural Organization, Rome, 1959).

conditions conducive to the spread of malaria and those favoring the cultivation
of fava beans, it is unlikely that such a coincidence would be distributed so
widely and consistently over the region, particularly if the beans had only negative effects.

Nutritional and Agricultural Potential

Although the epidemiological data show a clear association between the seasonal occurrence of malaria and the consumption of fava beans, this evidence is
not conclusive, since the extensive distribution of the fava bean could be explained, for example, by its agricultural and nutritional advantages. In this context it is clear that fava beans are highly suited to many of the environments in
which they are grown. Likewise, their nutritional value is in the same range as
that of other regionally grown pulses and legumes, which tend to be relatively
high in lysine and low in tryptophan and the sulfur-containing amino acids.
Hence, while clearly a highly productive crop, their presence is not additionally
explainable on the basis of any significant nutritional advantages over other
pulses and legumes found in these regions. Moreover, these other regional
legumes do not contain constituents that trigger hemolytic crises in G6PD-
deficient individuals (Table 5.1 and Katz and Schall 1979).

Population Genetics

In order to test the hypothesis that fava beans provide selective advantages for
the normals of both sexes and heterozygous females and disadvantages for
hemizygous deficient males, I carried out analyses of the available genetic data

on population distributions of the GdB^- genotype. The usefulness of these rather extensive data is limited by the difficulties in classifying female hetero-zygotes because of the deactivation of one of the X chromosomes during em-bryonic development, according to the Lyon hypothesis (Motulsky 1965). The data are also complicated by the fact that other genes for acid phosphatase B (Bottini et al. 1971), thalassemia in females (Carcassi 1974; Friedman 1978), and possibly tyrosinase variation (Beutler 1970) all play roles in mitigating the hemolytic effects of fava beans. Another factor that is likely to be important in the expression of GdB^- in females is associated with the onset of adrenarche. Since adrenarche is associated with increased secretion of dehydroe-piandrosterone (DHEA), which directly inhibits G6PD activity, it is highly likely that the unusual variation in the age at which favism is prevalent in females is closely associated with this developmental event, which occurs at age six to seven (Katz et al. 1983) and is particularly significant in children with higher body mass indexes (Katz et al. 1985). Since these interactions and other unknown factors tend to limit the data, it is more useful to compare the actual ranges of gene frequencies with various hyopthetical outcomes based upon variation in consumption patterns. If we assume that fava bean consumption confers no advantage, then we should see a trend that rapidly proceeds to-wards a very high frequency of the G6PD-deficiency gene; conversely, if there was a high selective advantage for the consumption of fava beans by normal individuals, the GdB^- gene would merely disappear over time. However, if fava bean consumption was somewhat advantageous for the normals and slightly more advantageous for the heterozygotes, which would be the case if fava beans were not consistently available in areas of endemic malaria, then a balanced polymorphism could be maintained in the same range that is widely reported in the circum-Mediterranean region. Hence, the fact that the popula-tion genetic data tend to support a balanced genetic polymorphism suggests additional evidence in favor of an anti-malarial effect from fava bean consump-tion. A more detailed explanation of the population genetics of this phenomenon can be found in Katz and Schall (1986; see Figure 5.6).

The Evolution of Cultural Information

I postulated that if fava beans were consumed over a long enough period of time, the cultural information about them would evolve toward an optimal fit with the cumulative biological effects of the beans. The model would predict a significant growth of cultural mechanisms to prevent the continued consump-tion of the beans if their net effects were negative. The accumulation of knowl-edge would proceed to the point where they would no longer be consumed, since danger of death and illness would be correlated with their consumption. On the other hand, if in addition to their negative hemolytic effects on G6PD-

FIGURE 5.6. Selection Models: Favism, Malaria, and G6PD Deficiency, by Sex

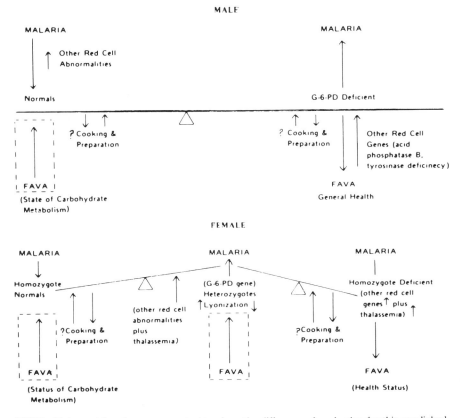

NOTE: Males and females are separated to show the differences in selection for this sex-linked gene. The arrows refer to factors that theoretically increase (upward arrow) and decrease (downward arrow) the frequency of the C1G6PD Mediterranean gene.

deficient individuals, they had some benefit such as promoting "good health" (i.e., absence of disease due to malaria), we would expect to see a mixture of culturally evolved traditions, both prescriptive and proscriptive, governing the behavior surrounding their consumption.

Before the cultural and historical evidence for the pattern of consumption can be evaluated, the time frame of these biocultural evolutionary hyeptheses has to be considered. Fava beans were one of the first plants to be intensively gathered by Indo-European populations. Probably coincident with or anteceding any kind of grain cultivation, they are found in association with neolithic pile dwelling sites in Switzerland and open-air sites in northern Italy, Spain, and Hungary. Even before their human use in Europe, fava beans were established in a range that extended from Persia and the Himalayas to the East and ultimately to the Atlantic coast in the West. There is other evidence of their use in Bronze age Troy and 12th-Dynasty Egypt, and there are many references to them in classical Greek and Roman literature (Andrews 1949; Arie 1959; Celsus 1935; Giles 1962; Herodotus 1947; Rowlett and Mori 1970). Currently they are known to extend through China and as far as Taiwan.

Extensive archaeological and historical data allow for a more careful analysis of our hypothesis, since the period of their continuous cultivation and apparent consumption is so considerable. Given this time dimension, it seems likely that had the effects of fava beans been only negative, their use as a human food would have long since disappeared among populations with G6PD-deficiency. Yet it could be argued that no implicit or explicit knowledge ever evolved about their toxicity. This argument, as it applies to the mode of X-linked inheritance (Papavasiliou et al. 1972) of favism, has been made by Giles (1962), who hypothesized that the Indo-European kinship pattern of patrilineality and patrilocality at least tends to preclude the correlation of favism with maternal inheritance in males. That is, the females who carry this X-linked trait to their sons are continually separated out by exogamy from the lineage, which makes it difficult to correlate the illness with family lines. Thus, data about favism could also be used to test hypotheses concerning the ways in which knowledge spreads when knowledge of the disease is carried by women versus men. Presumably women would have observed that their brothers were susceptible to the disease. Therefore, if their sons had the same symptoms as their brothers, it is reasonable to suggest that the women would have drawn some conclusions about the disorder. This knowledge could have given rise to various beliefs and behaviors among women that were different from those of men. A careful investigation of historical data and the roles of women in the transmission of knowledge from one generation to the next under patrilineal, patrilocal, and a partial matrilateral cross-cousin marriage kinship system could yield fruitful tests of hypotheses concerning this aspect of the biocultural evolutionary process.

Although favism as a specifically defined disease was first described in the mid-19th century, it is not clear whether it was known by other names or clusters of symptoms at the folk level. For example, through interviews I conducted in areas of Sardinia with very high rates of favism, I uncovered—contrary to the local medical belief—a well-founded folk knowledge of favism that extended back to the childhood of the oldest members of the community, some of whom were over 70. One distinctly recalled being warned about fava beans during childhood by his grandparents. This suggests that knowledge of the beans' negative effects went back well into the 19th century. Nevertheless, it is difficult to trace explicit knowledge before the 19th century, and this may also explain why favism was not directly correlated with fava consumption earlier. However, this does not rule out the possibility that earlier prescription or proscription of fava beans could evolve without any explicit knowledge of the relationship between bean consumption and favism.

More recently, studies have been conducted to determine whether traditional cooking, processing, and other dietary activities significantly alter the toxicity of the bean for individuals with G6PD deficiency (Belsey 1973; Jamalian 1978; Jamalian, Aylward, and Hudson 1977). In other words, it is reasonable to suggest that certain appropriate processing techniques may have evolved to decrease the possibility of fatalities from favism. Since there are considerable variations in processing, only two of these pathways will be considered here. However, before considering processing per se, it is important to point out that many, but not all, populations tend to consume the beans raw without any processing. In the event of an impending fava crisis, it is reported that the folk medical treatment of Iran is a high "sweet" diet consisting of naturally occurring sweet foods. This is believed to reduce the significance of the crisis. Indeed, there may be some medical rationale for this prescription, since the increased availability of glucose to a G6PD-deficient individual may provide sufficient saturation with glucose-6-phosphate to optimize the remaining G6PD activity, which is involved in the production of NADPH and in turn maintains a necessary level of GSH (Katz and Schall 1986; Katz et al. 1978). The GSH in turn prevents the toxic build-up of cellular peroxides and thus lessens the probability of a fava-induced hemolytic crisis.

The first step in processing fava beans is soaking. Most ethnic groups studied do soak their dried beans, and it is likely that soaking is sufficient to trigger the first reactions of germination. Although significant changes in the biochemical constituents could result from this germination process, little is known about its effects upon the toxicity of the beans, except that the toxic constituents are partially water soluble and would be discarded with the soaking water. It is known that the sprouting of soybeans, another legume, rapidly eliminates the anti-trypsin protein activity that prevents insect predation. Since the principal mechanism that the fava bean has evolved to protect its seed is the production of pyrimidines, it is likely that germination would produce a significant change in its oxidant activity.

A second widely practiced step in processing consists of removing the skin of the bean. This has been studied by Jamalian and associates (Jamalian 1978; Jamalian, Aylward, and Hudson 1977), who report high toxicity for all parts of fresh mature seeds, but higher activity in the seed coats than in the fresh seed flesh, although the overall toxicity was lower in the dried beans.

Both major processing steps make a difference in the outcomes, and both are widely used. Jamalian and his associates (Jamalian 1978; Jamalian, Aylward, and Hudson 1977) also report that the GSH levels of the processed beans were lowered by incubation, and that the level remaining was sufficient to avoid spontaneous hemolysis. This raises an important and as yet unanswered question: if the oxidant activity is lowered sufficiently to improve the survival of G6PD-deficient individuals, is it still sufficient to add any protection against malaria in the hemizygous males and homo- and heterozygous females? This question suggests that the model of the relations between fava bean consumption, favism, and the genetic factor requires a separate model for males and females, since males are hemizygous and either have or do not have the gene and the potential for the disease, whereas females have three classes of phenotypes, each with varying susceptibility. If the model also includes the potential interaction with malaria and the effects of fava bean consumption on the genetic frequency of the GdB^- gene, then the model begins to take on the characteristics of a more formal quantitative model of genetic change. Elsewhere Katz and Schall (1986) have developed a heuristic model of this phenomenon, which is presented here as Figure 5.6.

Folklore and Fava Bean Consumption

The fact that fava beans have had sufficient time to come to some kind of equilibrium with population groups strongly favors the accumulation of many specific beliefs about their effects. Consistent reports in the classical Greek, Roman, Egyptian, and Indian literature associate them with death (Andrews 1949). Andrews has conducted an intensive study of the ambivalence about fava beans. Although he was unable to conclude which factors besides the flatulence associated with fava bean consumption gave rise to the ambivalence of the belief that the beans were occupied by the souls of the dead, he determined that beliefs about the beans were not associated with some ancient vestige of Indo-European totemism, nor did they stem from some historical accident. The evidence he developed is extensive and relevant to the complex evolution of cultural knowledge about fava beans:

> The ancients felt toward beans a mingled respect and dread, a complex of emotions suggested by the Greek term ἱερόσ, which apparently was generally applied to an object believed to be charged with some supernatural force, contact with which might be either beneficial or harmful. Today we generally call this mysterious power mana in its helpful aspect and taboo in its harmful aspect. Beans belonged in the category of objects possessing both mana and taboo. (Andrews 1949:277)

Such beliefs in turn led to the notion that fava beans had enormous generative power—a power to be avoided by those members of society whose social functions required avoidance of death and sought by those whose functions were closely associated with death. Andrews has also documented that the ambivalence and controversy surrounding the consumption of fava beans are both ancient and widespread. He was able to accumulate evidence from the Greco-Roman era, ancient Egypt, India, and 19th- and 20th-century Africa. In addition, Rowlett and Mori (1970) have accumulated data for English folklore. These cultural data may be briefly summarized by area and time period.

GREECE

Despite the strong proscriptions against the beans in classical Greece, there is evidence of their continued use and consumption. The strictest aviodance of fava beans there appears to have been practiced by the Pythagoreans. Andrews relates that "the Pythagorean taboo was so stringent that it extended even to treading down the growing bean vine. According to one account . . . Pythagoras, pursued by Syracusan soldiers, could not bring himself to escape by crossing a field of beans, preferring to let himself be taken and killed. According to another . . . some Pythagoreans, fleeing from hostile soldiers, stopped when they came to a bean field in flower and defended themselves to the death" (1949:276).

Bean avoidance extended to other elements of the Greek population as well, although no one at that time seems to have known why the custom existed. Aristotle reported that the Pythagoreans, who were partisans of the oligarchical regime, detested the beans because they were used to cast a vote in elections for magistrates and were therefore a symbol of democracy. Nevertheless, Andrews notes that Aristotle supplied four more explanations for fava bean avoidance without settling on any one of them. Plutarch also offered various explanations, as did Lydus. Arie (1959) hypothesizes that at the root of the Pythagorean aversion was Pythagoras's own G6PD deficiency and possibly some knowledge about favism. What is evident is that although many ancient Greeks continued to eat fava beans, others shunned them, and those that avoided them had a plethora of reasons for doing so.

ROME

Judging from such information as Andrews provides, the prevailing rationale for fava bean avoidance among the ancient Romans was that the beans caused bad dreams. For this reason, Pliny, Diogenes Laertius, and Amphiaraus, a mythical dream interpreter, suggested abstention (1949:285). Plutarch noted that consumption of the beans was associated with increased male sexuality, restlessness, dreams, and flatulence. At the same time, others (particularly physicians) felt that fava beans were a good, healthful food. They were popular with artisans, farmers, builders, and gladiators (1949:281n).

151

ENGLAND

Rowlett and Mori note the presence of "unmistakable references to the magical effects of fava beans—or at least their deleterious ones"—in English folklore (1970:100). In many bean stories and superstitions, of course, it is nearly impossible to determine the identity of the bean or beans involved; but there are some stories in which the involvement of fava beans is quite beyond doubt. One of these is Ralph of Coggershall's tale of the Green Children, in which children eat beans, turn green (which is diagnostic of favism), and die. Similarly, the identification of fava beans in the Jack and the Beanstalk story is certain, as the beans in the story are very large and the stalk is tall and strong. Other folk conceptions concerning fava beans in England include the popular idea that more cases of lunacy occur when the plant is in bloom than at any other time of the year, a notion among coal miners that accidents in the pits occur more frequently when the bean plants are in bloom, and a general reluctance to have bean blossoms in the house. There is also a saying: "Sleep in a bean field all night if you want to have awful dreams or go crazy" (Rowlett and Mori 1970:101), as well as the idea that eating fava beans can harm one's senses of smell and vision and can be harmful to the blood. Rowlett and Mori suggest that "some of the most persistent English folktales" deal principally with the effects of *Vicia fava* (ibid.).

ANCIENT EGYPT

Andrews (1949:277n) notes the existence of bean avoidance in Egypt, but it is not clear how extensive or stringent the taboo was. Herodotus states that Egyptians would neither grow these beans nor eat them raw or cooked, and that they were so strongly proscribed for the priests that they could not even tolerate the sight of them; yet archaeological evidence and papyrus records at least as far back as the 12th Dynasty suggest their widespread and long-term use as a food and in funerary rites. "There is no doubt," says Andrews, "that a taboo of some kind did exist, and various implausible explanations have been advanced" (ibid.). Here again, we seem to have a situation in which fava bean taboos and widespread fava bean consumption exist side by side in the same society. Currently, fava beans are a major staple food for the vast majority of the Egyptian population.

INDIA

Other evidence for fava bean avoidance comes from Vedic India and the ethnographic present: "A bean taboo imposed on those rendering sacrifice is mentioned in the oldest Indian ritualistic text, the Yajurveda, as well as in the

Maitrayani Samhita and the Kathaka. The Bagdis of central and western Bengal are apparently of Dravidian descent. In the territory of Bankura, where the original caste structure seems to be particularly well preserved, they are divided into nine endogamous subcastes, which in turn are subdivided into exogamous clans or septs. Many of the latter are totemic, for example, the Patrischi or Bean Clan, members of which will not touch beans" (Andrews 1949:277n). Once again, it is my experience that fava beans are still widely consumed in western India today.

AFRICA

Andrews has one short but noteworthy comment on Africa: "Among the Baganda in the vicinity of Lake Victoria Nyanza, the Bean Clan will not eat or even cultivate beans. One of them is said to have eaten beans and died on the spot" (ibid.).

Other Biological Effects of Fava Beans

Fava beans have a considerable concentration of indigestible oligosaccharides, which are digested by bacteria of the lower gastrointestinal tract, the likely cause of the flatulence reported in the cultural data presented above. However, they also contain a high concentration of L-DOPA (approximately 0.25 percent by weight). L-DOPA is a potent psychoactive neurotransmitter that is known to be associated with the other symptoms Plutarch described and is consistent with English folklore. Moreover, the dose of L-DOPA obtained from one or two meals of fava beans appears to be in the range that can be effective in treating Parkinson's disease, which is the principal source of clinical data on the effects of L-DOPA (Jamalian 1978; Jamalian, Aylward, and Hudson 1977). Thus, it is conceivable that beside their agricultural efficiency and nutritional value, their possible psychoactive effects may be associated with their continued consumption. This combination of effects appears to fit well with the Greek word *hieros,* which Andrews (1949) suggested conveys the mixture of dread and respect that was applied to the harmful or beneficial supernatural force associated with the consumption of fava beans. Andrews sums up the magnitude and complexity of the "information pool" that was accumulated in ancient and historic times by concluding that "no plant or animal known to the Indo-Europeans produced a more luxuriant growth of beliefs than fava beans" (1949:290).

Conclusion

The evidence suggests that fava bean consumption throughout the circum-Mediterranean region fits a complex model of interacting biological and cultural evolution. The beans undoubtedly have highly toxic effects for many G6PD-deficient individuals, and hence there is extensive evidence for the development of taboos surrounding their use, particularly in children. In addition, many recipes for preparing the beans lower their toxic effects. However, consumption of the beans has continued since neolithic times, and it is clear that neither the taboos nor the processing techniques have mitigated this problem sufficiently to prevent a high incidence of favism. Even though their agricultural potential in the circum-Mediterranean region is high, it is still difficult to explain their continued use in light of the high morbidity and mortality rates in G6PD-deficient individuals. Hence, the evidence tends to support the addition of increased resistance to malaria as another major factor adding selective advantage to their continued consumption.

Several classes of pharmacologically active compounds in fava beans that appear to be responsible for the favism crisis in G6PD-deficient individuals produce similar increases in the oxidant sensitivity of the RBCs in normal individuals without toxic effects. Various epidemiological and biochemical evidence supports the hypothesis that an increase in RBC oxidant sensitivity as a result of fava bean consumption could lower rates of infection with malarial parasites and, therefore, be highly advantageous (Papavasiliou et al. 1972). If this hypothesis is fully substantiated, it would provide the first evidence that the biological and cultural evolution of disease resistance are linked through dietary practices.

This paper has also attempted to demonstrate the complex interactions between changes in the gene pool and changes in cultural knowledge, which accumulates over time a set of adaptive practices and information about the effects of fava bean consumption. Topics that call for further exploration in light of these cultural data include quantitative aspects of the evolution of the Mediterranean type of G6PD deficiency; folk knowledge of the sex-specific effects of the beans on males but not females, and the folk behavior and beliefs about females as carriers of the potentially lethal condition; and further research concerning the efficiency of folk medical practices for treating favism and the relations of these practices to the anti-malarial potential of the beans. The mechanism of transfer of this folk knowledge from one generation to the next and the roles of rituals and ideologies in this process could provide important clues for the assembly of a more sophisticated model. Finally, fava beans are still very widely consumed, and there is a need to integrate these findings with knowledge of contemporary social, agricultural, and food practices. The apparent net effect of these interactions is a dynamic equilibrium between biological and sociocultural dimensions, which, I suggest, provides a test case for understanding the co-evolution of genes and culture as it relates to the human food chain.

Acknowledgments

The ideas and data presented in this revised and updated paper are largely derived from Katz (1979). A more extensive discussion of the human biological aspects of the problem is given in Katz and Schall (1986), in which Figure 5.4 appeared. Figures 5.1b, 5.2, 5.3, and 5.6 appear courtesy of AVI Publishing, from Katz: Food, Behavior and Biocultural Evolution, in L. M. Barker, ed., *The Psychobiology of Human Food Selection,* pp. 171–88, © 1982 by the AVI Publishing Company, Westport, CT 06881. Figure 5.5 and Table 5.1 appear courtesy of *Medical Anthropology* (see Katz and Schall 1979), © 1979 Redgrave Publishing Co., Bedford Hills, N.Y.

Note

1. This wide range of enzyme variants has given rise to several notation systems for G6PD deficiency, such as Gd$^-$, which refers to the deficient variant of the enzyme.

References Cited

Andrews, A. C.
    1949   The Bean and Indo-European Totemism. *American Anthropologist* 51:274–92.
Arie, T. H. D.
    1959   Pythagorus and Beans. *Oxford Medical School Gazette* 2:75–81.
Belsey, M. A.
    1973   The Epidemiology of Favism. *Bulletin of the World Health Organization* 48:1–13.
Beutler, E.
    1970   L-Dopa and Favism. *Blood* 36:523–25.
Bienzle, U.; A. O. Lucas; O. Ayemi; and L. Luzzato
    1972   G6PD and Malaria. *Lancet* 1:107–10.
Bottini, E.
    1973   Favism: Current Problems and Investigations. *Journal of Medical Genetics* 10:213–19.
Bottini, E., et al.
    1970   Presence in *Vicia faba* of Different Substances with Activity in vitro on Gd$^-$ Med Red Blood Cell Reduced Glutathione. *Clinica Chemica Acta* 30:831–34.

Bottini, E., et al.
   1971   Favism: Association with Erythrocyte Acid Phosphotase Phenotype. *Science* 171:409–11.
Carcassi, L. E. F.
   1974   The Interaction Between B-Thalassemia, G6PD Deficiency and Favism. *Annals of the New York Academy of Sciences* 232:297–305.
Celsus
   1935   *De Medicina,* W. G. Spencer, trans. Cambridge: Harvard University Press.
Chevion, M., and T. Novak
   1983   Favism. *Annals of Biochemistry* 128:152–53.
Crosby, W. H.
   1956   Favism in Sardinia. *Blood* 11:91–92.
Eaton, J. W., and J. R. Eckman
   1977   Glutathione Metabolism in Malaria Infected Erythrocytes. *Clinical Research* 25:610.
   1979   Plasmodial Glutathione Metabolism: Dependence Upon the Host Cell. *Nature* 278:754–56.
Eaton, J. W.; J. R. Eckman; E. Berger; and H. S. Jacob
   1976   Suppression of Malaria Infection by Oxidant Sensitive Host Erythrocytes. *Nature* 264:758–60.
Etkin, N. L., and J. W. Eaton
   1975   Malaria Induced Erythrocyte Oxidant Sensitivity. In *Erythrocyte Structure and Function,* G. J. Brewer, ed., pp. 219–32. New York: Liss.
Friedman, J. M.
   1978   Increased Oxidant Sensitivity of Malaria Parasites Glucose-6-Phosphate Dehydrogenase Deficient and Thalassemia Trait Red Cells. *Blood* 52 (suppl. 1):64.
Giles, E.
   1962   Favism, Sex Linkage, and the Indo-European Kinship System. *Southwestern Journal of Anthropology* 18:286–90.
Golenser, J.; J. Miller; D. T. Spiro; T. Novak; and M. Chevion
   1983   Inhibitory Effect of a Fava Bean Component on the In Vitro Development of *Plasmodium falciparum* in Normal and Glucose-6-Phosphate Dehydrogenase Deficient Erythrocytes. *Blood* 61:507–10.
Herodotus
   1947   *The Persian Wars.* New York: Random House.
Huheey, J. E., and D. L. Martin
   1975   Malaria, Favism, and G6PD Deficiency. *Experientia* 30:1145–47.
Iversen, L. I.
   1975   Dopamine Receptors in the Brain. *Science* 188:1084–89.
Jamalian, J.
   1978   Favism-Inducing Toxins in Broad Beans (*Vicia faba*) Determination of Vicine Content and Investigation of Other Nonprotein Nitrogenous Compounds in Different Broad Bean Cultivars. *Journal of the Science of Food and Agriculture* 29:136–40.

156

Jamalian, J.; F. Aylward; and B. J. F. Hudson

    1977a   Favism-Inducing Toxins in Broad Beans (*Vicia faba*): Biological Activities of Broad Bean Extracts in Favism Sensitive Subjects. *Plant Foods for Human Nutrition* 27:213–19.

    1977b   Favism-Inducing Toxins in Broad Beans (*Vicia faba*): Estimation of the Vicine Contents of Broad Bean and Other Legume Samples. *Plant Foods for Human Nutrition* 27:207–11.

Katz, S. H.

    1973   Evolutionary Perspectives on Purpose and Man. Symposium on Human Purpose. *Zygon* 8:325fl–40.

    1979   Un Exemple d'Evolution Bioculturelle: La Feve. *Communication* 31:53–69.

    1981   Favism, G6PD Deficiency and Malaria: The Evolution of G6PD Deficiency. Unpublished Manuscript.

    1982   Food, Behavior and Biocultural Evolution. In *The Psychobiology of Human Food Selection*, L. M. Barker, ed., pp. 171–88. Westport, Conn.: AVI.

Katz, S. H.; L. Adair; and J. Schall

    1975   Fava Bean Consumption, Malaria and G6PD Deficiency. *American Journal of Physical Anthropology* 44:189.

Katz, S. H., and E. F. Foulks

    1970   Calcium Homeostasis and Behavioral Disorders. In Symposium on Human Adaptation, S. H. Katz, ed. *Journal of Physical Anthropology* 32:225–316.

Katz, S. H.; M. L. Hediger; J. Schall; and L. Valleroy

    1983   Growth and Blood Pressure. In *Clinical Approaches to High Blood Pressure in the Young*, T. and M. Kothchen, eds., pp. 91–132. Boston: John Wright/PSG Inc.

Katz, S. H.; M. L. Hediger; and L. Valleroy

    1974   Traditional Maize Processing Techniques in the New World: Anthropological and Nutritional Significance. *Science* 184:765–73.

    1975   The Anthropological and Nutritional Significance of Traditional Maize Processing Techniques in the New World. In *Symposium on Biosocial Interrelations in Population Adaptation, Wayne State University, 1973*. In *Biosocial Interrelations in Population Adaptation,* E. S. Watts, F. E. Johnson, and G. W. Lasker, eds., pp. 195–234. The Hague: Mouton.

Katz, S. H., and J. Schall

    1977   Fava Bean Consumption, Malaria and G6PD Deficiency. *American Journal of Physical Anthropology* 46:178.

    1979   Fava Bean Consumption and Biocultural Evolution. *Medical Anthropology* 3:459–76.

    1986   Favism and Malaria: A Model of Nutrition and Biocultural Evolution. In N. Etkin, ed., *Plants Used in Indigenous Medicine and Diet: Biobehavioral Approaches*. New York: Redgrave Press.

Katz, S. H.; J. Schall; P. Sundick; and J. Coleman

    1978   Fava, Biocultural Evolution and Favism. *American Anthropological Association Abstracts*, no. 78.

157

Katz, S. H., et al.
    1985   Adrenal Androgens, Body Fat and Advanced Skeletal Age in Puberty: New Evidence for the Relations of Adrenarche and Gonadarche in Males. *Human Biology* 57:401–403.

Kirkman, H. N.
    1968   G6PD Variants and Drug Induced Hemolysis. *Annals of the New York Academy of Sciences* 151:753–64.

Kosower, N. S., and E. M. Kosower
    1967   Does 3,4-dihydroxyphenyalanine Play a Part in Favism? *Nature* 215:285–86.
    1970   Molecular Basis for Selective Advantage of G6PD Deficient Individuals Exposed to Malaria. *Lancet* 2:1343–45.
    1974   Effect of Oxidized Glutathione on Protein Synthesis. In *Genetic Polymorphisms and Diseases in Man,* B. Ramot, ed., pp. 349–57. New York: Academic Press.

Liebowitz, J., and G. Cohen
    1968   Increased Hydrogen Peroxide Levels in Glucose Erythrocytes Exposed to Acetylphenylhydrazine. *Biochemical Pharmacology* 17:983.

Lin, J. Y.
    1963   Studies on Favism, 4: Reactions of Vicine and Divicine with Sulfhydrl Group of Glutathione and Cytesine. *Journal of the Formosan Medical Association* 62:777–81.

Lin, J. Y., and K. H. Ling
    1962a   Studies on Favism, 1: Isolation of an Active Principle from Fava Beans (*Vicia faba*). *Journal of the Formosan Medical Association* 61:484–89.
    1962b   Studies on Favism, 2: Studies on the Physiological Activities of Vicine in vivo. *Journal of the Formosan Medical Association* 61:490–94.
    1962c   Studies on Favism, 3: Studies on the Physiological Activities of Vicine in vitro. *Journal of the Formosan Medical Association* 61:579–83.

Livingston, F. B.
    1964   Aspects of the Population Dynamics of the Abnormal Hemoglobin and G6PD Deficient Genes. *American Journal of Human Genetics* 16:435–50.
    1967   *Abnormal Hemoglobins in Human Populations.* Chicago: Aldine.
    1973   Data on the Abnormal Hemoglobins and G6PD Deficiency in Human Populations. University of Michigan Technical Reports, no. 3, pp. 12–16. Ann Arbor: University of Michigan.

Luzzatto, L.; E. Usanga; and S. Reddy
    1969   Glucose 6 Phosphate Dehydrogenase Deficient Red Cells: Resistance to Infection by Malarial Parasites. *Science* 164:839–42.

Mager, J.; M. Chevion; and G. Glaser
    1980   Favism. In *Toxic Constituents of Plant Foodstuffs,* I. E. Liener, ed., pp. 265–94. 2nd ed. New York: Academic Press.

Mager, J.; A. Razin; and A. Hershko
    1969   Favism. In *Toxic Constituents of Plant Foodstuffs,* I. E. Liener, ed., pp. 293–318. New York: Academic Press.

Motulsky, A. G.
1965   Theoretical and Clinical Problems of Glucose-6-Phosphate Dehydrogen-
        ase Deficiency. In *Abnormal Haemoglobins in Africa: A Symposium Or-
        ganized by the Council for International Organizations of Medical Sci-
        ences Established Under the Joint Auspices of UNESCO & WHO,* J.
        H. P. Jonxis, ed., pp. 143–96. Philadelphia: Davis.
Mourant, A. E.; A. C. Kopec; and K. Domaniewska-Sobczack
1976   *The Distribution of Human Blood Groups and Other Polymorphisms.*
        London: Oxford University Press.
Papavasiliou, P. S.; G. C. Cotzias; S. E. Dueby; A. J. Steck; C. Fehling; and M. A. Bell
1972   Levodopa in Parkinsonism: Potentiation of Central Effects with a Pe-
        ripheral Inhibitor. *New England Journal of Medicine* 285:8–14.
Rowlett, R. M., and J. Mori
1970   The Fava Bean in English Folklore. *Ethnologia Europea* 4:98–102.
Sartori, E.
1971   On the Pathogenesis of Favism. *Journal of Medical Genetics* 8:462–67.
Siniscalco, M.; L. Bernini; G. Fillipi; B. Latte; P. Meera Khan; S. Piomelli; and M.
Rattazzi
1966   Population Genetics of Hemoglobin Variants, Thalassemia and G6PD
        Deficiency with Particular Reference to the Malaria Hypothesis. *Bul-
        letin of the World Health Organization* 34:379–93.
Siniscalco, M.; L. Bernini; B. Latte; and A. G. Motulsky
1961   Favism and Thalassemia in Sardinia and Their Relationship to Malaria.
        Nature 190:1179–80.
Spielberg, S. P.; L. A. Boxer; L. M. Corash; J. D. Schulman
1979   Improved Erythrocyte Survival with High Dose Vitamin E Therapy in
        Chronic Hemolyzing G6PD and Glutathione Synthetase Deficiencies.
        Annals of Internal Medicine 90:53–54.

PART III

Nutritional and Biopsychological Constraints

THE ESSAYS OF PART III DEAL WITH GENETICALLY DETER-mined biopsychological factors that affect foodways from the standpoint of nutritional adequacy and "taste." From a materialist perspective, it is axiomatic that human foodways that lead to severe malnutrition will tend to be selected against during both biological and cultural evolution. But this leaves us with the question of how much of what kinds of nutrients in what proportions and at what stage of life for males and females (including pregnancy and lactation) with different somatotypes and under varying conditions of health will result in a severely malnourished population. As the essays by Pellet and Lieberman make clear, nutrition is far from being an exact science. Not only are recommended daily allowances extrapolated from experiments on non-human models and from causally ambiguous epidemiological data, but to a considerable extent they express the outcome of political infighting between representatives of developed and developing nations as well as that between the vested interests of the agri-businesses and medical-nutritional establishments.

Attempts to relate foodways to minimum nutritional requirements are further complicated by the existence of some innate taste preferences and avoidances. It is possible that these biopsychological features account for the overconsumption of certain foods (e.g., sugar) or the selection of certain less nutritious foods when more nutritious ones are available (e.g., candy versus grains). Yet, as Rozin's essay shows, cultural conditions can readily turn innately aversive substances like hot chili peppers into the dominant taste signature of whole cuisines.

The interplay between cultural conditioning and nutritional requirements is especially baffling in relation to the widespread preference for animal food, whose existence is documented in Abram's essay. As Lieberman's essay shows, from a strictly nutritional point of view, neither animal nor plant foods can be said to be more suitable as a source of essential nutrients, nor can either be said to be free of nutritional risks and penalties when overconsumed. But it should be kept in mind that the evolution of foodways is probably subject to selection by costs and benefits that encompass more than the strictly nutritional composition of foods. Thus, the preferences for animal foods, especially for meat, may be a response to the higher "density" of calories and nutrients packed into a gram of meat versus a gram of plant food. We will return to this issue in Part IV.

P. L. PELLETT

Problems and Pitfalls in the Assessment of Human Nutritional Status

MORE THAN 40 SEPARATE ELEMENTS OR COMPOUNDS HAVE NOW been identified as necessary for life, together with at least 40 grams per day of amino acids as protein and more than 200 grams per day of a mixture of carbohydrate, protein, and fat that can be metabolized for energy. Although all these materials are required for daily metabolism to proceed, it is not necessary that they all be provided daily in the diet. The ability of the body to draw on reserves or stores allows varying amounts of time to elapse before deficiencies may be recognized. Oxygen (if that be a nutrient) is needed continuously, water deprivation cannot last for more than a few days; total food deprivation can last for weeks to months, depending on fat reserves; whereas vitamin A stores may last for more than a year on essentially zero intake (Hume and Krebs 1949). Daily requirements for nutrients also vary enormously, ranging from microgram quantities for Vitamin B_{12}, milligram quantities for many minerals and most vitamins, gram quantities for individual essential amino acids, calcium and phosphorus, and, of course, several-hundred-gram quantities of energy-providing materials.

The distinction between required and non-required nutrients is not always clear-cut. Fiber is necessary in the diet for optimal health, yet it is not a nutrient; its function, indeed, is *not* to be absorbed. Several mineral elements— for example, zinc, copper, and selenium—have only relatively recently been demonstrated as essential nutrients, but nickel, tin, and vanadium remain in the uncertain category. Of the essential amino acids, histidine is now known to be required by adults, but the demonstration of deficiencies can take months, since the amino acid can be synthesized in the body, but only at a rate somewhat below requirements. Normal individuals can manufacture as much cystine and tyrosine, as they need; thus, these two amino acids are termed non-essential (non-essential amino acids are so essential that the body has learned to synthesize them!). Under conditions of liver damage, however, cystine and

163

tyrosine can no longer be synthesized fast enough from methionine and phenylalanine respectively, so that they become essential and must be supplied in the diet (Horowitz et al. 1981). With some vitamins, synthesis may occur (invalidating some of our definitions): the well-known example of nicotinic acid, synthesized from the amino acid tryptophan, complicated the search for the cause of pellagra (Horwitt et al. 1955). Vitamin D (cholecalciferol) can be synthesized in the skin, and it functions more as a hormone than as a vitamin (DeLuca 1974). Even vitamin C, the first discovered if not first named of the vitamins, whose lack has probably influenced human history more than any other deficiency, may be synthesized to a very limited degree in pregnancy and lactation (Rajalakshmi et al. 1965).

Diets (and most individual foods) are mixtures of nutrients, in varying proportions, along with other compounds such as fiber (of various types), phytates, cholesterol, natural toxicants, and trans-fatty acids, which may be harmful or beneficial. No single food can supply all our needs for long, and the lack of intake of a single food may or may not affect the intake of nutrients. A safe rule of thumb is that the more components there are in a dietary, the greater the probability of balanced intake. The corollary of this is that monotonous dietaries with few components are more likely not only to show deficiencies, but to be seriously affected by dietary avoidances.

The assignment of credit or blame to dietary intake for the development or prevention of malnutrition is much less straightforward than many assume, both inside and outside the field of nutrition. Nutritional status and health status overlap; adaptation to high or low intakes may occur; nutritional requirements, although based on scientific facts, depend on informed judgments and are subject to a wide range of individual variability; and, finally, estimates of nutrient intakes are only approximate except under controlled metabolic conditions that are hardly normal. It is thus not surprising that the role of food preferences and food aversions in nutrition must often remain anecdotal and equivocal.

It is now increasingly recognized that malnutrition may be caused less by nutrient deficiency as such and more by many interrelated social, political, and economic factors (Johnsson 1981; Pellett 1983); the widespread prevalence of malnutrition is usually a symptom of a very sick society (Maletnlema 1980). Because of this multifactorial causation, solutions must also be multifaceted, even if such measures as the elimination of poverty and improvement of living standards are basic. Malnutrition affects the growth, development, and survival of children and the health, activity, and well-being of adults. Conventional solutions in the form of specific programs are usually inadequate, and their effects are transitory, since they do not reach causes. Nutrition can be improved through upgrading living standards—particularly the level of real income, food availability, and health services. Solutions will be found, therefore, mostly outside the traditional nutritional field, in economic and social development.

Although the term "malnutrition" strictly should include overnutrition and some of the diseases of affluence, it is often used only to refer to the condition resulting from a deficient intake of energy or of a particular nutrient. Four especially important and broad causes of malnutrition are the following:

1. Insufficient supply of the foods necessary for a balanced diet, often due to production failure, poor soil, climate, and farming techniques, or overpopulation

2. Uneven distribution of the available food (both between and within families)

3. Lack of knowledge about nutrition and health

4. Poor health and sanitation, including infectious diseases that are synergistic to malnutrition (Latham 1979)

It must, of course, be recognized that these causes are not separate and distinct causes, but overlap with each other.

The characteristics of the major world nutritional disorders are summarized in Table 6.1. The fundamental roles of health, wealth, and sanitation factors must be recognized. Nevertheless, depending on the disorder, actions can be taken to improve the nutritional status of the most vulnerable groups, which are women of child-bearing age and young children.

The causes of malnutrition for individuals or communities can be grouped into the levels summarized in Figure 6.1. These levels are related to money-based societies, but similar levels, overlapping in various ways, exist in other societies. Under present-day economic conditions, causes of malnutrition start with overall food availability. This is affected by international and national political-economic activities as well as agricultural policy both within and external to the country. The next determinant is family purchasing power. This also is dependent on political and economic factors, but at a more local level. Thus, what food is purchased is determined both by food availability and by economic status and money availability. At the next level comes food choice. Within any economic group, the pattern of food purchases is dependent on likes and dislikes as well as the relative prices of the various foods. Nutrition education can work at this level by encouraging selection of nutrient-rich foods over nutrient-poor sources with the same cost. However, nutritional education has been far less effective than we would wish (Schürch 1983).

The next level below the family food-purchasing pattern, and overlapping it to some degree, is the pattern of food distribution within the family. This is dependent on culture and is frequently a major cause of malnutrition in the vulnerable groups. Women's and children's greater need for protein and micro-

TABLE 6.1. The Characteristics of Hunger and the Major Nutritional Disorders

| Characteristics | Hunger[a] | Protein-Energy Malnutrition (PEM[b]) | |
		Nutritional Marasmus	Kwashiorkor
Causation/ precipitation			
Long-term	Poverty, poor agriculture		Low-protein diet
Immediate	Poverty, crop failure, war	Early weaning, infections	Infections
Vulnerable groups and main age of incidence	All ages	Children under 1 year	Children between 1 and 2 years
Major features	Growth failure, wasting, lethargy	Wasting	Edema, fatty liver, reduced serum albumin
Consequences	Reduced growth, reduced work capacity, high mortality	High mortality, impaired mental development	High mortality, impaired mental development
Areas of incidence	All areas of poverty	Urban areas, large families with low incomes and poor education	Rural Africa, areas with low-protein weaning foods
Prevalence	High	Widespread in poor areas	Increasingly rare in Middle East and North Africa

Xerophthalmia	Goiter	Iron-deficiency Anemia	Low Birth-Weight (LBW) Infants[c]
Low intakes of carotene and/or retinol	Low intakes of iodine	Low intake/ absorption of iron	Poor dietary intake since conception, infections of mother
Early weaning, infections		Blood loss from infestations	Low weight gain in pregnancy
Preschool children	Older children, females	Children (<3 years) and females of child-bearing age	Mothers of poor socioeconomic status
Night blindness, xerosis of conjunctiva and cornea, keratomalacia, low serum retinol	Enlarged thyroid	Low hemoglobin (microcytic hypochromic anemia if severe)	Hypoglycemia, hypothermia, poor resistance to infection (low IgG)
High mortality especially when associated with PEM, blindness	Cretinism	Pallor, reduced work and learning efficiency	High mortality, suboptimal development, high incidence of infection
Rice staple areas, areas of poverty	Areas with low soil iodine, mountain areas and certain oases	Ubiquitous	Low socioeconomic areas with high prevalence of infections
Not widespread in wheat-staple areas of Middle East and North Africa	High in localized areas	High	Incidence highly correlated with socioeconomic indicators—possibly 20 percent of all births in poor areas

(continued)

TABLE 6.1. (cont.)

| Characteristics | Hunger[a] | Protein-Energy Malnutrition (PEM[b]) | |
		Nutritional Marasmus	Kwashiorkor
Measures to eliminate	Major socioeconomic, agricultural, and educational improvements	Major socioeconomic and educational improvements, control of infections	Control of infections, higher protein in weaning foods

SOURCE: Pellett (1983).

[a]There is a considerable degree of overlap of causation, consequences, and prevalence of protein-energy malnutrition with low birth weight infants.

[b]PEM when early or of mild to moderate severity is usually sub-clinical and can only be diagnosed by anthropometric criteria (weight/age, height/age, and weight/height).

[c]Infants of birth weight below 2,500 grams. In developing countries the majority of cases are due to fetal growth retardation.

nutrients, despite their lower food-energy needs—that is, their need for a higher concentration of nutrients—is often difficult to impart, since nutritional education will frequently conflict with cultural norms. Finally, because of the now well-known inter-relationship between malnutrition and infection (Chen, 1983; Scrimshaw, Taylor, and Gordon 1968), consumed food may not be fully utilized. An individual suffering from infection (or infestation) may not only have a reduced food intake, but may also have poorer utilization for a range of nutrients. Sanitation and the availability of clean water thus profoundly affect nutritional status.

Techniques for evaluating the nutritional status of populations can also come from a consideration of various levels of information. These can be separated into two major categories, the first pertaining to agriculture and food availability, the second pertaining to the health of the population. These are shown in Table 6.2. Agriculture and food production data have limitations, but they can indicate the approximate availability of food supplies and nutrients to a population. Close examination of agricultural production data can also allow judgments on the success or failure of agricultural techniques. The next level of information concerning food derives from dietary surveys and food consumption patterns within the society and provides data about socioeconomic variables and

Xerophthalmia	Goiter	Iron-deficiency Anemia	Low Birth-Weight (LBW) Infants[c]
Increased consumption of green vegetables, fortification, improved socioeconomic conditions	Iodine enrichment	Iron enrichment, control of infestations	Maternal nutrition programs, prevention of infections, major socioeconomic and educational improvements

FIGURE 6.1. Major Factors Affecting Nutritional Status

Sequence	Causes/Solutions
Food availability	International and national politics and economics, agricultural policy, production and distribution
Family purchasing power	Political and economic factors at a local level Targeted economic assistance → Improved purchasing power
Family food-purchasing pattern	Poor nutrition knowledge Nutrition education → Improved food selection
Within-family food distribution	Poor nutrition knowledge Nutrition education, targeted food assistance → Improved food distribution
Utilization of foods by consumer	Infection, infestation, poor sanitation Health advice and services → Improved food utilization
Individual nutritional status	

SOURCE: Sequence adapted from Pinstrup-Anderson (1982).

169

TABLE 6.2. Information Needed for the Assessment of Nutritional Status

	Food-Related Data		Health-Related Data	
Category	Country	Individual	Country	Individual
Method	Food balance sheets	Dietary surveys	Vital and health statistics	Anthropometric, biochemical, clinical testing
Information	Approximate availability of food supplies per capita	Approximate nutrient intakes of individuals and comparison with nutritional requirements	Morbidity and mortality data and degree of risk to the community	Effect of nutrition on physical development, biochemical function, and development of clinical abnormalities

the distribution and storage of foods. Dietary surveys, though difficult to perform with accuracy, can give the most detailed information on food and nutrient consumption at the family level. Conversion of food intake to nutrient intake is now performed rapidly through the use of computers, but is still dependent on both judgment and the accuracy of food-table data.

Once nutrient intake data are established, these must be compared with standards before decisions can be made concerning the nutritional value of the diet. Derivation of the appropriate requirement standards and comparison with intake values does not always allow clear-cut conclusions concerning either the nutrient or the diet as a whole.

A recent definition of nutritional requirements comes from the Canadian recommended nutrient intakes (Bureau of Nutritional Sciences 1983). "Requirement" is taken to mean that level of dietary intake of a nutrient that meets an individual's need, defined as the establishment and maintenance of a reasonable level in tissues or stores in the body. In the case of energy, the requirement is considered to be the level of intake needed to maintain appropriate body size and composition and expected work and leisure activity. For infants, children, and pregnant women, the requirement is meant to include needs for the deposition of new tissues, and for lactating women, the production of milk. A similar definition is used for the recommended dietary allowances (RDAs) in the

United States, which appear at four- to five-year intervals. The most recent of these appeared in 1980 (NAS–NRC 1980) although a 1985 version has been prepared and is awaiting publication. All of these definitions refer to the nutrients needed to maintain health in already healthy individuals.

Among normal individuals, requirements for many nutrients are affected by the nature of the diet, body size, activity, age, sex, and physiological state. There is thus individual variability, and the requirements for a group will show a range, although in tabular presentations an average for a set of reference individuals is often shown. RDA is supposed to take into account individual variability and to meet the requirements of almost all individuals in a group of specified characteristics. For food energy, in contrast, average requirements are specified because both inadequate and excess intakes of energy sources may present a risk to health. Because of this major difference, food energy was removed from the main summary table of the 1980 edition of the RDAs, and average food energy allowances are now tabulated in the energy section, where they are shown together with a range for adults of ±400 kilocalories per day. Thus, the approach to drawing conclusions from the average intakes of groups of individuals will differ for energy and for other nutrients.

Human protein and energy needs are addressed in depth about every decade by an international group under the auspices of the Food and Agricultural Organization (FAO) and the World Health Organization (WHO). The United Nations University (UNU) collaborated in the most recent report (FAO/-WHO/UNU 1985).

Although the actual recommended allowances for protein and energy do not differ greatly from previous recommendations, the basis used for both recommendations has changed. The new report notes the apparent paradox of the survival of populations that consume only 80 percent of their estimated energy needs. These populations adapt to these lower energy intakes by a reduction in activity. This has been documented by Viteri (1976) for Guatemalan plantation workers, whose productive capacity is limited by their food intake but who remain almost inactive when their day's work is completed. After additional food was provided, both consumption and activity increased. The new report emphasizes the importance of adequate food for discretionary as well as work activities and underlines the obvious (but often ignored) fact that it is impossible to establish an appropriate average figure for a population's energy requirements unless their activity level is also specified. Not only do individuals adapt, but whole societies may develop patterns compatible with low food intakes, which may not, however, be compatible with their long-term interests. The report suggests a simplified approach to estimating energy needs in which needs are defined as follows:

$$\text{food energy need} = \text{basal needs} \times \text{activity},$$

171

where basal needs are calculated from a formula that includes sex, age, and weight and an appropriate activity factor is either calculated from daily activity patterns or assigned. These assigned factors would range from 1.4 for light activity to 2.2 for heavy activity.

It has been recognized for some years that the daily allowance of 0.57 grams per kilogram of high-quality protein (egg, fish, milk) recommended by the FAO/WHO (1973) committee was too low (Garza, Scrimshaw, and Young 1977). The FAO/WHO/UNU (1985) committee reviewed a number of short (in terms of weeks) and long (in terms of months) protein requirement experiments in humans and concluded that the new safe protein allowance should be 0.75 grams per kilogram, again expressed in terms of eggs, fish, or milk. This is an apparent increase of 30 percent. In practice, recommended allowances will increase far less, because there had previously been an excessively large correction factor for protein quality, net protein utilization (NPU), a measure that takes into account digestibility and amino acid composition (see Chapter 9). If the NPU for mixed ordinary diets is assumed to be 70 percent, then the allowance of 0.5 grams per kilogram for high quality protein is increased to 0.8 grams for mixed dietary protein. Newer values for adult human amino acid requirements would now increase the NPU of the same mixed dietary protein to 90 percent, and thus the new allowance becomes 0.83 grams per kilogram, almost identical to the previous value. An interesting outcome for a rather divisive dispute—protein requirements have been increased, yet remain the same.

The overall discussions have not significantly changed the now widely accepted view that many population groups can obtain adequate protein if they are able to obtain sufficient food; thus, agricultural policy should remain centered on total yields, and increases in protein concentrations in plant-breeding programs are not required (Nygaad and Pellett 1986). Despite this it remains true that there are many population sub-groups, especially among the poor, where protein intake may indeed be limited and increased protein is desirable.

Direct comparison of dietary intakes with other standards, such as the RDAs, may still, however, lead to inaccurate conclusions. The problems categorized by the 1980–85 Committee on Dietary Allowances (NAS–NRC 1986), reached the following conclusions. (1) RDAs are for reference individuals and must be adjusted for individuals with other physical characteristics. (2) The RDAs are guidelines for separate essential nutrients, whereas people eat food, and rarely for the express purpose of consuming nutrients. No set of nutrient guidelines can adequately address these nonnutrient factors. (3) The guidelines are often incorrectly interpreted. RDAs cannot be used to determine the adequacy of the average consumption of a group. If a group's average consumption meets the RDAs, it cannot be concluded that all members of the group are well nourished, because the distribution within the group may be skewed; that is, some may be consuming more and some less. However, if the average intake is much below the RDAs, then it can be concluded that there may be a significant risk of malnutrition. Failure to meet the RDA in any one day should not be interpreted as indicating poor nutrition, since the RDAs are set for intakes over time. Individual intakes below the RDA also cannot be interpreted as indicating poor nutritional status, since RDAs are set above the needs of many individuals.

It is often assumed that the RDAs (except for energy) are set to meet the needs of 97.5 percent of the population. This is strictly true only for protein, where the coefficient of variation from a large number of requirement studies is known. For other nutrients the "safety factor" used is not consistent and differs in derivation and magnitude from nutrient to nutrient. A policy analogous to *"caveat emptor"* probably applies to all users of all RDAs. In addition to simple extraction of allowances from the summary table, careful reading of the text is required.

The question whether the dietary survey method followed is appropriate may also arise. Vitamin A/carotene, for example, is present in high levels in relatively few foods and may thus be consumed only infrequently. For such nutrients, ordinary dietary recall methods, even when three-day recalls are used, may be misleading. Some vitamins are stored in the liver, so that nutritional status can be maintained if high levels of intake occur perhaps once or twice per month. The metallic micro-nutrient copper may also be in this category. For circumstances such as these, food frequency determination may permit more accurate predictions of nutritional status than dietary surveys.

Vitamin A status can also be used as an example of how overall dietary circumstances may affect the relative importance of dietary preferences. Many children throughout the world have an aversion to green leafy vegetables. This aversion to the only cheap source of vitamin A activity (in the form of several carotenes of varying potency) may be life-threatening to children in Asian rice-eating communities and can also lead to high levels of xerophthalmia and blindness. For a child in the United States or Europe whose vitamin A is readily obtained from animal foods, the same aversion is of little consequence. The paradox of blindness and vitamin A deficiency in individuals surrounded by lush, green vegetation rich in pro–vitamin A activity has been noted by McLaren (1963).

Observations on the health of populations are also used to indicate nutritional status, although impairment of health can usually be directly ascribed to faulty nutrition only when corresponding food and nutrient intake data are available to correlate with the health data. These data start at the regional or country level, including vital and health statistics when they are available. These can identify the extent of risk to the community. At a more individual level, nutritional assessment includes anthropometric, biochemical, and clinical studies. Consideration of the results of such surveys can give information on the effects of nutrition on physical development, on the impairment of biochemical function, and on the deviation from health due to malnutrition. Assessment of nutritional status by newer functional tests (Solomons and Allen 1983) is an important innovation that may allow more specific conclusions to be drawn concerning nutrient deficiency and health.

Poor apparent nutritional status—for example, as measured by inadequate growth and development of children—may be related more to infective disease or inadequate water supply and sanitation than directly to food availability and food selection. Analysis is further complicated by the synergistic relationship among these factors. Even the type of measurement used for anthropometry will often allow varying conclusions to be drawn (Table 6.3). Weight-for-age measurements in children may overestimate the prevalence of malnutrition when compared with weight-for-height measurements. Children from poor environments may weigh less than well-nourished children of the same age but, having adapted to the situation, may be apparently healthy. Are these children suffering from malnutrition or not? The answer depends on the definition used. Smaller overall size but balanced weight for height may be a reflection of adaptation to a lower level of total food energy intake.

Adaptation can also occur for other nutrients. Two populations with large differences in protein intake may both be in nitrogen balance and meeting their requirements. Similarly, the population of New Zealand attains selenium balance at an intake much below that of the United States with no apparent effects on health (Levander 1982).

For iron, the situation is even more complex. The RDA for iron is given as 10 milligrams per day for an adult male and 18 milligrams for an adult female. This, however, tells very little about how much iron is required in diets, because both the source of iron and the presence of phytates, oxalates, tannins, and crude fiber will greatly influence the biological availability of dietary iron. In general, iron of vegetable origin is poorly available, ranging from as low as 1 to 5 percent for leaf sources such as spinach, lettuce, and cassava leaves. In contrast, the heme iron in red meat is at least 10 to 20 percent absorbed and also improves the absorption of vegetable iron in the diet (Monson et al. 1978). Iron absorption is enhanced by ascorbic acid in the diet and reduced by protein deficiency.

The adequacy of dietary iron intake is complicated still further by environmental factors. Hookworm, schistosomiasis, and malaria can increase iron loss from the body, and enteric infections may further decrease iron absorption. Clearly one can tell little about the adequacy of dietary iron intakes per se or the probability that they will be associated with the known consequences of iron deficiency, which can include reduced physical capacity and work performance and impaired resistance to infection, resulting in increased sickness.

TABLE 6.3. National Nutrition Survey of Egypt: Anthropometric Criteria Used, in Percent

Diagnosis	Weight for Height	Height for Age	Weight for Age
Normal	95	78	53
Moderately malnourished	2	17	38
Severely malnourished	<1	5	9

SOURCE: AID (1978).
NOTE: The subjects of the survey were 8,016 children (4,240 males and 3,776 females) below the age of six. "Normal" was defined as above 85 percent of the reference standard population for weight/height and above 90 percent for height/age and weight/age. "Moderately malnourished" was between 80 and 84.9 percent of the standard for weight/height, 85 to 89.9 percent for height/age, and 75 to 89.9 percent for weight/age. "Severely malnourished" was less than 80 percent of the standard for weight/height, less than 85 percent for height/age, and less than 75 percent for weight/age. The last category thus includes Gomez's second and third degree malnutrition (Gomez et al. 1956).

Errors in the assessment of vitamin A nutriture from food intake values can readily occur, since the values given for the vitamin A content of vegetable foods in some food tables may be misleading. The biological requirement for vitamin A can be met either from pre-formed vitamin A (retinol), present in animal foods, or from various carotenoids, such as α carotene, β carotene, and cryptoxanthin. The degree of conversion to retinol for various carotenes differs markedly and ranges from zero to about 17 percent (β carotene). Of over 500 carotenoids found naturally, only about 50 show pro-vitamin activity, and of these β carotene is the most important quantitatively in human nutrition (Olson 1983). From this it follows that color bears no direct relation to vitamin A activity: for example, a pale yellow corn may supply more pro–vitamin A than some more deeply colored varieties, and although red palm oil is a good source of β carotene, the majority of the pigments present are non-active. Newer food table values attempt to allow for the varying activities of vegetable carotene sources by giving retinol equivalents for vitamin A activity: different factors are used to convert each of the carotenes present to retinol. Yet problems arise here too, since few complete analyses exist showing the distribution of the various carotenes in vegetable foods. Conversions are also complicated by the fact that the international unit (IU) for carotene is not the same as the IU for retinol. Guidelines for conversion are given in the 1980 RDA manual (NAS–NRC 1980). Knowledge that vitamin A may be toxic at excessive levels may also lead to problems. Although it does not follow that vegetables with high levels of carotene pigments (e.g., sweet potatoes) are also toxic, the high vitamin A scores given such foods in some food tables may lead to that impression. In addition, values, especially for minerals and vitamins, differ from region to region within a foodstuff (e.g., outer and inner leaves), and marked seasonal variations in content may also occur. Thus, complexities exist even in apparently simple food tables, and judgment and experience are needed in the interpretation of these data.

Certainly food habits, including preferences and aversions, may affect nutritional status, but positive or negative relationships may be extremely difficult to prove except in extreme instances. Among the factors that may make conclusions difficult are the following:

1. The multifactorial etiology of malnutrition
2. The ability to adapt to higher or lower than optimal intakes, and the varying definitions of optimal
3. The varying bioavailability of nutrients
4. The difficulty of assessing food intake with accuracy
5. Problems related to the accuracy, variability, and availability of nutrient composition data, especially for unusual foods
6. The relatively "soft" nature of requirement values for many nutrients

The general tenor of this brief paper may seem to be negative and to lead to the conclusion that everything is too complicated and that no relationships between food preferences and nutritional status can be drawn. General views on the causation of malnutrition have undergone considerable change over the last two decades, and vast numbers of inter-relationships and inter-dependences have been recognized. The science of nutrition, in common with many other disciplines, has undertaken much soul-searching with regard to its place and role in the world. Perhaps the expectations were too high, but the difficulty of action in the real, highly complex world is now recognized. Problems of malnutrition are so closely related to the major problem of society that it is easy to be overwhelmed by the size of the problem and to feel that one is powerless to make any impact. The pessimistic, perhaps realistic, view is that the elimination of malnutrition will be accomplished only when poverty and injustice are overcome and health care is available for all. This is likely to be far in the future, and problems of malnutrition persist and are increasing. Suggestions for nutritional improvement are thus now returning from vast planning endeavors to smaller targeted-assistance programs aimed at those at most risk in society, such as the mother and the young child. To paraphrase a biblical saying, man may live by bread alone, but his wife and children cannot. Here, an understanding of the role of food preferences and aversions in the selection of an adequate diet for the mother may be of supreme importance. This can not only decrease the prevalence of low-birth-weight infants but also help with the continuance of breast-feeding and thus positively influence infant nutrition and reduce infant mortality from two directions simultaneously.

References Cited

Agency for International Development (AID)
 1978 Arab Republic of Egypt National Nutrition Survey. Washington, D.C.: U.S. AID, Department of State.

Bureau of Nutritional Sciences
 1983 Recommended Nutrient Intakes for Canadians. Ottawa: Canadian Government Publishing Centre.

Chen, L.
 1983 Planning for the Control of the Diarrhea-Malnutrition Complex. In *Nutrition in the Community*, 2d ed., D. S. McLaren, ed., pp. 134–60. Chichester and New York: Wiley.

DeLuca, H. F.
 1974 Vitamin D: The Vitamin and the Hormone. *Federation Proceedings* 33:2211–19.

Food and Agriculture Organization/World Health Organization (FAO/WHO)
 1973 Energy and Protein Requirements. Report of a Joint FAO/WHO Ad Hoc Expert Committee. World Health Organization Technical Report Series no. 522. Geneva: WHO.

Food and Agriculture Organization/World Health Organization/United Nations University (FAO/WHO/UNU)
 1985 Energy and Protein Requirements. Report of a Joint FAO/WHO/UNU Expert Consultation. Geneva: WHO.

Garza, D.; N. S. Scrimshaw; and V. R. Young
 1977 Human Protein Requirements: A Long-Term Metabolic Nitrogen Balance Study in Young Men to Evaluate the 1973 FAO/WHO Safe Level of Egg Protein Intake. *Journal of Nutrition* 107:335–52.

Gomez, F., et al.
 1956 Mortality in Second and Third Degree Malnutrition. *Journal of Tropical Pediatrics* 2:77–83.

Horowitz, J. M.; E. B. Rypins; J. M. Henderson; S. B. Heymsfield; S. D. Moffitt; R. P. Bain; R. K. Chawla; J. C. Bleier; and D. Rudman
 1981 Evidence for Impairment of Trans-Sulfuration Pathway in Cirrhosis. *Gastroenterology* 81:668–75.

Horwitt, M. K.
 1955 Niacin-tryptophan Relationships in the Development of Pellagra. *American Journal of Clinical Nutrition* 3:244–45.

Hume, E. M., and H. A. Krebs (comps.)
 1949 Vitamin A Requirement of Human Adults. Report of the Vitamin A Subcommittee of the Accessory Food Factors Committee. Medical Re-

search Council (Britain), Special Report Series no. 264. London: HMSO.

Johnsson, U.
1981   The Causes of Hunger. (UNU/WHP) *Food and Nutrition Bulletin* 3(2):1–9.

Latham, M. C.
1979   Human Nutrition in Tropical Africa. Food and Nutrition Series, no. 11, rev. 1. Rome: Food and Agricultural Organization.

Levander, O. A.
1982   Selenium: Biochemical Actions, Interactions and Some Human Health Implications. In *Clinical, Biochemical, and Nutritional Aspects of Trace Elements: Current Topics in Nutrition and Disease,* vol. 6, A. S. Prasad, ed., pp. 345–68. New York: A. R. Liss.

McLaren, D. S.
1983   *Malnutrition and the Eye.* New York: Academic Press.

Maletnlema, T. N.
1980   How Europe Can Contribute to Nutrition Research for Developing Countries. In *Nutrition in Europe: Proceedings of the Third European Nutrition Conference,* Leif Hambraeus, ed., pp. 10–15. Stockholm: Almqvist and Wiksell International.

Monsen, E. R. L.; L. Hallberg; M. Layrisse; D. M. Hegsted; J. D. Cook; W. Mertz; and C. A. Finch
1978   Estimation of Available Dietary Iron. *American Journal of Clinical Nutrition* 31:134–41.

National Academy of Sciences–National Research Council (NAS–NRC)
1980   *Recommended Dietary Allowances.* 9th rev. ed. Washington, D.C.: NAS.
1986   *Recommended Dietary Allowances.* 10th rev. ed. Washington, D.C.: NAS. (Publication delayed.)

Nygaad, D., and P. L. Pellett (eds.)
1986   *Dry Area Agriculture, Food Science, and Human Nutrition.* New York: Pergamon Press.

Olson, J. A.
1983   Formation and Function of Vitamin A. In *Polyisoprenoid Synthesis,* vol. 2, J. W. Porter, ed., pp. 371–412. New York: Wiley.

Pellett, P. L.
1983   Commentary: Changing Concepts on World Malnutrition. *Ecology of Food and Nutrition* 13:115–25.

Pinstup-Andersen, P.
1982   Introducing Nutritional Considerations Into Agricultural and Rural Development. *Food and Nutrition Bulletin* 4:33–41.

Rajalakshmi, R.; A. D. Doedhar; and C. V. Ramakrishnan
1965   Vitamin C Secretion During Lactation. *Acta Scandanavia* 54:375–82.

Schürch, B. (ed.)
1983   Evaluation of Nutrition Education in Third World Communities. A Nestle Foundation Workshop. Bern and Vienna: Hans Huber.

Scrimshaw, N. S.; C. E. Taylor; and J. E. Gordon
    1968   Interactions of Nutrition and Infection. World Health Organization Monograph Series no. 57. Geneva: WHO.
Solomons, N. W., and L. M. Allen
    1983   The Functional Assessment of Nutritional Status: Principles, Practice and Potential. *Nutrition Reviews* 41:33–50.
Viteri, F. E.
    1976   Definition of the Nutrition Problem in the Labor Force. In *Nutrition and Agricultural Development: Significance and Potential for the Tropics,* N. S. Scrimshaw and M. Behar, eds., pp. 87–98. New York: Plenum Press.

7

PAUL ROZIN

Psychobiological Perspectives on Food Preferences and Avoidances

OUR WORK ON FOOD PREFERENCES AND AVOIDANCES COMES from a psychobiological perspective, but has been aided and enriched by information and perspectives from anthropology. I hope in this paper to show how a psychobiological approach can ask questions and provide information and points of view that can enrich the anthropological approach. I shall deal first with the biological roots of food choice in the human omnivore and then discuss the psychological dimensions of preference and avoidance. I will then describe what we know about how foods get to be liked or disliked and, in particular, how people come to like one innately aversive food, chili pepper. This is followed by discussion of a series of somewhat unrelated topics: disgust, the interaction of psychology, biology, and culture in determining food preferences, and the importance of traditional flavorings in understanding food choice, and then by some questions about the ways in which cultural institutions may be accounted for in terms of individual human psychology and biology. (See Barker 1982 for an excellent collection of papers representing the approaches presented here.)

The Mouth: Focus of Food Choice

Almost all material transactions for incorporating substances in the external world into the self involve the mouth, which serves as a guardian of the body (Rozin and Fallon 1981). It plays a pivotal role in accepting nutrients into the body and rejecting toxins. For most purposes, it is the last site at which reversible decisions about acceptance or rejection can be made. Once swallowing has occurred, the ingested substance is difficult to reject voluntarily. Given the special position of the mouth as the last reversible checkpoint and the great benefits and risks of putting food into the body, it should not be surprising that humans and other animals display a great deal of affect about things in the mouth. Our aim is to discover what gets into the mouth of any particular human, and why.

The Human Omnivore: The Biological Basis of Food Choice

Humans are quintessential omnivores. They are able and inclined to exploit a wide variety of food sources. Since it is not possible to specify in advance what sensory properties will characterize sources of nutrition (or toxins) in any particular environment, the omnivore must discover what is edible (P. Rozin 1976). That is, it is a fundamental part of omnivore biology to have only a few biologically based behavioral constraints or predispositions about foods.

However, there are some genetically determined predispositions in all humans that promote adaptive food choice. The best-documented biological constraints are: an innate preference for sweet tastes and an avoidance of bitter tastes or irritation of the oropharyngeal surface (e.g., as produced by irritant spices or tobacco smoke) (Steiner 1979; see Cowart 1981 for a review); an interest in new foods, coupled with a fear of them; and some special abilities to learn about the delayed post-ingestional consequences of ingested foods (Booth 1982; P. Rozin 1976). The adaptive value of these biases is quite obvious, except perhaps the ambivalent attitude to new foods. This is simply a reflection of the risks and benefits of trying new foods: the great advantage of discovering a new source of nutrition, versus the danger of ingesting a toxin— the "omnivore's dilemma" (P. Rozin 1976; E. Rozin and P. Rozin 1981).

Davis's (1928) classic work on the free selection of foods by three infants immediately after weaning confirms a strong preference for sweet items and an interest in variety in foods. These children did not show any evidence of a preference for meats. However, given the widespread preference for meat among adults, it is possible that there is a genetically programmed preference for meat that appears at some time after early childhood.

Extensive research on food choice in rats, dating from the classic work by Curt Richter (1943), reveals the same biological biases we have discussed in humans as well as other biological biases that may be present in humans. Most notable is a genetically programmed enhanced liking for sodium salts under conditions of sodium deficiency (Beauchamp, Bertino, and Engelman 1983; Richter, 1956; P. Rozin 1976 for reviews).

Use, Preference, and Liking

We must distinguish among three often confounded terms: use, preference, and liking (P. Rozin 1979). "Use" refers to whether and how much of a particular food a person or group consumes. "Preference" assumes a situation of choice and refers to which of two or more foods is chosen. One might prefer lobster to potatoes but eat more potatoes because of price or availability. "Liking," usually measured with verbal scales, refers to an affective response to foods and is one determinant of preference. Liking for a food almost invariably means that a person is pleased by its sensory properties (taste, smell, etc.). A dieter might prefer (choose) cottage cheese over ice cream, but like ice cream better. We tend to eat (use) what we prefer, and we tend to prefer what we like. However, availability, price, and convenience are critical determinants of use, but not of preference or liking. And the perceived health value of a food, while a potent determinant of preference and use (Krondl and Lau 1982), may have little to do with liking.

A Psychological Taxonomy of Preferences and Avoidances

Distinctions such as these require us to look systematically at what motivates people to accept or reject foods. By early adulthood, every human in every culture comes to adopt a culturally based set of beliefs and attitudes about objects in the world with respect to their edibility. We (Fallon and Rozin 1983; Rozin and Fallon 1980, 1981) have explored this psychological categorization of substances in American culture through interviews and questionnaire studies and concluded that there are three basic types of reasons (motives) for acceptance or rejection of potential food objects. Each of these reasons (Table 7.1) in one form motivates acceptance and in the opposite form motivates rejection. This simplified system emphasizes the principal feature motivating acceptance or rejection. We now briefly consider each of the three basic reasons.

Sensory Affective Factors

Some items are rejected or accepted primarily because of their sensory effects in the mouth (or sometimes their odor or appearance). We call such accepted items "good tastes" and those rejected, "distastes." Good tastes and distastes, by definition, produce appropriate positive and negative affect (like or dislike).

TABLE 7.1. Psychological Categories of Acceptance (+) and Rejection (−)

Dimensions	Rejections			
	Distaste	Danger	Inappropriate	Disgust
Sensory-affective	−			−
Anticipated consequences		−		
Ideational		?	−	−
Contaminant		−		−
Examples	beer, chili, spinach	allergy foods, carcinogens	grass, sand	feces, insects

SOURCE: Fallon and Rozin (1983). Reprinted with slight modifications, courtesy of *Ecology of Food and Nutrition*.

Sensory-affective reactions can be innately attached to certain objects (acceptance of sweet tastes, rejection of bitter) or can be acquired. Substances that fall into the sensory-affective category for any individual are almost always acceptable foods in his or her culture. Individual differences on sensory-affective grounds (e.g., liking or disliking lima beans) probably account for most variations in food preferences within a culture.

Anticipated Consequences

Some substances are accepted or rejected as food primarily because of anticipated consequences of ingestion. These could be rapid effects, such as nausea or cramps, or the pleasant feeling of satiation. More delayed effects involve beliefs and attitudes about the health value of substances (such as vitamins or low-fat foods on the positive side, or potential carcinogens on the negative side). Anticipated consequences may be social, such as expected changes in social status as a consequence of eating a food. We place all acceptances based on anticipated consequences in the beneficial substances category, and all rejections for similar reasons in the danger category. There may or may not be a liking for the taste of these items. If a liking (disliking) is present, it would be considered a secondary cause of acceptance (rejection).

Ideational Factors

Some substances are rejected or accepted primarily because of our knowledge of what they are and where they come from. Ideational factors predominate in

Acceptances			
Good Taste	Beneficial	Appropriate	Transvalued
+			+
	+		
	?	+	+
			+
saccharine	medicines	ritual foods	Leavings of heroes or deities

many food rejections, but are less common in acceptances. Two clearly distinct subcategories of food rejection based primarily on ideational grounds can be distinguished.

A large group of items can be classified as *inappropriate*. They are considered inedible within the culture and are refused simply on this basis. Grass and paper are examples. In such cases, there is not typically a presumption that these items taste bad, and the items are usually affectively neutral. They are inoffensive.

In contrast, the category of *disgust* carries a strong negative affective loading. The nature or origin of the substance makes it offensive, nauseating, and contaminating (tiny amounts in an acceptable food render that food unacceptable). The sensory properties, including the taste, are disliked, even though in most instances the substance has never been tasted. Feces are a universal disgust. Within American culture, the category includes insects and dogmeat.

We believe that this taxonomy has some cross-cultural validity in the sense that it captures the major motivations for accepting or rejecting foods. Of course, different items would fall into the various categories in different cultures. We explicitly recognize three limitations. First, some motivations for acceptance or rejection may have been overlooked. In particular, in some cultures a food is rejected on ideational grounds because of *respect* for it, as in the avoidance of some animals as food in parts of India (see, e.g., Eichinger Ferro-Luzzi 1975). Second, the taxonomy is not a classification of foods, but rather of motivations. The same food may fall into different psychological categories for the same person in different contexts, as when a charcoal-broiled hamburger moves from a distaste at breakfast to a good taste at dinner. Third, many foods are accepted or rejected for a combination of reasons and hence are not pure illustrations of the categories we have carved out.

The Multiplicity of Motives in Acceptance and Rejection

The taxonomy lays out an array of motives that must be acknowledged if one wishes to understand and manipulate preferences. A food rejected because it causes illness has a very different psychological status from one that is rejected because it is offensive or tastes bad. Procedures to promote acceptance of a food would depend on the nature of the rejection. The set of anticipated consequences of ingestion alone contains many sub-motivations (a variety of negative or positive physiological or social effects). But the motivational frame for accepting or rejecting any potential food is yet more complex.

Let us consider the case of coffee (Cines and Rozin 1982; Goldstein and Kaizer 1969). The motivations for consuming hot coffee are many in the United States, and include taste, a variety of positive caffeine effects, avoidance of caffeine withdrawal symptoms, social interaction (as in the coffee break), a desire to fill the stomach with a low-calorie substance, warming up, and so on. Most people in the United States consume a particular cup of coffee for a number of reasons, though for some there is a dominant reason. But even within the individual there is motivational variation. The first cup of the day, in the early morning, is often motivated primarily by its wakefulness-inducing properties, whereas later cups may have primarily social or other motivations.

Ethnic groups in the United States differ in the motivational base for consuming coffee; for example, in the Philadelphia area, sensory (taste-smell) motivations are particularly important among Jews, whereas social factors seem more important among Italian Americans (Cines and Rozin 1982). Cross-culturally, there are differences in both specific motivations and the complexity of the motivation. In a Mexican highland village (Rozin and Cines 1981) weak but hot coffee is drunk once a day, an hour or so after awakening. The motivation for doing so is rather simple and uniform: to warm up in the morning. The point of this is that we must understand the motivational structure of consumption before attempting further analyses and general explanations. In terms of motivational structure, coffee is more complex than many other foods. The motivation for consuming rice, fish, or chili pepper is less variable, both among individuals within a culture and across cultures.

The Development of Likes and Dislikes

We will next consider the acquisition of likes and dislikes for foods. We will consider three contrasting pairs of categories (from Table 7.1). In each case, the first member of the pair involves an affective (taste like or dislike) response, and the second does not.

Distaste Versus Danger

Aversion to bitter foods is innate. But many items that are initially acceptable come to be rejected, some because they come to taste bad, others because we learn that they are dangerous. We can understand that people avoid a food because they have been told that it will make them sick, but what makes them come to dislike its taste?

When ingestion of a food is followed by nausea, humans develop a strong aversion to it (Garb and Stunkard 1974; Logue, Ophir, and Strauss 1981; Pelchat and Rozin 1982). This acquired bad taste can occur after a single negative experience with a delay of some hours between ingestion and its consequences. There is a strong tendency to develop a dislike for the taste or smell (as opposed to the appearance) of the food in question. There is also a tendency for a novel, as opposed to a familiar, taste to become the subject of such a learned taste aversion. Taste aversions will occur even if a person "knows" that the food he or she has eaten did not cause the illness.

Nausea and vomiting are particularly potent in causing the acquired distaste (Pelchat and Rozin 1982). Other negative events such as hives, respiratory distress, headache, and cramps following eating usually induce avoidance motivated by danger rather than distaste. This contrast can be illustrated by the typical cases of two individuals who avoid shrimp. One has an allergy to shrimp and gets skin symptoms or respiratory distress after eating it. Such a person will avoid shrimp as dangerous but like its taste. If his allergy could be treated, he would be delighted to consume shrimp. The other person originally liked shrimp but got sick and vomited after eating it. This person will typically dislike the taste of shrimp and avoid it though realizing that it is in fact not dangerous, and was perhaps not even the cause of the sickness.

There are limits to the explanatory power of the distaste-nausea linkage. It seems very unlikely that most acquired distastes have a history of association with nausea. Somewhat less than half of the people surveyed could remember even one instance of a food-nausea experience that led to an aversion. So we must presume that many people who dislike lima beans, fish, broccoli, and so on do so for reasons as yet undiscovered, and there are unfortunately no sound theories as to what the other paths to distaste might be.

Good Tastes Versus Beneficial Substances: The Acquisition of Likes for Foods

There is much more research and information about acquired likes than dislikes, but no single factor as potent as nausea for dislikes has been identified (see Beauchamp 1981; Booth 1982; P. Rozin 1983 for reviews). The overriding empirical relation in the study of acquired likes in all domains is that exposure tends to increase liking. Zajonc (1968) has suggested that exposure is a sufficient condition for liking—the mere "exposure" theory. Such effects have been demonstrated with foods (e.g., Pliner 1982), but there are limits; for example, overexposure can lead to dislike. Since cultural constraints normally arrange for the exposure of a child to available foods prepared in the traditional manner, mere exposure could account for a good part of the acquisition of liking for one's native cuisine. Alternatively, exposure could provide an opportunity for other processes to operate and produce liking. I will briefly review here the incomplete evidence we have on processes that might induce liking.

The simplest explanation of increased liking with exposure is that exposure allows fear of a new food to dissipate; one learns that the food is safe (P. Rozin 1979). This does occur but by itself cannot account for a liking for (as opposed to lack of fear of) a food.

The most straightforward parallel to the creation of distastes would be that some physiological consequence of ingestion, most appropriately an upper gastrointestinal effect (parallel to the nausea-distaste linkage), induces liking. Booth (1982; see also Booth, Mather, and Fuller 1982) has demonstrated a clear effect of rapid satiety: under some circumstances, hungry humans will come to prefer (in laboratory settings) a food with higher satiety value. Other positive effects of foods seem less potent in inducing liking, as indicated by the fact that people do not usually come to like distinctive-tasting medicines, even though they produce positive effects (Pliner et al. 1983).

Pairing of a food with an already liked food can also lead to an enhanced liking for it. This Pavlovian-type process has been demonstrated once, for humans, in the laboratory. Flavors served with sugar (an already liked substance—a Pavlovian unconditioned stimulus) tend to become more liked (Zellner et al. 1983). There would certainly be cultural constraints to such a process: it is unlikely that a new meat could be made more acceptable for Americans by sweetening it with chocolate syrup.

The production of enhanced liking through positive consequences or pairing with positive tastes is a process that should occur in animals as well as humans. In the animal literature on preferences, a consistent finding is that it is much harder to establish preferences than aversions (Rozin and Kalat 1971; Zahorik 1979). The difficulty in establishing food preferences in animals, in contrast to the many strong likes for foods in humans, suggests that some important factors operate only in humans. Sociocultural influences are the obvious candidate.

We believe that social factors operate at two levels. First, social pressures (custom, the behavior of elders, the foods made available to the child) essentially force exposure, and as we have seen, exposure fosters liking. Second, the perception that a food is valued by respected others (e.g., parents) may itself be a mechanism for the establishment of liking. This has been directly demonstrated in a number of studies, the most convincing being experimental studies on pre-school children (Birch, Zimmerman, and Hind 1980). Preference for a snack is enhanced if it is given to the child in a positive social context, or used by the teacher as a reward. It is the teacher's indication that she values the food (using it as a reward) that seems to be critical. If the same food is given to other children, at the same frequency, in a non-social context, there is no enhancement of preference. The importance of the perception of social value in acquired liking is emphasized by the converse phenomenon. Research by Birch and her colleagues (Birch et al. 1982) indicates that the perception by the child that others do not value the food per se and that they must be bribed to eat it (e.g., rewarded, told how healthy it is) seems to reduce the liking for the food. In other words, using the food as a reward indicates that it is valued and enhances liking. Rewarding the ingestion of the food is an indication that it is not valued for itself and tends to decrease liking for it.

These results are compatible with self-perception theory (Bem 1967) in social psychology. The basic idea is that people "infer" their attitudes (e.g., liking a food) from their own behavior (e.g., choosing a food). If ingestion occurs without clear extrinsic motivation, there is a tendency to justify the behavior by increasing the value of the object. However, this relation would not hold if people interpret their behavior as externally constrained (e.g., they were forced to eat a food or there was nothing else to eat). The decline in value of an object when extrinsic reward is employed is called the "overjustification effect" (Lepper 1980). The notion that reward decreases or perhaps blocks liking is consistent with the fact that people are less likely to come to like oral medicines than foods, since medicine ingestion is clearly motivated by anticipated beneficial consequences (Pliner et al. 1983). It also "explains" the common claim that if something really tastes good, it is unlikely to be good for you.

Getting to Like Chili Pepper

Almost uniquely among animal species, humans regularly come to like substances that are innately aversive. Tobacco, coffee, the irritant spices, and the various forms of alcohol are among the more popular foods of humans around the world (P. Rozin 1978). The conversion of an aversion to a liking is one of the more striking phenomena in the area of human food selection. I will consider the processes at work in one of these instances, the acquired liking for chili pepper.

Chili peppers produce oral pain and, at moderately high levels, induce defensive reflexes, including salivation, running of the nose, and tearing of the eyes. They have been consumed in Meso-America and other parts of the New World for thousands of years and were incorporated into many Old World cuisines following their discovery in the 16th century. The circumstances under which such an aversive food was rather readily adopted are mysterious, especially in light of the reluctance to adopt seemingly more nutritive and palatable products of the Americas, like corn and tomatoes. Chili peppers are among the most commonly consumed flavorings in the world and are probably eaten on a daily basis by over one-quarter of the adults in the world (P. Rozin 1978, Maga 1975 for general background).

My emphasis will be on the mechanisms responsible for reversal of innate aversions. However, one can hardly refrain from discussing the possible adaptive value of consuming this popular spice. Chili peppers, per unit weight, are among the best sources of vitamins A and C in the world. Capsaicin, the substance that causes the mouth burn, activates the gastrointestinal system, stimulating salivation, gastric secretion, and gut motility. The role of any of these features in the adoption of chili pepper into new cultures or the acquisition of a liking for it is not known (see "Adaptation, Mechanism, and the Explanation of Culinary Practices" below).

We have studied the liking for chili pepper in a Mexican highland village and in the University of Pennsylvania community (P. Rozin 1978; Rozin and Schiller 1980). At this time we do not know how this aversion reversal occurs, but I will summarize some of its basic features, and some constraints on theories of acquisition. A basic first point is that people consume chili pepper because they like it. It is a "good taste," and according to self-reports, is rarely consumed primarily because of its anticipated effects. Furthermore, people who like chili come to like the very same sensation (the mouth burn) that initially puts people off. In a Mexican village, children in the two- to six-year-old range receive gradually increasing amounts but are permitted to refuse it when it can be removed (e.g., by omitting the hot sauce on the tortillas). They are not rewarded in any obvious way for eating it; rather they observe that it is enjoyed by their elders. By age five to eight, most children in the village were voluntarily adding piquancy to their foods; they had come to like the "hot" stuff after months to years of exposure to it in a natural family setting. (American adults sometimes acquire likings for chili peppers very rapidly, after a few experiences.) Some of the mechanisms I have discussed may be at work, with initial exposure "forced" by mild social pressure to do what other members of the family do and the fact that moderate levels of chili are cooked into some of the foods. The mouth burn is paired with the repletion produced by the food in the rest of the meal, and with the already good tastes of the main food staples. Furthermore, the salivation facilitates mastication of an otherwise rather dry and mealy diet and may enhance the flavor of the food as well. The saliva and the pepper flavor and burn added to a rather bland diet seem to improve the taste of the food significantly, explaining why the most frequent explanation for chili eating offered by Mexicans is that it adds flavor or zest to food.

Two possible explanations of the acquired liking for chili (and perhaps other innately unpalatable substances) depend on its initial unpalatability. The mouth pain of chili may become pleasant as people realize that it is not really harmful. This puts the pleasure of eating chili pepper in the category of thrill-seeking, in the same sense that the initial terror of a rollercoaster ride or parachute jumping is replaced by pleasure. People may come to enjoy the fact that their bodies are signaling danger while their minds know that there really is no danger (Rozin and Schiller 1980). Alternatively, the many painful mouth experiences produced by chili may cause the brain to attempt to modulate the pain by secreting endogenous opiates, morphine-like substances produced in the brain. There is evidence that, like morphine, these brain opiates do reduce pain. At high levels, they might produce pleasure. Hundreds of experiences of chili-based mouth pain may cause larger and larger brain opiate responses, resulting in a net pleasure response after many trials (P. Rozin 1982; Rozin, Ebert, and Schull 1982; see Solomon 1980 for a statement of opponent process theory that could account for this hypothesized effect).

We are very far from an understanding of the development of liking for foods. My experience in trying to understand the liking for chili pepper convinces me that there are multiple routes to liking. We can find convincing arguments against every single mechanism we have been able to suggest. This indicates not that these mechanisms play no role in acquisition, but that there may be more than one way of producing an acquired liking. In the case of chili pepper and most other acquired likings, I am inclined to emphasize the importance of the social matrix and the valuation of the food by important others. A major role for social valuation might help to explain why non-human omnivores seem to develop acquired likings for food rather rarely, and why it is extremely difficult to get animals to like chili pepper. A few cases of chili-liking in animals have been reported; however, in all such cases, the animals (chimpanzees, dogs, macaque monkeys) were adored pets in homes where chili pepper was a frequent part of the diet. Perhaps these personal domesticates participated in the human social matrix that may be so important in the reversing of aversions and development of likings (Rozin and Kennel 1983).

Disgust Versus Inappropriateness

All of the categories we have considered up to this point probably exist in animals as well as humans. Disgust and inappropriateness—two ideationally based categories—require the mediation of culture. Inappropriate items (e.g., grass, paper, or sand) are those that are simply classified as non-foods by the culture. Their non-food status is learned by the child along with the acquisition of other types of information about these items. In the case of disgust, information provided through cultural mechanisms links up with a strong negative affective response. Objects falling into either category are rejected because of the idea of what they are and not necessarily because of their sensory properties or because they are dangerous. Disgusting objects have a number of other characteristics, in contrast to inappropriate objects.

The critical difference between inappropriateness and disgust is that although inappropriate items are essentially neutral, disgusting items are offensive (Rozin and Fallon 1981). This offensiveness extends to the idea of the disgusting substance in the body, and to its sensory properties: taste, smell, and appearance. The thought of consuming disgusting substances—but not inappropriate ones—typically leads to nausea. Objects of disgust are contaminants. For example, most Americans would refuse a liked beverage if they believed that there was even a microscopic trace of urine in it. More generally, physical traces of disgusting substances render otherwise liked foods undesirable (trace contamination). Even pure ideational associations of a liked food with a disgust item, in the absence of any possible physical trace, can motivate rejection. For example, many Americans will not eat an otherwise liked soup if it is stirred by a *brand new* fly swatter (Fallon and Rozin 1983; Rozin, Fallon, and Mandell 1984). (Contamination seems to be essentially the same concept as Frazer's [1959] general principle of sympathetic magic, "contagion"—"once in contact, always in contact" [see Rozin and Fallon 1986 and Rozin, Millman, and Nemeroff 1986 for an elaboration of the relation between disgust and the laws of sympathetic magic].)

There is also a distinct difference between the disgust and inappropriateness categories in terms of the items that fall into each. Objects of disgust are almost always of animal origin, and hence usually of substantial nutritive value (Angyal 1941; Rozin and Fallon 1980). Most tabooed foods, which we believe would usually have disgust properties, are animals or animal products (Angyal 1941; Tambiah 1969). Inappropriate items, by contrast, are usually vegetable or inorganic in nature. We (Fallon and Rozin 1983; Rozin and Fallon 1980) developed psychological profiles for the various psychological categories. Thus, disgust and inappropriateness induce different responses to items concerning nausea, contamination, negative sensory properties, and so on. Using this profile, we examined the psychological status of a number of foods. We found that pork for most kosher Jews, and meat for some vegetarians, had disgust properties. On the other hand, vegetables that some subjects describe as disgusting (e.g., brussels sprouts) actually have distaste, rather than disgust, properties (by our definition).

Angyal (1941) suggests that disgust is fundamentally a fear of oral incorporation of an offensive substance. This is in keeping with the facial disgust response, which seems designed to keep offensive substances from the face, and particularly the area of the nose and mouth. In general, the more intimate the contact with a disgust substance, and hence the more real the threat of incorporation, the greater the disgust (Fallon and Rozin 1983).

We do not have a satisfactory explanation of the origin of disgust. A major feature of such an explanation should be an economical description of the general nature of the objects of disgust (presumably more specific than identification of them as animals and animal products). I will briefly discuss here some conceptions of the basic nature of disgust objects and the mode of acquisition implied by each conception (see Rozin and Fallon 1986 for more details).

One view is that at its core, disgust is an innate aversion to spoiled and decaying matter. From an adaptive point of view, this aversion could be related to the fact that decaying food is more likely to contain pathogenic organisms. However, we know of no evidence that non-humans (including other primates) systematically avoid decaying substances. Furthermore, there is evidence indicating an attraction to feces and to decay odors in young children (Senn and Solnit 1968; Stein, Ottenberg, and Roulet 1958), which disappears in the two- to seven-year age range.

A second view focuses on feces as the primary disgust substance but, consistent with the development data, holds that the disgust is acquired (see, e.g., Angyal 1941 and the Freudian position generally). The universality of disgust for feces in adult humans argues in favor of this view (Angyal 1941). Given the initial attraction to feces, the emotionally laden toilet-training experience seems like the natural source for the origin of disgust. The conversion of an attraction into a strong aversion is a paradigmatic instance of what Freud described as a reaction formation (Senn and Solnit 1968). This position predicts the appearance of disgust around the time of toilet training and a generalization of disgust to other objects similar to feces on perceptual or conceptual grounds.

A third view emphasizes filth or disorder as opposed to the narrower concept of decay or reference to a primal disgust substance. Association with filth (e.g., garbage, feces) would be a means for the extension of the category. Douglas (1966) explicitly identifies "filth" as disorder, anomaly, or matter out of place, taking a more conceptual-symbolic approach to this idea.

A fourth view focuses on animalness (Angyal 1941). Angyal notes that as the animalness is removed from the offensive object, as by cooking or chopping, the object becomes less disgusting. Attempts have been made to describe what particular features of animals lead to disgust, with ideas such as anomaly (Douglas 1966), or closeness to humans in form (e.g., primates) or relation (e.g., domesticated pets) (Ortner 1973; Tambiah 1969). We have argued in accord with this view that all animals and their products have the potential to elicit disgust (Rozin and Fallon 1986).

Finally, disgust can be related to the human social system, where it can be viewed as an emotionally laden aspect of human social relations. Many objects of disgust are human products or involve human mediation of one sort or another. Food is clearly a major means of social expression, a fact most clearly seen in the use of food in India (Appadurai 1981) or New Guinea (Meigs 1978, 1983). Incorporation of food produced, touched, or handled by a specific other can entail some notion of incorporation of this other. If so, the value of the food would depend on the nature of and the relation to that other (Appadurai 1981; Meigs 1978, 1983). With respect to hostile others, the food can have dangerous and sometimes disgusting properties.

It is quite possible that all of the views described contain part of the truth. All, except the innate spoilage view, entail some sort of acquisition or enculturation process. It would seem most likely that verbal and non-verbal signals from parents and others—and perhaps negative facial expressions (disgust faces) in particular—play a role in communicating disgust to children. We are currently exploring the development of disgust and the idea of contamination in children (Fallon, Rozin, and Pliner 1984); surprisingly, we find that contamination does not appear until about 7 years of age in American children.

We do not pretend that we have explained the mystery of how certain cognitions tap into the strong negative affect system that we call disgust. We know that when they do, a strong aversion results, which tends to be permanent and to resist modification by rational means. It is ironic that disgust presupposes a rather sophisticated cognitive base (in terms of categorization of the world and, perhaps, contamination) and yet is so resistant to further cognitive influence.

"Positive Disgust" and the Positive-Negative Balance

I noted above that, especially in animals, there is a strong bias to more rapid and more substantial learning about the negative properties of foods. An innate positive response to sweet tastes in rats can be changed into a strong aversion in one learning trial, but an innate aversion (as to bitter substances or irritants) is very difficult to reverse, and when there is success, the effect is small and the training extensive (e.g., Rozin, Gruss, and Berk, 1979; Zahorik, 1979). Presumably this bias is related to the destructive potency of many foods and other items in the environment and the adaptive importance of rapid learning about toxins, predators, and so on. The question then arises: how about humans? As I have pointed out, humans readily learn to reverse innate dislikes. Not only do humans come to like or even love many foods, but they develop strong likings for many types of objects (pets, people, sports teams, music, etc.). We seem in many ways to have overcome the negative bias. But have we? We still learn aversions much more rapidly than preferences. Most critically, although there are a large number of items in the world that we reject as offensive (disgusting), and that can contaminate good food, there are practically no instances in American culture of the opposite of disgust—that is, substances eaten because of their nature or origin (as opposed to their sensory properties or the anticipated consequences of eating), which have the peculiar property that, in trace amounts, they can make a disliked food likable. As succinctly put by a garage mechanic in Nebraska (in a remark conveyed to me by R. L. Hall): "A teaspoon of sewage would spoil a barrel of wine, but a teaspoon of wine would do nothing at all for a barrel of sewage." What we might call the positive transvaluation of food does occur in a more salient way in other cultures. The clearest example comes from the work of Meigs (1978, 1983) on the Hua of New Guinea. For these people, the vital essence of a person, or *nu*, extends into all of the things he or she interacts with. Hence, the food one has grown, shot, killed, or cooked contains some of one's vital essence (in the sense that we might say one's fingernail parings are part of the self). For the Hua, food that contains the *nu* of those in a positive relation to the eater (e.g., for a male initiate, elder males) can nourish, while food that contains the *nu* of those in a potentially hostile relation to the eater (e.g., for the male initiate, mature females) can harm. Here we have, in a potent and salient way, something like positive contamination. The Hua conception that such positively or negatively contaminated foods are beneficial or harmful may well be masking or coexisting with a "positive disgust" response to them. The general suggestion is that with the possible exception of a few core disgusts (e.g., feces), disgust is a context-sensitive response (Meigs, 1978, 1983).

Regardless of the status of positively transvalued food, the weakening of the negative bias in humans is clear. I would suggest that the gain in strength of the positive system in humans is related to culture (P. Rozin 1982). Enculturation amounts to the learning of many rules, at least some of which become internalized as positive and negative values. What better way to ensure enculturation than to have the culture members want (like) what the culture values, and dislike what it rejects? Such internalization obviates the necessity for rules and proscriptions to ensure compliance. It is possible that the unique presence of both culture and plentiful acquired likes in humans is not accidental.

Sources of Variance in Food Preferences and Attitudes

The major determinant of what is eaten is probably availability, a factor that is to a large extent independent of any individual's behavior. Economic factors also severely constrain food choice. However, working from a psychological perspective, I will focus on differences among people in the absence of availability and economic constraints.

The determinants of individual differences in food choice can be categorized as biological, cultural, or individual (psychological). If one was interested in determining as much as possible about an adult's food preferences and attitudes, and could only ask him one question, the question should undoubtedly be: what is your culture or ethnic group? But what is responsible for the substantial differences in food preferences and attitudes among members of the same culture? Surprisingly, we do not know. There is not a very informative second question to ask our hypothetical person. Sex and biological factors such as differences in taste sensitivity account for very little variance. The family should be a potent force. But studies on parent-child resemblance in food preferences (within a more or less homogeneous culture) have found either no relation or a very small one (correlations usually below 0.3) between children's preferences and those of their parents (Birch 1980; Pliner 1983; Rozin, Fallon, and Mandell 1984). The only substantial within-culture parent-child resemblance that we know of has to do with a particular food attitude: disgust sensitivity—the degree of concern for cleanliness of foods and the possibility that they have contacted offensive substances (Rozin et al. 1984). Although family resemblance can be caused by genetic factors or experience, the meager evidence we have implicates experience as the more important factor. For example, mother-father correlations in preferences or attitudes are equal to or higher than parent-child correlations (see, Rozin, Fallon and Mandell 1984), and heritabilities for taste preferences are very low (Greene, Desor, and Maller 1975).

However, there are well-documented genetically based differences in sensitivity to some bitter compounds in humans (Fischer et al. 1961), and these show some weak relationship to preferences for bitter foods. Metabolic differences among individuals and ethnic groups may account for different preferences in some individuals, and some differences in cultural practices (Katz 1982; Simoons 1982). A case in point is lactose intolerance. In this case, a genetically determined metabolic difference sets up different contingencies related to eating (the presence of gastrointestinal distress after drinking milk), and this consequence influences food preferences through learning mechanisms that I have already discussed.

Biology and Culture as Interacting Constraints

We can view biological and cultural factors as establishing constraints or predispositions within which any individual develops a particular unique set of preferences and attitudes. We have discussed some of the factors accounting for these individual differences in terms of mechanisms for producing likes or dislikes for foods. The psychological (individual), cultural, and biological domains interact in complex ways. In particular, biological factors are expressed in individuals, and culture is created by individuals (see P. Rozin 1982 for a detailed treatment). One might reasonably expect biological and behavioral features of

196

human food selection to be represented in cultures, and they are. (I leave aside the ways in which culture represents and adapts to nutritional as opposed to behavioral universals or individual differences; see Harris 1974, Katz 1982; or Simoons 1982 for examples of this approach.)

There are rather few examples of the representation of genetically based and food-related behavioral biases in cultural institutions, largely because there are very few biological biases. However, the extraordinary popularity of sweets worldwide is represented in many cultural institutions and can be traced to a simple, genetically based preference for sweet substances. The domestication of plants producing sweet edibles and ultimately sugar refining itself, the colonial slave system, and the development of artificial sweeteners are all instances of cultural institutions prompted by our basic urge for sweets (Mintz 1985; P. Rozin 1982). Similar arguments can be made for avoidance (at the level of culture) of bitter foods, or removal of the bitterness. However, there are many counterinstances, such as the widespread ingestion by humans of foods that taste bad innately (coffee, tobacco, alcohol, chili pepper, etc.). Here, sociocultural forces arrange for a pattern of exposure to these initially undesirable items that ultimately induces a preference for them and reverses a biological bias (P. Rozin 1982).

The Psychological Importance of Flavorings: The Omnivore's Dilemma and Culinary Themes and Variations

Although flavorings make up a trivial portion of the human dietary in terms of calories or weight, their psychological importance is disproportionate. They account to a substantial degree for the distinctiveness of cuisines. Elisabeth Rozin has pointed out that most of the world's cuisines add characteristic flavor combinations called flavor principles to all of their staple foods (E. Rozin 1982, 1983). ("American" cuisine and some other temperate and Arctic cuisines do not have distinctive flavor principles.) Examples would be soy sauce, ginger root, and rice wine throughout China, chili pepper and tomato or lime in Mexico, and the spice combinations called "curries" in the different regions of India. The presence of these flavorings is essential to the satisfaction one gets from one's native cuisine; immigrant groups go to great lengths to obtain these flavorings (P. Rozin 1978).

Flavor principles impart a characteristic flavor to most of the dishes in a cuisine. This culinary institution can be somewhat speculatively traced to a bit of human biology, the omnivore's dilemma. Fear and curiosity about new foods are represented in individual humans by a desire for familiarity in foods, an indicator of safety, and an opposing desire for variety and reaction against monotony in diets. Flavor principles may be a response to the desire for familiarity, since they give almost all foods a characteristic and familiar flavor. But what about the other side of the omnivore's dilemma, the desire for variety? Careful analysis indicates that the flavor principle of a cuisine is usually a group of flavorings that vary from dish to dish while maintaining a common identity or family resemblance. Thus, while chili pepper appears in almost all Mexican food, a wide variety of peppers with different flavors are used, and there is some systematic variation of these peppers from dish to dish. Similarly, the curries of any region of India are families of flavors that are mixed in varying ways in the menu cycle. In short, the practice of flavor principles can be seen to represent both sides of the omnivore's dilemma: variety within a general familiar constraint, or culinary themes and variations (E. Rozin and P. Rozin 1981; P. Rozin 1978). This may be a case where a culinary institution can be accounted for as a transformation of a basic bit of food selection biology.

Adaptation, Mechanism, and the Explanation of Culinary Practices

We move next to a home-base of "nutritional anthropology": the explanation of features of cuisine by explicating their adaptive value. As I have indicated, this enterprise has had its greatest successes in linking universal features of human nutrition (the need for protein, etc.), or genetically based metabolic differences among humans, with appropriately adapted culinary practices (see. e.g., Harris 1974; Katz 1982). A full explanation of these practices would require a historical reconstruction of how they came to be and an account of how they are passed along from generation to generation. This brings us to the contrast between adaptation and mechanism (see P. Rozin 1982 for a more extended discussion of this issue). The problem is: to what extent is an adaptive explanation of a culinary practice a representation of the selective force that caused it to become part of a cuisine, and to what extent is it a representation of how the practice is justified by contemporary users? Let us consider the latter question first. For some adaptive culinary practices, it is likely that the current motivation (psychology) overlaps the adaptive value. For example, the leaching of cyanide from bitter manioc may well be understood for what it is by contemporary users: the effects of the cyanide are rapid and striking. On the other hand, the elaborate and adaptive tortilla technology (Katz, Hediger, and Valleroy 1974) may be another story. The nutritional benefits of this technology, including the production of a better amino acid balance in the corn, are not obviously perceptible in the nutritional effects of the food over short periods of time. In fact, I asked a number of women in a Mexican highland village why they boil their corn with lime (calcium hydroxide) (P. Rozin 1982). The uniform response was that it was hard to roll out a tortilla made with corn cooked without lime. This, of course, is a much more concrete and observable consequence of the technology. The question is, what is the relationship between the adaptive explanation and the explanation of the contemporary user, and which of these (if not both) is involved in the adoption of the technique in the culture? The same question arises for the nutritionally and medically beneficial effects of cooking, as opposed to the fact that it makes food easier to chew and better tasting, and for the relationship between the vitamin content of chili pepper and the fact that it facilitates the chewing of mealy diets. The point is simply that we have an interesting problem in attempting to relate some individual, psychological, motivational, and mechanistic explanations with adaptive ones.

Psychology, Anthropology, and Reconstructing History

In an attempt to explain culinary practices, the hardest step is to account for origins and early stages. (For example, how were the first steps in the tortilla technology discovered and institutionalized?) The problem is, of course, that we rarely have records of such events. Seemingly insignificant chance events, as in evolution, can have far-reaching consequences. For instance, I have speculated that the history of corn in Western Europe might have been very different if Cortez had had a European woman in his party (P. Rozin 1982). What was brought back to the Old World was a collection of corn kernels, with perhaps some very, very stale tortillas. But Mexicans eat their corn in the form of the highly palatable (fresh) tortilla, made with a technology practiced almost exclusively by women. It is likely that none of Cortez's men took the time to learn the technology, as a woman would have, and that the technology was never established in Europe. Therefore, a highly palatable form of corn did not have a chance to take root on the continent.

The frustrations of dealing with such problems are not unique to the nutritional anthropologist. The nutritional psychologist interested in accounting for an individual's preferences faces the same problem. Experiences like taste aversions (eating a food and getting sick) are often unique, one-time occurrences and often cannot be traced. In fact, we cannot account for most within-culture variation and must consider the possibility that many preferences are caused by unique and/or chance events. Our only solace is that, in contrast to the situation of the culture historian or anthropologist, the history of an individual's food preferences is a part of his past and is locked somewhere in his head—and perhaps as well in the heads of some members of his family. It is likely that anthropologists and psychologists will both have a great deal of trouble in excavating these histories. Fortunately, both disciplines have many other very important things to do, and hopefully they will do some of them together.

Acknowledgments

This paper is, in large part, constituted from three earlier publications by the author (Rozin 1982, 1983; Rozin and Fallon 1981). The author thanks April Fallon, Marcia Pelchat, Patricia Pliner, and Elisabeth Rozin for their contributions to the research discussed and for comments on the three papers mentioned above. The research described here was supported by National Science Foundation Grant BNS 76 80108 and National Institutes of Health Grant HD 12674.

References Cited

Angyal, A.
  1941   Disgust and Related Aversions. *Journal of Abnormal and Social Psychology* 36:393–412.
Appadurai, A.
  1981   Gastropolitics in Hindu South Asia. *American Ethnologist* 8:494–511.
Barker, L. M. (ed.)
  1982   *Psychobiology of Human Food Selection.* Westport, Conn.: AVI.
Beauchamp, G. K.
  1981   Ontogenesis of Taste Preferences. In *Food, Nutrition, and Evolution,* D. Walcher and N. Kretchmer, eds. New York: Masson.
Beauchamp, G. K.; M. Bertino; and K. Engelman
  1983   Modification of Salt Taste. *Annals of Internal Medicine* 98:763–69.
Bem, D.
  1967   Self-Perception: An Alternative Interpretation of Cognitive Dissonance Phenomena. *Psychological Review* 74:183–200.
Birch, L. L.
  1980   The Relationship Between Children's Food Preferences and Those of Their Parents. *Journal of Nutrition Education* 12:14–18.
Birch, L. L.; D. Birch; D. W. Marlin; and L. Kramer
  1982   Effects of Instrumental Consumption on Children's Food Preference. *Appetite* 3:125–34.
Birch, L. L.; S. I. Zimmerman; and H. Hind
  1980   The Influence of Social-Affective Context on the Formation of Children's Food Preferences. *Child Development* 51:856–61.

Booth, D. A.
1982   Normal Control of Omnivore Intake by Taste and Smell. In *The Determination of Behavior by Chemical Stimuli,* J. Steiner, ed., pp. 233–43. London: Information Retrieval.

Booth, D. A.; P. Mather; and J. Fuller
1982   Starch Content of Ordinary Foods Associatively Conditions Human Appetite and Satiation. Indexed by Intake and Eating Pleasantness of Starch-Paired Flavors. *Appetite* 3:163–84.

Cines, B., and P. Rozin
1982   Some Aspects of the Liking for Hot Coffee and Coffee Flavor. *Appetite* 3:23–34.

Cowart, B. J.
1981   Development of Taste Perception in Humans: Sensitivity and Preference Throughout the Life Span. *Psychological Bulletin* 90:43–73.

Davis, C.
1928   Self-selection of Diets by Newly-weaned Infants. *American Journal of Diseases of Children* 36:651–79.

Douglas, M.
1966   *Purity and Danger: An Analysis of Concepts of Pollution and Taboo.* London: Routledge and Kegan Paul.

Fallon, A. E., and P. Rozin
1983   The Psychological Bases of Food Rejections by Humans. *Ecology of Food and Nutrition* 13:15–26.

Fallon, A. E.; P. Rozin; and P. Pliner
1984   The Child's Conception of Food: The Development of Food Rejections, with Special Reference to Disgust and Contamination Sensitivity. *Child Development* 55:566–75.

Ferro-Luzzi, G. E.
1975   Food Avoidances of Indian Tribes. *Anthropos* 70:387–427.

Fischer, R.; F. Griffin; S. England; and S. M. Garn
1961   Taste Thresholds and Food Dislikes. *Nature* 191:1328.

Frazer, J. G.
1959   *The New Golden Bough: A Study in Magic and Religion* (abridged). New York: Macmillan.

Garb, J. L., and A. Stunkard
1974   Taste Aversions in Man. *American Journal of Psychiatry* 131:1204–7.

Goldstein, A., and S. Kaizer
1969   Psychotropic Effects of Caffeine in Man, III: A Questionnaire Survey of Coffee Drinking and Its Effects in a Group of Housewives. *Clinical Pharmacology and Therapeutics* 10:477–88.

Greene, L.; J. A. Desor; and O. Maller
1975   Heredity and Experience: Their Relative Importance in the Development of Taste Preferences. *Journal of Comparative and Physiological Psychology* 89:279–84.

Harris, M.
    1974   *Cows, Pigs, Wars and Witches: The Riddles of Culture.* New York: Random House.
Katz, S.
    1982   Food, Behavior and Biocultural Evolution. In *The Psychobiology of Human Food Selection,* L. M. Barker, ed., pp. 171–88. Westport, Conn.: AVI.
Katz, S.; M. L. Hediger; and L. A. Valleroy
    1974   Traditional Maize Processing Techniques in the New World: Anthropological and Nutritional Significance. *Science* 184:765–73.
Krondl, M., and D. Lau
    1982   Social Determinants in Human Food Selection. In *Psychobiology of Human Food Selection,* L. M. Barker, ed., pp. 139–51. Westport, Conn.: AVI.
Lepper, M. R.
    1980   Intrinsic and Extrinsic Motivation in Children: Detrimental Effects of Superfluous Social Controls. In *Minnesota Symposium on Child Psychology,* vol. 14, W. A. Collins, ed., pp. 155–214. Hillsdale, N.J.: Lawrence Erlbaum.
Logue, A. W.; I. Ophir; and K. F. Strauss
    1981   The Acquisition of Taste Aversions in Humans. *Behavior Research and Therapy* 19:319–33.
Maga, J. A.
    1975   Capsicum. *Critical Reviews of Food Science and Nutrition* 7:177–99.
Meigs, A. S.
    1978   A Papuan Perspective on Pollution. *Man* 13:304–18.
Meigs, A. S.
    1984   *Food, Sex, and Pollution: A New Guinea Religion.* New Brunswick, N.J.: Rutgers University Press.
Mintz, S.
    1985   *Sweetness and Power: The Place of Sugar in Modern History.* New York: Viking.
Ortner, S. B.
    1973   Sherpa Purity. *American Anthropologist* 75:49–63.
Pelchat, M. L., and P. Rozin
    1982   The Special Role of Nausea in the Acquisition of Food Dislikes by Humans. *Appetite* 3:341–51.
Pliner, P.
    1982   The Effects of Mere Exposure on Liking for Edible Substances. *Appetite* 3:283–90.
Pliner, P.
    1983   Family Resemblance in Food Preferences. *Journal of Nutrition Education* 15:137–40.
Pliner, P.; P. Rozin; M. Cooper; and G. Woody
    1985   The Minimal Role of Specific Post-Ingestional Effects in the Acquisition of Liking for Foods. *Appetite* 6:243–52.

Richter, C. P.
    1943   *Total Self-Regulating Functions in Animals and Human Beings.* Harvey Lecture Series 38:63–103.
    1956   Salt Appetite of Mammals: Its Dependence on Instinct and Metabolism. In *L'Instinct Dans Le Comportment des Animaux et de L'Homme,* Fondation Singer Polignac, ed., pp. 577–629. Paris: Masson.

Rozin, E.
    1982   The Structure of Cuisine. In *The Psychobiology of Human Food Selection,* L. M. Barker, ed., pp. 189–203. Westport, Conn.: AVI.

Rozin, E.
    1983   *Ethnic Cuisine: The Flavor Principle Cookbook.* Brattleboro, Vt.: Stephen Greene.

Rozin, E., and P. Rozin
    1981   Culinary Themes and Variations. *Natural History* 90(2):6–14.

Rozin, P.
    1976   The Selection of Food by Rats, Humans and Other Animals. In *Advances in the Study of Behavior,* vol. 6, J. Rosenblatt, R. A. Hinde, C. Beer, and E. Shaw, eds., pp. 21–76. New York: Academic Press.

Rozin, P.
    1978   The Use of Characteristic Flavorings in Human Culinary Practice. In *Flavor: Its Chemical, Behavioral and Commercial Aspects,* C. M. Apt, ed., pp. 101–27. Boulder, Colo.: Westview.

Rozin, P.
    1979   Preference and Affect in Food Selection. In *Preference Behavior and Chemoreception,* J. H. A. Kroeze, ed., pp. 289–302. London: Information Retrieval.

Rozin, P.
    1982   Human Food Selection: The Interaction of Biology, Culture and Individual Experience. In *The Psychobiology of Human Food Selection,* L. M. Barker, ed., pp. 225–54. Westport, Conn.: AVI.

Rozin, P.
    1984   The Acquisition of Food Habits and Preferences. In *Behavioral Health: A Handbook of Health Enhancement and Disease Prevention.* J. D. Matarazzo et al., eds., pp. 590–607. New York: John Wiley.

Rozin, P., and B. M. Cines
    1981   Multiple Motives for Drinking Coffee. Unpublished Manuscript.
    1982   Ethnic Differences in Coffee Use and Attitudes to Coffee. *Ecology of Food and Nutrition* 12:79–88.

Rozin, P.; I. Ebert; and J. Schull
    1982   Some Like It Hot: A Temporal Analysis of Hedonic Responses to Chili Pepper. *Appetite* 3:13–22.

Rozin, P., and A. E. Fallon
    1980   The Psychological Categorization of Foods and Non-Foods: A Preliminary Taxonomy of Food Rejections. *Appetite* 1:193–201.

Rozin, P., and A. E. Fallon
    1981   The Acquisition of Likes and Dislikes for Foods. In *Criteria of Food*

     Acceptance: How Man Chooses What He Eats, J. Solms and R. L. Hall, eds., pp. 35–48. Zurich: Forster.

  1986 A Perspective On Disgust. *Psychological Review* (in press).

Rozin, P.; A. E. Fallon; and R. Mandell

  1984 Family Resemblances in Attitudes to Foods. *Developmental Psychology* 20:309–14.

Rozin, P.; I. Gruss; and G. Berk

  1979 The Reversal of Innate Aversions: Attempts to Induce a Preference for Chili Pepper in Rats. *Journal of Comparative and Physiological Psychology* 93:1001–14.

Rozin, P., and J. W. Kalat

  1971 Specific Hungers and Poison Avoidance as Adaptive Specializations of Learning. *Psychological Review* 78:459–86.

Rozin, P., and K. Kennel

  1983 Acquired Preferences for Piquant Foods by Chimpanzees. *Appetite,* 4:69–77.

Rozin, P.; L. Millman; and C. Nemeroff

  1986 Operation of the Laws of Sympathetic Magic in Disgust and Other Domains. *Journal of Personality and Social Psychology* 50:703–12.

Rozin, P., and D. Schiller

  1980 The Nature and Acquisition of a Preference for Chili Pepper by Humans. *Motivation and Emotion* 4:77–101.

Senn, M. J. E., and A. J. Solnit

  1968 *Problems in Child Behavior and Development.* Philadelphia: Lea & Febiger.

Simoons, F. J.

  1982 Geography and Genetics as Factors in the Psychobiology of Human Food Selection. In *The Psychobiology of Human Food Selection,* L. M. Barker, ed., pp. 205–24. Westport, Conn.: AVI.

Solomon, R. L.

  1980 The Opponent-Process Theory of Acquired Motivation. *American Psychologist* 35:691–712.

Stein, M.; P. Ottenberg; and N. Roulet

  1958 A Study of the Development of Olfactory Preferences. *American Medical Association Archives of Neurology and Psychiatry* 80:264–66.

Steiner, J.

  1979 Human Facial Expressions in Response to Taste and Smell Stimulation. *Advances in Child Development and Behavior* 13:257–95.

Tambiah, S. J.

  1969 Animals Are Good to Think and Good to Prohibit. *Ethnology* 8:423–59.

Zahorik, D.

  1979 Learned Changes in Preferences for Chemical Stimuli: Asymmetrical Effects of Positive and Negative Consequences, and Species Differences in Learning. In *Preference Behaviour and Chemoreception,* J. H. A. Kroeze, ed., pp. 233–46. London: Information Retrieval.

Zajonc, R. B.
    1968   Attitudinal Effects of Mere Exposure. *Journal of Personality and Social Psychology* 9 (Part 2):1–27.
Zellner, D. A.; P. Rozin; M. Aron; and C. Kulish
    1983   Enhancement of Human's Liking for a Flavor by Pavlovian Processes. *Learning and Motivation* 14:388–50.

8

H. LEON ABRAMS, JR.

The Preference for Animal Protein and Fat: A Cross-Cultural Survey

FROM BOTH A DIACHRONIC AND A SYNCRHONIC PERSPECTIVE, the preference for some type of animal protein and animal fat in human diets is a cultural imperative (Abrams 1979). Usually animal fat accompanies animal protein in foods (USDA 1975). Hence, when humans consume animal proteins, they also automatically consume some animal fats (although at certain seasons of the year non-domesticated animal species may be a poor source of fat).

The origin of the human preference for some type of animal protein and animal fat may be found in the evolutionary antecedents of the species. Although predominantly vegetarian, most contemporary primate species include in their diet some animal protein from such sources as small animals, birds, eggs, insects, and lizards. Even primates that do not purposely seek animal protein may eat small amounts of it adventitiously in the form of insects, insect eggs, and larvae that are present in consumed fruits and plants (S. Campbell 1978; Eimerl, DeVore, et al. 1965; Galdikas-Brindamour 1975; Harding 1981; Perry 1976; Starin 1981; Van Lawick–Goodall 1971). Observed baboons and chimpanzees have been found to hunt, often cooperatively, for small animals such as monkeys, baby gazelles, and other young ungulates, and to share the bounty. In contrast, joint search for or sharing of abundant plant food would be unusual (Eimerl, DeVore, et al. 1965; Hamilton 1978; Harding and Strum 1976; Strum 1981; Teleki 1973, 1981; Van Lawick–Goodall 1971).

Uncertainty still exists regarding specific features of the social organization and food habits of the australopithecines and *Homo habilis*. However, there is general agreement that the earliest humans were omnivorous (Dart 1969; Johanson and White 1979; Potts and Shipman 1981; Zihlman 1983). The ability of early hominids to survive through a hunting-gathering-scavenging mode of subsistence has been tested by experiments carried out in the australopithecines' ancient habitat, in conditions thought to resemble those of the early Pleistocene. Schaller and Lowther (1969), traveling without modern weapons, were able to secure ample meat supplies. During the course of several days and over many miles, they stumbled upon two gazelle carcasses. They encountered a cheetah making a kill, and they could easily have partaken of the prey. They found bits of brain remaining from another kill that had been almost entirely consumed. In addition, they were able to secure many small animals. In all, they found more than 655 pounds of meat.

The case for meat eating by early humans or proto-humans is further strengthened by evidence that between the late Pliocene (three million years ago) and the mid-Pleistocene (one million years ago), there was a significant reduction in the varieties of carnivorous species inhabiting southern Africa. It is suggested that the decrease was due, at least partially, to the arrival and subsequent evolutionary success of meat-eating hominids (Klein 1977). A clue as to the diet of the australopithecines can be deduced from that of the contemporary Australian Aborigine, who eats whatever edible food is available in the natural habitat. In addition to plant food, the selections range from worms and insects to the six-foot-high kangaroo (Birdsell 1972; D. Harris, 1978; Chapter 14).

It has been postulated that meat played an important role in the development of *Homo sapiens* (Washburn 1961). By consuming animals that live on plant foods, humans obtained a highly concentrated and complete form of protein that contains all of the essential amino acids, converted from plant into animal protein (White et al. 1973). Animal protein is far more complete and concentrated than plant protein. In addition, animal protein reduces the bulk needed for energy requirements and reduces by two-thirds the time necessary for eating. More time could thus be invested in hunting, especially in the pursuit of larger animals, which required higher levels of cooperation and the development through natural selection of an increased ability to postpone immediate desire (Bronowski 1972).

The selective adaptations that resulted in the emergence of *Homo erectus* included the hunt for wild game. *Homo erectus* developed specialized tools and, as a skillful hunter, was able to spread from tropical Africa into Europe and Asia, the availability of game being relatively constant from season to season in temperate regions, unlike the situation with plant food (B. Campbell 1976; Chard 1975). The driving force that led Cro-Magnon to occupy all of the world's continents except Antarctica was the constant quest for game. The modern Lapps apparently follow reindeer herds much as early man followed game (Bronowski 1972).

Diverse archaeological excavations reveal that *Homo erectus* had mastered the hunting of large game (Butzer 1971, 1977). Examples include finds at Ambrona and Torralba in Spain (White et al. 1973), Terra Amata in France (Lumley 1972), Olduvai Gorge in Africa (Leakey 1971), and Choukoutien in China (Braidwood 1975; Treistman 1972). With the advent of *Homo sapiens,* the quest for game became more efficient, perhaps so efficient that many large species were predated to the point of extinction (Martin 1967).

The central theme of the paleolithic food quest was the hunt for meat (Grivetti 1978). Both archaeological finds (B. Campbell 1976; Solecki 1971) and cave art (Gotham 1950) reflect the preoccupation with the quest for game. The debate may continue about the extent to which hunters and gatherers depended on animal protein. Most likely the plant-animal ratio varied. However, evidence seems to indicate a distinct preference for animal protein in the paleolithic hunting and gathering economies (Harding and Teleki 1981; Lee and DeVore 1968).

Current paleoanthropological data indicate that hominids have existed for at least three to four million years (Johanson and White 1979). For more than 99 percent of this time span, hominid societies depended on hunting and gathering food. This period came to an end only in the last ten thousand years, with the adoption of agricultural modes of production. Meat had been the mainstay for paleolithic humankind. Due to growing population pressure, grains became the staff of life in horticultural and agricultural societies (Cohen 1977). Nevertheless, in virtually all societies, meat and other animal products remain preferred foods. In most of the contemporary world, when people entertain guests for a meal, meat or some form of animal protein is usually featured as an expression of cordiality and friendship.

According to Lee and DeVore (1968), the hunting and gathering lifestyle represents the most successful and enduring adaptation ever achieved by humankind. Hunters and gatherers probably possessed the knowledge that plants grow from seeds from earliest times (Cohen 1977). No known human population is ignorant of the relationship between plants and the seeds from which they grow (Flannery 1968). Bronson (1975) maintains that activities resembling cultivation existed as early as the Pleistocene period. The growing of useful plants was neither a unique nor a revolutionary event of recent origin.

Murdock's (1934) and Service's (1958, 1971, 1978) profiles of non-industrial societies all reflect a preference for animal protein, albeit protein of various types. Among the Tasmanians, for example, although fish was taboo, the consumption of oyster, crab, and other shellfish was favored. In addition to ants and grubworms, snake, lizard, kangaroo, wallaby, bandicoot, and wombat were relished (Basedow 1925; Bourne 1953; Murdock 1934). Australian Aborigines ate practically any animal they could find. They especially prized kangaroo and other marsupials, and also ate grubworms, which have a high fat content. The Yahgan of Tierra del Fuego favor seal and whale and subsist largely on mussel, conch, shellfish, and limpet (Basedow 1925; Bourne 1953; Cooper 1946; Mountford 1974; Tonkinson 1978; Warner 1958). Andaman Islanders prefer pig, civet cat, large lizard, snake, rat, dugong, turtle, fish crab, crayfish, and mollusk. The distribution and eating of turtle and pig are important in their ceremonies. The turtle is highly valued for its fat. A young bachelor who kills a pig must distribute the choicest parts to the elders. This illustrates their preference for pork, which is also high in fat (Radcliffe-Brown 1964; Service 1971). The Dobe-area Bushmen of the Kalahari desert consider 54 species of animals edible, and relish 17 of them as choice (Lee 1968). In other areas, Bushmen include many more animals in their diet (Bleek 1928; Knobel 1952; Lee 1972, 1974; Marshall 1965; Silberbauer 1981). The effort expended to obtain a certain amount of animal food reflects a strong preference for it.

Traditionally the Eskimos subsisted almost entirely on the flesh of animals such as caribou, seal, fish, and bird (Stefansson 1957, 1960). The mainstay of the Lapp diet was the flesh and milk of reindeer (Bronowski 1972; Weyer 1961).

Although the Jivaro of the Amazon jungle depend primarily on crops, game is highly prized. The Jivaro actively hunt for wild hog, peccary, bird, crocodile, tortoise, snail, snake, lizard, and frog, as well as ant larvae for their fat content (Service 1958; Steward and Metraux 1948). Among the Mehinaku of the Brazilian Amazon jungle, fish is the mainstay of the diet, but meat from wild animals is highly cherished (Gregor 1981). Fishing is of prime importance to the Kalapalo of central Brazil (Basso 1973). Because of the Kalapalo taboo against killing most animals, few are eaten. The Yanomamo include monkey, wild turkey, wild pig, armadillo, anteater, tapir, deer, alligator, rodents, and several bird species among their valued foods (Chagnon 1968).

Andean and Meso-American staples were plant foods such as maize, white potato, beans, and squash. Animals that might have been suitable for domestication had been hunted to extinction as these societies were beginning to develop. The Andean civilizations domesticated the llama and alpaca. But these creatures, valuable as pack aniamls as well as for their wool, were rarely used as food. The Andeans domesticated the muscovy duck, dog, and guinea pig and ate fish and wild animals. All were highly regarded but, being scarce, were limited to festive occasions (Rowe 1946; Service 1978).

In Meso-American cultures, exemplified by the Aztecs, only two animals were domesticated: the Mexican hairless dog and the turkey. Both were highly valued (Duran 1964; Peterson 1959; Sahaguń 1963). Harner (1977) maintains that in order to augment their meager supply of animal foods, the Aztecs turned to cannibalism, legitimated through religious sanction as a sacrifice to the gods. The Aztecs ate ants, mosquito eggs, toasted grasshoppers, and many types of worm, including the well-known maguey worm. They used the stingless honey bee for its honey. Such items are still prized and eaten in many Mexican Indian villages (D. Heyden, pers. comm.; Taylor 1975).

Predominantly horticultural societies esteem animal proteins and animal fats, although the types consumed may vary in different cultures because of ecological factors and cultural values. For example, the Ganda of Uganda, a horticultural people of east Central Africa, supplement their predominantly plant food diet with wild game, such as antelope, buffalo, elephant, and smaller animals. They also keep chickens, goats, sheep, and cattle. Their cows yield little milk and its consumption is surrounded by many taboos. Barren cows and bulls may be slaughtered for food. Animals that die from natural causes may also be eaten. Animal protein would be eaten more frequently if it were available (Murdock 1934; Roscoe 1911). In contrast to the Ganda, the horticultural Dahomeans of West Africa engage in fishing and hunting of wild game. These animal protein sources are supplemented with pig and poultry (Murdock 1934, 1959).

The subcontinent of India is usually characterized as predominantly vegetarian. Despite this view, and the diversity of the diets of various religious and tribal groups, some types of animal proteins and animal fats are preferred foods (see Chapter 18). The Hindus, who constitute the overwhelming majority of the population, universally reject beef. Yet all Hindus regard milk and ghee (clarified butter) as preferred foods. Moreover, the Hindus eat certain types of meat. The lower their caste, the less frequently they can afford to include costly meat in their diet (HRAF 1964; Moore 1970; Vaidyanathan 1983; and see Chapter 18).

Agricultural societies differ from horticultural ones in that they utilize draft animals in farming. Frequently animals that are no longer useful in the field are eaten. The Kalinga rice-farmers of the Philippines eat the water buffalo after it is too old for plowing. The Kalinga value the domesticated pig, beef animal, and fowl (Service 1958). In contrast, the Aymara of Bolivia supplement their basic potato diet with fish, pork, mutton, guinea pig, and eggs only during festivities (Buechler 1971). In Morocco, which is typical of Middle Eastern farming societies, mutton and goat are highly esteemed foods, and beef, chicken, and milk are favored (Service 1958).

Generally in pastoral and nomadic herding societies the diet consists mainly of animal foods. The Kazaks of Central Asia subsist almost entirely on their sheep and goat herds. Their prime summertime sustenance is provided by milk from the goat, cow, ewe, mare, and camel (Murdock 1934). The culture of the Todas in southern India revolves around the water buffalo. The Todas subsist almost entirely on dairy products derived from buffalo milk, along with some plant foods (Murdock 1934; Rivers 1906). Among the Nuer of East Africa, milk, blood, and meat from their cattle provide the main source of food. Milk is their year-round staple (Evans-Pritchard 1940). For the nomadic Rwala Bedouins of Arabia, camel milk is the staple food (Service 1978).

A survey of the autochthonous Amerindian societies of North America reveals that all cultures preferred some type of animal protein and animal fat. The Eskimos, the Northwest Coast Amerindians, and the Plains societies all subsisted primarily on animal protein and animal fat. In the Southwest, where these were scarce, cultures such as the Hopi and Zuni consumed little animal protein and animal fat. The Navaho obtained more by hunting wild game. The Amerindian societies of the Eastern Woodlands cultural areas valued wild game such as deer, bear, and smaller mammals, as well as fowl, fish, shellfish, and fresh water mollusk (Owen, Deetz, and Fisher 1967; Spencer, Jennings, et al. 1965). The basic diet of the contemporary Navaho is bread and mutton or goat flesh (Kluckhohn and Leighton 1974). Often the near depletion of game by one Amerindian tribe in an area has led to incursions into the hunting areas of others. The wars between the Chippewa and Dakota typify the conflicts that ensued (Hickerson 1962).

A survey of the indigenous cultures of South American reveals a similar pattern, with all cultures using and prizing some animal protein in the diet. The range runs the gamut from an almost totally animal diet, as in the Tierra del Fuego area, to the use of small amounts of animal protein, as among the people of the Andean cultural area (Lyon 1974; Steward and Faron 1959; Steward and Metraux 1948). Autochthonous cultures in Africa reveal a similar pattern. The type and amount of protein and fat consumed correlates with ecological and subsistence patterns ranging from those of the Pygmies and Bushmen to those of horticultural and pastoral or herding societies (Moore 1970; Murdock 1959; Ottenberg 1960). The cultures of Asia and Oceania reflect similar patterns (Moore 1970). Apparently all contemporary pre-state peoples parallel the practice of prehistoric societies in devoting various amounts of their economic activity to the procurement of some type of animal protein and animal fat (Gabel 1967; Herskovits 1965).

The importance of insects, spiders, and other small creatures in the diets of many cultures throughout the world is frequently overlooked. Such food is esteemed by many peoples and sometimes relished as a delicacy. These small animals augment the intake of other animal protein and animal fat. Insect foods consumed may include the egg, larva, pupa, and adult (Brothwell and Brothwell 1969; Myers 1982; Oliver 1967).

Some of the small creatures eaten in various areas and by different societies have been noted by Bates (1959; 1967), Bodenheimer (1951), Bourne (1953), Bristowe (1932), Brothwell and Brothwell (1969), Curran (1937), Downs (1966), Essig (1934), Gibbs (1965), Gelfand (1971), Hallet (1966), D. Harris (1975, 1983), Hitchcock (1962), Hoffman (1947), Meyer-Rochow (1973), Pyne (1983), Quin (1959), Remington (1946), Ruddle (1973), Steward (1963a, 1963b), Taylor (1975), and Williston (1883a, 1883b). This research may be summarized as follows:

Ants: Australian Aborigines, Amerindian tribes (Digger, Onondaga, Jivaro, Miskito, Marquiritares, Yukpa), segments of populations (in Colombia, Thailand, Papua, West Irian, Tasmania, Zimbwawe, South Africa)

Bees and wasps: China, Burma, Malaya, Australian Aborigines, Sri Lanka,

Thailand, parts of Japan, Pedi of South Africa, Aun district in East Sudan, Khoisen people in South Africa, Amerindian tribes (Waro, Chaco, Yanomami, Yukpa)

Beetles: Papua, West Irian, Pedi of South Africa, Shona, Java, Sumatra, Burma, Malaya, Madagascar, New Zealand, Turkey, Australian Aborigines

Butterflies and moths: Eskimos, Amerindian tribes (Washo, Klamath, Modoc, Mono, Paiute), Australian Aborigines, Indonesia, Burma, Japan, China, Zambia, Congolese, Papua, West Irian, Polynesia, Madagascar, Shona, or Zimbwawe

Centipedes: Guahibo Amerindians of Venezuela

Cicadas: Australian Aborigines, Papua, West Irian, southern Thailand, ancient Greece

Cockroaches: China, Thailand, Australian Aborigines, Bushmen of the Kalahari desert

Crickets: Burma, Shone of Rhodesia (in times of famine), Papua, West Irian, Uganda, Thailand, Jamaican Amerindians, Japan (prior to use of insecticides)

Dragonflies: Indonesia (Bali and Island of Lombok), Thailand (Ubon district), Nigeria, China, Papua, West Irian, Madagascar, Japan

Flies: Paiute, Mono and Koso of the Sochone tribes, Washo, Modoc, Dog Rib of Canada, Nambicuara, Yukpa

Praying Mantis and Walking Sticks: Papua, West Irian, China, Japan (prior to use of insecticides)

Spiders: Papua, West Irian, Yanomami Amerindians, Diyarua Amerindians, Thailand, Burma, Annam, Cambodia, Maniana (south of Gambia), Madagascar, Bushmen

Termites: Pemon Amerindians, Yanomami Amerindians, many Hindu groups in India, Indonesia, Thailand, Palawi, Rhodesia, Pgymies of Africa, Congo, Australian Aborigines, Burma, many Bantu tribes of South Africa

Extensive data on food types, prestige values, and preferences were collated in the Food Habits Survey of the Human Relations Area Files (HRAF 1964), which was commissioned by the U.S. Quartermaster Corps. The survey encompassed 383 cultures, of South Asia and East Asia (except China), Oceania, the Middle East, Africa, and Latin America. About a half-million informational items were gathered. Data were compiled for 38 types, categories, or aspects of foods, with an average of 35 characteristics for each culture.

All societies consumed animal foods. As part of the study, these foods were ranked by order of occurrence, and their "acceptability" was rated according to the following scale:

1. *Highly preferred:* This category includes delicacies with great cultural value: for example, watermelons among the Aymara. Usually this rating does not apply to primary foods.

2. *Preferred:* These dishes are more highly valued than most, but not necessarily favorites.

3. *Accepted readily:* Positive evaluations are noted in some written source.

4. *Acceptable substitute:* These dishes are not preferred but will be consumed in lieu of preferred dishes when the latter are not available.

5. *Disliked:* Disfavor is expressed in some written source.

6. *Variable:* The preference for a dish may not be the same for different parts of the group, or the preference may vary from time to time.

7. *No preferences:* An author explicitly states that the people have no marked liking or dislike for a certain dish—for example, "They are indifferent" or "They can take it or leave it."

8. *Other:* A form of preference that cannot be classified in any of the above categories (HRAF 1964).

Table 8.1 lists the most commonly consumed animals and animal products.

Some hunting and gathering societies placed a premium on animal fats and marine oils. For example, the Eskimos utilized blubber (Stefansson 1960), and the Northwest Coast Amerindians used fish oil (Carbarino 1976; Service 1971). All horticultural and agricultural societies also favor oil or fat for use in food preparation—for example, in cooking, baking, or as a flavor enhancer, in spreads, and as cream in foods and in beverages. Tannahill's (1973) and Brothwell and Brothwell's (1969) histories of food demonstrate the important role of animal protein and animal fat throughout human history. Many contemporary cultures continue to use and to prefer animal fats, as demonstrated by Barer-Stein (1980) in her study of the following contemporary cultures:

Argentina: Beef fat, butter

Australia: Butter (being replaced by margarine)

Austria: Sour cream, whipped cream, lard, butter

Brazil: Beef fat, butter, lard

Belgium: Butter, lard

Bulgaria: Butter

China: Lard, strained pork suet for pastry

Czechoslovakia: Butter, rendered pork and goose fat

Denmark: Butter

Egypt: Butter

England: Lard, butter

Estonia, Latvia, and Lithuania: Lard, bacon fat, butter, sour cream, cream, whipped cream

Finland: Butter, salt pork, bacon fat

France: Butter, cream, lard, chicken and goose fat

Germany: Lard, bacon fat, rendered fat from geese, ducks, chickens, horses

Greece: Butter

Holland: Butter

Hungary: Lard, butter

Iceland: Cream, butter, sheep fat, horse fat

India: Butter, ghee

Iran: Butter, fat from "fat-tailed sheep"

Ireland: Bacon fat, butter

Israel (and Jewish cooking generally): Butter

Italy: Cream, butter

Korea: Fat eaten from pork cracklings and chicken skin

Lebanon: Clarified butter from sheep or goat milk

Malta: Lard, butter

Mexico: Lard, some butter

Morocco: Clarified butter

214

TABLE 8.1. Commonly Consumed Animals and Animal Products

Animal Protein Type	Occurrence[a]	Acceptability[b]
Chicken (flesh and eggs)	363	2
Cattle (meat and milk)	196	3
Pig (domesticated)	180	2
Goat	166	3
Fish (not including specified small species)	159	2
Sheep	108	2
Duck (primarily flesh)	67	2
Zebu, (primarily milk)	49	3
Turtle (meat and eggs)	46	3
Zebu (meat and milk)	43	3
Dog	42	3
Rat	42	2

[a]Number of societies.

[b]The acceptability scale ranges from 1 ("highly preferred") to 5 ("disliked"). A score of 2 indicates that a food is preferred; a score of 3 indicates that it is accepted readily (HRAF 1964). A rating of 1 ("highly preferred") is rarely applied to primary foods.

New Zealand: Butter, cream, lard, salt pork

Norway: Butter, cream, sour cream, rendered duck and goose fat, lard, salt pork

Philippines: Lard, butter

Poland: Butter, lard, salt pork, bacon fat, rendered chicken, goose, and duck fat

Portugal: Lard

Romania: Lard, butter

Russia: Butter

Scotland: Butter, lard, suet

Spain: Butter (mainly pork fat in Basque region)

Sweden: Butter, lard, cream

Switzerland: Butter, beef drippings, chicken fat, lard, bacon fat

Syria: Clarified butter from sheep or goat milk

Turkey: Butter

Ukraine: Lard, rendered salt pork, bacon ends, butter

Uruguay: Beef fat, butter

Vietnam: Pork fat

Wales: Lard and Drippings, bacon fat, butter

West Indies: Lard, butter, ghee

Yugoslavia (Croats, Serbs, Slovenes, Macedonians): Pork and sheep fat, butter, cream, sour cream

Although environment is not a determining factor in diet, it is a limiting one. An ecologically adaptive cultural relationship exists between the foods available

215

and those selected. For various reasons, most societies place taboos on some types of foods. The prominence of animal food in the diet of a people is limited by its availability or scarcity. For example, the Hopi Indians, a group typical of the Southwestern cultures of the United States, were predominantly vegetarian because of the paucity of animal foods available to them. The rabbit, antelope, and prairie dog, which were available in limited numbers, contributed a small amount of eagerly sought animal protein and fat to the Hopi diet (Murdock 1934).

At times, the general economic status of the population determines how much animal protein and fat are eaten. In countries such as China, because of the subsistence-level income of the masses, little animal protein and fat may be consumed per capita. Although the affluent may indulge frequently in meat, fish, and eggs, the masses can afford such foods only occasionally (Wittfogel 1960). This pattern is found worldwide in varying degrees.

In conclusion, cross-cultural data clearly demonstrate that all human cultures include some types of animal proteins and animal fats in their diets and esteem them highly. Consumption of these foods is determined, or limited, by ecological and economic factors. No exclusively vegetarian society has ever been discovered (Abrams 1980; Farb and Armelagos 1980). The preference for and use of animal protein and fat appears to have been a dominant human dietary trait from the earliest times. Both diachronic and synchronic cross-cultural data unequivocally reveal that animal protein and animal fat, as preferred foods, are universally present in human diets.

References Cited

Abrams, H. L.
    1979   The Relevance of Paleolithic Diet in Determining Contemporary Nutritional Needs. *Journal of Applied Nutrition* 31:34–59.
    1980   Vegetarianism: An Anthropological/Nutritional Evaluation. *Journal of Applied Nutrition* 32:53–87.
Barer-Stein, T.
    1980   *You Eat What You Are, A Study of Ethnic Food Traditions.* Toronto: McClelland and Stewart.
Basedow, H.
    1925   *The Australian Aboriginal.* Adelaide: F. W. Preece.
Basso, E. B.
    1973   *The Kalapalo Indians of Central Brazil.* New York: Holt, Rinehart and Winston.
Bates, M.
    1959   Insects in the Diet. *American Scholar* 29:43–52.
    1967   *Gluttons and Libertines.* New York: Random House.

Birdsell, J. B.
  1972   *Human Evolution.* Chicago: Rand McNally.
Bleek, D. F.
  1928   *The Naron: A Bushman Tribe of the Central Kalahari.* Cambridge: Cambridge University Press.
Bodenheimer, F. S.
  1951   *Insects as Human Food.* The Hague: Dr. W. Junk.
Bourne, G. H.
  1953   The Food of the Australian Aboriginal. *Proceedings of the Nutrition Society* 12:58–65.
Braidwood, R. J.
  1975   *Prehistoric Men.* Glenville, Ill.: Scott Foresman.
Bristowe, W. S.
  1932   Insects and Other Invertebrates for Human Consumption in Siam. *Transactions of the Entomology Society* (London) 80:387–404.
Bronowski, J.
  1972   *The Ascent of Man.* Boston: Little, Brown.
Bronson, B.
  1975   The Earliest Farming: Demography as Cause and Consequence. In *Population, Ecology and Social Evolution,* Steven Polgar, ed., pp. 53–78. The Hague: Mouton.
Brothwell, D., and P. Brothwell
  1969   *Food in Antiquity.* London: Thames and Hudson.
Buechler, H. C., and J. M. Buechler
  1971   *The Bolivian Aymara.* New York: Holt, Rinehart and Winston.
Butzer, K. W.
  1971   *Environment and Archaeology: An Ecological Approach to Prehistory.* Chicago: Aldine.
  1977   Environment, Culture and Human Evolution. *American Scientist* 65:576.
Campbell, B. G.
  1976   *Humankind Emerging.* Boston: Little, Brown.
Campbell, S.
  1978   Noah's Ark in Tomorrow's Zoo: Animals Are A-comin', Two by Two. *Smithsonian* 8:42–50.
Carbarino, M. S.
  1976   *Native American Heritage.* Boston: Little, Brown.
Chagnon, N. A.
  1968   *Yanomamo, The Fierce People.* New York: Holt, Rinehart and Winston.
Chard, P. S.
  1975   *Man in Prehistory.* New York: McGraw-Hill.
Cohen, M. N.
  1977   *The Food Crisis in Prehistory.* New Haven: Yale University Press.
Cooper, J. M.
  1946   The Yahgan. In *Handbook of South American Indians.* Bulletin 14, vol. 1, J. H. Steward, ed. Bureau of American Ethnology. Washington, D.C.: Smithsonian Institution.

217

Curran, C. H.
   1937   On Eating Insects. *Natural History* 43(2):84–89.
Dart, R.
   1969   *Adventures with the Missing Link*. New York: Viking.
Downs, J. F.
   1966   *The Two Worlds of the Washo: An Indian Tribe of California and Nevada*.
            New York: Holt, Rinehart and Winston.
Duran, Fray D.
   1964   *The Aztecs: The History of the Indies of New Spain*. Translated with
            notes, D. Heyden and F. Horcasitas; Introduction, I. Bernal. New York:
            Orion.
Eimerl, S.; I. DeVore; and the editors of *Life*
   1965   *The Primates*. New York: Time.
Essig, E. O.
   1934   The Value of Insects to the California Indians. *Science Monthly* 38:181–
            86.
Evans-Pritchard, E. E.
   1940   *The Nuer*. Oxford: Oxford University Press.
Farb, P., and G. Armelagos
   1980   *Consuming Passions: The Anthropology of Eating*. Boston: Houghton
            Mifflin.
Flannery, K. V.
   1968   Archaeological Systems Theory and Early MesoAmerica. In *An-
            thropological Archaeology in the Americas*, B. Meggers, ed., pp. 67–87.
            Washington, D.C.: Anthropology Society of Washington.
Gabel, C.
   1967   *Analysis of Prehistoric Economic Patterns*. New York: Holt, Rinehart and
            Winston.
Galdikas-Brindamour, B.
   1975   *Search for the Great Apes*. A National Geographic documentary film.
            Washington, D.C.: National Geographic.
Gelfand, M.
   1971   *Diet and Tradition in an African Culture*. London: E. and S. Livingstone.
Gibbs, J. L., Jr.
   1965.   *Peoples of Africa*. New York: Holt, Rinehart and Winston.
Gotham
   1950   *Lascaux: Cradle of Man's Art*. A documentary film. Gotham.
Gregor, T.
   1981   *We Are Mehinaku*. A Public Broadcasting System documentary film.
            Boston: Public Broadcasting Associates.
Grivetti, L. E.
   1978   Culture, Diet and Nutrition: Selected Themes and Topics. *Bioscience*
            28(3):171–77.
Hallet, J.
   1966   *Congo Kitabu*. New York: Random House.

Hamilton, W. J.
    1978   Primate Carnivory and Its Significance to Human Diets. *Bioscience* 28:761–66.

Harding, R. S. O.
    1981   An Order of Omnivores: Nonhuman Primate Diets in the Wild. In *Omnivorous Primates: Gathering and Hunting in Human Evolution.* R. S. O. Harding and G. Teleki, eds., pp. 191–214. New York: Columbia University Press.

Harding, R. S. O., and S. C. Strum
    1976   The Predatory Baboons of Kekopey. *Natural History* 85(3):46–53.

Harding, R. S. O., and G. Teleki (eds.)
    1981   *Omnivorous Primates: Gathering and Hunting in Human Evolution.* New York: Columbia University Press.

Harner, M.
    1977   The Ecological Basis for Aztec Sacrifice. *American Ethnologist* 4:117–35.

Harris, D. R.
    1978   Adaptation to a Tropical Rain-Forest Environment: Aboriginal Subsistence in Northeastern Queensland." In *Human Behaviour and Adaptation,* N. Blurton-Jones and V. Reynolds, eds., pp. 113–34. London: Taylor and Francis.

Herskovits, M. J.
    1965   *The Economic Life of Primitive Peoples.* New York: Norton.

Hickerson, H.
    1962   *The Southwestern Chippewa: An Ethnohistorical Study.* American Anthropological Association memoir no. 92, part 2, 64(3).

Hitchcock, S. W.
    1962   *Insects and Indians of the Americas. Bulletin of the Entomological Society of America* 8:181–87.

Hoffman, W. E.
    1947   Insects as Human Food. *Proceedings* (of the Entomological Society of America) 49:233–37.

Human Relations Area Files (HRAF)
    1964   *Food Habits Survey.* New Haven: U.S. Quartermaster Corps.

Johanson, D. C., and T. D. White
    1979   A Systematic Assessment of Early African Hominids. *Science* 203:321–30.

Klein, R. G.
    1977   The Ecology of Early Man in Southern Africa. *Science* 197:115–26.

Kluckhohn, C., and D. Leighton
    1974   *The Navaho.* Cambridge: Harvard University Press.

Knobel, L.
    1952   *Remnants of a Race.* A Documentary film on the Bushmen of the Kalahari: Kalahari Films, Educational Distributors (PTD) Ltd., Encyclopedia Britannica Educational Corp.

219

Leakey, M. D.
    1971   *Olduvai Gorge.* Vol. 3. New York: Cambridge University Press.
Lee, R. B.
    1972   The !Kung Bushmen of Botswana. In *Hunters and Gatherers Today,* M.
             G. Bicchieri, ed., pp. 327–68. New York.
    1968   What Hunters Do for a Living; or, How to Make out on Scarce Re-
             sources. In *Man the Hunter,* R. B. Lee and I. DeVore, eds., pp. 30–48.
             Chicago: Aldine.
Lee, R. B., and I. DeVore
    1968   Problems in the Study of Hunters and Gatherers. In *Man the Hunter,* R.
             B. Lee and I. DeVore, eds., pp. 3–20. Chicago: Aldine.
Lumley, H. de
    1972   A Paleolithic Camp at Nice. *Scientific American* 220:42–50.
Lyon, P. J. (ed.)
    1974   *Native South Americans.* Boston: Little, Brown.
Marshall, L.
    1965   The !Kung Bushmen of the Kalahari Desert. In *Peoples of Africa,* J. L.
             Gibbs, Jr., ed. New York: Holt, Rinehart and Winston.
Martin, P. S.
    1967   Pleistocene Overkill. *Natural History* 76:32–38.
Meyer-Rochow, V. B.
    1973   Edible Insects in Three Different Ethnic Groups of Papua and New
             Guinea. *American Journal of Clinical Nutrition* 26:673–77.
Moore, F.
    1970   Food Habits in Non-Industrial Societies. In *Dimensions of Nutrition,* J.
             Dupont, ed., pp. 181–220. Boulder: Colorado Associated University
             Press.
Mountford, C. P.
    1974   *Walkabout.* (A documentary film on the Australian Aborigines in the ear-
             ly 1940s.) Sydney: Film Australia.
Murdock, G. P.
    1934   *Our Primitive Contemporaries.* New York: Macmillan.
    1959   *Africa: Its People and Their Cultural History.* New York: McGraw-Hill.
Myers, N.
    1982   "Homo Insectivorous." *Science Digest,* May.
Oliver, D. L.
    1967   *A Solomon Island Society.* Boston: Beacon Press.
Ottenberg, S., and P. Ottenberg (eds.)
    1960   *Cultures and Societies of Africa.* New York: Random House.
Owen, R. C.; J. J. F. Deetz; and A. D. Fisher (eds.)
    1967   *The North American Indians: A Sourcebook.* New York: Macmillan.
Perry, R.
    1976   *Life in Forest and Jungle.* New York: Taplinger.
Peterson, F.
    1959   *Ancient Mexico.* New York: G. P. Putnam.

Potts, R., and P. Shipman
    1981   Cutmarks Made by Stone Tools on Bones from Olduvai Gorge. *Nature* 291:577–80.

Pyne, S. J.
    1983   Indian Fires. *Natural History* 92(2):7–10.

Quin, P. J.
    1959   *Foods and Feeding Habits of the Pedi.* Johannesburg: Witwatersrand University Press.

Radcliffe-Brown, A. R.
    1964   *The Andaman Islanders.* New York: Free Press.

Remington, C. L.
    1946   Insects as Food in Japan. *Entomology News* 57(5):119–21.

Rivers, W. H. R.
    1906   *The Todas.* New York: Macmillan.

Roscoe, J.
    1911   *The Baganda.* London: Macmillan.

Rowe, J. H.
    1946   Inca Culture at the Time of the Spanish Conquest. In *Handbook of South American Indians,* Bulletin 143, vol. 2, J. H. Steward, ed., pp. 183–330. Bureau of American Ethnology. Washington, D.C.: Smithsonian Institution.

Ruddle, K.
    1973   The Human Use of Insects: Examples from the Yukpa. *Biotropica* 5(2):94–101.

Sahagún, B. de
    1963   Earthly Things. In *General History of the Things of New Spain,* book 11. Sante Fe: School of American Research and University of Utah.

Schaller, G. B., and G. Lowther
    1969   The Relevance of Carnivore Behavior to the Study of Early Hominids. *Southwest Journal of Anthropology* 25:307–41.

Service, E. R.
    1958   *A Profile of Primitive Culture.* New York: Harper and Row.
    1971   *Profiles in Ethnology.* New York: Harper and Row.
    1978   *Profiles in Ethnology.* 3d ed. New York: Harper and Row.

Silberbauer, G.
    1981   Hunter/Gatherers of the Central Kalahari. In *Omnivorous Primates: Gathering and Hunting in Human Evolution,* R. S. O. Harding and G. Teleki, eds., pp. 455–98. New York: Columbia University Press.

Solecki, R. S.
    1971   *Shanidar: The First Flower People.* New York: Knopf.

Spencer, R. F.; J. D. Jennings; et al.
    1965   *The Native Americans.* New York: Harper and Row.

Starin, E. D.
    1981   Monkey's Moves. *Natural History* 90:37–43.

Stefansson, V.
  1957   *The Fat of the Land.* New York: Macmillan.
  1960   Food and Food Habits in Alaska and Northern Canada. In *Human Nutrition: Historic and Scientific,* Iago Galston, ed., Institute of Social and Historical Medicine, Monograph no. 3. New York: International Universities Press.
Steward, J. H.
  1963a   *Handbook of South American Indians,* Vol. 4. New York: Cooper Square Publishers.
  1963b   *Handbook of South American Indians.* Vol. 6. New York: Cooper Square Publishers.
Steward, J. H., and L. C. Faron
  1959   *Native Peoples of South America.* New York: McGraw-Hill.
Steward, J. H., and A. Metraux
  1948   Tribes of the Peruvian and Ecuadorian Montaña, In *Handbook of South American Indians,* vol. 3, J. H. Steward, ed., pp. 535–656. Bureau of American Ethnology. Washington, D.C.: Smithsonian Institution.
Strum, S. C.
  1981   Process and Products of Change: Baboon Predatory Behavior at Gilgil, Kenya. In *Omnivorous Primates: Gathering and Hunting in Human Evolution,* R. S. O. Harding and G. Teleki, eds., pp. 255–302. New York: Columbia University Press.
Tannahill, R.
  1973   *Food in History.* New York: Stein and Day.
Taylor, R. L.
  1975   *Butterflies in My Stomach.* Santa Barbara: Woodbridge.
Teleki, G.
  1973   *The Predatory Behavior of Wild Chimpanzees.* Cranbury, N.J.: Bucknell University Press.
  1981   The Omnivorous Diet and Eclectic Feeding Habits of Chimpanzees in Gombe National Park, Tanzania. In *Omnivorous Primates: Gathering and Hunting in Human Evolution,* R. S. O. Harding and G. Teleki, eds., pp. 303–43. New York: Columbia University Press.
Tonkinson, R.
  1978   *The Mardudjara Aborigines.* New York: Holt, Rinehart and Winston.
Treistman, J. M.
  1972   *The Prehistory of China.* Garden City, N.Y.: Natural History Press.
U.S. Department of Agriculture
  1975   *Handbook of the Nutritional Content of Foods.* New York: Dover.
Vaidyanathan, A.
  1983   Vegetarianism and Animal Protein Consumption in India. Paper read to the Symposium on Food Preferences and Aversions, sponsored by the Wenner-Gren Foundation for Anthropological Research.
Van Lawick–Goodall, J.
  1971   *In the Shadow of Man.* Boston: Houghton Mifflin.

Warner, W. L.
    1958   *A Black Civilization.* New York: Harper and Row.
Washburn, S. L.
    1961   *Social Life of Early Man.* New York: Wenner-Gren Foundation.
Weyer, E., Jr.
    1961   *Primitive Peoples Today.* New York: Doubleday.
White, E.; D. Brown; and the editors of Time-Life Books.
    1973   *The First Men.* Boston: Little, Brown.
Williston, S. W.
    1883a   Dipterous Larvae from the Western Alkaline Lakes and Their Use as Human Food, I. In *Transactions* (Connecticut Academy of Arts and Sciences) 4:83–86.
    1883b   Dipterous Larvae from the Western Alkaline Lakes and Their Use as Human Food, II. In *Transactions* (Connecticut Academy of Arts and Sciences) 4:87–90.
Wittfogel, K. A.
    1960   Food and Society in China and India. In *Human Nutrition: Historic and Scientific,* I. Galston, ed. Institute of Social and Historical Medicine, Monograph no. 3. New York: International Universities Press.
Zihlman, A.
    1983   Dietary Divergence of Apes and Early Hominids. Paper read to the Symposium on Food Preferences and Aversions, sponsored by the Wenner-Gren Foundation for Anthropological Research.

LESLIE SUE LIEBERMAN

Biocultural Consequences of Animals Versus Plants as Sources of Fats, Proteins, and Other Nutrients

THIS CHAPTER DESCRIBES THE PHYSIOLOGICAL AND SOCIO-cultural consequences of widely divergent diets based on either high animal or high plant intake. I examine variability in nutrient needs and nutrient sources and the benefits and liabilities of deriving nutrients from either animals or plants, using an evolutionary-adaptational framework to discuss population variability and the biochemical consequences of over- or under-consumption of protein, fats, and other nutrients.

Human Nutrient Needs

The long-established broad classification of the functions of nutrients in the body is still valid. Nutrients function (1) to supply energy; (2) to promote the growth and repair of body tissues; and (3) to regulate body processes. The nutrients that perform these functions are divided into five main categories: carbohydrates, lipids, proteins, minerals, and vitamins. A classification of the essential nutrients in each of these broad groupings is presented in Figure 9.1 (Guthrie 1975). There is one essential carbohydrate: glucose; one essential lipid: linoleic acid; nine essential amino acids; 15 essential minerals; and 13 essential vitamins. In addition, both water and fiber are needed. Sources of energy are provided by carbohydrates, lipids, and proteins, but minerals and vitamins are also necessary to catalyze the use of these nutrients.

The nutrients that humans need have been well established. However, the quantities needed of these different nutrients have been under revision for a number of years and are still an area of controversy. The estimates of nutrient

FIGURE 9.1. Essential Nutrients for Humans

Water

Fiber

Carbohydrate
  Glucose

Fat or Lipid
  Linoleic acid

Protein (Amino Acids)

Histidine	Phenylalanine
Isoleucine	Threonine
Leucine	Tryptophan
Lysine	Valine
Methionine	

Minerals

Calcium	Manganese
Chlorine	Molybdenum
Chromium	Phosphorus
Copper	Potassium
Fluorine	Selenium
Iodine	Sodium
Iron	Zinc
Magnesium	

Vitamins

FAT-SOLUBLE

A	E
D	K

WATER-SOLUBLE

Ascorbic acid (C)	Pyridoxine (B_6)
Biotin	Riboflavin (B_2)
Folacin	Thiamine (B_1)
Niacin	Vitamin (B_{12})
Panthothenic acid	

SOURCE: Guthrie (1975:10–11).

requirements are determined by a number of techniques: (1) collection of data on nutrient intake from the food supply of normal, healthy people; (2) review of epidemiological observations when clinical consequences of nutrient deficiencies are found; (3) biochemical measurements that assess degree of tissue saturation and molecular function; (4) nutrient balance studies that measure nutritional status; (5) studies of subjects maintained on diets containing marginally low or deficient levels of nutrients followed by corrective measures; and (6) extrapolation from animal experiments in which deficiencies are not corrected.

The results of these studies indicate that there is tremendous individual and population variability in all the biochemical processes involved in processing food. The biologist Rene Dubos has stated that "every person has a nutritional-metabolic pattern that is characteristic, indeed as unique as a fingerprint" (1980:14).

One classic study of inter-population differences evaluated the protein requirements of American Caucasian males and Taiwanese Oriental males. Urinary nitrogen loss was significantly greater among the American students (Scrimshaw and Young 1978). In other studies comparing individuals, protein utilization differences of over 100 percent were observed for some essential amino acids. The reasons for variation in protein needs might include the following: (1) differences in absorption capacity; (2) differences in urinary nitrogen excretory rates; (3) differences in hormonal response to anxiety or stress; (4) differences in sweat loss during physical acdtvity; (5) differences in energy or carbohydrate intake and need; and (6) unknown genetic and environmental variables (Scrimshaw and Young 1978). (See Chapter 6 for further discussion of biochemical variation.)

Because of these and other experimental findings, in the early 1970s the commissions on nutrition of the World Health Organization and the Food and Agricultural Organization scaled down the protein requirements of healthy persons some 30 percent (FAO 1973). As Dubos (1980) points out, this eliminated, by administrative decision, the international "protein gap" that had been postulated in earlier decades. It did not, however, eliminate the controversy over protein needs.

The Quantification of Nutrients (Recommended Dietary Intakes)

A brief discussion of the U.S. recommended dietary allowances (RDAs) for proteins and amino acids will serve to illustrate the points of controversy concerning the establishment of appropriate nutrient intake levels. The RDAs prescribe daily amounts of essential nutrients for population groups described

227

by age, sex, weight, and physiological state (i.e., whether pregnant or lactating or not) (Committee on Dietary Allowances 1980). Special conditions that are not considered by those who establish the RDAs include body stores, physical activity, climate, and clinical or pathological problems of individuals (Jackson 1983; Rennie and Harrison 1984).

Nine amino acids—histidine, isoleucine, leucine, lysine, methionine, phenylalanine, threonine, tryptophan, and valine—are not synthesized or (in the case of histidine) are synthesized in inadequate amounts. They are, therefore, indispensable dietary nutrients for humans: the essential amino acids. Three steps were involved in establishing the RDA for protein: (1) estimation of the minimum amount of good-quality protein needed for maintenance of nitrogen equilibrium in healthy individuals; (2) adjustment of the requirements to allow for poor utilization of proteins from a mixed diet of good- and poor-quality protein (i.e., primarily plant foods with unbalanced amino acid ratios); (3) adjustments in protein allowance to meet the added needs of growth, pregnancy, and lactation. The amino acid patterns for high-quality proteins in milligrams per gram of protein are presented in Table 9.1, with requirements for infants and adults. Requirements are high for leucine and for phenylalanine. However, the sulpha-containing amino acid methionine is the one most often in limited supply. Since a specific ratio of amino acids is needed to produce a specific protein, when one amino acid is in low concentration the other amino acids, although

TABLE 9.1. Estimated Amino Acid Requirements of Humans

Amino Acid	Requirements (mg/kg body weight/day)		Amino Acid Pattern in High-Quality Protein (mg/g of protein)
	Infant (<4 yrs)	Adult	
Histidine	33	—	17
Isoleucine	83	12	42
Leucine	135	16	70
Lysine	99	12	51
Methionine and cystine	49	10	26
Phenylalanine and tyrosine	141	16	73
Threonine	68	8	35
Tryptophan	21	3	11
Valine	92	14	48

SOURCES: Committee on Dietary Allowances (1980:43); Nutrition Search, Inc. (1975:222).

TABLE 9.2. Average Percentage[a] of Methionine Supplied in an Average Serving of Foods by Food Group

Food group	No. of Foods in Each Group	Mean % of Methionine	Highest Source of Methionine
Breads, cereals, grains, and grain products	52	10.6	Soy flour: 84%/cup
Dairy products	30	30.0	Cottage cheese: 166%/cup
Fish and seafood	18	174.8	Flounder: 268%/8 oz.
Fruits	17	2.7	Dried dates: 8%/cup
Meats and poultry	21	130.1	Leg of lamb: 196%/8 oz.
Nuts and seeds	14	77.6	Sesame seeds: 192%/cup
Vegetables	51	22.6	Soybeans: 46%/cup

SOURCE: Nutrition Search, Inc. (1975:223–29).
[a]Percentage of RDA for an adult male weighing 160 pounds.

abundant, will not be used in the production of proteins. Table 9.2 lists the mean percentage of methionine supplied in an average serving of food from each of the seven major food groups. Fish, seafood, red meat, and poultry provide over 100 percent of the RDA of this nutrient. These foods provide approximately six to eight times the methionine found in an average serving of vegetables. Fruits, breads, and cereal grains provide very little methionine.

The protein allowance that serves as the basis for the recommendations of the U.S. National Academy of Sciences/National Research Council (NAS/NRC) is the 0.57 grams of protein per kilogram of body weight per day recommended by the Food and Agricultural Organization/World Health Organization (1973). But the NAS/NRC's Committee on Dietary Allowances has raised this figure 30 percent to take account of the lower efficiency of different types of proteins compared with the reference protein, which is that derived from eggs (Table 9.3). In addition, there is a correction of 7 percent to allow for variations in the efficiency of protein utilization in mixed diets. These adjustments lead to the RDA of 0.80 grams per kilogram of body weight per day. This is 56 grams of protein for a 70-kilogram man and 44 grams of protein for a 55-kilogram woman. This pattern of tinkering with established dietary allowances has a long history. (See Chapter 6 for an update of the FAO/WHO position.)

In this connection it is instructive to review the protein requirements for one-year-olds issued by the NAS/NRC. In 1948 they established the need as

TABLE 9.3. Protein Quality

Protein Source	Amino Acid Score[a]	Biological Value[b]	Net Protein Utilization[c]	Protein Efficiency Ratio[d]
Egg	100	94	94	3.92
Meat, fish, poultry	66–70	74–76	57–80	2.30–3.55
Whole-wheat flour	44	65	40	1.53
Corn	41	60	51	1.12
Soybeans	47	71	61	2.32
Legumes	28–43	55	48	1.65

SOURCE: After FAO (1970, 1973).

[a] $\dfrac{\text{mg. of amino acid in 1 gm. test protein}}{\text{mg. of amino acid in reference protein}} \times 100$

[b] $\dfrac{\text{dietary nitrogen} - (\text{urinary nitrogen} + \text{fecal nitrogen})}{\text{dietary nitrogen} - \text{fecal nitrogen}} \times 100$

[c] $\dfrac{\text{nitrogen retained}}{\text{nitrogen intake}}$

[d] $\dfrac{\text{weight gain}}{\text{gm. protein}} \times \text{number of weeks}$

3.30 grams of protein per kilogram of body weight. In 1964 this was reduced to 2.50 grams, in 1968 to 1.80 grams, and in 1974 to 1.35 grams; finally, in 1980, it was raised again to 2.00 grams (Committee on Dietary Allowances 1980; Waterlow and Payne 1975).

In general, the RDAs for other nutrients have not fluctuated as widely as those for proteins, although the establishment of RDAs has been more difficult for some nutrients than for others. Nevertheless, all of the RDAs call for overabundant quantities of nutrients rather than marginal levels. One rationale for maintaining high RDAs is to take into account the loss of nutrients through such processes as cooking, freezing, refining, and fermenting foods. The essential fat linoleic acid may be lost through high-temperature cooking, and a number of other vitamins are also heat-labile. Refining of grains, in particular, leads to a loss of fiber, vitamins, and minerals. Table 9.4 displays the reduction in specific nutrients through common processing techniques. In spite of these nutrient losses, our nutrient needs, even at the generous levels of the RDAs, are generally met by a "well-balanced" diet. But what happens when diets are not "well-balanced," when there is not a nutritionally appropriate mix of plant and animal foods?

TABLE 9.4. Reduction in Nutrient Content Through
Processing

Nutrient	Cooking	Freezing	Refining/Other
Fiber			X
Fat (linoleic acid)	X		
Vitamin E		X	X
Vitamin B_1	X		
Vitamin B_2			X[a]
Vitamin B_6			X
Folic acid	X		
Vitamin B_{12}			X
Pantothenic acid	X		X
Biotin	X		
Vitamin C	X		X
Magnesium			X
Zinc			X
Iodine			X

SOURCE: Harris and Karmis (1975); Wing and Brown (1979:62).
NOTE: Nutrients not listed are usually stable under these conditions.
[a]Exposure to acid or alkaline pH.

The Biocultural Consequences of Diets High in Animal Foods

The heterogeneity of human diets reflects our omnivorous preferences and our biochemical flexibility. The shapes and functions of our digestive organs, our enzymes, and those of our resident intestinal bacteria enable us to extract the necessary nutrients from a wide variety of foods. Harris (1979) and others (see Chapter 8) have noted that in spite of our alimentary flexibility, there is a pan-human preference for meat and other animal products (i.e., milk, eggs, blood).

This meat-eating preference, which is evident in the earliest hominid records, may be explained, in part, by the metabolic efficiency of meat as a source of human nutrition (Stini 1971). Meat provides amino acids in the appropriate proportions; essential minerals (e.g., iron and zinc); vitamins that are often difficult to obtain elsewhere (e.g., B_{12}); fat (although meat is relatively low in the essential fat linoleic acid); and some glucose, especially in raw muscle meat and liver. Moreover, meat provides these nutrients in an easily digested form and is nutrient-dense. That is, meat is a concentrated form of macro- and micro-nutrients; and therefore much smaller quantities of meat and other animal foods than of vegetables are needed to fulfill the RDAs for protein, fat, iron, zinc, and other nutrients. For example, to obtain eight grams of protein you could eat as little as one ounce of cooked lean meat or one extra large egg but you would need to eat four slices of enriched bread or four medium-sized potatoes for the same protein intake.

Finally, the preference for meat and animal foods may involve specific organoleptic properties that appeal to our senses (see Chapter 7). Although our selections are culturally mediated, a number of traits transcend cultural differences. Humans, other primates, and rats are capable of learning to accept or reject foods on the basis of metabolic consequences. Primates are suspicious of new foods, but they also wish to explore and sample them (E. Rozin and P. Rozin 1981). Humans have a strong taste preference for sweet items. This preference is evident prenatally and is reinforced by the sweet taste of mothers' milk, which is high in lactose. The preference for sweet substances shows cross-cultural (Moskowitz et al. 1975) and age differences (Desor, Greene, and Miller 1975). Younger humans prefer higher concentrations of sucrose and lactose than do adults. They also prefer greater saltiness (Desor, Greene, and Miller 1975). The Rozins (1981) suggest that the preference for sweet tastes and the aversion to bitter or irritant tastes may be an important pressure in the course of human evolution. Potential human toxins often have a bitter taste.

Other specific organoleptic preferences in humans involve food texture, temperature, and smell. Rosenbaum (1976) focuses on "mouthfeel." He suggests that humans like foods that are crispy, chewy, crunchy, and smooth. These are foods that can be controlled. We, in general, find unpleasant foods that are gummy, rubbery, stringy, slimy, mushy, or slick. Some of these textures require a great deal of mastication, while others may give the individual a feeling of being out of control as they slide down the throat. Food preparation techniques alter textures. Meat may be rubbery and stringy, but it is rarely slimy or mushy, and cooking may render meat more desirably chewy, crispy, or even crunchy.

Nutrients from Animal Foods

Diets that are high in animal foods usually provide abundant protein, fat, and calories (see Chapter 8). The American diet is high in both calories and nutrients derived from animal products. The "average" American family of four annually consumes 400 pounds of beef, 229 pounds of other red meat, 260 pounds of poultry, 1,233 pounds of dairy products, 1,056 eggs, 81 pounds of seafood, 336 pounds of fresh fruit, 400 pounds of fresh vegetables, and 498 pounds of flour and other cereal products (Gainesville Sun, June 1982). Foods of animal origin provide most of the 75 grams of protein comsumed daily by the "average" American, but account for a mere 12 percent of the daily caloric intake. At the low end of the scale, estimated intakes of protein range from 10 to 40 grams per day for populations in Papua, New Guinea (Robson and Wadsworth 1977) to 200 grams of protein per day for some Inuit males (Draper 1977; Dubos 1980; Schaefer 1981). For the traditional hunting Inuit, protein supplies approximately 32 percent of the daily caloric intake. Fat intake is also very high, averaging 185 grams per day and representing 66 percent of the daily caloric intake (Draper 1977). In contrast, the first National Health and Nutrition Examination Survey indicates that U.S. males have an average daily intake of 100 grams of fat, and females 67 grams. For both groups fat accounts for 38 percent of the daily caloric intake (NCHS 1979). Other studies cite higher fat intakes, up to an average of 117 grams per day for adults (Draper 1977). Males consume more meat than females; and, as a consequence, a high percentage of their fat intake comes from meat. Children and adolescents of both sexes consume more dairy products than adults, and a larger proportion of their total fat and saturated fat comes from these animal sources. Eggs, meat, and dairy products contribute 73 percent and 67 percent of the cholesterol intake in males and females, respectively, in all age groups. Children and adults get the largest percentage of cholesterol from eggs, whereas adolescents report more cholesterol intake from meat. Linoleic acids are provided by fats and oils (36 percent) and poultry, particularly fried chicken (12 percent), for Americans of all ages. Meat is the major source of oleic acid (another important unsaturated fatty acid) for adults, and milk and milk products the major source for children (NCHS 1979).

Lipids or fats provide the most concentrated source of dietary energy, containing twice the number of calories per gram as protein or carbohydrates. Fats are usually obtained from animal sources and oils from plant sources. As lipid-protein complexes, they are found as components of cell membranes and as components of steroid hormones. Fat serves as a fuel when glycogen stores are depleted. Subcutaneous layers of fat are energy reservoirs and insulate the body against cold. Fat also serves to insulate vital organs. Recent evidence indicates that there are individual and possibly population differences in the amount and activity levels of thermogenic brown fat. These differences are under genetic control and account for substantial differences in basal metabolic rates and, hence, nutrient and caloric needs (Bray 1983).

The high-energy-yielding diet of Inuits is necessary to maintain basal metabolic rates that are 13 to 33 percent higher than those of populations in temperate climates (Draper 1977; Speth and Spielman 1983). The task of keeping warm in cold climates is calorically costly as indicated by estimated daily caloric intakes of 3,600 kilocalories for adult males (Draper 1977). These needs are about one-third greater than the United States RDA for energy. Furthermore, protein metabolism itself is energetically costly. Nearly one-third of all ingested protein calories are used to metabolize protein and in the process produce body heat. This specific dynamic action is about two to three times higher than one finds in a diet consisting largely of fat and about five times higher than one finds in diets high in carbohydrates (Speth and Spielman 1983). Additionally, proteins, once digested, may be used in the production of carbohydrate energy sources when carbohydrate intake is very low. Again the traditional Inuit diet serves as an example, with an estimated intake of 10 grams of carbohydrates per day accounting for only 2 percent of the daily caloric intake (Draper 1977). Although fatty acids may be used for most energy needs, glucose is the metabolically preferred source of energy, and some organs, such as the brain, are obligate glucose-users. Not surprisingly, the Inuit are extremely efficient at the production of glucose from amino acids: that is, the process of gluconeogenesis (Draper 1977; Lieberman n.d.). This metabolic adaptation to a long-term nutrient imbalance represents a genototrophic adaptation among Inuit and Aleuts. Unfortunately, it becomes maladaptive when carbohydrate intake rapidly increases as part of other dietary and lifestyle changes (Schaefer 1971; Weiss, Ferrell, and Hanis 1984). As Schaefer (1971) notes, for one group of urbanized Canadian Eskimos, 50 percent of the total caloric intake came from carbohydrates. There was a corresponding decrease in animal protein consumption.

Although deficits in energy and nutrients usually occur when animal protein intake is low, some hunter-gatherers in northern latitudes who suffer deficiencies in spite of high meat intake are exceptions. Speth and Spielman (1983) describe a fall and winter diet high in lean meat but low in fat and carbohydrates for some Canadian and northern U.S. natives. Traditional food animals (e.g., deer, bison, moose, caribou) lose body fat as a result of the fall rut for males, reduced forage for both sexes in the winter, and pregnancy and lactation for females in the early spring. The whole-body fat content in wild ungulates ranges from a high of 15 to 30 percent to a low of 1 to 2 percent. The protein content of lean meat remains relatively constant at about 21 percent (Speth and Spielman 1983:12).

As noted above, diets high in protein have a high specific dynamic action that requires additional energy for metabolism. The estimated caloric increase is 20 percent above basal metabolic rates. For example, if the basal metabolic rate required 1,600 kilocalories, an additional 320 kilocalories would be needed for specific dynamic action (Speth and Spielman 1983:5–7). These authors estimate that to meet daily energy needs of approximately 3,600 kilocalories, a hunter would need to consume 7.5 to 7.9 pounds of lean meat. When caloric needs are not met, the body uses available stores of fat and then skeletal muscle protein for energy. Both fat and carbohydrates have a protein-sparing effect, but because glucose is a required energy source for the central nervous system, carbohydrates provide a more efficient and protein-protective source (Speth and Spielman 1983:13–15).

A diet high in lean meat without additional carbohydrate and fat sources presents the possibility of linoleic acid deficiency. Meat is only a fair source of this essential fatty acid. Better sources are oil-rich seeds and grains. Low fat intake results not only in reduced energy sources, but also in a reduction of lipoprotein production and the absorption, transportation, metabolism, and storage of fat-soluble vitamins (Reed 1980). Furthermore, diets high in animal protein inhibit the absorption of calcium. Even Americans have low intakes of calcium, and these low intakes, perhaps coupled with a reduction in absorption ability, have been implicated in both osteoporosis and high blood pressure (Tufts University Newsletter 1984b; McCarron et al. 1984).

Speth and Spielman (1983) suggest a number of specific strategies employed by hunter-gatherers to offset the dietary deficiencies of high-protein, low-carbohydrate, low-fat diets. For example, there may be selective hunting of individuals or species with higher body fat or the consumption of fat-rich portions of the animal. Labor-intensive techniques may be employed to render fat from bones or to preserve fat. There may be selective gathering of oil-rich foods and the trading of animal items for high-fat or high-carbohydrate foods. Finally, humans may consciously gorge on fatty foods when they are available so that their fat stores may be drawn on in times of energy deficiencies (Wilmsen 1978). This latter strategy has been useful in populations confronted with the unusual circumstances described above, but in sedentary, Westernized populations the periodic or chronic overconsumption of protein and fat have been linked to a number of disorders.

Animal Foods: Dangers and Disorders

There are many dangers inherent in keeping and consuming animals and animal products. Herd animals may transmit diseases to humans (e.g., anthrax and brucellosis) or parasites such as *Trichinella spiralis*. Animal muscle and fat may be contaminated by plant substances ingested by the animal; by antibiotics, hormones, and other drugs in animal feed; by pesticides and herbicides; by radioactive substances; by naturally occurring fungi and bacteria producing human toxins; and by the addition of potential carcinogens during preparation and cooking (Liener 1974). In the United States both diary products and eggs have been contaminated with pesticides and radioactive substances, and milk has been contaminated with pathogenic bacteria and fungal mycotoxins (ibid.). Furthermore, nutrients and their metabolites may prove to be pathogenic in humans if consumed in large amounts. The classic example is hypervitaminosis caused by the high levels of consumption of the livers of marine mammals, known as "polar bear liver disease."

Humans are not infrequently allergic to milk and egg proteins and metabolically intolerant of lactose, the primary sugar in milk (Harrison 1975; McCracken 1971; Simoons 1969, 1970, 1980). Lactose intolerance results from the reduction in older children and adults of the production of the enzyme lactase. Lactase splits the disaccharide lactose into the component sugars galactose and glucose. Some individuals with lactose intolerance can consume other dairy products without gastric and intestinal distress because bacteria reduce the lactose content of cheese, yoghurt, ghee, and other dairy products.

Anthropologists are interested in lactose intolerance because its frequency varies so widely in human populations. Lactose tolerance or lactase sufficiency, unlike other diet-related polymorphisms, shows marked geographical differences. These differences are specifically related to a history of milk consumption and dairying. Among populations with high milk production and high consumption by adults, there is very low frequency of lactase deficiency (approximately 15 percent). Among groups with no or low consumption of milk, over 80 percent of the population may be lactase-deficient (Harrison 1975; McCracken 1971).

The advantage of consuming milk is that it enhances the absorption of both calcium and protein when lactose can be digested. Harrison (1975) argues that this enhanced calcium absorption has been a particularly powerful selective force under environmental conditions with limited sunlight and limited sources of vitamin D. The utilization of milk would have an advantage in reducing the risk of rickets, which is known to directly affect the pelvic as well as the lower limbs, enhancing both infant and maternal mortality. Calcium is also needed for various neurological functions whose impairment may compromise fertility. Harrison (1975) has indicated that a very small selective advantage of 1 percent for individuals carrying the gene for lactase production in adulthood would have caused the prevalence of lactose intolerance to decline from 90 percent to 16 percent of the population in 400 generations, or since the domestication of sheep and goats. This would mean an increase in the gene frequency for lactase production from 5 percent to 60 percent. Lactose comes only from animal sources, and therefore selection pressure is heaviest on those individuals who use milk and milk products as adults to obtain calcium and other nutrients. Although milk drinking has nutritional advantages, Simoons (1981) notes an increased risk of cataracts in milk-drinking populations. He suggests that this might be related to the high concentration of galactose in milk and milk products.

Of all the diet-health issues, for decades the most conspicuous has been the possibility of a dietary influence on coronary heart disease (National Livestock and Meat Board 1983). The hypothesis most widely investigated is that saturated fats or dietary cholesterol or both are high-risk factors for heart disease.

A fairly consistent epidemiological finding has been a positive correlation between elevated blood cholesterol levels and chances of developing atherosclerosis. Consistent findings demonstrate that egg-, milk-, and meat-eaters are at higher risk for heart disease. These sources account for 73 percent of the daily intake of cholesterol and 57 percent of the saturated fat intake in the U.S. diet (NCHS 1979). The average daily U.S. diet contains about 500 milligrams of cholesterol for men and 350 milligrams for women (National Livestock and Meat Board 1983), in both cases about 60 percent more than is recommended by the American Heart Association. In actuality, humans are poor digestors of cholesterol, and as little as 10 to 50 percent of it is absorbed. The body can manufacture from 800 to 1,500 milligrams of cholesterol daily even if no cholesterol is consumed in the diet.

A national long-term study that followed men with elevated cholesterol levels for a period of 7 to 10 years found that those on a moderately cholesterol-lowering diet plus blood-cholesterol-lowering drugs reduced their cholesterol levels by 8.5 percent (Tufts University Newsletter 1984a:3–5). The researchers concluded that for each 1 percent reduction in cholesterol there was a 2 percent reduction in the rate of heart attacks. However, other long-term studies have not shown these results (MRFITRG 1982). Rosch concluded in a letter to the *Lancet:* "It seems quite clear that reduction of fat, in contrast to caloric restriction, has little to do with blood cholesterol. In addition, the incidence of heart attacks is lowest in midwest U.S.A. farming areas, where fat consumption is the highest" (1983:851). He suggests that the results of studies that have shown reduction in heart attacks may be due to the effective lowering of stress-related catecholamines. These hormones can cause cardiac damage (Rosch 1983).

The stress-reducing value systems and lifestyles found among some vegetarian groups may be partially responsible for the finding that vegetarians have not only lower overall cholesterol levels but a higher percentage of protective high-density lipoproteins than meat-eaters (Liebman 1983; Sims 1978). One large-scale study of 25,000 Seventh-Day Adventists over a 20-year period shows that lacto-ovo-vegetarians were much less likely to die of heart attacks than meat-eaters. Within this group of Seventh-Day Adventists, meat-eaters were twice as likely to die of heart disease as vegetarians (Snowdon, Phillips, and Fraser 1984; West and Hayes 1968). Their lower plasma cholesterol concentration and rate of heart attacks are most likely due to a number of factors, including: (1) lower caloric consumption; (2) lower consumption of saturated fats and higher consumption of polyunsaturated fats; (3) higher consumption of fiber; (4) lower salt intake; (5) lower body weight; and (6) lifestyle factors such as more exercise and less stress (Flynn 1978; Krey 1982).

The above factors are also causally related to the prevalence of hypertension among populations of meat-eaters and non-meat-eaters. For example, there is an impressive positive relationship between salt intake and the incidence of hypertension across populations (Luft, Weinberger, and Grim 1982). Most populations exhibiting a high frequency of hypertension have a diet high in animal food (Gleibermann 1973). Meat contains more sodium (1 g of salt = 400 mg of sodium) than most plants, but, paradoxically, Americans get 24 percent of their sodium from grain products and only 9 percent from meat. The reason is that grain products are processed with salt as well as other sodium-based additives (NCHS 1979).

Gleibermann (1973) has linked the history of salt consumption and nutritional behaviors to the high incidence of hypertension among New World black populations. She argues that the high prevalence of hypertension in blacks with a moderate salt intake is related to past selection pressures in tropical Africa. She hypothesizes a tremendous selection pressure to develop salt retention mechanisms in populations living in areas with high temperatures and low salt availability. Dietary salt intake would have decreased as populations moved from a gathering-hunting economy to horticulture. Although salt is a very early trade item, Gleibermann notes that individuals who were most likely to be stressed through heat exhaustion were less likely to participate in the exchange and consumption of salt. Under these circumstances, therefore, there would be a selective advantage to conserving salt. Salt retention is mediated through the renin-aldosterone system. Recent research has shown consistently low renin activity levels among black Americans. The result is that blacks excrete less sodium during the day and more at night than white subjects, and their 24-hour sodium excretion is significantly less than that of whites (Luft, Weinberger, and Grim 1982). The increased fluid volume leads to increased blood pressure.

Although there is no specific genetic model for hypertension as there is for lactase deficiency, one interpretation of the link between hypertension and dietary sodium indicates that there may be a genetic factor in the absorption and retention of this mineral. If sodium retention is a phenotype that has been selected for, then hypertension may be seen as the disgenic outcome of a once-favorable physiological adaptation. Increased salt sensitivity becomes disgenic in environments with moderate and frequent salt intake and low excretory rate through sweat and urine. Hypertension fits my model of a hyperefficiency disease (Lieberman n.d.).

Recent studies using the large U.S. data base of over ten thousand individuals compiled in the first National Health and Nutrition Examination Survey have shown that hypertension is consistently associated with low calcium intake. Individuals with high blood pressure also have diets low in linoleic acid, carbohydrates, calories, potassium, and vitamins A and C. Surprisingly, lower mean systolic blood pressure and lower absolute risk for hypertension were associated with *higher* sodium intake (McCarron et al. 1984). When intakes were controlled for age, race, sex, and body mass index (weight in kilograms/height in meters squared), intakes of calcium, potassium, and vitamins A and C were still found to be low in hypertensive individuals. The food group most highly correlated with blood pressure was dairy products. The greater the individual's consumption of dairy products, the less likely he or she was to be hypertensive (McCarron et al. 1984:1396). Low sodium intake is also associated with lower intakes of dairy products. In this study, individuals reporting low sodium intakes were at two to three times greater risk for hypertension than those reporting high intakes. These authors suggest a number of biochemical and physiological mechanisms by which low levels of these nutrients could cause elevated blood pressures. Finally, obesity, as assessed by weight or body mass index, was positively correlated with hypertension but negatively correlated with caloric and other nutrient intakes. McCarron et al. (1984) conclude that nutritional deficiencies, and not excesses, distinguish overweight or hypertensive individuals in the United States. They warn that standard weight reduction diets may actually exacerbate conditions leading to hypertension by further reducing nutrients that are essential for maintaining normal blood pressures.

Both excesses and deficiencies have been implicated in the etiology of New World syndrome, found among Native Americans and Mexican Americans (Weiss, Ferrell and Hanis 1984). The syndrome includes early-age adult obesity, type II (adult-onset, non-insulin-dependent) diabetes mellitus, the formation of cholesterol gallstones, and gallbladder cancer. Cancers at other sites and the complications of these primary diseases also occur in elevated frequencies. Weiss, Ferrell, and Hanis (1984) refer to this syndrome as an epidemic that has been dramatically increasing since World War II. They have formulated a thrifty genotype hypothesis to account for it because, like other "diseases of Westernization," it results from an interaction of susceptible genotypes and rapidly changing environments, including significant dietary changes. The now unfavorable metabolic phenotypes were selected for under the earlier conditions of northern hunter-gatherers. The relevant observations indicate that obesity is associated with New World syndrome; that the syndrome involves aspects of nutrient absorption, deposition, metabolism, and storage; that it is exacerbated at puberty and during pregnancy; and that it involves lipid physiology and hepatic function (Weiss, Ferrell, and Hanis 1984:171). The authors suggest that genes related to the storage of food in the form of fat might have conferred a selective advantage on women during times of nutritional and physiological stress. This genotype was previously suggested as the mechanism by which diabetes manifested its thriftiness (Neel 1962). However, obesity alone does not account for the other components of the syndrome, and therefore the authors suggest that there may be another metabolic abnormality that predisposes the system to both obesity and increases in lithogenic bile leading to gallbladder stones.

The diets implicated in the etiology of New World syndrome are high in fats, particularly saturated fats; low in fiber; high in carbohydrates. The first two components are characteristic of highly animal-based diets, whereas the third is characteristic of both contemporary and traditional diets. However, although both types of diets are high in carbohydrates, traditional diets are also high in dietary fiber and often low in fat and total calories. The biocultural consequences of diets either high or low in fat have been discussed above. The low fiber content of meat-based diets has also received a lot of attention. A diet low in fiber increases the amount of time food stays in the intestines. Although this allows more time for the absorption of nutrients, many scientists have argued that enhanced absorption and increased transit time can lead to obesity, diabetes, atherosclerosis, colon cancer, and other diseases of "civilization" (Anderson and Ward 1978; Trowell and Burkitt 1981).

The relationship between specific dietary components and cardiovascular and metabolic diseases is not always clear. The relationship of diet to a second disease cluster, cancer, is even more tenuous. Many cancers have been linked to specific dietary components (e.g., fat) consumed in high amounts in animal-based diets. Other cancers have been linked to food preparation techniques and food additives. Cancer is second to heart disease as a cause of death in the United States. Yet the epidemiological data present problems. For example, the U.S. gastric cancer rate of 9.2 per 100,000 deaths has declined more than 80 percent since 1930. In the same period of time, the U.S. per capita consumption of processed meat products has more than doubled. This means that an increase in nitrates and nitrites, food colorings, and additives has been accompanied by a reduction in cancers of the digestive tract organs.

It is important to note that both animal products and plants have been cited as potentially carcinogenic. For example, we are urged to decrease our consumption of barbecued foods because of the benzopyrine that is formed when animal fat is burned at high temperature. On the other hand, the high nitrate content in vegetables such as spinach may be converted in the body to nitrite, react with the amino acids, and produce nitrosamines, which are known carcinogens. Common green vegetables contain as much as 2,000 parts per million of nitrate or more. Cured meats customarily contain 100 parts per million or less of nitrite and nitrate combined. Like nitrites and nitrates, nitrosamines are also widely distributed in the environment (National Livestock and Meat Board 1983).

Even heating proteins at high temperatures may result in amino acid reactions leading to carcinogens. The essential amino acid tryptophan is especially susceptible to this reaction. Unsaturated fats, since they oxidize and form free radicals, can destroy or change RNA and DNA. Vegetables high in natural estrogens, like brussels sprouts and cabbage, may be considered potential inducers of genetic and carcinogenic changes (Alcantara and Speckman 1976).

240

Alcantara and Speckman (1976) review the literature on diet and nutrition and cancer. They state that diet and nutrition are more appropriately seen as modifiers rather than initiators of tumorigenesis. In addition to dietary factors, exposure to environmental carcinogens, genetic and immunological background, stress, the aging process, and obesity may be etiologic variables for specific cancers.

These findings tend to bring into question the relationship between certain dietary components and specific cancers (National Livestock and Meat Board 1983). However, Phillips and Snowdon's work on Seventh-Day Adventists as reported by Liebman (1983) shows that Seventh-Day Adventist vegetarians are only about one-half as likely as other Americans to develop colon and rectal cancer. There is also a lower incidence of breast, prostate, pancreatic, and ovarian cancer. Phillips and Snowdon note that vegetarians not only eat less or no meat but also eat more beans, whole grains, vegetables, and other fruits. The fiber and vitamin A, C, and E content of their diet may be important in terms of preventing the developing of specific cancers.

The findings on both cardiovascular diseases and cancer reveal that an over-intake of calories leading to obesity, rather than an excess or deficit of any specific nutrient, from either an animal or a plant source, may be the key risk factor in these diseases. The disadvantage that animal-eaters have is that they are generally fatter than vegetarians. The relationship between leanness per se, dietary constituents, nutrient status, and diseases may be further investigated through an examination of diets high in plant foods.

Biocultural Consequences of Diets High in Plant Foods

Most of the world's populations live on diets characterized by very high intakes of plant foods and based on a starchy, bland staple (Robson and Wadsworth 1977). Most diets contain both plant and animal products. However, some traditionally vegetarian groups such as Orthodox Hindus, Buddhists, and Seventh-Day Adventists, and a few smaller religious orders such as Trappist monks, maintain exclusively vegetarian diets. Moreover, the last two decades have seen the emergence of what Abrams (1980) and others have called the "new vegetarian." Whether traditional or new, vegetarianism is practiced in many forms. Strict vegetarians, often referred to as "vegans," eat diets that contain no animal products but consist of fruits, vegetables, seeds, nuts, and so on. Some vegans limit their diets to fruits, nuts, honey, and oil. More commonly, vegetarians will eliminate only meat, often red meat. There are a number of varieties: ovo-vegetarians, who include eggs; polo-vegetarians, who include poultry; pesco-vegetarians, who include fish; lacto-vegetarians, who include

TABLE 9.5. Sources of Nutrients Frequently Lacking in Vegan Diets

Nutrient	Usual Sources	Alternative Sources
Riboflavin (B_2)	Dairy products, meat, eggs	Brewer's yeast, leafy vegetables
Vitamin B_{12}	Dairy products, meat, eggs, fish	None (some foods may be fortified or contaminated with B_{12}-producing bacteria)
Vitamin D	Fortified milk, fish, sun	Sun, fortified foods
Calcium	Dairy products, fish, leafy vegetables	Soy products, leafy vegetables
Iron	Meat, eggs, leafy vegetables	Legumes, leafy vegetables, dried fruit, cookware
Zinc	Meat, liver, eggs, seafood, cheese	Legumes, nuts, wheat germ, whole grains

SOURCE: After Liebman (1983:11).

dairy products; and ovo-lacto-vegetarians (Abrams 1980). As previously noted, vegans can achieve a balanced diet if they are careful about the consumption of specifically limited micro-nutrients such as B_{12}, vitamin D, iron, and zinc (Table 9.5) and the balance of proteins (Bergan and Brown 1980; Committee on Nutrition 1977).

Nutrients from Plant Foods

Plant foods offer a variety of tastes, textures, colors, and aromas not found in animal foods. Vegetables and fruits and the condiments made from plants not only add nutrients to starchy staples (e.g., sorghum, wheat, corn, manioc, potatoes) but impart specific flavor characteristics (Rozin and Rozin 1981; see also Chapter 7). In addition, Rozin argues, certain foods may have specific desirable psychopharmacological effects. Common examples include coffee, for the stimulant effect of caffeine, and chili peppers, as possible inducers of endogenous opiate-like substances.

Nutrient needs are generally met by a "well-balanced" vegetarian diet. Although plants, by volume or weight, are primarily sources of digestible and indigestible carbohydrates, they also supply protein, fat, and the micro-nutrients. It is possible to obtain enough protein, with appropriate amino acid ratios, from a vegetarian diet, but it requires more than one plant food, which is not the case with meat. Plant proteins do not have the same composition as animal protein and are therefore deficient in some amino acids or have inappropriate amino acid ratios for the production of human proteins. If an amino acid is not available in the amino acid pool when it is needed for protein synthesis, the synthesis stops.

The limiting amino acid in the human diet is usually methionine (see Table 9.3). Foods that are low in methionine are primarily of plant origin. The lowest percentage of methionine occurs in fruits, followed by breads and other grain products and by vegetables. There are also differences in the quality of proteins and the net protein utilization value (see Table 9.4). The lowest net protein efficiency ratios occur for corn, whole wheat flour, and legumes.

The notion of complementary proteins, whereby one protein supplies the limiting amino acid not found in the other, is familiar to nutritionists and individuals in the health-food movement (Lappé 1975). Many traditional cuisines, such as those in Latin America, combine corn and beans to provide complete protein. The limiting amino acid in corn is lysine, whereas the limiting amino acid in beans and other legumes is methionine. On the other hand, the combination of corn and wheat produces an incomplete protein because lysine is low in both corn and wheat.

Katz and his co-workers have investigated a number of food-processing techniques that enhance nutrient quality and quantity and reduce concentrations of toxic chemicals as a means of cultural accommodation to important dietary staples (Katz 1980; Katz, Hediger, and Valleroy 1975; Katz and Schall 1979; and see Chapter 5). Much of their work is relevant to the discussion of amino acid complementation (Katz, Hediger, and Valleroy 1975). Corn (i.e., maize), a widely distributed New World staple crop, undergoes a processing technique in which it is soaked in an alkali or lime solution. The lime liberates the vitamin niacin from an indigestible complex and improves the amino acid quality of the digestible protein fraction. This treatment actually lowers the quantity of amino acids except lysine, in which corn is generally low, so that there is a relative enhancement of lysine in comparison with the other amino acids. Corn also has a very high concentration of the amino acid leucine. An imbalance of the ratio of isoleucine to leucine has been implicated in the etiology of the niacin deficiency disease pellagra. In societies that traditionally treat corn with an alkali, there is little or no pellagra present. Overall there is an enhancement of the amino acid ratio so that the bioavailability of the amino acids is increased. Corn is a fairly good source of protein, which makes up 6.8 to 12.0 percent of the kernel weight.

Soybeans are widely used in Asia. They are high in protein and calcium but contain a potent anti-trypsin factor that can only be deactivated by long exposure to high temperatures. Trypsin is an important digestive enzyme, found

243

in pancreatic juices, that breaks down proteins into smaller polypeptides. A reduction in trypsin means a decreased efficiency of protein digestion. An investigation of the food preparation techniques employed in the manufacture of soybean products indicates that soy proteins (curd) were traditionally precipitated with magnesium in Japan to produce tofu and with calcium in China to produce doufu (Katz 1980). The curd is produced without the anti-trypsin factor. In the production of soy sauce, fermentation deactivates the anti-trypsin factor and enhances other nutrients, such as vitamin B_{12}. Other traditional preparation processes include sprouting the beans and the production of soy milk. Soybeans are an important dietary constituent, contributing a major portion of protein in a vegetarian diet. Katz (1980) points out that in cuisines where soybean curd is used extensively, so is rice. These foods provide complementary amino acid compositions.

Recent work by Sirtori and Lovati (1984) has demonstrated that the substitution of soybean protein for animal protein in a diet increases the favorable polyunsaturated/saturated fatty acid ratio and decreases plasma cholesterol levels in people with hypercholesterolemia. In their study the reductions in cholesterol levels always exceeded 15 percent and were independent of dietary cholesterol intake. The authors propose a mechanism by which soy proteins act on the liver receptors for lipoproteins. These receptors maintain normal or heightened affinities for lipoproteins and do not show the decreased activity level usually induced by excess dietary cholesterol. Other mechanisms operating on neutral steroids are also possible. These authors strongly endorse the use of soy protein diet therapy for people with hypercholesterolemia. Soy protein has little effect on people with normal cholesterol levels.

Studies tend to indicate that circulating levels of cholesterol, the low-density lipoproteins that are associated with cardiovascular disease, and triglyceride levels tend to be lower for vegetarians than for non-vegetarians (Snowdon, Phillips, and Fraser 1984). Yet individuals on complete vegetarian diets (vegans) have little trouble obtaining appropriate dietary fats. As noted above, the essential dietary fat, linoleic acid, is found in greater concentrations in plant than in animal foods. Linoleic acid is a polyunsaturated fatty acid. Polyunsaturated fatty acids predominate in vegetable oils, whereas saturated fats occur primarily in animal fat. Once lipids are absorbed by the intestine, they undergo further breakdown by additional enzymatic action. These glycerides and fatty acids are then absorbed into the blood system for transport. The amount absorbed is about 50 percent of intake. Since proteins can be transported more readily than lipids in a watery medium, combinations of lipoproteins are formed. These lipoproteins are then transported to a number of sites, where they are active in a variety of metabolic processes. Lipids are an important energy source. They have twice the number of calories per gram of food as either proteins or fats, so that diets low in calories may be low in fats.

Carbohydrates form the third macro-nutrient class that is readily obtained from plant sources. There are a number of types of carbohydrates. Monosaccharides are often referred to as simple sugars. Glucose, the most abundant of these, is essential for energy metabolism. Most foods contain disaccharides. These are found in sugar (sucrose), fruits (fructose), milk (lactose), vegetables, and malt products. Glucose is the major simple sugar in the polysaccharides of seeds, grains, cereals, legumes, fruits, and vegetables. Free glucose (as a monosaccharide) is found in some fruits and vegetables, honey, and corn syrup. The polysaccharides include starch, which is found extensively in grains, cereals, legumes, root vegetables, and fruits.

Carbohydrate digestion is quite efficient: about 98 percent of digestible carbohydrates in the diet are ultimately available for biological use. The chemical digestion of carbohydrates is accomplished primarily through specific enzymes in the mouth and small intestine. In general, the simpler sugars are soluble in water and impart sweetness. Fructose has the highest relative sweetness, followed by sucrose and glucose. Cellulose and starch lack this taste property.

Other carbohydrates are indigestible for humans. The most common of these are cellulose and pectin, which serve as bulk in the human digestive tract. Cellulose is the major component of cell walls of plants and is ingested with all fruits and vegetables. Pectin is a jelly-like material that acts as cellular cement in plants. It is found abundantly in unripe fruit. Glycogen is sometimes referred to as "animal starch" because it is the principal carbohydrate storage material in animals.

Foods with dietary fiber content greater than 20 percent of their dried weight include wheat bran, rye bread, endive, kale, and cabbage. Foods with low dietary fiber (less than 10 percent) include soybeans, peanuts, oats, rice, white bread, potatoes, and carrots (Guthrie 1975; Reed 1980). Dietary fibers decrease transit times, reducing the time for nutrient absorption. They also add bulk to the diet, so that infants and children on primarily low-processed vegetarian diets may have difficulty obtaining the RDAs for protein and other nutrients because of the high fiber content of the diet, their small digestive tracts, and their relatively higher nutrient needs.

Carbohydrate consumption, primarily from vegetable sources, has been linked to a number of diseases in Western societies. Although these diseases have continued to increase in incidence, the actual consumption of carbohydrates in the United States, for example, has decreased approximately 25 percent since the turn of the century. Recent work by Jenkins (1982) and others has demonstrated that the distinction between simple and complex carbohydrates—that is, sugars and starches—is not meaningful metabolically. The concentration of blood glucose and the rise of the blood glucose curve after ingestion of specific carbohydrate loads are unrelated to this distinction. These findings have confounded the previous dietary prescriptions for the diabetic diet. For example, potatoes and bread produce very steep rises in blood glucose, whereas corn and rice do not. The increases in blood glucose with potatoes and bread are equal to or exceed those caused by the ingestion of sugars. Furthermore, simple explanations based on the different fiber contents of foods and their different absorption times do not hold up under examination. Whole-grain bread and refined white bread, for example, have about the same blood glucose curve (Jenkins 1982). Other physical properties of the molecules of starches and sugars may be important in the glucose response curve. It is clear that consuming carbohydrate foods with higher protein and fat content (e.g., ice cream, high in sugar and fat) decreases the blood glucose response. Both Type II diabetics and non-diabetics initially respond in the same way to these foods, but in individuals with diabetes the elevated glucose levels persist longer.

Snowdon and Phillips (1985) have asked whether a vegetarian diet reduces the occurrence of diabetes. Since 1960 they have studied over 25,000 white Seventh-Day Adventists. Approximately 50 percent of the members of this religious group are lacto-ovo-vegetarians. They do not have the high rate of diabetes characteristic of Amerindians and black Americans and are generally at low risk for the disease. The risk of diabetes as an underlying cause of death for Seventh-Day Adventists is about half the risk for all U.S. whites. When comparing the two Adventist samples of meat-eaters and non-meat-eaters, the investigators found that vegetarians had a lower risk of dying with diabetes as an underlying cause and lower self-reports of diabetes. When the investigators controlled for the possible confounding factors of weight, physical activity, and other dietary factors (e.g., fat and sugar intake), the risk of diabetes remained lower for vegetarians. Interestingly, all the associations between meat eating and diabetes were stronger in males than females in this study (Snowdon and Phillips 1985).

Six micro-nutrients have been shown to be more difficult to obtain from natural food sources if an individual has a diet exclusively composed of plant foods (see Table 9.6). In most cases supplements or fortified vegetable foods will provide the nutrient, as in the case of riboflavin (vitamin B_2) and vitamin D. The nutrient that is most difficult to obtain on a vegan diet is vitamin B_{12}. The natural sources of B_{12} are dairy products, meats, eggs, and fish; there are no plant sources. Individuals on a vegan diet must get vitamin B_{12} either through the contamination of the food by B_{12}-producing bacteria that live in the soil or through fortified foods or dietary supplements.

Iron deficiencies are common in both meat-eaters and vegetarians in the United States (Guthrie 1975; Reed 1980). The primary source of readily available iron comes from animals. This is the heme iron found in meat. It is absorbed more readily than iron of vegetable origin (Scrimshaw and Young 1978).

Some incompatible dietary combinations lead to a decrease in iron absorption. These include the commonly found phytates in whole grains and oxalates in spinach and other green leafy vegetables. These phytates and oxalates bind iron and other minerals such as zinc and calcium and make them unavailable for absorption. Absorption of iron can be enhanced when small amounts of red meat are added to the diet. The extent to which a diet is high in phytates and oxalates and low in heme iron from meat depends primarily on social, economic, and cultural factors. The RDAs based on age, sex, and physiological state do not take account of these other factors, which may contribute substantially to population and individual variation in iron needs. For example, enhanced sweating and high environmental temperatures increase the loss of iron from the body. Bacterial and viral disease as well as certain parasites such as hookworm, schistosomiasis, and malaria increase blood loss.

In spite of these potential nutritional difficulties, early studies of the dietary and nutritional status of vegetarians (e.g., Hardinger and Stare 1954) and later studies as represented by Taber and Cook (1980) and Bergan and Brown (1980) indicate that vegetarians who maintain a diet with diverse food sources are not nutritionally deficient. Some studies have indicated that the caloric intake particularly among "new" vegetarians was low (Bergan and Brown 1980) and that adult men and women who had recently become vegetarians were generally quite lean. However, measurements of serum vitamins and cholesterol were within the normal range.

A well-publicized study by Dwyer and her colleagues of the nutritional status of pre-school vegetarian children indicated that such babies were heavier than the age/sex norms for the general U.S. population but that older children tended to be somewhat leaner and shorter. In general, children on a vegetarian diet are of normal height and weight. The children who were of shorter stature and underweight were following macrobiotic or very restricted vegetarian diets (Dwyer, Andrew, et al. 1980).

Nitrogen balance studies of humans on various diets (e.g., Register et al. 1967) indicate that individuals on vegetarian regimens are in appropriate nitrogen balance and are not deficient in amino acids. More specific studies looking at hard-to-get nutrients in the diet of long-term vegetarians have shown that women, both pregnant (King, Stein, and Doyle 1981) and non-pregnant (Anderson, Gibson, and Sabry 1981), show normal levels of iron and zinc in spite of relatively low intake of these minerals (Freeland-Graves, Bodzy, and Eppright 1980; Freeland-Graves, Ebangit, and Bodzy 1980). An additional concern related to the intake of minerals is the use of food items that may be high in phytates, oxalates, and fiber, all of which may interfere with nutrient absorption. However, the individuals studied were clearly not suffering from deficiencies in these minerals.

A study by Marsh et al. (1980) of the cortical bone density of vegetarian and omnivorous women shows no differences in bone mineral mass of 200 lacto-ovo-vegetarians and 71 omnivores of comparable ages in the third, fourth, and fifth decades of life. These researchers, therefore, propose that calcium and phosphorus absorption and utilization are adequate for these vegetarian women.

Dwyer, Miller, and their colleagues (1980) investigated the mental functioning of predominantly vegetarian children. Although the sample was small (N = 28), the results clearly indicate that the children consuming vegetarian diets had an average IQ that was in the 85th percentile of IQ scores of a standardized sample (mean IQ = 116).

Studies of the food-related value-orientations, attitudes, and beliefs of vegetarians and non-vegetarians have shown some significant differences (Hufford 1971; Krey 1982; Sims 1978). Vegetarians share: (1) a greater belief in the benefit of health foods; (2) a greater distrust of food processing and additives; (3) a belief that nutrition is important in the maintenance of health; (4) a belief in vitamin supplementation; (5) a strong commitment to weight control; and (6) a belief that they are more knowledgeable about nutrition than non-vegetarians. Tests of knowledge and the use of information sources on nutrition and diet planning did not show significant differences between the American vegetarian and non-vegetarian groups investigated by Sims (1978). Read and Thomas (1983) also found that vegetarians augmented their diet with vitamin and mineral supplements. Eighty-five percent of those studied used food supplements and tended to believe (incorrectly) that naturally occurring vitamins are more nutritious than synthetically produced vitamins.

The American Dietetic Association cautiously recommends a non-meat-based or vegetarian diet including eggs and dairy products (1980b). They strongly advocate nutrition education for vegetarians and careful meal planning. In addition, they recommend dietary supplements and the use of fortified products such as soybean milk and flour in a well-balanced multi-item menu. They do not recommend a restricted food intake in terms of nutrient amounts or specific food items.

In summary, individuals on non-restricted vegan or ovo-lacto-vegetarian diets have adequate nutrient intake, do not show signs of nutritional deficiencies, do not show signs of mental or intellectual impairment, and may be at reduced risk for cardiovascular diseases and cancers. However, in populations with a more restricted intake, nutritional deficiencies can be common, especially among children and women. Some of these deficiencies are due not to the amount of food ingested but to endogenous chemicals in the foods or to food preparation techniques or to the complicated biological interactions of particular foods. The next section examines some of these biocultural interactions.

Plant Foods: Dangers and Disorders

Many human toxins occur naturally in plant foods. These toxins are often destroyed by cooking. Exogenous toxins include pesticide and herbicide residues. Some fungi produce toxins (e.g., aflatoxin) that interfere with DNA, RNA, and protein synthesis. This section will briefly review some of the naturally occurring toxins. Of particular interest are the widely distributed oxalates and phytates mentioned previously.

The oxalates are found in high concentration in members of the cabbage family, in spinach, beet greens, carrots, peas, rhubarb, mushrooms, and also in tea and cocoa (Committee on Food Protection 1973). These substances bind soluble potassium, sodium, and calcium and make them unavailable for use by the body. Oxalates are also involved in the production of calcium-based kidney stones. Oxalates are heat-sensitive, as are most other toxins, including the phytates.

The phytates are found primarily in mature cereal grains, but nuts, legumes, potatoes, corn, strawberries, and figs are also sources. Phytates form insoluble complexes with metals—copper, zinc, iron, magnesium, and so on—so that they become unavailable for metabolic functions. Plant polyphenols include phenolic acids, flavanoids, and tannins. They are widely distributed in the leaves, stems, roots, flowers, fruits, and seeds of many plants. These substances, like the goitrogens, can pass into animal products like milk and be ingested by humans as secondary consumers. Phenolic acids and tannins can reduce protein digestibility (Committee on Food Protection 1973). Goitrogens are found primarily in plants of the cabbage family, including turnips, kale, and brussels sprouts. These substances bind iodine. The biocultural consequences of a low iodine–high goitrogen diet are presented below. A number of alkaloids may interfere with the digestion and absorption of nutrients, and some staple foods contain varying amounts of poisons, such as arsenic in potatoes and cyanide in manioc. The potato alone contains some 150 distinct chemical substances, and orange oil has 42 (Coon 1973).

The legumes and pulses (e.g., black beans, kidney beans, soybeans, lentils) are some of the best plant protein sources, yet they contain harmful substances called lectins that cause red blood cells to agglutinate and can destroy the walls of intestines, leading to decreased nutrient absorption. Kidney beans also have a substance that inhibits starch digestion. Lectins are destroyed by cooking, and the germination of beans reduces their concentration. Lectins also occur in foods like tomatoes that are frequently consumed without cooking.

Finally, foods contain a number of psychoactive agents. For example, substantial amounts of the neurotransmitter serotonin are found in bananas, plantains, and pineapples. The flavor-enhancer monosodium glutamate (MSG), made from beets, is a variant of the neurotransmitter glutamic acid (Lieberman n.d.) Glutamic acid may be responsible for the symptoms in Chinese restaurant syndrome. Perhaps fortunately, many of these neurotransmitters do not cross the blood-brain barrier into the central nervous system. These psychoactive components make up only one of the many classes of drugs derived from plant sources in traditional pharmacopeias.

Many techniques have been developed to reduce or eliminate food toxins. Dry storage kills fungi and molds, and the desiccation or drying of foods may eliminate toxins and other potential pathogens. Exposure to light and heat, acid or alkaline environments, fermentation, germination, cooking, and freezing all change the chemical composition of foods (see Table 9.5). Selective breeding for reduced levels of toxins, soil conditions, temperature, humidity, and other environmental factors alter nutrient composition. Certain combinations of food can act synergistically to detoxify harmful chemicals.

An example of a significant processing technique involves the preparation of bitter manioc (Katz 1980). Manioc (*Manihot esculenta*) contains cyanate, which is bound to glycosides distributed throughout the tuber. Any physical damage to the manioc releases a potent glycosidase, which immmediately acts to free small amounts of cyanide (HCN). The processes of squeezing and cooking the manioc release these toxins and volatilize the HCN into the air. These processes are traditionally used by South American Indians. Manioc is also consumed in sub-Saharan Africa, where, in addition to its role in the diet, it has a more complex relationship with the hemoglobin variant HbS, or sickle cell hemoglobin. The cyanate that remains in the manioc is associated with a breaking of the chemical bonds that cause the sickling of red blood cells. This has the advantage of decreasing the risk of anemia due to HbS. At the same time, cells that maintain a sickle shape are more resistant to the malarial parasite. Katz (1980) proposes that the rapid spread of manioc in sub-Saharan Africa over the last 400 years is due to the ability of this crop to reduce the frequency and severity of sickle cell anemic crises.

Malaria has been a potent selective agent in human evolution, changing not only the frequency of genes that alter hemoglobin but also the genes for the red cell enzyme glucose-6-phosphate dehydrogenase (G6PD). A deficiency in this enzyme is common in malarial endemic areas, where the deficiency confers some anti-malarial advantage. However, people with G6PD deficiency are susceptible to a potentially lethal attack of a hemoagglutination or of favism caused by the ingestion of the fava bean (Katz 1980; see also Chapter 5).

Another important example of the biocultural consequences of the ingestion of potentially pathogenic substances is found in the work of Greene (1977). He investigated the relationship between goiter, goitrogenic plants, and social organization in highland Ecuador. Greene found that a number of indigenous plants contained goitrogens, which bind dietary iodine and make it unavailable to the organism. Moreover, at high altitudes people are far from the traditional source of iodine, sea salt. In the two communities studies by Greene, the prevalence of goiter was 52.8 percent and 69.7 percent. In general, these populations had poor supplies of high-quality protein. Many communities contained a significant proportion of cretins, neurologically deficient and behaviorally limited individuals. Cretinism occurs when thyroid function is limited during development. Greene (1977) succinctly documents the severe reduction in the transmission of cultural knowledge when a significant proportion of the population is intellectually and physically impaired. The economic and political ramifications of the subordinate-impaired sub-population's dependence on the dominant-healthy sub-population are starkly portrayed.

As with favism and lactase deficiency, an underlying genetic variable is related to the distribution pattern of goiter. This is the genetically inherited ability to taste the manufactured chemical compound phenylthiocarbamide (PTC). PTC is related to the naturally occurring goitrogens. Individuals who are taste-sensitive—that is, those who have inherited a dominant allele for PTC tasting—are more likely to avoid or to reduce their intake of bitter-tasting plants containing goitrogens. Non-tasters—individuals who cannot taste this bitter substance—will consume larger quantities of goitrogenic plants. Greene noted a positive correlation between non-tasting and goiter.

The final example also shows genotype-diet or genetotrophic interactions. As in the cases above, food items that are regularly consumed components of dietaries may cause adverse biological reactions—we have noted above, for example, the increased risk of developing cataracts in milk-drinking societies (Simoons 1981). Celiac disease, or gluten sensitivity, is found in populations that are on the margins of wheat-cultivating areas. Populations who are long-time consumers of wheat and other cereal products have a low prevalence of celiac disease. People with celiac disease are sensitive to the substance gliadin, which is a fraction of the gluten in cereal grains. These people suffer from intestinal damage, malabsorption, wasting, and a high frequency of gut and lymphoid cancers (Simoons 1981). Gluten is found in wheat and rye and in lesser concentrations in barley and oats. *Triticum* wheat has the highest percentage of protein that is gliadin (40 to 60 percent) and therefore causes the most severe reactions in celiacs. Therapy involves the consumption of a gluten-free diet. The mechanism by which symptoms are produced by gliadins is not known (Simoons 1981). Although there is no single gene that can account for celiac disease, there is a genetic marker that is part of the immune system. Celiac disease is related to the human leukocyte antigen HLA-B8. This serves as a good genetic marker in U.S. and northwestern European groups. Eighty-eight percent of adult celiacs in the United States and England have HLA-B8, compared with a frequency of 22 to 30 percent in the general population. HLA-B8 appears to be linked to some unidentified gene or gene complex that is selected against in wheat- or cereal-eating populations.

The above examples of genetotrophic adaptations indicate the tremendous nutritional and metabolic variability found in contemporary members of our species. These genetotrophic adaptations represent an extreme form of adjustment to selective pressures. Humans, like other animals, more readily adapt by changing behavior or modifying the environment rather than changing themselves. The most time-consuming and inflexible form of change is genetic. Short- and long-term physiological changes offer an intermediate level of flexibility, whereas cultural and behavioral changes can be mustered readily and have the greatest flexibility. As omnivores, our dietary diversity provides both pleasures and pitfalls.

Conclusions

There is great diversity in human nutrient needs and even greater diversity in human diets. The first fact has, in part, accounted for the continuing assessments and revisions of the RDAs. It is also clear that human populations have undergone and continue to undergo physiological modifications in response to "new" foods. These accommodations are often both cultural and biological. Accommodations have been made to nutrients from both animal sources (lactose, high meat diets) and plants sources (wheat, goitrogen-containing plants, soybeans, maize). Yet our variable and flexible metabolisms are being strained by rapid change. New Westernized lifestyles and dietaries are associated with new diseases like New World syndrome, cancers, and cardiovascular disease. Our genetic adaptations are designed for diets containing a wide range of plant and animal foods, moderate energy intakes, a fair amount of dietary fiber, and an energetically more costly lifestyle than is pursued today by most people. As Stini (1971) and many others have indicated, perhaps 99 percent of our evolution has occurred within a hunting, gathering, and scavenging niche. It has allowed for increases in body size and brain development leading to a number of behavioral and physiological characteristics that make our species unique.

With the adoption of a more sedentary mode of life approximately ten thousand years ago, a simplification of the diet took place as a preoccupation with crop and animal husbandry reduced the opportunity for hunting and gathering. Usually the diet was and is based on a starchy staple (Robson and Wadsworth 1977). As humans specialized in different environments, the digestive, absorptive, metabolic, and excretory functions of different groups underwent differential selection, leading to the enormous variability in nutritional processes

252

and needs at the population and individual level that has been explored in this chapter.

The macro- and micro-nutritional excesses and deficiencies of diets high in either animal or plant foods have been presented. Even lean meat, one of our cultural superfoods, can disrupt normal metabolic processes when too few calories or not enough fat and carbohydrates are consumed with it. On the other hand, even relatively unbalanced protein sources, if subjected to special treatments (e.g., the lime preparation of maize) and eaten with other complementary plant protein, can provide the same amino acids as lean meat. Humans are ingenious in their approach to solving dietary problems. Of particular importance has been the cooking of foods. Heat, although it may destroy some nutrients, also destroys pathogens and toxins, makes grains palatable, enhances the bioavailability of nutrients, and improves the texture of meat. Our legacy of metabolic and behavioral adaptability has allowed us such abundant dietary choices that whether nutrients come from plants or animals is less important than whether one obtains adequate amounts. The biocultural conditions that create this flexibility are phenomenally diverse.

References Cited

Abrams, H. L.
    1980   Vegetarianism: An Anthropological/Nutritional Evaluation. *Journal of Applied Nutrition* 32:53–87.
Alcantara, E. N., and E. W. Speckman
    1976   Diet, Nutrition and Cancer. *American Journal of Clinical Nutrition* 29:1035–47.
American Dietetic Association
    1980a   Improving the Amino Acid Profile of Vegetable Proteins. *Journal of the American Dietetic Association* 76:141.
    1980b   Position Paper on the Vegetarian Approach to Eating. *Journal of the American Dietetic Association* 77:61–68.
Anderson, B. M.; R. S. Gibson; and J. H. Sabry
    1981   The Iron and Zinc Status of Long-Term Vegetarian Women. *American Journal of Clinical Nutrition* 34:1042–48.
Anderson, J. W., and K. Ward
    1978   Long-Term Effects of High Carbohydrate, High Fiber Diets on Glucose and Lipid Metabolism: A Preliminary Report on Patients with Diabetes. *Diabetes Care* 1:77–82.
Bergan, J. G., and P. T. Brown
    1980   Nutritional Status of "New" Vegetarians. *Journal of the American Dietetic Association* 76:151–55.

Bray, G. A.
    1983   The Energetics of Obesity. *Medicine and Science in Sports and Exercise*
            15:32–40.
Committee on Dietary Allowances, Food and Nutrition Board
    1980   *Recommended Dietary Allowances.* 9th rev. ed. Washington, D.C.: Na-
            tional Academy of Sciences.
Committee on Food Protection, Food and Nutrition Board
    1973   *Toxicants Occurring Naturally in Foods.* 2d ed. Washington, D.C.: Na-
            tional Academy of Sciences/National Research Council.
Committee on Nutrition, American Academy of Pediatrics
    1977   Nutritional Aspects of Vegetarianism, Health Foods and Fad Diets. *Pedi-
            atrics* 59:460–64.
Coon, J.
    1973   Toxicology of Natural Food Chemicals: A Perspective. In *Toxicants Oc-
            curring Naturally in Food,* 2d ed., pp. 573–91. Washington, D.C.: Na-
            tional Academy of Sciences/National Research Council.
Desor, J. A.; L. S. Greene; and O. Miller
    1975   Preference for Sweet and Salty in 9–15-Year-Old and Adult Humans.
            Science 190:686–87.
Draper, H. H.
    1977   The Aboriginal Eskimo Diet in Modern Perspective. *American An-
            thropologist* 79:309–16.
Dubos, R.
    1980   Nutritional Ambiguities. *Natural History* 89(7):14, 16, 20–21.
Dwyer, J. T.; E. M. Andrew; J. Valadian; and R. B. Reed
    1980   Size, Obesity and Leanness in Vegetarian Preschool Children. *Journal of
            the American Dietetic Association* 77:434–39.
Dwyer, J. T.; L. G. Miller; N. L. Arduino; E. M. Andrew, W. N. Dietz; J. C. Reed; and
H. B. C. Reed
    1980   Mental Age and I.Q. of Predominantly Vegetarian Children. *Journal of
            the American Dietetic Association* 76:142–47.
Flynn, M.
    1978   The Cholesterol Controversy. *Contemporary Nutrition* 3:3–4.
Food and Agricultural Organization (FAO)
    1970   Amino Acid Content of Foods and Biological Data on Proteins. FAO
            Nutrition Studies, no. 24. Rome: FAO.
    1973   Energy and Protein Requirements. FAO Nutrition Meeting, Series no.
            52. Rome: FAO.
Food and Agricultural Organization/World Health Organization (FAO/WHO)
    1973   Energy and Protein Requirements. Report of the Joint FAO/WHO Ad
            Hoc Expert Committee. Technical Report Series no. 522. Geneva:
            WHO.
Freeland-Graves, J. H.; P. W. Bodzy; and M. Eppright
    1980   Zinc Status of Vegetarians. *Journal of the American Dietetic Association*
            77:655–61.

Freeland-Graves, J. H.; M. L. Ebangit; and P. W. Bodzy
 1980 Zinc and Copper Content of Foods Used in Vegetarian Diets. *Journal of the American Dietetic Association* 77:648–54.
Gleibermann, L.
 1973 Blood Pressure and Dietary Salt in Human Populations. *Ecology of Food and Nutrition* 2:143–56.
Greene, L.
 1977 Hyperendemic Goiter, Cretinism, and Social Organization in Highland Ecuador. In *Malnutrition, Behavior and Social Organization,* L. Greene, ed., pp. 55–94. New York: Academic Press.
Guthrie, H.
 1975 *Introductory Nutrition.* 3d ed. Saint Louis: C. V. Mosby.
Hardinger, M. G., and F. Stare
 1954 Nutritional Studies of Vegetarians, I: Nutritional, Physical and Laboratory Studies. *Journal of Clinical Nutrition* 2:73–82.
Harris, M.
 1979 Our Pound of Flesh. *Natural History* 88(7):30–36.
Harris, R., and E. Karmas
 1975 *Nutritional Evaluation and Food Processing.* 2nd ed. Westport, Conn.: AVI.
Harrison, G. G.
 1975 Primary Lactase Deficiency: A Problem in Anthropological Genetics. *American Anthropologist* 77:128–35.
Hufford, D.
 1971 Organic Food People: Nutrition, Health and World View. *Keystone Folklore Quarterly* 16(4):179–84.
Jackson, A.
 1983 Aminoacids: Essential and Non-Essential? *Lancet* 1:1034–37.
Jenkins, D. J.
 1982 Lente Carbohydrate: A Newer Approach to the Dietary Management of Diabetes. *Diabetes Care* 5:634–41.
Katz, S. H.
 1982 Food, Behavior, and Biocultural Evolution. In *The Psychobiology of Human Food Selection,* L. M. Barker, ed., pp. 171–88. Westport, Conn.: AVI.
Katz, S. H.; M. L. Hediger; and L. A. Valleroy
 1975 The Anthropological and Nutritional Significance of Traditional Maize Processing Techniques in the New World. In: *Biosocial Interrelations in Population Adaptation,* E. S. Watts, F. E. Johnston, and G. W. Lasker, eds., pp. 195–234. The Hague: Mouton.
Katz, S. H., and S. Schall
 1979 Fava Bean Consumption and Biocultural Evolution. *Medical Anthropology* 3:459–76.
King, J.; T. Stein; and M. Doyle
 1981 Effect of Vegetarianism on the Zinc Status of Pregnant Women. *American Journal of Clinical Nutrition* 34:1049–55.

Krey, S. H.
    1982   Alternate Dietary Lifestyles. *Primary Care* 9:595–603.
Lappé, F. M.
    1975   *Diet for a Small Planet.* Westminster, Md.: Ballantine Books.
Lieberman, L. S.
    n.d.   Nutrition, Behavior and Adaptation. Manuscript.
Liebman, B.
    1983   Are Vegetarians Healthier Than the Rest of Us? *Nutrition Action,* June,
                pp. 8–11.
Liener, I.
    1974   *Toxic Constituents of Animal Food Stuffs.* New York: Academic Press.
Luft, F.; M. Weinberger; and C. Grim
    1982   Sodium Sensitivity and Resistance in Normotensive Humans. *American
                Journal of Medicine* 72:726–36.
McCarron, D.; C. Morris; H. Henry; and J. Stanton
    1984   Blood Pressure and Nutrient Intake in the United States. *Science*
                224:1392–98.
McCracken, R. D.
    1971   Lactase Deficiency: An Example of Dietary Evolution. *Current An-
                thropology* 12:495–517.
Marsh. A.; T. V. Sanchez; O. Mickelsen; J. Keiser; and G. Mayor
    1980   Cortical Bone Density of Adult Lacto-Ovo-Vegetarian and Omnivorous
                Women. *Journal of the American Dietetic Association* 76:148–51.
Moskowitz, H. W.; V. Kumaraiah; K. N. Sharma; H. L. Jacobs; and S. D. Sharma
    1975   Cross-Cultural Differences in Simple Taste Preferences. *Science*
                1:1217–18.
Multiple Risk Factor Intervention Trial Research Group (MRFITRG)
    1982   Multiple Risk Factor Intervention Trial: Risk Factor Changes and Mor-
                tality Results. *Journal of the American Medical Association* 248:1465–
                77.
National Center for Health Statistics (NCHS)
    1979   Fats, Cholesterol and Sodium Intake in the Diet of Persons 1–74 Years:
                United States Advance Data 54:1–12. DHEW Pub. no. 80-1250
                Hyattsville, MD.: Department of Health, Education and Welfare.
National Livestock and Meat Board
    1983   *Exploring the Unknown: Meat, Diet and Health.* Chicago: NLMB.
Neel, James U.
    1962   Diabetes Mellitus: A Thrifty Genotype Rendered Detrimental by "Pro-
                gress"? *American Journal of Human Genetics* 14:353–62.
Nutrition Search, Inc.
    1975   *Nutrition Almanac.* New York: McGraw-Hill.
Read, M., and D. C. Thomas
    1983   Nutrient and Food Supplement Practices of Lacto-Ovo-Vegetarians.
                Journal of the American Dietetic Association 82:401–4.
Reed, P. B.
    1980   *Nutrition: An Applied Science.* St. Paul: West.

Register, U. D., et al.
    1967   Nitrogen Balance Studies in Human Subjects on Various Diets. *American Journal of Clinical Nutrition* 20:753–59.
Rennie, M., and R. Harrison
    1984   Effects of Injury, Disease and Malnutrition on Protein Metabolism in Man. *Lancet* 3:323–25.
Robson, J. R. K., and G. R. Wadsworth
    1977   The Health and Nutritional Status of Primitive Populations. *Ecology of Food and Nutrition* 6:187–202.
Rosch, P.
    1983   Stress, Cholesterol and Coronary Heart Disease. *Lancet* 2:851–52.
Rosenbaum, R.
    1976   Crunch. *Esquire,* July, pp. 57–60, 114.
Rozin, E., and P. Rozin
    1981   Some Surprisingly Unique Characteristics of Human Food Preferences. In *Food in Perspective,* A. Fenton and T. Owen, eds., pp. 243–52. Edinburgh: John Donald.
Schaefer, O. H.
    1971   When the Eskimo Comes to Town. *Nutrition Today* 6:8–16.
    1981   Eskimo (Inuit). In *Western Diseases: Their Emergence and Prevention,* H. Trowell and D. Burkitt, eds., pp. 113–28. Cambridge: Harvard University Press.
Scrimshaw, N. S., and V. R. Young
    1976   The Requirements of Human Nutrition. *Scientific American,* September, pp. 51–64.
    1978   Biological Variability and Nutrient Needs. In *Progress in Human Nutrition,* vol. 2, S. Margen and R. Ogar, eds., pp. 102–31. Westport: AVI.
Simoons, F. J.
    1969   Primary Adult Lactose Intolerance and the Milking Habit: A Problem in Biological and Cultural Interrelations, I: Review of the Medical Research. *American Journal of Digestive Diseases* 14:819–36.
    1970   Primary Adult Lactose Intolerance and the Milking Habit: A Problem in Biological and Cultural Interrelations, II: A Cultural Historical Hypothesis. *American Journal of Digestive Diseases* 15:695–710.
    1982   Geography and Genetics as Factors in the Psychobiology of Human Food Selection. In *The Psychobiology of Human Food Selection,* L. M. Barker, ed., pp. 205–24. Westport: AVI.
    1981   Celiac Disease as a Geographic Problem. In *Food, Nutrition and Evolution,* D. Walcher and N. Kretchmer, eds., pp. 179–99. New York: Masson.
Sims, L.
    1978   Food-Related Value-Orientations, Attitudes, and Beliefs of Vegetarians and Nonvegetarians. *Ecology of Food and Nutrition* 7:23–35.
Sirtori, C., and M. Lovati
    1984   Soybean Protein Diet: Experimental and Clinical Studies on the Mode of Action and Therapeutic Efficacy. In *Diet, Diabetes and Atherosclerosis,*

G. Possa, P. Micossi, A. Catapano, R. Paoletti, eds., pp. 241–53. New York: Raven Press.

Snowdon, D., and R. Phillips
1985   Does a Vegetarian Diet Reduce the Occurrence of Diabetes? *American Journal of Public Health* 75:507–12.

Snowdon, D.; R. Phillips; and G. Fraser
1984   Meat Consumption and Fatal Ischemic Heart Disease. *Preventive Medicine* 13:490–500.

Speth, J., and K. Spielmann
1983   Energy Source, Protein Metabolism, and Hunter-Gatherer Subsistence Strategies. *Journal of Anthropological Archaeology* 2:1–31.

Stini, W.
1971   Evolutionary Implications of Changing Nutritional Patterns in Human Populations. *American Anthropologist* 73:1019–30.

Taber, L. A., and R. A. Cook
1980   Dietary and Anthropometric Assessments of Adult, Omnivores, Fish-Eaters and Lacto-Ovo-Vegetarians. *Journal of the American Dietetic Association* 76:21–29.

Trowell, H., and B. D. Burkitt
1981   *Western Diseases: Their Emergence and Prevention.* Cambridge: Harvard University Press.

Tufts University Newsletter
1984a   Cholesterol: Is the Verdict Finally In? Special Report. *Tufts University Diet and Nutrition Newsletter* 2:3–50.
1984b   The Estrogen-Calcium Gap. *Tufts University Diet and Nutrition Newsletter* 2:1.

Waterlow, J. C., and P. R. Payne
1975   The Protein Gap. *Nature* 258:113–17.

Weiss, K.; R. Ferrell; and C. Hanis
1984   A New World Syndrome of Metabolic Diseases with a Genetic and Evolutionary Basis. *Yearbook of Physical Anthropology* 27:153–78.

West, R., and O. B. Hayes
1968   Diet and Serum Cholesterol Levels: A Comparison Between Vegetarians and Nonvegetarians in a Seventh-Day Adventist Group. *American Journal of Clinical Nutrition* 21:853–62.

Wilmsen, E.
1978   Seasonal Effects of Dietary Intake on Kalahari San. *San Federation Proceedings* 37:65–72.

Wing, E. S., and A. B. Brown
1979   *Paleonutrition: Method and Theory in Prehistoric Foodways.* New York: Academic Press.

PART IV

Pre-State Foodways: Past and Present

GRANTED THAT THERE ARE INNATE BIOPSYCHOLOGICAL RE-straints on human diets, we are still left with the problem of accounting for the enormous variability of foodways and their divergence and convergence during the course of cultural evolution. The essays in Part IV deal with these diachronic and synchronic variations in foodways among pre-state societies, from the perspective of archaeology (Cohen and Yesner), from the perspective of ethnohistory (D. Harris), and from the perspective of ethnography (Winterhalder, Hawkes, Johnson and Baksh, and Good). The archaeological issue addressed by Cohen is the transition from hunting-gathering to agricultural modes of production with the attendant "revolutionary" consequences for human foodways. Yesner addresses an equally important but less well known aspect of the evolution of human foodways—namely, the increased utilization of maritime resources at the end of the Pleistocene that paralleled and sometimes preceded the shift to domesticated plant and animal species.

Both Cohen and Yesner invoke aspects of optimal foraging theory in relation to resource depletion and population growth in order to explain why apparently abundant species and simple food production technologies were neglected for tens of thousands of years prior to the Neolithic. In addition, Cohen presents data that indicate that the transition to neolithic modes of food production was actually accompanied by a deterioration in nutritional standards—a paradoxical consequence, but one that is not incompatible with optimal foraging theory.

Two chapters devoted entirely to optimal foraging theory follow. Winterhalder defends the basic epistemological and theoretical principles that underlie this approach, reviews some of its applications to the explanation of diet breadth and foraging patterns among several contemporary foraging groups, and offers new models that incorporate opportunity costs and sensitivity to risks. Hawkes then addresses the question of why Kalahari !Kung men do not spend as much time as the men of the Aché of Paraguay in hunting, and why Aché women do not spend as much time as !Kung women in gathering. Of special interest in these two

259

papers is the central theoretical significance Hawkes attaches to foodways selected for by their consequence for reproductive success and Winterhalder's explicit denial that the analysis of optimality in foraging behavior is inextricably bound to reproductive success models.

In a different vein, David Harris describes the broad-spectrum subsistence regimen of northern Australian Aborigines. This is of special interest not only for its ecological interpretation of ethnohistorical sources, but for its treatment of cannibalism as an integral feature of a foraging economy.

The final two essays in Part IV are concerned with the foodways of two Amazonian tropical forest village societies, the Machiguenga of Peru and the Yanomami of Venezuela. Johnson and Baksh find that despite the existence of some aversions that apparently cannot be reduced to ecologically utilitarian costs and benefits, the Machiguenga exploit the possibilities of their technology and habitat in an overwhelmingly pragmatic fashion. Although Good's study of Yanomami hunting patterns does not address the adaptive efficiency of their foodways, it does provide valuable new information on the extent to which preoccupation with scarce animal food results in semi-migratory settlement patterns and intra-village factionalism associated with village fissioning.

10

MARK N. COHEN

The Significance of Long-Term Changes in Human Diet and Food Economy

HUMAN BEINGS INHERIT FROM THEIR PRIMATE ANCESTORS A common set of nutritive needs as well as a set of limited physiological capabilities for intake, absorption, storage, and excretion and a sensory apparatus that guides food choice. All appear in part anachronistically geared to the ancestral primate environment, with some modifications from the period of early hominid adaptation. We also inherit from our ancestors the capacity for flexible, widely ranging, omnivorous solutions to nutritive problems and a habit, already observable in other primates, of forming culturally determined food lists – that is, of *learning* food habits, which are determined as much by the experience of our parents and peers as by our physiological limits.

Given this heritage, the range of human dietary habits can be viewed as an aggregation of localized, idiosyncratic cultural solutions to common nutritive problems (minor, recently evolved differences in food tolerance and utilization, such as variations in lactase or sucrase production or the tasting/non-tasting of goitrogenic compounds notwithstanding). Each "successful" solution must approximate adequate and balanced nutrition for enough members of the population, particularly those in critical roles or at critical life periods, to live and reproduce; and it is the requirements for this success that selectively limit the range of idiosyncratic variation in diet. [1] But it is clear that to be "successful" a solution need not provide equally for all and need not provide what we would consider a "healthy" diet. Moreover, it is clear that any group's choices serve a number of functions other than good nutrition and thus that nutritional values are always compromised by competing functions in the design of food strategies. Indeed, part of a group's successful adaptation may lie in the nutritional deprivation of some of its members (Cassidy 1980, 1983, 1984).

Local variations in strategy occur in part because of local variations in the distribution and timing of potential resources. "Optimal foraging" theorists have, during the past few years, given us a handle with which to approach these local variations by asserting a series of propositions about common animal behavioral tendencies through which the adjustment of common human needs and predilections to different environmental circumstances can be assessed (Winterhalder and Smith 1981). But optimal foraging theory can, at best, recognize limited parallels among varying local economies. It can identify the expression of basic needs and of common adaptive strategies and common behavioral principles, such as the "principle" of maximizing calorie returns for labor. In this way it can explain the "systematic" fraction of any food economy; however, it can at best isolate, but not explain, the non-systematic (or "noise") fraction of any local adaptation resulting from competing cultural purposes or the baggage of taste, tradition, and habit.

The noise fraction represents, I suspect, a far larger portion of human behavior than most anthropologists are willing to allow. Much behavior witnessed much of the time, whether through archaeological or ethnographic techniques, is, I believe, noise at the level of most of our explanatory paradigms. We cannot hope to explain the specifics of what people eat through any means other than a study of the histories of individual cultures. What we *can* do is recognize some limited parallels across systems that are expressible as statistical trends and tendencies across populations. Optimal foraging theory is in fact a set of such statements recognizing common solutions to certain adaptive problems across species and across living human cultures. At least two other major sets of predictive statements have been offered describing alternative sets of limited parallels among human food economies (sets that complement one another and the theorems of optimal foraging rather than being contradicted by either). These are statements about regional or latitudinal variations (such as the latitudinal predictions of Lee 1968) and statements of temporal or sequential variation (Cohen 1977; Hayden 1981a, 1981b). The latter, which provide the focus of this paper, suggest that amidst the variety of human cultures, and cutting across regularities of both latitude and local optimization, there are recognizable trends in human food preferences over time.

Human Food Economies Through Time

Recent syntheses of world prehistory (see Cohen 1977; Fagan 1983; Hayden 1981a, 1981b) largely agree about what the archaeological record *appears* to show concerning changes in human food habits through time. The earliest fully human groups in most world regions appear to have been selective in their use of biomes, preferring open savanna-like biomes, regardless of latitude, to more heavily vegetated ones; and these early populations appear to have focused relatively heavily (though in unknown proportions) on the taking of large game and a limited range of vegetable foods. Smaller game, non-mammalian (particularly avian) fauna, fish, and shellfish, and a broader range of vegetable foods, particularly small seeds and starchy tubers, seem increasingly to have been exploited only in relatively recent prehistory. The roots of these trends are traceable into the Pleistocene in the Old World; the trends culminate in the post-Pleistocene "broad-spectrum revolution." The attention newly paid to small seeds and starchy tubers then seems to have resulted repeatedly in the domestication of crops, whereby such foods were caused to grow in high densities in the vicinity of human settlements, altered genetically to grow and be harvested at human convenience, and further altered to produce enlarged and often detoxified and otherwise unprotected edible parts. Simultaneously, however, human habits were domesticated to the convenience of the reproductive cycle of the plants in question. Human groups were forced (or permitted) to be sedentary, and work habits were altered to fit the growth cycles of the plants.

This sequence appears to have been replicated with fair regularity on each of the world's major continents. (Australian prehistory has often been cited as an exception to this rule because it has been said to display an essentially static adaptation, but in at least one recent synthesis [Lourandos 1983], the Australian sequence is said to show a pattern of intensification of resource use very similar to that of other continents.) Significantly, the sequence seems to be replicated whether it is played out over hundreds of thousands of years, as in most of the Old World, or telescoped into thousands, or at most tens of thousands, as in the New.

The meaning of this apparent pattern, however, is in dispute on at least two levels. First, it is uncertain to what degree the archaeological record is to be taken at face value or must be modified by considerations of differential preservation and/or biases in the reporting and interpretation of data. Second, even if the evidence has been correctly read, it is uncertain how the sequence is to be interpreted—that is, what it implies in terms of changing human behavior.

A number of authors have criticized the sequence of changing food habits described above, suggesting that it is primarily a sequence of archaeological preservation rather than one of actual dietary change (e.g., Dahlberg 1981; Kamminga 1981). They note that most modern human hunter-gatherers (outside extreme latitudes) eat a wide range of (predominantly vegetable) foods; that the range of foods at least occasionally preserved at very early human sites suggests a similar broad spectrum of exploitation; that the items usually considered late additions to the human diet are archaeologically fragile and may simply have been removed from the early part of the record by differential destruction; and that on seacoasts, where much of the recent broad-spectrum revolution is observed, early sites have now largely been destroyed by rising sea levels.

It is clear that a sufficient record of broad-spectrum food use from early human history does indeed exist to indicate that there has been no simple sequence of *pure* economic types from the legendary "big-game hunters" of the Middle Pleistocene to the broad-spectrum gatherers at the end of the Pleistocene and after. The evidence of primate omnivory itself (Harding and Teleki 1981) is sufficient to cast the image in doubt, and I would agree that there is clear evidence of fairly omnivorous foraging early in the human record. Yet I would argue that a good case can still be made for a real *quantitative* trend in human diets over time—as a statistical tendency across diverse economies. I would suggest that our diets have shifted in the ways the record suggests even though that trend may be exaggerated by differential preservation. As I have argued elsewhere (Cohen 1977), the trend occurs not only along coasts but also inland, where sea level, despite its indirect effects on rivers, does not exert the profound and uniform influence on the preservation of archaeological sites that it does on the coast. The trend also occurs in regions of the coast where sea level change can be ruled out (see Chapter 11); it occurs over the relatively short span of New World prehistory, through which differential preservation necessarily is far less important as a selective factor than it is over the long span of Old World prehistory; and it occurs also in patterns of changing tool frequencies (particularly with regard to the frequencies of grinding tools) not subject to differential preservation.

Since I initially wrote and presented the arguments above, moreover, a number of new lines of argument have become available that tend to help establish the reality of the trends described. One possible line of evidence, discussed at the Wenner-Gren Foundation Conference on Food Preferences and Aversions, concerns the human ability to absorb dietary iron.

Human beings are inefficient absorbers of iron from vegetable sources. Iron deficiency is a common problem among modern human beings and among archaeological populations beginning with the adoption of agriculture (Cohen and Armelagos 1984; see discussion below). This pattern may bespeak an evolutionary heritage somewhat richer in iron sources (and particularly animal products) than are recent agricultural diets. (In much the same manner, our inability to synthesize ascorbic acid is commonly attributed to an earlier stage of our ancestry in an environment rich in vitamin C.)

Another, firmer line of argument is provided by optimal foraging theory and its application to living populations. Several such models have suggested that a widening of the foraging base (the broad-spectrum revolution) is a predictable response by organisms to an increase in their own density, the decline of prey species, an improvement in food-getting technology, the deterioration of the environment, or all of these (Christenson 1980; Earle 1980; Hespenheide 1980; Winterhalder 1981). Moreover, specific studies of exploitative efficiency have suggested that in the expansion of the food base of human groups, large game animals should be (and commonly are) a preferred resource, whereas small seeds, small game, avifauna, shellfish, and vegetable resources requiring more than minimal processing should be (and commonly are) low-priority resources that foragers take increasingly as returns from hunting decline (Hames and Vickers 1982; Hawkes, Hill, and O'Connell 1982; O'Connell and Hawkes 1981; Perlman 1983). Such observations increase the likelihood that the observed archaeological sequence represents a real pattern of adaptive changes rather than a mere artifact of preservation.

A further point is that human skeletal remains themselves display a history of changes throughout the Pleistocene that appear to represent either micro-evolution or plastic responses to changing diets and food economies. Wolpoff (1980) has speculated, for example, that changes in skeletal size and in tooth structure in the *Homo* line in the Early and Middle Pleistocene reflect readaptation of a foraging ancestral line to a more carnivorous diet at the same time that my own reading of the archaeological data suggests that efficient hunting first emerged (see Cohen 1977). A firmer case can be made for a very widespread reduction in skeletal size and robusticity (Angel 1984; Frayer 1981; Kennedy 1984; Meiklejohn et al. 1984; Smith et al. 1984) that began, at least throughout the Old World, at the end of the Pleistocene. The trend has been alternately considered a response or adaptation to declining nutrition or a result of increased dependence on shellfish or a relaxation of selective pressures on robusticity. But whatever interpretation is selected, very broadly parallel trends in food use and/or food acquisition are probably implicated.

A further test of the reality of the apparent economic change is now emerging in the form of trace element and isotope analysis of bones, which has successfully demonstrated short-term changes as well as intra-site variations in diet but which so far has had only limited success in reconstructing dietary changes of any time depth. One published study (Schoeniger 1982) appears to demonstrate a long-term decline (from the Middle Paleolithic to the Mesolithic) in the quantity of meat in human diets in the Middle East. However, this argument has been criticized by others (Smith et al. 1984).

If the observed trends in the archaeological record are thus at least partly real (if partly exaggerated by preservation), their significance is still in dispute. In recent years, as indeed through much of the history of the discipline, there have been two major schools of thought concerning these trends. One of these schools celebrates the improvement in human life brought about by the advancement of technology. Childe (1951) is probably the most famous proponent of this position among prehistorians; Hayden (1981a, 1981b) is its most recent major spokesman. Its models tend to eqaute changes in food economy with advances in technology that permitted new resources to be exploited.

Others have proposed that the increasingly broad spectrum of resources utilized was more a function of need than of progress. These latter models propose that new resources were adopted not so much as technology *permitted* but as the relative scarcity of preferred resources *demanded*. The scarcity of preferred resources is in turn seen as a function of the increasing size and density of (or demand generated by) human populations and the decline in the populations of preferred prey species resulting either from the inroads of human predation or from the detrimental effects of post-Pleistocene patterns of climate change (see Binford 1983; Cohen 1977; Harris 1977, 1979). The same issue exists between "stress" and "progress" models of the adoption of agriculture itself. The adoption of agriculture, once considered clearly a technological advance (e.g., Childe 1951), has in recent years itself been viewed by some as an adaptation to stress generated by population growth or a decline in the productivity of wild resources (Cohen 1977; Harris 1977, 1979).

The two schools of thought largely agree that increases in the size and density of human populations are associated with changing technology. Where they differ, primarily, is in interpreting the effects of increasing density and new technology on the quality of human life and in characterizing the motives behind economic change. Models emphasizing technological progress (e.g., Hayden 1981a, 1981b) tend to assume that greater numbers of people were supported with increasing ease and with increasing reliability (if not quality) of food supplies and to assume that such technological improvements were positively sought by our forebears. A stress model (Cohen 1977) implies, on the contrary, that economic changes necessitated by population growth or resource decline most commonly resulted in diminished returns for labor and in declining quality and reliability of food supplies. A model offered by Harris (1977, 1979) suggests something of an intermediate pattern in which economic stress motivates change but occasionally promotes changes of sufficient magnitude (such as the adoption of cultivation) temporarily to relieve stress, producing short-lived periods of relative prosperity before population growth initiates a new cycle of stress.

One possible means of differentiating between these stress and progress models is to consider human food preferences. Both Harris and I have argued that the meat (and, as we must now concede, even more the fat) of large animals is a preferred food for most human groups, suggesting that the expansion of the diet away from this resource is likely to represent stress rather than progress in the eyes of those making the change. This assertion is supported by two lines of evidence that emerged at the Wenner-Gren conference. First it was argued (see Chapter 4) that although non-human primates commonly consume less animal food than do people, they do nonetheless treat it as a preferred food when available. In addition, there was a consensus among ethnographers in the group that, among modern human beings, the consumption of animal products was highly correlated with social class (and the ability to choose resources), suggesting that human beings tend to consume higher amounts of animal food when they can, higher amounts of vegetable food when they must. Both sets of observations suggest that the broadening of the food spectrum away from animal products represents necessity, not choice.

The optimal foraging theories described above seem to me to distinguish between progress- and stress-related theories at least for the foraging (pre-agricultural) part of the sequence. The broadening of the resource base itself is ambiguous in this regard, since a wider resource based is predicted to result either from an increased population of predators (or a decline in prey) or from increased technological capabilities (Winterhalder 1981). However, the studies of resource *ranking* cited above suggest that, quite independent of taste, preference, and the quality of the nutrient package, the meat of large animals provides a more efficient caloric return for labor than do most other wild resources, even among modern foragers utilizing an essentially mesolithic (post-Pleistocene) technology. If these results can be extrapolated back into the past (when, if anything, large game was more plentiful and hence more easily taken), they suggest that the broad-spectrum revolution, despite its new technology, was probably accompanied by declining returns for labor (decreasing caloric efficiency). The results thus suggest that necessity, not progress, motivated economic change. (These data, of course, do not directly compare the efficiency of foraging strategies to the efficiency of *cultivation,* two broadly different economies whose relative labor costs are also widely debated. The results do suggest, however, that cultivation focusing on small seeds and tubers was initially directed at one of the least efficiently exploited and least valued parts of the foragers' repertoire.)

The Evidence of Skeletal Pathology

The last decade has seen explosive growth in the field of skeletal analysis and paleopathology, growth that promises to help resolve many of the issues presented above and already provides substantial evidence on several of them (see Buikstra and Cook 1980; Cohen and Armelagos 1984; Huss-Ashmore et al. 1982). The growth in these fields includes not only an enormous increase in the number of studies done, but also a new, ecological, population-oriented (rather than specimen- or pathology-oriented) approach and the appearance of new analytic techniques. Supplementing the traditional identification of specific pathologies, modern skeletal analysis now recognizes and *quantifies* a number of more general conditions of biological stress. Both quantification itself and the identification of non-specific indicators of stress facilitate comparisons between populations with regard to overall health and nutrition. It is possible to describe populations with regard to the incidence and severity of infection, inflammation,

267

and malnutrition, and to combine this description with quantitative analysis of the frequency of growth-disrupting stresses experienced by individuals and analysis of the age distribution of deaths. Using these techniques, it is then possible to begin to evaluate the quality of the diet provided by different food economies; the degree to which different economies (or concomitant features of settlement) exposed their participants to infection, illness, physical stress, and trauma; the frequency of periodic starvation or other growth-disrupting events; and the life expectancy offered to participants.

In recognition of this potential, Cohen and Armelagos (1984) invited scholars who possessed such comparative data for hunter-gatherers and farmers in various regions of the world to make comparative assessment, where possible, of populations at four broadly defined economic stages: early (paleolithic or Paleo-Indian) hunter-gatherers; late, broad-spectrum (mesolithic or Archaic) hunter-gatherers; transitional or incipient agricultural populations; and established agriculturalists.

We obtained 18 regional sequences of varying degrees of completeness and detail, distributed as follows. There were eight regional sequences from the United States, including one each from California (Dickel et al.), Ohio (Perzigian et al.), Kentucky (Cassidy), Georgia (Larsen), the lower Mississippi (Rose et al.), the Southwest (Palkovich), and two from Illinois (Goodman et al.; Buikstra and Cook). The New World was further represented by one study from Central America (Panama and Costa Rica by Norr et al.); one from Ecuador (Ubelaker), and two from Peru-Chile (Benfer, Allison). Two sequences were reported from Europe (Western Europe by Meiklejohn; the Mediterranean by Angel), two from the Middle East (the Levant by Smith et al.; Iran-Iraq by Rathbun), one from South Asia (Kennedy), and one from North Africa (Nubia by Martin et al.). (All are listed in the References Cited section with 1984 citations.)

The comparison of these sequences poses a number of problems. Each sequence involves comparison of several distinct populations; thus representing, in effect, a series of snapshots of a continuous process of economic evolution in the region. Moreover, because of the nature of archaeological preservation and recovery, each sequence is composed of a slightly different series of snapshots, so that it is difficult to isolate precisely equivalent stages of transition for comparison. In addition, each sequence involves its own unique series of confounding factors, such as changing climate, the movement of people, or the action of political systems; and in each sequence the interaction of dietary change, population growth, population nucleation, and sedentism (factors that might exert independent effects on health) is unique. The studies also suffer from the fact that skeletal populations are often skewed representations of living groups, and from the fact that different analyses have been performed (or the same analyses have been performed in a different manner) in different regions and often on different populations from the same region, making both inter-regional comparisons and inter-population comparison within a region more difficult.

Perhaps the most important limitation of the studies as a whole, from the point of view of the questions raised here, is that skeletal remains of truly early, mobile, hunter-gatherers (paleolithic or Paleo-Indian populations) are either unrepresented or are represented only by scattered, often fragmentary finds. Most statements about hunter-gatherers offered here, therefore, reflect relatively late pre-agricultural groups, groups that may have adopted the sedentism, class-stratification, and relatively large population aggregates that are usually considered more typical of farmers. Only tantalizing glimpses are offered of the earlier groups, and conclusions about hunter-gatherer lifestyles must be tempered accordingly, although the existing data often show clear trends that might be extrapolated back into the past.

A further problem is that skeletal populations occasionally lack association with sufficient organic archaeological refuse to permit nice discriminations between stages of economic change. In a few instances, associated economies are postulated almost entirely from associated artifacts and site distributions, supplemented by data from skeletons themselves (including data on the frequency of tooth caries or the trace-element and isotope composition of bone that are considered indicative of diet). Even under the best circumstances, *quantified* estimates of diet are generally unavailable.

Given these caveats, the most reliable conclusions drawn from the data are those which relate to the simplest, crudest distinctions. In a simple comparison of hunting and gathering populations with the agricultural populations that came after them, for example, a number of fairly clear trends emerge. But attempts to describe trends in health across subtler transitions—that is, attempts to make finer distinctions among economic stages—rapidly encounter problems of poor sampling or poor resolution.

The Health of Hunter-Gatherers as Compared with Farmers

Infection

The clearest major trend in the comparison of hunter-gatherers and farmers concerns the incidence of infection as measured by the frequency of generalized infectious lesions of bone and specific infectious diseases. Twelve of the 18 studies report on the incidence of infection (Allison; Angel; Buikstra and Cook; Cassidy; Goodman et al.; Larsen; Meiklejohn et al.; Norr; Perzigian; Rathbun; Rose et al.; Ubelaker). Almost all conclude that infection was a more serious problem for farmers than for their hunting and gathering forebears, and most suggest that this resulted from increasing sedentism, larger population aggregates, and/or the well-established synergism between infection and malnutrition. Conversely, a decline in the incidence of infection among farmers as opposed to hunter-gatherers is reported only by Norr and Rose et al. (and by the latter for only one of three sub-areas in their study.) Rathbun, while reporting a higher rate of infections for neolithic and chalcolithic populations than for hunter-gatherers in Iran, reports, surprisingly, that later Bronze and Iron age populations showed the lowest infection rates.

In addition to reporting on generalized lesions of infection, two studies (Buikstra and Cook; Perzigian) note an increase in the frequency of mycobacterial (tubercular) infections identifiable in the skeletons of farming or later populations; and one (Allison), working with mummies, has been able to document an increase in rates of gastrointestinal infections with sedentism and agriculture, although he finds no trend in respiratory diseases.

Nutrition

The studies also suggest fairly consistently that farming resulted in a decline in the overall quality of nutrition. The clearest indicator of this is provided by the incidence of porotic hyperostosis and cribra orbitalia (porosity of the skull and orbits), considered indicative of anemia. Such anemia is most commonly attributed to iron deficiency and may reflect low-meat, high-cereal diets or the competition of parasites such as hookworm for available iron. (In the Old World such lesions may also reflect genetic anemias not directly related to diet but tied to malaria, which in turn has been shown to be responsive to changing human economic strategies.) Sixteen studies (Allison; Angel; Buikstra and Cook; Cassidy; Goodman et al.; Kennedy; Larsen; Martin et al.; Meiklejohn et al.; Norr; Palkovich; Perzigian et al.; Rathbun; Rose et al.; Smith et al.; Ubelaker) estimate rates of porotic hyperostosis, and most (12 of 16) conclude that the lesions appear or increase with farming, suggesting that anemia, whether nutritional, parasite-related, or genetic, is primarily a farmers' disease. The remaining four studies (Allison; Larsen; Martin et al.; Meiklejohn et al.) either provide no hunter-gatherer data or find no trend in their data.

Other indicators of chronic malnutrition are more sporadically reported and, in some cases, are less certain of interpretation; but these other indicators seem generally to support a similar conclusion. Four of the studies (Buikstra and Cook; Cassidy; Goodman et al.; and Smith et al.) employ either the cortical thickness or relative length-for-age of long bones to assess nutrition, and all four found that chronic malnutrition was more common among farmers than among their hunting and gathering forebears. Angel, using measurements of skull-base height and pelvic-inlet depth as indices of nutrition, found a decline in the overall quality of nutrition from the Paleolithic through the Neolithic in the Mediterranean region.

Several of the studies also suggest that the smaller stature and reduced skeletal robusticity among farmers as compared with hunter-gatherers might be indicative of declining quality of nutrition (Angel for the Mediterranean; Kennedy for India; Larsen for Georgia; Meiklejohn for Europe), but not all of the studies agree on the significance of this indicator, and not all show similar trends. For example, Meiklejohn et al. report a decrease in stature from Paleolithic through Mesolithic to Neolithic in Europe, followed by a rebound, but cautiously concludes that the trend might reflect either dietary stress or altered activities. Smith et al. show a decline in stature from paleolithic to mesolithic groups in Israel but argue against considering this an index of declining nutrition, since there are no accompanying stress indicators. They note a rebound in stature in the Neolithic. Rose et al. suggest that an *increase* in size in the Caddoan region of the lower Mississippi valley might reflect an increase in available protein with farming while noting that a decline in size, reflecting declining nutrition, occurred in the lower Mississippi valley proper.

Episodic Stress

One of the most interesting and, in some ways, most problematic sets of data is provided by indicators of episodic stress sufficient to produce disruptions in growth. Two such indicators were commonly reported, with surprisingly conflicting results. Harris lines (growth disruption lines in long bones) are reported in seven studies comparing hunter-gatherers and farmers (Allison; Buikstra and Cook; Cassidy; Goodman et al.; Perzigian et al.; Rathbun; Rose et al.). Most conclude that the lines are more common in hunter-gatherers than in the farmers who followed them, suggesting that farming reduced the frequency of episodic stress. Rathbun, in contrast, reports an increase in these lines through time; Allison finds regional differences but no trend among different economies; and Cook notes that the lowest frequency of Harris lines occurred in her transitional group.

Linear enamel hypoplasias and enamel micro-defects of the teeth tell a very different story, however. Ten studies (Allison; Angel; Buikstra and Cook; Cassidy; Goodman et al.; Kennedy; Perzigian et al.; Smith et al.; Ubelaker; and, very tentatively, Rathbun) report that the frequency or the severity of this indicator of growth disruption increased in farming and later populations in comparison with hunter-gatherers, suggesting more frequent and more severe episodes of stress in later groups. One study finds no trend (Rose et al., for one of their three sub-areas), and the other studies do not report this index. In other words, no study finds a decline in the frequency of this index over time. Three studies (Cassidy; Perzigian et al.; and Smith et al.) also report that hypoplasias of *deciduous* teeth (indicating episodes of pre-natal stress presumably reflecting poor maternal health) were more common in later agricultural groups than in hunting and gathering groups.

The apparently contradictory pattern of Harris lines and enamel defects may be resolved in various ways. One possibility is that the two represent stresses of differing etiology. Both are considered general indicators of stress sufficient to cause growth disruption, but in neither case is the range of possible stressing agents well defined. Hence, it is possible that the contradictory trends indicate a trade-off of one form of stress for another. Cassidy suggests that minor, regular periods of hunger among hunter-gatherers may have been traded for the more irregular and more severe stresses of farming life, involving bouts of infection and the more serious famine associated with crop failure. It was also pointed out in several of the papers and in discussion that enamel hypoplasias are almost certainly the more reliable indicator of the two. Harris lines are subject to subsequent erasure during growth, whereas enamel hypoplasias are not. Moreover, Harris lines record not so much the cessation of growth as the subsequent compensatory acceleration of growth. It can be argued, therefore, that the lower frequency of Harris lines in farming populations reflects chronic malnutrition and the resulting failure of the acceleration phase as much as the actual incidence of growth arrest. (This interpretation is supported by a recent study of laboratory monkeys [Murchison et al. 1983] that demonstrates that chronic malnutrition does indeed prevent the body from developing Harris lines in response to stress episodes.)

At best, therefore, the two indicators taken together suggest that no relaxation of episodic stress resulted from the adoption of farming in most regions. They may indicate the trade-off of one type of stress for another; and they may indicate a net increase in such episodes that is not recorded in Harris lines because of a concomitant decline in overall "background" levels of nutrition.

Physical Stress

The data on physical stress (work stress and physical injury) are more mixed but seem to argue, on balance, for a reduction in physical stress and therefore a probable reduction in workload associated with the adoption of agriculture. Lower levels of arthritis and skeletal robusticity are reported for farmers in comparison with hunter-gatherers in several studies (Kennedy; Larsen; Meiklejohn; Perzigian; Smith et al.). Others report more complex patterns (Rathbun; Rose et al.) or note an increase in rates of arthritis with the adoption

272

of farming (Goodman et al.). Cassidy suggests, however, that the arthritis she observed was of infectious etiology.

It should be pointed out that both arthritis and muscular robusticity are likely to reflect the severity of peak or intermittent demand on muscles and joints rather than simply the number of hours of work involved in the two economies. The data thus suggest that, generally, such peak demand was greater for hunter-gatherers than for farmers, but they do not necessarily indicate that farming resulted in a reduction in the time invested in the food quest.

The incidence of trauma, both accidental and violence-related, shows a similarly mixed picture, generally decreasing with the adoption of agriculture in some study regions (Meiklejohn et al.; Perzigian et al.; Rathbun) and increasing in others (Goodman et al.; Kennedy).

Life Expectancy

Perhaps the most interesting results concern the changes in life expectancy associated with the transition to agriculture. Thirteen of the regional studies provide data (of varying quality) bearing on this issue. Of these, 10 either conclude, or provide fragmentary data suggesting, that the life expectancies of farming populations were *lower* than those of preceding hunter-gatherers. Working with relatively good, well-controlled samples (N = 114, 224, 219, respectively) from a single well-defined location, Goodman et al. suggest that there was a progressive decline in life expectancy for all age classes as hunter-gatherers first adopted and then intensified agriculture in Illinois. Buikstra and Cook, from large and well-controlled samples (N = 800+, 500+, 336), describe a decline in life expectancy with the adoption of agriculture, followed by a recovery of life expectancy for adults (but not for children) late in the sequence as agriculture was intensified. Cassidy finds that a maize-farming group in Kentucky (N = 296) had a lower life expectancy for both sexes and for all age groups than did an earlier hunting and gathering group (N = 295). Ubelaker notes that life expectancy at birth was relatively high in an early hunter-gatherer group (N = 192); rose slightly in what might be an agricultural group (N = 199), which, however, still exhibited a low caries rate, leading him to question their degree of reliance on agriculture; and then fell sharply in an intensive agricultural group (N = 30) before a partial rebound occurred (N = 435). He suggests that there was a trend toward increasing infant mortality through his sequence. Life expectancies at more advanced ages (E_5 and E_{15}) fluctuated more irregularly over time, but the earliest clearly hunting and gathering population had life expectancies at both ages comparable to the average of later groups.

273

Larsen, while cautioning that available samples (N = 152, 177) are unlikely to be truly representative because both showed too high a percentage of survivors to adulthood, nonetheless notes that the age distribution of the available sample of farmers was lower than that of the earlier hunter-gatherers in Georgia. He reports a higher percentage of individuals dead in all age classes below 25 for farmers and a higher percentage of hunter-gatherers in all age classes over 25, with the exception of the 30- to 35-year age bracket. Even if sub-adult mortality is discounted, the pre-agricultural adults had the higher average age at death. In the conference version of their paper, Rose et al., working with samples of similar size, suggested that in the Caddoan region of the lower Mississippi, hunter-gatherers had a lower probability of dying either as children or as young adults than did later farmers. In the lower Mississippi valley proper, they also suggest, the lowest probability of dying was associated with a hunter-gatherer group.

Working with more fragmentary or scattered data, a number of other studies report similar trends. Angel notes a decrease in adult life expectancy from Paleolithic (N = 53) to Mesolithic (N = 120) and Neolithic (N = 106) for males in the Mediterranean. For females he reports an increase in adult life expectancy from Paleolithic (N = 53) to Mesolithic (N = 63), followed by a decline to levels at or below that of the Paleolithic for the Neolithic (N = 200). Kennedy notes that the aggregate pre-agricultural sample from India (N = ± 100) display higher ages at death than do later agricultural populations. Rathbun, who claims no trend because his samples are so small, cites figures on average age at death of known adult specimens that are higher for pre-agricultural individuals (N = 9) than for early agricultural (neolithic) groups (N = 69). According to his tables, 10 small samples of neolithic burials all had average ages at death for adults below those of the Shanidar Neanderthals and the pre-neolithic Hotu population (although the Hotu sample may not be representative). And Allison suggests that childhood mortality was lowest in his earliest population (although recovery bias is probably involved in this sample).

These latter studies, which suffer from very poor sampling of early hunting and gathering populations, mean relatively little individually, but collectively and in combination with the larger and better-controlled samples discussed above, they begin to suggest a fairly widespread pattern of declining longevity with the adoption of farming. Certainly they at least challenge the prevailing reverse presumption. Three studies, however, suggest an increase in life expectancy with farming. Smith et al. report a general increase in life expectancy from late pre-agricultural (Natufian) populations in the Levant through the Bronze age; Perzigian et al. cite a comparison suggesting better survivorship for an agricultural (N = 44) group in Ohio than for pre-agricultural groups (N = 1,327), but they noted that the later, smaller sample almost certainly underestimated sub-adult mortality, accounting at least in part for the difference in life expectancy. Figures provided by Norr might also be read as suggesting greater survivorship to adulthood in agricultural populations compared with pre-agricultural populations in Panama; but she adds several disclaimers about both the size (N = 87, 28, 32) of her samples and probable age biases related to known burial practices.

Taken as a whole, these indicators suggest an overall decline in the quality— and probably in the length—of human life among farmers as compared with earlier hunter-gatherer groups. Farmers seem fairly commonly to have suffered more infection and more chronic malnutrition than their forbears living on wild resources, and they seem to have suffered as many or more episodes of growth-disrupting stresses and to have had reduced life expectancies. On the other hand, there is evidence that farming often placed fewer physical demands on the skeleton (in terms of peaks of mechanical stress) than did hunting and gathering.

It should be reiterated here that the hunter-gatherer/farmer comparison masks a number of separate adaptive shifts whose importance in accounting for differences in health is not always clear. The effects of new foods per se, of farming as an activity, of sedentism, of the dispersal and nucleation of settlement, and of altered politics should all be considered separately, but these separate effects are necessarily lumped together in any simple comparison (see especially Rose et al. 1984).

Biological Stress and the Broad-Spectrum Revolution

The data available for assessing conflicting interpretations of the broad-spectrum revolution are fewer (because of the relative dearth of early hunter-gatherers), and the results are necessarily far more tentative. The clearest pattern in the studies, already alluded to, is a decline in stature from paleolithic to mesolithic populations, which occurred through much of the Old World (as reported by Angel; Kennedy; Meiklejohn et al.; and Smith et al.). Unfortunately this widespread trend toward reduced body size at the end of the Pleistocene can be read two ways: either as a sign of a general decline in nutrition or as a function of reduced workloads and reduced muscular, physical stress. A concomitant decline in arthritis and robusticity (Kennedy; Meiklejohn et al.; Smith et al.) seems to argue for the latter explanation. A concomitant increase in other indicators of malnutrition would support the former one; and such is reported in one region (by Angel for the Mediterranean). Such evidence is not noted in the other regions (where the indices of malnutrition used by Angel were not employed), but if reduced body size resulted from *selection* for survival with a poor diet rather than from *plastic* individual growth response, surviving individuals might not show signs of distress in their own skeletons even though the population was evolving to adapt to nutritional deprivation.

Indicators of growth disruption (Harris lines and enamel hypoplasias) should hold the key to distinguishing between "stress" and "progress" models of the broad-spectrum revolution, but the data are extremely scanty. Comparative Harris line data generally are not reported among Old World populations from this time period, and only Smith et al. report on the relative frequencies of enamel hypoplasias (noting no trend). An earlier study (Brothwell 1963), with an extremely small sample from Europe, notes an increase in the frequency of hypoplasias from the Paleolithic to the Mesolithic.

In the New World there are again no data comparing Paleo-Indians with archaic and later groups. Dickel et al. (1984), however, report on indicators of health among California Indians, who, although they never became farmers, did display a pattern of changing economic exploitation of wild resources similar to the evolution of broad-spectrum exploitation elsewhere. They report that Harris lines declined through the sequence, possibly suggesting improved homeostasis as a broader spectrum of resources was utilized, but they note steady or increasing rates of enamel hypoplasia and declining life expectancies for most age classes through time. In a study of pre-agricultural populations on the coast of Peru, Benfer (1984) finds improvement in a number of indices of health (Harris lines, stature, life expectancy) in a population that moved first toward increased use of vegetable resources and then back toward increasing use of marine fauna. Benfer also notes that the group appeared to be degrading its resources.

In sum, there are not yet sufficient data (nor are the existing data sufficiently consistent) to permit interpretation of the meaning of the broad-spectrum revolution in terms of human health. There is no clear pattern either of increasing stress or of improving homeostasis.

The Harris Hypothesis: Temporary Amelioration of Stress Through Adoption of Agriculture

The Harris (1977; 1979, and Chapter 2) hypothesis that the adoption of agriculture would have resulted in temporary improvement in the quality of life meets with only mixed success. In the Old World, Smith et al. report two trends that appear to support this hypothesis. Early neolithic populations in the Levant display an increase in stature over preceding mesolithic (Natufian) populations, and analyses of strontium content in the bones of these same populations suggest that there was an increase in the consumption of animal products by the neolithic group, presumably as a result of animal domestication. At the same time, however, these authors also suggest that chronic malnutrition was first evidenced more generally in the Neolithic in the form of thinned cortical layers of long bones, and they note that rates of enamel hypoplasia are higher for neolithic groups than for earlier ones. In Rathbun's data from Iran, moreover, the Neolithic appears to be a period of *peak* stress in terms of rates of infection, arthritis, and at least one indicator of malnutrition, porotic hyperostosis. In Rathbun's figures, later populations seem to have adjusted more successfully to farming than did the Neolithic populations. Angel's figures for the Mediterranean suggest a similar pattern. Several indicators of malnutrition in this study suggest that nutrition declined into and through the Neolithic and that a rebound in nutrition occurred only beginning with the early Bronze age. In Europe, Meiklejohn et al. note that the decline in stature that began in the Mesolithic extended into the Neolithic, with rebound beginning only late in the Neolithic. Martin et al. suggest that early farming populations were healthier than later farmers, but they offer no pre-farming groups for comparison.

In the New World, Cassidy notes that in Kentucky a (poorly reported) transitional (incipient agricultural) group may have enjoyed good health in contrast to both the hunter-gatherers before them and (more strikingly) the farmers who followed, as the Harris hypothesis would suggest. Perzigian also finds some suggestion of an improvement in health in Ohio with the initial adoption of farming. He notes that there was an increase in stature with the transition to farming followed by a later decrease; rates of enamel hypoplasia did not increase significantly until the later agricultural periods. Rose et al., discussing various portions of the Mississippi valley, find a complex picture that varies from region to region. For the Caddoan region they note a temporary decline in rates of arthritis associated with the adoption of farming, suggesting that the new economy temporarily reduced the workload. But they also note that both rates of infection and rates of porotic hyperostosis peaked in this transitional group. In their sequences from Illinois, Buikstra and Cook suggest that the early farming population showed the generally poorest health and nutrition; and Goodman et al. find a steady decline in most health indicators without any indication of a temporary improvement. In Latin America, Norr notes a steady increase in rates of porotic hyperostosis but a reduced rate of infection in the early agricultural group. And Ubelaker finds that a group generally regarded as early farmers displayed various indications of relatively good health (compared with people before them, and especially people after). But the rate of caries in this group led him to question whether they were truly agricultural.

Harris's expectation of a temporary amelioration in health and nutrition following the adoption of farming is therefore only occasionally or partially fulfilled (in part perhaps because of the difficulty of identifying and differentiating the various stages of economic change with precision and consistency). Equally common is a pattern in which early farmers display *poor* health in comparison

277

with populations both before and after them. It may be that the amelioration Harris predicts is offset by the stress associated with economic change per se and that adoption of a new economy results in poor health until appropriate adjustments are made.

It is interesting that there is no clear difference between Old and New World populations with regard to the stresses experienced by early farmers. The presence of large domesticable animals in the Old World might lead us to expect that the adoption of farming would be less nutritionally stressful there than in the New World, where no large animals were domesticated. But the data, at present, allow no such simple distinction.

Summary

Beginning in the Middle Pleistocene, the archaeological records of the various regions of the world display broadly similar patterns. Groups appear first to focus relatively heavily on the exploitation of large mammals and then to expand the range of resources utilized to include increasing amounts of small game, avian and other non-mammalian fauna, fish and shellfish, and small seeds and other vegetable material. These trends, which culminate after the end of the Pelistocene, are now commonly referred to as the "broad-spectrum revolution." The attention paid to small seeds and vegetable sources of calories then appears to have resulted in various regions of the world in the domestication of crops and in the commitment of human populations to dependency upon them as primary sources of calories.

Although our perception of these trends may be affected by differential preservation in the archaeological record, which may exaggerate the differences in economy between different periods, various lines of evidence suggest that these patterns do not result solely from differential preservation. In particular, there is evidence that the archaeological sequence corresponds to known patterns of resource preference among primates and modern human beings; and it appears that the sequence conforms fairly well to "optimal foraging" predictions (and related ethnographic observations) about the sequence in which various types of resources should be and are utilized by optimizing populations. These same data seem to suggest that both the broad-spectrum revolution and the subsequent focus on small seeds and other vegetable sources of calories by farmers were more a function of necessity (resulting from either increasing human population or declining resources) than a function of improved technological capacity.

The meaning of these trends in terms of the quality of human life, nutrition, and life expectancy can now be assessed by means of skeletal pathology. The data from skeletal analysis suggest fairly consistently that the adoption of farming commonly resulted in declining health and nutrition, steady or increasing rates of episodic stress, and declining life expectancies in comparison with earlier hunting and gathering, although it often resulted, too, in reduced physical stress. The data do not yet allow us to determine what the broad-spectrum revolution implied for human health. The extant data simply show no clear pattern either of increasing stress or of improved nutritional homeostasis. Similarly, among archaeological farming populations there is no clear, consistent trend in health and nutrition when incipient and established farmers are compared.

Note

1. In contrast with the stricter cultural materialism of the editors of this volume, I hold a view of human cultural evolution adopted from Campbell (1965). Campbell asserted that cultural evolution parallels biological evolution in being a two-stage process. New variations are created or introduced to a population by a series of mechanisms (invention and diffusion in cultural evolution, mutation and gene flow in the biological context). These variations are then secondarily channeled by differential survival or selection. The second, selective phase of this process eliminates dysfunctional or competitively unsuccessful variations and thus imposes limits on the potential range of variation. Surviving cultures (or parts of cultures), like surviving organisms, must therefore display some minimum degree of adaptive design, the degree being dependent on the stiffness of the competition. But the largely random nature of the original creative forces and the existence of competing sets of selective forces suggest that, within the limits imposed by selection, a good deal of random, non-adaptive, or even mildly dysfunctional variation is possible and is to be expected. Cultural evolution theory can no more predict all of the features of cultural design than the rules of biological evolution can predict the design of specific organisms.

References Cited

Allison, M.
    1984   Paleopathology in Peruvian and Chilean Populations. In *Paleopathology at the Origins of Agriculture,* M. N. Cohen and G. Armelagos, eds., pp. 515–29. New York: Academic Press.
Angel, J. L.
    1984   Health as a Crucial Factor in the Changes from Hunting to Developed Farming in the Eastern Mediterranean. In *Paleopathology at the Origins*

of Agriculture, M. N. Cohen and G. Armelagos, eds., pp. 51–73. New York: Academic Press.

Benfer, R.
1984   The Challenges and Rewards of Sedentism: The Preceramic Village of Paloma, Peru. In *Paleopathology at the Origins of Agriculture*, M. N. Cohen and G. Armelagos, eds., pp. 531–58. New York: Academic Press.

Binford, L. R.
1983   *In Pursuit of the Past.* New York: Thames and Hudson.

Brothwell, D.
1963   The Macroscopic Dental Pathology of Some Earlier Populations. In *Dental Anthropology*, D. R. Brothwell, ed., pp. 271–88. Oxford: Pergamon.

Buikstra, J.
1984   The Lower Illinois River Region: A Prehistoric Context for the Study of Ancient Diet and Health. In *Paleopathology at the Origins of Agriculture*, M. N. Cohen and G. Armelagos, eds., pp. 215–69. New York: Academic Press.

Buikstra, J., and D. C. Cook
1980   Paleopathology: An American Account. *Annual Review of Anthropology* 9:433–70.

Campbell, D.
1965   Variation and Selective Retention in Sociological Evolution. In *Social Change in Developing Areas,* H. R. Barringer et al., eds., pp. 19–49. Cambridge, Mass.: Schenkman.

Cassidy, C. M.
1980   Benign Neglect and Toddler Malnutrition. In *Social and Biological Predictors of Nutritional Status, Physical Growth and Neurological Development,* L. S. Greene and F. Johnston, eds., pp. 109–39. New York: Academic Press.

1983   Commentary on "Food: Past, Present and Future" by N. S. Scrimshaw. In *How Humans Adapt,* D. Ortner, ed., pp. 253–57. Washington: Smithsonian Institution.

1984   Skeletal Evidence for Prehistoric Subsistence Adaptation in the Central Ohio River Valley. In *Paleobiology at the Origins of Agriculture,* M. N. Cohen and G. Armelagos, eds., pp. 307–45. New York: Academic Press.

Childe, V. G.
1951   *Man Makes Himself.* New York: Mentor.

Christenson, A. L.
1980   Changes in the Human Niche in Response to Population Growth. In *Modeling Change in Prehistoric Subsistence Economies,* T. K. Earle and A. L. Christenson, eds., pp. 31–72. New York: Academic Press.

Cohen, M. N.
1977   *The Food Crisis in Prehistory.* New Haven: Yale University Press.

Cohen, M. N., and G. Armelagos (eds.)
1984   *Paleopathology at the Origins of Agriculture.* New York: Academic Press.

280

Dahlberg, F. (ed.)
    1981   *Woman the Gatherer.* New Haven: Yale University Press.
Dickel, D., et al.
    1984   Central California: Prehistoric Subsistence Changes and Health. In *Paleopathology at the Origins of Agriculture,* M. N. Cohen and G. Armelagos, eds., pp. 439–61. New York: Academic Press.
Earle, T.
    1980   A Model of Subsistence Change. In *Modeling Change in Prehistoric Subsistence Economies,* T. K. Earle and A. L. Christenson (eds.), pp. 1–29. New York: Academic Press.
Fagan, B.
    1983   *People of the Earth.* 4th ed. Boston: Little, Brown.
Frayer, D. W.
    1981   Body Size, Weapon Use and Natural Selection in the European Upper Paleolithic and Mesolithic. *American Anthropologist* 83:57–73.
Goodman, A., et al.
    1984   Health Changes at Dickson Mounds, Illinois (A.D. 950–1300). In *Paleopathology at the Origins of Agriculture,* M. N. Cohen and G. Armelagos, eds., pp. 271–305. New York: Academic Press.
Hames, R. B., and W. T. Vickers
    1982   Optimal Diet Breadth Theory as a Model to Explain Variability in Amazonian Hunting. *American Ethnologist* 9:358–78.
Harding, R. S. O., and G. Teleki
    1981   *Omnivorous Primates: Gathering and Hunting in Human Evolution.* New York: Columbia University Press.
Harris, M. R.
    1977   *Cannibals and Kings.* New York: Vintage.
    1979   *Cultural Materialism.* New York: Random House.
Hawkes, K.; K. Hill; and J. F. O'Connell
    1982   Why Hunters Gather: Optimal Foraging and the Aché of Eastern Paraguay. *American Ethnologist* 9:379–98.
Hayden, B.
    1981a   Research and Development in the Stone Age: Technological Transitions Among Hunter-Gatherers. *Current Anthropology* 22:519–48.
    1981b   Subsistence and Ecological Adaptations of Modern Hunter/Gatherers. In *Omnivorous Primates: Gathering and Hunting in Human Evaluation,* R. S. O. Harding and G. Teleki, eds., pp. 344–422. New York: Columbia University Press.
Hespenheide, H. A.
    1980   Ecological Models of Resource Selection. In *Modeling Change in Prehistoric Subsistence Economies,* T. H. Earle and A. L. Christenson, eds., pp. 73–78. New York: Academic Press.
Huss-Ashmore, R., et al.
    1982   Nutritional Inference from Paleopathology. *Advances in Archaeological Method and Theory* 5:395–474.
Kamminga, J.
    1981   Comment on B. Hayden. *Current Anthropology* 22:535–36.

Kennedy, K. A. R.
   1984   Growth, Nutrition and Pathology in Changing Paleodemographic Setting in South Asia. In *Paleopathology at the Origins of Agriculture,* M. N. Cohen and G. Armelagos, eds., pp. 169–92. New York: Academic Press.

Larsen, C.
   1984   Health and Disease in Prehistoric Georgia: The Transition to Agriculture. In *Paleopathology at the Origins of Agriculture,* M. N. Cohen and G. Armelagos, eds., pp. 367–92. New York: Academic Press.

Lee, R. D.
   1968   What Hunters Do for a Living; or, How to Make Out on Scarce Resources. In *Man the Hunter,* R. B. Lee and I. DeVore, eds., pp. 30–48. Chicago: Aldine.

Lourandos, H.
   1983   Intensification in Australian Prehistory. Paper read to International Congress of Anthropological and Ethnological Sciences, Vancouver.

Martin, D., et al.
   1984   The Effects of Socioeconomic Change in Pehistoric Africa: Sudanese Nubia as a Case Study. In *Paleopathology at the Origins of Agriculture,* M. N. Cohen and G. Armelagos, eds., pp. 193–214. New York: Academic Press.

Meiklejohn, C., et al.
   1984   Socioeconomic Change and Patterns of Pathology and Variation in the Mesolithic and Neolithic of Western Europe: Some Suggestions. In *Paleopathology at the Origins of Agriculture,* M. N. Cohen and G. Armelagos, eds., pp. 75–100. New York: Academic Press.

Murchison, M. A., et al.
   1983   Transverse Line Formation in Protein Deprived Rhesus Monkeys. Paper presented to the annual meeting of the Paleopathology Association, Indianapolis.

Norr, L., et al.
   1984   Prehistoric Subsistence and Health Status of Coastal Peoples from the Panamanian Isthumus of Lower Central America. In *Paleopathology at the Origins of Agriculture,* M. N. Cohen and G. Armelagos, eds., pp. 463–90. New York: Academic Press.

O'Connell, J. F., and K. Hawkes
   1981   Alyawara Plant Use and Optimal Foraging Theory. In *Hunter-Gatherer Foraging Strategies: Ethnographic and Archeological Analysis,* B. Winterhalder and E. A. Smith, eds., pp. 99–125. Chicago: University of Chicago Press.

Palkovich, A.
   1984   Agriculture, Marginal Environments and Nutritional Stress in the Prehistoric Southwest. In *Paleopathology at the Origins of Agriculture,* M. N. Cohen and G. Armelagos, eds., pp. 425–38. New York: Academic Press.

Perlman, S.
   1983   Optimum Diet Models and Return Rate Curves: A Test on Martha's

Vineyard Island. In *Ecological Models in Economic Prehistory*, G. Bronitsky, ed., pp. 115–67. Anthropological Research Papers, no. 29. Tempe: Arizona State University.

Perzigian, A. J.
1984   Prehistoric Health in the Ohio River Valley. In *Paleopathology at the Origins of Agriculture*, M. N. Cohen and G. Armelagos, eds., pp. 347–66. New York: Academic Press.

Rathbun, T.
1984   Paleopathology and Economic Change in Iran and Iraq. In *Paleopathology at the Origins of Agriculture*, M. N. Cohen and G. Armelagos, eds., pp. 137–67. New York: Academic Press.

Rose, J., et al.
1984   Paleopathology and the Origins of Maize Agriculture in the Lower Mississippi Valley and Caddoan Culture Areas. In *Paleopathology at the Origins of Agriculture*, M. N. Cohen and G. Armelagos, eds., pp. 393–424. New York: Academic Press.

Schoeniger, M.
1982   Diet and the Evolution of Modern Human Form in the Middle East. *American Journal of Physical Anthropology* 58:37–52.

Smith, P., et al.
1984   Archaeology and Skeletal Evidence for Dietary Change During the Late Pleistocene/Early Holocene in the Levant. In *Paleopathology at the Origins of Agriculture*, M. N. Cohen and G. Armelagos, eds., pp. 101–36. New York: Academic Press.

Ubelaker, D.
1984   Prehistoric Human Biology of Ecuador: Possible Temporal Trends and Cultural Correlations. In *Paleopathology at the Origins of Agriculture*, M. N. Cohen and G. Armelagos, eds., pp. 491–513. New York: Academic Press.

Winterhalder, B.
1981   Optimal Foraging Strategies and Hunter-Gatherer Research in Anthropology: Theories and Models. In *Hunter-Gatherer Foraging Strategies: Ethnographic and Archeological Analysis*, B. Winterhalder and E. A. Smith, eds., pp. 13–35. Chicago: University of Chicago Press.

Winterhalder, B., and E. A. Smith (eds.)
1981   *Hunter-Gatherer Foraging Strategies: Ethnographic and Archeological Analyses*. Chicago: Aldine.

Wolpoff, M.
1980   *Paleoanthropology*. New York: Knopf.

283

11

DAVID R. YESNER

Life in the "Garden of Eden": Causes and Consequences of the Adoption of Marine Diets by Human Societies

IN EXAMINING THE BIOCULTURAL BASIS OF HUMAN FOOD PREFER-
ences and aversions, it is important to document not only short-term idiosyncratic aspects of human foodways, but also longer-term historical trends
underlying the acceptance and rejection of food types. Both the causes and the
consequences of such major transformations in human foodways need to be
assessed. It is in this spirit that this paper attempts to address the question of
the causes and consequences of the relatively late adoption of seafood diets by
human societies, using some current research being conducted in Maine and
Alaska.

The historical fact that maritime resources were not exploited until relatively
late in the prehistoric record has been recently discussed by Osborn (1977) and
others, and has attracted a general consensus of agreement. Very few coastal
sites predate the late Upper Paleolithic in the Old World, even in areas (such as
England) with emergent shorelines in which earlier sites are not likely to have
been erased by subsequent coastal erosion. Those sites that *do* predate the
late Upper Paleolithic show only very scanty evidence of the use of coastal
resources (e.g., at Terra Amata; see de Lumley 1969) or certainly much less
use of those resources than in Upper Paleolithic or later times at the same
location (e.g., at Klasies River mouth in South Africa; see Singer and Wymer
1982; Volman 1978). The overall pattern of these sites suggests that a real
commitment to maritime lifeways did not precede late Upper Paleolithis times.
Similarly, in the New World, early occupants (Paleo-Indians and hypothetical
pre-Clovis occupants) have not been found to have used marine resources, and
in most parts of North America a real commitment to maritime lifeways post-
dates the mid-Holocene (Yesner 1983). What is it in the nature of marine re-

sources, then, that prevented their exploitation until relatively late in pre-historic times, and what conseqeunces did this use have on the development of human societies?

Binford (1983) suggests that coastal resources have been characterized by many archaeologists, including myself, as a "Garden of Eden" in which there is "plentiful food just for the picking," providing "a setting for the beginnings of sedentary life." Binford finds this proposition distasteful because it leads to what he terms a "historical problem": "If aquatic resources are to be considered Gardens of Eden, why did early populations apparently not realize this fact?" This, in turn, seems to lead to the implication that, in terms of the seacoast, "some peoples were 'more perceptive' or 'smarter' . . . while others ignored its self-evident advantages" (Binford 1983:202). If, indeed, such mentalistic notions are to be rejected in favor of ones based on natural selection, then we are left asking two questions. First, is the Garden of Eden model accurate, or must we replace it with a model that suggests that coastal resources are "second rate" (Osborn 1977) in order to explain why coastal environments were not initially exploited in either the Old or the New World? If neither model should prove to be accurate, however, what alternative forces may have led to a failure to exploit marine resources until relatively late?

A second paradox that needs to be addressed has to do with the set of constraints imposed upon a society by its resource base. Binford (1983) notes that some have used the Garden of Eden principle to suggest why hunter-gatherers have *rejected* agriculture in some places (e.g., coastal California), whereas in other places (e.g., coastal Peru), the sedentism associated with intensive harvesting of seafoods has been viewed as a *causative* agent underlying the development of agriculture. In addition, the range of political organization that has been attributed to maritime hunter-gatherers ranges from band-level societies (e.g., among the Yahgan of Tierra del Fuego) to "big-man" types of societies (e.g., among coastal Californians or New Englanders), hereditary chiefdoms (e.g., among Aleuts or Northwest Coast Indians), and even incipient state-level societies (e.g., in coastal Peru). How, then, do the constraints of the productive process help us to understand these seemingly divergent consequences of maritime adaptation for the development of cultural complexity?

The "Garden of Eden" Versus the "Second-Rate Resource" Model

Recently a number of archaeologists—including myself (Yesner 1981)—have argued that optimal foraging theory presents a robust model that allows one to explain why certain resources are or are not included in the diet (as well as how much time or energy is devoted to the exploitation of those resources). Following the tenets of this theory, an item is included in the "optimal diet" if it is "valuable" in energetic terms, usually expressed as the difference between its per-unit caloric yield and its caloric cost (including search, pursuit, and "handling" costs such as retrieval and processing). Whether or not an item is to be included in the diet has little to do with its own abundance but depends solely on its ranking as a resource in terms of "value" and the abundance of more "valuable" or highly ranked resources. As a result, a lower-ranked resource will often not be exploited until more highly ranked resources decline in abundance. Thus, Hayden (1981) has noted that human beings rarely eat field mice in spite of their abundance, because the per unit cost of exploiting such resources is extremely high. Nevertheless, hunter-gatherers living in marginal environments such as deserts do end up eating a lot of rodents, lizards, snakes, insects, and grubs, not necessarily because they are more available, but because more "valuable" resources (such as large mammals) may be *less* available. Hill (1982) and O'Connell and Hawkes (1981) have recently shown that hunting in general produces a per unit benefit that far outweighs that of plant collecting, and Simms (1983) has also shown that large-mammal hunting produces an energy benefit that outweighs small-mammal hunting (which, in turn, generally outweighs plant collection). If, as Hill (1982) has suggested, optimal foraging theory can be used to show why human beings originally became hunters—particularly big-game hunters—then it could potentially be used to suggest why marine resources were not used until late: that is, because they are high-cost, low-benefit, "secondary" resources.

The major problem with this approach, of course, involves estimating the costs and benefits associated with marine resource exploitation. Furthermore, lumping of seafoods into a single category obscures the analysis of costs and benefits. In terms of cost, for example, it is clear that complex technology of any sort is rarely required to collect shellfish or other marine invertebrates (which are successfully harvested with rakes, forks, hooks, or spades), but even here, species that burrow or live in high-energy environments may be more "costly." The same applies to fish, which range from more easily exploited nearshore varieties to "costlier" (although often high-yielding) deep-sea varieties. Sea birds may be planktonic feeders with generally smaller ranges, which are more easily caught, or diving fish-eaters, which are more difficult to exploit. Sea mammals are considered to be "high-cost" resources that generally require complex technology to obtain, but this is certainly much more true of migratory whales than basking seals.

Cross-cutting all of these differences is the fact that nearly all marine resources are aggregated, or obtainable in large concentrations under certain conditions, which allows reduced search and retrieval costs. Shellfish beds, fish schools, anadromous fish runs, sea bird colonies, ice leads, and sea mammal rookeries all offer conditions in which these resources can be taken at reduced cost. Archaeological evidence from numerous coastal regions, furthermore, suggests that within each category of sea life, less costly harvesting methods tend to be replaced over time by more costly ones. For example, in coastal California, early emphasis on picking surface shellfish, hooking nearshore schooling fish, and clubbing seals at haulouts was replaced by digging clams, trolling for offshore solitary fish species, and (in some areas) actively hunting large sea mammals (Meighan 1983; Tartaglia 1976). In the Old World, long-term sequences of coastal occupation—such as at Klasies River mouth—reveal a gradual shift from strandlooping to more "costly" marine hunting techniques (Singer and Wymer 1982) and certainly Arctic prehistory can be interpreted as a developmental sequence in which there was increased hunting of more "costly" species such as large baleen whales. On the Maine coast, where I have been working most recently, one shift in late prehistoric times apparently involved increased exploitation of a small coastal mammal called the "sea-mink," which is now extinct (Loomis 1911).

Clearly the "cost" of exploiting marine resources depends upon the class of resources and often upon the individual species involved. However, the use of boats for "central-place" foraging among marine hunters reduced many search and particularly retrieval costs for a wide variety of resources, and many improvements in maritime technology were largely directed toward increasing the range of boats and thus reducing mobility costs per unit of time. Much of the real cost of marine hunting, however, involves not so much the technology as the social relations of production, ranging from the cost of maintaining family or clan territories in order to restrict access to areas where resources aggregate (anadromous fishing locales, productive shellfish beds, sea mammal haulouts) to the cost of maintaining the structure of whaling crews and the ceremonial apparatus necessary for effective whale hunts.

If the energetic "costs" of marine resource exploitation are difficult to calculate, the "benefits" are equally so. Here again it is difficult to deal with marine resources in any kind of monolithic fashion. For example, some seafoods, such as shellfish, are notoriously low in calories (about 0.6 to 1.0 kilocalories per gram), but sea mammals are certainly equal to terrestrial mammals in the caloric content of their flesh, and the fact that they often come in very large packages increases the benefit of exploiting them per unit of effort. Marine fish vary greatly on both counts, ranging from about 0.95 to 3.38 kilocalories per gram (Arimoto 1962).

The caloric differences observed among seafoods are related in part to their fat content, since fats have twice the caloric density of either proteins or carbohydrates. Sea mammals are obviously high in fat content, ranging from about 22 to 24 percent fat (Heller and Scott 1962). Shellfish, at the other end of the spectrum, range from only 0.4 to 1.3 percent fat, while marine fish range widely from less than 1 percent fat among species like haddock to 25 percent among species like tuna (Arimoto 1962; Heller and Scott 1962). Speth and Spielman (1983) have recently emphasized the dietary role of fats in energy production among hunter-gatherers, particularly in places where cold stress is prevalent all or part of the year, and at times when carbohydrate energy sources are unavailable. In addition, triglycerides allow for transport of fat-soluble vitamins, while essential fatty acids serve as precursors for the manufacture of phospholipids and prostaglandins with hormone-like functions, as well as cholesterol, which is required for steroid and bile salt formation (Shodell 1983). An important distinction, however, is that marine foods generally contain larger amounts of *unsaturated* fatty acids such as eicosapentaenoic acid (EPA), which not only produce as much energy as saturated fatty acids but also tend to have a depressive effect on blood cholesterol levels (Toyama and Kaneda 1962). Thus, it has recently been suggested that the I_3 prostaglandins produced by EPA have protected coastal peoples who consume substantial amounts of marine fats (including fish oils) from high blood pressure, atherothrombotic disorders, and other cardiovascular disease (Fischer and Weber 1984). However, problems with blood clotting and other physiological processes may occur if dietary sources of cholesterol are insufficient. Furthermore, marine fatty acids tend to have an antagonistic effect on tocopherol (vitamin E), and an important fatty acid, linoleic acid, is generally less prevalent in marine diets (Toyama and Kaneda 1962).

Clearly latitudinal variation is important in this whole picture. Although marine species diversity—particularly fish species diversity—is generally higher in tropical regions, many of these species have a lower fat and caloric content. This is particularly true of reef fish, although other fish and sea mammals may also be affected. In higher latitudes, although marine species diversity is lower, fattier sea mammal and fish species are more available, including both anadromous and catadromous fish. (Salmon, for example—an anadromous fish—averages 17 percent fat content, and eels—catadromous fish—average 18 percent fat content; these species produce about 2.25 kilocalories per gram of body weight [Arimoto 1962].) In the Arctic, shellfish tend to disappear above the southern boundary of pack ice, since ice scouring greatly affects their ability to reproduce and maintain their habitat. These latitudinal effects are compounded by the fact that "plants edible by man decrease in diversity and abundance poleward from the tropics through the temperate zones" (Harris 1982:19). This has led to an inverse latitudinal trend in human utilization of the two most abundant types of high-calorie foods—terrestrial plants and marine animals—such that occupants of different latitudinal zones tend to substitute one resource for the other.

If the use of particular seafoods in different latitudinal zones is viewed in historical perspective, additional patterns emerge. For example, in northern temperate and Subarctic zones such as the Maine-Maritimes region or the Pacific coast from southwestern Alaska to Washington state, sea mammals were exploited earlier than anadromous fish or shellfish. One might well argue that the caloric benefits for these populations outweighed the considerable costs associated with sea mammal hunting and that shellfish were not exploited until pressures on more "valuable" sea-mammal resources necessitated the inclusion of shellfish in an optimal diet. Optimal foraging theory thus appears helpful in explaining such phenomena, but it is important to be careful that what we are observing is not simply the result of environmental change—for example, the fact that shellfish beds could not initially form because of rapid post-glacial sea-level rise, particularly in nothern glaciated coastal zones with isostatically active coastlines. (The same caution is necessary if we attempt to adopt wider-scale energetically based explanations for the initial exploitation of marine resources in late Pleistocene times in Europe, North Africa, and the North Pacific region. However, the work of Clark et al. (1980) on the north coast of Spain has clearly demonstrated that initial involvement with marine resources in that region occurred under a situation of little or no environmental change.) Optimal foraging theory also helps to explain why lower-calorie, low-fat seafoods may sometimes be *dropped* from an optimal diet—as, for example, in the famous case of the prehistoric Tasmanians, who stopped eating fish when sea mammals became more abundant under cooler water temperature conditions (Allen 1979; Bowdler 1980; Horton 1979; see also Jones 1977, 1978). Eventually, similar phenomena may help to explain the fish taboos that exist in a number of human societies (Aschmann 1975; Simoons 1974a, 1974b).

The purely energetic concerns of optimal foraging theory may, in fact, be more powerful in helping to explain why *particular* seafoods are utilized than in explaining the use of coastal resources in general. Seafood exploitation can provide net caloric returns in excess of 5,000 kilocalories per hour, and under exceptional circumstances (e.g., the netting of migratory, schooling fish in estuaries during annual runs), it can provide net caloric returns in excess of 18,000 kilocalories per hour (Lischka 1979:5; Perlman 1976:117), mostly because search times are relatively low. Terrestrial mammals such as deer generally provide net caloric returns of about 3,000 to 5,000 kilocalories per hour (Perlman 1976), but, again, short-term concentrations of aggregated species such as caribou may yield values as high as 27,000 kilocalories per hour (Yesner n.d.a). In fact, if the distinction between coastal and terrestrial resources were truly substantial, it would be difficult to explain why coastal resources in so many parts of North America, for example, were utilized virtually as soon as they became available. Of course, large Pleistocene megafauna may have exceeded the energetic returns of modern terrestrial fauna, at least on a short-term basis; hypothetically, this could have necessitated the exploitation of "secondary resources," including marine foods, when the megafauna became extinct. However, the encounter rates with these species may have been so low as to make these energetic calculations almost meaningless, unless significant food storage was taking place.

In addition, per unit energy yield is not the only factor—nutritional or otherwise—that needs to be considered in evaluating the importance of marine diets. Additional factors include those discussed below.

Protein Yields

Osborn (1977) has greatly overemphasized the distinction in protein yields between marine and terrestrial resources. For example, the value that he cites for marine fish flesh (17 percent protein) is close to a minimum value; some marine fish species (such as dogfish and flounder) range as high as 25 percent in protein content, equivalent to or exceeding terrestrial mammals such as caribou, moose, and deer (Arimoto 1962). Osborn's (1977) figure for whalemeat is also fallacious; whalemeat averages about 23.3 percent in protein content, not 10 percent as he suggests. Finally, species of shellfish other than those cited by Osborn (1977) range as high as 24.6 percent in protein content (Borgstrom 1962), and crustaceans such as crab contain up to about 20 percent protein (Arimoto 1962). Furthermore, a great deal of protein is present in shellfish liquids, which are frequently discarded in modern nutritional analyses but would have been important to prehistoric consumers, particularly if the shellfish were eaten raw. There is also evidence to suggest that the digestibility of marine protein is enhanced if eaten raw (Borgstrom 1962). Even certain seaweeds (e.g., eelgrass) harvested by coastal hunter-gatherers contain up to 13 percent protein by weight (Felger and Moser 1973).

Beyond simple percentages, marine fish and shellfish yield high-quality proteins, with nitrogen values greater than or equal to that of casein. Both marine fish and shellfish are particularly good sources of lysine, histidine, and arginine. They are somewhat deficient in valine, phenylalanine, and the sulfur-containing amino acids (cystine and methionine), but these are found in greater concentrations in shellfish than in marine fish. It has also been found that specific body parts such as fish eyes or sea mammal flippers—parts that are often considered delicacies—may have particularly favorable amino acid ratios (Bergstrom 1962) and may contain larger amounts of fat (Heller and Scott 1962).

Nietschmann (1972, 1973) has demonstrated that a marine diet produces adequate protein to supply coastal populations in Central America, and Meehan (1977) has demonstrated the same for coastal Aborigines in Australia. Experimental evidence from both California (Lischka 1979; Lischka and Sheets 1980) and Alaska (Erlandson 1983) has shown that shellfish collected by a single individual are sufficient to provide for the protein needs of 100 to 500 persons per

291

day. In low-latitude regions, the protein supply generated by marine resources is generally sufficient to permit trade with interior-adapted peoples for high-calorie foods such as grains or other plant foods (Stark and Voorhies 1978). Tropical groups in coastal environments are often taller, on average, than neighboring interior groups, and clinical evidence for protein malnutrition among coastal groups is rare (Borgstrom 1962). In fact, the case has been made that among hunter-gatherers in tropical environments, the protein provided by marine foods may have been critical to subsistence in some areas, at least after the extinction of the Pleistocene megafauna and the evolution of the modern biotic zones. One reason for this is the relatively low nitrogen content (and therefore relatively low biological vlaue) of proteins in tropical plants, which use C_4 metabolic pathways (Russell-Hunter 1970), as well as the limited secondary productivity of tropical forests. It has also been suggested that horticulture involving low-protein root crops in areas such as Polynesia would have been difficult without the existence of a marine food base (Harris 1982).

Vitamins and Minerals

Seafoods are excellent sources of a number of vitamins, including vitamins A, D, and niacin (Heller and Scott 1962). Vitamin A is particularly plentiful in sea mammal organs, and vitamins A, B_1, and B_2 are concentrated in many fish roes, although they are subject to loss in dried or otherwise stored seafoods (Borgstrom 1962). Mollusks and crustaceans contain large amounts of thiamine, as well as electrolytes such as sodium. Eating whole fish provides a good source of fluorine (up to 250 parts per million), while iodine and Vitamin B_{12} are also obtainable from seaweeds (Felger and Moser 1973).

Maximum Sustained Yield

As noted previously (Yesner 1980), migratory marine species can often be intensively exploited with a high maximum sustained yield. In addition, even non-migratory marine species can withstand culling rates of about 10 to 14 percent, higher than the maximum sustained yield of most terrestrial species (Yesner 1980). It is true, of course, that a good deal of evidence of overexploitation of marine resources has been observed, both ethnographically and archaeologically (Botkin 1980; Shawcross 1975; Swadling 1976, 1977a; 1977b). This seems logical, given that marine hunters tend to be relatively sedentary, exploit relatively large territories, and have relatively high population densities (see "Consequences of the Adoption of Marine Diets" below). Modern marine hunters have certainly been held accountable for the extinction of slow-reproducing species such as the northern sea-cow in Alaska (Domning 1972) and captive residents of offshore islands such as the sea-mink in Maine (Loomis 1911).

In my own research in Maine, I have found evidence for overexploitation of shellfish, indicated both by size diminution and by a switching back and forth between the species collected (Yesner 1983). Undoubtedly the diminution in shellfish size is the result of a characteristic harvesting pattern of selecting larger individuals (Yesner 1983), a practice guaranteed to affect shellfish during their period of maximum fertility. However, most of the effect of shellfish over-exploitation seems to occur within a few hundred years after the initial colonization of a site, suggesting that exploitation patterns stabilize, possibly as groups develop schedules that allow "fallowing" of individual sites for some years while exploitation of alternative sites continues; this is made possible by the more or less ubiquitous distribution of shellfish as well as the mobility permitted by the use of boats. In addition, shellfish populations are extremely difficult to extirpate completely, because small individuals with low net yields are rarely collected at all; thus, populations can almost always regenerate if abandoned for short periods of time. Sedentary sea mammals and sea birds obtained from rookeries on offshore islets can also be subjected to overexploitation, requiring a shift to the exploitation of alternative prey types, as is demonstrated in the archaeological record of the Aleutian Islands (Yesner 1977; Yesner and Aigner 1976). However, these types of resource exploitations are, again, highly localized processes, solutions for which are well within the capabilities of the shifting resource exploitation strategies of individual hunting bands.

Lower Dependency Ratios

Because both old people and children are able to engage in activities such as shellfish collection, and because they have lower caloric requirements, they are virtually able to support themselves in coastal zones and do not act as a sump for the population's resources. This may be what has led to the greater life expectancies and more broadly based population pyramids characteristic of regions that depend almost exclusively on marine resources, such as the Aleutian Islands (Laughlin 1972; Yesner 1980).

On the basis of the above factors, it should be clear that although coastal resources cannot be considered a Garden of Eden, neither are they entirely second-rate resources as suggested by Osborn (1977). A third model, therefore, needs to be considered—one that offers a more satisfying explanation for the adoption of seafood diets by human societies. This model is based on a feature of those diets not previously discussed: their spatial and temporal *reliability.*

The Third Model: Risk Reduction, Resource Seasonality, and Energy Flow

Perhaps the greatest contrast between terrestrial and marine foods lies in the much greater spatial and temporal reliability of the latter. Numerous sea mammals, for example, are locally sedentary residents that can be exploited at predictable locations (haulouts and rookeries). Many bottomfish are year-round residents of predictable locations and are thus easily exploited with the proper equipment. Many sea birds have localized colonies at which they can be easily obtained; this is often attested to by the high proportions of immature individuals of these species in the archaeological record. However, sessile invertebrates (e.g., shellfish and crustaceans) are the most "reliable" marine resources of all, both spatially and temporally. Their spatial reliability (predictability) is attested to by the frequently close association of coastal occupation sites with shellfish beds, reefs, and strandflats (Yesner 1980, 1983). Their temporal reliability is due to their relatively low fluctuation in numbers, particularly in areas free from ice scour and not subject to frequent changes in currents or movements of sediment. The resistance of shellfish populations to total depletion, as noted above, is another factor in their temporal reliability; Lischka (1979), for example, has noted that shellfish of "harvestable" size (i.e., over about five centimeters in length) often still exceed densities of 1,200 grams per square meter in areas intensively exploited by humans today.

Even migratory marine species are highly reliable in space and time. Migratory sea mammals, birds, and fish (including anadromous fish) follow predictable migration routes at specific times of the year. In the case of sea mammals, lower search costs make the interception of migrating individuals an efficient hunting strategy. On the opposite end of the spectrum, anadromous fish have high search costs along their migratory routes and are therefore generally exploited only at their point of arrival (i.e., spawning streams). Sea birds tend to be intermediate in terms of both search and retrieval costs.

The *storability* of seafoods—primarily through drying or smoking—vastly enhances their reliability. The high salinity of these meats facilitates the storage process, but the high fat content of some marine species often makes it more difficult. Methods therefore tend to depend on fat content; drying is apparently the method of choice for preserving lean fish like bottomfish, whereas smoking (or freezing, where possible) is used to preserve fattier fish such as salmon and other anadromous species. Semi-subterranean storage pits or cache pits for fish, such as the ones recently discovered on the Maine coast (Yesner 1984a), also attest to the important process of cold storage during winter and spring months in Arctic or northern temperate zones.

In sum, seafoods tend to be highly reliable resources. Paradoxically, some of the highest-ranked resources in terms of net caloric yield (e.g., anadromous fish) are less reliable than lower-ranked resources (e.g., shellfish). This yields a significant "trade-off" potential in coastal zones between highly caloric but less reliable foods and those that are less caloric but more reliable.

Hayden (1981) has suggested that the history of cultural evolution has involved continuing efforts by humans to increase the reliability of their subsistence (and thus the security of their existence). Hayden included the initial exploitation of seafoods as a part of that security-seeking pattern. Whether or not his analysis is valid, it is important to note that there is a difference between increasing the reliability of subsistence in a total sense (i.e., through expanding dietary breadth) and seeking out individually reliable food resources (such as seafoods) for exploitation.

Utilizing this notion of seafoods as reliable resources, I suggest the following as a realistic scenario for the development of coastal lifeways. First, with the extinction of the "valuable" Pleistocene megafauna, diet breadth expanded at the bottom to encompass a number of resources with lower net yields. During the early Holocene, this primarily meant the exploitation of a wider variety of smaller terrestrial fauna. Then, during mid-Holocene times, as the thermal maximum developed, the width of the temperate zone (which had been compressed under previous glacial conditions) began to expand. This in turn resulted in the expansion of the area characterized by strong resource seasonality. At the same time, these environments were becoming increasingly patchy, thus increasing the exploitation costs for terrestrial resources.

Under these conditions marine resources became advantageous, not only because of net caloric yields, fat, and protein content, but also because they were available at the times of the year when terrestrial resources were least productive (in terms of plants) or least accessible (in terms of animals): late winter and spring. It is undoubtedly no accident that seasonal coastal sites throughout the world tend to be occupied during precisely this period (Yesner 1980). It is also noteworthy in this regard that many shellfish species (in North America, oysters and scallops, for example) tend to have a "spring peak" in protein and fat content that appears to be related to the timing of upwelling events (Borgstrom 1962). Thus, the worldwide pattern of spring utilization of coastal resources may be related as much to peaks in the protein and fat content of shellfish as to declines in the availability of terrestrial resources at this time of year. Under these more seasonal conditions, the storability of marine resources would also have made them attractive. A precondition for this possibility was the development of storage technology itself in late Pleistocene and early Holocene times.

In short, the wide adoption of coastal resources during mid-Holocene times may have been a function of the increased seasonality of environmental perturbations as well as environmental patchiness. These features are particularly notable in some of the regions where coastal adaptations first developed (e.g., South Africa, the circum-Mediterranean region, Japan). The addition of seafoods to the diet served a function similar to the evolution of storage techniques in that it allowed the evening out of energy flow during the annual cycle, thus minimizing subsistence risk and contributing to population survival. Stabilization of the food supply, including the use of aquatic resources, appears to have been a general goal of late glacial and postglacial hunter-gatherer economies, particularly those in seasonal, patchy, and/or marginal environments such as temperate forested regions (Zvelebil 1986).

Why did this phenomenon not occur during earlier (inter-glacial?) periods that may have been characterized by similar circumstances? Ultimately the answer may be found in Binford's (1983) and Cohen's (1977) model of continuous, worldwide population growth during the Pleistocene period. The eventual result of this population growth was greater population packing and corresponding diminution of habitat, which in turn limited the alternatives available when highly ranked resources declined in abundance. The adoption of coastal resources thus allowed an expansion of dietary breadth when increased population density removed the opportunity to survive by continuing to exploit more "valuable" resources. In earlier periods the relatively high-cost resources could be ignored because population "pressure" was not as great.

Associated with this transition toward coastal lifeways must have been a significant "retooling" cost in terms of both technology and socioeconomic organization. This would include the costs involved in the development of efficient boat transportation and the complex technology required for harvesting sea mammals and large fish species, as well as the organization of the communal search, pursuit, retrieval, and division of the kill necessitated by the exploitation of those species. It has also been suggested that because many marine species (particularly sea mammals) are largely submerged, their characteristics would have been less discernible to hunting and gathering peoples, thus delaying any automatic transfer of hunting techniques from terrestrial to marine animals. These retooling costs are related to what Binford (1983) has recently termed the "inertia" principle: the idea that once a population adapts to a particular lifeway, it is difficult for it to face the energetic and behavioral demands of adapting to a completely new one. This has certainly been argued for the origins of agriculture, and Binford (1983) implies that it might be applied to the use of the oceans as well. Nevertheless, cases such as the Tanaina Athapaskans of southcentral Alaska demonstrate that maritime adaptation, involving the hunting of at least medium-sized sea-mammals as well as shellfish collection, can be developed among terrestrial hunter-gatherers within a relatively brief period of time (no more than a few hundred years).

At the same time, it is important to recognize that, just as with the development of agriculture, the intensification of maritime adaptation often did take place over a considerable period of time, and often proceeded by a series of stages. A common scenario, for example, involves an initial exploitation of sea-mammals, followed by an increased exploitation of anadromous fish and/or other large or schooling fishes, and finally a relatively late concentration on shellfish and other marine invertebrates, depending upon the relative availability of these species (Ames 1985). Further intensification of fish exploitation may involve attempts to widen the resource base by obtaining smaller fish, non-schooling fish, or those located further from the coastal zone (often with the use of more complex fishing equipment) and/or it may involve changes in social organization that allow further intensification of anadromous fishing. Further intensification of shellfish exploitation may similarly involve exploitation of harder-to-obtain species, as well as smaller individuals of more "valuable" species—i.e., those that normally provide higher returns for energy invested in exploiting them (Yesner 1984b). Among societies that are buffered by a wide variety of marine resources, intensification of sea-mammal hunting (e.g., the hunting of large baleen whales) is not often observed (Ames 1985). This seems to have occurred primarily in the Arctic zone, beyond the northern limits of both anadromous fish and shellfish populations.

In sum, coastal resources do not make up a Garden of Eden, but neither are they clearly second-rate resources in the sense proposed by Osborn (1977). The relatively late adoption of this class of foods is not explained by appealing to such simple models, but instead by developing more complex models relating the use of marine resources to environmental change, technological development, and human population growth. As noted above, the frequent use of coastal resources during the spring season suggests that at least one purpose of utilizing those resources was to minimize subsistence risk at times of the year when other resources were either unavailable or inaccessible; this appears to have occurred in environments with significant seasonal or longer-term fluctuations in the food supply. At the same time, such foods contained important nutrients that might otherwise have been limiting factors in the food supply, even though they may have been relatively low in per unit energy yield. However, because of that energy cost, the exploitation of coastal resources did not occur until population growth had reduced locally available alternatives and forced an expansion of dietary breadth and "retooling" costs had been met. (In keeping with the tenets of optimal foraging theory, at no time was the relative abundance of these resources an issue.) Once the above set of processes is understood, the fact that coastal resources, often highly productive as well as reliable, were not exploited until relatively late should not be considered any more of a paradox than the fact that agriculture, which also greatly increased both the productivity and the security of human subsistence, was even later in its adoption.

Perhaps the lack of a clear-cut advantage or disadvantage to the use of marine resources, however, is the reason why, even in those temperate zones where aquatic resources were more prevalent in the diet (Lee 1968), seafoods rarely appear to have formed the greater part of that diet. Meehan's (1977, 1982) work suggests that shellfishing, for example, never provided more than about 15 percent of the diet of coastal peoples. The major exceptions here, of course, are high-latitude populations with a high degree of dependence on coastal resources, particularly sea mammals and fish. In many cases the dependence on marine resources was a function not only of the productivity of the coastal zone itself, but also of the productivity, stability, and nutrient yields of interior environments adjacent to the coast.

Unfortunately the degree of dependence of prehistoric populations on marine resources can be assessed with confidence only when very detailed archaeological faunal and floral analyses can be undertaken and sampling effects can be sufficiently controlled to allow rigorous quantitative dietary estimates. However, the advent of stable carbon, nitrogen, and strontium isotopic ratio analyses for human bone has allowed us to reconstruct the contribution of marine resources to prehistoric diets with a greater degree of precision. Recently, for example, it has been established that about 90 percent of the protein intake on the British Columbia coast was from marine resources (Chisholm, Nelson, and Schwartz 1983), which exceeds available ethnographic estimates (Murdock 1967), as well as archaeological estimates (Boucher 1976), by about 35 percent. These discrepancies are worth noting, particularly for areas in which little or no quantitative ethnographic data exist. For example, I have recently undertaken analyses of both stable carbon and nitrogen isotopes from a series of skeletons from Moshier Island in Casco Bay, Maine (dated to ca. 1000 A.D.), which suggest that 80 percent of the diet was from marine resources; this appears to exceed the estimates from faunal analysis by about 20 percent. However, such statistics may be meaningless unless we know how much seasonal movement and food storage was undertaken by these groups. In the case of our research in coastal Maine, fish vertebra and shellfish sectioning has demonstrated a pattern of seasonal transhumance; the coast was occupied primarily during the spring (i.e., from late winter to early summer), and codfish were stored in the large pits found in some coastal sites. Unfortunately, since the preservation of faunal remains in interior sites is very poor, it is impossible to fill out the seasonal round in the same rigorous fashion. It is doubtful, therefore, whether ecofactual analyses from coastal sites will ever be as rigorous as the chemical analyses now being developed for the examination of human bone.

Consequences of the Adoption of Marine Diets

To this point I have focused primarily on the causes, rather than the consequences, of the adoption of marine diets by human societies. In this section, I want to turn instead to four related aspects of human society affected by the shift to seafood diets: (1) population mobility; (2) population density; (3) population health; and (4) sociopolitical complexity. Let me deal with each of these in turn.

Population Mobility

Elsewhere (Yesner 1980) I have characterized coastal lifeways as "semi-sedentary," typified by "communities whose members shift from one to another fixed settlement at different seasons, or who occupy more or less permanently a single settlement from which a substantial proportion of the population departs seasonally to occupy shifting camps" (Binford 1980:13). Coastal settlement allows "central-place foraging," primarily with the use of boats, a strategy that promotes sedentism and thereby reduces mobility costs in the exploitation of resources. However, a great deal of variation in settlement pattern among coastal societies is encompassed within the general framework of "semi-sedentary," central-place foraging. For example, on one extreme the Yahgan of southern Patagonia used canoes for daily outings but returned to different camps every few days, possibly to prevent overexploitation of shellfish beds in an area where marine invertebrates were rather scantily distributed, sea mammal resources were limited and anadramous fish resources were absent (Stuart 1972, 1977). On the other extreme, Northwest Coast Indians and Bering Sea Eskimos were characterized by relatively little mobility, primarily of task groups and nuclear family units; such sedentism seems to be related in particular to the availability of anadromous fish (Schalk 1977).

Among the factors determining the degree of mobility necessary to obtain marine resources are the following:

1. The diversity and abundance of resources available within the coastal zone

2. The productivity of terrestrial environments adjacent to the coastal zone

3. Temporal variations in the strength of nutrient upwelling systems

4. The frequency and timing of migrations of marine species, and the importance of these migratory species in the overall diet

5. Variations in marine resource aggregation (e.g., the number of rookeries, colonies, or haulouts, and their spatial distribution)

The nutritional quality of coastal resources also has important constraining effects on population mobility. Several years ago I argued (Yesner 1979) that mesolithic coastal populations that focused almost exclusively on shellfish would have been forced into some degree of transhumance in order to supply some important nutrients that would otherwise be missing in the diet. It is equally important to consider fluctuations in the nutritional quality of seafoods, something that affects nearly all coastal populations regardless of diet, but again particularly affects those dependent on marine resources. The fat content of sea mammals and sea birds fluctuates seasonally, like that of terrestrial mammals and birds. Among anadromous fish and shellfish, fluctuation in fat content is related primarily to spawning or reproductive cycles, which vary among species. As noted above, shellfish also vary in protein content, having a "protein peak" that, again, differs by species. These variations in protein and fat content could well be limiting factors on coastal populations and need to be taken into account more often in developing models of seasonal population movements by these peoples. An additional factor to be considered in developing such models is the timing of "red tide" infestations in shellfish and other seafoods during the late spring and early summer.

Population Density

The constraints of coastal lifeways on human population densities are more difficult to assess. High local population densities among coastal groups may in some cases be less a function of ecosystem richness per se than of local concentrations of resources ("species packing") in areas such as estuaries, island passes (where upwelling takes place), peninsulas (which funnel migratory sea-mammals), or areas where streams, lakes, or marshes about the coast (where there is a high diversity of fish, birds, and small mammals). In addition, the productivity of the terrestrial zone adjacent to the coast may have as much to do with aboriginal coastal population density as the richness of the coast itself, particularly in lower latitudes where the major function of coastal resources may be as a dietary protein supplement (Osborn 1980).

On the basis of both the archaeological and ethnographic records, it has been argued that population densities are higher in coastal regions. Numerous authors have argued that increased sedentism alone offers a robust explanation for population growth, resulting from increased fertility associated with changes in exercise patterns, male absenteeism, female work load (including carrying of infants), and desire for children.

If population growth potential is indeed higher for coastal societies, this suggests that pressure on resources would be likely to occur every so often. Seeking objective evidence for such population pressure, however, is difficult at best. If we follow Cohen's (1975) caveat, however, that one of the best dicators of population pressure is the increasing use of more marginal habitats, then my research in both the Aleutian Islands and on the coast of Maine has demonstrated that, indeed, continued population growth and pressure on resources have been occurring since mid-Holocene times. This expansion involves the use of microenvironments with less species diversity, such as straighter, less complex (and hence less biotically diverse) coastlines, as well as areas with lower species abundance, such as small, offshore islands (Yesner 1984b; Yesner and Aigner 1976). Even for North America as a whole, it is possible to show that areas such as the California Channel Islands or the Florida Keys were occupied relatively late in the prehistoric record, at the end of a period of continuous local population growth.

Population Health

The diets of coastal peoples generally provided enough calories to support relatively large population densities (Yesner 1980) and may be related to an earlier menarche as well as greater life expectancy among coastal societies. This does not mean, of course, that no health problems were created by occasional population "pressure" on resources or by inadequacies in the marine diets themselves. There is, however, very little evidence of nutritionally related disease among coastal groups. For example, the only major forms of paleopathology consistently associated with coastal peoples are activity-related ones, particularly dental attrition (and its consequences), and degenerative and traumatic disorders (e.g., osteoarthritis). These are found with particularly high frequency in Arctic populations but are also high in other coastal populations, such as aboriginal California (Jurmain 1983; Leigh 1928; Walker 1978). We have found a similar pattern in our skeletal series from Moshier Island on the Maine coast (Yesner n.d.b). In areas in which skeletal indicators of acute nutritional deficiency (such as Harris lines) have been found, as in coastal California (McHenry 1968), they have been associated with periods in which *less* use of marine foods was taking place.

However, it is still possible that *chronic* nutritional stress may have been occurring in these populations. The fact that the frequency of enamel hypoplasia (16.7 percent) is somewhat higher than that of Harris lines (10.4 percent) in these coastal California groups may indeed suggest some nutritional stress (McHenry and Schulz 1975; but see Chapter 10). Additionally, cribra orbitalia has been noted among groups such as California coastal Indians (Walker 1986) and Northwest Coast Indians (Cybulski 1978; Gordon 1974), but "it is difficult to reconcile the findings in terms of possible deficiency in dietary intake of iron in the earlier British Columbia population," since the aboriginal diet of fish, shellfish, and sea mammals was iron-rich (Cybulski 1978:37). Other factors, such as hereditary patterns or infectious diseases, might be at fault, and infectious diseases or metabolic disorders might also explain some of the "growth-arrest" indicators seen in human skeletons from coastal areas. In this case, of course, an increased load of infectious disease might reflect the effects of higher population density, although no evidence has been found of infectious

301

disorders associated with iron-deficiency anemias (e. g., tuberculosis), which *do* leave their mark on bone.

Sociopolitical Complexity

As noted earlier, the range of cultural complexity associated with maritime populations ranges from band-level organization (e. g., among the Yahgan) to incipient state-level societies (e. g., on the prehistoric coast of Peru). However, these extremes appear to be associated with an unusual paucity and abundance of resources, respectively (Jackson and Popper 1980; Osborn 1977; Stuart 1972). The most commonly cited models for coastal societies involve "big-man" types of political organization or chiefdoms characterized by incipient social stratification. A greater degree of cultural complexity seems likely to occur where anadromous fish are a significant element in the diet of coastal peoples, since their predictability in space and time allows for a good deal of control over these resources, including the restriction of access to the more productive fishing locales (Schalk 1977). Hierarchical leadership may have evolved in such regions in order to coordinate the complex scheduling required for catching, processing, and storing spatiotemporally aggregated anadromous fish resources (Ames 1985). In general, coastal groups tend to display a greater degree of sociocultural complexity than other hunter-gatherers, and Cohen (1981) has suggested that this may directly result from the higher population density achieved in coastal regions. He cites the following connections between high population density and increased cultural complexity: (1) less room for spatial adjustment to resource failure; (2) fewer "emergency" food resources available; and (3) less "social flexibility" in adjustment to resource variations. Thus, "the elaboration of material culture and of social hierarchies . . . may reflect a social response to economic vulnerability in the face of resource failure—the vulnerability resulting from high population density" (Cohen 1981:275).

Two commonly employed archaeological indices of greater cultural complexity found among coastal peoples are the elaboration of grave goods and the presence of exotic items, reflecting an elaboration of ritual and the development of widespread trade networks managed by an elite group. On the basis of these indices, King (1978) and others have demonstrated that a cultural complexity above the band level existed in aboriginal California. Zvelebil (1986) has developed similar arguments for Mesolithic Europe. In northern New England as well, the widespread appearance of exotic materials such as Lake Superior copper in coastal burials suggests some evolution of cultural complexity. (In all three cases however, there is relatively little difference in the quantity or quality of grave goods buried with different individuals, suggesting the presence of only incipient social stratification.) These archaeological data from coastal societies help us to make sense out of ethnographic accounts of, for example, the so-called sagamores and sachems on the New England coast, and the doyons of the Aleutian Islands.

Although marine resources may have most commonly supported only incipient stratified societies, there is evidence to suggest that they may have helped to support more complex societies as well. Lange (1971), for example, has made an excellent case for the importance of marine resources in supporting the framework of the lowland Maya civilization, and, as suggested earlier, these resources were also important to highland Meso-American civilizations (Stark and Vorrhies 1978). Coastal Peru, however, still appears to be unique in the degree of cultural complexity that was supported by a marine food base there (Moseley 1975; Osborn 1977). In that area, original interest in the coast may have been fed by a tremendous local seasonal variation in terrestrial food supply, as well as by the availability of a rich coastal zone. An unusual degree of fluctuation in *coastal* resources (which, as noted above, are generally more reliable over time), due to the phenomenon of El Niño, in turn promoted increased cultural complexity in Peru. In addition, the juxtaposition of a relatively rich coastal zone with a depauperate interior zone created unique ecological conditions favorable to the evolution of redistributive systems, which in turn contributed to cultural complexity in that area; Kelly (1983) has recently offered a similar argument for the origin of the Northwest Coast cultural pattern. Population "spillover" from densely populated coastal zones to adjacent resource-poor interior zones may also have promoted an increased interest in horticulture, whether in Peru or in the U.S. Southwest (Glassow 1972). Thus, to return to Binford's (1983) original question about the apparent differences in receptivity to agriculture in coastal regions, it may well be that the reasons that California Indians did not adopt agriculture had more to do with the relative richness of both the coast *and* the (acorn-using) interior zone than with the richness of the coast alone.

One final element needs to be considered as well: that of resource failure. Zvelebil (1986:114) has recently noted that "farming was not necessarily advantageous . . . for communities that specialized in exploiting aquatic resources," and that this may have led to a delay in commitment to a farming way of life among such littoral hunter-gatherers in temperate Europe. Yet, paradoxically, it was the commitment to such a coastal lifeway that led these mesolithic Europeans down the road toward agriculture. Although their lifeway "was capable of supporting relatively high population densities and of absorbing some fluctuations in resources," when major crises occurred in sea-mammals and a shellfish in various parts of Scandinavia—whether as a result of climate change or culturally-induced factors—such coastal foraging economies could no longer be maintained, and were quickly replaced by farming populations. In this light, the "Garden of Eden" principle can be seen *both* as the reason for the original rejection of agriculture *and* as the eventual causative agent for the acceptance of agriculture. Risk-reducing strategies are apparently maintained by human societies until the risks themselves make them no longer tenable; at that point, other risk-reducing strategies are implemented. Certainly, like the maritime adaptations that preceded them, the ostensibly risk-reducing farming strategy contained within it the seeds of even greater risks for growing human populations.

Conclusion

Coastal resources are neither a "Garden of Eden" nor second-rate resources; they allow neither total mobility nor permanent settlement; and a wide variation in degree of social stratification is found among societies exploiting these resources. Variations in these phenomena may have more to do with the relationship of coastal and interior zones than with the nature of coastal resources alone. However, while recognizing this variability in subsistence, settlement, and sociopolitical organization, we can discern a number of consistent patterns in the preceding analysis of coastal adaptations. To begin with, the pattern of delayed adoption of marine diets is observable worldwide. This phenomenon can best be explained as a result of concurrent forces of environmental change (especially increased seasonality and environmental patchiness) and population growth, during a period of rapid technological change, including the development of food storage technology. The consequences of the adoption of marine diets included more sedentary lifestyles and further increases in population density; these increases may have had some consequences for individual health as well as for the generation of social complexity. Our work on the Maine coast is also beginning to suggest that, in a feedback fashion, the population growth associated with semi-sedentary coastal societies forces an even greater commitment to a coastal diet. As with the origins of agriculture, an element of irreversibility seems to be associated with this important transition in human lifeways.

Acknowledgments

Much of the fieldwork in the Aleutian Islands and the Maine coast was supported by grants from the National Science Foundation and the Maine Historic Preservation Commission. I would like to thank all of the conference participants who commented on my paper, and particularly Jane Buikstra, who suggested revisions that were extremely helpful in the redrafting of some of the ideas.

References Cited

Allen, H.
    1979   Left Out in the Cold: Why the Tasmanians Stopped Eating Fish. *Artefact* 4:1–10.

Ames, K.
    1985   Hierarchies, Stress, and Logistical Strategies Among Hunter-Gatherers in Northwestern North America. In *Prehistoric Hunter-Gatherers: The Emergence of Cultural Complexity,* T. D. Price and J. A. Brown, eds., pp. 155–80. Orlando: Academic Press.

Arimoto, K.
    1962   The Role of Fish in the Japanese Diet. In *Fish as Food,* G. Borgstrom, ed., pp. 370–71. New York: Academic Press.

Aschmann, H.
    1975   Culturally Determined Recognition of Food Resources in the Coastal Zone. *Geoscience and Man* 12:43–47.

Binford, L. R.
    1980   Willow Smoke and Dogs' Tails: Hunter-Gatherer Settlement Systems and Archaeological Site Formation. *American Antiquity* 45:4–20.
    1983   *In Pursuit of the Past.* New York: Thames and Hudson.

Borgstrom, G.
    1962   Shellfish Protein—Nutritive Aspects. In *Fish as Food,* G. Borgstrom, ed., pp. 115–47. New York: Academic Press.

Botkin, S.
    1980   Effects of Human Exploitation on Shellfish Populations at Malibu Creek, California. In *Modeling Change in Prehistoric Subsistence Economies,* T. K. Earle and A. L. Christenson, eds., pp. 121–40. New York: Academic Press.

Boucher, N. D.
    1976   Prehistoric Subsistence at the Helen Point Site. M.A. thesis, Simon Fraser University, Burnaby, British Columbia.

Bowdler, S.
    1980   Fish and Culture: A Tasmanian Polemic. *Mankind* 12:334–40.

Chisholm, B. S.; D. E. Nelson; and H. P. Schwartz
    1983   Determination of the Relative Intakes of Marine and Terrestrial Protein by the Prehistoric Inhabitants of the British Columbia Coast. *Current Anthropology* 24:396–98.

Clark, G.; L. Straus; J. Altuna; and J. Ortea
    1980   Ice Age Subsistence in Northern Spain. *Scientific American* 242 (June):142–53.

Cohen, M. N.
    1975   Archaeological Evidence for Population Pressure in Pre-Agricultural So-cieties. *American Antiquity* 40:471–75.
    1977   *The Food Crisis in Prehistory.* New Haven: Yale University Press.
    1981   Pacific Coast Foragers: Affluent or Overcrowded? In *Affluent Foragers: Pacific Coasts East and West,* S. Koyama and D. H. Thomas, eds., pp. 275–95. Osaka: National Museum of Ethnology.

Cybulski, J.
    1978   Cribra orbitalia, a Possible Sign of Anemia in Early Native Populations of the British Columbia Coast. *American Journal of Physical Anthropology* 47:31–40.

Domning, D. P.
    1972   Steller's Sea Cow and the Origins of North Pacific Aboriginal Whaling. *Syesis* 5:187–89.

Erlandson, J.
    1983   The Role of Shellfish in Coastal Economies: A Protein Perspective. Paper read at the meeting of the Alaska Anthropological Association, Anchorage.

Felger, R., and M. B. Moser
    1973   Eelgrass (*Zostera marina*) in the Gulf of California: Discovery of Its Nutritional Value by the Seri Indians. *Science* 181:355–56.

Fischer, S., and P. C. Weber
    1984   Prostaglandin I_3 Is Formed *in vivo* in Man After Dietary Eicosapentaenoic Acid. *Nature* 307:165–68.

Glassow, M.
    1972   Changes in the adaptations of Southwestern Basketmakers: A Systems Perspective. In *Contemporary Archaeology,* M. P. Leone, ed., pp. 289–302. Carbondale: Southern Illinois University Press.

Gordon, M. E.
    1974   A Qualitative Analysis of Human Skeletal Remains from Gabriola Island, British Columbia. M.A. thesis, University of Calgary.

Harris, D. R.
    1982   The Prehistory of Human Subsistence: A Speculative Outline. In *Food, Nutrition, and Evolution: Food as an Environmental Factor in the Genesis of Human Variability,* D. N. Walcher and N. Kretchmer, eds., pp. 15–35. New York: Masson.

Hayden, B.
    1981   Research and Development in the Stone Age: Technological Transitions Among Hunter-Gatherers. *Current Anthropology* 22:519–48.

Heller, C. A., and E. M. Scott
    1962   The Alaska Dietary Survey. Washington, D.C.: Government Printing Office.

Hill, K.
    1982   Hunting and Human Evolution. *Journal of Human Evolution* 11:521–44.

Horton, D. R.
    1979   Tasmanian Adaptation. *Mankind* 12:28–34.

Jackson, H. E., and V. Popper
    1980   Coastal Hunter-Gatherers: The Yahgan of Tierra del Fuego. In *The Ar-chaeological Correlates of Hunter-Gatherer Societies: Studies from the Ethnographic Record,* F. E. Smiley et al., eds., pp. 40–61. Ann Arbor: University of Michigan Museum of Anthropology.

Jones, R.
    1977   The Tasmanian Paradox. In Stone Tools as Cultural Markers, R. V. S. Wright, ed., pp. 189–204. Canberra: Australian Institute for Aboriginal Studies.
    1978   Why Did the Tasmanians Stop Eating Fish? In *Explorations in Eth-noarchaeology,* R. Gould, ed., pp. 11–47. Albuquerque: University of New Mexico Press.

Jurmain, R. D.
    1982   Paleoepidemiology of a Native Californian Skeletal Population. *American Journal of Physical Anthropology* 51:211–12.

Kelly, R. L.
    1983   Hunter-Gatherer Mobility Strategies. *Journal of Anthropological Research* 39:277–306.

King, T. F.
    1978   Don't That Beat the Band? Nonegalitarian Political Organization in Pre-historic Central California. In *Social Archaeology: Beyond Subsistence and Dating,* C. Redman et al., eds., pp. 225–48. New York: Academic Press.

Lange, F. W.
    1971   Marine Resources: A Viable Subsistence Alternative for the Prehistoric Lowland Maya. *American Anthropologist* 73:619–39.

Laughlin, W. S.
    1972   Ecology and Population Structure in the Arctic. In *The Structure of Human Populations,* G. A. Harrison and A. J. Boyce, eds., pp. 379–92. Oxford: Clarendon Press.

Lee, R. B.
    1968   What Hunters Do for a Living; or, How to Make Out on Scarce Re-sources. In *Man the Hunter,* R. B. Lee and I. DeVore, eds., pp. 30–48. Chicago: Aldine.

Leigh, R. W.
    1928   Dental Pathology of Aboriginal California. *University of California Pub-lications in American Archaeology and Ethnography* 23:399–423.

Lischka, J. J.
    1979   On the Evaluation of Marine and Terrestrial Food Resources. Manu-script. Department of Anthropology, University of Colorado, Boulder.

Lischka, J. J., and P. D. Sheets
    1980   Comments on "Maritime Hunter-Gatherers: Ecology and Prehistory." *Current Anthropology* 21:739–40.

Loomis, F.
    1911   A New Mink from the Shell-Heaps of Maine. *American Journal of Science* 181:227–29.

Lumley, H. de
    1969   A Paleolithic Camp at Nice. *Scientific American* 220 (May):42–50.
McHenry, H.
    1968   Transverse Lines in Long Bones of Prehistoric California Indians. *American Journal of Physical Anthropology* 29:1–18.
McHenry, H. M., and P. D. Schulz
    1975   The Association Between Harris Lines and Enamel Hypoplasia in Prehistoric California Indians. *American Journal of Physical Anthropology* 44:507–12.
Meehan, B.
    1977   Man Does Not Live by Calories Alone: The Role of Shellfish in a Coastal Cuisine. In *Sunda and Sahul: Prehistoric Studies in Southeast Asia,* J. J. Allen et al., eds., pp. 493–531. New York: Academic Press.
    1982   *Shell Bed to Shell Midden.* Canberra: Australian Institute of Aboriginal Studies.
Meighan, C.
    1983   Maritime Adaptation and Midden Analysis in California. Paper read at the meeting of the Society for American Archaeology, Pittsburgh, Pa.
Moseley, M.
    1975   *The Maritime Foundations of Andean Civilization.* Menlo Park, Calif.: Cummings.
Murdock, G. P.
    1967   Ethnographic Atlas. Pittsburgh: University of Pittsburgh Press.
Nietschmann, B.
    1972   Hunting and Fishing Focus Among the Miskito Indians, Eastern Nicaragua. *Human Ecology* 1:41–67.
    1973   *Between Land and Water.* New York: Seminar Press.
O'Connell, J. F., and K. Hawkes
    1981   Alyawara Plant Use and Optimal Foraging Theory. In *Hunter-Gatherer Foraging STrategies: Ethnographic and Archaeological Analyses,* B. Winterhalder and E. A. Smith, eds., pp. 99–125. Chicago: University of Chicago Press.
Osborn, A. J.
    1977   Strandloopers, Mermaids, and Other Fairy Tales: Ecological Determinants of Marine Resource Utilization. In *For Theory Building in Archaeology: Essays on Faunal Remains, Aquatic Resources, Spatial Analysis, and Systemic Modeling,* L. R. Binford, ed., pp. 157–205. New York: Academic Press.
    1980   Aboriginal Coastal Population Density: Toward the Resolution of a Paradox. Paper read at the meeting of the Society for American Archaeology, Philadelphia, Pa.
Perlman, S.
    1976   Optimum Diet Models and Prehistoric Hunter-Gatherers: A Test on Martha's Vineyard. Ann Arbor: University Microfilms.
Russell-Hunter, W. D.
    1970   *Aquatic Productivity.* New York: Macmillan.

Schalk, R. F.
  1977   The Structure of an Anadromous Fish Resource. In *For Theory Building in Archaeology: Essays on Faunal Remains, Aquatic Resources, Spatial Analysis, and Systemic Modeling,* L. R. Binford, ed., pp. 207–50. New York: Academic Press.

Shawcross, W. F.
  1975   Some Studies of the Influences of Prehistoric Human Predation on Marine Animal Population Dynamics. In *Maritime Adaptations of the Pacific,* R. W. Casteel and G. I. Quimby, eds., pp. 39–66. The Hague: Mouton.

Shodell, M.
  1983   The Prostaglandin Connection. *Science* 83:78–82.

Simms, S. R.
  1983   The Evolution of Hunter-Gatherer Foraging Strategies. Paper read at the meeting of the Society for American Archaeology, Pittsburgh, Pa.

Simoons, F. J.
  1974a   Fish as Forbidden Food. *Ecology of Food and Nutrition* 3:185–201.
  1974b   Rejection of Fish as Human Food in Africa: A Problem in History and Ecology. *Ecology of Food and Nutrition* 3:158–64.

Singer, R., and J. Wymer
  1982   *The Middle Stone Age at Klasies River Mouth in South Africa.* Chicago: University of Chicago Press.

Stark, B. L., and B. Voorhies
  1978   *Prehistoric Coastal Adaptations.* New York: Academic Press.

Stuart, D. E.
  1972   Band Structure and Ecological Variability: The Ona and Yahgan of Tierra del Fuego. Ann Arbor: University Microfilms.
  1977   Seasonal Phases in Ona Subsistence, Territorial Distribution, and Organization: Implications for the Archaeological Record. In *For Theory Building in Archaeology: Essays on Faunal Remains, Aquatic Resources, Spatial Analysis, and Systemic Modeling,* L. R. Binford, ed., pp. 251–86. New York: Academic Press.

Swadling, P.
  1976   Changes Induced by Human Exploitation in Prehistoric Shellfish Populations. *Mankind* 10:156–62.
  1977a   Implications of Shellfish Exploitation for New Zealand Prehistory. *Mankind* 11:11–18.
  1977b   Depletion of Shellfish in the Traditional Gathering Beds of Pari. In *The Melanesian Environment,* J. H. Winslow, ed., pp. 182–87. Canberra: Australian National University Press.

Tartaglia, L. J.
  1976   Prehistoric Maritime Adaptations in Southern California. Ann Arbor: University Microfilms.

Toyama, Y., and T. Kaneda
  1962   Nutritive Aspects of Fish Oils. In *Fish as Food,* G. Borastrom, ed., pp. 149–73. New York: Academic Press.

309

Volman, T. P.
    1978   Early Archaeological Evidence for Shellfish Collecting. *Science* 201:911–13.
Walker, P. L.
    1978   A Quantitative Analysis of Dental Attrition Rates in the Santa Barbara Channel Area. *American Journal of Physical Anthropology* 48:101–6.
    1986   Porotic Hyperostosis in a Marine-Dependent California Indian Population. *American Journal of Physical Anthropology* 69:345–54.
Yesner, D. R.
    1974   Population Pressure in Coastal Environments: an Archaeological Test. *World Archaeology* 16:108–27.
    1977   Resource Diversity and Population Stability Among Hunter-Gatherers. *Western Canadian Journal of Anthropology* 7:18–59.
    1979   Nutrition and Cultural Evolution: Patterns in Prehistory. In *Nutritional Anthropology,* N. Jerome et al., eds., pp. 85–116. Pleasantville, New York: Redgrave.
    1980   Maritime Hunter-Gatherers: Ecology and Prehistory. *Current Anthropology* 21:727–50.
    1981   Archaeological Applications of Optimal Foraging Theory: Harvesting Strategies of Aleut Hunter-Gatherers. In *Hunter-Gatherer Foraging Strategies: Ethnographic and Archaeological Analyses,* B. Winterhalder and E. A. Smith, eds., pp. 148–70. Chicago: University of Chicago Press.
    1983   On Explaining Changes in Prehistoric Coastal Economies: The View from Casco Bay. In *The Evolution of Maritime Cultures on the Northeast and Northwest Coasts of America,* . J. Nash, ed., pp. 77–90. Burnaby, B.C., Department of Archaeology, Simon Fraser University.
    1984a   The Structure and Function of Prehistoric Households in Northern New England. *Man in the Northeast* 28:51–72.
    n.d.a   Comparative Hunting Efficiencies for Arctic and Subarctic Species. Manuscript. Portland: Department of Geography-Anthropology, University of Southern Maine.
    n.d.b   Prehistoric Maritime Adaptation in Southwestern Maine: Isotopic Evidence from the Moshier Island Burial Site. Paper presented to Chacmool Conference, Calgary, 1986.
Yesner, D. R., and J. S. Aigner
    1976   Comparative Biomass Estimates and Prehistoric Cultural Ecology of the Southwest Umnak Region, Aleutian Islands. *Arctic Anthropology* 13:91–112.
Zvelebil, M.
    1986   Postglacial Foraging in the Forests of Europe. *Scientific American* 254 (5):104–15.

BRUCE WINTERHALDER

The Analysis of Hunter-Gatherer Diets: Stalking an Optimal Foraging Model

MY TITLE ALLUDES TO HUNTING. THE IMAGERY IS DELIBERATE: I intend a somewhat predatory engagement with the subject. How do ecological factors affect hunter-gatherer decisions about the harvest of non-produced food resources? What are the ecological strategies of the food quest? And, especially, how does one go about asking these questions? What is a productive or heuristically useful research procedure? I will suggest that the analytic process is a little like foraging itself. The inquiry is, in a sense, the quarry.

This paper has three parts: (1) a brief statement about the methodology of evolutionary ecology that focuses on assumptions and attempts to convey a particular attitude toward this kind of invesgiation; (2) a quick summary of applications, giving evidence that the assumptions are not so unrealistic nor the effort so unrewarding as they may seem after the first part; and (3) an exploration that attempts to extend the models while showing more precisely what they cannot do.

A Brief Historical Digression

I will begin indirectly, with an older but similar biological model, the logistic equation, developed first by Verhulst in the 1840s but promoted and popularized by Pearl in the 1920s. The history of the equation (Kingsland 1982) contains lessons about the strengths and limitations of foraging models.

The logistic is a systematic expression of a set of biological relationships (Figure 12.1). It has an easily visualized graphic form, the s-curve. It can be stated as an intuitively appealing equation of several variables. It also raises some hard, though usually implicit, questions. What kind of scientific status do we give to a creature like this? For what is it best used?

FIGURE 12.1. The Logistic Curve and Equation

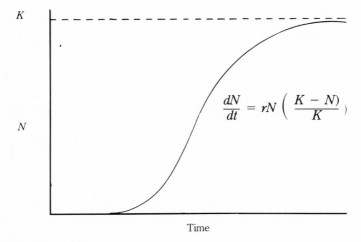

$$\frac{dN}{dt} = rN \left(\frac{K - N)}{K} \right)$$

Time

NOTE: See Hutchinson (1978) for a definition of the terms in the equation.

Verhulst was after a calculating device (*"logistique"*) derived from first princi-ples. He had practical problems in mind—the limitations of Belgian farmland, for one. In contrast, Pearl developed the formula directly from empirical data and promoted it as a Law, comparable "in a modest way" to Boyle's and Kep-ler's laws. Pearl devoted much of his scientific work to showing that population-growth data sets fit the logistic curve. This required second-order corrections in the equation and some creative attention to the data as well. Pearl's pro-mulgation of the equation in this manner led to clamorous debates, as econo-mists, statisticians, and demographers pointed out that its assumptions were artificial and that the fudging required to preserve its lawfulness was counter-productive.

Others approached the equation differently. Lotka realized the potential of closely investigating the r term. His pursuit of that component led to formulas relating population growth rates to age structure. The logistic gave Lotka entry to demographic questions going beyond the equation itself. He said of it: "An empirical formula is . . . not so much the solution of a problem as the challenge to such a solution. It is a point of interrogation, an animated question mark" (quoted in Kingsland 1982:42). Gause (1934) realized that the growth-resistance term—$(K - N)/K$—expressed competitive processes like those envisioned in Darwinian natural selection. He extended the model to two com-peting species and used it as a tool for the analysis of resource competition and co-existence. In his experimental work he attempted to estimate model parameters directly, but he did not confuse the equation with a realistic portrayal of nature.

The debates provoked by Pearl are forgotten; the approaches developed by Lotka and Gause permeate evolutionary biology. Kingsland's summary indicates why:

> The logistic curve cannot be tested by comparison with observations, as one would test a scientific hypothesis, for it is neither a law nor a hypothesis, but a logical argument based on a variety of assumptions. By looking at deviations from the logistic curve, however, one can refine these assumptions to gain a more accurate understanding of how a population behaves. The logistic can therefore be useful as a tool of research even though it is not a realistic description of growth. (Kingsland 1982:41)

Optimal foraging models are valuable in much the same way—not as lawful statements about reality, but as structured forms of inquiry, more interesting to stalk than to live by.

Assumptions, Procedures, and Two Basic Models

Optimization as a Working Principle

Optimization is the outcome of selection in a finite environment. Resource competition gives the edge to organisms more efficient at gaining energy and nutrients to expend on more foraging, the search for mates, or avoidance of predators and hazards. This is a neo-Darwinian article of faith, although competition is remarkably difficult to observe in nature (Connell 1975; Schoener 1982; Wiens 1977).

The extensive use in evolutionary ecology of optimization and cost-benefit assessments has led to a serious debate about their validity and merits (Gould and Lewontin 1979; Lewontin 1978; Maynard Smith 1978). I argue (Winterhalder 1981a:15) that optimization principles provide a structured, contingent, and partial guide: an entry to inquiry rather than an acceptable proposition about nature. They are structured because they allow one to devise hypotheses or predictions about adaptive behaviors in well-defined conditions. They are contingent because no set of conditions has complete theoretical generality. They are partial because they assist one in speculating about selection at the expense of attention to other aspects of the evolutionary process. In general, they make explicit and thus open to scrutiny a widespread form of functionalist reasoning (Smith and Winterhalder 1981).

The optimization principle relevant to what follows is this: human foragers

313

will adopt behaviors that allow them to achieve the highest possible net rate of energy capture *while foraging*. Note the phrase "while foraging." It circumvents the assumption that hunter-gatherers attempt to maximize (or minimize) resource use in general. It leaves open the question of how long an organism forages. It is a postulate of scarcity for analytic purposes, not a statement about actual scarcity. It is a formal, operational way of stating a commonsense hypothesis: hunter-gatherers will have developed behaviors that make them as skillful and successful as is possible in the capture of game or harvesting of plants, relative to their effort. I will return below to the question of how long they forage.

The expectation of optimal results is more heuristic than realistic. Natural design highlights the efficacy of selection, but a careful look often shows that nature is "tinkered" together, to use Jacob's (1977) metaphor. Constraints arise from history, chance, and competing goals (Cody 1974). The appropriate pre-adaptations or phenotypic variance may not be present. Environmental fluctuations may impede or reverse directional evolution. Or the optimal responses for concurrent goals may conflict. Nature is less facile, it is messier, and it is not so single-minded as the methods of the evolutionary ecologist. Thus, the constraints themselves may be "more interesting and more important in delimiting pathways of change than the selective force that may mediate change when it occurs" (Gould and Lewontin 1979:581). Optimization analysis sensitive to this possibility is the best way to uncover the effects of such constraints.

The issue of constraints raises one of mechanism. Although Darwinian in origin, optimal foraging models can predict the effects of the selection of behavioral variants not associated with genetic variance (see discussion in Durham 1976; Orlove 1980; Pulliam 1981; Pyke, Pulliam, and Charnov 1977; Richerson 1977).

Simple and Compound Currencies

An optimization assumption requires a currency. Here again there is debate. A simple energy currency is used widely. It addresses several possibilities (Smith 1979): (1) energy may be periodically or chronically scarce; (2) foraging may expose the hunter-gatherer to greater-than-average hazards; or (3) foraging may divert valuable time from other activities. Energy, unlike some nutrients, is an immediate, recognizable need and hence a likely proximate guide to foraging behavior.

If, however, resources have several significant nutritional or non-food attributes, or complementary effects, then compound or linear programming models are required. Resources assessed by multiple attributes are not easily ranked; those with complementary effects cannot be assigned a value independently of one another (Rapport 1980; Westoby 1978). Few researchers have asked in what circumstances simple or compound currency models are more appropriate. In general, the foods of carnivores are of a high quality and roughly comparable in their nutrient mix. Attaining sufficient energy is likely to subsume other requirements (but see Speth and Spielmann 1983). The mixed diet of an omnivore may be nutritionally adequate even if "chosen" on the basis of an energy currency, but here nutrient considerations are more salient. The low and uneven quality of plant foods makes a presumptive case for compound currencies when these predominate in the diet.

Compound currencies require linear programming models, but I am wary of the view that complex nutritional models are more desirable because they appear to be more realistic. They incorporate more elements, but whether they accurately take account of them is more difficult to decide. Few of the input variables are known precisely (see Chapter 6), and although detailed, results can quickly become sensitive to these poorly understood parameters. Ethnographic study (Johnson and Behrens 1982) has shown that specific auxiliary information is needed to "calibrate" a linear programming model to particular circumstances and questions. Simple models are hedged with analytically penetrable uncertainties. As structured questions, their virtues diminish as their structure escapes comprehension.

Whatever the currency, most foraging models are deterministic. They are based on average or "expected" values and do not allow for the possibility that decisions respond to stochastic variability in the factors affecting foraging. I will return below to the question of stochasticity and risk (see Jochim 1982).

Models as Creatures That Are Good to Think

We seek, then, simple models that are good to think. These are not theories or hypotheses. Neither are they true or false in the manner of a lawful statement. Rather, they are valuable because they "generate good testable hypotheses relevant to important problems" (Levins 1966:430). A comprehensive theory about a subject is composed of a family of these models, each with its idiosyncracies. Thus, for modeling purposes "foraging" is artificially divided into "decision sets" (Krebs and Cowie 1976:100; Pyke, Pulliam, and Charnov 1977:140) related to such factors as diet breadth, foraging space, foraging period, and group size. Each model is uniquely relevant to a few questions and a small set of conditions. Models are not always clearly hierarchical, overlapping, or complementary. It is disconcerting to some that foraging theory works with such a motley set of individually limited tools, as if restricted applicability and the necessity to be selective were themselves a rebuke to the whole approach.

But this confuses something like a law, which is meant to be an accurate and universal representation, with something like a structured question. If models are the latter—good to think—then better many thoughts than a few.

The methodology, then, is built on (1) an optimization (or scarcity) assumption, to be distinguished from a belief that actual scarcity is a general condition; (2) a simple energy currency, tractable to those of us who can think about only a few things at a time; and (3) simple models meant to guide inquiry about a phenomenon, not to depict it.

The Diet-Breadth Model and the Marginal-Value Theorem

To exemplify this approach I will describe two key models. Consider a predator with prey scattered randomly through its environment. The diet-breadth model specifies the set (which and how many types) of resources this forager should pursue in order to achieve the highest net rate of energy intake while foraging (MacArthur and Pianka 1966; Pyke, Pulliam, and Charnov 1977:141). The assumptions of this model are as follows:

Currency:

1. The organism has the goal of maximizing its net rate of energy intake while foraging.

Constraints:

2. Prey are encountered randomly; the type encountered is independent of the last type encountered.

3. At a particular diet breadth, the organism always does or does not take a prey item; that is, there are no partial preferences.

4. Prey types have a stable ranking by net energy value per unit of pursuit and handling costs; that is, the quality of each prey type can be evaluated independently of other types.

5. Foraging can be divided into searching and pursuit phases, which are independent; that is, the predator searches for all prey jointly but pursues them singly.

6. Prey density is constant in a foraging interval; that is, the forager does not reach the end of its foraging range or overtake a constant rate of prey renewal during a foraging interval.

7. The benefits and costs associated with resources are treated as expected values, without relevant stochastic variance.

Despite its appearance, this is not a paralyzing list.

In graphic form (Figure 12.2), addition of each potential prey type reduces average search costs by an increment (ΔS) that can be plotted. The average

316

FIGURE 12.2. The MacArthur and Pianka (1966) Diet-Breadth Model and Equation

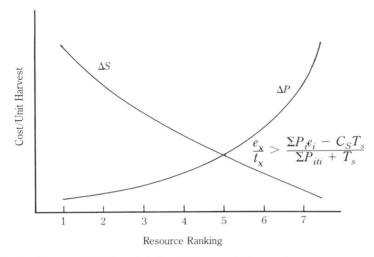

NOTE: See Schoener (1974) for a definition of the terms in the equation.

pursuit and handling time per unit of prey increases by an increment (ΔP) because the less desirable prey added are more difficult to capture or less rewarding when secured. The optimal diet includes all ranked prey types down to the last for which the incremental savings in search costs are larger than the incremental loss due to added pursuit costs (i.e., the last before the intersection of the curves). Virtually any factors that might affect foraging can be adapted to this "systematic argument" to form a hypothesis. Thus, decreased overall habitat richness raises average search costs and expands diet breadth by stepwise addition of items of lower rank. Or, increased pursuit capabilities lower average pursuit costs, with the same effect. An especially important prediction is the following: presence of a resource in the optimal diet is independent of its abundance. It depends rather on its rank, and on the abundance of items of higher rank.

The algebraic form specifies that an item x should be added to the diet only if its return relative to pursuit and handling costs (e_x/t_x) is greater than the average for the diet containing all items of higher rank. In other words, the optimal forager elects to pursue an item if and only if it does not expect, in the same interval of time, to both locate and capture a more valuable item.

The second model is the marginal-value theorem (Figure 12.3; Charnov 1976; Charnov, Orians, and Hyatt 1976). This model answers the question,

317

FIGURE 12.3. The Marginal-Value Theorem

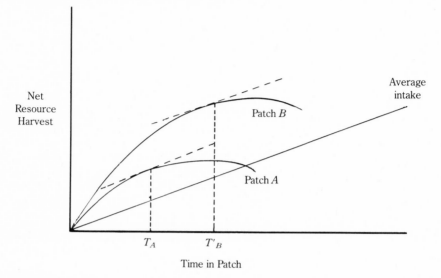

Time in Patch

NOTE: See Charnov 1976.

when should a forager leave one discrete patch to travel to another? The assumptions are:

Currency:

1. The forager attempts to maximize its net rate of energy intake.

Constraints:

2. Food is encountered within habitat patches.

3. Patches are encountered randomly.

4. Patches are not revisited before their resources recover from exploitation.

5. Travel between one or more patch types is non-productive or lost time.

6. As an organism forages within a patch, it depresses the rate of food intake because the prey become scarce or wary, or because they flee to other locations.

7. The relevant variables are characterized by expected value.

The model predicts that the optimal forager will leave a patch being harvested when the marginal capture rate there drops to the average rate of intake for the habitat. At this margin, the predator will do as well or better by seeking out an unexploited locale, even though some effort will be lost in traveling there. The optimal forager abandons particular spots before prey are fully depleted, and the higher the overall quality of the environment, the sooner it abandons them.

Anthropological Studies

I have tried to convey the assumptions and constraints that give optimal foraging theory its strength and also rather strongly restrict the range of issues that it may help to resolve. Whatever its attractiveness as an exercise in structured inquiry, or problem stalking, the success of optimal foraging theory depends on the guidance it offers in actual analyses. I will restrict a brief discussion to several ethnographic analyses that use simple currency models, and I will stress relevance to important problems rather than testability of hypotheses (see also Chapter 13). Smith (1983) presents a detailed review of the ethnographic research based on foraging theory; Keene (1979, 1981) and Reidhead (1979, 1980) focus on linear programming models and archaeological research. Yesner (Chapter 11) and Cohen (Chapter 10) give additional examples of the use of the models.

Cree Foraging

The first anthropological fieldwork guided by these models was my work with the boreal forest Cree-Ojibwa in 1975 (Winterhalder 1981b, 1983a, 1983b). For a year I traveled with Cree-Ojibwa foragers, timing and assessing the energy expenditure of foraging activities, mapping on airphotos their movement through the vegetation mosaic, weighing game captured, and discussing the tactics of foraging with my companions. The results were a modest confirmation of the diet-breadth and marginal-value theorem hypotheses and a more certain demonstration that the assumptions of another model, the patch-choice model (MacArthur and Pianka 1966), were frequently violated in the Cree-Ojibwa case.

For instance, historical changes in diet breadth give comparative evidence that fits the predictions of the diet-breadth model (Winterhalder 1981b, 1983b), and the qualitative dynamics of Cree-Ojbiwa foraging appear to confirm the marginal value theorem hypothesis. A forager nearly always leaves a localized patch of beaver, muskrat, or hare in search of another location before that patch is exhausted of capture opportunities. Equally interesting is the negative result. Using the MacArthur and Pianka (1966) model for patch choice, I predicted that habitat use would be quite generalized. In fact, not all patches containing sought game can be exploited. Anyone who has attempted to walk in thawed muskeg or to hunt a large, skittish herbivore like a moose in thick brush will understand immediately. And contrary to model assumptions, patches are not encountered randomly. The Cree-Ojibwa forager knows a wide landscape of vegetation communities intimately. Moreover, Cree-Ojibwa foragers do not always adopt the patch-to-patch pattern incorporated into the model. Because they know that some prey move in this manner, the foragers search for tracks in the interstices between patches, a practice that is more efficient and improves the chances of successful pursuit.

Fortified with these limited successes, I suggested that foraging theory might also shed light on a key issue in hominid paleoecology (Winterhalder 1981c). Using the competitive exclusion principle, some paleoanthropologists have argued that there could be no more than one sympatric hominid species. In this view, the response of a partially cultural hominid to a like competitor would be to expand its use of resources and hence to exclude the less efficient of the two species. However, a derivative result of the diet-breadth and patch-choice models, the "compression hypothesis" (Schoener 1974), shows that although the diets of the two competitors might become more general, their use of habitat patches would specialize, producing the ecological and ultimately the evolutionary divergence necessary for joint survival. Cultural flexibility would only facilitate the selective processes for the optimal response of each species: niche divergence in the use of micro-habitats.

I have argued as well that the Pleistocene overkill hypothesis of Martin—that human foragers newly arrived in North America around 11,000 B.P. caused massive extinctions of big game species (review in Webster 1981)—can be questioned using the marginal value theorem. The situation outlined by Martin—highly efficient hunters in a heterogeneous environment rich in game species and with a virtually unlimited frontier—are exactly those in which depletion of localized patches of prey is least likely. Such foragers would have moved quickly through the habitat, skimming the most easily obtained prey in each location before moving on. Each patch left behind would retain a breeding population.

Inuit Foraging and Group Size

In fieldwork with the Inuit on the northeast coast of Hudson Bay, Smith (1981) has used optimization approaches to analyze ecological determinants of hunter-gatherer group size and structure. The Inuit provide a classic but untested example of ecological adaptation—the winter aggregation of small hunting parties to engage in cooperative hunting of seals at their breathing holes. Since studies by Boas in the 1880s, anthropologists have noted that a seal visits several breathing holes unpredictably. It has been argued that a successful harvest requires that hunters station themselves at as many of the holes as possible. By plotting group sizes against measurements of their energy efficiency, Smith was able to test this proposition. For seal hunting, his evidence shows a peak of individual efficiency at 3 hunters, corresponding to a winter camp of about 20 persons (1981: 62). This is much smaller than the 50 to 200 persons observed by Boas and others, suggesting the influence of factors besides this one. Overall, in 5 or 10 hunt types, Smith found a positive and statistically significant correlation between hunting group size and foraging efficiency. Where the energy optimization hypothesis failed, alternative factors like apprenticeship of children or partnerships to reduce foraging hazards apparently were operating.

Tropical Foragers: The Aché

Hawkes, Hill, and O'Connell (1982) have shown that foraging choices of neotropical Aché living in Paraguay match reasonably well those predicted by the optimal diet model. Whether plant or animal, a resource appears to enter the optimal diet set of the Aché by virtue of its pursuit and handling costs and the abundance of foods of higher rank as expected. That set will usually include some plants as well as animals. This answers the central question, "Why do hunters gather?", especially those that apparently could live well on meat alone.

These conclusions are qualified somewhat by the Aché division of labor, in which males pass up encounters with highly ranked plants and females with highly ranked animals, lowering the average foraging of each . Where the energy-optimization hypothesis failed, alternative factors like apprenticeship of youths or partnerships to reduce foraging hazards apparently were operating.

Tropical Foragers: The Yanomamo, Ye'kwana, and Siona-Secoya

In a neotropical example, Hames and Vickers (1982) have examined data on the diet choice of Yanomamo, Ye'kwana, and Siona-Secoya foragers. These people forage radially (see Orians and Pearson 1978) from their gardens and villages. Hames and Vickers have made comparative observations on diet choice as prey are depleted adjacent to the village and as radial foraging effort grows. The observed practices of taking only more valuable game at greater distances from the village are broadly in accord with predictions. Resolution of disputes (Ross et al. 1980) about the effects of ecology on the lifeways of tropical horticulturalists may well come from interpretations and data like these.

Marine Fishermen in New Jersey

Finally, McCay's (1981) analysis of a marine inshore fishery on the east coast of the United States is the first explicitly to set optimal foraging theory into the context of a market economy. Some optimal foraging predictions were consistent with harvest decisions made by the fishermen, but these were a rather restricted part of a complex of choices influenced by personal values, economics, and politics. McCay argues that New Jersey fishermen *are* foragers, but they exist in an enveloping political economy that rather strongly restricts the insights available from foraging theory alone.

Opportunity-Cost Models

The above-mentioned studies are instances in which an optimal foraging approach has resulted in different, more complete, or better-substantiated conclusions about hunter-gatherer subsistence practices.

Are there dangers in this type of exercise? I see several. It is easy to overextend the purview of optimal foraging models, or to misapply them, individually or collectively. The emaciated expository style of theoretical ecologists often does not make assumptions and constraints accessible to those of us who must be enlightened by the prose between the equations. Collectively the models are bound by the individual-level food acquisition focus and the restriction to a material currency. In their present form, they help to examine food procurement but do not readily extend to supra-individual aspects of economy, such as exchange, wherein social and cultural valuation of goods becomes especially important. And they do not have the character of lawful statements.

For the remainder of this paper I will address two questions mentioned earlier—total foraging effort and risk—while trying to balance among these dangers. This means recognizing limits even while trying to push the models beyond their present limitations. I am interested first in the optimization statement stipulation: "while foraging."

The Opportunity-Cost Foraging Model

The diet-breadth model identifies the prey set giving the maximum net rate of energy intake while foraging. It does not indicate how long the organism should forage, nor how much energy it should harvest. Establishing the latter requires that foraging be evaluated relative to other behaviors. Foraging takes time away from those activities; it also provides the energy needed to engage in them.

I have been working on a model that addresses the question of how long to forage (see Winterhalder 1983c). It begins with several definitions. The *opportunity cost* of an activity (X) is the value of some alternative activity forgone because resources were invested in X rather than the alternative. This concept assumes that resources are limited relative to potential uses, that different courses of action are evaluated relative to one another, and that one activity among all the foregone activities can be identified as providing the relevant substitute measure. *Marginal value* recognizes that the value (or cost) of an activity can change as a function of its duration. An economic decision to cease or continue will focus on the value (or cost) of the next, the marginal, unit of that behavior (see Charnov 1976). Finally, an *indifference curve* connects points of equal utility or preference; a *value isocline* points of equal sociocultural valuation; and a *fitness isocline* points of equal fitness.

Foraging is represented in the right-hand portion of this model (Figure 12.4); all non-foraging activities are aggregated in the left-hand portion. The right-hand vertical axis measures the net acquisition of energy (E_a) while foraging; the left-hand vertical axis measures the total energy expenditure (E_e) in non-foraging activities. For the interval considered, acquisition must balance expenditure ($E_a = E_e$). The horizontal axis extending from the right shows the time spent foraging (T_f); that extending from the left shows the time spent in non-foraging activities (T_{nf}). Note that increasing foraging times are read from right to left, and increasing non-foraging times from left to right, subject to the constraint that $T_f + T_{nf} = T_t$, where T_t represents an appropriate interval for analysis.

Combinations of time and energy consumption in non-foraging activities that have the same utility are connected by the indifference curves. Initially, take the configuration of the curves to be consistent with the standard conventions of micro-economic theory (e.g., Stonier and Hague 1972):

• They are convex to the origin, implying that the scarcer of two jointly used resources is likely to be the more valuable. The marginal value of activity X increases (or its relative rate of substitution for Y decreases) as the quantity of Y grows. Thus, an organism with much non-foraging time but relatively little expendable energy will probably value an additional unit of energy more than one of time.

• The indifference (or isocline) map is independent of foraging intake.

• Indifference curves or isoclines more distant from the origin have higher value. In principle, the capacity for increased utility is insatiable.

• And the forager is knowledgeable, has stable preferences, and acts rationally by attempting to obtain the greatest possible utility.

FIGURE 12.4. The Opportunity-Cost Foraging Model for a Time-Minimizer

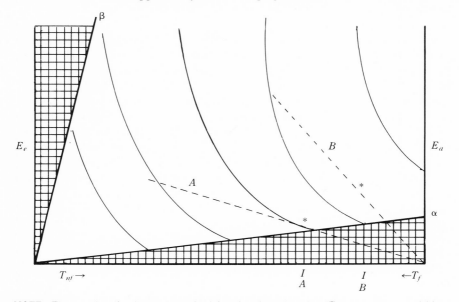

NOTE: The asterisk (*) shows the optimal foraging time allocation (T_f) and energy acquisition (E_a) for two foraging constraint lines, A and B. The vertical bars below the X-axis show how time is partitioned between non-foraging activities (T_{nf}) and foraging (T_f) in each case.

The 0-to-α line shows the minimum survivable rate of energy expenditure; the 0-to-β line shows the maximum rate attainable in non-foraging activities.

A set of indifference curves can be very sensitive to a forager's circumstances. The model offers distinctions that pass continuously from the strictly time-limited to the strictly energy-limited cases. If the marginal gain in utility from a unit of time freed from foraging is greater than that attached to an additional unit of energy gained by foraging, then the organism is time-limited and will act as a "time-minimizer" (Schoener 1971). The indifference curves will tend toward the vertical (Figure 12.4). Conversely, if the marginal gain associated with a unit of energy is larger, the organism is energy-limited (i.e., it will act as an "energy-maximizer") and has a indifference map that tends toward the horizontal (Figure 12.5). A forager may act as an energy-maximizer in one portion of its indifference map and as a time-minimizer in another. It may switch from one to the other with seasonal or other temporal factors.

The left and right portions of this model are linked in the following way. Each foraging option is associated with a net gain of energy (E_a) for each unit of foraging time (T_f). This is represented by a *foraging-constraint line* on the indifference map. The optimal time investment (and thus the optimal energy

FIGURE 12.5. The Opportunity-Cost Foraging Model for an Energy-Maximizer

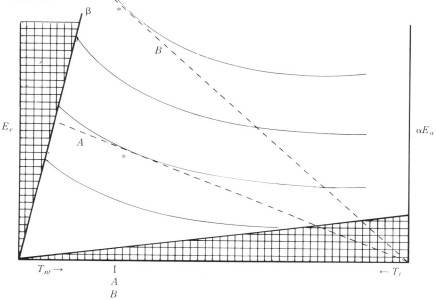

NOTE: The asterisk (*) shows the optimal foraging time allocation (T_f) and energy acquisition (E_a) for two foraging constraint lines, A and B. The vertical bar below the X-axis shows how time is partitioned between non-foraging activities (T) and foraging (T_f) in each case.

acquisition) is determined by the point on the foraging-constraint line that is tangent to the highest indifference curve (or value/fitness isocline). This linkage establishes the opportunity costs (time) and benefits (energy) of foraging by evaluating them relative to alternative uses in other activities.

If foraging conditions vary, so will the diet choice and efficiency of the optimal hunter-gatherer. This change will alter the slope of the foraging-constraint line. Rotating that line over the indifference map (Figure 12.6) generates a *consumption curve* (*cc*) that characterizes the forager's effort and harvest for all ecological circumstances.

An Opportunity-Cost Currency

The opportunity-cost approach directs attention beyond the diet-breadth model to some related and here exploratory lines of inquiry. What is the relevant currency for the opportunity costs experienced by a human forager? Is there an

325

FIGURE 12.6. An Opportunity-Cost Model that Depicts the Forager's
Consumption Curve (cc)

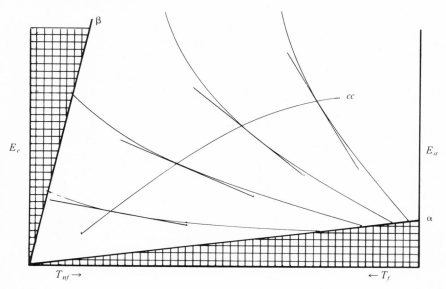

expected form for a hunter-gatherer opportunity-cost map? What determines
that configuration?

Some anthropologists using foraging models (Hawkes et al. n.d.) state flatly
that fitness is the sole appropriate currency. I do not find that position compelling. First, fitness has a special, limited, theoretical meaning: differential reproductive success of phenotypic traits expressed variably among the individuals of a population, for those phenotypes tied more or less directly to a
corresponding inter-individual genotypic variance. Given our ignorance about
mechanisms of biocultural evolution, appeals to fitness outside this biological
setting are analogies carrying heavy loads of ambiguity. Second, it is nearly
impossible to make a quantitative assessment of the incremental contribution of
a particular phenotype/genotype linkage to relative fitness. For those seeking a
rigorous, operational measure of segments of human behavior, fitness is a poor
candidate. Fitness in the abstract, even the fitness of individuals, will not help,
because the analysis actually considers fitnesses associated with a restricted
set of activities extracted from the totality of behavior. Finally, Mayr (1974)
argues that resource-acquisition behavior has evolved toward "open" behavioral programs based on generalized abilities to accumulate and interpret experience, to learn, and to make choices. It is based in the "cultural retention of

individually adaptive behavior" and "cognitive evaluation and retention of beneficial customs" (Pulliam 1981:62). We should expect, then, that foraging decisions are heavily influenced by sociocultural information that may be independent of fitness considerations.

In a context in which it cannot be defined or measured, and in which even its relevance is at issue, invocations of fitness must entail some other kind of adaptive judgment, usually related to material utility. The alternative, however, is not particularly attractive. Biologists discomforted by ambiguities in a central concept (e.g., Stearns 1976:4) will find company with the economists and anthropologists when it comes to preference and utility. Despite this, I propose that the appropriate currency for this opportunity-cost map is utility.

In economics utility theory has a convoluted history (Page 1968). Bentham, in his own words, "planted the tree of utility . . . deep, and spread it wide" (quoted in Stigler 1965:66) in the late 18th century, a calculus for an introspective but measurable quantity that could be used for designing efficacious moral legislation. Over the next hundred years the concept changed profoundly. Bernoulli and others formalized the idea of marginal utility. Edgeworth introduced the convention of indifference curves, here adapted to ecological analyses. Marshall got the curves firmly linked to a theory of consumer demand. Pareto showed that utility was not measurable—that, in effect, utility maps represented only ordinal relationships of preference. Hicks and Allen argued that introspective ideas like utility were unnecessary if one replaced marginal utility with marginal rate of substitution. And Samuelson completed the program by showing that behaviorist analysis of "revealed preference" freed the theory of all unscientific notions, like utility. The utility in utility theory extinguished itself. From a social theory it has been transformed into an idea strictly tied to price-demand theory, ordinal, thoroughly behaviorist, and therefore presumably free of any base sociocultural content or psychological assumptions. Despite the Nobel Prize attached to the end of this sequence, I am most comfortable with the utility of the pre-Samuelson period (see Sen 1977; Wong 1978).

I define utility as the worth people attribute to things or actions, either because they are useful, in an adaptive or fitness-enhancing sense, or because they have status within sociocultural systems of meaning or exchange. Preference is the expression of such rankings, revealed in choice or evident in action.

Fitness draws on the deductive power of evolutionary theory; sociocultural valuation on the surety that learned beliefs and experience exert a strong and more or less independent influence on the variability in the specific forms of human foraging choices. Both are necessary for human adaptation research, but neither in the abstract is very helpful. To interpret them (as isocline maps) or evaluate their combined action (in the form of utility), we are forced to consider empirical understandings of behavior and environment, to generalize from facts about the meaning of our deductive postulates, to inquire about,

327

observe, and, if need be, assume preferences. This is necessary to translate those abstract currencies into an indifference map that will produce interesting, testable hypotheses. Utility and preference are messy concepts, but until we have sound theories of biocultural evolution, their use is unavoidable.

An Idealized Hunter-Gatherer Indifference Map

I will also propose a normative or idealized form for the indifference map of a hunter-gatherer. Consider the following question: How would we represent the case in which there is a social stigma or material disadvantage associated with too much or too little success in the harvesting of food? Note that this allows social phenomena an explicit influence on individual preference. Note also that this map will portray long-term averages or behavioral tendencies, ignoring day-to-day vagaries of motivation and success in the food quest.

Social controls come into effect when a person exceeds or falls short of a consumption norm. Controls might have three effects. First, they might cause the person to reevaluate his or her preferences toward greater conformity with the norm. Second, if the person adamantly holds to certain preferences, the group, by withdrawing assistance or otherwise impeding the performance of non-foraging tasks, could reduce that individual's ability to derive utility from various time and energy combinations. Finally, they might reduce the foraging efficiency of the recalcitrant, perhaps by withholding information, thus depressing his or her foraging-constraint line and reducing energy intake (if not the commitment to consumption).

Graphically, a social consumption norm will take the form of a line intermediate between minimum and maximum non-foraging expenditure rates. It can be derived as follows. Begin with a garden-variety indifference map (Figure 12.7), with an individual consumption curve different from the social consumption norm. Social pressures (the second alternative above) can be represented by arrows transforming the indifference map. Above the consumption norm these cause the indifference curves to pivot upward and to the right because the utility that the person can derive from various time-energy combinations is lowered. Below the consumption norm, disapproval of insufficient harvest will also lower the utility of various time-energy combinations, again pivoting the indifference curves upward and to the right. Whether this individual begins as a time-minimizer or an energy-maximizer, his or her individual consumption curve will approach the accepted norm.

The indifference map generated by this exercise is an intuitively reasonable hypothesis about individual preferences as such. If energy shortfalls approach sustenance levels, tactics will tend toward energy maximization and longer foraging. If intake grows to or above a comfortable level, people will tend to

FIGURE 12.7. Generation of a Consumption Norm (cn) by Group Pressure on an Individual's Preferences (Indifference Map)

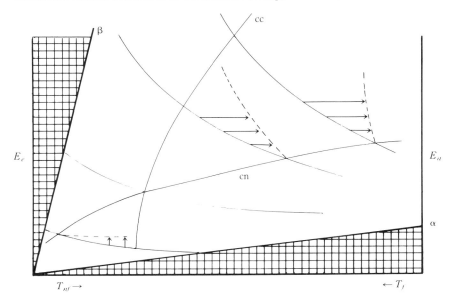

adopt time-minimizing strategies and engage in less foraging. This hypothesis also recognizes that the coercive powers of fitness and sociocultural factors over human behavior are not evenly distributed over the indifference map. In the lower and left-hand portions, for instance, sufficient food assumes more importance. Health and survival (and perhaps, but not necessarily, fitness) may be at stake. In the upper and right-hand portion, basic needs have been satisfied, and historically specific, sociocultural determinants of needs and wants may prevail. People are guided sometimes by the belly and sometimes, quite independently, by the head.

This idealized indifference map should be viewed as a baseline hypothesis. The actual map of any particular forager or foraging group may be different in ways that must be given a situational explanation. Deviations will be a function of various factors, including the following:

1. The number and value of the non-foraging activities performed, including the support of dependents, and their collective demands on energy and time

2. The potential for satiety with respect to energy and time, and their use in non-foraging activities

3. Differences in age, sex, and individual competence in non-foraging tasks

4. Physical hazards and perceived comforts or discomforts of foraging, relative to those for non-foraging activities

5. Uses of resources aside from immediate consumption by foragers or their dependents (perhaps in exchange or for storage)

6. Temporal and situational factors that influence the opportunity costs of behaviors through scheduling constraints on alternative activities

This last point is quite important. The "cost" of an activity is not necessarily the actual time or energy expended on it. For instance, tool manufacture in the secure warmth of one's hut, after the evening's reproductive fitness has been secured and while hunting and gathering are on hold until the following day, has no cost except the increment of energy expenditure above the resting metabolic rate.

Satiety

Economists have no qualms about the assumption that human wants for goods are unlimited, that ever greater amounts of utility can be gained from ever larger baskets containing, for instance, potatoes and grapes (Stonier and Hague 1973:53). The notion of surfeit is absent from the workings of microeconomics, which has formalized the ignorance of excess. But even if we accept insatiability for combinations of goods in a market economy, the combination of time and energy represented in a hunter-gatherer indifference map is a different matter. The time of the model refers to a finite interval, and the metabolic use of energy has a limit at the point of exhaustion. The foraging mode may itself place structural constraints on the use of energy (Lee 1981). Thus, for foragers, consumption of energy is tied to physiological and socioeconomic constraints quite unlike those affecting the consumption of goods in a market economy (where the object is not acquisition of potatoes and grapes to eat but competitive transformation of commodities to sustain a profit or retain a wage).

This brings us to Sahlins's (1972) proposition that hunter-gatherers are in business for their health (a not un-Darwinian statement), and a new question: How would satiation affect the model? It is possible and perhaps likely that foragers have, and readily attain, an upper bound for energy/time utility, and express it in their preferences. If non-foraging leads to boredom, which impels the forager to hunt or gather, or if the social constraints on material acquisition or aggrandizement through accomplishments cause an unusually successful forager to forgo the food quest temporarily (R. B. Lee, pers. comm.), then maximum utility may actually be a curved ridge, or it may reach a plateau (Figure 12.8). More time foraging and greater energy harvest may reach a point of

FIGURE 12.8. An Indifference Map with a Utility/Fitness Plateau, Generating a Consumption Space (cs)

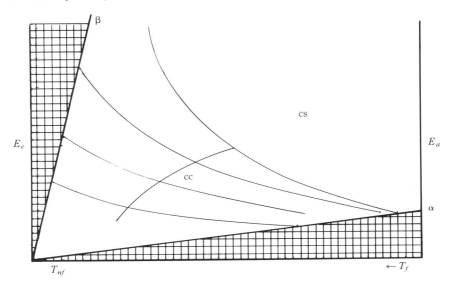

disutility or an indeterminant zone of like utility. A ridge would cause the consumption curve to bifurcate into two optimal harvest options; a plateau would generate a set of equivalent options, a *consumption space*. There is no longer a single equilibrium, but a set of alternatives among which pressures for adaptive optimization carry no determinancy.

These latter two indifference maps (Figures 12.7 and 12.8) are important because they provide a link between optimal foraging theory and some more traditional analyses of foragers, including the "original affluence" and "limited needs" proposals of Sahlins (1972) and Lee (1979; cf. Hawkes and O'Connell 1981). It is a revealing link because some (Hawkes et al. 1985) have claimed, incorrectly I believe, that an evolutionary ecology approach is theoretically incompatible with this earlier work. Sahlins and Lee inquire principally about the political economy of foraging, raising questions that cannot be answered by foraging theory per se. "Original affluence" and "limited needs" are mainly concepts of sociocultural valuation. They enter an opportunity-cost foraging analysis through their effect on the shape of the individual's indifference map. To have limited needs with respect to foraging is to be, in effect, a time-minimizer. A forager may seek to be optimal in the choice of a foraging strategy in order to be a time-minimizer and energy satisfier in the food quest. There are no theoretical impediments to this possibility, nor does it seem unlikely, given the ethnographic record of hunter-gatherer preferences and foraging efficiencies. The proposition that there is always more utility to be gained from hard productive work is more aptly ascribed to Calvin than to Darwin.

Risk-Sensitive Foraging Models

A second body of recent work focuses on the effects of stochasticity in foraging decision variables (e.g., encounter rate). Most existing models, including those discussed above, are deterministic, based on the simplifying assumption that expected (or average) values adequately characterize the important factors in foraging decisions. But, in fact, foragers may respond to the mean *and* variance in the rewards associated with each diet choice. They may be "risk-sensitive," depending on their preference for variance or certainty in combination with differing mean food reward expectations. A simple result of this work is the prediction that a forager will make choices that avoid variance if its current energy budget is positive, but seek variance if that budget is negative. Figure 12.9 is a simplified depiction of this prediction. There are four possible foraging decisions (A through D), each with a different mean/variance combination in the associated food reward. For positive mean expected intakes (u_t), those above the net minimum survivable requirement (R_{net}), minimizing variance (var_t) is optimal (A is preferable to B); for u_t below R_{net}, maximizing variance will result in at least some positive outcomes (D is preferable to C).

Stephens and Charnov (1982) have derived a model that generalizes the results depicted in Figure 12.9. The probability of starvation (Z') may be given as follows (in a form that avoids mathematical details to the extent possible):

$$Z' = (R_{net} - u_t)/(var_t)$$

Risk diminishes as Z' decreases, with the troublesome mathematical quirk that the organism is in positive energy balance when Z' is negative. Reference to the equation will show that for positive values of Z'

$$R_{net} - u_t > 0$$

That is, there is a negative energy balance; increasing variance decreases risk. For negative values of Z'

$$R_{net} - u_t < 0$$

332

FIGURE 12.9. The Extreme Variance Rule for Risk-Sensitive Foraging Decisions in a Stochastic Environment

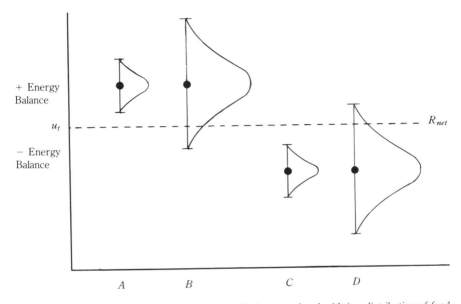

NOTE: Each of the foraging choices (A through D) has associated with it a distribution of food rewards, characterized by a mean and a variance.

There is a positive energy balance; decreasing variance decreases risk. Large expected values relative to minimum requirements ($R_{net} - u_t \ll 0$; Z' is a large negative number) also reduce risk. The equation can be reorganized as:

$$u_t = R_{net} - Z'(var_t),$$

the standard slope-intercept equation, and then depicted graphically as in Figure 12.10. The full set of mean/variance combinations associated with the available foraging choices can be represented by points (var_t, u_t) on this plane. The optimal diet is that combination intersected by the line extending from R_{net} with the greatest slope. (This is because the greater the slope ($-Z'$), the lower the value of Z, which we want to minimize.)

Stephens and Charnov derive the mean/variance combinations for the marginal-value theorem that result from stochastic variance in the time required to locate a patch. They get an oblong curve with these properties: (1) the

FIGURE 12.10. Generalized Stephens/Charnov (1982) Model for Foraging Decisions with Stochastic Elements

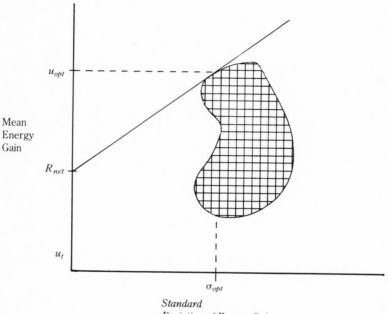

NOTE: The greatest slope $(-Z')$ of the line that intersects one of the available mean/variance pairs (shaded area) minimizes Z' and hence risk.

stochastic result will usually approximate the deterministic outcome; but (2) if minimum requirements are less than the expected maximal intake predicted by the deterministic model, then the forager should remain in patches somewhat longer than predicted by the deterministic model. That the complicated stochastic outcome approximates the simple deterministic one is encouraging, but the unusual set of mean/variance combinations that gives rise to this consequence suggests caution in extrapolating to other situations.

Conclusions on the Process of Stalking

To summarize, optimal foraging models may provide one answer to Bettinger's (1980) "impending crisis" in hunter-gatherer studies—the need for new "predictive/explanatory" models to guide research and interpretation. They may provide a "consequence law"—in the restricted sense of Cohen (1978)—and hence a method for mitigating some shortcomings of functionalism (see Smith and Winterhalder 1981).

By attention to the history of the logistic equation and by carefully listing the assumptions of optimal foraging theory, I hope to have conveyed a particular and somewhat cautious attitude toward models. Partial skepticism is the best favor one can do a favorite theory. The fieldwork examples were meant to demonstrate that this is a heuristically rewarding type of inquiry. The section on opportunity costs and risk was meant to further develop the theory, and to define its boundaries. Extensions of opportunity-cost models may allow us to use formalist approaches in hunter-gatherer foraging and diet studies even while clinging to substantivist insights on forager goals. The initial results of risk-sensitive analyses suggest that we may be able to retain the simplicity of some deterministic models even while acknowledging the presence of stochasticity. In combination with fieldwork, these and other developments using evolutionary ecology theory may eventually generate a rigorous understanding of the ecological component of the foraging mode of production.

References Cited

Bettinger, R. L.
 1980 Explanatory/Predictive Models of Hunter-Gatherer Adaptation. *Advances in Archaeological Method and Theory* 3:189–255.

Charnov, E. L.
 1976 Optimal foraging: The Marginal Value Theorem. *Theoretical Population Biology* 9:129–36.

Charnov, E. L.; G. Orians; and K. Hyatt
 1976 Ecological Implications of Resource Depression. *American Naturalist* 110:247–59.

Cody, M. L.
 1974 Optimization in Ecology. *Science* 183:1156–64.

Cohen, G. A.
 1978 *Karl Marx's Theory of History: A Defence.* Princeton, N.J.: Princeton University Press.

Connell, J. H.
 1975 Some Mechanisms Producing Structure in Natural Communities: A Model and Evidence from Field Experiments. In *Ecology and the Evolution of Communities,* M. L. Cody and J. M. Diamond, eds., pp. 460–90. Cambridge: Harvard University Press.

Durham, W. H.
 1976 The Adaptive Significance of Cultural Behavior. *Human Ecology* 4:89–121.

Gause, G. F.
  1934   *The Struggle for Existence.* Baltimore: Williams and Wilkins.
Gould, S. J., and R. C. Lewontin
  1979   The Spandrels of San Marco and the Panglossian Paradigm: A Critique
            of the Adaptationist Programme. *Proceedings of the Royal Society of Lon-
            don* B 205:581–98.
Hames, R. B., and W. T. Vickers
  1982   Optimal Diet Breadth Theory as a Model to Explain Variability in Ama-
            zonian Hunting. *American Ethnologist* 9:358–78.
Hawkes, K.; K. Hill; and J. F. O'Connell
  1982   Why Hunters Gather: Optimal Foraging and the Aché of Eastern Para-
            guay. *American Ethnologist* 9:379–98.
Hawkes, K., and J. F. O'Connell
  1981   Affluent Hunters? Some Comments in Light of the Alyawara Case.
            American Anthropologist 83:622–26.
Hawkes, K.; J. F. O'Connell; K. Hill; and E. Charnov
  1985   How Much Is Enough: Hunters and "Limited Needs. *Ethology and So-
            ciobiology* 6:3–15.
  n.d.   Why Reduce It to Fitness? Optimal Foraging and Hunter-Gatherers.
            Manuscript.
Hutchinson, G. E.
  1978   *An Introduction to Population Ecology.* New Haven: Yale University
            Press.
Jacob, F.
  1977   Evolution and Tinkering. *Science* 196:1161–66.
Jochim, M.
  1982   Optimization and Risk. Manuscript.
Johnson, A., and C. A. Behrens
  1982   Nutritional Criteria in Machiguenga Food Production Decisions: A Lin-
            ear-Programming Analysis. *Human Ecology* 10:167–89.
Keene, A. S.
  1979   Economic Optimization Models and the Study of Hunter-Gatherer Sub-
            sistence Settlement Systems. In *Transformations: Mathematical Ap-
            proaches to Culture Change,* C. Renfrew and K. Cooke, eds., pp. 369–
            404. New York: Academic Press.
  1981   Optimal Foraging in a Nonmarginal Environment: A Model of Prehistoric
            Subsistence Strategies in Michigan. In *Hunter-Gatherer Foraging Strat-
            egies: Ethnographic and Archaeological Analyses,* B. Winterhalder and
            E. A. Smith, eds., pp. 171–93. Chicago: University of Chicago Press.
Kingsland, S.
  1982   The Refractory Model: The Logistic Curve and the History of Popula-
            tion Ecology. *Quarterly Review of Biology* 57:29–52.
Krebs, J. R., and R. J. Cowie
  1976   Foraging Strategies in Birds. *Ardea* 64:98–116.

Lee, R. B.
1979   *The !Kung San: Men, Women and Work in a Foraging Society.* Cambridge: Cambridge University Press.
1981   Is There a Foraging Mode of Production? *Canadian Journal of Anthropology* 2:13–19.

Levins, R.
1966   The Strategy of Model Building in Population Biology. *American Scientist* 54:421–31.

Lewontin, R. C.
1978   Fitness, Survival and Optimality. In *Analysis of Ecological Systems,* D. J. Horn, G. R. Stairs, and R. D. Mitchell, eds., pp. 3–21. Columbus: Ohio State University Press.

MacArthur, R. H., and E. R. Pianka
1966   On Optimal Use of a Patchy Environment. *American Naturalist* 100:603–9.

McCay, B.
1981   Optimal Foragers or Political Actors? Ecological Analysis of a New Jersey Fishery. *American Ethnologist* 8:356–82.

Maynard Smith, J.
1978   Optimization Theory in Evolution. *Annual Review of Ecology and Systematics* 9:31–56.

Mayr, E.
1974   Behavior Programs and Evolutionary Strategies. *American Scientist* 62:650–59.

Orians, G. H., and N. E. Pearson
1978   On the Theory of Central Place Foraging. In *Analysis of Ecological Systems,* D. J. Horn, G. R. Stairs, and R. D. Mitchell, eds., pp. 155–77. Columbus: Ohio State University Press.

Orlove, B. S.
1980   Ecological Anthropology. *Annual Review of Anthropology* 9:235–73.

Page, A. N.
1968   *Utility Theory: A Book of Readings.* New York: John Wiley.

Pulliam, H. R.
1981   On Predicting Human Diets. *Journal of Ethnobiology* 1:61–68.

Pyke, G. H.; H. R. Pulliam; and E. L. Charnov
1977   Optimal Foraging: A Selective Review of Theory and Tests. *Quarterly Review of Biology* 52:137–54.

Rapport, D. J.
1980   Optimal Foraging for Complementary Resources. *American Naturalist* 116:324–46.

Reidhead, V. A.
1979   Linear Programming Models in Archaeology. *Annual Review of Anthropology* 8:543–78.
1980   The Economics of Subsistence Change: Test of an Optimization Model.

In *Modeling Change in Prehistoric Subsistence Economies,* T. K. Earle and A. L. Christenson, eds., pp. 141–86. New York: Academic Press.

Richerson, P. J.
1977 Ecology and Human Ecology: A Comparison of Theories in the Biological and Social Sciences. *American Ethnologist* 4:1–26.

Ross, E. B.; J. B. Ross; N. A. Chagnon; and R. B. Hames
1980 Amazonian Warfare (Letter). *Science* 207:590–93.

Sahlins, M.
1972 *Stone Age Economics.* Chicago: Aldine.

Schoener, T. W.
1971 Theory of Feeding Strategies. *Annual Review of Ecology and Systematics* 2:369–404.
1974 The Compression Hypothesis and Temporal Resource Partitioning. *Proceedings of the National Academy of Sciences, USA* 71:4169–72.
1982 The Controversy Over interspecific Competition. *American Scientist* 70:586–95.

Sen, A. K.
1977 Rational Fools: A Critique of the Behavioral Foundations of Economic Theory. *Philosophy and Public Affairs* 6:317–44.

Smith, E. A.
1979 Human Adaptation and Energetic Efficiency. *Human Ecology* 7:53–74.
1981 The Application of Optimal Foraging Theory to the Analysis of Hunter-Gatherer Group Size. In *Hunter-Gatherer Foraging Strategies,* B. Winterhalder and E. A. Smith, eds., pp. 36–65. Chicago: University of Chicago Press.
1983 Optimal Foraging Theory and Hunter-Gatherer Societies. *Current Anthropology* 24:625–51.

Smith, E. A., and B. Winterhalder
1981 New Perspectives on Hunter-Gatherer Socio-Ecology. In *Hunter-Gatherer Foraging Strategies: Ethnographic and Archaeological Analyses,* B. Winterhalder and E. A. Smith, eds., pp. 1–12. Chicago: University of Chicago Press.

Speth, J. D., and K. A. Spielmann
1983 Energy Source, Protein Metabolism, and Hunter-Gatherer Subsistence Strategies. *Journal of Anthropological Archaeology* 2:1–31.

Stearns, S. C.
1976 Life History Tactics: A Review of the Ideas. *Quarterly Review of Biology* 51:3–47.

Stephens, D. W., and E. L. Charnov
1982 Optimal Foraging: Some Simple Stochastic Models. *Behavioral Ecology and Sociobiology* 10:251–63.

Stigler, G. J.
1965 The Development of Utility Theory. In *Essays in the History of Economics,* G. J. Stigler, ed., pp. 66–155. Chicago: University of Chicago Press.

Stonier, A. W., and D. C. Hague
    1973   *A Textbook of Economic Theory.* New York: Wiley.

Webster, D.
    1981   Late Pleistocene Extinction and Human Predation: A Critical Overview. In *Omnivorous Primates: Gathering and Hunting in Human Evolution,* R. S. O. Harding and G. Teleki, eds., pp. 556–94. New York: Columbia University Press.

Westoby, M.
    1978   What Are the Biological Bases of Varied Diets? *American Naturalist* 112:627–31.

Wiens, J.
    1977   On Competition and Variable Environments. *American Scientist* 65:590–97.

Winterhalder, B.
    1981a   Optimal Foraging Strategies and Hunter-Gatherer Research in Anthropology: Theory and Models. In *Hunter-Gatherer Foraging Strategies: Ethnographic and Archeological Analyses,* B. Winterhalder and E. A. Smith, eds., pp. 13–35. Chicago: University of Chicago Press.
    1981b   Foraging Strategies in the Boreal Forest: An Analysis of Cree Hunting and Gathering. In *Hunter-Gatherer Foraging Strategies,* B. Winterhalder and E. A. Smith, eds., pp. 66–98. Chicago: University of Chicago Press.
    1981c   Competitive Exclusion and Hominid Paleoecology: Limits to Similarity, Niche Differentiation and the Effects of Cultural Behavior. *Yearbook of Physical Anthropology* 24:101–21.
    1983a   History and Ecology of the Boreal Zone in Ontario. In *Boreal Forest Adaptation: The Algonkians of Northern Ontario,* A. T. Steegmann, Jr., ed., pp. 9–54. New York: Plenum Press.
    1983b   Boreal Foraging Strategies. In *Boreal Forest Adaptations: The Algonkians of Northern Ontario,* A. T. Steegmann, Jr., ed., pp. 201–41. New York: Plenum Press.
    1983c   Opportunity Cost Foraging Models for Stationary and Mobile Predators. *American Naturalist* 122:73–84.

Wong, S.
    1978   *The Foundations of Paul Samuelson's Revealed Preference Theory.* London: Routledge and Kegan Paul.

KRISTEN HAWKES

How Much Food Do Foragers Need?

AN INTERESTING EMPIRICAL PUZZLE IS POSED BY RECENT OBSER-
vations on foraging effort among hunter-gatherers. In the mid-1960s, the Dobe
!Kung of Botswana reportedly spent no more than 20 hours per week collecting resources that yielded an average of 2,100 kilocalories per consumer day
(Lee 1968, 1969). Many anthropologists take these figures to be typical of
hunter-gatherers. They expect that work effort is set to meet some general
and specifiable consumption need, so that when this need is easily met, foragers work little. When it takes more effort to reach the same goal, workloads
increase. Yet, in contrast to Lee's reports on the !Kung, the Aché of eastern
Paraguay have recently been observed to work, averaging male and female
foragers, at least 35 hours per week for a mean return of 3,800 kilocalories per
consumer day (Hill et al., 1984). They procure *more* food than Lee reports for
the !Kung, and they work *longer* hours to get it. The Aché data are inconsistent
with what has become the received wisdom on hunter-gatherer foraging, and
they raise an obvious and important theoretical question: what determines the
amount of time hunter-gatherers devote to foraging and the quantity of food
they consume?

The Problem

Largely because of the rich ethnographic descriptions (e.g., Lee 1968, 1979;
Marshall 1976; Thomas 1959; and films by John Marshall), the !Kung are often
identified as prototypical hunter-gatherers—well-nourished foragers who work
relatively short hours, rely on the widely available plant foods collected by
women for the bulk of their diet, and maintain low birthrates, which prevent
population growth from threatening local resources. Though this characterization has been challenged, as applied both to the !Kung themselves and to other
hunter-gatherers (e.g., Ember 1978; Lee and DeVore 1968; Truswell and

Hansen 1979; Wilmsen 1978), it remains remarkably persistent. When anthropologists write about hunter-gatherers, more often than not they write about the !Kung (e.g., Cohen 1977; Harris 1977, 1983; Leakey and Lewin 1978).

The Aché are very different. The per capita daily consumption rates they sustain while foraging are quite high, averaging 2,600 to 5,400 kilocalories, depending on the season (Hill et al. 1984). More than half this total comes in the form of meat. This is especially surprising in view of generalizations about tropical hunter-gatherers (Lee 1968), particularly those of the South American lowlands (Lathrap 1968). These figures are not the result of unusually high local capture rates. Hourly returns for Aché hunters average only 10 to 15 percent higher than those calculated for the !Kung (Hawkes, Hill, and O'Connell 1982; Hill and Hawkes 1983). The difference in return is almost entirely a function of the time Aché men devote to hunting—nearly 50 hours per week per hunter while on foraging trips, more than *twice* the figure reported by Lee (1969) for !Kung men. The contrast becomes even more striking when one considers the difference in women's work effort. !Kung women spend about 12 to 19 hours per week collecting food (Lee 1968; but see recalculation by Hawkes and O'Connell 1981); yet for Aché women, the figure seldom exceeds 10 hours per week.

Stimulated by Lee's description of the !Kung, Sahlins characterized hunter-gatherers as "the original affluent society" (1968, 1972). Wanting little, they could work little to have all their needs met. Yet neither the differences in overall time investment in foraging between the !Kung and the Aché nor the differences in relative time investment between men and women show the pattern that might be expected if some fixed food total were the goal. The !Kung and Aché are both of small stature. They are of about the same height. Yet the Aché eat a great deal more, and they are almost 20 percent heavier (Hill et al. 1984; Howell 1979). If needs were a function of some standard nutritional goal, patterns of caloric intake should be more similar than they apparently are.

Moreover, the Aché are not an isolated case, an oddity among hunter-gatherers with respect to foraging. Other groups described within the past few years (Harako 1981; Hawkes and O'Connell 1981; Tanaka 1980), including the !Kung themselves (Yellen 1977), display patterns of work effort and food consumption quite different from those reported by Lee. These data underline the problem of interest here: how much food will hunter-gatherers eat, and how much time will they spend getting it? Recommended daily allowances and minimum daily requirements do not provide answers to these questions. To label the differences as "cultural" only begs the question. Can we account for the variation in some nomothetic way that will allow us to predict other cases, including patterns in the past?

A Sociobiological Perspective

There is wide agreement among anthropologists that variation in hunter-gatherer behavior is, in some sense, an adjustment to local circumstances—that it is "adaptive." However, opinions differ about the meaning of adaptation. If the direction and the means of adjustment are not specified, adaptation is an empty notion. Supposing that people who depend on local environments suit their pattern of exploitation to the resources available gives us no way to predict which plants and animals they will use as resources, how much they will crop, or what patterns of movement they will display. As circumstances change, what sort of adjustment to suit these changes do we expect? Without some specification of the goal of adjustments, the direction and form they will take cannot be predicted. However, a strict biological notion of adaptation does specify a goal: maximizing fitness. Adaptations are features of living organisms spread by natural selection (Williams 1966), that is, features spread according to the fitness—the relative reproductive success—they confer. If we can take advantage of this rigorous notion of adaptation, we have a powerful explanatory and predictive theory with which to work. The warranting argument is straightforward and simple.

Past selection has shaped capacities and tendencies for enormous flexibility in humans. This flexibility spread in ancestral populations because it was adaptive; it provided a fitness advantage to its carriers. This means it is a flexibility of a particular kind—not flexibility to do anything at all, but flexibility to track locally changing fitness opportunities. Tendencies to do otherwise would lower reproductive success and so continually be extinguished whenever they appeared. If this is so, the changes, the differences, we see in human behavior over time and space need not be the consequence of changing gene frequencies to allow explanation in terms of natural selection. They are the consequence of individuals adjusting to take advantage of changing fitness options. This means that we can use a strict biological definition of adaptation to apply to patterns of human behavior and a fortiori the behavior of hunter-gatherers. Adaptations are features that maximize the (inclusive) fitness of those displaying them. This allows us to set questions about variation in the behavior of hunter-gatherers in a fundamental theory that applies not only to *Homo sapiens* and not only to behavior but to all the changes in hominids throughout the Pleistocene.

From this perspective the key question in the analysis of any particular behavioral trait is how that trait contributes to the inclusive fitness of the individuals who display it. To address this question, one must construct a series of specific hypotheses about the fitness-related goal of the behavior in question, the alternative means available to achieve that goal, and the costs and benefits associated with each.

It is important to note that in such an analysis neither adaptation, selection, nor optimality is directly under test (Maynard Smith 1978). They provide the theoratical motivation for and links of coherence among various hypotheses. Nor is fitness itself usually measured directly. Rather, attention is directed to "design for fitness" (Williams 1966)—that is, to measurable criteria, such as energetic efficiency, that are likely to be closely related to fitness (Pyke, Pulliam, and Charnov 1977; Smith 1979).

If we apply this perspective to the analysis of food acquisition patterns among the !Kung, Aché, and any other hunter-gatherers, our attention is immediately directed to the fitness-related costs and benefits of foraging—that is, to the relative advantages and disadvantages of alternative foraging strategies under different circumstances. To the extent that we can correlate these fitness costs and benefits to features of local ecology, we develop understanding applicable not only to the present but to the Pleistocene as well.

The !Kung

It is ironic that Lee's work on the !Kung, which set a new standard for ecological anthropology, seems to show that !Kung behavior is inconsistent with a biological definition of adaptation. !Kung women, so the data suggest, work relatively little, never exhaust local resources, yet have comparatively few children. This is paradoxical. If there is plenty of food available and plenty of time to acquire it, they could comfortably feed more children than they have. Under these circumstances any tendency to shorten the birth interval and increase the number of offspring would increase parents' fitness. Why don't the !Kung work harder, eat more, and turn more resources into babies? Could it be that in spite of appearances the !Kung are working as hard and eating as much as will give them the maximum number of grandchildren?

Following a lead from Lee (1972), Blurton Jones and Sibly (1978) asked precisely this question some time ago in an essay that remains curiously underappreciated. They measured the labor costs of alternative inter-birth intervals given five assumptions: (1) that women seasonally provide about 60 percent of family caloric intake in the form of mongongo nuts; (2) that mothers usually take children under the age of four on foraging trips; (3) that these children depend heavily on mother's milk; (4) that women could not gather nuts daily because of the processing time these nuts require; and (5) that dry-season camps must be up to six miles from nut groves because of the distribution of groves and permanent water holes. Blurton Jones and Sibly found that with these constraints, the *maximum* backload that did not threaten thermal exhaustion is sustained by carrying the nut-and-baby load set by a four-year birth interval. In other words, !Kung women seem to be working as hard as they safely can in order to get food to support as many children as possible under the prevailing ecological circumstances. The apparent challenge to a biological perspective is provisionally rebutted, at least as far as women's work effort and reproductive strategy are concerned.

But what about *men's* work effort? If more food means more surviving offspring, why don't !Kung men hunt more frequently? It would certainly seem as if their wives should try to persuade them to do so. Can it be that the low level of hunting effort is one that maximizes men's reproductive success given the options available?

If Blurton Jones and Sibly are right, the heat and humidity constraints that limit women's work effort may impede the men's as well. Although hunters do not carry heavy burdens, except when bringing game to camp, the faster pace they sustain in tracking and pursuit may increase the danger of heat exhaustion and raise water requirements. Lee (1979:105–7) notes that "a person walking in the sun at 38°C (100°F) sweats at the rate of roughly 800 cc of water loss per hour, an equivalent of over 3 liters (over 6 lb of water) in a typical working day." If either high temperatures or a relative lack of water limit men's hunting efforts, we might expect to see a pattern of seasonal variability in this activity.

Lee (1968, 1969, 1979) presents quantitative data on hunting for a four-week period in July–August, the coolest and nearly the driest time of year. He says that tracking conditions during this period "encourage more hunting and the setting up of snare lines" (Lee 1979:104), but his data show that men actually hunt on only 31 percent of all possible days.[1]

Additional data are available in Yellen's activity reports for 15 Bushmen camps (1977:appendix B), covering a 28-day period in May–June (cool-dry) and a 42-day period from December to March (warm-wet). No complete data are available for July to November. Yellen shows that men hunted on 47 percent of all days in May and June, and on 73 percent of all days in December through March (Table 13.1). In other words, the !Kung hunt more than five days a week on average in the hot, relatively wet summer, but only about two days a week in the cool, dry weather. The !Kung summer pattern is more like that of the Aché than it is like the !Kung winter pattern. This suggests that it may be water rather than heat stress that limits Kalahari hunters.[2] Only more quantitative information on seasonal hunting effort, water and temperature factors, and variations in prey distribution can clarify the seasonal costs and benefits of hunting. Empirical tests of hypotheses about specific trade-offs are clearly in order. Still, the very high hunting effort evident during the summer is sufficient to encourage the suggestion that !Kung men may well be working as hard and providing as much food as they safely can under the circumstances.

TABLE 13.1. Hunting Effort Among !Kung Men in a
Sample of 15 Camps

Season	Month	Camp number indentification	Adult man days of occupation
Dry Winter	May	7.2	21
		13	25
	June	2	18
		12	15
		16	31
Dry Winter **Totals**			**110**
Wet Summer	December	4.3	21
	January	4.4	13
	February	1.2	10
		3.1	24
		4.5	4
		5	4
	March	3.2	6
		6	9
		7.1	15
		9	6
Wet **Summer** **Totals**			**112**

SOURCE: Tabulations from Yellen (1977: appendix B).

The Aché

Also low-latitude foragers, the Aché of Paraguay are not as well known as the
!Kung. There are several references to the Aché (also called Guayaki) in historical accounts before the 1960s (see Metraux and Baldus 1963; O'Leary
1963), but the first modern ethnographic reports that were widely available are
those of Clastres (1968, 1972), who studied two of the four living Aché groups.
The data used here pertain to the northern Aché, who have come into unarmed
contact with outsiders only during the past decade (Hill 1983). Full-time hunter-
gatherers until that time, they currently live primarily at a Catholic mission

Adult man days of hunting	Adult man days of gathering or honey collecting	% of days men hunted	% of days men spent in food acquisition
8	1		
13	7		
9	5		
8	1		
14	7		
52	**21**	**47%**	**66%**
14	4		
8	4		
4	2		
15	6		
4			
2			
6			
9			
15			
5			
82	**16**	**73%**	**88%**

(Chupa Pou) but continue to forage frequently in the nearby forest. These foraging trips have been described in reports that include figures on time costs and quantities of resources acquired, as well as analyses of the efficiency of Aché foraging strategies (Hawkes, Hill, and O'Connell 1982; Hill and Hawkes 1983), the seasonal pattern of food acquisition (Hill et al. 1984), the sharing of food resources (Kaplan et al. 1984; Kaplan and Hill 1985), and men's and women's time allocation (Hill et al. 1985; Hurtado et al. 1985).

During the 10 years prior to their first peaceful contact with outsiders (1960–1970), the northern Aché probably numbered between 600 and 800 (Hill 1983). Their traditional range is an area of about 12,000 square kilometers between 54 and 56 degrees west and 24 and 25 degrees south. This is a well-watered region with many rivers and streams. Most of the area is covered with tropical broad-leaf evergreen forest, which the Aché prefer to open grassland. Rainfall is quite unpredictable from month to month and year to year, although there is a statistically significant difference between wet and dry seasons. Annual average precipitation is approximately 1,600 millimeters. Fluctuations in temperature are much more regular, with an annual January maximum around 40°C and a July minimum of about -3°C. Ecology and climate are more fully described in Hill et al. (1984).

The Aché take a wide variety of animal species. Among the most important are peccaries (*Tajassu tajacu* and *Tajassu pecari*), paces (*Cuniculus paca*), coatis (*Nasua nasua*), armadillos (*Dasypus novemcintus*), and capuchin monkeys (*Cebus apella*). They also exploit numerous plant products, especially those of the palm *Arecastrum romanzolfianum,* from which they take the fruit, the heart, and starch from the trunk. Fruits and honey are also major resources with insects providing a small but consistent component of the diet.

Hunting in closed, sub-tropical forest, cross-cut by many small streams, the Aché are at much less risk of heat stress or dehydration than are the !Kung. Here, too much water can limit hunting. Rain ruins bow strings, blurs tracks, makes the animals difficult to hear or see. The 15 percent of the study days on which men hunt less than two hours are days of heavy rain. Otherwise, and with surprisingly low variance (Hill et al. 1985), men hunt an average of seven hours a day, day after day, in every season.

The simple proposition implicit in the discussion of the !Kung was that more food generally gives higher fitness benefits. Thus, acquisition will not stop when some "minimum needs" are met. Instead, work effort and procurement totals will be limited by the costs (and benefits) imposed by local ecological circumstances. Where these costs are lower, foraging investment should increase accordingly. The higher work effort of Aché men, throughout the seasons, is consistent with this. Two specific findings relevant here are that better hunters spend more time hunting (Hill and Hawkes 1983; Hawkes et al. 1985), and that better hunters have higher reproductive success (Kaplan and Hill 1985).

Why then, if heat and water stress are unlikely and more food is generally better than less, should Aché women spend so little time gathering, an average of less than two hours per day (Hurtado et al. 1985)? The answer to women's low food-related work effort may lie partly in the fact that Aché move camp nearly every day in pursuit of game. The women are responsible for carrying all household equipment and at least some of their children between camps. This suggests the hypothesis that women and their children do better by following the men than they would by establishing a more permanent camp in which gear and children could be deposited while they gathered food in the surrounding forest. Two implications of this are (1) that men should do better hunting on days when camp moves, and (2) that on days when camp is not moved, women's foraging effort should increase. In fact, if the days when camp is not moved are separated from the "normal activity" days, the difference in the time women spend acquiring and processing food is substantial. Their foraging time increases 77 percent on the rare days when camp does not move (93 versus 165 minutes).

In addition to trading off foraging for carrying, Aché women face another problem. In an environment where the "safe area" for small children is never larger or more substantial than the temporary camps, the local exigencies of child care may constrain women's foraging. Women's collecting activities may reduce the quality of their child care or significantly increase its cost where there is high probability of danger to children who are not attentively monitored. That child care does constrain foraging is indicated by the kind of foraging women do. They collect those items out of the larger set the Aché exploit whose acquisition is most compatible with child care. The trade-off is quantitatively demonstrated by the reductions in women's foraging efficiency (calories acquired per unit of time) when they are nursing, and also when the number of weaned dependents they have goes up (Hurtado et al. 1985). These data are consistent with the view that more foraging imposes a fitness cost on women, unmatched by its fitness benefit. What women "need" to collect is not set by nutritional minima, but by the fitness opportunity costs of foraging.

Conclusion

Even though provisional and illustrative, this argument about the determinants of variation in foraging effort and food acquisition among the Kung and Aché should be sufficient to suggest the potential utility of a sociobiological perspective in the analysis of human behavior. With respect to foraging, this perspective suggests that features of local ecology such as the presence of injurious flora and fauna, the distribution and availability of water and food resources, and seasonal changes in these will affect the costs and benefits associated with food acquisition. The expectation is that variable patterns are adaptations in the narrow sense—that is, they tend to maximize (inclusive) fitness. Whether arguments like this are ultimately compelling will depend on the results of further analyses of these and larger, more comprehensive data sets, especially those collected specifically for the purpose of testing sociobiologically derived hypotheses about behavioral variability.

From a sociobiological perspective, patterns of behavior are expected to favor options that tend to have the highest fitness payoffs. Leisure, food, com-

349

fort, security, health, power, affection, are not ends in themselves but means. More food generally means more grandchildren. If and when it does not, we expect acquisition to be limited accordingly. From this perspective many differences among modern foragers, and differences within and between local groups and across time among our Pleistocene ancestors, may be the result of fitness-enhancing adjustments to fairly immediate local constraints.

It is not enough to see the rather different work effort and consumption patterns of the !Kung and the Aché as the adventitious results of recent history. By taking advantage of the concept of adaptation in the strictest biological sense, we may be able to account for some of the variety in the present in the way that will help us understand the past. Among other things, it may prevent us from giving up on the simple answers too soon.

Appendix

The foregoing description of the variation in foraging patterns between the !Kung and the Aché does not attend to the larger political and economic network in which both populations are embedded. This is an important general issue, independent of the merits of sociobiological perspectives. Can it be useful and clarifying to focus on the behavior of modern hunter-gatherers, and their local ecology, to the exclusion of wider historical contexts? In fact, given the special features of the modern world, can research on modern hunter-gatherers ever inform us in any general way about human foragers, especially in the prehistoric past?

It is widely recognized that modern hunters are not pristine living relics of the Pleistocene. As Schrire (1980) has shown, the !Kung have alternately made their living as farmers and pastoralists as well as hunter-gatherers for at least the past four centuries and have often been the clients of more powerful neighbors, just as they are today.

The Aché case is somewhat less clear but has some similar features. The northern Aché have been economically independent of its agricultural neighbors in the recent past, having only hostile contact with them until the establishment of local mission-sponsored settlements in the early 1970s. At that time the Aché suffered enormous losses from disease. In 1978 the mission colony of Chupa Pou was created and is now home to more than two hundred Northern Aché. From here many continue to take extended foraging trips, sometimes longer than two weeks, into the surrounding forest, where they support themselves entirely by hunting and gathering in a manner they claim to be like their full-time foraging of a few years ago. The more distant past remains clouded. Their language is closely related to that of the surrounding horticultural Guaraní Indians. It may be that they have ancestors in common, the Aché having been displaced by warfare to become refugee foragers sometime before the arrival of the Spanish in the 16th century. Such a pattern is probably not uncommon among lowland South American hunter-gatherers (Isaac 1977; Lathrap 1968).

Some (notably Isaac 1977 and Schrier 1980) have argued that the historical circumstances of the !Kung and the Aché and other 20th-century foraging groups make them inappropriate sources of information and inference about "real" hunter-gatherers, especially those of the remote past. It is as though their recent history, with its episodes of disease, depopulation, and displacement, and its periods of dependence on horticulture or pastoralism, has somehow tainted them, made them "unrepresentative" as foragers. Moreover, it is argued that the social, political, economic, and ecological circumstances in which modern foragers are encountered are so much the product of colonialism and the reach of industrial capitalism, and so unlike the prehistoric past, that one cannot hope to learn anything useful from them apart from documenting the disastrous results of their contact with state societies. From that perspective studies of the foraging patterns of modern hunters that do not focus on the play of wider regional economic and political forces in their lives are, at best, deeply misguided.

This conclusion can be challenged on several grounds. Most importantly, it implies little hope for a nomothetic understanding of human behavior. All societies differ from each other and change over time. Each occurs in a unique social and ecological setting. Any synchronic description slices out a unique set of events. It is the variability within and between societies and over time, the pattern in the differences observed ethnographically or inferred archaeologically, that we seek to explain. The descriptive convenience of typing societies—as "hunter-gatherers," for example—should not divert us into a search for archetypes in which the variability, the original object of inquiry, is cast aside as an imperfection, due to the damage of recent history, in some representations of the type. Any society anywhere has a recent history, and disease, depopulation, and displacement are not unique to the modern world.

The question is, how do we go about explaining the variety? Although any particular instance of human behavior has some unique shape, we also expect that there are common processes that dictate this shape. How else do we account for the remarkable commonalities in the evolution of human behavior worldwide over the past hundred thousand years? If common processes are not at work in such phenomena as the independent near-simultaneous emergence of agriculture in several parts of the world at the beginning of the Holocene, or the subsequent, again more or less simultaneous and independent, emergence of state societies in a smaller number of cases, the coincidence can only be seen as astonishing.

If we expect general principles to govern the larger pattern of temporal changes, we must also expect them to govern short-term patterns. The apparent uniqueness of modern circumstances must be accountable as well. We *might* use our sociobiological perspective to focus on the effects on modern foragers' behavior of particular features of their current state of dependence. The Aché mission shapes the opportunities available to individual Aché. We might seek to identify these alternatives, and the fitness-related costs and benefits of each, and make testable predictions about which of the array individual Aché will pursue. We might expect, for example, that variations in the amount of time individuals choose to spend at the mission or in the forest will depend on the respective fitness-related costs and benefits of each, and that these may vary with such factors as the age, sex, and health of those individuals, as well as with the changing mix of other individuals in either place, including potential mates, kin, and rivals. In this way a series of testable hypotheses can be developed about the effects of the mission on Aché behavior. The mission has changed the array of behavioral opportunities, but the process of choosing among them continues.

In general, as in this paper, our focus of attention in studying the Aché has not been on the effects of the mission. Instead, we have focused on the behavior of the Aché observed away from the mission, in the forest. We have made the working assumption that certain behavioral strategies in the forest are shaped by the behavioral options in the forest. In other words, we assume that once Aché leave the mission to live entirely dependent on hunting and gathering for a week or two, some aspects of their behavior are shaped by the opportunity costs of foraging for different resources in different ways, and by the opportunity costs of foraging itself relative to other activities. We expect that people who spend significant portions of their time foraging in familiar habitats for their own subsistence in the company of kin, with mating opportunities largely limited to local groups, are likely to shape much of their behavior to these conditions. Such expectations are empirically vulnerable. If other factors—such as mission activities, features of the larger regional or world economic system, or historical circumstances not embodied in currently measurable options and constraints—overwhelmingly influence their choices, then correlations with local foraging conditions will be swamped.

Surely many Aché (and !Kung) behaviors depend entirely on the opportunities shaped by the larger state society in which they are embedded. But some behavior may be more powerfully governed by local ecology. If it is possible to account for much of the difference in work effort and food procurement by focusing on the opportunity costs set by such features as temperature and the distribution and abundance of water and wild plant and animal resources, we have a strong foundation for constructing expectations about foragers elsewhere, including behavior in particular times and places in the Pleistocene. As long as we construct and test theoretically motivated hypotheses about behavioral variety, we will check any tendency to give too much weight to the costs and benefits of immediate foraging options. It is important to know how much of the variation we can account for in this way. Unless we try, we may forfeit the richest line of evidence we have about human behavior in the Pleistocene.

Acknowledgments

James F. O'Connell is responsible for much of this paper and eludes co-authorship only at his firm wish. I thank Kim Hill, Nicholas Blurton Jones, Kevin Jones, Mark Cohen, Eric Charnov, Eric Smith, Eric Ross, Seymour Parker, Robert Anderson, and especially Hillard Kaplan for stimulating criticism and advice.

Notes

1. The alternative work opportunities for men at Dobe during Lee's 28-day sampling period may have made hunting significantly less attractive than during the same season in other years (Hill 1983).

2. There are, however, some puzzling inconsistencies. For example, Lee (1979: 104–5), citing observations reported by Marshall (1976:140), says that in the dry, hot spring (August–November), "the men say the heat makes the animals less wary and their movements are more predictable, so they are easier to stalk and kill. This fact is reflected in the kill statistics: October was a consistently good hunting month in terms of number of large animals killed." If water stress was a danger, one would have expected relatively *low* hunting effort during this period. Unfortunately, no data are available on the average number of days men actually hunt during this season.

References Cited

Blurton Jones, N., and R. Sibly
    1978   Testing Adaptiveness of Culturally Determined Behavior: Do Bushmen Women Maximize Their Reproductive Success by Spacing Births Widely and Foraging Seldom? In *Human Behaviour and Adaptation,* N. Blurton Jones and V. Reynolds, eds., pp. 135–58. London: Taylor and Francis.

Clastres, P.
           Ethnographie des Indians Guayaki (Paraguay-Brésil). *Journal de la Société des Americanistes de Paris* 57:9–61.
    1972   The Guayaki. In *Hunters and Gatherers Today,* M. B. Bicchieri, ed., pp. 138–174. New York: Holt, Rinehart and Winston.

Cohen, M.
    1977   *The Food Crisis in Prehistory.* New Haven: Yale University Press.

Ember, C.
    1978   Myths About Hunter-Gatherers. *Ethnology* 17:439–448.

Harako, R.
    1981   The Cultural Ecology of Hunting Behavior Among Mbuti Pygmies in the Ituri Forest, Zaire. In *Omnivorous Primates: Gathering and Hunting in Human Evolution,* R. S. O. Harding and G. Teleki, eds., pp. 499–556. New York: Columbia University Press.

Harris, M.
    1977   *Cannibals and Kings: The Origins of Cultures.* New York: Random House.
    1983   *Cultural Anthropology.* New York: Harper and Row.

Hawkes, K.; K. Hill; and J. F. O'Connell
    1982   Why Hunters Gather: Optimal Foraging and the Aché of Eastern Paraguay. *American Ethnologist* 9:379–98.

Hawkes. K., and J. O'Connell
    1981   Affluent Hunters? Some Comments in Light of the Alyawara Case. *American Anthropologist* 83:622–26.

Hawkes, K.; J. F. O'Connell; K. Hill; and E. Charnov
    1985   How Much Is Enough: Hunters and "Limited Needs." *Ethology and Sociobiology* 6:3–15.

Hill, K.
    1983   Adult Male Subsistence Strategies among Aché Hunter-Gatherers of Eastern Paraguay. Ph.D. dissertation, University of Utah.

Hill, K., and K. Hawkes
    1983   Neotropical Hunting Among the Aché of Eastern Paraguay. In *Adaptive Responses of Native Amazonians,* R. Hames and W. Vickers, eds., pp. 139–88. New York: Academic Press.

Hill, K.; H. Kaplan; K. Hawkes; and A. M. Hurtado
    1984   Seasonal Variance in the Diet of Aché Hunter-Gatherers in Eastern Paraguay. *Human Ecology* 12:145–80.

Hill, K., et al.
    1985   Men's Time Allocation to Activities Among Ache Hunter-Gatherers. *Human Ecology* 13:29–47.

Howell, N.
    1979   *Demography of the Dobe Kung.* New York: Academic Press.

Hurtado, A. M.; K. Hawkes; K. Hill; and H. Kaplan
    1985   Female Subsistence Strategies Among the Aché of Eastern Paraguay. *Human Ecology* 13:1–28.

Isaac, B.
    1977   The Siriono of Eastern Bolivia: A Reexamination. *Human Ecology* 5:137–54.

Kaplan, H., and K. Hill
    1985   Hunting Ability and Reproductive Success Among Male Ache Foragers: Preliminary Results. *Current Anthropology* 26:131–33.

Kaplan, H.; K. Hill; K. Hawkes; and A. M. Hurtado
    1984   Aché Food Sharing. *Current Anthropology* 25:113–15.

Lathrap, D.
    1968   The "Hunting" Economies of the Tropical Forest Zone of South America: An Attempt at Historical Perspective. In *Man the Hunter,* R. Lee and I. DeVore, eds., pp. 23–29. Chicago: Aldine.

Leakey, R., and K. Lewin
    1978   *People of the Lake: Mankind and Its Beginning.* Garden City, N.Y.: Anchor Press/Doubleday.

Lee, R. B.
    1968   What Hunters Do for a Living; or, How to Make Out on Scarce Resources. In *Man the Hunter,* R. B. Lee and I. DeVore, eds., pp. 30–48. Chicago: Aldine.

    1969   Kung Bushmen Subsistence: An Input–Out Analysis. In *Environment and Cultural Behavior,* A. P. Vayda, ed., pp. 47–79. Garden City, N.Y.: Natural History Press.

    1972   Population Growth and the Beginning of Sedentary Life Among the !Kung Bushmen. In *Population Growth: Anthropological Implications,* B. Spooner, ed., pp. 329–42. Cambridge: MIT Press.

    1979   *The !Kung San: Men, Women and Work in a Foraging Society.* Cambridge: Cambridge University Press.

Lee, R. B., and I. DeVore (eds.)
    1968   *Man the Hunter.* Chicago: Aldine.
Marshall, L.
    1976   *The !Kung of Nyae Nyae.* Cambridge: Harvard University Press.
Maynard Smith, J.
    1978   Optimization Theory in Evolution. *Annual Review of Ecology and Systematics* 9:31–56.
Metraux, A., and H. Baldus
    1963   The Guayaki. In *Handbook of South American Indians,* Vol. 1, J. Steward, ed., pp. 435–44. New York: Couper Square.
O'Leary, T.
    1963   *Ethnographic Bibliography of South America.* New Haven: Human Relations Area File Press.
Pyke, G.; R. Pulliam; and E. L. Charnov
    1977   Optimal Foraging: A Selective Review of Theory and Tests. *Quarterly Review of Biology* 52:137–54.
Sahlins, M.
    1968   Notes on the Original Affluent Society. In *Man the Hunter,* R. B. Lee and I. DeVore, eds., pp. 85–89. Chicago: Aldine.
    1972   *Stone Age Economics.* Chicago: Aldine.
Schrire, C.
    1980   An Inquiry Into the Evolutionary Status and Apparent Identity of San Hunter-Gatherers. *Human Ecology* 8:9–32.
Smith, E. A.
    1979   Human Adaptation and Energetic Efficiency. *Human Ecology* 7:53–74.
Tanaka, J.
    1980   *The San: Hunter Gatherers of the Kalahari—A Study in Ecological Anthropology.* Translated by D. W. Hughes. Tokyo: University of Tokyo Press.
Thomas, E. M.
    1959   *The Harmless People.* New York: Knopf.
Truswell, A. S., and J. D. L. Hansen
    1979   Medical Research Among the Kung. In *Kalahari Hunter-Gatherers,* R. B. Lee and I. DeVore, eds., pp. 166–94. Cambridge: Harvard University Press.
Williams, G.
    1966   *Adaptation and Natural Selection: A Critique of Some Current Evolutionary Thought.* Princeton: Princeton University Press.
Wilmsen, E.
    1978   Seasonal Effects of Dietary Intake on Kalahari San. *Federation of American Societies for Experimental Biology Proceedings* 37:65–72.
Yellen, J.
    1977   *Archaeological Approaches to the Present: Models for Reconstructing the Past.* New York: Academic Press.

355

14

DAVID R. HARRIS

Aboriginal Subsistence in a Tropical Rain Forest Environment: Food Procurement, Cannibalism, and Population Regulation in Northeastern Australia

In this chapter an indigenous, non-Westernized dietary pattern is analyzed as a contribution to the understanding of human food procurement and nutrition in tropical rain-forest environments. The example is drawn from northern Queensland, specifically the southeastern Cape York Peninsula, where an Australian Aboriginal population of foragers, fishers, and hunters continued to exist, unaffected by European influences, until the second half of the 19th century. The descriptive data on which the analysis is based are derived partly from 19th-century historical sources and partly from ecological and ethnographic fieldwork (Harris 1975, 1978). There is as yet little archaeological evidence relating to the antiquity and temporal development of the 19th-century dietary patterns (Campbell 1980; Harris 1978:132; Hersfall 1983, 1984), but palynological investigation has demonstrated that tropical rain forest has been established in the area for approximately the last ten thousand years (Kershaw 1974, 1976).

Methodological Assumptions

The methodological assumptions on which this Australian case study rests accord with the adaptational and evolutionary perspective that underlies this volume as a whole. They can be enumerated as follows:

1. Persistent human dietary patterns consist of sets of behaviors involving food procurement, production, processing, and consumption that are them-

357

selves part of larger subsistence systems composed of interacting ecological, physiological, demographic, technological, and sociopolitical variables.

2. Dietary patterns result from processes of evolutionary selection, the spatial and temporal dimensions of which need to be specified as precisely as possible.

3. Persistent (i.e., evolutionarily "successful") dietary patterns vary widely in relation to food availability and choice, but only within physiologically determined limits set by the basic nutritional requirements of humans for a dietary mix of proteins, carbohydrates, fats, and essential minerals and vitamins sufficient to provide energy and to sustain growth and reproduction.

4. A dietary pattern is definable in terms of behavioral norms in food-related activities that are common to, and the result of ecophysiologically optimizing behavior by, a group as a whole, but . . .

5. Group dietary behavior may incorporate socially prescribed food preferences and avoidances that take effect within or between groups and are keyed to differences in age, sex, status, or ethnicity.

In analyzing the example presented in this Chapter, I focus on how the food-getting and food-using activities of the Aboriginal population meshed with ecological, demographic, and social variables that form part of the subsistence system as a whole, giving special attention to how basic nutritional requirements were satisfied. Less attention is paid to the temporal development of the dietary patterns described because there is as yet so little chronological evidence available; and ethnograhic information on socially prescribed food preferences and avoidance is also too meager to allow more than causal reference to them.

The Cultural Context

Prior to the penetration of northeastern Queensland by European prospectors, loggers, and settlers in the second half of the 19th century, the mountains, plateaus, and coastal lowlands between Cardwell and Cairns were clothed in structurally complex and floristically diverse rain forest. The pre-European distribution of rain forest coincided closely with the east coast area, which receives more rainfall annually (1,500–ca. 4,000 millimeters) than any other part of Australia, although even here the winter months (June–November) are relatively dry. In the mid-19th century, the rain-forest region of approximately 11,660 square kilometers was occupied, according to Tindale (1974:164–90), by 12 Aboriginal tribal groups whose territories were, with one exception, restricted to coastal and inland rain-forest habitats. There is uncertainty over the precise number and distribution of "rain-forest tribes" (Dixon 1976; Peterson 1976), but there is little doubt that the Aboriginal populations of the region were in many ways physically and culturally distinct from the tribal groups of the open-woodland savanna habitats farther inland.

Nineteenth-century European observers were impressed by the small stature and slender limbs of the rain-forest Aborigines, and Tindale and Birdsell (1941), who worked with a remnant population on the Atherton Plateau in 1938, identified the 12 tribal groups of the rain-forest region and argued that they constituted a distinctively pygmoid racial type. This led to a controversy about their racial affinities and putative role in the initial peopling of Australia, which lies outside the scope of this paper, but later linguistic studies by Dixon (1972, 1976) have tended to support the view that the rain-forest tribes were clearly differentiated from their neighbors, although at least five distinct languages were spoken in the region and linguistic links existed with peripheral groups.

It is in their material culture, however, that the rain-forest tribes exhibit their greatest distinctiveness. Several items of their material culture are unique within Aboriginal Australia and directly reflect features of the rain-forest habitat. These include dome-shaped, rainproof, thatched huts occupied mainly in the wet season (December–May), but lasting from year to year; bark cloth hammered from the inner bark of fig trees (*Ficus pleurocarpa*), which was used to make blankets as well as containers both for carrying water and honey and for leaching bitter yams; baskets made from lawyer cane (*Calamus australis*) and rush (*Xerotes longifolia*), which were used as sieve bags for leaching toxic nuts; huge wooden swords and shields, the latter made from the flange buttresses of fig trees and painted with intricate designs when a boy was initiated into manhood (McConnel 1935); and, of potential archaeological significance, very large stone axes used, for example, to lop off the fig tree buttresses, and two unique types of specialized nut-processing stone tools. The first of these was a large anvil stone pitted with small, spherical depressions, accompanied by a small hammer stone, used to crack open the exceptionally hard nuts of the Queensland almond (*Elaeocarpus bancroftii*). The other was an ovate or rectangular grooved slab (the *morah*), associated with a smaller crushing stone (the *moogi*), used to macerate nut kernels, especially those of the yellow and black walnuts (*Beilschmiedia bancroftii* and *Endiandra palmerstonii*).

In addition to these items of material culture, several non-material aspects of rain-forest culture also appear to have been distinctive—for example, the holding of fighting corroborees to settle disputes, the practice of partial mummification prior to cremation, and, of particular interest in the context of this volume, cannibalism. The last trait was frequently—and avidly—commented upon by early European observers, but it is difficult to determine from the historical sources what role it may have played in pre-European rain-forest society. Its possible significance is discussed below.

Food Procurement

It is possible to reconstruct in outline the pre-European pattern of food procurement of those rain-forest tribes who occupied the inland basaltic, granitic, and metamorphic plateaus and mountains, as opposed to the alluvial coastal lowlands, and who did not apparently have direct access to the coast and its resources. Four main historical sources provide information on the Aborigines of this area, all dating from the 1880s. They are the records left by Christie Palmerston (1883, 1886, 1887), a pioneer prospector; Carl Lumholtz (1889), a Norwegian zoologist and ethnographer; Archibald Meston (1889, 1904), who led two scientific expeditions to the Bellenden Ker Range; and Walter Roth (1901–10), the pioneer ethnographer who became the Queensland Government's first Northern Protector of Aborigines in 1897. Useful additional information on Aboriginal subsistence can be gleaned from a series of newspaper articles written by Robert Johnstone (1903–5), who served in the Native Police and traveled extensively in the rain-forest region in the 1870s and 1880s. On the basis of these historical sources, together with limited information from living descendants of the rain-forest tribes and ecological observations in the few remaining tracts of uncleared forest, it is possible to construct a broad picture of pre-European subsistence.

The most detailed descriptions of Aboriginal food procurement are contained in Meston's reports on his two expeditions to the Bellenden Ker Range. They are worth quoting in full because they provide the most comprehensive picture of subsistence in the rain forest:

> Their food is chiefly vegetarian, varied occasionally by the flesh of the wallaby, the tree-climbing kangaroo, fish, birds, eggs, and three or four varieties of opossums. The koa nut and other large nuts not yet botanically named, are the chief articles of diet. Some of the nuts and roots they eat are poisonous in their raw state, and these are pounded up and placed in dilly bags in running water for a couple of days to have the poisonous principle washed out. Of edible nuts of various kinds they have an unlimited supply. In pursuit of tree-climbing animals they display an agility probably unsurpassed in the world, and probably not rivalled by any other Australian black. It would severely tax the reader's credulity to describe how these natives take a vine and run up the tallest trees, walk on to others across the branches, and descend sometimes a considerable distance from the starting point. Their main camps are always built on some healthy dry situation, beside or very near a running stream. These are the "wet weather camps," where they remain during the wet season, and store large supplies of nuts. . . . We saw no camps higher than 2,000 feet, and very rarely any above 1,000 feet. These camps on high altitudes are only temporary, and usually consist of a few bent boughs covered over by fern or palm leaves. At certain times they go up the mountains after the "mappee," the tree-climbing kangaroo, but

never remain long. The nuts they chiefly live on are only found on the flats and in the valleys. There is little or no food on the mountains. (Meston 1889:8)

They use three kinds of yam, and so far as I could learn they eat about twenty varieties of nuts, eight species of beans, and thirty species of fruit, large and small. . . . A majority of the nuts used are subjected to roasting and purification by running water. Some are merely roasted and eaten, and a few are eaten raw. . . . Some of the nuts, when roasted and ground, and placed in water, deposit an arrowroot which is roasted and eaten in that shape, and can be boiled and sweetened. . . . Among the fruits eaten raw are at least four varieites of figs, all excellent, even in their wild state, and promising highly satisfactory results in cultivation. The Bellenden-Ker blacks wear no covering of any kind. Their camps in the scrub on the mountain are usually roofed with the fronds of the lawyer palm (*Calamus australis*), and on the edge of the forest they roof with blady grass. The camps are dome-shaped, with one or two entrances, and on the mountain I found three or four connected, one entrance going through them all. In the wet season the nuts are collected by the women, who gather them every second or third day, regardless of the state of the weather. . . . I found these blacks living through the wet season almost exclusively on two kinds of nut, "Cankkee" and "Tekkel," and a majority were in fair condition. This diet was supplemented at very irregular intervals by the eggs of the scrub turkey and scrub hen (*Megapodius tumulus*). In the winter they got a few eggs of the cassowary. Animal food is scarce, though there are three opossums and four iguanas, one tree-climbing kangaroo, two bandicoots, five species of rats, and various other small animals, apart from the dingo and two species of native cat. (Meston 1904:6)

Although these two descriptions refer specifically to the Bellenden Ker Range, many of Meston's statements about particular foods are corroborated independently by the writings of Palmerston, Lumholtz, and Johnstone, which relate to more extensive areas south and west of Bellenden Ker. Meston's descriptions can, therefore, be taken as broadly representative of the inland rain-forest tribes as a whole. In one particular, however, his comments are slightly misleading, probably because his first-hand observations were restricted to the Bellenden Ker Range itself. He barely mentions fish, but it is clear from the other historical sources that fish and other freshwater aquatic resources, such as eels and crayfish, made an important contribution to the food supply, as is reflected in the range of Aboriginal fishing techniques recorded, which included spearing, hooking, trapping, netting, and stupefaction.

Meston's descriptions of food procurement, and the less detailed accounts provided by other early observers, give a vivid impression of the diversity of plant and animal foods exploited in the rain forest, but they also pose problems of interpretation. In particular they raise the question of the botanical identity of the nuts and other plant products that were apparently staple foods. Careful study of the Aboriginal plant names recorded by early observers, and their correlation with the scientific binomials given by Bailey (1899–1905, 1909) and other botanists, allows at least tentative identifications to be made of most of them, identifications that can sometimes be confirmed by checking early descriptive statements against modern specimens. Analysis of the historical data yields a minimal total of 59 species (or 48 genera in 18 families) used for food in the inland rain forest, and classification of them into four categories according to the part of the plant consumed shows that 28 species were exploited for their fruits, 15 for their "nuts" or other seeds, 9 for their stems, buds, or shoots, and 7 for their roots or tubers.

Although fruits form the largest group of plant foods, it is clear from the historical sources that nuts, and to a lesser extent roots and tubers, made a more important contribution to the daily diet because they provided a large and assured supply of carbohydrates. Tree nuts in particular provided a ready source of starchy "bulk" food, comparable, for example, to the role of wild grass and cycad seeds, or roots and tubers, in the diets of non-forest populations elsewhere in Aboriginal Australia, and they had the added merit of also yielding appreciable quantities of protein and fat. Most of them, however, are bitter or even toxic, and require laborious processing to render them palatable. The historical accounts abound in references to the abundance, processing, and storage of tree nuts, and the large numbers of nut-processing stones that have been discovered in the course of forest clearance during this century further confirm the status of this resource as the staple plant food in the rain forest.

Despite the difficulty of securely identifying all the plant foods referred to in the historical accounts, it has proved possible to identify eleven tree species, the seeds of which provided substantial quantities of starchy food and, in some cases, also protein and/or fat. They are listed in Table 14.1, where their status—inferred from the historical accounts—as primary or secondary staples, or as supplementary food sources, is also indicated. Seven of the species listed

TABLE 14.1. Principal Nut-Yielding Rain-Forest Trees

| Botanical names | English names | Preparation | | Inferred status as aboriginal food |
		Leached	Eaten raw	
Lauraceae				
Beilschmiedia bancroftii (syn. *Cryptocarya bancroftii*)	Yellow walnut, Red walnut, Yellow nut, Canary ash	+		ps

Botanical names	English names	Preparation		Inferred status as aboriginal food
		Leached	Eaten raw	
Endiandra palmerstonii (syn. *Cryptocarya palmerstonii*)	Black walnut, Queensland walnut, Australian walnut	+		ps
Endiandra pubens (syn. *E. insignis, Cryptocarya muelleri*)	Hairy walnut, Rusty walnut	+		ss
Endiandra tooram	Brown walnut, Tooram walnut	+		ss
Proteaceae				
Macadamia whelanii (syn. *Helicia whelani*)	Whelan's silky oak, Silky oak	+		ss
Hicksbeachia pinnatifolia (syn. *H. pinnatifida*)	Ivory silky oak	+		ss
Helcia diversifolia	White oak		+	ss
Elaeocarpaceae				
Elaeocarpus bancroftii	Queensland almond, Johnstone River almond, Kuranda quandong		+	ps
Euphorbiaceae				
Aleurites moluccana (syn. *A. triloba, Jatropha moluccana*)	Candlenut		+	sup
Leguminosae				
Castanospermum australe	Moreton Bay chestnut, Moreton Bay bean, Bean tree, Black bean	+		sup
Podocarpaceae				
Podocarpus amarus (syn. *P. Pedunculatus, P. Pedunculata*)	Black pine		+	sup

NOTE: ps = primary staple, ss = secondary or local staple, sup = supplementary source of starchy food.

in Table 14.1 are toxic, or at least bitter, and require roasting, either pounding or grating, and soaking or washing in water, before they can be safely eaten. The kernels of all four of the walnuts listed contain sufficient hydrocyanic acid in the form of amygdalin to make them inedible, or at least unpalatable, raw. The historical accounts contain many reference to the processing of these nuts to produce "meal" and "flour," which was then either eaten raw or baked into "damper." The yellow and black walnuts were primary staples, particularly important in the wet season (Meston 1904:6), and the yellow walnut appears to have been the single most important source of nut-derived starchy food (Bailey 1901:1302; Flecker, Stephens, and Stephens 1948:11). Analysis of its shell-to-kernel weight ratio (2.9 to 1.0), and of its nutrient status, shows it to have a relatively high yield per fruit, and high food value per kernel (Tables 14.2 and 14.3), which, together with the abundance and prolific nut production of the trees, goes far to explain its status as a primary staple. It and the other walnuts have relatively thin, easily removed shells, which can, as Palmerston remarks (1886:242), be broken by hitting "against some hard substance . . . allowing the nut to roll out cleanly." This suggests that the large nut-cracking stones found in the rain forest were not designed to process walnuts, although it is known (from a living descendant of rain-forest Aborigines) that the *morah* and *moogi* stones were used to macerate walnut kernels.

The technique of using the massive, pitted nut-cracking stones probably developed as a means of processing the third primary staple, the Queensland almond. The nut has an exceptionally thick and hard shell that contains a single small kernel. The great thickness and weight of the shell relative to the kernel (the shell-to-kernel weight ratio is 13.6 to 1.0; see Table 14.2), and the effort required to crack the shell, do not suggest that the Queensland almond would be a staple food. There are, however, three reasons that favor its exploitation:

TABLE 14.2. Average Weights in Grams of the Seeds of Four Species of Nut-Yielding Rain-Forest Trees

	Elaeocarpus bancroftii	*Beilschmiedia bancroftii*	*Aleurites moluccana*	*Castanospermum australe*
Average weight per kernel	1.2	5.5	3.2	23.1
Average weight per shell	16.4	16.0	6.0	18.5
Ratio of shell to kernel	13.6:1.00	2.9:1.0	1.9:1.0	1.0:1.2

TABLE 14.3. Proximate Nutrient Analysis in Percent of the Kernels of Four Species of Nut-Yielding Rain-Forest Trees

	Moisture	Protein	Carbohydrate	Fat	Fiber	Ash	Calories per 100 g.
Aleurites moluccana	6.05	17.71	7.87	63.72	1.54	3.11	678.36
Elaeocarpus bancroftii	9.48	7.23	19.85	45.11	16.18	2.25	516.61
Beilschmiedia bancroftii	12.13	7.96	71.82	0.59	6.44	1.06	322.41
Castanospermum australe	81.40	1.46	15.78	0.03	0.87	0.46	70.95

first, the very high yield per fruiting tree, which results in large accumulations of nuts beneath individual trees (for example, I counted 40 nuts in an area of 30 square centimeters beneath one tree); second, the durability, and therefore the storability, of the nuts; and third, the palatability and high food value of the kernel. In fact, nutrient analyisis of the kernels revealed that they are rich in fat and also contain an appreciable amount of protein as well as carbohydrate (Table 14.3). The contrast in nutrient balance between the two primary staples, yellow walnut and Queensland almond, the former starchy and the latter more oily, suggests that their emergence as staples may also have been a result of their contrasting taste and their nutritional complementarity.

None of the other species listed in Table 14.1 appears to have been a primary staple, but the candlenut, *Aleurites moluccana,* provided palatable kernels that were particularly valued for their oiliness. Nutrient analysis of the kernels shows that they contain more fat (and protein) than any of the other species sampled and that consequently they have an exceptionally high caloric value (Table 14.3). They also have a favorable shell-to-kernel ratio of 1.9 to 1.0 (Table 14.2). However, they are too emetic to be eaten in quantity, and it is likely that they were valued mainly for their oil content, which would have improved the palatability of foods prepared from the many forest products, plant and animal, that are low in fat. For example, I was told that in the rain forests near Lockhart, farther north in the Cape York Peninsula, candlenuts were traditionally eaten, raw or cooked, with roasted wild banana.

Collectively, the nut-yielding trees listed in Table 14.1 made a massive contribution to Aboriginal subsistence in the inland rain-forest region. The evidence suggests that the yellow and black walnuts and the Queensland almond were primary staples; that the candlenut, Moreton Bay chestnut, and black pine were supplementary foods; and that the remaining species were secondary staples that varied in importance locally. Nutritionally the tree nuts contributed mainly carbohydrate, but also appreciable quantities of protein and fat. They thus added to proteins and fats derived from animal foods and at the same time provided the "bulk" food necessary to satisfy daily hunger, especially in the wet season. Supplementary supplies of starchy vegetable food were also obtained from a wide variety of other rain-forest plants that yielded roots, tubers, stems, shoots, leaves, fruits, and seeds.

The contribution of animal foods to the diet is difficult to assess from the historical sources. References to hunting and fishing tend to be less precise and more opinionated than the accounts of plant use. For example, Lumholtz (1889:128) claims that the Aborigines "subsist chiefly on vegetables" and that "those that live near bodies of water, and have an opportunity of securing fish in addition to game and other animal food, are more vigorous physically than those who have to be satisfied with snakes, lizards, and indigestible vegetables—the latter affording little nourishment." This statement may reflect no more than the carnivorous traditions of a European (whose staple food on his travels in northern Queensland was salt beef!), but the claim that the Aborigines "subsist chiefly on vegetables" does echo Meston's more circumstantial statement (quoted earlier) about their food being "chiefly vegetarian, varied occasionally by the flesh of the wallaby, the tree-climbing kangaroo, fish, birds, eggs, and three or four varieties of opossums."

All the animals referred to as sources of food by early European observers can be listed and classified according to three types of rain-forest habitat: forest floor, forest canopy, and freshwater rivers, lakes, and swamps within the forest. The forest floor is the habitat of fewer animal taxa (15) than either the canopy (21) or the freshwater bodies (8 specified as well as numerous but unspecified "fish"). The most important animal foods of the forest floor were evidently the ground-living scrub fowl, scrub turkey, and cassowary, particularly the former two, the large, durable, nest mounds of which were easily found and provided large numbers of highly nutritious eggs. The cassowary, despite its great size, probably contributed less to the food supply because it is comparatively rare. None of the mammals, reptiles, and insects of the forest floor were major sources of food, although some, such as beetle larvae, were relished for their fatty quality.

The meager supply of animal flesh that could be procured on the forest floor was added to by foraging in the tree canopy and up its supporting trunks and branches. The tree-climbing ability of the rain-forest Aborigines greatly impressed the early European observers, as the opening quotation from Meston illustrates, and Lumholtz (1889:89–90) gives a detailed description of how the trees were climbed by a means of a *kamin* or length of lawyer vine looped around the trunk. This ingenious means of reaching the canopy gave the Aboriginal forager access to a greater variety of animal species than live on the forest floor. However, most of the canopy-living creatures are small, many are nocturnal and difficult to catch, and few can have made a major contribution to the diet. The largest animal of the canopy is the tree kangaroo, and there is some suggestion in Lumholtz's account of its hunting (1889:231–32) that it was a preferred food, subject to overexploitation, at least at the southern limit of its restricted range. The possums probably provided the most constant supply of animal food from the canopy layer, but because of their relatively small size and elusiveness, they cannot have been a staple food. One niche within the canopy layer—the large epiphytic ferns and orchids that cluster around the upper tree trunks—sheltered many kinds of animals and was a valued source of food. Lumholtz describes (1889:294) how "these ferns . . . are constant objects of interest to the natives, for in them they find not only snakes, but also rats and other small mammals. . . . They therefore, as a rule, take the trouble to climb the trees to make the necessary search."

The giant white-tailed rat would have been one of the principal objects of these searches, as it is the largest rain-forest rodent, reaching 60 centimeters in length and about 1 kilogram in weight. The most important snakes hunted in the canopy layer were pythons, which Lumholtz describes (1889:294) as a favorite food hunted mainly during the winter (i. e., the dry season). Both he and Palmerston emphasize how highly pythons were valued as food, particularly for their fat. Palmerston, describing (1887:351) how two pythons were cooked, comments that they were "extremely fat" and that "several quarts of oil could easily have been obtained from them"; while Lumholtz states (1889: 298) that "nothing is wasted, for even the back-bone is crushed between stones and eaten, and the blacks lick and suck the small amount of juice which drops from the meat, and enjoy themselves hugely. But the greatest delicacy is the fat."

Birds and bats that nest and roost in the canopy contributed small amounts of animal food to the diet, chiefly flying foxes, which were killed in large numbers at their summer (late dry/early wet season) "camps" in the forest, and some species of pigeons, parrots, and cockatoos, which were hunted and their young and eggs collected.

Although much of the animal life of the rain forest is concentrated in the canopy layer, few arboreal species offered the Aborigines sizable and readily accessible quantities of food. It is not surprising, therefore, that freshwater habitats within the forest were foci of animal food procurement. The importance of fish and other aquatic creatures in the diet and the elaboration of fishing techniques have already been mentioned. There is little precise historical information on the preferred species, but among the more important were barramundi, catfish, garfish, bream, perch, eel, and crayfish. A few semi-aquatic animals were exploited—for example, Merten's water monitor, which was valued for its eggs as well as its flesh—but these creatures were less important sources of food than waterfowl, particularly geese and ducks.

The Aborigines of the inland rain forest do not seem to have had regular access to animal (or plant) foods of the open-canopy woodland and grasslands beyond the margins of the forest. They did hunt in the small areas of woodland, grassland, and swamp that occur within the main forest tracts and that are the preferred habitat of such animals as the swamp and river wallabies, but these habitats are limited in size and number and cannot have made a major contribution to Aboriginal subsistence. Despite the diversity of species in the rain forest as a whole, what emerges from this review of the historical data on subsistence is that very few animals had the status of staple foods. With the exception of fish, which were obtained in variety and quantity, the overall picture of animal food procurement confirms the comments of Meston, already quoted, that "animal food is scarce" and that the food of the Aborigines is "chiefly vegetarian." This in turn raises the questions of whether the rain-forest tribes may have suffered from a lack of protein and fat in their diet, and whether the practice of cannibalism could have had a nutritional basis.

The Role of Cannibalism

There is no doubt that in the late 19th century Aborigines living in the inland rain forests ate human flesh, but it is very difficult to assess the extent of cannibalism and its role in rain-forest culture. European travelers in the region responded to it with varying degrees of shock, horror, and fascination. Interpretation of their comments demands a greater awareness of the moral climate of the time and a keener sensitivity to variations in outlook between individuals than interpretation of European comments on less emotive matters, such as the capture and preparation of plants and animals for food. Four of the late 19th-century witnesses on whose testimony we depend—Lumholtz, Meston, Palmerston, and Roth—refer to cannibalism, and in so doing they reveal contrasting attitudes. Roth emerges as the coolest and most objective commentator. Palmerston betrays a certain relish in his two references to cannibalism, but retains that prosaic, factual style that gives value to so many of his descriptions. Meston's account of cannibalism among the Bellenden Ker Aborigines is more heavily loaded with moral repugnance, although he is clearly fascinated by the details; while Lumholtz—scientist though he was—overgeneralizes and comes closest to indulging in sensationalism, as the title of his book implies. Before I attempt to assess the role of cannibalism, it is best to let these witnesses speak for themselves.

Palmerston first mentions (1883:557–58) the eating of human flesh when, on his return journey from Herberton to Mourilyan Harbour in 1882, he

> came into a large niggers' camp, the blacks clearing out and leaving everything; baskets all loaded with red berries, also a great quantity of their rough meal. The boys continued on the main track, and I stopped to gratify my curiosity. There being a fleshy smell arising from an oven, I opened the latter and there saw a female child, half roasted. The skull had been stove in, the whole of the inside cleaned out and refilled with red-hot stones. The hideous habit of murdering and eating little girls is carried on far more in these jungles than in any other part of the colonies, which accounts for the female children being so scarce. One of the Mourilyan Aborigines informed me that they catch the unsuspecting child by the legs, and dash its head against a tree; also, that picaninny makes quite a delicious meat—he had assisted in eating many.

Palmerston's second description (1887:433) refers to the consumption of members of another tribe, presumably adult males:

> My boys report that a distant tribe waylaid and massacred two of them, carrying away the two bodies for cannibal purposes. I took a few trackers, and went in pursuit for some two or three miles, to the top of a high and densely jungled pinnacle. Here the savages were preparing their horrible meal. However, they heard us coming and eluded us. The dead bodies had been decapitated; the lower jaw severed from the head; the hands and feet cut off; trunks disembowelled; and some of the intestines were roasting on the embers. The savages had been feasting on these while large stone ovens were being heated close by for the large-jointed portions. I ordered my aborigines to put the whole of it in the fire, and we waited until it was reduced to a cinder.

Meston is not content merely to describe cannibalism among the Aborigines of Bellenden Ker but speculates about its possible cause (1889:8–9):

> All these blacks were cannibals of a particularly bad type. They kill and eat their women and children, and occasionally they kill and eat their men. It is possible the custom arises out of an irrestrainable craving for flesh food, in a violent reaction against prolonged vegetarianism. . . . On many occasions I have seen conclusive proofs of cannibal feasts. They are in no way ashamed of the habit, and will sometimes chat about it in quite a jocular manner, and tell you what a great delicacy is a roast foot or a grilled hand. No women or boys are allowed to witness or join in the feast. When a gin is to be killed she is taken away to some secluded spot, one man seizes and crosses her hands in front, and another hits her on the back of the head with a nulla or wooden sword. Then she is disembowelled, and cut up and roasted.

Infidelity in a gin is punished by death. If a native falls from a tree or is seriously injured, he is generally killed and eaten.

Lumholtz gives a more general account of the phenomenon (1889:271–72):

The natives of Northern Queensland and of many other parts of Australia are cannibals. My people never made any secret of this, and in the evenings it was the leading topic of their conversation, which finally both disgusted and irritated me. The greatest delicacy known to the Australian native is human flesh. The very thought of *talgoro* makes his eyes sparkle. When I asked my men what part of the human body they liked best, they always struck their thighs. They never eat the head or the entrails. The most delicate morsel of all is the fat about the kidneys. By eating this they believe that they acquire a part of the slain person's strength and so far as I could understand, this was even more true of the kidneys themselves. For according to a widespread Australian belief, the kidneys are the centre of life. . . . As a rule the Australian natives do not eat persons belonging to their own tribe. Still, I know instances to be contrary, and I have even heard of examples of mothers eating their own children. . . . I know of examples of their killing their children because they were a burden to them. . . . the father is the one who determines whether a child is to live or not, so that when the mother kills the child she usually obeys the orders of her husband.

Elsewhere Lumholtz elaborates on the theme of infanticide (1889:134–35):

The advent of a baby is not always regarded with favour, and infanticide is therefore common in Australia, especially when there is a scarcity of food, as under such circumstances they even eat the child. In their nomadic life children are a burden to them, and men particularly do not like to see the women, who work hard and procure much food, troubled with many children.

Lumholtz's conclusion (1889:274) on the importance of cannibalism is that "human flesh, however, is not the daily food of the Australian. On the contrary, he seldom gets a mouthful of this delicacy."

Roth summarizes (1901:30) information on cannibalism both in "North-West Central Queensland" (i.e., southwest of the Cape York Peninsula) and on the "Eastern Coast" at Cape Bedford north of Cooktown, in the Bloomfield River area, and on the lower Tully River. Only the latter area lies within the inland rain-forest region, and there Roth attributes differences in cannibalistic behavior to coastal and inland, or "scrub," tribes:

On the lower Tully River, though the natives may actually kill to eat, the practice is exceptional, and met with only among the scrub blacks, not the coastal ones. In response to inquiries, the following reasons are given for its observance: As a punishment assigned to a woman for leaving her husband, etc.; for spite, *e.g.*, their enemies killed in war used formerly to be eaten; for pure devilment. This last is really a true explanation, so as to give cause, for instance for the commencement of a row at the next "run" [regular organized fights for which special days are set apart]. A man has thus been known to purposely eat a woman in order to provoke a quarrel with her father: indeed, women are generally the victims in these cases. All parts of the body are eaten, though the legs and arms are considered delicacies, any remains being generally burnt. There are no special ceremonies or cooking-places connected with cannibalism, nor is any particular term applied to human flesh. It is only the men who indulge in the practice, and when relating its occurrence, etc., only to do so in whispers; from an objective point of view, they apparently possess some idea of its being "uncanny" even amongst themselves.

Though carefully sought for, I have obtained no reliable evidence of cannibalism being practised in order to acquire any qualities, etc., of the deceased [brackets in original].

These quotations are in part congruent and in part contradictory, which makes interpretation doubly difficult. But several points of at least partial agreement emerge: that cannibalism was a relatively rare or unusual event (Lumholtz, Roth); that victims came (not necessarily exclusively) from other tribes (Palmerston, Lumholtz, Roth); that women and children were eaten more often than men (Meston, Lumholtz, Roth); and that only adult men indulged in cannibalism (Meston, Roth). It is also of interest that Palmerston regards female infanticide as a feature of rain-forest culture and that Lumholtz links infanticide with the demands on female mobility inherent in the food quest.

Meston's surmise that cannibalism arose "out of an irrestrainable craving for flesh food, in a violent reaction against prolonged vegetarianism" naturally accords with his belief (1904:6) that on the Bellenden Ker Range "animal food is scarce," but is a difficult suggestion to sustain. As we have already seen, animal foods, including such staples as fish and the flesh and eggs of scrub turkey and scrub fowl, were rather more abundant and varied than Meston supposed; in addition, significant quantities of protein as well as carbohydrate were obtained from tree nuts. It might be argued that this last point is irrelevant, since it is only animal-derived proteins that contain many of the essential amino acids necessary for balanced growth; but even if the contribution of plant foods to the diet is excluded, it cannot be convincingly demonstrated that there was a critical shortage of animal protein.

A more telling argument in favor of the supposition that cannibalism arose from nutritional requirements might be based on the need—or preference—for fat in the diet. Adult human bodies consist on average of about 15 percent fat by volume, and a pronounced liking for fat is a common human trait. That the Aboriginal populations of the rain-forest region shared this preference is vividly illustrated, for example, in the description by Lumholtz, already cited, of the python feast in which "the greatest delicacy is the fat." The fact that most of the animals, including fish, procured by the rain-forest Aborigines are low in body fat per unit volume relative to humans (and pythons) might be said to strengthen this argument, as might Lumholtz's observation that his cannibals regarded kidney fat as "the most delicate morsel of all." But a craving for fat can hardly be regarded as a primary cause of cannibalism when it is recalled that there were several alternative sources of animal and plant fat available in the rain forest. In addition to pythons, cassowaries and some of the larger rodents and possums yielded considerable quantities of fat, although not with sufficient frequency to provide a regular input to the diet. The largest and most dependable supply of fat came from the tree nuts, particularly from the candlenut and the Queensland almond (Table 14.3), and, indeed, the high fat content of the latter, combined with its protein yield and other non-nutritional advantages, helps to account for its status as a primary staple.

Given that alternative sources of protein and fat were available in the rain forests, the proposition that cannibalism was nutritionally necessary carries little conviction. Human flesh would undoubtedly have ranked high in terms of food value per person eaten, but the evidence suggests that cannibalism was relatively rare and that it did not make a regular contribution to the food supply. Although Lumholtz and Meston remark on the absence of secrecy surrounding cannibalism, and Roth states that no special ceremonies were connected with it, it was evidently not a wholly mundane activity. It is difficult to know what credence to attach to Roth's opinion that eating human flesh was regarded as in some sense "uncanny," but the fact that he and Meston both state that the practice was restricted to adult men, together with Meston's additional comment that no women or boys were allowed even to witness a cannibal feast, does imply that it had some ceremonial significance. According to Dixon (1972:28), whose informants among the surviving members of the Dyirbal-speaking tribes living at Murray Upper included the man who was "prime mover," in 1940, in the last known case of cannibalism (when a man was deliberately killed for excessive sexual misconduct), it was necessary that a man drink the blood of a cannibalistic victim before he could attain the status of a *gubi* ("wise man" or "doctor"); it was also reported that anyone who had persistently broken the social code might be killed by senior men of the tribe, the flesh eaten, and the blood offered to younger men to drink, and that, although no particular ritual was involved, people were not killed just for the sake of being eaten but only after considerable discussion of the crime of the wrong-doer.

This information from living descendants of rain-forest dwellers tends to confirm Meston's and Roth's claims that sexual infidelity was punished—in women at least—by cannibalistic killing. But it does not throw any light on the other two occasions for cannibalism to which the historical sources refer: infanticide and inter-group fighting. There is insufficient evidence on which to judge the relative importance of these three apparently distinctive forms of cannibalism, but it is probable that—as Lumholtz states explicitly—victims came more commonly from outside the group. Indeed, Palmerston's description of a distant tribe massacring and eating two members of his companions' tribe may exemplify the most usual mode of cannibalism in the rain forest.

Without more precise information about the social organization and attitudes of the rain-forest tribes, the role of cannibalism must remain enigmatic. Its institutionalization in the region may be due fundamentally to ecological conditions and nutritional needs, but its relative infrequency and the social contexts in which it occurred argue against the notion that cannibalism made a decisive, direct contribution to subsistence. Whether it had an indirect effect on food procurement by helping to regulate population is considered in the next section.

Population Regulation

Systemic analysis of pre-European Aboriginal subsistence in the rain-forest region demands knowledge of tribal population sizes, density, and social structure; unfortunately, however, detailed information on these topics is extremely meager. The historical sources provide limited data on tribal demography and social organization, and these data can be supplemented by reference to more general knowledge of Australian Aboriginal society. Lumholtz (1889:176–77) distinguishes the "family tribe" of 20 to 25 individuals from the "tribe" of 200 to 250, and he comments that "individuals belonging to the same tribe are usually on the best of terms, but the different tribes are each other's mortal enemies," although "the small subdivisions of the tribes that live nearest the border are on amicable terms with their neighbours." His distinction between tribes and sub-tribes or family tribes corresponds to the commonly recognized distinction in Australian Aboriginal society between larger tribes that shared a common language or dialect, and the smaller kin-based bands or hordes. His estimate of band and tribal sizes, implying an average of 10 bands per tribe, is reasonable for the early post-contact situation that he witnessed, but it obscures ecologically based variations in population density.

In a previous analysis (Harris 1978:122–25), I demonstrated that there was a consistent correlation between pre-European population density and habitat type, whereby, among the inland rain-forest tribes, the highest density (0.7 square kilometer per person) occurred on the fertile basaltic tableland of the Atherton Plateau, which supported the most floristically and structurally complex type of rain forest, whereas on the neighboring granitic and metamorphic highlands, which supported less complex rain forest, population densities were

373

much lower (3.9 to 5.2 square kilometers per person). The nut-yielding trees on which rain-forest subsistence focused are most abundant in the more complex type of forest, which, together with the presence on the Atherton Plateau of many freshwater streams and lakes, helps to explain the high population density of the basaltic tableland. The figure of 0.7 square kilometers per person is among the highest extrapolated for any pre-European Aboriginal population in Australia, but it does not imply that the population of the Atherton Plateau, or that of other, less densely peopled parts of the rain-forest region, attained a maximum density in relation to the available food supply and the technology of food procurement. On the contrary, the historical evidence suggests that band and tribal populations were regulated by varied cultural practices that maintained densities below any upper level set by eco-technological limiting factors.

According to the historical sources, such cultural practices included late marriage, postpartum abstention, infanticide, prolonged weaning, inter-group killing, and cannibalism. Lumholtz refers to all these practices (1889:134–35, 163, 184), and in his comment on infanticide (quoted in the previous section), he makes an explicit connection between the demands of mobility in food procurement and the wish to limit the number of children. The specific demographic effects of all these cultural practices are difficult to gauge, but those associated with inter-group killing and cannibalism are particularly problematic. Palmerston, Meston, and Lumholtz all refer to the hostility that existed between tribes and to the risk of death that attended transgression of tribal boundaries, but Lumholtz implies (1889:270) that inter-tribal killing was unusual: "they content themselves with hating and fearing one another, except when the opportunity of taking life is, so to speak, forced upon them. There is much talking and loud boasting, but the words seldom ripen into action."

The pattern of inter-group hostility seems to have been one of enmity between widely separated tribes, leading to occasional killing and cannibalism, in the general context of intra-tribal and proximate-tribal friendliness. Movements of individuals from band to band, and of bands within their own and neighboring tribal territories, were part of the normal pattern of economic and social interaction that sustained the autonomous, exogamous bands. Polygyny was also practiced. Lumholtz states (1889:162) that the men

usually have two, frequently three, sometimes four wives, and I saw one man who had six. All the wives live in the same hut with their husband. He who has many is envied by the others. . . . As the women perform all the labour, they are the most important part of the property of an Australian native, who is rich in proportion to the number of wives he possesses.

This statement tallies with Lumholtz's comment (1889:163) that "the majority of young men wait a long time before they get wives," and it implies that women were valued more as food-procurers than as child-bearers, a point also made in his (previously quoted) comment on infanticide. The practice of polygyny would thus have tended to limit rather than to increase population growth.

Viewed together, the historically attested practices of polygyny, late marriage, infanticide, prolonged weaning, inter-tribal killing, and cannibalism can be regarded as a set of interacting variables, the overall effect of which would have been to regulate populations in the rain-forest region at levels below the maximum densities attainable with the food resources and technology available. Without fuller and more precise data, it is not possible to specify the relative importance of the different variables, but it is likely that those operating mainly within bands and between bands of the same tribe (polygyny, late marriage, infanticide, and prolonged weaning), rather than those operating mainly between tribes (killing in raids and cannibalism), were the more effective in limiting population. Other variables may also have checked population growth, such as contraception or abortion induced by the use of rain-forest plants, but I have found no evidence of such in the historical or ethnographic record. One interesting possibility is that low fertility may have been general among the women because they were less well nourished than the men. For example, Lumholtz states (1889:161) that the hunter "very often keeps the animal food for himself, while the woman has to depend principally upon vegetables for herself and her child." If the women were systematically deprived of animal protein, and especially fat, as seems likely, then this dietary inequality between the sexes would have tended to limit population, especially by delaying the onset of menstruation and suppressing ovulation during lactation. Disease may also have acted as a population regulator, but there is almost no reference to it in the historical sources, whereas there are numerous comments on the Aborigines' agility and general physical prowess.

The demographic variables discussed, particularly polygyny, late marriage, infanticide, and prolonged weaning, can thus be envisaged as having had negative feedback effects, within and between bands, that checked any tendency for populations to increase above an average size of about 40 to 50 per band or 400 to 500 per tribe (i.e., twice Lumholtz's post-contact estimate). These approximations assume a pre- to early post-European decline in the Aboriginal population of 50 percent, which may, however, be a slight underestimate (Harris 1978:125). We cannot know if and how the limitation of family and group size was perceived as advantageous by the individuals concerned, although Lumholtz's comment on the conflict between mobility and child bearing is suggestive; but we can confidently postulate that the demographic sub-system, with its negative feedback effects operating at family and band level, was regulated indirectly by spatial and seasonal patterns of movement of individuals, family groups, and bands: patterns that articulated with spatial variation and seasonal changes in the rain-forest ecosystem through the annual cycle of subsistence activities.

The Annual Cycle of Settlement and Subsistence

The historical sources contain few explicit references to the seasonal movements of the rain-forest Aborigines, but they do yield enough information to generate a broad reconstruction of the annual cycle of settlement and subsistence. Lumholtz states (1899:207) that "the natives usually have regular places for camping," and elsewhere (1889:161, 194) he refers to the mode of travel between camps. Meston, in his account of the Bellenden Ker Aborigines (already quoted), comments on their "wet weather camps," which are "always built on some healthy dry situation, beside or very near a running stream . . . where they remain during the wet season, and store large supplies of nuts." And Palmerston often remarks on the paths that ran through the forest between camps as well as to and from fisheries and other important locations, such as the ceremonial *bora* grounds where dance festivals and fighting corroborees were held. One quotation from Palmerston's diary (1883:558) gives a particularly vivid impression of one of the bora grounds in the wet season, when vegetable foods were stored there:

> Passed over beautiful chocolate soil as level as one could wish, also through many native camps; saw many paths, leading from and junctioning with this one. In two miles it led me into a small pocket, or open space, of about an acre or less, and in which I found my boys waiting. This corroboree ground presented a clean orderly appearance, the smallest shrub even having been plucked out by the roots, to all appearance the preceding day. Its shape was circular, with a few large trees in its centre; mi-mis [huts] built all round it, at the edge of the scrub, and equal distances apart, adorned inside with skulls, some painted. A tremendously long vine stretched across the centre of this pocket, about 2 ft. high from the ground, and supported by small stakes; it looked like a miniature telegraph line. Large paths, similar to the one followed by me, branched from this pocket in all directions. There was a fine illustration in these camps of the abundance and variety of good food these jungles contain, flesh excepted, which I believe the natives here taste but seldom, and which partly accounts for their cannibalistic propensities. They had red berries heaped up in hundredweights [and] . . . many bushels of newly-ground [nut] meal were piled up on their leather-like [bark] blankets . . . of which they have a great number.

Palmerston also traveled in the rain forest in the drier winter months, and those parts of his journals that relate to the dry season lack evidence that the bora-ground camps were occupied at that time. His testimony in fact supports Roth's description (1910:55–59) of the relatively elaborate dome-shaped thatched huts used in the wet season, which contrasted with the simpler, temporary shelters used in the dry season. Palmerston's accounts also demonstrate that the thatched huts lasted from one wet season to the next, when, presumably, they were reoccupied.

If the historical sources are scrutinized for evidence of seasonal variations in social and economic activity, and if that evidence is related to seasonal changes in the rain-forest ecosystem, it is possible to develop a simple but plausible model of the pre-European subsistence cycle. The chief natural variation that pulsed the cycle was the seasonality of flowering and fruiting among the rain-forest plants that provided staple foods. The major seasonal contrast was between the main fruiting peak in the late dry/early wet season and the relatively lean period of the main wet season. This seasonal flux in the supply of many plant foods was paralleled by similar variations in animal populations, some of which, such as late dry/early wet season peaks in rain forest mammal (especially rat) and bird populations, may have been particularly important in the subsistence cycle.

The band was the basic subsistence unit, which, in pre-European times, probably contained on average 45 people divided into seven or eight family or hearth groups, each consisting of six or seven individuals. Although a band exercised customary rights over the use of resources in its own "country" or territory, it did not always act as a single food procurement unit. Part of the time individuals and family groups foraged on their own, and at other times bands came together in tribal and even supra-tribal congregations. All subsistence activities, at family, band, and tribal level, were permeated by an emphatically unequal division of labor between the sexes. This inequality is described in some detail by Lumholtz (1889:160–61):

> Among the blacks it is the women who daily provide food, and they frequently make long excursions to collect things to eat. . . . [The woman] must do all the hard work, go out with her basket and her stick to gather fruits, dig roots, or chop larvae out of the tree-stems. . . . [She] is often obliged to carry her little child on her shoulders during the whole day, only setting it down when she has to dig in the ground or climb trees. . . . when she comes home again, she usually has to make great preparations for beating, roasting, and soaking the fruits, which are very often poisonous. It is also the woman's duty to make a hut and gather the materials for the purpose. . . . She also provides water and fuel. . . . When they travel from place to place the woman has to carry all the baggage. The husband is therefore always seen in advance with no burden save a few light weapons, such as spears, clubs, or boomerangs, while his wives follow laden like pack-horses with even as many as five baskets containing provisions. There is frequently a little child in one of the baskets, and a larger child may also be carried on the shoulders.

This passage demonstrates clearly the disproportionate domestic burden placed on the women. It reinforces the point already made that the men regarded the women's role as food-procurers and -processors as more important than their role as mothers. A general result of the sexual division of labor would thus have been to reinforce the negative feedback effects that regulated band and tribal populations at low levels.

In following the sequence of a band's subsistence activities through the year, it is convenient to begin with the situation in the dry season. According to Lumholtz (1889:294), "it is easy to procure subsistence during this season of the year. Fruits are not so abundant, but, on the other hand, animal food is easily obtained. During this season the natives are much occupied in hunting snakes, which during the winter are very sluggish, and can be slain in great numbers."

The contribution of snakes, particularly pythons, to rain-forest nutrition has already been discussed, and the passage just quoted demonstrates that they were principally a dry-season food. But Lumholtz's generalization that "animal food is easily obtained" in the winter requires qualification. Certain rain-forest taxa, particularly herbivorous and insectivorous mammals and birds, tend to be more abundant in the dry season, when insect populations have built up following late wet/early dry season peaks in leaf and flower production, whereas fruit- and seed-eating animals are most abundant and best nourished in the late dry/early wet season, when many rain-forest trees reach their fruiting peaks.

During the dry season the band acted more autonomously and was more mobile than during the wet season. The men made hunting trips to the more open habitats both for terrestrial game and for honey. They fished in lakes and rivers, using techniques of fish stupefaction in the quieter reaches and water holes formed at this season of reduced stream flow. They also procured goannas and cassowaries' eggs on the forest floor and hunted for arboreal birds and their eggs in the forest canopy. The women spent a good deal of time locating and digging yams, principally *Dioscorea transversa,* and other tubers such as *Vitis clematidea.* The vines and leaves of these climbing plants had withered, and the tubers had completed the process of bulking, early in the dry season, and they were harvested as required through the drier months. Other tuberous plants, such as *Bowenia spectabilis,* were also harvested at this time.

Family groups were probably more independent of the rest of the band during the dry season, foraging within the band's territory and sometimes building temporary lean-to shelters at night, although it is likely that some of the more permanent wet-season huts were occupied by part of the band for most or even all of the year. In the dry season, too, longer journeys were probably made, especially by adult men, to visit neighboring bands or friendly tribes. When a family or larger group moved from one camp to another they split up for the journey and reassembled at night. As Lumholtz points out (1889:194):

> On their journeys the natives seldom carry provisions with them, but depend for their subsistence on what they can find on the way. They therefore take different routes, not very wide apart, and assemble in the evening in the place agreed upon for a camp, bringing with them the possums, lizards, eggs, honey, and whatever else they may have collected during the day.

In general, the dry season was a period of partial dispersal and relative social isolation, during which there was heavy dietary dependence on proteins and fats obtained mainly from fish, terrestrial animals, and birds, balanced by carbohydrates obtained chiefly from tuberous plants and tree nuts.

Toward the end of the dry season and into the early wet season (October–December), production of wild food in the rain forests reached its seasonal peak. This was the time of most prolific fruiting among rain-forest trees, particularly those nut-bearing species that provided staple foods (Table 14.1). The seeds of forest lianes, such as *Omphalea queenslandiae*, and of understorey plants, such as *Lepidozamia hopei*, were also available at this season. There is ample evidence in the historical sources that the abundance of tree nuts at this time of year correlated with the coming together of groups for corroborees and other social purposes. The congregation of people at bora grounds and elsewhere during the late dry season and on into the wet season was also correlated with the maximum availability of many rain-forest fruits.

Among the fruit- and seed-eating rain-forest animals that were relatively more abundant at this time of year were rats, including the giant tree rat, and probably the musk rat–kangaroo. Lumholtz states (1889:149) that the scrub fowl was most abundant in November and implies that the scrub turkey was too, at higher elevations. Palmerston's references (1883:518; 1886:243; 1887:651) to the collection of scrub hen and scrub turkey eggs relate to late October, early November, and late January, which accords with the fact that the birds deposit eggs in their mounds at intervals from the late dry/early wet season onward. Cassowary eggs were, by contrast, a dry-season food. Flying foxes were also an important if less constant source of animal food in the late dry/early wet season, being captured in large numbers when roosting at their "camps" in the forest.

At the beginning of the wet season, when rainfall, temperature, and humidity all increased, individuals, family groups, and bands became less mobile. The more elaborate and permanent wet-season camps were reoccupied, or more fully occupied, at locations that bore strategic relationships to spatially predictable and seasonally abundant resources. Easy access to running water was a primary locational requirement for these camps. Most of the tree nuts that provided staple starchy food required leaching in fresh, preferably running, water, and access to rivers and streams also favored the exploitation of fish, including eels and crayfish, which yielded dependable supplies of protein. Thus, the exploitation of starch-rich, toxic nuts and of fish was functionally as well as spatially related. Not only was the starch obtained from nuts complemented by the protein from fish, but the leaching of nuts and other toxic plants in streams and water holes was related to—and may even have generated—the use of plant toxins to stupefy fish. Both saponin and rotenone can paralyze the muscular system without poisoning the fish, which then rise helpless to the surface and can be "gathered." Saponin was leached from the seeds of Moreton Bay chestnut and other tree nuts exploited for food, and as this was normally done along streams, the effects of saponin on fish would easily have been discovered. Other genera that contain saponin in their roots and bark, such as *Barringtonia, Ternstroemia,* and *Pongamia,* were specifically used as fish stupefacients by Aborigines, together with rotenone-containing genera such as *Derris* and *Tephrosia* (Webb 1973:292).

Riparian sites were favored locations for permanent or semi-permanent camps also because along the banks there were frequent rock outcrops, often pitted with water-worn holes and depressions convenient for crushing, macerating, and leaching plant products. Pebbles and boulders provided suitable raw material for making nut-processing stones, and large exposures of bedrock offered sites for the grinding of axes and other stone tools, for fishing, and for general social interaction. It is less humid in the open beside the water than under the rain-forest canopy, and there are fewer leeches, flies, and other noxious creatures. Many of the nut-bearing trees thrive better on the deeper soils of the valleys than on the intervening slopes and ridges, and this would have reinforced a natural preference for streamside living. Access to running water was probably the principal factor influencing the location of the main wet-season camps, but the hunting or harvesting of particular resources led to the establishment of more casual, short-term camps. For example, Meston refers (1889:19) to temporary camps that were built during hunting trips in pursuit of the tree kangaroo, and such camps were also made close to fruiting Queensland almond trees to allow the nuts to be gathered quickly before they were eaten by rats.

The late dry/early wet season was the time of the year when social activity was most intense and inter-band, and possibly inter-tribal, corroborees took place. They did so at traditional bora grounds, the location of which probably optimized both access to staple resources and strategic position within or on the margins of group territories. Unfortunately there is no direct evidence by which to determine the location of bora grounds in relation to specific resources and boundaries, but the frequency with which Palmerston refers to them suggests that, at least on the Atherton Plateau, where poulation density was high, they were closely spaced and related primarily to band rather than to tribal territories. For example, it is clear from Palmerston's account (1886:232–33) that two of the bora grounds he visited in December 1884 lay slightly less than seven miles apart.

Palmerston and Lumholtz seldom refer to the numbers of people present at corroborees, but their descriptions imply that these gatherings were normally of bands rather than tribes. They evidently fulfilled at least two distinct social functions: the settling of disputes and the performance of dance ceremonies. In Lumholtz's description (1889:119) of "a great *borboby*" to settle disputes, he gives a figure of two to three hundred coming from many "lands" and various tribes. The general context of the description and the way in which Lumholtz customarily uses the term "tribe" show that he is describing a meeting of bands, probably about 10 of them, given his own estimate of 20 to 25 individuals per band in the 1880s. This number of bands accords closely with the inference of an average of nine bands per tribe in pre-European times and suggests that Lumholtz's *borboby* was a gathering of most or all of the Keramai tribe in whose territory he traveled. This particular gathering took place in the dry season (November) and lasted two days, after which each band returned to its own "land." Lumholtz also adds (1889:127) that while he "remained at Herbert river four borbobies occurred with three to four weeks intervening between each, in the month of November, December, January, and February—that is, in the hottest season of the year. During the winter no borboby is held."

From the end of the dry season on into the wet season, the life of a rainforest band was thus punctuated by brief periods of intense social activity when some or all of them joined a population aggregate of tribal dimensions assembled for a fighting corroboree. Dance ceremonies also occurred at this time of year and involved more prolonged periods of intensified social life. In September 1886 Palmerston witnessed a cockatoo dance at a bora ground in the upper Mulgrave valley. His account (1887:467) indicates that the bora ground was located beside the river and at narrows that probably facilitated both crossing and fishing; that there were at least one hundred people assembled for the ceremony; and, by implication, that several separate camps were positioned around the ground. It thus suggests that several bands had assembled, no doubt by invitation of the "host" band, to witness the ceremony. Lumholtz's description (1889:236–41) of a dance "festival" suggests that these ceremonies occurred less frequently but lasted longer than fighting corroborees and that they were dependent on the availability of yellow walnuts—and no doubt other staple foods—to sustain such relatively large assemblies of people for several weeks. From the context of Lumholtz's description, it can be inferred that the dance festival took place in the middle of the wet season and that the dancers moved from one bora ground to another at intervals determined by the need to gather fresh supplies of food.

As the wet season advanced, the seasonal peak in food availability passed and there was a corresponding decline in social activity. The latter half of the wet season (February–March) was evidently the leanest period of the year, although there is no evidence in the historical sources that bands experienced sustained hunger at this (or any other) time. Tree nuts, collected and stored at the main camps, remained a staple plant food, and some forest species continued to fruit, at least through January. No doubt perennially available foods were exploited relatively heavily during this lean period. Aquatic species, particularly fish, contributed protein and some fat to the nutrient input from tree nuts, and additional quantities of carbohydrate were available from such perennial plant foods as palm stems and wild gingers. Bands remained at the main camps, occupying their relatively large and rainproof wet-season huts, although the women continued to forage, as Meston says (1904:6), "every second or third day, regardless of the state of the weather." As the rains gradually diminished in intensity and duration through April and May, bands, family groups, and individuals once again becamse more mobile. And, with the arrival of the dry season, another annual cycle began.

Conclusion

Although the historical evidence on which this analysis of subsistence in a tropical rain-forest environment is based is inadequate in many respects, it is sufficient to demonstrate how closely the cultural system was integrated with the rain-forest ecosystem. Family groups, bands, and tribes adapted their foraging, fishing, and hunting activities to the complex forest ecosystem, with its "fine-grained" distribution of component species, by following an annual cycle of movement, and of group aggregation and disaggregation, that harmonized with the seasonal reproductive cycles of the principal rain-forest biota that were used for food. Mobility was maximized in the dry season and minimized in the wet season, but semi-sedentism existed, in the sense of the wet-season occupation and reoccupation by the whole band of a perennially maintained site or "home-base."

Semi-sedentism was based on the abundance of wild foods, particularly the nutritions and storable tree nuts, but it also allowed, and was itself favored by, the elaboration of material culture, especially the development of specialized nut-processing tools. The relationships between semi-sedentism and material culture represent a sub-system within which positive feedback effects promoted a degree of specialization in the use of resources that allowed a relatively dense population to be sustained. But the tendency toward specialization was held in check by a demographic sub-system that linked mobility with the sexual division of labor and with marraige and child-rearing practices in a network of negative feedback effects that regulated populations at densities below the maximum attainable with the food resources and technology available. It is clear that trends toward sedentism, toward specialization in the use of resources, and toward the build-up of relatively large populations existed among the rain-forest tribes; but it is also evident that the negative factors checking such trends remained sufficiently strong to maintain the subsistence system as a whole at a level of selective fishing and hunting that nevertheless provided a sufficiently ample and well-balanced diet to sustain what appear to have been the highest population densities of any inland tribes in Aboriginal Australia.

In accordance with the second methodological assumption outlined at the beginning of this chapter, I have attempted to specify, as precisely as the patchy historical evidence allows, the spatial and temporal dimensions of the subsistence system in the late 19th century, just before Aboriginal culture disintegrated under the impact of European penetration of the rain-forest region. The temporal dimension of this analysis is necessarily limited to the sequence of seasonal activities summarized in the reconstruction of the annual cycle of settlement and subsistence, but, ideally, the whole should be seen not just as a snap-shot in time but as the last phase of an evolutionary process, the duration of which cannot yet be specified.

Unfortunately, as was pointed out at the beginning of this chapter, there is at present little archaeological evidence available with which to trace the pre-19th century development of rain-forest subsistence. A recent trial excavation of stratified deposits in Jiyer Cave on the banks of the Russell River (which Palmerston himself visited in 1886), has, however, yielded the first direct chronological evidence of human occupation of the rain-forest region (Horsfall 1983, 1984). Here a charcoal sample from the lowest of three excavated occupation layers gave a radiocarbon age of 2160 ± 60 years (Beta 5801; Horsfall 1983:173). Interestingly, fragments of nutshell provisionally identified as from the black and yellow walnuts were recovered from all three layers, suggesting that the practice of mascerating and leaching the toxic walnut kernels goes back at least two millennia. This may imply, as Horsfall postulates (1984:169), that low population density characterized early human occupation of the rain-forest region and that at some later time population density increased and the use of resources became both more intensive and more specialized, including the application of the technique of leaching to toxic plant products.

Such a trend in the evolution of rain-forest subsistence would accord with the principles of optimal foraging theory in that it implies a temporal shift from the initial exploitation of high-ranked (low cost–high return) resources to the later exploitation of lower-ranked (high cost–low return) resources, in particular in this case toxic tree nuts. It could even be argued that the small stature of the rain-forest Aborigines, which distinguished them physically from the taller Aboriginal populations of the open-canopy woodlands beyond the confines of the rain forest, is a result of nutritional selection in an environmentally circumscribed habitat of realtively low animal biomass. This speculation cannot be pursued further here, but it does suggest that a promising direction for future research would be to compare the Queensland rain-forest population with other small-statured "pygmoid" groups in rain-forest environments in Southeast Asia and elsewhere in terms of their physical characteristics, demography, subsistence behavior, and settlement history.

References Cited

Bailey, F. M.
    1899   *The Queensland Flora.* 7 vols. Brisbane: Queensland Government.
    –1905
    1909   *Comprehensive Catalogue of Queensland Plants Both Indigenous and
             Naturalized.* 2d ed. Brisbane: Queensland Government.

Campbell, J. B.
    1980   Human Adaptation in the Quaternary. In *The Geology and Geophysics of
             Northeastern Australia,* R. A. Henderson, and P. J. Stephenson, eds.,
             pp. 402–7. Brisbane: Geological Society of Australia, Queensland
             Division.

Dixon, R. M. W.
    1972   *The Dyirbal Language of North Queensland.* Cambridge: Cambridge
             University Press.
    1976   Tribes, Languages and Other Boundaries in Northeast Queensland. In
             Tribes and Boundaries of Australia, N. Peterson, ed., pp. 207–38. Can-
             berra: Australian Institute of Aboriginal Studies.

Flecker, H. G. B.; Stephens, S.; and Stephens, S. E.
    1948   *Edible Plants in North Queensland.* Cairns: North Queensland Natu-
             ralists' Club.

Harris, D. R.
    1975   *Traditional Patterns of Plant-Food Procurement in the Cape York Penin-
             sula and Torres Strait Islands.* Fieldwork report. Canberra: Australian
             Institute of Aboriginal Studies.
    1978   Adaptation to a Tropical Rain-Forest Environment: Aboriginal Subsis-
             tence in Northeastern Queensland, In *Human Behaviour and Adapta-
             tion,* N. Blurton Jones and V. Reynolds, eds., pp. 113–34. London: Tay-
             lor and Francis.

Horsfall, N.
    1983   Excavations at Jiyer Cave, Northeast Queensland: Some Results. In
             Archaeology at ANZAAS 1983, M. Smith, ed., pp. 172–78. Perth: West-
             ern Australian Museum.
    1984   Theorising about Northeast Queensland Prehistory. *Queensland Ar-
             chaeological Research* 1:164–72.

Johnstone, R.
    1903–5   Spinifex and Wattle: Reminiscences of Pioneering in North Queensland.
             Queenslander May 2, 1903–March 11, 1905.

Kershaw, A. P.
    1974   A Long Continuous Pollen Sequence from North-eastern Australia.
             Nature 251:222–23.
    1976   A Late Pleistocene and Holocene Pollen Diagram from Lynch's Crater,
             North-eastern Queensland, Australia. *New Phytologist* 77:469–98.

Lumholtz, C.
    1889   *Among Cannibals.* London: John Murray.
McConnel, U. H.
    1935   Inspiration and Design in Aboriginal Art. *Art in Australia,* May 15, pp. 49–57.
Meston, A.
    1889   *Report on the Government Scientific Expedition to the Bellenden-Ker Range (Wooroonooran), North Queensland.* C.A. 95. Brisbane: Queensland Government.
    1904   *Report on Expedition to the Bellenden-Ker Range.* C.A. 36. Brisbane: Queensland Government.
Palmerston, C.
    1883   From Mourilyan Harbour to Herberton. *Queenslander,* September 11, pp. 477–78; September 29, pp. 518–19; October 6, pp. 557–58.
    1886   From Herberton to the Barron Falls, North Queensland. *Transactions and Proceedings of the Royal Geographical Society of Australia, New South Wales Branch* 4:231–44.
    1887   The Diary of a Northern Pioneer. *Queensland Figaro,* February 12, pp. 265–66; February 19, pp. 291, 295; February 26, pp. 346, 351; March 5, p. 385; March 12, p. 433; March 19, p. 467; March 26, p. 491; April 2, pp. 545–46; April 9, p. 596; April 23, p. 651.
Peterson, N.
    1976   The Natural and Cultural Areas of Aboriginal Australia. In *Tribes and Boundaries of Australia,* N. Peterson, ed., pp. 50–71. Canberra: Australian Institute of Aboriginal Studies.
Roth, W. E.
    1901–   North Queensland Ethnography, Bulletins 1–8 (1901–5). Brisbane: De-
    10   partment of the Home Secretary. Bulletins 9–18 (1907–10). *Records of the Australian Museum* 6–8.
Tindale, N. B.
    1974   *Aboriginal Tribes of Australia.* Berkeley and Los Angeles: University of California Press.
Tindale, N. B., and Birdsell, J. B.
    1941   Results of the Harvard-Adelaide Universities Anthropological Expedition, 1938–1939: Tasmanoid Tribes in North Queensland. *Records of the South Australia Museum* 7:1–9.
Webb, L. J.
    1973   Eat, Die, and Learn: The Botany of the Australian Aborigines. *Australian Natural History* 17:290–95.

ALLEN JOHNSON
and MICHAEL BAKSH

Ecological and Structural Influences on the Proportions of Wild Foods in the Diets of Two Machiguenga Communities

A MAJOR THEME ADDRESSED IN THIS VOLUME CONCERNS THE usefulness of competing or alternative explanatory frameworks in accounting for the observed patterns of food procurement and food consumption among different human populations. In this paper we compare and contrast dietary patterns in two subsistence-oriented Machiguenga communities of the Peruvian Amazon. We will argue that the similarities and differences we observed in their diets are largely to be explained as reflections of the cost of obtaining each food given the nutritional value of that food. By "cost" we refer to such etic constraints on food production as time and energy inputs, soil fertility, and resource availability. We have demonstrated elsewhere (Baksh 1982; Johnson 1980, 1981) that the Machiguenga are sensitive to the relative costs and benefits of alternative procurement strategies, and that their behavior is adjusted in the direction of efficient or economically rational strategies. Here we will show that this is specifically true with regard to the choices that determine which foods are consumed in Machiguenga households.

We will also present evidence of food preferences and beliefs—that is, structural data—that are related to ecological costs and benefits. These emic influences do not contradict or override etic ecological constraints, but rather help organize behavior to be efficient in the sense just described. The residue of the dietary pattern that remains, and appears only to reflect structural processes, will be shown to be of great symbolic significance but of minor importance to the biological health and well-being of the population.

We also give detailed attention to the question of exactly what it is that motivates the Machiguenga to pay very high costs in order to obtain animal foods (Baksh 1984). We will argue (1) that fat is a better candidate than protein as the element in meat that people crave to taste, and (2) that fat is actually more scarce in the Machiguenga diet than protein, relative to the levels of intake that have been recommended for good health.

The Machiguenga Indians of the Peruvian Amazon are well adapted to their environment, and a major aspect of their adaptation is the successful procurement of food resources. The Machiguenga, like all cultural groups, have access to a unique array of potential foods, yet not all are considered edible. Why some foods predominate over others in the diet, why some "costly" foods are preferred over "cheap" ones, and why some edible foods are avoided are questions addressed in this paper.

Two Communities

As a result of recent migration, the Machiguenga communities of Camana and Shimaa are separated by 50 miles of tropical forest, but they originated in adjacent river valleys, the Kompiroshiato and the Mantaro Chico, tributary to the Upper Urubamba River of southeastern Peru. Typologically they inhabit the same environment and share the same language and culture. Indeed, there are close kinship ties between some members of the two communities. Both communities are subsistence producers of horticultural products and wild foods obtained through hunting, gathering, and fishing. Their members are mostly monolingual speakers of Machiguenga and share similar social structures based on bilateral kinship reckoning and centered on nuclear family households and extended-family clusters or hamlets. During our studies of Shimaa (1972–75) and Camana (1976–81), most Machiguenga still wore their homemade *cushmas* and were economically self-sufficient except for trade goods, mainly axes, machetes, cooking pots, and medicines.

Despite basic similarities, there remain many differences in ecological and structural features (Baksh 1982, 1984; Johnson 1981, 1983). The community of Camana in 1976 migrated from a settlement at an altitude of about 4,000 feet, which most members viewed as impoverished and perhaps spiritually contaminated, in order to colonize a sparsely inhabited site at about 1,500 feet, where wild foods, and fish in particular, were far more abundant. Shimaa, at an altitude of 2,300 feet, is viewed by the Machiguenga as intermediate between the two Camana sites in the availability of wild foods. Each community had formed around a public school approximately three years before major research began.

Shimaa is a comparatively traditional community, localized by its members' desire to live near the government-appointed Machiguenga schoolteacher.

They still retain their preference for single-family households or small clusters of such households and their emphasis on the economic autonomy of the household. Indeed, a chronic complaint of the schoolteacher is that the aggregate of households, which numbers around 100 individuals in 15 households, rarely acts in unity on the community projects he attempts to promote. By contrast, Camana is a relatively unified community under the direction of a strong, charismatic leader (who is also the schoolteacher). Although households tend to cluster in small, extended-family groups, he has been able to hold together a stable community of some 250 individuals in 41 households. Following his lead, they have made a commitment to cooperative growing of cash crops in addition to their traditional subsistence practices.

In a typological sense, we would say that the Machiguenga of Shimaa and Camana are identical in their major features: the environment presents them with similar levels of rainfall, wild food resources, and raw materials; they speak the same language and have the same culture history; they share the same range of technological skills; and the division of labor by sex and the economic organization of the household are similar. In Table 15.1, however, we see that the emphases of the two economies are very different. Briefly, Shimaa emphasizes the production of garden foods over the production of fish and

TABLE 15.1. Labor Productivity and the Calorie and Protein Efficiencies of Subsistence Strategies in Shimaa and Camana

	Strategies			
Category/Location	*Horticulture*	*Fishing*	*Hunting/Gathering*	*Cash Crops*
% of labor time invested				
Shimaa (1972–73)	64	17	19	—
Camana (1979–80)	31	48	16	5
Labor productivity (kg./hr., average household)				
Shimaa	3.7	0.4	0.3	—
Camana	3.5	0.5	0.35	0.35
Calorie efficiency (cals. out/kcals. in)				
Shimaa only	18.5	1.4	0.8	—
Protein efficiency (g. protein/kcals. in)				
Shimaa only	0.22	0.14	0.03	—

other wild foods, whereas Camana emphasizes the production of fish over garden foods and other wild foods. In the next section we examine the ecological (etic) costs and benefits that account for this major difference in emphasis between such similar peoples.

Labor Productivity and Diet: Etic Analysis

The determinants of diet may be sought in both the production and the consumption ends of food getting. We begin with a description of factors that shape the ecological costs and benefits of the three main production strategies: horticulture, fishing, and hunting/gathering.

Horticulture

In terms of the sheer weight of production, Machiguenga horticulture is far more productive than any of their wild food strategies (Table 15.1). For example, in kilograms of food produced per hour of productive labor, Machiguenga gardens are about 10 times more productive than hunting and gathering or fishing. And as sources of food energy, garden foods predominate in the diet: about 90 percent of the food the Machiguenga eat comes from horticulture.

In Shimaa, of the total labor a household invests in food production, nearly two-thirds is in gardens, the remainder being allocated about equally to foraging (hunting and gathering) and fishing. With this they manage to produce more than twice as many calories of food energy as they will consume in a year. They could probably do well in most years by reducing their garden efforts, and get by in bad years by sharing within a large, supra-familial community. But in Shimaa strong emphasis is placed on household economic independence, and the "overproduction" of garden foods is actually a security margin ensuring such independence. Most families do share with other families, including some that are not particularly close friends or kin, but recipients of such help are uncomfortable at having to ask for it and will expand their gardens to avoid such dependence in succeeding years.

We have seen that Camana differs to some degree. Camana's unity, focused on its leader, is based on a commitment to "advance ourselves" through cash crop production and market participation. The productivity of an hour of labor invested in agriculture is about the same in both places (Table 15.1), as is the productivity of garden land per hectare. But the people of Camana spend much less time gardening than those in Shimaa, and therefore subsistence gardens in Camana are smaller, as is the per capita production of garden surplus. Their security derives more from obligations to share in a large, unified village than from the surplus subsistence production of individual households.

The differences in social organization between Shimaa and Camana, which account for part of the difference in the amount of labor invested in horticulture, are not arbitrary. They represent the two poles of response to modern change that are encountered throughout the Machiguenga region. The origin of the present community of Camana illustrates the process. The population originally resided as scattered family groups along the valley of the Mantaro Chico River. With the arrival of their strong-willed and admired schoolteacher, they united into a village of nearly 300 members in a few years. But not all were satisfied with the arrangement, and when the schoolteacher asked them to move with him to Camana, to take advantage of a richer environment and continue the development of a cooperative for the production of beans and peanuts for market sale, only about 200 members followed him (the additional 50 individuals in Camana in 1979–80 are largely offspring born after the move, but also include the members of two families who were already living in the Camana region). The other hundred or so in Mantaro had had their fill of dense community life and reverted to their old ways, living in scattered families. This was a serious decision, for in doing so they lost access to medicines, trade goods, and education for their children. Likewise, those who did move with the schoolteacher thereby proved their willingness to compromise their individualistic, family-oriented loyalties in order to be part of a close-knit, cooperative community. Given the uncertainties that characterize the shift to market production in the Machiguenga setting, each alternative has its own costs and benefits, and it would be difficult to prove that one is clearly better than the other. But once the decision is made, the family must accept the implications, which in the cooperative village means exchanging some family autonomy for a far greater economic interdependence between family groups.

This difference in commitment to community life, however, is not in itself enough to account for the large difference in emphasis on garden foods between Shimaa and Camana. The other major factor is the greater emphasis on maize production in Shimaa (Table 15.2). In both places maize only grows well in first-year gardens. Baksh (1984) has shown that this is due to the rapid changes in the soils that take place during the first year of maize production, including a decline in pH levels and the loss of nitrogen and other soil nutrients. In order to grow large amounts of maize, therefore, it is necessary to plant large gardens each year. This is the pattern in Shimaa, where first-year gardens are very large, second-year gardens are smaller, and gardens are usually abandoned after the second or third year, despite clear evidence that root crops like manioc and cocoyam will grow well in Machiguenga gardens for five or more years. In Camana, by contrast, first-year gardens are small but are maintained in size after the maize harvest and kept in production longer, pri-

TABLE 15.2. Maize in Shimaa and Camana

Category	Shimaa	Camana
Average size of new garden (in hectares)	0.56	0.21
Per capita maize produced (in kilograms)	72	34
Maize as % of total calories produced	20	7

marily for manioc. In Shimaa, therefore, maize, which is a comparatively rich source of protein and vegetable oil in contrast to manioc, is so desirable that it encourages a much larger investment in gardens than in Camana. It can be shown that maize is a much more efficient source of protein than wild foods in the Machiguenga environment (Johnson 1977), but this is as true in Camana as in Shimaa. We must seek further, therefore, for an explanation for the prominence of maize in Shimaa as compared with Camana.

Wild Foods

The Machiguenga fish and hunt and gather for several reasons, even though these activities are less productive per unit of time or energy than gardening. The reasons are of ecological significance and contribute to the overall quality of adaptation that the Machiguenga maintain. Although horticulture is extremely productive and efficient, it does not replace foraging and cannot provide for all the nutritional, material, social, and psychological requirements of the Machiguenga level of adaptation. (These needs are discussed below). The production of horticultural products and the procurement of wild foods are not competitive strategies in the Machiguenga view. Rather, they are complementary; both are essential, and the loss of either would lower their quality of life.

The production of wild foods is, in most respects, similar in Camana and Shimae. Both communities spend about the same amount of time in hunting and gathering and are rewarded with similar returns. Although rates of return are comparatively low, the quality of returns is high, as we will see when we consider emic influences on decision making below. The rates of return for fishing are somewhat higher and, again, are roughly similar in both communities. The dramatic difference in food production between the two communities is that three times as much time is devoted to fishing in Camana.

The reason is that the potential for large harvests of fish is far greater here than in Shimaa. This is not immediately evident in the quantitative figures given in Table 15.1. To be sure, fishing in Camana is 25 percent more productive per hour of labor than in Shimaa, but this is not a great enough difference by itself to explain such a reversal in the allocation of labor. In Shimaa, most fishing takes place fairly close to home because at this altitude, and under scattered settlement, there is little value in traveling to distant fishing spots. Fish are scarce everywhere, returns are meager, and families are reluctant to intrude on the favorite fishing spots of other families. Travel time is a small part of the cost of fishing in Shimaa, and returns are low primarily because fish are scarce.

In Camana, however, beyond the village there are no other humans competing for fishing areas (the complex historical reasons for this are beyond the scope of this paper). Thus, as fish become scarce close to the village, people do not accept lower harvests but continue to travel farther and farther to fishing spots. Once there, yields of fish can be prodigious. Fishing expeditions have a high probability of success, and the fishers usually return laden with backloads and canoeloads of hastily smoked fish. Because of their community commitment, however, families typically must be in the village four days each week, so they cannot simply move out to good fishing areas and stay to enjoy inexpensive fish. Thus, travel time makes up a major share of the cost of fish in Camana.

This raises a point of theoretical significance. On the basis of simple supply and demand economics, the situation in Shimaa is what we would expect after an extended period of settlement (Earle 1980). When colonizing a new area, foragers can be expected to focus their energies on the most productive food procurement strategies. Over time, as they deplete these abundant resources, production costs rise relative to the costs of alternative foods, making the latter more attractive. Thus, a diet in which a single species dominates evolves into a diet in which diverse foods are represented more equally. In Camana both fish and game were exceptionally abundant in 1976 when the first settlers arrived, and the people enjoyed an unprecedented consumption of wild foods. The game quickly gave out, but fish continued to make a major contribution to most meals. Although today fishing is still more productive than hunting/gathering, the gap between the two has been narrowing as fishers must travel to ever more distant fishing spots to maintain high yields. In 1979–80, for example, travel time per fishing trip was doubling every five months, so that by the end of our fieldwork in 1981, travel to fishing sites occupied as much time as fishing itself. As a consequence, the contribution of fish to the diet was at that point declining as costs were rising, and theory predicts that this trend will continue until a "broad spectrum" (Flannery 1969) of wild foods characterizes the diet in Camana as it does in Shimaa.

The traditional response to such declining productivity in favorite foods, of course, was scattered settlement and frequent shifting of residence. This is still a popular response in Shimaa. In Camana, however, at the end of the fieldwork in 1981, serious strains were arising as local resources were depleted, and we have since received word that the village fissioned, with the majority of the community following the leader downstream to a rich, unexploited new location.

In sum, the major etic reason why Camana and Shimaa give the opposite priorities to gardening and fishing is that in Camana people have come to expect large harvests of fish and the inclusion of fish with most meals. As fishing productivity has declined in their vicinity, rather than give up fish, they have traveled farther and farther away from their home-base in order to have plentiful harvests. This they can do because beyond their village there are no neighboring communities to compete for fishing grounds, and fishing continues to be very successful. In Shimaa, this potential for abundant harvests is nowhere present. A low average productivity has been created everywhere by long-term, scattered settlement and continuous exploitation of fishing areas. We conclude that the Machiguenga of Shimaa must emphasize maize production more than those of Camana because maize provides a source of protein and fats that they cannot obtain from fish. Furthermore, because in Shimaa the residence pattern is scattered and "competitive" (Steward 1977:76), household economic autonomy is a high priority and is achieved by a substantial overproduction of garden foods for security. In Camana, security is achieved by widespread sharing of garden foods and continuous trading of fish by successful fishers in exchange for garden food.

In this context, a major etic reason why the Machiguenga do not rely exclusively upon horticultural production for protein and fat, despite the observation that this activity is highly productive and the Machiguenga cultivate crops that hypothetically could meet their estimated nutritional requirements (Johnson and Behrens 1982), is that maize and beans are difficult to produce and store year-round in the tropical rain forest. At present maize and a few varieties of beans are planted together and mature simultaneously. Beans are an extremely minor crop, and the harvest can be consumed in a few meals; maize, even when dried, is available for consumption for only six to eight months. Maize production is limited to one crop annually, and the long-term storage of maize or beans beyond the small amounts required for seed would risk failure as a result of pest infestation and spoilage. Finally, a diet based on maize and legumes would require a much greater labor investment, since the Machiguenga say maize only produces well in a first-year garden in the best soils. High-quality soils are already scarce, and under current methods are used efficiently to produce calorie-rich root crops for several years after the maize has been harvested. Although the maize-beans complex is common throughout Latin America, particularly among peasant societies, it is more labor-intensive and land-intensive than the current Machiguenga subsistence system. It seems plausible that such a system developed experimentally and was found to be nutritionally sound when the population in these areas became too great to be supported by wild foods. The Machiguenga still enjoy adequate wild foods, however, making further dependence on agriculture unnecessary.

Protein, Fat, and the Preference for Fish

Much recent Amazonian cultural-ecological research has focused on the potential scarcity of animal foods and, particularly, high-quality protein (see Hames and Kensinger 1980 for a review). Proponents of protein scarcity have argued that the limited availability of meat and fish is responsible for such cultural and demographic features as small village size, low population density, high settlement mobility, and so on. Other researchers, however, have found that some communities actually consume more than twice the amount of protein recommended as a daily allowance. Yet it is apparent that native Amazonians are unaware of protein per se, as it is not visible or directly related to food flavor. In view of these observations, it is interesting that other chapters in this volume have suggested the potential role of dietary fat in the food search. The consumption of some fat is essential for human health, and there is a general relationship between the fat content and the protein content of most foods. Thus, a "selection of fatty foods for their taste usually results in consumption of high protein foods as well" (Jochim 1981:82). Yet, unlike protein, fat provides a major contribution to food taste, and, emically, human groups generally associate the good taste of animal foods with their content of visible fat.

Dietary fat is important for several biological reasons. Fat is an important source of energy, a carrier for the fat-soluble vitamins A, D, E, and K (elimination of fats from the diet could result in vitamin deficiencies), and, most importantly, the source of essential fatty acids. Certain fatty acids are known to be necessary for various physiological functions and especially child development; they are probably also necessary for the healing of surgical wounds and severe burn cases (Food and Agriculture Organization [FAO] 1980:23). Effects of deficiencies that have been observed in humans include "abnormal skin conditions, reduced regeneration of tissues, increased susceptibility to infections" (FAO 1980:23) and "hair loss, and in children, a failure to grow properly" (Los Angeles Times 1982:sec. 8). A recent FAO/World Health Organization (WHO) study on the role of dietary fats in human nutrition states that the "minimum energy content of essential fatty acids (EFAs) in the human diet is 3%. Because EFA requirements are higher in pregnancy and lactation, this energy value is raised to 4.5% in pregnancy and 5–7% in lactation." (FAO 1980:85).

"Essential fatty acids" are not equivalent in weight to "dietary fat." According to data provided on selected foods (FAO 1980:appendix 1), "fatty acids" (not all of which are "essential") constitute 94 percent of the fat in human milk, an average of 95 percent of beef, mutton, and pork fat, 97 percent of chicken fat, 83 percent of the fat in hen eggs, 89 percent of catfish fat, 88 percent of maize fat, and 95 percent of peanut fat. Thus, to meet EFA requirements, measured either by percentage of total energy consumption or by weight (grams), a proportionately higher amount of actual fat must be consumed. The same FAO/WHO committee also notes that (1) "in the developing countries, there is evidence that in the lowest income groups, with dietary fat comprising about 10% of the energy, an increase to 15–20 energy % of fat, with adequate regard for essential fatty acids, would have beneficial effects" (ibid.:13), and (2) there is universal agreement by scientific and nutritional committees that "a dietary intake of 30–35% of the energy as fat and a saturated/polyunsaturated fatty acid ratio of 1 to 1 are in fact generally recommended" (ibid.:38).

Cultural ecologists have overlooked the role of dietary fat in human behavior, perhaps because EFA deficiency appears to be rare for humans. According to the National Academy of Sciences (NAS): "Studies with both human subjects and animals indicate that, to prevent deficiency, the required intake of essential fatty acids . . . in the diet is not difficult to achieve" (1974:50). Indeed, since fat provides over 40 percent of the total calories consumed by residents of North American and European countries, it is difficult to imagine a diet that fulfills energy requirements yet approaches the minimum fat requirements. Yet, as we describe in more detail below, the fat component of the Machiguenga diet is close to if not below the recommended minimum requirement.

First, however, it is important to return to the point that dietary fat is intimately related to the taste of foods. Thus, "on the most practical level, fat is what makes eating really enjoyable because it is the fat, more than anything else, that gives different foods their distinctive tastes and aromas. Therefore, if you eliminate the fat, you also do away with much of the flavor—leaving yourself with little more than a variety of shapes and textures" (Los Angeles Times 1982:sec. 8). For meats in particular, the fat content affects flavor and aroma, juiciness, and tenderness (Smith and Carpenter 1976). Aside from enhancing palatability, fat also delays gastric emptying and contributes to a feeling of satiety (Burton 1965:76; NAS 1974:34).

Two observations are relevant here: (1) there is an almost universal preference for meat over plant foods, and (2) the reasons for preferring certain foods (i.e., those that taste good) are often related to the presence of visible fat, despite the fact that these foods are normally the most costly to obtain (Jochim 1981:81–87). Although most meats are generally higher in fat than most plants, most fat is invisible, particularly in plant foods. The most valued foods of the Machiguenga are fish and other meats, and within these categories the fattiest specimens are the most enjoyed. When fish or other faunal products are not available, maize, high in invisible fat, is the next most preferred food. Peanuts, extremely high in fat content, have recently been adopted as a cash crop. They have traditionally been a very minor crop, undoubtedly because of their comparatively high cost of production.

From a preliminary analysis of the diet in Camana, it is obvious that the consumption of dietary fat is extremely low (Baksh 1984). The total fat content of consumed foods provided an average of 6.3 percent of the total calories (one-fourth of this, it should be noted, was from peanuts, which supposedly are produced not for local consumption but as a cash crop). As suggested above, the total fatty acid content of this intake would be even less, and the "essential" fatty acids lower yet. Thus, the essential fatty acid content of meals in Camana is close to if not below the recommended minimum requirement. Given the current mix of crops, a diet based solely on subsistence agriculture would provide a total fat content of only 2.5 percent of caloric energy.

If we return to the differences in food production between Shimaa and Camana, it is apparent that Shimaa is unable to sustain wild food procurement at a level that would satisfy their desire for the tastiest foods. The scarcity of faunal foods, in short, has forced residents of Shimaa to place a greater emphasis upon maize production. Camana, on the other hand, is able to maintain the production of comparatively large amounts of fish on a frequent and regular basis, although the increased local scarcity of this resource is making it more costly to obtain.

The shift in consumption from fish and other faunal foods to maize involves not only acceptance of a less desirable food, but also a higher overall cost of food production (Table 15.2). Machiguenga soils support only a single crop of maize, so larger areas must be cleared to meet projected needs. In Shimaa, where maize provides at least 20 percent of the calories in the diet, as opposed to 7 percent in Camana, new gardens (where maize is the dominant crop) are almost three times as large as in Camana. Manioc and other root crops may be cultivated in the larger area as well, but since caloric needs are met with the cultivation of a smaller area, the labor necessary for planting these crops and weeding the area after the harvest of maize is to some extent wasted. Indeed, new gardens in Shimaa are 50 percent larger than are older gardens from which maize has been harvested.

Emic Influences on Diet

We will group the many emic factors influencing wild food procurement strategies into two broad categories: first, the subjective evaluation of the costs and benefits of wild food production, and second, the existence of taboos and other restrictions on foods in the diet.

397

Subjective Costs and Benefits of Wild Food Production

Factors that increase the subjective value of what is produced include food preferences, dietary diversity, access to valued non-food resources, and general information about the environment. These factors are discussed below. We then turn to factors that reduce the subjective costs of production, reflecting enjoyment of the forest and streams as loci of many pleasurable activities.

FACTORS INCREASING THE SUBJECTIVE VALUE OF WHAT IS PRODUCED (OUTPUT)

The Machiguenga highly value game, fish, and other wild foods, and a meal without some form of meat is subdued, unless a favorite garden crop such as maize is available. Even if maize is abundant, however, a few consecutive meatless meals give rise to household tension, which invariably lingers until a fishing or hunting and gathering trip is successfully completed. For example, in Camana both the presence of fish in the household and the quest for it saturate all aspects of daily life. Fish is eaten almost every day, and on those days when fish, or some other animal product, has not been eaten, it is frequently commented that people are hungry. In fact, although there is abundant garden produce, this is often literally true; when fish is not available for a meal, little manioc, the staple, is eaten. In October 1980, when meat and fish were scarce, the amount of manioc consumed in one household was only three-fourths of that consumed in April 1980, when fish and game were relatively abundant (1.7 kilos per day, of which 17 percent was in the form of beer, versus 2.2 kilos per day, of which 3 percent was in the form of beer). In October adults complained, "Everyone is hungry, there is no meat or fish." People simply find it difficult to eat manioc without fish or meat, and when serving a one-course meal of manioc, a host inevitably notes sadly: *"Mameri ivatsa"* ("there is no meat"). The importance of fish may also be underscored by the timing of sexual relations, which increase in frequency in direct proportion to the abundance of fish (Baksh 1982: 7).

The procurement of wild foods is also worthwhile because it accompanies the procurement of important non-food resources. The construction of a single house, for instance, requires the leaves of hundreds of palm trees, and certain varieties are sought for their effectiveness and durability. These trees must be located, as must numerous other manufacturing or otherwise useful materials, and the hunting and gathering of wild foods is a practical strategy for accomplishing this. And, conversely, when setting out specifically to obtain a particular non-food resource, it is advantageous to take a bow and arrows; it is not rare for such a trip to yield a bird, and it is often during these trips that grubs are obtained or the feeding sites of game observed.

Finally, the procurement of wild foods, while not as efficient as the production of domesticated crops, is unquestionably advantageous in a general adaptive sense. The pursuit of wild foods takes individuals out beyond the immediate vicinity of a village, into settings where the physical and biological environment is different and constantly changing. Machiguengas do not reside in the same location all their lives, and in fact many migrate to different valleys or river systems for various reasons. The knowledge and awareness of different agricultural soils and animal and plant communities that is brought about largely through foraging activities contributes to adaptive success.

FACTORS REDUCING THE SUBJECTIVE COST OF PRODUCTION (INPUT)

In the field we have repeatedly observed that wild food getting has a special quality for the Machiguenga. Men are eager to tell and listen to stories about their hunting ventures, and they plan new ones with open anticipation of enjoyment. To some degree this may simply reflect the enjoyment of walking alone or with a single companion through the forest. More often, whole families travel together in search of whatever wild foods present themselves, and the atmosphere is that of a picnic. One man even used the Spanish word for "vacation" to describe his plan to forage with his family.

The possibility of making a "big catch" is also anticipated with pleasure. Large game animals are occasionally shot and killed, and enormous catches of fish do occur. Unlike gardening, in which workers basically know what they will produce for their efforts, hunting, gathering, and fishing are in this sense gambles. The chance of sighting a large animal or poisoning a large pool of fish is a compelling motivation, and the experience of past success undoubtedly plays a major role in motivating men to pursue these activities. When successful, they offer unparalleled excitement for the Machiguenga. When involved in cooperative fishing or, more rarely, hunting, a sort of "social high" develops, full of boisterous good spirits, during which the anthropologist finds it nearly impossible to carry on a conversation or even get simple answers from participants.

Before turning to the subject of food restrictions, we wish to emphasize that although we have been discussing emic influences on the production of wild foods, we do not regard these as non- or anti-ecological in nature. Clearly the preference for animal fats and proteins, the serendipity of finding essential raw materials in addition to foods, and the prospects of a windfall catch are potentially etic ecological factors, in the sense of being ultimately measurable and relatable to ecological theory. Even the social high of cooperative fishing, the enjoyment of hunting, and the picnic atmosphere of family outings, strictly speaking more psychological than ecological, do not contradict the underlying ecological motivation of the events and could reasonably be considered sources of motivation that make them more likely to be successful.

Food Restrictions

Every cultural system restricts consumption of certain animal and plant foods. The difficulty in explaining such restrictions is compounded by cross-cultural variability. It seems that virtually every digestible and nutritional animal or plant food available on earth is eaten by somebody somewhere; certain potential foods that are prohibited, found disgusting, or even feared by one cultural group are often relished by another. This opens the door to the possibility that food restrictions are arbitrary "cultural" artifacts that have little relation to ecology. Although we began work on this paper with this possibility in mind, in working through our data we have become convinced that the Machiguenga food restrictions are not arbitrary and often have adaptive significance.

Our data show very little impact on the diet from food prohibitions. None of the restricted foods by themselves would constitute more than a small proportion of the wild foods in the diet, even if they were pursued without restriction. This is not to say that a certain amount of potentially nutritious food is not lost as a result of dietary restrictions, only that what is lost is probably not more than a minuscule percentage of the total wild food supply.

Typologically, we find it useful to distinguish "tabooed" foods from foods classified as "inedible." Although many foods seem to fall in both categories, some are prohibited primarily because of the spiritual danger believed to be associated with eating them, whereas others are avoided primarily because they are thought to taste bad or because their animal sources are believed to have dirty or disgusting habits. Some of the more important restricted foods are snake, howler monkey, jaguar, dog, vulture, hawk, vampire bat, deer, fox, *moritoni* (smooth-billed ani), and *soromai* (a poisonous caterpillar).

TABOO FOODS

The most dramatic example of a tabooed food is snake. Although snakes are eaten in other parts of the world, even in Amazonia (e.g., the Eastern Timbira), the Machiguenga avoidance of snake is absolute. All snakes are assumed to be poisonous and hence extremely dangerous to people. Whenever a snake is sighted, an effort is made to kill it on the spot, and if that is not possible, a party of men will often return to the spot to try to kill it later. If it is killed, someone picks it up with the end of a long stick held at arm's length and either buries it deep in the ground, stamping on the earth to make sure it is well buried, or else hurls it into the river, counting on the current to carry it so far away that its spirit will be unable to return to seek revenge through its snake kin. A great deal of labor is spent in clearing gardens, trails, and yards of all rubbish where snakes could hide.

This categorical fear of snakes is intensified by the belief that snakes kill through spiritual means. Their bites are actually thought to be wounds inflicted by the magical arrows of their spirit ruler, *inato*, who uses this means to obtain the souls of humans for his consumption. Snake is the clearest example of an animal that, while presumably edible and capable of making a real, if small, contribution to the diet, is absolutely proscribed for ideological reasons.

Jaguar is in a similar position. Jaguar is greatly feared, both for its real ferociousness and for its attributed spiritual powers, which enable it to track and steal a soul at night. In the four cases we observed of jaguars or wildcats being killed, only one was eaten, and it is our impression that this meat is rather strongly prohibited on the grounds of the great spiritual strength associated with it, although poor taste may also be a factor.

Perhaps the most intriguing case of a food taboo among the Machiguenga is the howler monkey. Opinion is strongly divided: some Machiguengas regard it as harmful and do not eat it, others regard it as edible but slightly unpalatable, and still others regard it as desirable. On one occasion when we had howler monkey meat to distribute, two households refused it and three welcomed it.

Howler monkeys are moderately common in both Shimaa and Camana. We have sighted families of three to five members on many occasions. The male's distinctive roar is a common accompaniment to the chorus of early morning sounds. The howler monkey is unusual among the monkeys hunted by the Machiguenga in being slow and seemingly lethargic. No doubt this is related to its style of food getting, which depends heavily on the consumption of large quantities of "low-quality" foods (e.g., leaves), as distinct from that of other monkeys, such as the spider monkey, which feed on "high-quality" fruits and seeds that are widely dispersed and require greater mobility (see Chapter 3). Howler should be an easy monkey to hunt, since it wanders lazily in the treetops or stolidly sits watching the hunter below. Yet the Machiguenga often pass howler monkeys by in pursuit of other game.

Etically, this may be a good case of what Ross (1978) sees as cultural practices that preserve vulnerable species from extinction. Thus, the easily killed howler monkey is less often sought than other, more elusive, prey. Emically, the Machiguenga give both physical and spiritual reasons for avoiding howler monkey. People who do not eat howler monkey meat claim that it causes them gastric and chest pains. They do not say "it is prohibited" or "it is inedible," but simply "we do not know how to eat it." When asked to elaborate, they will explain that "my father [male speaking] or mother [female speaking] did not eat it, and so I never learned how." This allows them to explain others' consumption of the meat as a matter of learning or being accustomed.

The howler monkey is also surrounded by magicoreligious beliefs. He is considered the epitome of laziness, and this property can be magically transmitted in various ways. Giving howler monkey meat to a child can "spoil" the child so that it will grow up dissatisfied; if a pregnant woman eats it, her child will grow up lazy; if a man eats it when his new corn is still young, the corn will never produce seeds. It is also believed that the adult male, with a fully developed howler pouch, is a sorcerer (*seripigari*). Thus, pregnant women, young children, and men with immature corn plants are enjoined from eating it.

The case of deer is similar. It holds spiritual danger for women and children, who are supposed to avoid it. But deer are so rare in these parts that the issue of whether or not to eat deer meat seldom arises.

More often than not, food restrictions like those on howler monkey are applied individually. Many foods that are normally considered edible, such as peccary, spider monkey, tapir, and certain fish, are prohibited to anyone in an especially vulnerable condition, such as infancy, pregnancy, or exposure to spiritual danger (especially soul loss). These foods do not go uneaten, however, because most people are unaffected by the taboos. This becomes evident during the family's investigation when someone falls ill: either the victim or some close relative will frequently be found to have eaten one or more "dangerous" foods.

An interesting example of the "individualism" of food restrictions is reported by Betty Snell (pers. comm.). While at the river, she noticed that some women who were cleaning a large fish had discarded its plump liver. She asked the women, who were good friends of hers, if it would be all right for her to take the liver home and cook it for her family, and they said, "Fine." Her whole family became quite ill from eating the liver, but when she confronted the women with this they said, "Yes, well, it makes us sick too, but we thought perhaps you knew how to eat it."

INEDIBLE FOODS

Many of the animals on the list of restricted foods, such as vulture, vampire bat, *moritoni* (a crow-like scavenger), and dog, are not eaten because they are scavengers or, in the case of the bat, blood-suckers; that is, their feeding habits are disgusting (dogs, who eat human feces, are a main means of sanitation for the community). The counterpart in our culture would be "eating crow." We have noted that certain chickens gain the reputation of feeding in the outhouses, and, being well known locally, these are never slaughtered for home consumption but are given to the schoolteacher to sell on his trips downstream.

The foods in this category are not prohibited by injunctions so much as by a pervasive but unobtrusive agreement that they are not good to eat. There are no categories of people who can eat them while others cannot, for no one eats them. This practice is similar to our definition of dogs, cats, vultures, and similar animals as inedible.

There is also a non-magical category of poisonous foods (*okepigate*) that "can make us sick" without a specific spiritual mechanism. The caterpillar *soromai,* which is protected by a cocoon of poisonous spines or hairs, is one of these, as are certain frogs. Some kinds of honey are also known to cause hallucinations and disorientation. But honey is such a prized food that men continue to eat it when they find it, and many men tell stories of how they became lost for hours or days at a time after eating poisonous honey.

Conclusions

When we began work on this paper, we set out to examine the extent to which the patterns of Machiguenga food production and food consumption could be accounted for on ecological grounds, and whether significant features of the diet could only be accounted for by reference to structural features that were either unrelated to biological adaptation to their environment or else actually contradictory to adaptation. Although we expected ecological constraints to dominate the overall dietary pattern, we were surprised by the extent to which they do in the Machiguenga case.

Specifically, we find the following patterns of food production and food consumption to be ecologically explainable:

1. The dominance of agricultural foods in the diet results from the low cost of calories produced in gardens.

2. The relatively large amounts of time spent in wild food procurement, given the high labor costs associated with such foods, reflect cost-benefit considerations beyond low-cost calories. These include: higher levels of proteins, fats, and other nutrients; a no doubt related conviction that wild foods, especially animals, are superior in taste and indeed make a meal worth eating; procurement of non-food resources along with the foraging activities; a constantly renewed knowledge of the environment, including potential sites for new gardens, traps, and blinds, building materials, and so forth; and enjoyment of the effort expended in wild food getting. It might be argued that taste preferences and the enjoyment of certain kinds of work are not biological but cultural facts. We would not deny that they may be culturally shaped to some degree, but we assume that such important bases of motivation in the food quest as what tastes good and what feels good are part of the biological heritage of the species, which was formed, after all, in a foraging economy.

3. Even the specific kinds of foods sought in foraging reflect ecological costs. Shimaa, with sparser supplies of fish in the small, cold streams at its altitude, had reached the "broad-spectrum" phase somewhat sooner than Camana; hence, people in Camana were still focusing their efforts on fish. But

fish were declining in availability, and we presume that people in Camana averted the situation found in Shimaa by moving to a new location in order to preserve the abundance of fish they had come to appreciate and expect.

4. Taboos on foods like snake, jaguar, and howler monkey are partly explainable in terms of the real danger of exposure to those animals (jaguar and some snakes, like *loro machado* and bushmaster, are extremely dangerous), the unpleasant taste of the meat, or both. Other food restrictions, like those on vulture and vampire bat, seem intuitively obvious to us, at least until we learn that in some other culture these are eaten as delicacies, and we are forced to abandon our intuition that these are inherently disgusting foods.

Certainly food beliefs cannot be completely reduced to ecology. When one man explained the failure of his maize crop as a result of the monkey meat his co-planter ate *after* the maize was already a month old, and when another explained that his manioc failed to give a generous yield after smoke from his fire, over which peccary meat was roasting, blew across the young plants, both were referring to a general belief system whereby crop failures and other catastrophes acquire magicoreligious interpretations.

Ecologically, we do not accept either explanation. On the other hand, these beliefs tend to be applied after the fact, when crops have failed or someone has fallen ill. They have very little impact on the diet, since there are few edible and nutritious foods that are not eaten by somebody. The Machiguenga pragmatically make full use of the possibilities for a healthy life offered by their environment, and even as they imbue nature and work with emotional and magical significance, they do so not at the expense of their adaptation, but in harmony with and support of it.

References Cited

Baksh, M.
> 1982 The Impact of Increased Fish and Game Scarcity on Machiguenga Subsistence Behavior. Paper read to the annual meeting of the American Anthropological Association, Washington, D.C.
> 1984 Culture Ecology and Change of the Machiguenga Indians of the Peruvian Amazon. Ph.D. dissertation, University of California, Los Angeles.
> 1985 Faunal Food as a "Limiting Factor" on Amazonian Cultural Behavior: A Machiguenga Example. *Research in Economic Anthropology* 7:145–75.

Burton, B. T. (ed.)
> 1965 *The Heinz Handbook of Nutrition.* New York: McGraw-Hill.

Earle, T.
> 1980 A Model of Subsistence Change. In *Modeling Change in Prehistoric Subsistence Economies,* T. K. Earle and A. L. Christenson, eds., pp. 1–29. New York: Academic Press.

Flannery, K. V.
    1969   Origins and Ecological Effects of Early Domestication in Iran and the Near East. In *The Domestication and Exploitation of Plants and Animals,* P. Ucko and G. W. Dimbleby, eds., pp. 73–100. Chicago: Aldine.

Food and Agriculture Organization (FAO)
    1980   *Dietary Fats and Oils in Human Nutrition.* FAO Food and Nutrition Series, no. 20. Rome: FAO.

Hames, R. B., and K. M. Kensinger (eds.)
    1980   *Studies in Hunting and Fishing in the Neotropics.* Working Papers on South American Indians, no. 2. Bennington, Vt.

Jochim, M. A.
    1981   *Strategies for Survival: Cultural Behavior in an Ecological Context.* New York: Academic Press.

Johnson, A.
    1977   The Energy Cost of Technology in a Changing Environment: A Machiguenga Case. In *Material Culture,* H. Lechtman and R. Merrill, eds., 1975 Proceedings of the American Ethnological Society, pp. 155–67. St. Paul: West.

    1980   The Limits of Formalism in Agricultural Decision Research. In *Agricultural Decision Making: Anthropological Contributions to Rural Development,* Peggy F. Barlett, ed., pp. 19–43. New York: Academic Press.

    1981   Reductionism in Cultural Ecology: The Amazon Case. *Current Anthropology* 23:413–28.

    1983   Machiguenga Gardens. In *Adaptation in Amazonia,* R. Hames and W. Vickers, eds., pp. 29–63. New York: Academic Press.

Johnson, A., and C. A. Behrens
    1982   Nutritional Criteria in Machiguenga Food Production Decisions: A Linear Programming Analysis. *Human Ecology* 10:167–89.

Los Angeles Times
    1982   Good Nutrition Calls for Some Fat. *Los Angeles Times,* April 15, sec. 8.

National Academy of Sciences (NAS)
    1974   *Recommended Dietary Allowances.* 8th ed. Washington, D.C.: NAS.

Ross, E.
    1978   Food Taboos, Diet, and Hunting Strategy: The Adaptation to Animals in Amazon Cultural Ecology. *Current Anthropology* 19:1–36.

Smith, G. C., and Z. L. Carpenter
    1976   Eating Quality of Meat Animal Products and Their Fat Content. In *Fat Content and Composition of Animal Products.* Proceedings of a Symposium of the Board on Agriculture and Renewable Resources and the Food and Nutrition Board, National Academy of Sciences. Washington, D.C.: NAS.

Steward, J.
    1977   Evolutionary Principles and Social Types. In *Evolution and Ecology: Essays on Social Transformation,* J. C. Steward and R. F. Murphy, eds., pp. 68–86. Urbana: University of Illinois Press.

16

KENNETH R. GOOD

Limiting Factors in Amazonian Ecology

IN RECENT YEARS MUCH DEBATE HAS FOCUSED ON THE SIGNIFI-cance of protein in the diet of tropical forest populations. On the one hand a number of authors have emphasized the limited supply of animal protein and the significance of this limitation on village size and inter-village relationships (Gross 1975; Harris 1977; J. Ross 1980, 1971). As a reaction to these asser-tions, several papers have appeared denying, in various degrees, the impor-tance of proteins as a limiting factor in Amazonian subsistence (Beckerman 1979; Chagnon and Hames 1979; Lizot 1977). In this paper the issue will be addressed in light of data from three and one-half years of fieldwork over a six-year period on protein capture among the Yanomami of southern Venezuela.[1]

One of the most striking features of Amazonian subsistence systems is that the staple crops that supply the Yanomami with approximately 75 percent of their caloric intake, and approximately the same percentage of food by weight, are markedly deficient in protein. Manioc and plantains, the most common sta-ples in Amazonia, both contain about 1 percent protein. In both cases the pro-tein is deficient in essential amino acids. Since medical science recognizes the need for a daily supply of high-quality protein, and since the indigenous animal populations are present in small and dispersed numbers, a logical choice for a possible limiting factor in Amazonian subsistence would be animal protein.

If protein is a legitimate variable for analysis, the question remains as to the exact nature of its role in a model of sociocultural behavior. A basic misunder-standing of this role has led critics to attempt to refute it on grounds other than those crucial to the argument.

Rather than propose a "deficiency" or "scarcity" of protein, the model sim-ply states that as the size of a community grows, the amount of time and energy required to obtain a desired amount of meat will increase to a point where any of a number of processes will occur that have the net effect of maintaining or restoring previous levels of animal capture. It is the particular process that occurs among the Yanomami living within their traditional culture that is the subject of this paper.

407

Opponents of this model have tended to overlook the fact that it is constructed in terms of diminishing returns in the context of population growth. They have therefore tended to interpret it as meaning that there is an actual shortage or deficiency of protein (Chagnon and Hames 1979). Thus, the objective of much of the responses has been to demonstrate that the Yanomami have adequate protein consumption. As will be demonstrated in this paper, the number of grams of protein consumed is not the critical issue in the model of protein as a limiting factor among indigenous tropical forest communities.

Yanomami Subsistence Patterns

The role of protein capture among the Yanomami cannot be understood in isolation from the total subsistence pattern as practiced by traditional Yanomami. The Yanomami community consists of a single circular communal house called the *shabono*. This dwelling not only serves as a shelter but constitutes the locus for the community's most important economic, political, and social activities. Among these, one of the most critical because of its contribution to intra-village cohesion is the distribution of game and other foods.

The bulk of the Yanomami diet consists of plantains and bananas, which are grown in gardens located next to the communal house. Other contributions to the daily diet consist of plants and small animals gathered by women in the forest and small streams, and larger animals hunted exclusively by men.

Hunting

There are three kinds of hunts: the *rami, heniyomou,* and the *wayumi.* The *rami,* [2] or one-day hunt, is the most common form of hunting. Most men participate in a *rami* about twice a week.

The *heniyomou* is a multiday communal hunt during which most of the adult men of a village spend four to five days in the forest. The *heniyomou* often has the ceremonial objective of acquiring large quantities of meat for a funeral feast, but on numerous occasions the sole purpose is to satisfy a desire to eat meat. The *heniyomou* takes place farther from home than the *rami* and extends into territories that are very infrequently hunted (Figure 16.1). As a result the average yields per hunt are greater than those of the single-day *rami* (Tables 16.1 and 16.2). About 10 percent of the *heniyomous* produce virtually no game and are considered total failures by the hunters (*no breai*). An additional 20 percent produce so little game that quantities are insufficient for distribution at

FIGURE 16.1. Hunting territories of Hasubuwiteri Village

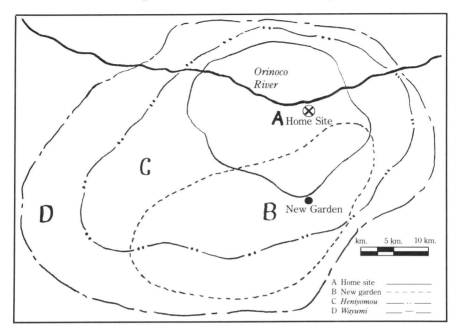

a funeral ceremony. Throughout the year a number of different areas are exploited on the *heniyomou* in a pattern that will be described below. Although the *heniyomou* hunters normally take two to three days to arrive at the most distant spot in which they will hunt, it takes them only 5 to 10 uninterrupted hours to walk back home.[3]

The *wayumi* is a sojourn of the entire community in the forest for several weeks. The *wayumi* brings the hunters to more remote areas than does the *heniyomou*. Usually the *wayumi* takes place in the vicinity of large stands of a fruit or legume that provide food during the outing. As women gather and prepare these foods, the men spend much of their time hunting in the surrounding forest. Since the hunters are in parts of the forest where they have not been for perhaps a year, they are enthusiastic about the prospects of a good hunt.

The Yanomami schedule the *wayumi* trips when foods in the forest are becoming ready to harvest. If an excessive number of plantains ripen before the planned departure, they eat them in larger quantities than they normally do, often boiling them down to a hot drink. Usually however, the opposite condition prevails, and while there may be numerous young plantains in the garden, none

TABLE 16.1. Yields for Single-Day (*Rami*) Hunts at the Home Site, at New Garden Sites, and on *Wayumi* Camping Trips

| | | New Garden Sites[a] | | |
Hunting Observations	Home Site	Months 1–3	Months 12–15	Wayumi
No. of hunts documented	361	225	282	248
No. of hunters/hunt	1.40	1.60	1.62	1.31
No. of hours/hunt	6.47	6.23	6.40	5.78
Weight (kg.) of dressed game/hunt	6.78	8.52	7.94	7.14
Weight (kg.) of dressed game/hunter	4.84	5.33	4.90	5.49
Weight (kg.) of dressed game/hunter/hour	0.75	0.86	0.77	0.95
Success rate (%)[b]	41.83%	48.96%	43.82%	53.51%

NOTE: The data are derived from 1,116 documented hunts between 1975 and 1981.
[a]The data represent hunts recorded during the first three months of camping at a new garden site and during the 12th through the 15th months of residence.
[b]A "failure" (*no breai* in Yanomami) is here defined as any hunt on which the hunters returned with less than two kilograms of meat.

are ready to be eaten. The headman then announces to the community that they will move out into the forest and live on whatever fare they may encounter. The villages I researched made four to six of these trips per year, each lasting from 25 to 40 days. As will be shown below, this time, combined with

TABLE 16.2. Productivity of Multiple-Day Hunts (*Heniyomou*) of a Community of 117 People at Two Sites from 1975 to 1981

Hunting Observations	Hashaawa (riverine)	Wawadoi (inland)	Both Locales
No. of hunts	31	18	49
No. of hunters/hunt	9	7	8.27
No. of days/hunt	4.87	4.25	4.56
Weight (kg.) of dressed game/hunt	76.23	104.43	86.59
Weight (kg.) of dressed game hunter/day	1.60	2.42	1.85
Success rate[a]	68.00	73.00	69.80

[a]A failure for purposes of comparison is here defined as a hunt that produces either no game or a quantity so small that distribution is not possible.

campouts at new garden sites, adds up to approximately one-half of the year during which the entire community is away from the home site.

Another reason the Yanomami give for departing on a *wayumi* is that hunting near the communal house has become less successful. Hunters begin to speak of more distant areas and how they would catch game there.[4] At these times it is not uncommon for individual hunters to go out for 6 to 10 hours at a time on several consecutive hunts and return with no game.

As seen in Table 16.3, hunting yields during the *wayumi* are higher than for equal periods at the home site. A number of factors contribute to this difference. First, the areas of the *wayumi* go unexploited for periods of up to a year or more. Moreover, since these are areas without permanent settlements, game are not scared off, and, in fact, the provisional shelters are sometimes unknowingly built next to dens, nests, and burrows.

Frequently the *wayumi* camp is made very close to an old *heniyomou* campsite, suggesting that the *wayumi* offers no real hunting advantage over the *heniyomou* in terms of territory covered. However, on the *wayumi* the entire community camps in this area for two to four weeks, whereas on the *heniyomou* only some of the men camp for four to five days. Thus, the exploitation of the area during the *wayumi* can be far more intensive.

Subsistence Patterns and Village Movement

When we consider the above-mentioned hunting practices, the following pattern of Yanomami subsistence activities emerges:

1. Approximately 50 to 60 percent of the yearly round is spent at a communal house (*shabono*) with adjoining plantain gardens. At this time the bulk of the

TABLE 16.3. A Size of Game Animals Killed on Single-Day Hunts (*Rami*) at the Home Site, *Wayumi* Trips, and Multiple-Day *Heniyomou*s

Size	Home Site		Wayumi		Heniyomou	
	Freq. (%)	Total Wt. (%)	Freq. (%)	Total Wt. (%)	Freq. (%)	Total Wt. (%)
Large[a]	18.2	36.6	24.4	44.2	28.3	61.9
Small[b]	81.8	63.4	75.6	55.8	71.7	38.1

NOTE: The data are derived from 1,116 documented hunts from 1975 to 1981.
[a]Large game includes peccaries, tapir, deer, and other animals over 10 kilograms.
[b]Small game includes birds, monkeys, and animals weighing 10 kilograms or less.

diet by weight (75 to 80 percent) consists of plantains, which are boiled or roasted while they are still green.

2. During the periods when they are living in the communal house, the women go out to nearby forest areas an average of five times per week to gather fruits and legumes or crab and fish in the small streams. The men spend two to three days a week hunting in areas from which they can return by dusk (*rami*).

3. Approximately every five weeks most of the men in the village (up to 30 individuals) go as a group to a distant forest area where they hunt all day for four to five days (*heniyomou*). This is usually somewhat more productive than the *rami*, but it may produce very little. Of 49 documented *heniyomou* hunts, the failure rate was approximately 30 percent (Table 16.2).

4. Periodically, as foods become ripe in the forest, plantains run short in the gardens, or local game becomes scarce, the entire community leaves for the *wayumi*, a sojourn of four to six weeks in the forest. This effectively removes the entire village to areas where the men can, on a long-term basis, exploit forest areas that would be difficult to hunt from the home-base. Hunting production tends to show a dramatic rise after the principal *wayumi* site is established. Large game is caught more frequently during the *wayumi* (Table 16.3). Sometimes the men go on *heniyomou* from the *wayumi* camp, which enables them to hunt even more remote areas.

5. A Yanomami village normally has two and sometimes three gardens in various stages of development at any given time. When the garden near the *shabono* is mature, the men begin to clear the ground and plant a new garden at a location two to four hours away. During this preparation the entire community camps out near the new garden site.

At the new garden site, the hunting yields increase as they do on the *wayumi* (Table 16.1). Over a longer term the yields show a different pattern. After permanent residence was established, yields during the first year at Boreya-nimobi were considerably higher than those at their former home-base. The yields then showed a downward trend, and eventually, in 1980–81, they were similar to those of the former home-base.

Hunting Ranges and the Yearly Round

From the preceding discussion it can be seen that the Yanomami reside at a number of different sites throughout an extensive region in the course of their yearly round. By residing at these sites the hunters are able to exploit a much more extensive forest area than would be feasible from a single stationary village. Not only is the total area increased, but the pattern of *rami, heniyomou,*

TABLE 16.4. Residence Time in the Sub-areas Occupied in the Course of the Yearly Round for Two Villages

Area[a]	Hasubuwiteri		Patahamiteri	
	No. of Days/Year	% of Year	No. of Days/Year	% of Year
Home site (area A)	175	48.0	180	49.3
Heniyomou (area B: adult hunters only)	41	11.2	50	13.7
New garden site (area C)	65	17.8	—	—
Wayumi (area D)	84	23.0	135	37.0
Total	365	100.0	365	100.0

NOTE: Data are based on 658 days of observation at Hasubuwiteri and 382 days at Patahamiteri.
[a]See Figure 16.1 for designated areas.

wayumi, and new garden camping enables the hunters to exploit the various parts of that area alternately throughout the yearly round. Table 16.4 shows the number of days spent in each area per year. It is evident that the one-day *rami* territory of the home-base (area A in Figure 16.1), that area which can be exploited on a regular basis without special communal hunts or the migration of the entire village, is actually exploited little more than one-half of the year. Villages that are not making a new garden (e.g., Patahamiteri; see Table 16.4) spend more time on *wayumi* trips. Thus, in either case there is a tendency to spend about half of the time away from the home site.

Residence Patterns, Biomass, and Hunting Yields

The interval spent away from the home site is four to six weeks for both the *wayumi* and the new garden camps. One would not expect these four to six weeks by themselves to have any significant effect on the animal populations. However, since the duration of these trips in combination with the *heniyomou* amount to a total of five to six months per year, the home site area in effect is exploited only about half the time, a fact that would indeed have a significant effect on the depletion pressure when compared with that of a fully sedentary village.

It would seem likely that uninterrupted hunting in the home territory would cause a decline in yields. From Table 16.1 it can be seen that the success rates on single-day *rami* hunts at both the new garden site and on the *wayumi* are higher than those at the home-base. But it is impossible to measure the change in these rates over a longer period of time in any given area because the Yanomami move their village to a new garden site every two to three years. However, it was observed that the initially high success rates of *rami* hunts at the new garden of Boreyanomobi and subsequently at Wawadoi after one year flattened to resemble the rates at the home site (Table 16.1). This sharp drop strongly suggests that were the Yanomami to remain in the same site for more than two or three years, the rates would continue to decline. This, in turn, suggests that such moves are a reaction to these declining rates.

The answer to the question of why the Yanomami (living within their traditional non-riverine habitat) most often establish their new gardens at a three- to six-hour walking distance from the old site instead of simply expanding their old gardens may also be related to a decline in the hunting success rate. (The different practices of the Yanomami who have moved to the major rivers and have had acculturative contracts will be discussed elsewhere (see Note 11). Garden measurement and land evaluation at all of the communities researched demonstrated that there was more than an adequate amount of land available for garden expansion. The fact that moving to the new garden site relocates the community in a part of the forest where hunting yields, particularly at the beginning of the period of residence, are markedly higher suggests a relationship that cannot be ignored. Moreover, as I indicated above, *wayumis* usually take place when the garden is low on plantains that are ready to be harvested. Although it is quite difficult to elicit statements from the Yanomami to this effect, it appears that the *wayumi* trips are taken into consideration in determining the size of the gardens. The Yanomami, in other words, could easily avoid running short of plantains and bananas by planting larger gardens. They do not plant larger gardens since they anticipate being away from the village for four to six months of the year.

Meat Consumption

Without a doubt the overriding daily preoccupation in a Yanomami village is the hunt. Not only is it a subject of discussion among the men during their leisure time, but they are reminded of it at almost every meal. The Yanomami have a strong preference for eating plantains and meat together. They do this by alternating bites of meat and plantains and chewing them together. To be without plantains when they have meat, a situation called *tehimi* in Yanomami, causes great dissatisfaction.

Most often the reverse situation prevails, and plantains are eaten alone. A Yanomami gets to eat meat only once every 3.4 days, or about twice a week. (This figure does not reflect quantity, since consumption of only 30 grams of meat was counted as a meat-eating event.) When the Yanomami have only plantains they often express their desire to eat meat (*ya naiki*). It is not uncommon for Yanomami to go five days a week without eating a piece of meat.

When meat is available, the portion per adult male amounts to no more than about 100 grams. Women and children receive even less.[5] To satisfy their hunger, they eat large quantities of roasted plantains (up to 10 at one meal) along with the meat. In fact, when a piece of meat is available, more plantains are eaten during a meal than when the meal consists solely of plantains (an average of 850 grams with meat, versus 510 grams when eaten alone). This enables them to prolong the delight of having meat to eat with their plantains. Even after a meal with meat, the Yanomami are never really satiated.

Intra-Village Meat Distribution

Probably the most important aspect of Yanomami protein consumption is the distribution of meat to adult males within the village. Although senior men eat freely of their own kill, younger hunters up to about 25 years of age believe that they will lose their hunting abilities if they do not share their catch. This distribution is the only village-wide form of reciprocal food exchange and therefore is one of the most important integrating mechanisms within the village. All other foods are consumed by the producer and his or her immediate family.

In villages with more than a hundred people, however, the portions must be divided into small pieces, and frequently some individuals are left out of the distribution (see Table 16.5). Resentments build when a man who thinks he has been given too little meat has a successful hunt and does not share it with the individual he thought had neglected him.

If a man is repeatedly slighted, he may out of anger take his immediate family and move to another village where he has relatives, hoping that he will be treated better there.[6] When the inequitable distribution of meat is perceived as a slight directed at the lineage as a whole, village cohesion begins to crack. This is most likely to occur in villages with 130 inhabitants or more.[7] Thus, the disharmony resulting from dissatisfaction with meat distribution patterns is principally a problem of numbers: too many people for any given distribution. The fact that meat is so highly desired and often unavailable intensifies this disharmony.

Wayumi Camping Trips and Village Splits

Three previously mentioned reasons for initiating a *wayumi* camping trip are the depletion of plantains in the garden, the presence of large stands of desirable foods in the forest, and the greater chance of hunting success. A fourth reason is the development of tensions between two factions in the village. As quarrels become more frequent and animosities and insults increase, the two groups desire to get away from each other. One solution is to set out on a *wayumi,* each group going its own way. This separation also obliges individuals who are not totally committed to either faction to decide which group they will accompany, which further dichotomizes the village.

After a period of three to five weeks in the forest, the two groups return to the *shabono* and reestablish co-residence. If the hostilities continue, the same process is repeated, with the two groups staying apart for longer periods. During these separations suspicion and animosity tend to rise; in part because Yanomami place great emphasis on communal living in a single residence as a measure of confidence and loyalty. When an individual chooses to move to another village, he is no longer considered a close ally. Even those who are closely related can become enemies.[8]

Finally, relations may deteriorate to the point that one group stays at a campsite for months and, in effect, splits itself off from the village without a formal declaration. This allows them the option of returning to the communal house should they reconcile their differences. During this time they are exploiting unfrequented regions of the forest. Game and other foods are distributed among a smaller number of people, and community harmony is restored. Table 16.5 shows the increase in the amount of meat per capita for 41 individuals after they separated from a community of 115 people. No men were omitted from the distributions in the separated group, as was the case in the pre-fission group.

If animosities continue, ultimately one or both groups will remain permanently in a new location. Thus, a village fission will have occurred as a gradual process motivated by an increasingly higher level of tensions but without hostilities. This is not a rare process. Often the fissioning occurs over a number of years as the village grows in size. In Table 16.6, village splits on *wayumi* are related to village size and subsequent permanent fissioning.

Summary and Conclusions

The data presented here lead us to a number of conclusions. First, slash-and-burn plantain gardens supply adequate calories for the existing Yanomami vil-

TABLE 16.5. Intra-village Distribution of Meat Before and After Village Fissioning

Animal	No. Distributions Recorded	Average Cooked Weight (kg.)	No. Pieces	Average Weight/ Piece (kg.)	Range of Weights (kg.)	No. Adult Men	No. Men Omitted
Before Fissioning[a]							
Tapir	5	30.14	33	0.91	0.09–3.64	38	2
Peccary							
(white-lipped)	15	7.37	22	0.34	0.11–0.88	24	7
Peccary							
(collared)	11	5.18	19	0.27	0.18–1.10	24	6
After Fissioning[b]							
Tapir	3	28.24	18	1.57	1.40–5.81	11	0
Peccary							
(white-lipped)	10	7.48	12	0.62	0.88–3.72	11	0
Peccary							
(collared)	9	4.98	12	0.41	0.75–2.58	11	0

[a]115 people.
[b]41 people.

TABLE 16.6. Villages that Separated into Two Groups during *Wayumi* Trips, 1975 to 1981

Village	No. of People	No. in Group A	No. in Group B	Fissioned by 1981
Hasubuwiteri	111	62	49	yes
Patahamiteri	109	59	50	no
Kobariwerteri	149	78	71	yes
Hiomisiteri	113	70	43	yes
Hawarowateri	132	76	56	no
Nanimabuwateri	151	96	55	yes
Yehiobiteri	83	44	39	no

lages of 40 to 250 inhabitants and probably could be extended to support larger communities of 500 to 600 inhabitants, although this never occurs.[9] Second, although their protein consumption is adequate, they are limited to game animals for most of this nutrient.[10] This condition imposes a number of demographic and residential constraints, one of which is the maintenance of village size at 125 to 150 people. There are exceptions, but most often villages fission when they grow to this level, and those that do not are very unstable, eventually fissioning at some later point.

The data on hunting productivity in this study demonstrate that when a village reaches 125 to 150 people, the yields at the home-base begin to drop. This strongly suggests that were the community to remain in the same area, yields would continue to decline. To maintain productivity levels, hunting excursions are carried out by the men. Extended trekking by the entire community into different areas of the forest also results in higher hunting yields. A third mechanism for relocating the community is to make the new gardens far enough away from the home-base to require a move to the new site. All the above practices bring the Yanomami into either new hunting territories or ones that are infrequently exploited. The net effect of these extralocal forays is to increase the hunting yields over those of the home site.

When a village grows to about 175 to 200 people, however, even the above-mentioned mechanisms of maintaining hunting yields become ineffective. Large villages are not suited for the migratory *wayumi,* and they most often split on these occasions. Likewise, when the village grows in number, hunting yields are too small for village-wide distributions. Thus, intra-village interpersonal strains and the limitations of the animal biomass tend to establish an upper limit to village size.

Finally, comparison of productivity rates at different locales strongly suggests not only that the *wayumi* trips and *heniyomou* hunts serve to increase hunting productivity, but that these periodic translocations into areas outside the home territory are essential to avoid permanently depressed hunting yields and the depletion of animal populations.

It is important to reiterate that the processes described here are found in those Yanomami communities which maintain their traditional lifeways. Communities that have relocated to the large rivers, attracted by missionaries and Western goods and technology, have adopted other means of obtaining meat.[11]

The purpose of this paper has been to examine the status of protein capture as a limiting factor in tropical forest communities. It was agreed that these communities, living within their traditional lifeways with little or no external influences, manifest sufficient protein intake. But the questions addressed in this chapter cannot be answered by demonstrating that the Yanomami consume a sufficient or insufficient number of grams per capita of protein per day. Rather, the objective here has been to demonstrate that the hunting strategy employed by the Yanomami is one that permits a steady harvest of game and prevents the diminishing yields that would occur if the community remained sedentary.

Such variations in yield at any given time or place are manifested not in dietary deficiencies but rather in the reaction of the hunters, the frequency of meat consumption, the time and energy required to procure game, and, most importantly, intra-village cohesion as a response to the distribution of meat.

Acknowledgments

Research was supported by the National Institutes of Mental Health and the Max Planck Institut.

Notes

1. The first phase of the fieldwork was carried out from March 1975 to May 1977. Subsequent field trips of two to five months were made in 1978, 1979, and 1980–81.

2. The terms used to describe Yanomami activities are actually verbs but are here used as nouns for purposes of discussion. Thus, *rami* in Yanomami means "to hunt," *heniyomou,* "to go on a hunting trip."

3. Distance in the Amazon is most easily measured in time rather than miles or kilometers, and time is of much more significance to native behavior than is distance. All quantities of time, unless stated otherwise, are given for the fastest rate—that of an unburdened adult male traveling alone. The rates of elderly people, women, and children would be slower to varying degrees.

4. The different locales where game might be present or where tracks have been spotted is a never-ending subject of conversation among men, especially in the early morning and late evening.

5. A detailed description of the diet will be presented in another report, now in preparation. Meat in most cases is distributed to men, who in turn allocate portions to the women and children.

6. In 1976, at Hashaawetaki, a young adult who had been repeatedly disappointed in village-wide meat distributions took his wife and two children and moved to a nearby community.

7. In 1977, when I arrived at the village of Kobariwerteri, a community of 154 people, the headman of one lineage was shouting at his counterpart in another lineage, accusing him and his relatives of consistently slighting his people in the distribution of meat. The latter was shouting back that his own people were also *naiki,* or meat-hungry, and there just was not enough to go around. On the following *wayumi* trip to the forest, the two lineages split up and went in different directions.

8. Younger men are more inclined to abandon kinship terms of address should an individual move to another village. Although some terms were fictive, others were not. In the case mentioned in n. 6 above, a young man who had previously addressed the man who moved away as "father" refused to continue doing so (the departer was a parallel cousin of his father, which defined him as a classificatory father): "If he lives here with us I will call him father, but if he lives with others I will *not* call him father."

9. The village of Patanowerteri consists of approximately 500 people who reside in two separate *shabonos*. The concentration of this many people within a small radius is evidence that larger communities can be supported by the plantain gardens.

10. Beckerman (1979) has argued against the overemphasis on game animals in tropical forest diets. Although there are numerous animal and vegetable sources of protein, the results of my studies nevertheless indicate that over 50 percent of Yanomami protein consumption is derived from game animals. Lizot (1977) also reports that 70 percent of the protein in one village is derived from game animals and over 60 percent in another.

11. Hames (1980), on the basis of his study of a small group of Yanomami who annexed themselves to a Ye'kwana Indian village, has asserted that the Yanomami have been able to remain sedentary by rotating hunting zones. The many atypical characteristics of this group is discussed elsewhere (Good and Lizot, n.d.). It is important to point out here, however, that this group of Yanomami, who call themselves Torobiteri, and the members of the much larger and highly acculturated Ye'kwana village of Toki live on a large river at the periphery of Yanomami settlements. Because of the integration of the Yanomami group into the Ye'kwana economic system, and the availability of Western goods from the Ye'kwana and the nearby missions, sedentary village life offers them unusually good facilities and strong attractions. A tendency observed in other Yanomami communities that live near missions on the major rivers is to alter their traditional subsistence activities, becoming more sedentary and benefiting from a steady flow of Western goods.

Perhaps most important, however, is the small size (approximately 35 people) of the village on which Hames bases his conclusions. A village of 35 individuals falls at the extreme lower limit of observed viable Yanomami communities. Thus, it is not surprising that this group is able to satisfy its protein needs without carrying out the normal activities of a Yanomami Village.

References Cited

Beckerman, S.
1979   The Abundance of Protein in Amazonia: A Reply to Gross. *American Anthropologist* 81:533–60.
Chagnon, N., and R. Hames
1979   Protein Deficiency and Tribal Warfare in Amazonia: New Data. *Science* 203:910–13.

Good, K., and J. Lizot
   n.d.   Unpublished Letter to *Science*. See Appendix 3.2 of A Cultural Mate-
             rialist Theory of Band and Village Warfare: The Yanomamo Test, by
             Marvin Harris in *Warfare, Culture, and Environment,* R. Brian Fer-
             guson, ed., pp. 111–40. New York: Academic Press.
Gross, D.
   1975   Protein Capture and Cultural Development in the Amazon Basin. *Ameri-
             can Anthropologist* 77:526–49.
Hames, R.
   1980   Game Depletion and Hunting Zone Rotation among the Ye'kwana and
             Yanamamo of Amazonas, Venezuela. *Working Papers on South American
             Indians,* no. 2:31–66. Bennington, Vt.: Bennington College.
Harris, M.
   1977   *Cannibals and Kings: The Origins of Cultures.* New York: Random
             House.
Lizot, J.
   1977   Population, Resources, and Warfare among the Yanomami. *Man*
             12:497–517.
Ross, J.
   1980   Ecology and the Problem of Tribe. In *Beyond the Myths of Culture: Es-
             says in Cultural Materialism,* E. Ross, ed., pp. 33–60. New York: Aca-
             demic Press.
   1971   Aggression as Adaptation. Manuscript.

PART V

The Political Economy and the Political

Ecology of Contemporary Foodways

THE SIX ESSAYS IN THIS SECTION ADDRESS SOME OF THE MANY
problems that arise in considering diet in state-level societies, with all the contra-
dictory and countervailing forces and intersecting social relations that such sys-
tems encompass. They all suggest that, whatever else, the emergence of the state,
and even the eventual global spread of the capitalist system with its trans-national
character, did not wholly divorce individual human beings from local ecological
pressures or dissociate their dietary patterns from immediate questions of risk,
cost, and benefit. In his paper on changing diet in the Andes, for example, Orlove
finds that although he is discussing a complex society that has been deeply influ-
enced for a long time through its political and economic linkages with the interna-
tional order, Andean dietary patterns must nonetheless be regarded as largely
determined by the nature of the environmental pressures that shaped regional
agriculture. Preferences and avoidances can generally be accounted for in a prag-
matic way, and their adaptiveness tends to induce an intelligible resistance to
innovation. Nonetheless, so-called traditional diet is not impervious to change,
precisely because of the inherent structural vulnerability of any peasantry. New
foods seem to find their entry easiest in times of ecological or economic crisis—
even though in the long run such foods, being less closely bound to the imperatives
of local subsistence and often of poorer quality, actually diminish the quality of
peasant life.

Such changes are described in the papers by Lindenbaum, Franke, and
Edelman. The first focuses primarily on the displacement of rice cultivation by
wheat in Bangladesh in very recent times. The explosive expansion of wheat grow-
ing is seen to have been in good measure the result of a massive financial, tech-
nological, and ideological campaign on the part of governmental and interna-
tional agencies, but, looking even farther afield, one finds that the single most
effective factor involved in creating a "preference" for wheat in Bangladesh was its

role as recipient of U.S. wheat surpluses. Most importantly, however, Linden-baum points out that neither such imports nor the escalation of wheat production, which was accompanied by a decline in more traditional crops, meant an improvement in dietary quality. On the contrary, the spread of wheat also entailed a transformation in the rural economy that drastically increased landlessness and exacerbated already existing nutritional disparities between the urban and rural sectors, rich and poor. Edelman provides an illuminating parallel to this scenario in his discussion of the way in which the U.S. demand for beef led to the development of a beef-export economy in Costa Rica, with the same result: local protein consumption declined.

Franke extends this argument to a wider consideration of the general impact on diet of colonialist relations of production, as Europeans, over several centuries, disrupted one traditional economy after another, substituting new foods for old, appropriating land and labor, and destroying the environment, as they themselves profited by the production for export of raw materials that were grown where subsistence crops had once predominated. Such profits commonly rested on the dietary immiseration of colonized populations. And, as Franke argues, transnational corporations have been no less disruptive than former colonial powers when it comes to displacing subsistence crops with more profitable ones destined for a more affluent market abroad. In contrast, those Third World countries which have been most successful in redressing these trends and in materially improving the diets of their people have been those which have reclaimed their political and economic autonomy.

Finally, the two other papers in this section, one by Nair and the other by Pelto, shed light on the internal distinctions in diet that are characteristic of state-level systems, illustrating how much depends on economic status. Examining dietary patterns in Mexico, Pelto parallels Orlove's discussion of the relationship of dietary change to income in contrasting the more traditional diet of the rural, low-income family with that of the urban, middle-class family, whose food consumption tends to conform to a newly emergent international cuisine that is much more variegated and less culture-specific. The contrast, while based on income, is also a reflection of a situation of internal colonialism, as circumstances have impelled small farmers in the Mexican countryside to replace subsistence crops with fodder to raise animals that they can sell for urban consumption. Nair, in his discussion of protein consumption in India, points to a similar divergence between the rural and urban sectors but demonstrates that once again the basic variable is income. Indeed, in the course of his examination of the factors underlying the phenomenon of the Hindu taboo on cow slaughter, he observes that in spite of ideological imperatives, beef consumption is spreading in some regions among upper-caste Hindus.

The bulk of Nair's paper, however, is concerned with the material considerations that underlie the sacred cow complex. Though still frequently regarded as a somewhat aberrant cultural feature, even after years of theoretical debate, the

424

resistance to slaughtering cattle for consumption is seen quite clearly to make economic and ecological sense if one examines it, not as an insolated trait, but as part of a complex processual cycle embedded in a specific history. It is within such a perspective that most human dietary preferences or avoidances must, in the end, be examined. For, as the other papers in this section also demonstrate, diet is less a distinctive domain of culture than the result of the intersection of many, often contradictory, economic, social, and historical forces.

17

SHIRLEY LINDENBAUM

Loaves and Fishes in Bangladesh

IN *AN INTRODUCTION TO COLLOQUIAL BENGALI,* PUBLISHED IN 1970, a farmer is asked, "What crops do you raise?" The hypothetical Bangladeshi villager replies, "I raise paddy, jute, chili and mustard," to which the enquirer responds, "Don't you raise corn or wheat?" This elicits the reply: "No sir, corn or wheat can't be raised in my farm" (R. Islam 1970:96).

Bangladesh is indeed a "land of paddy cultivation par excellence" (Ahmad 1976:63). The production of rice in Bangladesh exceeds the combined acreage of Thailand, Formosa, Java, and Madura (Ibid.:66). Rice is the "cultural superfood" (Jelliffe 1968) of the region, the dominant staple and the main source of calories. Its production and consumption occupy a major part of agricultural and domestic work time. In West Bengal, the sharing of cooked rice is said to define solidary relationships among Hindus. Shared rise is the substance of kinship, linking kin to kin and the humans to the gods (Inden and Nicholas 1977), and uncooked rice (paddy) is a key symbol of wealth and prosperity. Wealth in paddy confers mastery over others (Greenough 1983:840–41). Throughout the Bengal region, rice is the center of cultural and agricultural attention.

By 1983, however, wheat had become an important winter crop in Bangladesh, and most Bangalees had begun to eat wheat at least once a day. For some urban residents and many of the rural poor, wheat now provides the staple for two daily meals.[1] Nevertheless, Bangalees continue to think and speak of themselves as rice-eaters. The question "Have you had a meal?" is still phrased as "Have you eaten rice?"; a recent nutritional survey of Bangladesh describes the national diet as "rice plus trimmings" (INFS 1977:122), and the aura of rice is such that a dish of rice cooked with a potato "filler" is still said to be "rice."

This paper examines the rapid intrusion of wheat into a rice cultivation zone of some antiquity, and consider the ways in which cultural conceptions adjust to, incorporate, and contribute to dietary and social change. This requires an analysis of the problem at two levels: first, a historical approach that takes into account the political economy of the region, an evaluation of long-term food preferences and consumption patterns, and an estimate of the nutritional and demographic outcome of these matters; and, second, a simultaneous reading of shifting political and economic forms at the level of symbolic communication, on the assumption that people within and between populations have different commitments to facilitating or changing diet and modes of production. The recent incorporation of wheat into the Bangladesh diet provides one avenue for investigating this variable cultural embrace, avoidance, or taboo of foodstuffs.

Rice and Wheat in Bangladesh

Rice and wheat are crops with long histories in the sub-continent. By Vedic times (1200–900 B.C.), the Aryans are said to have included in their diet wheat, rice, and lentils, the indigenous grains of the Indus Valley (Prakash 1961:241). Rice remained the staple throughout the Epic period (300 B.C.–300 A.D.), although wheat was becoming somewhat more popular (ibid.:102–3). Between 750 and 1200 A.D., the consumption of wheat increased, and many luxurious dishes prepared from both wheat and rice flour and milk entered the cuisine (ibid.:246). Yet although wheat had become a major *Indian* food by the medieval period, it is not clear how popular it was in the eastern regions. The evidence suggests a very early predilection for wheat in northwest India, with rice much preferred in the east and south, a passion that continues to this day.

Wheat began to emerge as an important agricultural crop in East Bengal during the 1960s, although it was still described as late as 1976 as a "minor field crop," said to be raised mainly in the northern districts (Ahmad 1976:85). The expansion of wheat acreage during the second half of the 1970s, however, is astonishing. The great leap in production began in 1975, when the national department of agriculture is said to have supplied seeds, fertilizer, and water for irrigation, as well as extension workers to promote the production of high-yielding variety (HYV) wheat (Yearbook of Agricultural Statistics of Bangladesh 1975–76:18), a picture described in greater detail in a recent publication of the International Maize and Wheat Improvement Center (CIMMYT Today 1982). Since 1975–76 a number of international agencies linked to national institutions have jointly sponsored soil surveys, trained Bangalee wheat workers, and provided consultants, chemical fertilizers, pesticides, irrigation equipment, and loans for seed production and procurement. Research teams have identified methods of farm-level seed storage, composed educational bulletins to disseminate technical information, and trained and organized the extension agents who cooperate with local farmers. In addition, the Bangladesh government is said to have been "willing to devote scarce foreign exchange to import thousands of tons of seed of improved varieties to assure that sufficient seed was available to continue spurring the expansion in the national wheat area" (CIMMYT 1982:14). In this context of national and international cooperation, wheat production in Bangladesh has spread rapidly. In the 30 years between 1944–45 and 1975, the wheat acreage increased from about 105,000 to 148,000, producing by the latter period approximately 35,000 tons annually. By 1981 wheat covered 1,482,000 acres and yielded 1.1 million tons annually. Between 1973 and 1980, the sale of wheat seed to farmers increased nearly 10-fold (CIMMYT 1982:10).

Despite this evidence of the remarkable incorporation of wheat into an agricultural economy, Bangladesh is not self-sufficient in cereal production, and much foodgrain is currently imported. In 15 years foodgrain imports increased from an average of 0.6 million tons per year in 1960–65 to 1.4 million tons in 1970–75, the growth rate of food imports exceeding that of domestic production (Chen and Chaudhury 1975:207). Incoming grains consist overwhelmingly of wheat from the United States, although the Federal Republic of Germany, the United Kingdom, Canada, and Australia provide wheat in lesser amounts (New Nation 1983 [Feb. 4]:1, [March 30]:5).[2] Between Independence in 1971 and September 1982, the United States has provided $2 billion in bilateral assistance to Bangladesh, predominantly in the form of food aid and assistance for agricultural production (New Nation 1983 [March 22]:3).

The story of dietary change in Bangladesh in the 1970s thus begins in the productive wheatlands of the United States. Despite its more captivating image as the home of high technology, agriculture is the single largest dollar-earner in the U.S. balance of trade (Fribourg 1983).[3] During the 1970s, for instance, the United States produced 86 percent of the world's surplus food. By 1981 the product of one of every three harvested acres was exported (U.S. Department of Agriculture 1981). The success of American agriculture stems in part from the mechanization of agriculture in the Great Plains, but it also results from the creation of a national infrastructure of land-grant colleges, agricultural extension services, transportation, and rural credit. Farm subsidies from the federal government, which rose to $21.8 billion in 1983 (New York Times 1983b), also underwrite the position of the United States as the world's dominant agricultural exporter. When the world's main wheat-exporters (the United States, Canada, Australia, Argentina, and the European Community) met in 1983 to discuss ways of coping with the current price-depressing global surplus of wheat, the other exporters tried to dissuade the United States, which currently holds more than one-half of the world's grain stores, from the continued use of subsidies to sell grain (*New Nation* (1983) [April 28]:4).

Subsidized grain from the United States, however, is the means by which Bangladesh has largely attempted to overcome its food deficit. Food shipments, which took the form of food aid during the affluent 1960s, became food trade in the 1970s, following changes in the world economy and a shift of policy in the donor countries. U.S. food "aid" to Bangladesh, under a program known as Food for Peace (or P.L. 480, the Agricultural Trade Development Assistance Act), falls into three categories: Titles I, II, and III. In 1980 Bangladesh was one of the 10 top purchasers of Title I food, which is supplied on concessional terms (40 years at low interest), and allows the receiving government to sell the commodity on commercial markets (Lappe 1980:165). Foodgrain sales provided about one-fifth of the revenue budget of Bangladesh in fiscal year 1977 (Hartmann and Boyce 1978:5). Title II provides food through distributing agencies such as CARE and the Church World Service for relief and feeding programs and Food for Work projects. In 1978 Bangladesh was one of the largest recipients of Title II food, along with India, Egypt, Morocco, and the Philippines. Title III, also called Food for Development, allows the proceeds from the sale of food to be used for projects instead of being repaid by the recipient government. Bangladesh is one of five countries party to this five-year agreement. Most of the foodgrain shipped to Bangladesh comes in the form of concessionary loans. Between 1974 and 1979, for instance, Title I provided 94 percent of American food aid to Bangladesh, while only 6 percent came in the form of an outright grant for disaster relief and humanitarian purposes.

The important place of wheat in the contemporary Bangalee diet does not stem from the spontaneous choice of individual consumers. It is the outcome of the interlocking interests of a national government, the American farm bloc, the World Bank group of lending institutions, international grain dealers, and the operations of American diplomacy, which uses the shipment of food as an arm of foreign policy (see Morgan 1979). At one level, the massive transit of grain from one side of the world to the other appears to derive from a natural logic. The surplus products of one agricultural system resolve the deficits of a food-hungry region. At another level, however, the "gift" is seen to be a more complex prestation, giving rise to a relationship that transforms giver and receiver, "gastropolitics" on a grand scale. In two decades, a new kind of global interdependence has emerged, based most visibly on the transit of food, yet having significant political, economic, nutritional, and cultural connotations, particularly for Bangladesh. No longer a mere recipient of grain, Bangladesh now produces a sizable winter wheat crop and must import the technology and information to support it.

International agribusiness is interested in making capitalists out of peasant-producers (Feder 1977:58) and is thus a force aligned against the emergence of alternative social forms within the country. Moreover, there are dangers inherent in becoming the commercial customer of a single distant food-supplier. Shipments of food from the United States halted during the 1974 famine, for instance, until Bangladesh agreed to terminate the export of jute to Cuba (Morgan 1979:259). Unable to gain credit, Bangladesh was forced to cancel contracts to buy 230,000 tons of U.S. wheat, about one month's supply of grain. Following cancellation of the order, the U.S. government agreed to send its own aid, but the shipments arrived when the worst of the famine was over (Rothschild 1977).

There has been some suggestion that imported food does not reach the poorest segment of Bangladesh society. Imported grain is said to be used instead as an instrument for generating revenue and ensuring political stability by providing subsidized food to the urban middle class (Scott 1979:6). Thus, a public food distribution system that supplies rationed food at roughly 33 percent below open market prices has not had a major impact on nutrition or income distribution in Bangladesh (Karim and Levinson 1979:100).

Since 1973 a number of further developments have had unfavorable consequences for the future growth of the Bangalee economy. These include a substantial increase in the price of energy, worldwide inflation, and a slowing down of growth in the industrialized countries. As a consequence, the terms of trade for developing countries such as Bangladesh are expected to decline. Furthermore, Bangladesh faces the problem of the long-term availability of resources for development, since debt payments on loans seriously strain its balance of payments (ibid.:228), a situation that has been described as peonage or debt slavery on an international scale (Payer 1975). Nominally independent countries find that their debt and their inability to finance their needs out of current exports keep them tied to their creditors. Debtor countries are said to be doomed to the development of their exports in the service of multinational enterprises, and at the expense of development for the needs of their own citizens (ibid.).

In spite of international food assistance on an unprecedented scale during the past two decades, the nutritional status of the population has markedly declined. Three large-scale nutritional surveys (Government of Pakistan 1965; INFS 1977; INFS 1983) document the decline in some detail. The period between the first and second survey includes the 1971 revolution and the famine and near-famine of 1974 and 1975, periods of social and economic disruption. Moreover, the big leap in wheat production had only just begun. Still, by 1975–76 wheat intake is said to have increased by 81 percent while the average caloric intake had declined by 9 percent. Significantly, the consumption of pulse (lentils) had decreased by 15 percent (INFS 1977:130). Since wheat is a winter crop that tends to displace the cultivation of pulse, and since pulse contains a more efficient pattern of essential amino acids than wheat, the displacement of pulse by wheat appears to lead to a diet reduced in both variety and nutritional value (Lindenbaum 1986).

By 1983, 60 percent of rural households were judged to be deficient in calories; 30 percent of the rural population were thought to get insufficient protein, and the intake of fat, carbohydrate, and calcium was also considered inadequate; 78 percent of children under 10 were classified as suffering from various degrees of malnutrition; and more than 800,000 people had become blind due to a deficit of vitamin A. (See also Glimpse 1983). The daily rural intake of meat, cereals, and lentils had continued to decline, and the nutritional gap between urban and rural populations was said to be "widening alarmingly" (Holiday 1983: [February 26]:3).[4] In sum, recent nutritional surveys indicate that while the population continues to increase rapidly, the average Bangalee diet is deteriorating, with total caloric intake declining appreciably in the last decade.

Bangladesh has thus become increasingly dependent on imported food and food technology without any improvement in the general level of nutrition. The recent dietary change whereby a nation of rice-eaters has become semi-converted to another staple[5] shows that Bangladesh is now irretrievably a member of the global food network. As the archaeological record shows, however, processes of stratification accompanied by the development of unequal access to food have occurred in earlier times. The value of the present case is that it provides an opportunity to track cognitive shifts as people respond and contribute differentially to sociopolitical changes taking place at international, national, and local levels. If Bangalees are not born-again wheat-eaters, but continue to see themselves as rice people, where does wheat enter into daily life, cultural conception, and world view?

The Classification of Food

Food taxonomies are not innocent categories but the weighted expressions of what people consider it proper to consume. Food categories, knowingly and unknowingly formulated, are the coded language of ecological and political contest, debate, and reflection. Like people in other parts of the sub-continent (Katona-Apte 1975), Bangalees make a clear distinction between a meal (*khanna*) and a snack (*nasta*). Rice provides the basis of a meal, whereas wheat products constitute snacks. As in Tamil Nadu, however, the staple must be prepared in an accustomed form to be considered a meal. Thus, rice in Bangladesh becomes a meal when boiled in water or fried in butter, but puffed rice (*muri*) or flattened rice (*chirra*) join such wheat-based foods as *chapati* (unleavened flatbread or *atta ruti*), loaf bread (*pau ruti*), noodles, and biscuits in the category of snacks. Snack foods are considered most suitable for breakfast or late afternoon "tiffin," but beyond these two occasions, the consumption of wheat has a more varied set of meanings.

Almost all urban and rural Bangladeshis now eat bread (*atta ruti* or *pau ruti*) for breakfast with egg, sweet halva, left-over curry, or potato *bhaji* (fried spiced potato), or with salt and chili, depending on their economic circumstances. In rural areas, such as Shotaki in Comilla District, those who can afford it eat a rice meal at mid-day and another rice meal in the evening. The eating pattern for the less well-to-do, however, is *ruti, rice, ruti,* while extremely impoverished people may eat wheat three times a day. In the city, an eating pattern of *ruti, ruti,* and evening rice is not considered a hardship for the new professional and commercial classes, who may prefer to eat rice in its "rightful" place in the middle of the day but acknowledge the convenience of mid-day *ruti* as well as its less soporific effect. (Mid-day rice meals are said to cause drowsiness and to fit poorly into an urban workday.) A sweetened pap of boiled wheat flour, like its rice powder equivalent, is now a common supplemental infant food, particularly among the rural poor, as are manufactured biscuits.

The alignment of wheat foods with several dry rice preparations (*muri* and *chirra*) is reminiscent of an earlier food "debate" in Bengal, when the ground rules for an emerging sociopolitical order were presented in the coded language of the proper forms of food, drink, and social behavior. From the 9th to the 12th centuries, a coalition of artisans, hunters, fishermen, and slash-and-burn horticulturalists argued for a Tantric way of life based on the "five *M*s" (meat, fish, wine, parched grain, and sexual intercourse), in opposition to a Brahman-sponsored social order based on intensive rice agriculture (Lindenbaum 1979). The social compromise that emerged resulted in a hierarchical society with hunters, fishermen, and grain-parchers in the lowest strata, and the parched grains (*muri* and *chirra*) relegated to the less significant gastronomic cateogry of snacks. Thus, the apparently innocent classification of certain foods as meals and others as light morsels in present-day Bangladesh is a precipitate of earlier "ethnic" encounters and political debates. The staple of the colonized becomes the colonists' snack. The present status of wheat in Bangalee food categorization indicates a similar resistance to outside control, but as the story that follows illustrates, some political, economic, and cognitive barriers are breaking down.

A second level of food classification in Bangladesh stems from Hindu and Muslim perspectives on the social and culinary universe. The grouping of foods into pure (*pak*) and impure (*napak*), as well as vegetarian (*niramis*) and non-vegetarian (*amis*), is related to debates internal to Hinduism whereby the food transactions of different social groups define and maintain hierarchical ranking. The categories wet/dry and hot/cold, however, are common to both Hindu and Islamic conceptions of food, physiology, and the cosmos and are more closely related to the present consideration of the place of wheat in Bangalee social life.

Wheat is considered a "dry" (*sukna*) food and is therefore given to women following childbirth in order to dry out the birth canal. The same property makes it the food of choice for a mother whose breast-feeding child catches a fever. Persons suffering from typhoid should also take advantage of its status as a "hot" (*gorom*) food (in the conception of villagers) in order to keep the body warm. Urban residents seem less ready to place wheat in the hot food category. A lengthy discussion of the matter among a group of urban Muslim women was summarized by one participant who commented that "although we tend not to question whether *ruti* is hot or cold, it may be hot, because we usually think of it in association with meat."

Wheat is also considered to be a "hard" (*sokto* or *kasha*) food, like *dal* (lentils), meat, and potatoes, which keep hunger at bay for a longer period than "soft" (*rasha*) foods. Unlike rice, however, which is "cool" and is not considered a source of disease, wheat has properties that are believed to cause illness. Roasted wheat seeds are said to cause stomach upset, and persons with gastric trouble should not eat *ruti*, although it is frequently observed that poor people have no way of avoiding this problem. In addition, some people believe that perceived increased incidence of cancer stems from the fertilizers used to produce the crop, an agricultural innovation that increases production but is also said to dry out the "juices" in the soil. Thus, wheat has a drying effect on human flesh and the earth, the substance from which Allah created humankind (Thorp 1982:205).

Rural and urban residents agree that wheat is "not a Bangalee food." It is said to be "foreign," "American," "West Pakistani," or "Western," and was first encountered by many village people in "Ayub Khan's time"—that is, sometime around 1967–68. A few villagers at Shotaki first heard of the new food grain when a boatload sank in the nearby river.

Most farmers give an account of acquiring the knowledge of how to plant and process the crop from their local union council chairmen and council members, or from radio broadcasts that presented agricultural news following Independence. As a winter cash crop, farmers rank wheat below potatoes but above *dal* in terms of its productivity, although they are aware that *dal*, which it often supplants, is "better for health." If wheat, which is widely cultivated and consumed on a daily basis, is still perceived as a foreign food, what do people consider to be the foods of Bangladesh?

The first response of many people to this question is to say that the food of Bangladesh is *dal-bhat* (lentils-rice), an idiom used by the current political leadership, which promises to bring about the social conditions that will put rice and *dal* on every farmer's plate. The idiom is also part of the etiquette of hospitality, in which a host invites a guest to a humble repast of *dal-bhat*, but is expected to serve *pulao* (fine rice with ghee or butter) and an array of other dishes.

Dal-bhat may also be a diminished version of an earlier image of the Bangalee diet as *bhat-mach* (rice-fish) that prevailed when fish was less expensive, and more people assumed that they could afford to eat it. Whether or not this is the case, a more considered response to the question of the foods of Bangladesh adds *mach-mangsho* (fish-meat), although Hindus include only fish.

Some middle-class urban residents note that although they think of themselves as fish-eaters, they are in fact eating more meat, a feature of the urban diet to be discussed shortly. Milk is rarely mentioned in discussions of Bangalee diet; town-dwellers consider it a luxury food, a fond memory of their rural past. Vegetables are included, but wheat, significantly, does not occur at this level of food conceptualization.

As a specific topic of discussion, wheat has a dual image stemming from its manner of entry into the diet. Those who experienced their first meal of wheat flour as a relief food during the famine years, or who received it as payment in a Food for Work program, consider it inferior to rice and view their morning *ruti* or evening wheat-gruel as a deprivation. If rice supplies were sufficient, they would prefer to return to a breakfast of the dried rice preparations *muri* or *chirra,* or even *panta bhat* (cooked and soaked rice). Wealthier people, on the other hand, see wheat as a nourishing addition to the diet. They appreciate the relative cheapness of the grain, and they also eat it in a greater variety of forms, including bread (*pau ruti, atta ruti, paratha,* and *puri*), noodles, biscuits, cakes, and several sweetened (cream of wheat) concoctions. Among certain segments of the urban population, *atta ruti* is a diet food taken in place of mid-day rice, the yoghurt of the new middle classes.

Wheat thus occupies an ambiguous cultural position in contemporary Bangladesh, having different meanings for the urban and rural rich and poor, and perhaps even for men, women, and children. In an admittedly small sample, some well-to-do urban women say that they continue to prefer rice, whereas their husbands (whose workday may "demand" it) have accepted a second eating of *ruti*. Their children, however, show greater enthusiasm for breads, as well as for sliced and fried potatoes.

The attractiveness of wheat to the urban middle classes has to do with its association with a "Western" and "progressive" way of life. This association is encouraged in Dhaka by the emergence during the past two decades of many new food shops, restaurants, and hotels. New patterns of upper- and middle-class food consumption have been shaped by an efflorescence of Chinese restaurants in the 1960s and 1970s, by the Indian-style restaurants of the 1970s, and by the appearance in the 1980s of a few American "coffee shops" and the first hamburger joint (called the "Bargar House") in the commercial center of the city. In addition, urban elites frequent the new sweet and cake shops to "eat in" or "take home" milk-based delicacies or wheat confections. Although the sweet shops are identifiably Muslim in ownership and Bengali in character, the "French Pastry" shops have a more enigmatic quality. Despite the name, the French Pastry chain produces Anglo-American fare: loaf breads, fruit and pound cakes, many styles of sweet biscuits (cookies), and chicken- and meat-filled pastries. They regularly sell apple turnovers (to my knowledge apples do not grow in Bangladesh) and at Easter in 1983 sold hot-cross buns.

In Dhaka city three new luxury hotels have been constructed in the past two decades. The most recent, the super-luxury-class Sonargaon, draws its name and imagery from the once-famous Bengali capital city, located a few miles from Dhaka, but its management is Japanese and its architectural motifs transnational-Mogul. The menus of the Sonargaon's three restaurants encapsulate the recent history of Bangladesh: a Mogul garden-room rotating various Asian specialties; an architecturally clean-cut ground-floor "American" coffee bar, which serves Bangalee, Indian, and American cuisine; and an upstairs French restaurant, which provides more costly international-European fare. Although rice and fish are at times available in some form in all three dining areas, the combined menus represent a significant shift toward the consumption of breads and grain-fed poultry and meats.

Thus, international systems of production and finance are changing the ways that the rich and poor eat and lead their lives. Bangalees harbor an image of themselves as rice- and fish-eaters in the midst of evidence that this conception is becoming daily less tenable. Given the paucity of fish-based protein in the present diet of the poor, it is ironic that Bangladesh's current exports include frozen fish (to the United Kingdom) and shrimp and frog legs (to the United States) (New Nation 1983 [March 1]:3). Moreover, the shrimp beds in the Bay of Bengal are said to be suffering from the heavy trawling of chartered vessels registered in Thailand (Bangladesh Times 1983 [April 16]:1).

As wheat enters the Bangalee agricultural cycle, it also encourages new forms of social and productive relations in the countryside. A survey of agricultural employment in 1975–76 indicates that landless laborers are increasing more rapidly than the total agricultural labor force (Clay and Khan 1977). In 15 years the proportion of landless rural households has risen from 16 to nearly 50 percent (Fuller 1979). By 1983 the landless and near-landless formed a rural majority. National and international economic policies affect rural rates of unemployment, as do food grain prices, access to irrigation, fertilizer, credit, and HYV seeds. There is some evidence already that changes in the forms of rural social organizations have occurred where HYV crops have been introduced. Migrant workers begin to compete with local laborers, and the traditional share system of payment is partially replaced by the introduction of cash contracts and daily wages (Briscoe 1979; Wood 1981).

With increasing landlessness and poverty, women are also becoming participants in the rural labor force in novel ways. At Shotaki in 1983, I witnessed (for the first time in my experience) women harvesting a field crop. Wealthy farmers now hire women from landless families to cut as well as to process their wheat crops, although they do not yet employ women to harvest rice or jute.

This may be because wheat must be rapidly harvested and threshed from March to April before the monsoon rains destroy the grain, or because female labor is cheap. The inexpensiveness of female labor derives in part from the fact that women thresh wheat by beating the harvested plant with sticks, whereas men use the more costly method of trampling with bullocks. It could be said that this new employment is to women's advantage; female labor "lost" recently to men and machines when commercial rice mills began husking rice is restored by the high demand for women in the wheat harvest. This new shift in the sexual division of labor, however, is not without some drawbacks for women. Field labor is not a socially acceptable form of work in purdah-observing Bangladesh. Thus, only the poorest women are found "in the open," working for others. In addition, women (and men) agree that wheat harvesting is especially arduous work. After cutting the crop and separating the grain from the plant, the work of husking, winnowing, and drying begins, tasks similar to those demanded by rice. Women's rice-processing labors, however, are performed during the cool months of the year, whereas wheat is harvested and processed in the heat of April, when the sun is at a peak. Thus, the restoration to women of their social value in agricultural production may be at some cost to their precarious health status, a matter that remains to be evaluated. The issue may soon be moot, however, for a recent CIMMYT (1982) publication reports that research is under way to develop threshing equipment to overcome the predicted labor bottleneck in March and April when the area under wheat production increases. It remains to be seen whether women will become users of the new wheat-threshing technology or whether their current home-based labor will again be supplanted by men and machines. At Shotaki marketplace, commercial mills began husking rice in 1973 and powdering threshold grain in 1975. The use of men and machines is thus firmly established in the region.

Is wheat really changing the diet, the consumption habits, and the social relations of production without leaving its imprint on cultural categories or world view? The answer is, of course, no. Although Bangalees still speak of themselves as fish- (or *dal*-) and rice-eaters, and relegate wheat to the margins as a snack food, the new grain has slipped quietly into Muslim ceremonial consumption and entered unobtrusively into the theological domain.

In the eighth month of the Muslim calendar, the important Muslim festival Sab-e-Barat occurs. During this festival, Allah heals sickness, forgives sins, and, most importantly, decides the destiny of each person for the coming year. Family groups and residential brotherhoods gather to read the Koran and pray together, and charity is given to the poor. Families eat special dishes prepared by women for the occasion. In the past these consisted of sweet dishes and unleavened rice flour bread (*chauler ruti*). In 1972 or 1973, however, wheat flour breads (*atta ruti*) became an accepted festival food, and women now prepare both kinds of *ruti*. At the same time, the new pastry shops in Dhaka began selling sweetened breads, "often in decorated shapes" (Ellickson 1972:87), thereby devising in wheat foods a market equivalent to the indigenous sweet rice flour pastries (*pittha*) produced on festive occasions in every rural household. In one blow, wheat had entered the Muslim sacred calendar, become part of changing urban consumer habits, and issued yet another general challenge to female household production.

To Bangalees, wheat may always have had Muslim associations. Muslim preachers in the late 19th century had told their listeners that the rewards of heaven would include women, wine in full jars, hot *pulao* (fine rice with ghee), breads, and kebabs, evidence that the Bengali Muslim search for identity was based on vague notions of Middle Eastern and trans-Indian patterns (Ahmed 1981:87). The acquisition of a national identity based on Islamic values is still a concern in Bangladesh today, in political life, in architecture,[6] and perhaps in food. Thus, in 1983 a Dhaka university student surmised that wheat had been incorporated into Sab-e-Barat festivities because this was "the food of the Prophet, who was not a Bengali."[7]

The connotation of wheat as a Muslim food is confirmed also by the story of creation as told by the farmers of Pabna District in 1975–76 (Throp 1978:6). In this version of the story, Allah created Adam (from earth and water) and his wife Howa (from Adam's rib) and set them with the angels in heaven. He then warned them not to eat the fruit of one particular plant, the *gandamphal*, literally a smelly or perfumed fruit, which the Pabna farmers translated surprisingly as "wheat." Adam and Howa ate the "fruit," were banished from heaven, and were thus forced to begin cultivating the earth.

By 1976 Pabna was apparently already one of the main wheat-growing districts in Bangladesh (Ahmad 1976:85), although Thorp's farmers appeared reluctant to discuss the identity of *gandamphal,* saying merely that it did not grow in Bengal (meaning perhaps that it was not a native Bangalee plant). Thorp speculates that some of this reluctance was related to the farmers' general wariness in 1975–76 about discussing politics, since wheat was associated at that time with West Pakistani hegemony (pers. comm.), a connection raised less hesitantly by 1983.

The identification of wheat in 1975–76 as the forbidden fruit of heaven points once again to the historic ambiguity concerning what is Bengali and what is Islamic. This more recent attempt to come to terms with cultural identity is now complicated further by the supra-national forces that are intensifying wheat production in the region and changing the diet, behavior, and social relationships of the eaters and growers of the "forbidden" grain. These extra-national forces provide wheat with a new Muslim-free identity, reflected in the international "nutri-speak" of food scientists, who are the witting and unwitting arms of international finance and production.

Just as foods in the United States have been coded by official food guides that reflect the national and multinational interests of governments, producers, and grain-traders (Haughton 1982; Lindenbaum 1986), so health educators, nutritionists, and food researchers in present-day Bangladesh have begun to code Bangalee foods into seemingly neutral "scientific" categories. During the past 60 years in the United States, for example, food guides have presented 5, 12, 7, and finally 4 "basic food groups" (milk, meat, vegetables and fruits, bread and cereals). This last categorization gave a deliberate boost to the wheat and dairy industries, since wheat and dairy products now make up half the recommended daily diet. Moreover, grain-producers and -traders stand behind three of the four groups, providing fodder for meat and dairy animals and supplying the basis of bread and cereals. Similarly in Bangladesh, a recent publication (Rahman 1979) proposes that families be informed that the three basic food groups consist of (1) energy-giving, (2) body-building, and (3) protective foods. Rice, *chapati*, and potatoes are given equal weight as the energy-giving foods of category 1, thereby dislodging the "folk" status of wheat as a "hard" food in the same class as meat and *dal*. Meat and *dal* are said to be body-building, components of category 2. In addition, professional journals have begun to assess the nutritive value of wheat and to recommend it as a staple "ideally suited for human consumption" (Azim 1981:82).

A further stimulus to changing food conceptions comes from the daily newspaper lists of national market "prices and essentials." These "essentials" fall into eight categories: rice, pulses (lentils), edible oil, spices, miscellaneous (sugar and salt), milk, vegetables, and meat. Fish does not appear to be included. Moreover, the tables place wheat in the category of "rice," but potatoes remain with the vegetables.

Wheat is thus a moving counter in the national consciousness.[8] The attention it receives from professional counselors and the national media disallows a parochial discourse concerned with the qualities of "hot," "cold," "wet," and "dry." There is already a tendency among villagers to speak of the "vitamins" rather than the subtle qualities of foods (Maloney, Aziz, and Sarker 1981). This new food discourse provides cognitive categories not of local origin, which change the way reality is perceived. Statements about foods are intentional messages of political will, economic interest, nutrition, health, and pleasure, as well as cosmological reflections on the self, rightly situated in a moral world. Changing food conceptions thereby encapsulate meanings generated in the past and the present, as well as those at a distance and those of local origin. As the Bangalee economy is drawn further into supra-national realms of finance and production, nutrition educators and others may persuade Bangalees that wheat is indeed a meal, not a snack, and Bangalees may say, in addition, that it is not a food foreign to Bangladesh.

Acknowledgments

The data in this paper were gathered during my work for the International Center for Diarrhoeal Disease Research, Bangladesh. I would like to thank the center and its director, Dr. W. B. Greenough, III, for providing financial, intellectual, and logistic support.

Notes

1. I am aware that Bangladesh exhibits some regional variation with regard to changes in cultivation and diet. The data in this paper come mainly from Shotaki in Matlab Thana, where I have carried out fieldwork intermittently since 1963, from several villages closer to Matlab town, and from Dhaka city. I am indebted to Manisha Chakraborty and Mohammed Elias from the International Center for Diarrhoeal Disease Research, Bangladesh, for field assistance and companionship at Shotaki and Matlab.

2. Rice, milk powder, vegetable oils, and cotton are also imported, to a lesser degree.

3. This information is derived from a letter to the editor of the *New York Times;* the author is president and chief executive officer of the Continental Grain Company.

4. Recent nutrition reports note especially a high incidence of night blindness in young boys, due perhaps to their lower intake of green vegetables. The experience of the Bangalee population may also throw light on a condition known as celiac sprue (or gluten-induced enteropathy), an inherited condition in which gluten-containing foods, such as wheat, lead to the inflammation and destruction of the villae of the small intestine. It will be interesting to see whether celiac sprue will occur now that there is widespread exposure to wheat, although the disease may not be readily recognized because of the prevalence of other diarrheal conditions.

5. The story of the potato should also be told. Potatoes as well as wheat have recently made a massive entry into the winter growing season. Some farmers grow potatoes on land formerly allocated to *dal*. Potatoes are viewed, however, as a very productive market crop. On 1 *khet* of land, a farmer harvests perhaps 2 *maunds* of *dal* but 30 *maunds* of potatoes. International assistance in potato technology, seed, and cold storage facilities are again part of the picture. The nutritional advantages of this "addition" to the diet have not been studied, as far as I am aware.

6. Public and domestic architecture in the capital city is developing a local language based on Pan-Islamic themes. Much of it is based on the spectacular capitol building, designed by the American architect Louis Kahn, who formulated his own international vision in a Euro-Asian arena.

7. Calcutta Hindus in the late 1960s, who also had access to subsidized wheat grain, perceived it as a festive food of Muslims (M. J. Beech, pers. comm.).

8. It would be nice to know what food was provided for the Indian astronaut who accompanied two Soviet astronauts on the Soyuz mission in 1984: he was to have his own food, but in a 1984 report space officials of the two countries had not yet agreed on

the menu. The food must be dry and solid, lest it float from the cans. Moreover, the size and shape of the food cans must conform to Soviet specifications (*India Abroad,* July 29, 1983), a problem not yet posed by the terrestrial food network.

References Cited

Ahmad, N.
  1976   *An Economic Geography of East Pakistan.* London: Oxford University Press.
Ahmed, R.
  1981   *The Bengal Muslims, 1871–1906: A Quest for Identity.* Delhi: Oxford University Press.
Azim, Z. N.
  1981   Wheat and Its Nutritive Value. *Bijnan O Amra:*82–84.
Bangladesh Times
  1983   April 16, p. 1.
Briscoe, J.
  1979   Energy Use and Social Structure in Bangladesh. *Population Development Review* 5:615–41.
Chen, L. C., and R. H. Chaudhury
  1975   Demographic Change and Food Production in Bangladesh 1960–1974. *Population and Development Review* 1:201–27.
CIMMYT (Centro Internacional de Mejoramento de Maiz y Trigo) Today
  1982   Wheat in Bangladesh. *CIMMYT Today* (Mexico), no. 15.
Clay, E. J., and N. S. Khan
  1977   Agricultural Employment and Under-Employment in Bangladesh: The Next Decade. Rural Social Science Paper, no. 4. Dacca: Bangladesh Academy for Rural Development.
Ellickson, J.
  1972   A Believer Among Believers: The Religious Beliefs Practices and Meanings in a Village in Bangladesh. Ph.D. dissertation, Michigan State University.
Feder, E.
  1977   Capitalism's Last Ditch Effort to Save Underdeveloped Agricultures. *Journal of Contemporary Asia* 7:56–78.
Fribourg, M.
  1983   Letter to the Editor. *New York Times,* June 7.
Fuller, W. P.
  1979   Landlessness, Unemployment and Rural Poverty. Resource Paper, Agricultural and Resources Staff Seminar, Yoghakarta, Indonesia.
Glimpse
  1983   *Glimpse 1983:*5(4). International Center for Diarrhoeal Research, Dacca.

Goverment of Pakistan
  1965   Nutrition Survey, 1962–65.
Greenough, P. R.
  1983   Indulgence and Abundance as Asian Peasant Values: A Bengali Case in Point. *Journal of Asian Studies* 42:831–50.
Hartmann, B., and J. Boyce
  1978   *Needless Hunger: Voices from a Bangladesh Village.* San Francisco: Institute for Food and Development Policy.
Haughton, B.
  1982   The Cosmopolitan Radish: Procedures for Constructing a Food Guide for New York City and State in the Year 2000. Ph.D. dissertation, Teachers College, Columbia University.
Holiday
  1983   February 26, p. 3.
Inden, R. B., and R. W. Nicholas
  1977   *Kinship in Bengali Culture.* Chicago: University of Chicago Press.
INFS (Institute of Nutrition and Food Science)
  1977   *Nutritional Survey of Rural Bangladesh, 1975–76.* Ford Foundation Archives, Grant no. 75-27. Dacca: INFS.
  1983   *Nutritional Survey of Rural Bangladesh, 1982.* Dacca: Dacca University.
India Abroad
  1983   July 29.
Jelliffe, D.
  1969   *Child Nutrition in Developing Countries.* Washington, D.C.: U.S. Department of State.
Karim, R., and F. J. Levinson
  1979   A Missing Dimension of Food and Nutrition Policy in Bangladesh. *Bangladesh Development Studies,* 7:99–106.
Katona-Apte, J.
  1975   Dietary Aspects of Acculturation: Meals, Feasts and Fasts in a Minority Community in South Asia. In *Gastronomy: The Anthropology of Food and Food Habits,* Margaret L. Arnott, ed., pp. 315–26. The Hague: Mouton.
Lindenbaum, S.
  1979   Understanding Siva: An Anthropological Analysis. Paper read to the annual meeting of the American Anthropological Association, Cincinnati.
  1986   Rice and Wheat: The Meaning of Food in Bangladesh. In *Food, Society and Culture: Aspects of South Asian Food Systems,* R. S. Khare and M. S. A. Rao, eds., New Delhi: Manohar.
Maloney, C.; K. M. A. Aziz; P. C. Sarker
  1981   *Beliefs and Fertility in Bangladesh.* Dhaka: ICCDR-Bangladesh.
Morgan, D.
  1979   *Merchants of Grain.* New York: Viking Press.
New Nation
  1983   *New Nation,* Feb. 4, March 1, March 22, March 30, April 28.

New York Times
1982   Filipinos Turn Back From Green Revolution. *New York Times,* May 16.
New York Times
1983a   *New York Times,* July 6.
1983b   *New York Times,* August 21.
Payer, C.
1975   *The Debt Trap: The I.M.F. and the Third World.* London: Penguin.
Prakash, O.
1961   *Food and Drink in Ancient India.* Delhi: Munshri Ram Manshar Lal.
Rahman, S. H.
1979   Education for Housekeeping and Nutrition. In *Integrated Rural Develop-*
        ments and the Role of Education, vol. 2. Dhaka: National Foundation for
        Research on Human Resource Development.
Rothschild, E.
1976   Food Politics. *Foreign Affairs* 54:285–304.
1977   The Economics of Starvation—1: For Some, A Feast of Crumbs. *New*
        York Times, January 10.
Scott, M.
1979   Aid to Bangladesh: For Better or Worse? San Francisco, Institute for
        Food Development Policy.
Thorp, J. P.
1982   The Muslim Farmers of Bangladesh and Allah's Creation of the World.
        Asian Folklore Studies 41:201–15.
U.S. Department of Agriculture
1981   A Time to Choose: Summary Report on the Structure of Agriculture.
        Washington, D.C.: Government Printing Office.
Wood, G. D.
1981   Rural Class Formation in Bangladesh, 1940–80. *Bulletin of Concerned*
        Asian Scholars 13(4):2–17.
Yearbook of Agricultural Statistics of Bangladesh
1975–   Dacca: Bangladesh Bureau of Statistics.
76

K. N. NAIR

Animal Protein Consumption and the Sacred Cow Complex in India

PEOPLE IN INDIA EAT A PREDOMINANTLY VEGETARIAN DIET. AT the same time, roughly 70 percent of the population is estimated to be non-vegetarian. For vegetarians milk is practically the only source of animal protein, but the non-vegetarians consume a variety of other flesh foods as well. Such preferences for animal protein are found among all the world's societies (see Chapter 8). Despite the universal preference for animal protein, however, consumption of certain animal foods is a taboo in some societies. According to some scholars, such aversions are due to the influence of religious values; others attribute them to the human response to the objective conditions of food production. Both have adduced evidence in support of their arguments, and the debate is still on. The objective of this paper is to take these discussions further and to highlight the relative importance of various factors in shaping the animal protein complex.

Consumption of Animal Proteins

Animal foods contribute only a small fraction of the total per capita intake of protein in India. During 1961–62, the only year for which all-India estimates of animal protein intake are available, the average consumption per capita in rural areas was about 5 grams per day, which was then about 7 percent of the total per capita protein intake. The figure for the urban sector was slightly higher: 7 grams per day (Table 18.1).

Although the absolute level of animal protein intake is low in India, the fact that the nutritive value of plant protein is improved when consumed along with animal protein highlights the importance of animal protein. The cost per unit of plant protein is significantly lower than that of animal protein. Therefore poor

TABLE 18.1. Average Per Capita Intake of Protein per Day (in Grams) in Rural and Urban India, 1961–62

	Rural	*Urban*
Total protein	69.0	58.4
Animal protein	4.5	7.1
Animal protein as percentage of total	6.5%	12.1%

SOURCE: Government of India (1969).

NOTE: Independent estimates of the actual quantum of intake of milk, fish, meat, and eggs in India are available only from the 17th round of the National Sample Survey. The following procedure was adopted in deriving protein content:

1. Data on milk consumption were broken down in the original source into (a) per capita consumption of liquid milk; (b) per capita consumption of ghee; and (c) per capita consumption of butter. In order to estimate the per capita consumption of milk protein, we first converted ghee and butter into their liquid milk equivalent according to the average fat content of milk in each state. Since the fat content of cow and buffalo milk is different, and the relative importance of these varies across states, we have used a weighted average of fat content, the weight being the relative production of cow and buffalo milk in the respective states. In the process of converting liquid milk into butter, the protein is separated with buttermilk. We therefore estimated the quantity of buttermilk obtained from the liquid milk equivalents of ghee and butter and applied the standard protein content of buttermilk (0.8 percent) to obtain the protein derived from this. In the case of milk consumed as such, a weighted average of protein content was applied, the weight being the production of cow and buffalo milk.

2. In the case of meat, we applied an average protein content of 22 percent, which is a simple average of the protein content of chicken, beef, and mutton. For eggs we have applied a protein content of 13.5 percent.

3. In the case of fish, we used a protein content of 18.8 percent, a simple average of the protein content of 18 important seafood items consumed in India.

people derive a high proportion of their protein intake from plant sources. But as one moves up in the scale of income or expenditure classes, the consumption of animal protein also increases significantly (Table 18.2).

Among the various sources of animal protein, milk is the most important item, preferred by all sections of the population. It contributes about one-half of the total animal protein intake. Meat and egg together contributed another

TABLE 18.2. Per Capita Consumption of Animal Protein over 30 Days in Rural and Urban India by Expenditure Class, 1961–62 (in kilograms)

Expenditure Class[a]	Rural				Urban			
	Fish	Meat/ Eggs	Milk	Total	Fish	Meat/ Eggs	Milk	Total
0–8	0.009	0.005	0.004	0.018	0.010	0.101	0.007	0.118
8–11	0.002	0.008	0.012	0.022	0.017	0.031	0.015	0.063
11–13	0.019	0.014	0.019	0.052	0.026	0.025	0.023	0.074
13–15	0.030	0.017	0.030	0.077	0.019	0.060	0.042	0.121
15–18	0.040	0.017	0.041	0.098	0.028	0.042	0.052	0.122
18–21	0.038	0.030	0.054	0.122	0.035	0.056	0.066	0.157
21–24	0.044	0.037	0.069	0.150	0.038	0.066	0.078	0.182
24–28	0.051	0.050	0.077	0.178	0.049	0.061	0.091	0.201
28–34	0.056	0.040	0.113	0.209	0.060	0.068	0.118	0.246
34–43	0.058	0.057	0.165	0.280	0.058	0.071	0.140	0.269
43–55	0.058	0.109	0.180	0.347	0.072	0.083	0.168	0.323
55–75	0.056	0.091	0.243	0.390	0.091	0.129	0.208	0.428
75 + above	0.095	0.177	0.216	0.488	0.104	0.107	0.277	0.488
Average	0.038	0.033	0.062	0.133	0.047	0.100	0.099	0.246

SOURCE: Government of India (1969).
[a]Per capita monthly expenditure on food and nonfood items, in rupees.

fourth of the total per capita intake, and the remaining fourth comes from fish. The relative importance of the various sources of animal protein is similar in urban and rural areas.

Although the consumption of animal protein is low and most of the population is non-vegetarian, there is a strong aversion to the consumption of cattle and buffalo meat in India. In order to unravel the factors underlying this aversion, it is necessary to examine the management of livestock resources in India in a historical perspective.

Livestock Management

An important aspect of livestock management in India is the existence of communal grazing (Crotty 1980). Because of the continuous grazing of animals over centuries, the productivity of pasture lands has declined. The proportion of

447

land devoted to permanent pastures and grazing has also declined at an alarming rate with the growth of population and the expansion of the area under cultivation. At present only about 2 percent of the geographic area of India is permanent pasture and grazing land. Because of this, livestock keeping in India has become essentially a farmyard business. Since land has become very scarce, the extent to which farmers can afford to divert land from food crops to the cultivation of fodder is also limited. Therefore livestock are fed mostly with the by-products of agriculture. Most of the feedstuffs (except for concentrates) have very little opportunity cost outside the livestock sector. However, the availability of feedstuffs is far below the nutritional requirements of the livestock population.

Even in the face of the accute scarcity of feed resources, Indian farmers rear a large number of livestock species. Bovines which are mostly fed on agricultural by-products, supplemented by grazing, constitute the primary level of livestock production. In the farmers choice of bovinestock, preference is given to draught animals, without which it is difficult to sustain food production in the existing state of farming technology. But once the draught animals are fed, adult females needed to produce calves and milk and other follower stock come next in the farmers' order of priority. Small livestock like sheep, goat, pig, and poultry reared for their meat, wool, and eggs constitute a secondary level of livestock production. Pigs and poultry are reared as scavenging animals; goats and sheep are generally maintained on browsing and natural pasture and are given very little supplementary feed. They consume feeds that are not generally consumed by the large animals (Government of India 1973). The two levels of livestock production can co-exist, since there is no competition between the small and large animals for the available feed resources.

There is a widespread belief that the management of livestock resources in India is in general inefficient because of their very low productivity (Nair 1981). Low productivity is, in turn, attributed to a large extent to the low feed conversion efficiency of the stock. If we consider conversion efficiency strictly in terms of input-output ratios, Indian livestock management may indeed appear inefficient. But this is not the best criterion. An appropriate measure of conversion efficiency should take into account the type of food eaten by the animals and the competition between man and animal for land resources:

> When an animal eats something that we could not readily turn into food in some other way, or when it lives on fodder we could not have harvested, the question of efficiency does not arise. But when an animal eats something we could have used or something growing on land we could have used to grow human food, efficiency has a real meaning. It is the ratio of the amount of human food that is produced by an average population of animals (not just one animal at the peak of its productivity) to the amount that could have been produced by an alternative method of use. (Pire 1969:235)

In the world's advanced agricultural systems, a good part of the indirect consumption of grain is in the form of beef. Rearing beef cattle on roughages produced on land that is not suitable for the raising of crops is one way to produce a high-quality, much-sought-after protein product. When cattle are transferred from roughage to high-intensity feed-lot, they become extremely inefficient converters to protein. Cattle reared on grazing areas require no grain, but those on feed-lots consume about 10 pounds of grain for every pound of meat produced. The crucial point is that once all available grazing areas are being fully utilized, it is very costly in resource terms to satisfy any additional demand for beef without diverting to beef production crop lands and grains that could otherwise be used to meet human needs directly. In the world's poor countries, intensive beef production is carried on at the expense of land needed to cultivate grains for direct human consumption. The bulk of the beef produced in poor countries is exported to affluent ones, and even if intended for domestic consumption, it will not reach those who desperately need protein in their diets; more likely it will help to meet the consumer demand of the higher-income groups. In overpopulated and less developed agrarian economies like India's, therefore, the avoidance of large-scale slaughter of cattle and consumption of beef is a perfectly rational procedure for ensuring the proper use of agricultural resources in producing grains required for mass consumption.

It is important to bear in mind several other material benefits that are derived from bovine husbandry in India. The milk not only provides a source of nutrition but helps poorer farmers to earn extra cash income. Dung is used for manure and as fuel for cooking. The availability of bullocks is important in the timely cultivation of crops. (The death of a plough animal seriously upsets the small farmer's economy, particularly since he may have to sell part of his land to buy another to replace it.) Such economic and social benefits may account to a considerable extent for the taboo against cattle slaughter and beef eating in India, as a close look at the historical evolution of the cattle complex in India shows.

The avoidance of cattle slaughter originated in the Vedic period (1200–900 B.C.). The strategy adopted was to restrict animal sacrifice to ceremonial occasions and the entertainment of guests and to make the cow a sacred animal (Harris 1980; Srinivasan 1979). The sacredness of the cow was ensured by emphasizing the importance of milk in the diet, the cow's divine origin, the belief in the transmigration of the soul and the cow's role in helping humans along the path to salvation.

Nomadic Aryan people were highly pastoral people and reared large number of cattle for subsistence needs. Beef was a delicious food, but simultaneously, breeding on a large scale was necessary to maintain stocks of cattle in subsistence needs. On the other-hand nomadic Aryan tribes had limited capacity to maintain a given cattle stock

449

and constant culling of useless cattle in relation to breeding capacity was extremely necessary. Thus, in order to achieve a balance between maintenance capacity and need for beef an institutionalised method of saving was required in the form of resisting the temptation for beef. (Batra 1981:16—grammar as in original)

At a subsequent stage, the Jains and the Buddhists initiated social movements against the Brahmin practice of cow sacrifice and beef eating. At the same time, belief in the sacredness of the cow and in the transmigration of the soul continued to grow. During the last two centuries, many Hindu reform movements have exploited the "sacred cow" as a means of strengthening Hindu religious unity. Struggles against cow slaughter have resulted in communal riots in several parts of the country. Nationalist movements used it as an issue to fight the British. Since Independence, cow slaughter has remained an issue on which general elections are fought. In brief, the taboo on cow slaughter and beef eating that was developed in order to preserve several of the material advantages of the bovine economy and to prevent the inefficient use of resources became a fetish and an instrument for achieving religious and political gains for the Hindus.

Consequences of the Beef Eating Taboo

That the Hindu taboo on beef eating limits the market for beef in India is indisputable. But the extent to which it results in a waste of beef needs a close look because of the significant underestimation in several studies of the scale of bovine slaughter. Relative to other species, the slaughter of cattle and buffalo is on a small scale, clearly a reflection of preferences for and aversion to various sources of meat. Meat from smaller animals is consumed by a large section of the Hindu population, and consequently their slaughter is more widespread than that of large animals (Table 18.3). Muslims and Christians, who form a substantial proportion of India's population, have a strong preference for beef. As the traditional practice of carrion eating disappears among the low-ranking castes in states like Kerala and West Bengal, the consumption of beef is becoming more widespread among upper-caste Hindus. In the beef-scarce regions of the country, especially in Kerala and West Bengal, the demand for beef is well developed and has outstripped domestic supply (Nair 1981). In Kerala, beef in 1983 cost about one U.S. dollar per kilogram. About a million bovines are currently slaughtered in the state each year, roughly a third of the state's bovine herd. A large proportion of the slaughtered cattle are imported from neighboring states. Since a legal ban on cattle slaughter is in force in most other Indian states, it is difficult to judge the extent of cattle slaughter and beef eating

TABLE 18.3. Estimated
Percentage of Animals
Slaughtered in India per Year

Type of animal	% of animals slaughtered
Cattle	0.9
Buffaloes	1.4
Sheep	32.5
Goats	36.8
Pigs	22.0
Others	6.4

SOURCE: Government of India (1976).

nation-wide, but surveys conducted in many parts of the country indicate large-scale clandestine slaughter of cattle. In a Punjab survey, for example:

The birth rates of cattle, buffaloes, sheep, goats were estimated at 126, 251, 392, and 571 per thousand respectively. The corresponding death rates were 68, 163, 115, and 85 per thousand respectively showing thereby that both birth rate and death rate were the lowest among cattle. Among goats, although the birth rate was the highest, the death rate was very low; slaughtering of goats is most commonly practiced and this accounts for wide differences between the two rates. For similar reasons there was considerable differences between the birth and death rates among sheep also. Although slaughtering of cattle and buffalo is banned by law in this area, high differences between birth and death rates for these species of animals are not consistent with the annual rate of increase in the population, indicating the possibility of unreported unauthorised slaughtering of animals of these species. (Maini et al. 1979:13–14—grammar as in original)

Even if we allow for some unauthorized slaughter of cattle and buffaloes, a significant proportion of bovine mortality is due to natural death. If these cattle were slaughtered, the supply of animal protein in India would be augmented. The taboo on cow slaughter and the consumption of beef thus limit the supply of animal protein. But this potential wastage of animal protein needs to be weighed against the potential social damage that would follow from the development of a large-scale meat industry in India. To meet the nutritional requirements of the large population, simplification of diet is very important:

There is thus sound nutritional as well as economic and ecological logic behind India's traditional preference for vegetarian diet. It would be a great pity, if in the name of

451

modernity, we let ourselves in for a change in our diet habit towards the consumption of meat. It is one thing to supplement a cereal diet with milk and milk products, fish which require no land base and even a limited quality of egg in spite of the larger input of cereals it entails. But it is quite another thing to go in for meat, which makes a heavy draft on cereal output. (Rao 1982:148)

Fortunately, the bulk of the meat produced in India is obtained as an end product from livestock husbandry; animals are not reared for the sole purpose of slaughter. Meat is obtained from animals that are reared for draught power, milk, and wool. But this picture may disappear as the slaughter of bovines and consumption of beef spread. Fattening of animals to meet the consumer demands of high-income groups may emerge in this situation. Already symptoms of such a tendency are observed for poultry, the meat preferred by most of the non-vegetarian population. In the hinterlands of most of the urban centers, commercial production of broilers has developed on a large scale in recent years.

Other important advantages and disadvantages are associated with the taboo on cow slaughter and beef eating. In the absence of a well-developed market for beef in India, the prices of cattle and buffaloes remain relatively low, allowing vulnerable sections of society to acquire the animals and thus derive the benefits of their ownership. A serious disadvantage of the ban appears in the field of cross-breeding. The success of any cross-breeding program depends to a great extent on the elimination of animals that are useless or unproductive through selective culling and slaughter. These mechanisms are, however, largely absent in most parts of India as a result of both the legal ban and the taboo on cow slaughter. Continuing the restrictions on slaughter is bound to dilute the effectiveness of the cross-breeding program insofar as it facilitates the growth in the number of unproductive stock, which, besides competing with productive animals for the available supply of feed, will make it extremely difficult to maintain the genetic quality of the cross-bred stock. One way out of this situation is to implement the selective slaughter of cattle, supported by measures to prevent the growth of a large-scale beef industry in India.

Conclusion

The universal preference for animal protein consumption in India is evident from the pattern of consumption observed across various income groups. The animal protein intake, however, is very low, reflecting both the constraints on production and the aversion among Hindus to certain types of animal flesh, especially beef. We should remember that the taboo itself came into existence in the remote history of the country as a logical resolution of the ecological and economic conflicts of those times.

The economic, nutritional, and ecological reasons behind the taboo are not totally irrelevant even now. The production of beef is a highly energy-intensive process, and widespread cattle slaughter and beef consumption require a considerable diversion of resources from the direct production of grains for human consumption. Viewed from this angle, the Hindu taboo on beef eating has played a positive role in shaping consumption patterns in India along sound lines. It has also contributed to a more equitable distribution of cattle wealth by keeping down the capital cost of youngstock. However, the recent spread of cross-breeding of cattle has created a need for a higher level of efficiency in the culling of the stock. Slaughtering, on a limited and judicious scale, is required by the introduction of modern methods of cross-breeding. The sacred cow complex might continue, but with rather less sacredness than in the past.

References Cited

Batra, S. M.
    1981   *Cows and Cow Slaughter in India: Religious, Political and Social Aspects.* The Hague: Institute of Social Studies.

Crotty, R.
    1980   *Cattle, Economics, and Development.* Farnharm: Royal Commonwealth Agricultural Bureau.

Government of India
    1969   *National Sample Survey, 17th Round Tables with Notes on Consumer Expenditures.* New Delhi: Department of Statistics, Ministry of Planning.

Government of India
    1973   *Report of the Subgroup on Sheep and Goat Development.* New Delhi: National Commission on Agriculture, Ministry of Agriculture and Irrigation.

Government of India
    1976   *Report of the National Commission on Agriculture, Part VII, Animal Husbandry.* New Delhi: Ministry of Agriculture and Irrigation.

Harris, M.
    1980   *Cultural Materialism: The Struggle for a Science of Culture.* New York: Vintage Books.

Maini, J. S.; B. B. Goel; and D. C. Dahiya
    n.d.   Report of Sample Survey for Estimation of Production of Hides and Skins, Punjab (1974–76). New Delhi: Institute of Agricultural Research Statistics (ICAR).

Nair, K. N.
  1981   Bovine Holdings in Kerala: An Analysis of Factors Governing Demand and Supply. Ph.D. thesis, University of Kerala, Trivandrum.
Pire, N. W.
  1969   *Food Resources, Conventional and Novel.* Harmondsworth: Penguin Books.
Rao, V. K. R. V.
  1982   *Food Nutrition and Poverty in India.* New Delhi: Vikas Publishing House.
Srinivasan, D.
  1979   *Concept Cow in the Rigveda.* New Delhi: Motilal Banarsidas.

RICHARD W. FRANKE

The Effects of Colonialism and Neocolonialism on the Gastronomic Patterns of the Third World

THE EFFECTS OF COLONIALISM AND NEOCOLONIALISM ON THE Gastronomic Patterns of the Third World can be summed up in one word: contradictory. On the one hand, the capitalist economic system—the primary motivator of modern colonialism—has unleased powerful production forces based on intensified world trade, improved communications, and scientific and technological development that have the potential to improve the diets of all people. On the other hand, the accumulation needs of the capitalist system have caused large-scale dislocations and misallocations of resources that have left much of the colonized world enslaved or disenfranchised, underpaid, and underfed.

The end of colonialism in Latin America in the 19th century and most of Asia and Africa in the mid-20th century has altered these effects in some ways and continued them in others. Although capitalism still generates important technological innovations in food production, processing, and dietary mix, it has also engendered a new central contradiction deriving from the old colonial division of the world into accumulating nations and those that provide surplus for the accumulation. In the neocolonial world, agribusiness searches for cheap land and labor, additional profit through emphasis on luxury crop *production* in the former colonies, and *sales* in the rich consumer markets of the old colonial powers; the subsidized sale of grain produced in the rich nations keeps the underpaid Third World producers of these luxury crops alive. At the same time, fearing the political instability and threat of revolutions created by this exploitative system in an era of political awakening and the existence of powerful alternative production systems in the socialist bloc, capitalist states have sought to increase basic food production within certain of the poor countries through programs such as the green revolution.

These contradictory policies have produced a mosaic of outcomes, including dietary improvements in some Third World nations, but continued and even increasing vulnerability to famine, and stagnation or even further deterioration in general calorie and protein intake among the poorest groups in the Third World. In this essay I shall attempt to detail and specify as much as possible in the space allotted the most salient aspects of each of these major contradictions and their close relationship to the evolving food patterns in the Third World.

Colonialism and Dietary Patterns

One of the most dramatic effects of colonialism was the dissemination of many previously localized crops and animals to sites around the world. Chocolate, tea, coffee, cotton, pineapples, sugar, tobacco, nutmeg, peppers, maize, tomatoes, papaya, sweet potato, groundnuts, and many other foods were grown and marketed in only limited regions, sometimes even a specific island group, before about 1500. The early mercantile colonialism of the Spanish, Portuguese, Dutch, French, and English centered on expanding the markets for these crops and, later, introducing them into new fields in other parts of the world. Coffee, for example, is thought to have originated in Ethiopia. It appeared in Cairo and Istanbul before 1517, spread to Venice in 1615, and had reached London by 1650. The rapid growth in European consumption spurred the Dutch East Indies Company to plant the crop on Java in 1712, and other colonial interests led to its presence on Réunion in 1716 and Martinique in 1730. By 1789 Santo Domingo was producing 40 million pounds of coffee a year, and merchants and production investors were eyeing the possibility of selling coffee to approximately a third of the world's people in Europe and the Muslim world. As Braudel has noted, "An active capitalist sector had a financial interest in its production, distribution, and success" (1975:184–87; see also Wolf 1982:336–37).

Nutmeg was brought to Europe by Portuguese and then Dutch, traders. From just a few small islands in Eastern Indonesia, the Dutch were able by 1756 to export annually 300,000 pounds of nutmeg and 110,000 pounds of mace to Amsterdam. Their income was more than three times their expenses, suggesting a very high profit rate (Hanna 1978:87). By 1854 output had risen to 539,000 pounds of nutmeg and 134,000 pounds of mace, and income was a bit under three times expenses (ibid.:112).

One of the most adventuresome of the colonial crops was tobacco, which could be spread widely because of its adaptability to varied climates and soils. It seems to have been first sighted by a European when Columbus visited the New World in 1492, was planted in Spain in 1558, the Philippines in 1575,

Virginia in 1588, Java in 1601, and India and Ceylon by 1610 (Braudel 1975:189).

Other important crop disseminations included the taking of maize from Cuba to China by 1555 (Tannahill 1973:246), the spread of peanuts from Haiti and Peru to China and West Africa (ibid.:256), the movement of pineapples, papaya, and potatoes from the New World to Europe and Asia, where potatoes had reached Nepal by the 19th century (ibid.:241), and the spread of tea from China through the markets of Amsterdam (1609), and France (1635), and its first plantings on Java in 1827 and Ceylon in 1877. It is estimated that between 1693 and 1793 imports of tea into Europe increased 400-fold (Braudal 1975:180).

Perhaps the crop that most dramatically illustrates the colonial enterprise is sugar. This non-nutritious source of energy had its origins in either the Pacific islands or West Bengal. It is reported from Persia in the sixth century and was brought into European markets by Arab traders. Soon after the "discovery" of Brazil in 1500, sugar prices began rising in Europe after a long slump, and a gradual expansion of sugar into the Brazilian Northeast began (Taylor 1978:13–17). Production went from 2,470 tons in 1560 to more than 5 million tons in 1946 (Deerr 1949: vol. 1, 130–31). Sugar also appeared in many of the Caribbean islands between 1527, when first grown in Jamaica (ibid.:174), and 1638, when introduced into Guadaloupe (ibid.:228). It spread to Louisiana in 1751 (ibid.:248) and to Hawaii in 1825 (ibid.:252). Sugar was already in small-scale production when the Dutch arrived in Java in 1619. Production rose from 48 tons in 1622 to 2,000 tons by 1826, when a major expansion led to its increase to 534,000 tons in 1896 and a peak of just under 3 million tons in 1930 and 1931 (ibid.:213–26; see also Wolf 1982:332–36).

Another, more indirect effect of colonial trade should also be noted. In many of the colonized countries, root crops were major sources of energy. As trade became increasingly necessary in maintaining the diets of the colonized, the more perishable root crops were often replaced by grains that could be stored and thus shipped. Even before European colonialism speeded up the development of trade, this process was under way. In Indonesia, for example, as inter-island and international trade expanded eastward, rice replaced taro and yams as the staple crop; by 1500, it was only east of Lombok that taro and yams were staples (Missen 1972:73). The higher protein content of the grains over the tubers may not have been very important to forest populations that had access to pigs. A negative effect—an increase in famine vulnerability—accompanied increases in output and the benefits of trade: the seed-sown crops were initially less reliable than the tubers (ibid.:75).

The 450-year period of European colonialism thus transformed the distribution of crops, increasing the potential variety of people's diets and vastly increasing overall food production through the opening of new lands, intensification through technical improvements, and the vast accumulation of wealth in the colonial centers, many of which had undergone industrial transformations by the mid–20th century. But this very accumulation process, based on profits from the colonial enterprises, had as its counterpart several harmful effects on the diets of colonized peoples. These resulted from colonialism's division of the world into increasingly landless, impoverished producers and better-off consumers in the colonial centers. Several distinct, but often interrelated processes were involved, including the seizure of land and labor, the abuse of environmental resources for quick profits, control over markets to the detriment of producers, and the creation or exacerbation of inequalities that have persisted into the neocolonial era. The general effect of these interrelated processes seems to have been a deterioration in the calorie and protein content of the diets of substantial numbers of Third World people. Paradoxically the very people who produce food are victims of a shortage of it.

French colonialism in Vietnam provides a dramatic example of many of these processes. The first step was seizure of land. Village communal lands, which accounted for as much as 25 percent of the rice land in Tonkin, and as little as 3 percent in Cochin China, were confiscated by force and turned into concessions for French military officers and adventurers. In Cochin China, low population density allowed the French to dislodge peasants from their more isolated villages and proclaim the land "unused." Between 1860 and 1931, the French managed to confiscate 40 percent of the potential rice-producing land, using it for rubber, coffee, tea, and *export* rice (Long 1973, esp. pp. 16–19). The concessions also went in some cases to Vietnamese collaborators, simultaneously engendering an increase in landlessness at the bottom, which had affected 1,303,000 families by 1952 (ibid.:19), and a small elite of landlords at the top.

French colonial studies have documented the effects of these policies. In 1939, for example, data showed that in one province surveyed, 62 percent of the landowners had less than the amount necessary to produce the minimum diet of 230 kilograms per year of milled rice (calculated from Long 1973:20–22). Another study in Annam in 1952–53 showed that 53 percent of the families were landless; of the landholders, 94 percent held only 37 percent of the land, while 6 percent of the owners held 22 percent of the land; at the very top, 0.1 percent of the owners held 17 percent of the land. Another 24 percent was still in communal holdings. Tenant farming, sharecropping, and labor recruitment for mines in Tonkin and for rubber plantations in the south were also features of French colonial control in Vietnam. Although it is not detailed, available evidence suggests that such extreme forms of inequality were not present in pre-French Indochina (ibid.:5–6). The overall effects of the system can be seen in the declining availability of food: 262 kilograms per person per year in 1900; 226 by 1913; 182 by 1937. Finally, under the strain of war and the Japanese occupation, the entire food system collapsed in 1943, and during the next two years, more than 2 million people starved to death (ibid.:131–33).

On Java sugar expansion in the 19th century had similar if less dramatic effects. It now appears that, contrary to the thesis put forward by Geertz in *Agricultural Involution,* sugar in the 19th century was associated with a *decline* in rice production (Geertz 1963; White 1983). Instead of intensifying their rice production labor, peasants instead often resorted to faster-growing but lower-yielding varieties and used *less* labor-intensive methods on their rice fields (White 1983). Incompatibilities between the requirements of rice and sugar production may be seen in the ecological and technical spheres. Sugar, for example, requires a 15- to 18-month growing cycle in which water is mainly fed to the fields in the first 6 months. Rice, by contrast, grows in a 3- to 5-month cycle and requires a steady flow of water throughout. Sugar requires irrigation furrows, whereas rice requires basin irrigation; thus, "irrigation systems developed with the intention of maximizing sugar production are inappropriate for the maximization of rice production" (Alexander and Alexander 1978:210). Considerable labor is required each time a field is changed over from one crop to the other. By detailed reconstruction of cropping cycles, Alexander and Alexander concluded that a sugar village would suffer a 42 percent loss of rice land availability in each three-year cropping cycle, and another 14 percent loss due to the time needed for the conversion/reconversion of the irrigation system (ibid.:212), compared with a village that remained outside the sugar regime. By 1920, 8 percent of the entire wet rice land of Java was planted in sugar, and 25 to 44 percent of the best land; moreover, 73 percent of the irrigated land was subject to potential seasonal appropriation (Geertz 1963:72–74).

In addition to the land and labor seizures of the sugar regime, another powerful force was the destruction of the land itself. The Gunung Kidul or "southern mountains" region of south central Java was heavily wooded in the 1850s. Government decrees forcing peasants to plant coffee trees, however, led to cutting of the teak and other mixed tree species. The coffee trees did badly because of the climate and disease. By 1933 the hills were severely denuded, and they were further cleared during the Japanese occupation. By 1958 only 7.7 percent of the area had forest cover, and that was being lost to firewood as desperate peasants sought some form of income in the impoverished region. Rising population and sharply declining rice yields brought a move to cassava cultivation (Bailey 1962:248–50). In 1896 cassava was not a principal food in any part of Java, but 30 years later it had become an important hunger crop in the limestone hills, including Gunung Kidul (Smith 1974:25). The limestone underlay of the hills makes water retention difficult, and when nutrition studies were conducted at a regional hospital in the late 1950s, it was found that calories produced per person per day were only 1,264 in the better of two areas (Bailey 1961:298). Consumption figures were somewhat higher in some of the individual villages, but protein intake was extremely low; clinical signs of edema were present in from 9 to 100 percent of lactating women sampled in different villages (ibid.:305); and comparisons with data from 1938–39 indicated that men were shorter than those of the previous generation, suggesting dietary failure (Bailey 1962:230–37). The loss of trees from the coffee scheme of the 1850s was being reflected in the dietary patterns of cassava farmers and fire-wood-collectors in the 1950s.

As in Vietnam, colonialism in Java was associated with a worsening land situation for the majority. As early as 1903, reports indicate that over 70 per-cent of all farm owners had less than 0.7 hectare, while only 3.9 percent owned more than 2.8 hectares (Wertheim 1964:218, 230). A comparison between the years 1868 and 1928 in a village on the north coast of Java revealed that land-holdings had been nearly cut in half (ibid.). In the early 1950s, a village study in West Java showed that 44 percent of the population had become totally land-less, while another 25 percent owned only the land on which their houses stood (ten Dam 1966:349). Research in East Java in 1953 indicated in one village that 181 households held house and garden lands of less than 0.5 hectare, while four families held 5.1 hectares or more each (Jay 1969:16). The inequality in Jav-anese landholdings continues to haunt the countryside in the neocolonial devel-opment programs to be described later (Franke 1982).

In Brazil, sugar seems to have combined the various effects of different colonial crops in Java into one intensified attack on land, labor, and diet. The land of the Northeast was stripped of trees. Sugar mono-culture deprived the soil of nutrients. Denuded river banks became flood paths that carried away minerals and humus. Wildlife variety was also destroyed (de Castro 1966:31). As for labor, the local Indian population was partially enslaved, partially exter-minated, and partially driven deeper into the interior. By the early 16th cen-tury, slaves from Africa were becoming the main labor source: their loss to their home villages was likely a source of agricultural and thus dietary decline there (Franke 1981), but sugar had direct effects on diet in Brazil too. The single-minded colonial concentration on sugar production and the loss of en-vironmental diversity led to an unhealthy diet of manioc—a crop requiring little land or labor. The gastronomic monotony and poor health of the slaves thus helped finance the accumulation of capital by the sugar barons, who invested in the scientific development of sugar technology, leisure, luxury, British industry, and so on rather than the dietary needs of their workers (Taylor 1978:56).[1]

British colonialism, too, while spreading tea, coffee, and sisal to wealthy markets around the world, wrought harmful effects on local diets through land and labor seizures, ecological destruction, and increasing inequality. In the 1890s colonial military expeditions seem to have brought dislocations, famine, and a host of diseases such as smallpox, whooping cough, influenza, and polio to Kenya (van Zwanenberg 1975:9). The first dietary survey of the Kikuyu and Masaai, conducted in 1926–27, concluded that both groups suffered dietary deficiencies. In addition to the campaigns of the 1890s, British policies during World War I may have played a role (ibid.:13). In any case British interests in production for export led to a massive land grab that deprived African farmers of 18 percent of Kenya's best land (that which gets 30 inches of rainfall annually). The 7,560 square miles seized never supported more than 3,500 European families—about 14,000 persons—while the remaining 34,070 square miles had to support 2 million people in 1940 and 5 million by 1950 (ibid.:30). On average, the Europeans had about 26 times as much of the good land per person as did the Kenyans, many of whom became low-paid squatters on the margins of the British estates.[2]

Among those whose diets were most affected by British capital accumulation in Kenya were the nomadic herders. Kenya's ecology includes a dramatic dualism: well-watered highland valleys around Nairobi, and mostly dry pasture or desert in the remainder of the territory. Before colonial rule, pastoralists had a good diet that included meat, milk, and blood from their animals (van Zwanenberg 1975:80–81). European ranching interests, however, effected a series of policies including quarantines that kept herders from moving their animals across "European areas," forced auctions at low prices to European buyers, and other interferences in herder trek routes that led to localized overgrazing and loss of animals (Spencer 1983). As early as the 1930s, many of the semi-arid parts of Kenya began showing signs of erosion (van Zwanenberg 1975:85–100).

In southern Africa massive labor migration was a major vehicle of dietary decline. In Ovamboland (Namibia), for example, colonial ivory trading and control over cattle raiding combined with a local social order based on kingship to produce a progressive pauperization of vassals that drove many families' young males to work in railway construction and mining. This "labor-exporting peasantry" suffered a series of famines, unsuccessful revolts, and punitive military expeditions while local farm production was seriously undermined (Clarence-Smith and Moorsom 1977).

In Barotseland (Western Zambia) labor migration seems to have been the main factor in transforming what Livingston in 1853 described as a "fruitful" and "fertile" valley where "the people never lack abundance of food" to a place that Gluckman in 1965 called "notorious even beyond its borders as almost a permanent famine area" (quoted in van Horn 1977:144). Local flood recession fields were manured. Both the amount and the timing of labor inputs were critical. Colonial taxation and competition from colonial labor recruiters undercut the ability of all but the wealthiest farmers (i.e., the ruling elite) to keep up their fields. The result was abandonment of the intricate flood recession system and a shift to farming on more marginal, less productive lands. The colonial government, concerned only with getting workers for capitalist accumulation, primarily in mining, did nothing to protect or restore the farming potential of the region (van Horn 1977). In general, the picture of famine vulnerability throughout Africa may have been accurately summarized in Kjekshus's conclusion for Tanzania: "Periodic catastrophes due to structural imbalances and maladaptations to the new economic system of colonialism . . . replaced the random disasters that characterized the 19th century" (1977:19).

The West African Sahel further exemplifies the colonial contradiction. While French science developed improved varieties of peanuts and the French vegetable oil business prospered, African farmers were being coerced through taxation and physical brutality into peanut mono-cropping that depleted the soil, overuse of fallow areas, seasonal labor migrations that interfered with millet production, and a breakdown of mutually beneficial grain-milk exchanges with pastoralists from the Sahara desert fringe, whose animals had also manured the farmers' fields (Franke and Chasin 1980, esp. pp. 63–108). In 1949 a French colonel summed up the dietary situation: "The people in the whole territory [then French West Africa] lack balanced nutrition; and this is a permanent state" (quoted in ibid.:74). Caloric intake was found to drop from 3,000 per person per day right after harvest to 750 in the pre-harvest period. In Niger famines occurred in 1900–1901, 1903, 1913–14, 1920–21, 1927, and 1931. Overall food availability in Senegal dropped from 240 kilograms per person per year in 1920 to just 145 in 1959 (ibid.:74). The allocational irrationality of colonialism can be seen in the connections between the Sahel and Vietnam. So desperate did the food situation in the Sahel become that the French colonial regime began moving rice from its Indochina colonies to keep its West African peanut farmers alive long enough to produce and reproduce (ibid.:83).

Perhaps here the concept of "shared poverty" could be revived: Vietnamese farmers and workers, who were starving to subsidize French industrial growth, starved also to feed West African peanut farmers, who also starved to subsidize French industrial growth.

Neocolonialism and Dietary Patterns

The transition from direct colonial control to formal independence in most of the Third World has correlated with certain clear gains in the standard of living for Third World peoples overall. Enormous progress has been made in Third World literacy, which increased from 33 percent in 1950 to 56 percent in 1979. Life expectancy rose from 43 to 58 years in the same period (World Bank 1982:24). At the same time, the tremendous inequalities between the rich former colonial and developed socialist nations on the one hand and the Third World on the other have remained and even intensified in some respects. In 1982 the top 20 percent of the world's people had 71 percent of the world's income while the poorest 20 percent had only 1.6 percent of the income. The poorest 60 percent of the people held only 9.3 percent of the world's income (calculated from Sivard 1982:19). In 1980 Third World nations had 75 percent of the world's people, but only 50 percent of the cereal production, 35 percent of the arable land, 35 percent of the meat and eggs, 22 percent of the milk, and 15 percent of the tractors. Third World nations accounted for 6 percent *less* of the merchandise exports in 1980 than in 1955, suggesting a lag in industrialization and increasing use of their resources as primary products (ibid.:3, 26). Agricultural output per person increased only 0.3 percent per year in the Third World between 1960 and 1980, and in some areas, such as Subsaharan Africa, it actually declined, while in the Middle East and South Asia it remained absolutely stagnant (ibid.:41).

What has led to this contradictory pattern? The most likely explanation is that some improvements in education, medicine, and, in some areas, diet have been offset by processes undermining the development struggle of the past 30 years. The two most evident of these processes are the growing control of the world food system by transnational corporations and continuing or increasing inequalities within Third World nations that offset attempts to improve diet merely by introducing advanced technology.

Agribusiness, Inequality and Diet

Colonial regimes and colonial state trading companies have been replaced by transnational food firms, which have captured increasing portions of the world food supply. In 1980 the 15 largest transnationals marketed 85 to 90 percent of exported wheat, 60 percent of sugar, 85 to 90 percent of coffee, corn, cotton, tobacco, and jute, 90 percent of pineapples, and 70 to 75 percent of bananas (Clairmonte and Cavanagh, 1982a:161).

Transnationals are in business to make a profit, and profits are maximized by two major factors: the cheapest possible land and labor and the maximum amount of processing. Much processing is done in the developed world, but the search for cheap land and labor is increasingly bringing the transnationals to Third World nations. Profits from pineapple production, for example, are 17 times as high in the Philippines as in Hawaii for Castle and Cooke's Dole subsidiary (ICCR 1973:43). Gulf and Western's sugar operation utilized 11 percent of the arable land of the Dominican Republic (Clairmonte and Cavanagh 1982b:11); the banana-producing subsidiary of R. J. Reynolds holds access to 17,000 acres of prime land in the Philippines. A United Nations study shows that only 11.5 cents of each banana dollar spent in the United States goes to the producers. When input costs are added, only 0.2 percent of the final price could be counted as gross margin to the producers (ibid.: p. 16). The main profits go to packagers, insurance companies, shipping lines, and marketers, often owned by the same vertically integrated transnational. Large-scale increases in food production in a Third World country thus do not necessarily translate into either edible and affordable food *or* the foreign exchange required to purchase it.

An effect of these international arrangements is that land needed for local subsistence is being taken for overseas luxury crops. In the last 20 years, Africa, which has suffered as much as a 15 percent decline in per capita food production, has quadrupled its coffee production, tripled its sugar cane output, and increased tea production sixfold (Lappé and Collins 1977:227). Most of this production went for export. Similarly, in Latin America the per capita production of subsistence crops decreased by 10 percent between 1964 and 1974 while per capita production of export crops increased by 27 percent (Burbach and Flynn 1978:5). An often neglected aspect of the neocolonial production system is that the transnationals have a material interest in maintaining poverty, not in overcoming it.[3]

The agricultural growth of Brazil is a case in point. With over $6 million in agricultural exports and over $5 million in agricultural trade balance in 1978, Brazil ranked first among third world nations in net agricultural trade balance (Hawes 1982:29). The price for this export boom—mostly in soya and grain production—was a 14 percent per capita *decline* in bean production between 1960 and 1975 (Valente and Heimann 1978). Calorie consumption remained low, with 38.5 percent of the population below the reference standard of 2,450 calories per person per day in 1970, and a highly uneven regional distribution saw 29 percent malnourished in the south and 75 percent in the Northeast (ibid.), the region of the sugar estates described earlier. Furthermore, data collected in 1963 show a strong correlation between income level and caloric intake (ibid.: table 15), and income inequality in Brazil *increased* between 1960 and 1970, with the top 1 percent increasing its share of wealth by 6 percent while the bottom 80 percent of the population suffered a 9 percent decrease. Between 1968 and 1977 Brazil experienced a 5 percent drop in its protein consumption per capita (Szymanski 1981:357).

Some of the local mechanisms of pauperization have been studied by the anthropologist Daniel Gross. When a sisal scheme was introduced into a village in the *sertão,* the increased labor demands forced poor families to deprive their children of sufficient calories in order to make possible the productive activity of the male household heads (Gross and Underwood 1971). Inequalities among classes and within families are commonly reported dietary patterns in the Third World.

The important link between inequality and dietary patterns is further illustrated in another study from Brazil. In the brief active period of the peasant leagues of the Brazilian Northeast, a rural labor statute was passed resulting in increased incomes for sugar workers. Dietary surveys conducted in 1961 and 1964 allowed diets before and after the statute to be compared. They showed marked changes in the amount and pattern of food intake. With their higher incomes, workers increased their consumption of bread by 205 percent, rice by 71 percent, and meat and fish by 41 percent, but decreased by 8 percent their intake of root crops, of which white yams were a major element (Taylor 1978:109). These data suggest that reducing inequality could be an effective means of altering food patterns in the Third World.

Kenya provides another example in which export-led development by transnational corporations is correlated with continuing dietary insufficiencies. Although Kenya has been a major recipient of governmental and corporate investment, per capita food production declined by 14 percent between 1970 and 1979 (World Bank 1982:110), while protein consumption declined by 10.5 percent between 1966 and 1977 (Szymanski 1981:360). Malnutrition is regarded as the fourth leading cause of death in Kenya, with 30 percent of children suffering mild-to-moderate protein-energy malnutrition in the 1960s and 1970s (Leitner 1976; Wisner 1980:100). In a model study of the process of producing nutritional vulnerability, the geographer Ben Wisner examined the Kamba Gradient region. He was able to document an association between levels of malnutrition among children in particular villages and certain effects of capitalist economic penetration, including the drawing off of local labor and the loss of peasant control over land, partly as a result of the loss of a major part of the workforce (Wisner 1980:114–16). Wisner further found that loss of access to pasture lands (partly a result of colonial processes described earlier) had deprived one village of its ability to get milk and meat and forced too high a reliance on millet, resulting in a higher proportion of underweight children than in other nearby villages, where the situation was better but still bad (ibid.:118–19). A further strong relationship was found between access to good soil and better-nourished children (ibid.:121). Thus, several forms of inequality combined with the overall scarcity of food in Kenya to produce an uneven incidence of malnutrition: 40 percent in the worst village, and 15 percent in the best.

In other parts of Kenya similar processes appear to be at work. Clinical and anthropological studies suggest a deterioration in child nutrition in the area affected by the Mwea plains irrigation scheme (Wisner 1983:21). In sugar areas of Kenya, "field workers interviewed indicated that the current emphasis on cash crop production, especially of sugar cane, causes a decrease in food crop production and exacerbates existing nutritional problems" (quoted ibid.:15). The correlation between sugar and declining subsistence documented for colonial Java (as described earlier) appears to have repeated itself in neocolonial Kenya. A consultant study projected that the best way to meet the nutritional needs of the poorest Kenyans would be to shift 20 percent of the income of the richest 10 percent of the population to the poorest 60 percent. By contrast, a production-oriented strategy depending on transnational investments in sugar, coffee, pineapples, and so on would probably only worsen the distribution and fail to solve the problem (McCarthy and Mwangi 1982).[4] Only 7 percent of Kenya has good soil and adequate rainfall. Yet there are 3,200 large Kenyan-owned landholdings that contrast with 1.5 million small farms with an average size of 0.3 hectare. Kenyan policies to induce transnational investment in cash crops can therefore be expected to lead those transnationals into an alliance with the nation's large farmers (Dinham and Hines 1983:92; Langdon 1981). The allocational irrationality of transnational investment is highlighted by a case in Kenya in which the British firm Brooke Bond Liebig Kenya Ltd. set up "the world's biggest production area of asparagus plumosus, a fluffy foliage which is very popular as a green support for bouquets" (quoted in Dinham and Hines 1983:104). In order to guarantee only the best for the European bouquets, Kenyan workers are forbidden to keep livestock or have local gardens that might spread disease to the more valuable export crop.

The Green Revolution, Inequality, and Diet

While marginalization and poverty seem both to induce and to result from transnational investment, there is also grave concern in the high offices of both transnational companies and the capitalist states that instability and revolution could threaten the profit system. Such fears at the top have combined with the humanitarian concerns of scientists, the public, and middle-level bureaucrats to produce the "green revolution," a set of policies for increasing local subsistence foods in some of the poorest Third World nations (Cleaver 1972; Franke 1972; Oasa and Jennings 1982).

A major testing ground for the green revolution has been the island of Java. Following the mass slaughter of the leadership and middle cadre of a well-developed radical peasant movement in 1965, in which between 200,000 and one million people are believed to have been killed, the military regime of General Suharto oriented the nation toward transnational investment. Concern about political stability in the impoverished countryside of Java combined with interest in the valuable minerals and other wealth of the outer islands to produce a focus on increasing food production in Java. The green revolution there has gone through several unsuccessful stages.

From 1967 to 1970 transnational corporations contracted for seed and fertilizer delivery, aerial pesticide spraying, and "modern" management services that failed to improve the situation and led to the retreat of the companies. A second stage of the program began in 1971, when the entrepreneurial potential of the "small farmer" became the watchword, but this program, too, had serious difficulties (Franke 1972, 1974).

In the period since 1978, several years of good weather have combined with large—and unrepeatable—oil revenues to allow increased government investments that have led to substantial production increases: over 17 million tons of rice in 1978, rising to 20 million in 1980 (Dick 1982:26) and to 22 million in 1981 (Scherer 1982:25). Per capita food production also increased substantially, from 174 kilograms per person in 1977 to 202 in 1980 (still far below the 230 needed), with 137 of this in rice (Dick 1982:26). This spectacular rise came after a period of 11 years in which the green revolution had not improved food production per capita (ibid.:25), suggesting to critical observers that a run of good weather might be the most important factor in the sudden "success" of the green revolution, and that problems would reappear. A March 1983 Reuters report indicated that such was indeed the case, stating that Indonesia was expected to import about 2.3 million tons of rice to cover a drought-induced shortage that had entirely wiped out the gains made since 1978 (*Asia Record* 1983).

Continued rural and urban inequality leaves additional doubts about Indonesia's progress. Real agricultural wages, for example, fell slightly from 1977 to 1982 and were on a sharp downward trend in 1982 itself (Scherer 1982:23). In the urban manufacturing sector, the number of labor disputes rose from 11 in 1975 to 187 in 1980 (Scherer 1982:31), and the head of the government-controlled trade union federation stated publicly that at least 60 percent of the urban workforce received less than a subsistence wage (INDOC 1981:94).

Anthropological research confirms the close relationship between inequality and inadequate diet suggested by these national statistics. In the Central Javanese village of Kali Loro, households with 0.1 hectare or less of paddy land consumed 25 percent less food than those with 0.2 hectare, and "poorer households" in general consumed 65 percent less rice than their "wealthier" counterparts. As for protein, consumed mostly in the form of fermented soybean cake (*tempeh*), households of more than 0.2 hectare ate 45 percent more than their counterparts with 0.1 hectare or less (Stoler 1981:251). An ironic benefit to malnourished Javanese is that they do not suffer vitamin A deficiency, as leafy vegetables are a major element in their diet, replacing rice and *tempeh* (ibid.:250). Another study in East Java found that wealthier households eat more, and in particular more oils, sugar, and animal protein. Landless workers eat more corn and cassava (Edmundson 1981:257). On the basis of a dietary survey of 54 adult males, the researchers were also able to estimate that, generally, poor families were "barely" meeting minimum caloric needs and, furthermore, that intra-family decisions about the allocation of calories particularly disfavored two groups: children from 3 to 6 and persons over 45 (ibid.:264–65). Thus, families at the subsistence threshold were maximizing the work potential of the males aged 18 to 35, and the health needs of the youngest children. These findings are consistent with other data showing that the highest rates of anemia occur among women and especially pregnant women (Soekirman 1974).

What have been the effects over time? At the all-Java level, the anthropologist Ben White reported that between 1970 and 1976, the percentage of the population above poverty (total income equal to more than 320 kilograms of rice per year) increased from 39 percent of the rural population to 41 percent, but the percentage of destitute (180 kilograms) had increased far more, from 13 to 25 percent (1979:94). These figures suggest a polarization of the Javanese countryside consistent with the social analyses of a number of anthropologists and others, who have concluded that upper-income and a few middle-income farmers are benefiting from the green revolution while smallholders and landless laborers are dropping out of the bottom. The system may thus produce more food and, at the same time, more destitute and hungry people.

How is this possible? It appears that over the past 15 years, several social changes have been occurring in the Javanese countryside. Large landowners are using their increased earnings from the green revolution to bind poor villagers into a number of closed labor arrangements, including sharecropping, indebted labor (Franke 1972), "privileged" contractual arrangements whereby a family wishing to get work at harvest time must put itself on call for other tasks the landlord needs done (Kikuchi 1981), replacement of traditional villager harvest access rights and the stalk-by-stalk harvesting method with sickles that reduce labor needs (Collier, Wiradi, Soentoro 1973; buf cf. Hayami and Hafid 1979), and a general limiting of agricultural labor availability through the power and privilege of the landowners and merchants rather than through the organized power of agricultural workers themselves.

This social bonding, initiated and controlled from the top, may explain why agricultural wages could be declining when labor availability is restricted: there remains a substantial and growing class of marginalized rural poor (White's "destitute" category) who provide a reserve army for the landlords, merchants, and government officials who have benefited most from the green revolution. A telling figure comes from a study of the rural labor force in Java, indicating that only 9 percent of the men and 3 percent of the women are "adequately employed" (Rosenberg and Rosenberg 1980:50–51). The "success" of the green revolution in India, the Philippines, Mexico, and many other areas has similarly coincided with the intensified pauperization of the poorest groups and failure to distribute the benefits of increased food production, when such increases occur (Griffin 1974; Pearse 1980; but cf. Bayless-Smith and Wanmali 1984). We might say that even when an attempt is made to circumvent the effects of the international profit system, the economic and political alliances made by the capitalist "donor" states are with Third World ruling classes that interfere with the production and especially the distribution of food. The usual features of such a situation in a Third World country are (1) a military regime that suppresses the political organization of the poor; (2) substantial development investment through capitalist governments and/or transnational corporations; and (3) some combination of landlords, merchants, bureaucrats, and so on in a rural ruling group that has interests in common with the generals and their overseas allies and in opposition to the needs of the smallholders and landless laborers.

Even when a development program specifically *rejects* profit making as a key element in its strategy, international arrangements and local class structures reinsert it at the ground level. Realizing that the environmental and production needs of the Sahel countries after the devastating drought and famine of 1968–74 made further use of the region for accumulation purposes undesirable, development officials from the Western "donor" nations actually wrote profitability out of the criteria for evaluating projects in the early stages of the ambitious 25-year Sahel Development Program, launched in 1977 (Franke and Chasin 1980:154). As the projects began to take hold, however, Citibank became involved in financing rice production in an area of Senegal where several hundred villagers would have to be removed from their communal lands, only to return as hired laborers (ibid.:191–92); a subsidiary of Castle and Cooke attempted winter vegetable production for European markets, tearing down trees and threatening to reduce smallholders to proletarians in another part of Senegal (ibid.:184–91); and, in project after project, local class inequalities interfered with the production, distribution, and environmental protection policies that had looked so good on paper (ibid.:203–27). Only a few small private organizations incorporate into their projects some attempt to control the use of introduced resources by elite groups for their own accumulation of wealth, and even these are problematic (ibid.:228–39). Meanwhile, protein-calorie malnutrition averaged 30 percent in 46 dietary surveys in the Sahel through the 1960s and 1970s (calculated from IDRC 1981:77). Thus, a program hailed by its proponents as innovative and genuinely directed at the needs of the poorest people seems to have fallen prey to the same corporate interests and local landowners, merchants, and bureaucrats that interfere with the implementation of a reasonable diet for the poorest groups in Java, Brazil, Kenya, and other Third World regions. Are there alternatives to this scenario of corporate accumulation, military regimes, and local elite aggrandizement at the cost of supplying needed food to the farmers, landless laborers, and animal herders?

Reform and Revolution: Strategies Against Neocolonialism

A substantial body of evidence suggests that reforming the distribution of wealth in favor of the poorest groups may have the most significant impact on diet. Examples from Brazil in the 1960s and a projection for Kenya for the coming decades have been mentioned earlier. Other evidence for Chile suggests that more significant improvements in the diets of the poor were achieved through redistribution in three years under the Allende government than had been accomplished in the previous 40 years of capitalist neocolonial development (Hakim and Solimano 1978, esp. pp. 24–26; but cf. Brunser et al. 1984). The examples from Brazil and Chile, where anti-reform movements used massive violence and support from neocolonial capitalist states to destroy such reforms, suggest that revolution may be the most effective way to introduce and maintain them.

The most relevant case in this instance is Cuba, for Cuba is the only Third World country to have had a socialist revolution without substantial destruction of its infrastructural base and was thus able to move through a redistributional process without first having to reconstruct its basic production facilities. In this light, the achievements of the Cuban revolution in dietary changes constitute an instructive experiment. While the ration system has prevented nutritional resources from accumulating in the hands of a few, state investment and planning have given high priority to increasing production as well. The combination of redistribution and production advances represents the greatest potential of socialism. Between 1958 and 1980 overall food availability in Cuba increased by 33 percent. Before the revolution only 11 percent of the population drank milk; by 1980 this had reached 100 percent. The proportion of farm workers regularly eating eggs rose from 2 percent in the 1950s to 96 percent in 1979. Production of fish and potatoes increased substantially. Despite continued dependence on sugar for foreign exchange, 40 percent more land was in rice than before the revolution—on land that would theoretically be in direct competition with sugar (statistics from Benjamin, Collins, and Scott 1984).

Another way to measure the changes is based on the Physical Quality of Life Index (PQLI), a composite of statistics on life expectancy at age one, infant mortality, and literacy (Morris 1979). Out of a possible 100 points on the PQLI scale, Cuba, with a per capita GNP of only $640, scored 84 in the early 1970s. This was 30 to 40 percent higher than other countries with similar per capita GNPs. Cuba's 1981 PQLI rose to 95, although per capita GNP (for 1982) was only $700. By contrast, Brazil managed a PQLI of just 74, despite a phenomenal per capita GNP of $2,240 in 1981 (Sewell, Feinberg, and Kalb 1984). These data suggest that socialist policies may be the most efficient means of achieving nutritional improvements in low-income, underdeveloped countries (Table 19.1). Although the Cuban government does not make available income distribution statistics, even hostile observers concede that redistribution of wealth has played a major role in the country's undeniable eradication of malnutrition. In 1982, for example, a study compiled by the Office of East-West Planning in the U.S. Commerce Department concluded that there has been in Cuba "a highly egalitarian redistribution of income that has elimi-

TABLE 19.1. Comparative Statistics on Economics and Physical Quality of Life (PQLI) in Developing Countries

Country	Per capita GNP		PQLI		Infant Mortality per 1,000
	Early 1970s[a]	1982[b]	Early 1970s[a]	1981[b]	1983[c]
Vietnam	$189	$190	54	75	53
Indonesia	$203	$580	48	58	101
Kenya	$213	$390	39	56	81
Brazil	$912	$2,240	68	74	70
Cuba	$640	$700	84	95	20

[a]Morris (1979).
[b]Sewell et al. (1984).
[c]World Bank (1982).

nated almost all malnutrition, particularly among children" (Theriot 1982:105; cf. Ubell 1983; Valdes-Brito and Henriquez 1983).

Perhaps more typical than the Cuban case is that of Vietnam. Like the Soviet Union, East Europe, North Korea, Angola, and Mozambique, Vietnam achieved its revolution only after suffering devastation by the neocolonial powers. Fourteen million tons of bombs and shells were dropped on Indochina—not counting napalm and phosphorous. According to the Vietnamese government, there are 25 million bomb craters impeding food production. In one province, out of 2.5 million coconut palms, only half a million remain. Ten million hectares of cultivated land were bombed and defoliated while a million head of cattle were deliberately destroyed. Between 150,000 and 300,000 tons of unexploded munitions make agricultural work extremely dangerous (Government of Vietnam, 1979; Lewallen 1971). In the wake of this destruction, the Socialist Republic of Vietnam has also had to face several years of bad weather and continuing military harassment from China and the United States.

Nonetheless, redistribution has begun in the former South Vietnam, modeled in part on the 20 years' experience of the North, but with several innovations throughout the entire country. One of the most important of these innovations is the establishment of a National Institute of Nutrition, which has extensively surveyed the dietary needs of the population. Finding a 10 to 15 percent caloric deficiency and an even greater protein deficit, the institute has begun programs at two levels. At the national level, major efforts are being made to increase production of soybeans, peanuts, sesame, and eggs. Soybean production doubled in 1982 and was expected to increase sixfold by 1985. The

471

institute has further proposed a program in which each household would have a small plot on which to develop a closed ecosystem with vegetable garden, animals, and fish culture (Eisman 1982:9). Vietnamese planners have thus joined in the experiment currently spanning much of the socialist world in which combinations of household and collective farm production are utilized in search of the most effective mix of individual material incentives and socially balanced, egalitarian growth (Beresford 1985). Even proposing such a plan would be nonsensical in countries like Indonesia, Brazil, and Kenya, where landholding patterns and power relationships would preclude smallholders from gaining access to the inputs, and the substantial numbers of landless would, by definition, not be able to participate.

In the more socialist northern part of Vietnam, communes are being used to introduce the program on a pilot basis. The three-decade-old policy of breaking up large landholdings and then reconsolidating the parcels into communal village plots has created levels of equality and cooperation that may facilitate such innovations. A U.S. nutritionist describes one of the pilot villages, Da Ton Commune, 12 miles north of Hanoi: "I saw well-developed family gardens, fish ponds, pigs, and poultry. The collective has planted four ha. of orchard and over 100,000 trees to improve the ecology and provide fuel. Soybeans, peanuts, sesame, and medicinal plants are grown in private plots and collective fields" (Eisman 1982:9).

It is, of course, easier to achieve success with a single experiment than a national program. But the elements of a strategy for overcoming malnutrition are in place in socialist Vietnam: extensive dietary research, design of projects to produce appropriate foods presently lacking or insufficient in the diet, and a social structure that will distribute both production inputs and food outputs to those who are most in need of them. Along with the garden plots, the institute has propopsd to the government that mothers with malnourished children should be given three additional months of maternity leave so that they can breast-feed their children longer. A proposal for extended maternity leave for women agricultural workers can only be taken seriously in a socialist economy, where distribution of nutritional resources is not left to the logic of the marketplace.

Conclusions

The contradictory effects of colonialism and neocolonialism on the dietary patterns of the Third World show up in many forms and with great variety. In this paper it has been possible to survey only a limited sample of cases that illustrate some of the major features of these systems. The continuing dietary shortages for large numbers of people in the neocolonial world are in part a heritage of colonialism and in part the result of neocolonial corporate profit seeking and the development efforts of the neocolonial capitalist states, which operate through local ruling groups, usually made up of military officers, merchants, landlords, and government bureaucrats. Attempts to improve the diets of the poorest groups in the Third World through redistribution have shown that the reforms threaten powerful national interests in the Third World countries and their allies in the neocolonial states, who are able to destabilize and over-throw the reformers unless the latter have seized full control of the Third World state apparatus and, in most cases, have received economic and military assistance from the developed socialist states. In the neocolonial world as it is presently structured, struggles for socialist control of Third World states are probably the most effective and efficient means of reversing the dietary inequalities inherited from colonialism and reproduced by neocolonialism. Anthropologists can play an important role in such struggles by conducting detailed, village-, herding-group-, or band-level studies that incorporate, inasmuch as the data allow, both a historical perspective on the colonial background and awareness of the regional, class, state, and neocolonial contexts in which such local-level data are gathered. To view our research in this way is not simply to make a political choice to side with those who suffer protein-calorie malnutrition; it is a decision to integrate our small-scale studies with the larger studies of which they are a part and thus to produce intellectually and scientifically sounder and more thorough analyses. The correlation between these two choices may not be accidental, for science is an anti-authoritarian, democratic, egalitarian, and progressive form of thought.

Notes

1. Poor farmers and sugar workers of the Northeast today have numerous food taboos against some of the very fruits that would increase their vitamin intake. Josué de Castro suggests that these taboos may have originated from the ruling classes, to diminish "the possibilities that the poor would go so far as to touch the fruits that they were selfishly hoarding for their own exclusive use" (quoted in Taylor 1978:57). Taylor goes on to note that employees of the sugar estates are not allowed to plant trees on the land surrounding their houses.

2. This ratio is calculated from van Zwanenberg's (1975) data. Using the largest number of Europeans and the smallest number of Africans, this calculation gives the most conservative impression of the land differentials. By 1950, the imbalance was probably several times as great as stated in the text.

3. Another contradiction is that corporations may eventually want to develop these same underfed Third World peoples as markets. Although poor people generally are not

good markets for expensive, processed foods, some partially successful experiments have taken place. Probably the most widely debated of these is the sale of bottled baby formulas by Nestlé and other companies (see, for example, Greiner 1975 and Greiner, Almroth, and Latham 1979).

4. Concluding a detailed study of all types of multinational investments in Keyna, Langdon (1981:194) remarks: "Most fundamentally, this study implies that a marked reduction in the mnc [multinational corporation] role is essential to an egalitarian strategy."

References Cited

Alexander, J., and P. Alexander
    1978   Sugar, Rice and Irrigation in Colonial Java. *Ethnohistory* 25:207–23.
Bailey, K. V.
    1961–   Rural Nutrition Studies in Indonesia. *Tropical and Geographical Medi-*
    62   *cine* 13:216–55, 289–315; 14:1–19, 111–39, 230–78.
Asia Record
    1983   March:5.
Bayless-Smith, T., and S. Wanmali (eds.)
    1984   *Understanding Green Revolutions: Agrarian Change and Development*
    Planning in South Asia. Cambridge: Cambridge University Press.
Benjamin, M.; J. Collins; and M. Scott
    1984   *No Free Lunch: Food and Revolution in Cuba Today.* San Francisco:
    Food First.
Beresford, M.
    1985   Household and Collective in Vietnamese Agriculture. *Journal of Con-*
    temporary Asia 15:5–36.
Braudel, F.
    1975   *Capitalism and Matrial Life, 1400–1800.* New York: Harper and Row.
    [Orig. 1967.]
Brunser, O.; G. Figueroa; M. Araya; and J. Espinoza
    1984   Infections and Diarrheal Disease. In *Malnutrition: Determinants and*
    Consequences, Philip L. White and Nancy Selvey, eds., pp. 259–70.
    New York: Alan R. Liss.
Burbach, R., and P. Flynn
    1978   *Agribusiness Targets Latin America. NACLA Report* 12(1):5.
de Castro, Josué
    1966   *Death in the Northeast.* New York: Vintage Books.
Clairmonte, F., and J. Cavanagh
    1982a   Transnational Corporations and Global Markets: Changing Power Rela-
    tions. *Trade and Development* 4:149–82.
    1982b   Foods as Corporate Commodity. *Southeast Asia Chronicle,* no. 86, pp.
    10–17.

Clarence-Smith, G., and R. Moorsom
    1977   Underdevelopment and Class Formation in Ovamboland, 1844–1917. In *The Roots of Rural Poverty in Central and Southern Africa,* Robin Palmer and Neil Parsons, eds., pp. 96–112. Berkeley: University of California Press.

Cleaver, H.
    1972   The Contradictions of the Green Revolution. *Monthly Review* 24(2):80–111.

Collier, W.; G. Wiradi; and Soentoro
    1973   Recent Changes in Rice Harvesting Methods. New York: Agricultural Development Council.

Dam, H. ten
    1966   Cooperation and Social Structure in the Village of Chibodas. In *Indonesian Economics: The Concept of Dualism in Theory and Policy,* pp. 347–82. The Hague: W. van Hoeve. [Orig. 1956.]

Deerr, N.
    1949   *The History of Sugar.* 2 vols. London: Chapman and Hall.

Dick, H.
    1982   Survey of Recent Developments. *Bulletin of Indonesian Economic Studies* 18(1):1–38.

Dinham, B., and C. Hines
    1983   *Agribusiness in Africa.* London: Earth Resources Research Ltd.

Edmundson, W.
    1981   Nutrition and the Household Economy. In *Agricultural and Rural Development in Indonesia,* Gary E. Hansen, ed., pp. 255–69. Boulder, Colo.: Westview Press.

Eisman, B.
    1982   Focus on Nutrition. *Southeast Asia Chronicle,* no. 87, pp. 9–10.

Franke, R. W.
    1972   The Green Revolution in a Javanese Village. Ph.D. dissertation, Harvard University.
    1974   Miracle Seeds and Shattered Dreams in Java. *Natural History* 83(1):11ff.
    1981   Mode of Production and Population Patterns: Policy Implications for West African Development. *International Journal of Health Services* 11:361–87.
    1982   Being a Peasant in Java. *Southeast Asia Chronicle,* no. 86, pp. 18–24.

Franke, R. W., and B. H. Chasin
    1980   *Seeds of Famine: Ecological Destruction and the Development Dilemma in the West African Sahel.* Montclair, N.J.: Allanheld, Osmun.

Geertz, C.
    1963   *Agricultural Involution: The Processes of Ecological Change in Indonesia.* Berkeley: University of California Press.

Government of Vietnam
    1979   Those Who Leave: The Problem of Vietnamese Refugees. *Vietnam Courier* (Hanoi).

Greiner, T.
   1975   *The Promotion of Bottle Feeding by Multinational Corporations: How Advertising and the Health Professions Have Contributed.* Ithaca, N.Y.: Cornell International Nutrition Monograph Series, no. 2.
Greiner, T.; S. Almroth; and M. C. Latham
   1979   *The Economic Value of Breastfeeding.* Ithaca, N.Y.: Cornell International Nutrition Monograph Series, no. 6.
Griffin, K.
   1974   *The Political Economy of Agrarian Change: An Essay on the Green Revolution.* Cambridge: Harvard University Press.
Gross, Daniel R., and B. Underwood
   1971   Technological Change and Calorie Costs: Sisal Agriculture in Northeastern Brazil. *American Anthropologist* 73:725–40.
Hakim, P., and G. Solimano
   1978   *Development, Reform, and Malnutrition in Chile.* Cambridge: MIT Press.
Hanna, W. A.
   1978   *Indonesian Banda: Colonialism and Its Aftermath in the Nutmeg Islands.* Philadelphia: Institute for the Study of Human Issues.
Hawes, G. A.
   1982   Southeast Asian Agribusiness: The New International Division of Labor. *Bulletin of Concerned Asian Scholars* 14(4):20–29.
Horn, L. van
   1977   The Agricultural History of Barotseland, 1840–1964. In *The Roots of Rural Poverty in Central and Southern Africa,* R. Palmer and N. Parsons, eds., pp. 144–69. Berkeley: University of California Press.
Hayami, Y., and A. Hafid
   1979   Rice Harvesting and Welfare in Rural Java. *Bulletin of Indonesian Economic Studies* 15(2):94–112.
Indonesian Documentation and Information Center (INDOC)
   1981   *Indonesian Workers and Their Right to Organize.* Leiden: INDOC.
Interfaith Center for Corporate Responsibility (ICCR)
   1973   *The Philippines: American Corporations, Martial Law, and Underdevelopment.* New York: ICCR.
International Development Research Center (IDRC)
   1981   *Nutritional Status of the Rural Population of the Sahel. Report on a Working Group, Paris, France, 28–29 April, 1980).* Ottawa: IDRC.
Jay, R.
   1969   *Javanese Villagers: Social Relations in Rural Modjokuto.* Cambridge: MIT Press.
Kikuchi, M.
   1981   Changes in Rice Harvesting Systems in the Philippines and Indonesia: Village Structure and Choice of Contractual Arrangements. *Developing Economies* 19(4):291–304.

Kjekshus, H.
  1977   *Ecology Control and Economic Development in East African History.*
          London: Heinemann.
Langdon, S. W.
  1981   *Multinational Corporations in the Political Economy of Kenya.* New
          York: St. Martin's Press.
Lappé, F. M., and J. Collins
  1977   *Food First: Beyond the Myth of Scarcity.* New York: Ballantine Books.
Leitner, K.
  1976   The Situation of Agricultural Workers in Kenya. *Review of African Politi-
          cal Economy* 6:34–50.
Lewallen, J.
  1971   *Ecology of Devastation: Indochina.* Baltimore: Penguin Books.
Long, N. V.
  1973   *Before the Revolution: The Vietnamese Peasants Under the French.*
          Cambridge: MIT Press.
McCarthy, F. D., and W. M. Mwangi
  1982   *Kenyan Agriculture: Toward 2000.* Laxenburg, Austria: International In-
          stitute for Applied Systems Analysis.
Missen, G. J.
  1972   *Viewpoint on Indonesia: A Geographical Study.* Melbourne: Nelson.
Morris, D. M.
  1979   *Measuring the Condition of the World's Poor: The Physical Quality of Life
          Index.* Washington, D.C.: Pergamon Press–Overseas Development
          Council.
Oasa, E. K., and B. Jennings
  1982   Science and Authority in International Agricultural Research. *Bulletin of
          Concerned Asian Scholars* 14(4):30–44.
Pearse, A.
  1980   *Seeds of Plenty, Seeds of Want: Social and Economic Implications of the
          Green Revolution.* Oxford: Clarendon Press.
Rosenberg, J. G., and D. A. Rosenberg
  1980   *Landless Peasants and Rural Poverty in Indonesia and the Philippines.*
          Ithaca, N.Y.: Cornell University Center for International Studies, Rural
          Development Committee.
Scherer, P.
  1982   Survey of Recent Developments. *Bulletin of Indonesian Economic Stud-
          ies* 18(2):1–34.
Sewell, J. R.; E. Feinberg; and V. Kalb (eds.)
  1984   *U.S. Foreign Policy and the Third World: Agenda, 1985–86.* New
          Brunswick, N.J.: Transaction Books, Overseas Development Council.
Sivard, R. L.
  1982   *World Military and Social Expenditures.* Leesburg, Va.: World Prior-
          ities.

Smith, R. R.
    1974   Impasse in Java's Agriculture: A Case for Chinese Style Collectivization. M.A. thesis, Monash University, Australia.
Soekirman
    1974   *Priorities in Dealing with Nutrition Problems in Indonesia.* Cornell International Nutrition Monograph Series, no. 1. Ithaca, N.Y.: Cornell University.
Spencer, I. R. G.
    1983   Pastoralism and Colonial Policy in Kenya, 1895–1929. In *Imperialism, Colonialism, and Hunger: East and Central Africa,* pp. 113–40. R. I. Rotberg, ed., Lexington, Mass.: Lexington Books.
Stoler, A.
    1981   Garden Use and Household Economy in Java. In *Agricultural and Rural Development in Indonesia,* Gary E. Hansen, ed., pp. 242–54. Boulder, Colo.: Westview Press.
Szymanski, A.
    1981   *The Logic of Imperialism.* New York: Praeger.
Tannahill, R.
    1973   *Food In History.* New York: Stein and Day.
Taylor, K. S.
    1978   *Sugar and the Underdevelopment of Northeastern Brazil: 1500–1970.* Gainesville: University of Florida. University of Florida Social Sciences Monograph, no. 63.
Theriot, L. H.
    1982   Cuba Faces the Economic Realities of the 1980s. Hearings of the Joint Economic Committee, U.S. Congress. *East-West Trade: The Prospects to 1985,* pp. 104–35. Washington, D.C.: Government Printing Office (91–916-0).
Ubell, R. N.
    1983   High-Tech Medicine in the Caribbean: 25 Years of Cuban Health Care. *New England Journal of Medicine* 309:1468–72.
Valdes-Brito, J., and J. Henriquez
    1983   Health Status of the Cuban Population. *International Journal of Health Services* 13:479–85.
Valente, F., and L. S. Heimann
    1978   Political Economy of Agricultural Production and Nutrition in Brazil: 1500–1977. Manuscript.
Wertheim, W. F.
    1964   Social Change in Java, 1900–1930. In *East-West Parallels: Sociological Approaches to Modern Asia,* pp. 211–37. The Hague: W. van Hoeve.
White, B.
    1979   Political Aspects of Poverty, Income Distribution and Their Measurement: Some Examples from Rural Java. *Development and Change* 10:91–114.

1983 Agricultural Involution and Its Critics: 20 Years After. *Bulletin of Concerned Asian Scholars* 15(3):18–31.

Wisner, B.
 1980 Nutritional Consequences of the Articulation of Capitalist and Noncapitalist Modes of Production in Eastern Kenya. *Rural Africana* 8–9:99–132.
 1983 An African Food Dilemma? National Self-Sufficiency Versus Family Food Security. Manuscript.

Wolf, E. R.
 1982 *Europe and the People Without History.* Berkeley: University of California Press.

World Bank
 1982 World Development Report: 1982. New York: Oxford University Press.

Zwanenberg, R. M. A. van
 1975 *An Economic History of Kenya and Uganda, 1800–1970.* London: Macmillan.

BENJAMIN S. ORLOVE

Stability and Change in Highland Andean Dietary Patterns

Approaches to Andean Dietary Patterns

The diet of the highland Andean peasants reflects their complex history. The virtual isolation of South America before European conquest and the emergence of civilizations from pre-agricultural societies account in part for the strong presence in the diet of locally domesticated crops and animals capable of being produced in difficult environmental circumstances and of satisfying human nutritional needs. Some of those crops and animals are still found only in the Andes; others have spread through the world. With these unique elements and a long autonomous development, Andean dietary patterns have offered a satisfactory solution to many of the problems faced in trying to support human life in harsh environments at high altitudes.

Andean highlanders also resemble peasants in other parts of Latin America and elsewhere in the world. They seek to combine some household subsistence production with cash earnings obtained through wage labor or the sale of crops and animals. They are dominated, economically and politically, by elites linked to an international order. These peasants accommodate many features of their lives, including their diets, to this situation of subordination and control of certain productive resources. The interplay of the cash and the subsistence economies affects their diet and nutrition.

Dietary patterns in the Andes are also influenced by the differences in status between peasants and other groups. This separation of groups resembles ethnic differentiation in some ways. Although it is no longer accurate to describe the Andes as if its population could neatly be divided into Indians and mestizos, a simple class model would fail to recognize the objective and subjective distinctions between these groups.

These general features of Andean society—adaptation to environment, class domination, status differences—have parallels in other societies, although the nature of the environmental constraints and the class structure are unique to the Andes. The traditional diet may be considered adaptive in the general sense that it offers most of the population adequate and balanced nutrition. A general trend toward replacing locally produced native foods with purchased Western-style foods has been accompanied by a decline in nutritional status. This shift is the result of several forces: population pressure in the highlands, increasing participation in wage labor on the part of highland peasants, and national economic policy. Although the dietary patterns in the Andean highlands are in many ways representative of those of other peasant groups, the extreme nature of the environment and the particular history of the region have shaped food production and consumption along with many other aspects of economic and social life. Uniqueness may itself have parallels in other dietary patterns; a comparison of diets in many areas would reveal not only common characteristics, but a number of idiosyncratic ones as well.

This paper examines stability and change in Andean dietary patterns. Traditional diets, emphasizing locally produced starchy staples, met the nutritional needs of most peasants, despite some risk of insufficient levels of micro-nutrients, particularly vitamin A, and of inadequate caloric intake as a result either of unpredictable crises (e.g., disease and drought) or of low income. Some peasants have shifted away from a heavy reliance on subsistence production because of growing population pressure on the land or a desire to have higher cash incomes. The new foods in the Andean diet are ones whose prices are subsidized, whether imports such as wheat and cooking oil or coastal products such as sugar and rice. The production and consumption levels of highland products, whose prices have not been subsidized, have grown far less. The changes in dietary patterns reflect the influence of preferences on demand as well as that of price subsidies on supply. Prestige factors seem to influence the choice of new foods.

This shift away from a subsistence economy and diet has had two somewhat opposed effects on nutritional status. On the one hand, higher incomes (taking into account the cash value of subsistence production as well as monetary earnings) are associated with higher caloric intake and nutritional status. On the other hand, an increase in the proportion of purchased rather than home-produced food is tied to poorer nutrition. The latter effect appears to be the stronger one for the majority of highland peasants. However, this shift away from a traditional diet is not necessarily a permanent one. Under some circumstances, highland Andean peasants can expand the role of subsistence production in their diet and their economy. In this regard they are unlike peasants in many other parts of the world who cannot halt, let alone reverse, the twin movements toward greater participation in the cash economy and unimproved or declining nutritional status.

Problems in the Study of Andean Dietary Patterns

Two difficulties, one conceptual and one methodological, must be addressed in any discussion of changes in dietary patterns in the Andes. It is tempting to assume that one can describe the "traditional" Andean diet and then analyze patterns of change. Any such analysis would be both arbitrary and inaccurate. There is no period that one could safely pick as representative of a natural or equilibrium state of Andean society. European domesticates have been very widely distributed throughout the Andes since the 16th century. Even if good data were available for the Inca empire, dietary patterns from that period would differ greatly from those immediately before, since the Incas extended maize cultivation and the herding of llamas and alpacas and altered systems for the storage and transport of food. The Pax Incaica facilitated the transport of goods over long distances. The patterns that will be referred to as "traditional" in this paper are those practiced in this century by relatively remote populations with a low degree of involvement in the cash economy. It should be remembered, though, that these patterns are the product of centuries of change.

The methodological difficulty reflects the scarcity of data. Some ethnographies present general descriptions of the principal foods, the means of preparing and serving them, and broad accounts of nutritional status. Such descriptive accounts do not contain enough information to permit a detailed presentation of diet for comparative purposes. In recent years, some detailed nutritional surveys have been carried out. These suffer from somewhat different sorts of weaknesses. They often describe consumption during a period of days or weeks, missing the annual cycle of dietary patterns. In many cases they are conducted by individuals with little experience in communities or rapport with their members and therefore may contain data that are somewhat less reliable than the ethnographic studies. Furthermore, both sorts of data tend to describe patterns at one moment in time, making it difficult to trace patterns of change. These methodological difficulties are compensated for by the existence of an unusually rich data source for nutritional information in highland Peru. In 1972–73 the Peruvian Ministry of Agriculture conducted the National Food Consumption Survey (the *Encuesta Nacional de Consumo de Alimentos,* or ENCA); careful comparison of different regions permits some analysis of dietary change. This ENCA material has been analyzed both by the Ministry of Agriculture and in a recent Ph.D. dissertation (Ferroni 1980), which focuses in

483

particular detail on the department of Puno in southern highland Peru and Junin in the central Peruvian highlands. This data set is described in more detail in the appendix.

Traditional Dietary Patterns in the Andes

Tubers and grains are the main staples of the Andean diet. The most important of the former are potatoes, which are consumed both fresh and as *chuño,* a kind of freeze-dried potato. Certain varieties of potatoes are exposed to frost for several nights in a row. When the ice crystals melt, the water does not return into the cells of the potato but remains under the skin. Trampling the potatoes forces the water out and leaves a dry potato that can be stored for several years without spoilage. The other types of tubers—*olluco* (*Ullucus tuberosus*), *oca* (*Oxalis tuberosa*), and *isaño* (*Tropaeolum tuberosum*)—though frequently consumed, do not form as large a part of the diet. The most important grains are barley, maize, and two closely related native grains, both very high in protein: *quinoa* (*Chenopodium quinoa*) and *cañihua* (*Chenopodium pallidicaule*). Several legumes are consumed, including the European broad bean (*Vicia faba*) and the Andean *tarhui* (*Lupinus mutablis*); in some areas peas and other varieties of beans are also eaten. There is considerable local variation in the role of specific tubers, grains, and legumes in the diet; *chuñno,* for instance, is rarely consumed in Ecuador, where maize is more important. In general, most tubers that are currently cultivated are Andean domesticates, and legumes are European domesticates; plants originating in both areas are more evenly represented among the grains. A number of domesticated animals are eaten. Sheep are the most important, and others include cattle, llamas, alpacas, pigs, chicken, and guinea pigs. Some dairy products, particularly cheese, are consumed. Fresh fruit and vegetables are relatively scarce, although fruit brought to the highlands from the eastern lowlands and the desert coast is highly valued, and a number of leafy plants are added to other dishes. Condiments include salt, hot peppers, and a number of wild and domesticated plants. An important element of the traditional Andean diet is the mildly narcotic leaf of the coca plant (*Erythroxylon coca*), the topic of much criticism, first by those who viewed its use as a sign of the degeneration of the highland peoples and more recently by those who see its continued cultivation as a source of drug abuse in the United States. Recent ethnographic work shows that its use among Andean peoples is highly ritualized (Allen 1981), and other studies (e.g., Burchard 1976) show that it enhances rather than diminishes work capacity.

An early published description of the traditional cooking practices around Lake Titicaca applies to many other areas as well: "The majority of foods—

meat or fish cooked with potatoes, chuñu, quinoa, ocas, greens, etc.—are boiled and eaten either as stews and drained and eaten dry" (Tschopik 1946:525). A more recent source for a nearby village gives a detailed account of the meal pattern (Collins 1981:124–26): sugared hot tea and bread are served to the members of the household soon after they rise before dawn; the first cooked meal follows about three hours later, consisting of soup, porridge, or boiled potatoes or *chuño*. Members of the household carry with them a cold lunch, consisting of grains or legumes, which may be boiled or toasted, boiled tubers, or small *quinoa* cakes. They eat this meal around noon where they are working, and do not return home till the late afternoon, when they have another meal of sugared tea and bread. The second hot meal is served about an hour later. It usually consists of reheated leftovers from the morning meal. When groups of people are engaged in labor in the fields or pastures or in house construction, road maintenance, and the like, breaks for chewing coca are taken in mid-morning and mid-afternoon. This pattern of meals—sometimes with unsweetened tea and without the bread in the morning and the afternoon, and with different tubers and grains—characterizes most traditional Andean peasants. The dietary pattern for the department of Puno, which Ferroni extracted from the ENCA data, resembles that which Collins describes for the same region and the less detailed information on the topic in earlier ethnographies. The main difference between the first sources and the later ones is the increased presence of bread and sugar in recent years.

Agricultural activity in the Andean highlands is strongly conditioned by the seasonal variation in weather. Most of the rain falls in a specific season, from about November through March, and the long clear nights of the dry season, particularly in June and July, are accompanied by frost. Most of the harvest is gathered in the months after the rains end. In some areas, milder climates or irrigation permit double- and even triple-cropping, but the general pattern of a seasonal peak in harvest remains. This constraint on food availability is resolved in part by higher levels of consumption soon after the harvest of crops that tend to spoil. It has led to an emphasis on storage. Tubers, which otherwise tend to spoil, can be preserved by freeze-drying. The availability of pasture also follows the cycle of rainy and dry seasons; animal flesh is also harvested and preserved by freeze-drying at the time when it is most abundant, at the end of the period of rich pastures.

There is some annual variation in the diet, in terms of both specific food items consumed and total quantity. Some foods in the Andes are eaten fresh at harvest time (corn on the cob, green broad beans) or are prepared in special ways then; potatoes, for example, are roasted in small dome-shaped ovens made of clods of earth. There are shifts in the mix of food items consumed during the year. Ferroni notes that potatoes, which are more susceptible to spoilage than grains, are eaten more in the months immediately following the harvest; the percentage of the more storable grains in the diet increases after that (1980:111). There is some decline in food consumption in the months before the harvest, although this trend does not appear as marked as in many other peasant groups. Consumption levels of food, coca, and alcohol on ceremonial occasions can be quite high. The ceremonial cycle in each village adheres to an annual schedule (current rituals are linked to the Catholic calendar, although at least some of the major pre-Columbian rituals were also celebrated at a particular season). Although there is a great deal of ritual activity in the months following the harvest, fiestas are held throughout the year.

Within this general pattern, there is considerable local variation. Brush (1977:177) shows that wheat and field peas, both high-yielding crops, are more important in a community in northern highland Peru than in the central and southern highlands, where they do not grow as well. The areas in the southern highlands that are warm enough to facilitate adequate levels of gluten formation in wheat tend to be too dry to permit adequate yields (Gade 1975:138). In Brush's field site, a large proportion of the wheat is consumed as locally baked bread. Studies (e.g., Flores 1977) of high-altitude pastoral zones indicate a much higher, though by no means exclusive, reliance on meat, although even full-time herders sell and barter the products of their animals to obtain grains and tubers. In general, local products tend to dominate, so that villages at lower elevations will have higher rates of maize consumption, the inhabitants of certain portions of coastal valleys eat more fruit, and so forth.

The Nutritional Value of Traditional Diets

AGGREGATE LEVELS

The most detailed analysis of nutritional status in the Andean highlands is found in Ferroni's work (1980:48–141). He summarizes the ENCA data for the department of Puno to show that the average diet is generally adequate but that a certain percentage of the population is subject to malnutrition (Table 20.1). To summarize his discussion, this diet provides an average daily intake of 2,454 calories, 110 percent of the mean requirements set by the Food and Agriculture Organization/World Health Organization. The average daily protein intake is 66 grams, nearly 90 percent of which comes from plant sources. This quantity is nearly one and a half times the calculated local requirement of 45 grams per person per day. This high quantity compensates for the somewhat low quality of the protein. To a certain extent the grains and tubers provide complementary amino acids, the former lacking lysine and the latter methionine.

486

TABLE 20.1. ENCA—Categorization of Food Groups
According to Calorie and Protein Supply (Average
Values for Rural Puno)

		% of Total	
Class	Food Groups	Calories	Protein
High	cereals	49.0	50.0
	tubers, roots	39.0	26.0
Intermediate	legumes	4.0	11.0
	fats, oils	2.0	—
	sugar	1.0	—
Low	vegetables	1.0	1.0
	meat	2.0	6.0
	eggs	1.0	3.0
	fish	0.5	2.0
	milk and products	0.5	1.0
	condiments	—	—
	prepared foods	—	—

SOURCE: Ferroni (1980:53).

Lipid consumption also derives heavily from vegetable sources. Of the average daily intake of 21.3 grams per person per day, only 9.1 grams come from separated fats (butter, oil, and animal fat); 9.0 grams derive from cereals, 1.7 grams from meat, and 1.5 grams from milk. This mix provides enough unsaturated fats to meet minimum requirements, although the proportion of calories derived from fats—7.4 percent of the average daily caloric intake—is far below that of many other populations. Ferroni also notes that the starchiness of the diet (over 80 percent of the calories are carbohydrates) is not necessarily a sign of malnutrition. It could be seen as a sign of poverty, since low-income people around the world tend to consume large quantities of starchy foods and replace them with other foods as income rises. He also cites Picón-Reátegui (1976), who suggests, without strong quantitative support, that a high-carbohydrate diet is adaptive in the hypoxic environment of the Andes, since less oxygen is required to metabolize starches than would be used to obtain an equivalent amount of energy from protein or fats. This reliance on starchy staples does not make for as monotonous a diet as might be expected, at least to local palates. A number of species of tubers and grains are eaten. The numerous cultivars of potatoes bring diversity to the diet in addition to permitting efficient use of many micro-habitats and reducing the risk of attacks of pests on any one cultivar.

The diet in rural Puno also contains adequate amounts of micro-nutrients, with the exception of vitamin A, which is severely deficient. This vitamin A deficiency and its potential effect of reducing visual acuity at low levels of light intensity might account in part for the fear many Andean peasants express of walking outside at night, particularly when they are alone. This fear is usually justified in terms of the presence of supernatural beings. Although neofunctionalists (Orlove 1980a) might find this practice adaptive in reducing exposure to cold, and structuralists accord the contrast between day and night a place alongside other major Andean dualisms, it could also be noted that the nighttime visual field is simply more threatening to Andean peoples than to others who can distinguish more clearly among objects in the dim light of moonless nights.

Although some potential exists for calcium deficiency, Ferroni indicates that the ENCA surveys underestimated consumption of this essential mineral by neglecting to consider the use as a condiment of minerals that contain it, the consumption of *lloita* (a calcium-rich substance derived from the ashes of burnt *quinoa* stalks) with coca leaf, and the eating of clays. *Quinoa, cañihua,* barley, potatoes, and *chuño* are richer in protein, vitamins, and minerals than many other staples, such as rice, wheat, and maize. (There are relatively few areas in the Andean highlands where maize forms the dominant staple, as it does in other parts of the world.)

Other dietary practices contribute to the generally adequate nutritional status. These include the roasting of potatoes in earth ovens, the relatively brief cooking of potatoes, and the consumption of soups that contain the water in which potatoes have been boiled. These cooking practices, it might be added, conserve limited fuel supplies, the availability of which is reduced by the absence or scarcity of firewood, the use of dung as fertilizer, and the expense of kerosene and natural gas. Serving warm soups and stews early in the morning and late in the afternoon has other adaptive aspects. It provides boiled water, reducing the risk of dehydration in the dry season without incurring the danger of ingesting parasites from contaminated water sources. It may also warm the body at times of high risk of cold stress. (Other cooking practices, admittedly not as important as the preparation of soups, are more difficult to explain in adaptive terms. A striking example is the food known in Aymara as *thayachi*. It consists of boiled *isaño* tubers that are frozen by exposure to frost on clear, cold nights in the dry season. The icy, slightly sweet product, considered quite a treat, is eaten early in the morning, sometimes before sunrise, when the risk of cold stress is great.)

HOUSEHOLD AND INDIVIDUAL LEVELS

Ferroni also examines the ENCA data at a household level to see whether some individuals are undernourished, even though the average levels of consumption for the population as a whole are adequate. He discusses the difficulties of selecting among dietary, anthropometric, clinical, and biochemical criteria for assessing malnutrition and indicates that the ENCA data permit one to address only the first two. Approximately 37 percent of all highland households—urban as well as rural ones, and those in both more and less traditional areas—are "at risk" for calorie malnutrition; that is, their consumption lies between the minimum recommended levels and the ideal levels, as established by the FAO/WHO. Another 16 percent fall below the minimum levels. In general, the households whose caloric consumption is adequate are not in danger of protein insufficiencies.

The anthropometric data collected by the ENCA staff generally support this estimate. Two different analyses following the methods of Gomez and Waterlow suggest that 30 or 50 percent of the highland children between one and six show some signs of malnutrition, but that most of them experience the mildest of the three calculated degrees. The studies indicate similar levels of malnutrition in urban and rural areas. The malnourished children are about equally divided between those who have relatively low height for their age (suggesting chronic malnutrition) and those who have low weights for their height (suggesting acute malnutrition). The former type is apparently associated with poverty, and also a relatively urban diet in which foodstuffs produced by the household form a low percentage of the total caloric intake. It might be argued, though, that short stature is an adaptation to high elevation and that well-nourished individuals raised from birth in the mountains might be shorter, but no less healthy, than their counterparts who grew up at sea level. Small body size may be as much the product of cold stress, hypoxia, and genetic factors as of chronic malnutrition (Frisancho 1976). The latter type of malnutrition represents a temporary condition—loss of crops due to floods or drought, illness in the family, and so forth. Some of these risks might be associated with land scarcity; others are density-independent. One anthropometric study conducted by ENCA indicates similar levels of malnutrition for males and females, and the other indicates slightly higher levels for males. This point is of interest for several reasons. It helps overcome a weakness of the ENCA data—its aggregation at the household level—which makes it difficult to evaluate the distribution of food among members of the household. The Andean practice of serving from a common pot also makes it difficult to measure individual portions. This apparent relative lack of bias in favor of males is supported by Collins's description of an Aymara-speaking district in Puno where "the principle for the distribution of food within an Aymara household is that those who work eat more. One of the strongest criticisms of another family members is to call them *manq'a q'ara*, which can be roughly translated as 'eats for nothing.' Because men and women share equally in agricultural work, they are entitled to equal shares of food" (1981:138). Collins goes on to state that children and aged inactive adults receive somewhat less than working adults. This pattern is also of interest in that it suggests a contradiction of the "female infanticide by neglect" hypothesis which has been applied elsewhere. These data on malnutrition also indicate the vulnerability of Andean highland peasants to disaster, as reflected in the number of children who suffer from a mild degree of acute malnutrition. Despite the storage of crops, food supplies cannot always last through environmental disasters or economic hardships, even though these may be temporary in nature.

The Cultural Patterning of Traditional Diets: Preferences and Avoidances

The highland Andean dietary pattern not only generally satisfies nutritional needs but also shows some coherence in terms of cultural patterning. It does not appear to contain preferences or avoidances that are difficult to explain. The high value placed on coca may correspond in part to the nutritional and physiological benefits that accrue from chewing it (Burchard 1975). Some groups located at elevations too high to permit the cultivation of maize make considerable efforts to obtain this plant, either maintaining small plots at great distances or traveling to barter their own products for it. They use it for the preparation of *chicha,* a mild beer that is consumed on ceremonial occasions. The importance of *chicha* suggests that the value placed on maize in some cases goes beyond its nutritive qualities. It is obligatory for it to be served at work parties associated with activities such as harvesting and roofing houses and at certain ceremonies. Some households will thus make considerable efforts to cultivate maize, even though the returns in caloric and protein yields are much lower than those for other crops. In some cases unmarried individuals will seek marriage partners who own maize lands (Harris 1981). Murra's (1960) description of the role of maize in ritual during the Inca Empire shows a similar importance for the crop at an earlier time. Other sources confirm its importance in pre-Columbian times (e.g., Antúnez de Mayolo 1981). In some areas, however, peasants are content to brew *chicha* from barley, which can be grown at higher elevations. (Potatoes, by contrast, tend not to be a direct focus of ceremonial consumption, although potato planting rituals can hold great importance in establishing and maintaining social ties [Barstow

1979], and individuals who have not planted potatoes would be at a disadvantage.) In any case, the possibly inefficient allocation of effort to obtain maize is not a great paradox or "riddle" (Orlove 1980a): it does not appear to be that expensive in energetic terms, since the cultivation of maize plots does not always compete directly with other agricultural labor (Platt 1981). In general, one can view the emphases on maize and coca as part of the pattern Murra (1975) describes as verticality, the desire to maintain direct access to a maximum number of ecological zones located at different elevations. This pattern can be seen as adaptive: it allows labor to be used efficiently, since agropastoral activities are carried out at different times in different elevations, and it reduces the risk of crop loss by dispersing fields and herds in different areas. This pattern can also be seen as cultural in that it contains a perception of the environment structured in terms of different zones. Ceremonial uses of maize and coca could appear to be a symbolic mapping of the Andean economy, with specific products representing particular zones. Custred (1980) makes a similar argument for the use of llama fat as a symbolic representation of pastoral grassland zones, located above the lower agricultural zones. The high values placed on meat, potatoes, maize, and coca can been seen as a translation of the pattern of verticality into dietary preferences.

The avoidances also do not appear unusual. Horses are not eaten, but they are not efficient producers of meat, and it is important to reserve them for work. The avoidance of dogmeat similarly seems unproblematic. (In the one form of dogmeat consumption that I was told of, soup made of the head of a black dog is served to people considered in Quechua as *musphasqa* or "crazy." It is difficult to tell whether Sahlins or Skinner would be more likely to consider this practice as confirming his theoretical schemes.) The strongest avoidance that I encountered was horror at the thought of eating toadmeat. Simple word-play in Spanish on "toad soup" (*sopa de sapo*) would elicit a response of disgust, as would any other reference to eating toads. The general association in folklore of toads with negative forces might account for this avoidance, surely not a costly one in nutritional terms.

The spatial variation in diet also seems to reflect the fact that people like to eat what is readily available to them. Thus, herders who live in the high-altitude grasslands above the upper limits of cultivation pity the people lower down, who do not eat as much meat, while the residents of lower zones praise their potatoes, *ocas,* or maize. The inhabitants of the shores of Lake Titicaca prize the stalks of the lake reed *totora* (*Scirpus* spp.), an item that is little eaten in other places. In some cases this preference for local foods leads to reputations or nicknames (Orlove 1984). The inhabitants of Yunguyo in Puno, Peru, are known for eating *tarhui,* and the residents of Huanta in Ayacucho, Peru, are called in Quechua *lukma suphi* or "lucuma (*Lucuma bifera*) fart." Nevertheless, this emphasis on local foods does not eliminate the value placed on foods from other ecological zones, as in the instances of maize and coca just mentioned or such other lowland products as hot peppers and fruits.

Accounting for food preferences in adaptive terms, however, tends to present dietary practices as isolated traits whose coherence lies only in their nutritional or environmental significance. Without denying the importance of such constraints on Andean peasants and without suggesting an exclusively cultural interpretation of the Andean diet, it is worthwhile mentioned additional perspectives. The timing of food consumption is also structured culturally. Some foods are associated with particular religious festivals. To give only two out of many possible examples, a course of boiled meat, potatoes, and vegetables such as carrots and cabbage—an Andean version of the New England boiled dinner—followed by a plate of the broth in which the ingredients were cooked, is served in many highland villages at Carnaval. Peasants who visit the graves of recently deceased relatives on All Saints Day provide special foods to passers-by in exchange for prayers. One such dish, found in villages near Lake Titicaca, is a stew of peas and dried *ispi,* a small fish. (These fish are known in highland Spanish as *indios muertos,* or "dead Indians," in reference to this occasion.) Other foods, such as fried trout in the Lake Titicaca area, are delicacies eaten primarily at the weekly markets. Beliefs about hot and cold substances, common throughout Latin America, are found in the Andes as well, so that some foods are deemed dangerous at inappropriate times of the day or year, and foods that might otherwise be avoided in this system can often be rendered sae safe by the judicious use of seasonings.

In addition, Andean peoples place a high value on abundant food and on the sharing of food. Even La Barre, who tended to paint an unflattering portrait of the Aymara as hostile and distrustful, in describing ceremonial meals states that "in such a gathering one may observe many charming acts of gentle kindness, between members of the same ayllu [local kin group], such as one would not suspect even remotely possible for the otherwise sullen, dour, and taciturn Aymara" (1948:65). The importance placed on giving food to all the people who are present at a meal is reflected in the proverbial negative outcomes of hoarding food and secretly eating it alone, such as having the food stick in one's throat, and in such insults as *manka kirpa,* or "pot-coverer." Men and women who would be considered overweight in the United States and Europe are seen as attractive in the Andes. This perception may have many sources: an association between wealth and weight, the greater ability of heavy people to survive periods of scarcity, or, as one informant told me, the fact that fatter people are warmer to sleep with at night. Conversely, thinness is negatively perceived. I recall hearing a maid in the parish house of a provincial capital, a woman of peasant origin, discuss with a market woman three candidates for the position of Miss Peru whose photographs appeared on the front page of a major newspaper. They were amused that such scrawny women would appear in scanty bathing suits; they thought that no man would find these *k'aspi chaki* ("stick-legs") appealing.

Food, however, is not judged solely by quantity. Specific qualities are also valued; it is not only potatoes that are appreciated for being mealy (*haq'o*), but other items, such as fruit, as well. (A peasant once did me the honor of selecting a particularly mealy specimen from an entire sack of mealy apples, whose flavor and texture—in my judgment—had not been improved by a week-long trip on the back of a donkey from a distant coastal valley.) Although there is no real *haute cuisine* (Goody 1982) in the highlands at present, peasants do appreciate certain special dishes (one example that comes to mind is *tunta,* a variety of freeze-dried potato, which is sliced and filled with cheese and anise seeds and then steamed), and they recognize that some individuals prepare everyday soups and stews particularly well, with appropriate textures and use of condiments.

Change in Dietary Patterns in the Andes

The analysis of change in dietary patterns in the Andes is based on two principal types of sources. The ENCA data, which describe a set of households at one moment in time, can be used to examine change if one is willing to assume that all households follow the same pattern of change, and that the households that now appear to be less traditional have changed from earlier patterns to a greater extent than the present-day households that are more traditional. The latter may be assumed to have changed less or not at all. The second type of source is represented by studies carried out in one region at different points in time. Although these studies permit direct observation of change, they were not conducted as carefully as the ENCA study. Fortunately, these two types of studies complement rather than contradict one another, and point in the same general direction.

The ENCA Study: Shifts in Dietary Patterns

The ENCA data present "snapshot" descriptions of dietary patterns in Peru in 1971–72. Contrasts between different groups, though, can suggest the direction of trends. A contrast can be noted between the coast and the highlands, between urban and rural groups within the highlands, between rural groups in the central and the southern highlands, and between wealthier and poorer households in the highlands. In each of these contrasts, the latter group can be labeled more traditional. One could plausibly argue that the wealthier highland

493

households have undergone a process of change that the poorer households have not participated in as fully. It is slightly more difficult to presume that the central and southern highlands once shared an identical pattern of diet, but that the people in the central highlands have changed, since one can point to ecological differences between the two regions. In particular, the lower elevations of many portions of the central highlands encourage maize production, and the extensive grasslands of the southern highlands favor the raising of livestock. Nonetheless, central highland households appear to have shifted in a direction similar to that of the wealthier households in the south. The change consists primarily in a replacement of traditional highland staples (potatoes, *chuño,* maize, barley, *quinoa,* broad beans) with exogenous staples, either coastal items (rice, sugar) or imported ones (wheat flour in the form of bread and noodles, cooking oil). The structure of meals does not appear to have changed greatly in rural areas, but more calories are drawn from sweetened hot drinks and bread, and noodles and rice are used more in the soups and stews.

Ferroni's explanation of these changes rests on the interaction of three variables (Table 20.2). Because of the difficulties he had in utilizing ENCA data on income, he relies on the total expenditures (TEX) of a household as a substitute. This variable includes the value of the home-produced food that a household consumes. The other variables are the calorie subsistence ratio (CSR), which is the ratio of the calories from home-produced food to the total calories that a household consumes, and the expenditure subsistence ratio (ESR), which is the ratio of the monetary value of the home-produced food to the total expenditures. A household could have a CSR of 1.0 by producing all of its own food, but no highland households have a value of ESR equal to 1.0, because they spend money on items other than food.

In many cases, these variables are interrelated. Households that have high CSRs and ESRs tend to have low values for TEX, for instance. Nevertheless, the large number of cases in the sample allows an examination of the independent contributions of these variables to dietary patterns and nutritional status. Both the high TEX households and those with low CSRs and ESRs tend to consume the non-traditional items. Households with high subsistence ratios tend to consume primarily traditional foods, and those with low subsistence ratios consume primarily non-traditional foods. Within each of these categories, higher-income households have a higher average consumption of protein and calories, and they have lower risks of caloric deficiencies. It is also worth noting that for both income categories, an increase in the CSR also brings high levels of protein and calorie consumption and lower risks of caloric deficiencies.

Ferroni explains these patterns in economic rather than cultural terms. Peru has maintained food prices at low levels, satisfying in the short run both the urban masses, who consume the food, and urban employers, who can keep

TABLE 20.2. ENCA—Distribution of Rural Sample by Income and Subsistence Groups, Central and Southern Sierra: Food Intake, Calorie Satisfaction, and Incidence of Deficiency

| | Subsistence Level | |
	Low	High
Low income		
N	238	547
% of total N	17	38
Calorie Subsistence ratio (%)	16.8	83.8
Calories/person/day	1,850	2,045
Protein/person/day (grams)	48.2	56.1
% calories from traditional foods	37.4	60.4
% coefficient of calorie satisfaction	88.5	98.2
% of households with less than ideal calorie intake	70.2	62.0
% of households with less than minimum calorie intake	64.1	48.6
High income		
N	235	410
% of total N	16	29
Calorie subsistence ratio (%)	19.9	83.7
Calories/person/day	2,205	2,716
Protein/person/day (grams)	61.1	76.3
% calories from traditional foods	27.6	59.8
% coefficient of calorie satisfaction	100.6	126.7
% of households with less than ideal calorie intake	57.9	33.2
% of households with less than minimum calorie intake	30.3	11.9

SOURCE: Ferroni (1980:tables 6.3, 6.4).

wage levels low. These low prices have discouraged food production within Peru, so that food deficits are made up by imports. However, highland peasants receive little income from the sale of their own food. Peasants in the highlands who have high CSRs consume primarily local staples. Those with low CSRs, however, will tend to purchase foods in accordance with their necessities and means. Non-traditional foods tend to be cheaper because of the subsidies on food imports and the lack of incentives to highland producers. Ferroni shows that high ESRs are correlated positively with the consumption of potatoes, barley, maize, *quinoa,* and legumes (principally broad beans and *tarhui*)—all

495

traditional items—and negatively with the consumption of non-traditional items: rice, bread, noodles, vegetable oil, and sugar. CSR and ESR, though distinct, are closely relatd, since they measure the importance of home-produced food consumption in the caloric and economic budgets of the household.

The data on total expenditure elasticity (TEE) are also interesting (Table 20.3). This variable is a substitute for income elasticity. It measures the tendency of households to increase their consumption of a particular item as their total expenditures increase. An elasticity of 1.0 would mean that the amount of an item that a household consumes would rise it the same rate as their total expenditures. Elasticities below 1.0 indicate that the percentage of the total expenditures devoted to a particular item decreases as total expenditures increase; a classic instance of a commodity with low income and total expenditure elasticities is salt. Elasticity values higher than 1.0 mean that the item occupies a relatively larger proportion of the total budget as total expenditure rises. An elasticity of 0.0 would mean that changes in total expenditure do not influence the expenditures for a particular item, and a negative elasticity would mean that the expenditure for an item drops as total expenditures increase. The fact that most of the elasticities in Table 20.3 are positive means that highlanders tend to increase their absolute consumption of all items as total expenditures increase, which reflects unsatisifed demand and perhaps the high value placed on corpulence. In many other societies, the consumption of low-prestige starchy staples decreases as income or total expenditures increase. I am endebted to Mary Weismanzer for a cultural rather than an economic explanation of this phenomenon. Since there is no well-developed *haute cuisine* (Goody 1982) in the Andes, a meal is improved not by the addition of fancier items, but by greater abundance. This point recalls Hirschman's comment (1970) that there has been relatively little formal economic study of trade-offs by consumers between objective increases in the quantity of an item and subjective improvements in quality.

This situation has led to the apparently paradoxical result that increases in income can lead to actual declines in nutritional status. As Ferroni states,

> a clear and at first sight paradoxical, negative relationship between TEX and caloric intake appears to hold between rural sample strata (data for rural Puno as well as the complete Southern and Central Sierra samples). This relationship exists because the level of TEX (mostly imputed value [of subsistence production]) required for adequate or even abundant caloric intake is not high (cf. rural Puno), in situations of high CSR and low levels of the quantity $1 - ESR$, i.e., the budget proportion spent on purchased goods. Unless decreases in CSR and increases in $1 - ESR$ are accompanied by substantial increases in TEX (i.e., of the order of the rural/urban differences [in the combined southern and central highlands]), caloric intake will, however, decrease (Ferroni 1980:66).

This decrease in caloric intake will increase the risk of other nutritional deficiencies. Dewey (1981) has documented a similar situation in Tabasco in southeastern Mexico, where increasing commercialization of agriculture and wage labor have led to an increase in income without an improvement in nutritional status.

The low CSR and ESR households tend to have poorer nutritional status because of their lower caloric intake and because of the lower nutritional quality of non-traditional foodstuffs, which tend to be lower in protein quantity and quality and to have less vitamins. As Ferroni (1980) shows, undernutrition in the highlands is primarily a problem of insufficient caloric consumption, which in turn is related to low incomes and low subsistence ratios. His proposed solution would be to raise highland incomes, in part through food policies such as changing the food prices structure. Reducing current subsidies for imported food and encouraging the production of highland staples would increase incomes for the highland peasants. (This policy's concurrent effect of making purchased foods more expensive for them would not present a serious difficulty, because it would encourage them to increase subsistence production and because their incomes would grow faster than their costs.) He also supports food relief after disasters such as earthquakes or major droughts and floods. He does not recommend the more traditional policies of distributing supplements or providing nutritional education, except in the case of combating vitamin A deficiencies; these could be remedied by the encouragement of gardens and by education, and even in this case, the severity of the problem is not yet well established.

Corroboration of the ENCA Study: Other Sources from Puno

Several studies confirm Ferroni's analysis of the importance of relative food prices and subsistence ratios in influencing dietary patterns in the Andean highlands. These studies are of particular interest because they are diachronic and thus document change by examining the same group at different periods of time. However, they are not as detailed as the ENCA survey and therefore do not permit as thorough an analysis of dietary change as could be hoped for.

Appleby conducted a detailed study of the marketing system of the department of Puno in 1973 (Appleby 1976a, 1976b, 1978, 1979) and restudied it in 1979 (Appleby 1982). In the intervening years, the Peruvian economy suffered a growing foreign debt, high rates of inflation, and devaluations of the national currency. Municipal councils in the two principal cities of the department, under pressure from urban consumers, maintained the prices for locally produced

TABLE 20.3. ENCA—Daily per Capita Consumption and Total Expenditure Elasticity (TEE) of Principal Staples by Expenditure Strata: Urban and Rural Samples from Central and Southern Highlands.

	Total Expenditure					
	Low			Intermediate		
Commodity	Cal.	Kg.[a]	TEE	Cal.	Kg.	TEE
Rice[b]	51	.015	1.359	176	.052	.685
	(1)			(0)		
Wheat bread[c]	127	.039	.982	166	.051	.913
	(2)			(5)		
Noodles	61	.018	1.116	78	.022	.639
	(1)			(5)		
Sugar, sweets	94	.891	125	.037	.645	.645
	(6)		(8)			
Vegetable oil	53	.007	1.089	72	.011	1.032
	(4)			(9)		
Potatoes	271	.316	.821	467	.522	1.057
	(78)			(85)		
Barley	190	.057	.361	164	.049	−.195
	(90)			(90)		
Maize	365	.144	.147	328	.118	−.045
	(89)			(91)		
Quinoa	66	.020	.554	70	.021	.969
	(92)			(86)		
Legumes	97	.044	.316	114	.061	.419
	(86)			(88)		
Total staple-derived calories	1,375			1,760		
Other calories	552			467		
Total calories	1,927			2,227		

SOURCE: Ferroni (1980:tables 6.9, 6.10).

NOTE: Figures in parentheses give CSR for the particular commodity for each expenditure stratum.

[a]Figures under "kg." give weight "as purchased." They include waste during kitchen preparation, but not waste along the wholesale chain up to the point of retail.

[b]Home-produced rice may include that gleaned in coastal plantations during migratory wage labor.

[c]Wheat bread does not include subsistence-produced wheat grain, which is used in soups and stews, rather than for making bread.

			Strata		
High			*Average*		
Cal.	*Kg.*	*TEE*	*Cal.*	*Kg.*	*TEE*
181	.056	.668	136	.041	.917
(0)			(0)		
320	.099	.520	204	.063	.715
(0)			(2)		
118	.035	.535	87	.025	.646
(1)			(2)		
202	.061	.694	140	.043	.668
(9)			(8)		
129	.017	.698	85	.012	.676
(7)			(6)		
479	.612	.058	406	.494	.511
(70)			(78)		
88	.031	−.176	147	.046	−.014
(84)			(88)		
198	.085	−.361	297	.106	.016
(81)			(87)		
77	.024	.398	71	.022	.356
(84)			(87)		
84	.039	−.138	98	.048	.177
(68)			(81)		
1,876			1,671		
737			585		
2,613			2,256		

staples at low levels. The prices for imported foodstuffs rose in relation to those for the local staples. As a consequence, "farmers keep more of their staples for domestic use" (Appleby 1982:7) and market less of it. In addition, consumption of purchased items, notably the non-traditional ones, has declined. "Bread and spices, particularly the chili aji, which were ubiquitous market items before, are being eliminated from the rural diet as too expensive luxuries. Imported staples—flour, noodles, rice, sugar, salt—remain in the rural diet, but people are buying them less frequently" (Appleby 1982:7). Appleby's data do not address the possibility that overall agricultural production levels in the department of Puno may have changed, either increasing because of higher levels of effort in subsistence agriculture or declining because of increased out-migration. It does seem likely that peasant households are moving in the direction of high CSRs and ESRs. It is also likely that their nutritional status is improving somewhat, unless they are simultaneously experiencing dramatic declines in TEX, a possibility that cannot be excluded because of the decline in off-farm income associated with a contraction of the national economy and the sensitivity of their agriculture to climatic disasters.

Appleby's data are particularly striking in that they document a return to more traditional dietary patterns. Although the broad historical trend in recent decades has been a shift from traditional diets to ones including more purchased non-native foods, the shift is, in this case, a reversible one. This point reinforces the suggestion made earlier in the paper that the term "traditional" should be used in a provisional sense.

Other diachronic data are available for the district of Nuñoa, located in a part of the department of Puno farther away from Lake Titicaca and near the upper limit of agriculture. Dietary surveys were conducted there in the early 1960s by Mazess and Baker (1964) and later in that decade by Gurksy (1969). The first study documented a reliance on locally produced foodstuffs, with maize and wheat providing 2.5 percent of the bulk. The second study may be seen as documenting a shift away from the traditional pattern—a greater emphasis on imported foods such as wheat, rice, sugar, and cooking oil, particularly in the village that is the district capital, and lower overall bulk. Picón-Reátegui, however, warns against interpreting these data in too straightforward a fashion (1976:235). The potato harvest in 1969 had been unusually poor, and the region qualified for food aid, thus altering the consumption patterns in two of the three settlements that Gursky studied and perhaps influencing the inhabitants of the third to underreport consumption in the hope of obtaining such aid. These data thus do not support unequivocally a long-term move from traditional diets to more Western ones. They indicate, however, the susceptibility of highland diets to environmental fluctuations (thus calling into question the representativeness of most dietary surveys, even the year-long ENCA data set) and the importance of the variability in food prices induced by state agencies.

500

Other dietary surveys from Puno support this general view of the highland diet (Table 20.4). The *Proyecto Perú-Canadá,* a development project in Puno funded by the Canadian International Development Research Council, conducted two dietary surveys as part of its effort to stimulate the production of improved barley varieties and rapeseed. One study consisted of 263 interviews conducted in 20 communities, primarily in the lakeside portion of the department of Puno, in the months of September and October 1977 (Montoya, Ccama, and Izquierdo 1980). These months are characterized by relatively low levels of consumption, according to the ENCA data. The other is based on interviews with 59 households in the community of Huancho in Huancané, Puno, in 1977 and 1978 (Coaquira and Huarachi 1981). This community is located quite close to the provincial capital of Huancané and consequently has easier access to purchased foods.

These studies only partially support Ferroni's summary of the ENCA data, aggregated for the central and southern highlands. The Puno sources indicate higher levels of broad bean consumption and lower levels of maize consumption. These results are not surprising, since maize cultivation in the lakeside region is restricted to areas with particularly favorable micro-climates, but broad beans are a common crop. The higher levels of *quinoa* consumption in the 20-community study and the still high but somewhat lower levels of consumption in Huancho could also lend themselves to a simple ecological explanation, since the crop is generally grown in large quantities in Puno but is not abundant in Huancho. It might be suggested that maize and broad beans do

TABLE 20.4. Per Capita Daily Consumption of Selected Foods in Highland Peru (Kilograms per Day)

Commodity	Central and Southern Highlands	Puno: 20 Communities	Puno: Huancho
Potatoes	0.494	0.326	0.335
Quinoa	0.112	0.112	0.047
Broad beans	0.048	0.094	0.160
Barley	0.046	0.023	0.022
Maize	0.106	0.027	0.042
Noodles	0.025	0.036	0.039
Sugar	0.043	0.058	0.060
Cooking oil	0.012	0.019	0.018

SOURCES: Coaquira and Huarachi (1981); Ferroni (1980); Montoya, Ccama, and Izquierdo (1980).

501

somewhat better on the moist northeastern shore of the lake where Huancho is located. The higher levels for noodles and cooking oil might indicate an increase in the consumption of purchased foods, contradicting Appleby's results; it is more likely, however, that they reflect higher consumption in Huancho and greater reliance on these purchased items in the late post-harvest season. The low levels of barley consumption are more puzzling; it is unlikely that they reflect a desire of the project staff to emphasize the need for increasing barley consumption in Puno. Similarly, the low levels of potato consumption may reflect a less traditional diet in Huancho and lower levels of consumption many months after the March–July harvest. Ferroni (1980:109) shows a sharp drop in tuber consumption in rural Puno as a whole in July and August.

Factors That Promote Change

FOOD SUPPLY: IMPORTS AND PRICES

The ENCA survey and other studies support Ferroni's claims for the importance of prices in influencing both production and consumption in the Peruvian highlands. This analysis, however, does not explain the price levels themselves. Neoclassical economics provides one sort of explanation through the theory of comparative advantage; it is easier for Peru to import the products of countries better suited to agriculture than to make the effort to bring into production its arid desert coast, its cold highlands, or its remote eastern lowlands. Exports of minerals or other products could pay the bill. Such arguments cannot be entirely dismissed, but their weakness is that agriculture in all countries is strongly influenced by government policy, through both direct measures, such as the allocation of credit and regulation of prices, and less direct ones, such as exchange rate policies.

Ferroni (1980), recognizing the importance of such measures, indicates that Peruvian governments have tended to favor low food prices and food imports to satisfy the economic and political demands of urban consumers and employers. These policies, however, limit the scope of industrialization because of the lack of demand within the country as a result of low incomes in the wage sector and the rural peasantry. Other recent work has developed this sort of argument further. Reviewing four books on Peruvian agriculture and food policy, Painter (1983) shows that Peruvian agricultural policy is complex and at times contradictory. Nevertheless, it operates within certain limits. The first left-wing phase of the military government, which ruled from 1968 to 1980, carried out a thorough agrarian reform and sought to make Peru more self-sufficient in food. However, these efforts were limited to large-scale enterprises, showing the political weakness of highland peasants. The government did encourage some production of food crops on the large capitalized coastal plantations, but it did not allocate credit to small-scale producers in the highlands, nor did it end subsidies of imports. Painter documents the importance of foreign actors, particularly multinational corporations, in several key sectors of the food industry. Three corporations account for 80 percent of the oilseeds that are imported to Peru for production of cooking oil (1983:210). Nestlé and Carnation completely control the production of canned milk. Wheat imports are similarly dominated by large trading companies. The efforts of governments to assure the Peruvian people of cheap bread by subsidizing wheat imports are partially subverted by the milling companies, which encourage the sale of items like cookies and crackers, whose prices are not regulated, thus ensuring larger volumes and higher profits for the trading companies (Painter 1983:213). Government subsidies of some foods thus benefit a small number of corporations as well as masses of consumers.

The emergence of the policy that favors wheat imports can be related, as Painter writes, to

the passage of Public Law 480, the Food-for-Peace bill, by the U.S. Congress in 1954. Designed to reduce grain surpluses in the United States, this law authorized low-interest loans to developing countries for the purchase of American grain that could be repaid with local currency. Later, the local currencies received were one of several forms of low-interest loans made available to U.S. corporations interested in establishing operations in those countries. It was hoped that this arrangement would increase the local wage-earning population who might purchase U.S. grain products. (1983:215).

These processes can also be noted in the case of salt: the Peruvian National Salt Enterprise simultaneously places strong restrictions on traditional highland salt producers and grants favorable concessions to the Morton Salt Company (Orlove 1982b).

Painter is correct in pointing out the influence of multinational corporations and international policy on Peruvian agriculture. In fact, P.L. 480 wheat sent to Peru as temporary disaster relief during droughts in the 1950s led to an increased acceptance of bread and noodles that continues to the present. However, prices are not simply the product of these external forces. Platt (1983) documents the willingness of Bolivian elites to have their country flooded with cheap imported wheat. Once the market for domestic wheat was undercut, highland peasants in some areas moved to a more subsistence-oriented agriculture. Nor can the role of consumer preferences be eliminated entirely. The high consumption of wheat products in Peru and rice in Hong Kong, for instance, may immediately reflect price subsidies, but these subsidies in turn are the outcome of local pressures. Diets would appear to be susceptible to price

503

influences, but certain dietary preferences remain. (It can be difficult to separate cause and effect in these instances, since dietary patterns can recreate
themselves through the encouragement of certain price subsidies over other
ones.)

FOOD DEMAND: THE FORMATION OF PREFERENCES

If the erection of a system of prices is not entirely transparent, neither is the
response to this system of prices. By examining price, consumption, and nutritional data from the ENCA surveys, Ferroni (1980) shows that there is a
tendency for the people in the central and southern Peruvian highlands to purchase the foods that are the cheapest sources of calories and protein, but that
other factors operate as well (see Tables 20.5 and 20.6). In other words, consumption patterns are shaped not only by the availability of food but also by a
schedule of preferences. These preferences are influenced, but not deter-

TABLE 20.5. ENCA—Changes in Daily per Capita Food Demand Due to
Changes in the Subsistence Proportion of Income: Combined Central and
Southern Sierra Sample

| | Current Consumption | | Subsistence Ratio | | | |
| | | | 10% Decrease | | 10% Increase | |
Commodity	Cal.	Kg.	Cal.	Kg.	Cal.	Kg.
Rice	136	.041	140	.042	132	.039
Wheat bread	204	.063	210	.065	198	.061
Noodles	87	.025	89	.026	85	.024
Sugar, sweets	140	.043	143	.044	137	.042
Vegetable oil	85	.012	87	.012	83	.011
Potatoes	406	.494	398	.484	414	.504
Barley	147	.046	143	.045	151	.047
Maize	297	.106	290	.104	304	.108
Quinoa	71	.022	68	.021	74	.023
Legumes	98	.048	95	.046	101	.049
Other food	585		584		586	
Total calories	2,256		2,247		2,265	

SOURCE: Ferroni (1980:table 6.12).

TABLE 20.6. ENCA—Average Nutrient Prices of Major Staples:
Combined Central and Southern Sierra Sample

| Commodity | Price/100 calories | | Price/10 grams protein | |
	Soles (1971–72)	Index (Rice = 100)	Soles (1971–72)	Index (Rice = 100)
Rice	.314	100	1,772	100
Wheat bread	.329	105	1,142	64
Noodles	.330	105	1,082	61
Sugar	.235	75	—	—
Vegetable oil	.283	90	—	—
Potato	.477	152	2,048	116
Barley	.255	81	1,619	91
Maize	.266	85	1,181	67
Quinoa	.362	115	1,105	62
Legumes	.308	98	1,803	102

SOURCE: Ferroni (1980:table 6.13).

mined, by the nutritional content of particular foods. Subsistence ratios are negatively correlated with the consumption of non-traditional foods, which means that the households that produce less of their own food consume more purchased foods. The strength of the correlation does not directly reflect the nutritional value of the food. Other factors influence preferences. The fact that most households produce some of their own food means that, as Ferroni states, "nonquantifiable considerations such as the convenience and security of controlling the food supply through home production also bear on consumers' subjective valuation of subsistence" (1983:185). Another reason for favoring subsistence production is that it ensures the position of the household in social networks within the community. A household that produced little or no food, even if it was able to meet all its needs through purchases, would not participate in labor exchange networks (Barstow 1979). Other qualities of the foods themselves are important. Ferroni notes that bread has several advantages, since it stores well, does not need further preparation before it is ready to eat, and gives a greater sense of satiety than many other foods.

The preference for cooking oil indicates in many cases a shift in the type of cooking, since traditional clay pots and adobe stoves do not lend themselves well to frying with cooking oil, although rendered sheep or llama tallow can be used with these implements. Frying in cooking oil is often carried out in metal skillets over kerosene or bottled gas stoves. These require additional cash outlays, not only for utensils, but also for fuel, in contrast to the dung and brush used in adobe stoves, which can be gathered without monetary cost. The use of purchased fuels appears to reflect the price of fuels. In Bolivia, bottled gas has become relatively cheaper since the construction of pipelines to gasfields in the eastern lowlands, and this fuel is widely used in the region around Lake Titicaca. In that region population increases may have limited the availability of dung. There has also been a large expansion of rural schoolhouses following the 1952 revolution, and children, who used to collect dung, may now have less time available for that activity (Orlove 1982a:20).

Nevertheless, some food preferences remain difficult to explain in simple adaptationist terms, even when factors such as price, convenience, and the labor time involved in preparation are included. For instance, barley is a cheaper source of calories and protein than rice, and both can be prepared in generally similar ways (i.e., they can be added to soups or be boiled and drained). The difference may lie in the fact that barley is a typical peasant food and in some of its forms, such as toasted kernels and ground flour added to hot liquids, is seen as very rural, whereas boiled rice is a sophisticated urban dish (Orlove 1984). The role of prestige in influencing the formation of preferences is discussed in the next section.

Conclusion: Three Approaches to Changes in Andean Dietary Patterns

The discussion in the previous section allows an examination of the causes of changes in Andean dietary patterns. Different conceptualizations of the highland Andean peasants will give different explanations for these changes. A fundamentally adaptationist perspective would argue that traditional patterns of resource utilization allow Andean peasants to draw sustenance from their harsh and unpredictable environment. The pattern of "verticality," discussed earlier, can be seen as adaptive in that it allows efficient use of labor and reduces the risk of crop loss. The various foodstuffs that can be produced in this manner also satisfy human nutritional needs. In this view, diets change because traditional adaptations are no longer viable, primarily as a result of population pressure. This argument has some validity but is not strong enough to stand on its own. In some parts of the Andes, rural populations are increasing at the rate of 1.0 to 2.0 percent per year, and the existing agropastoral base is insufficient to maintain that population. In many other areas, though, the increase is slower, in part because of migration to cities and colonization areas. Between 1940 and 1972, for instance, the rural population in the province of Espinar in the department of Cuzco in southern Peru increased by 0.38 percent per year, hardly a high rate, but the expansion of the marketing system brought non-traditional foodstuffs to the province in large quantities (Orlove 1974). Furthermore, the acceptance of new foodstuffs does not rest simply on their nutritional value per unit cost, as adaptationist arguments would tend to assume.

A second argument, that adopted by Ferroni (1980), draws on political economy, presenting highland Andean peasants as impoverished. It explains their need for additional food by showing their position in the national economy. They are seen as a source of cheap labor and, to a lesser extent, cheap products. They can work for low wages because they provide themselves with much of their own food. Dietary change can be explained by the deteriorating position of the peasants within the national economy. Their subsistence base has eroded, due to population pressure, the lack of technical and economic aid to highland agriculture, the inability of the marginalized peasants to invest enough labor to maintain the land, and other such factors. This approach also can explain some of the dietary changes. It omits, however, a crucial component. This political economy argument would assume that households first tend to produce as much food as they can on their lands, and then seek additional income from other sources. In other words, subsistence ratios, as defined by Ferroni, are determined for peasant households by their factor mix, particularly the amount of land and labor which they control. This assumption, though common in discussions of peasant economies, requires further examination. First of all, a peasant household, given the land and labor at its disposition, has a variety of forms of cultivation at its disposal. Deciding how much labor to put into land is not like deciding how much paint to put on a wall. It seems likely that two peasant households in an identical economic position might choose to allocate their resources differently, one emphasizing subsistence agriculture by cultivating more carefully their fields and the other concentrating on migratory wage labor. Data on this topic are difficult to obtain. Collins (1981:119) notes that in 1979 purchased foods represented between 7 and 12 percent of the calories consumed in her research site on the Peruvian side of Lake Titicaca, a little below the figure of 13 percent that Ferroni reports for rural Puno as a whole in 1972–73. This difference might be due to the relative isolation and better climatic conditions of Collins's field site, to the withdrawal from the cash economy noted by Appleby (1982) or to other factors. A second point is that the subsistence sector and wage sector cannot be considered entirely separate, since all households use purchased inputs, notably tools, and many also buy fertilizer and other agrochemicals and, on occasion, hire laborers and oxen. In other words, a household that wishes to produce more of its own food might allocate some time to wage labor outside the highlands in order to be able to purchase inputs. Since the ENCA questionnaires did not contain detailed information on activities outside subsistence agriculture, Ferroni could not examine the differences between households with high and low subsistence ratios. Some households with low subsistence ratios might well have been able to produce enough crops and animals to feed themselves, but chose to allocate resources to non-subsistence activities.

The third approach emphasizes the highland peasants as a dominated ethnic group. Despite the loosening of rigid caste-like barriers between Indian and mestizo, a number of objective and subjective differences mark them as two separate groups. One might expect food items in some cases to acquire a significance associated more with prestige than with cost or nutritional value. Although these prestige factors may not be as important as the other two, ignoring them altogether or assigning them a minimal role may cause errors in interpretation. An examination of other cases of consumption could be useful. Three notable changes in the Lake Titicaca area have been the replacement of grass and reed roofs by ones made of sheet-metal, the use of purchased cloth rather than homespun, and the decline in the consumption of coca.

Metal roofs, though found disappointingly unpicturesque to many outsiders, possess a number of advantages. Not only do they last longer, but they can be installed more quickly. Putting on a roof of grass or reeds requires the as-sistance of a number of people who then can request at a future date assistance in roofing their own houses. Similarly, it takes a considerable investment of time to produce homespun cloth. In both cases, people who are involved in both subsistence agriculture and migratory wage labor may prefer to save time by minimizing other activities, although they incur higher monetary costs in doing so. Nonetheless, a certain ethnic component may also be involved. Mes-tizo elites deemed inappropriate, if not subversive, the use of certain items of consumption by Indians and placed strong restrictions on them. An extreme example is the reception given to the first Indian peasants who returned to the village of Acora on the shores of Lake Titicaca after having worked in Chilean mines in the early years of this century: the mestizos who saw them wearing shirts made of factory cloth rather than homespun beat them violently. The use of sheet metal roofs was similarly forbidden. It is not surprising that the lakeside area, where such domination was common, was marked by uprisings in the 1920s. This area was also fertile ground for Protestant missionaries, who represented an alternative to the power monopoly held by mestizos. The peas-ants who were converted were willing to give up certain practices, chewing coca among them. Many peasants who did not convert to Protestantism also began to chew coca much less often, and to omit it entirely on certain occasions where it previously had been obligatory. Like some of the other changes that the Protestants brought, such as the shifting from braided to short hair for men, the decreasing use of coca seems to have represented simultaneously a break with the old Indian way of life, the adoption of some formerly prohibited mestizo traits, and the construction of a new future in which the two caste-like social segments will not merge, but in which the peasants have many opportunities formerly denied them. In this context it seems to me possible that bread and cooking oil are valued not for their nutritional or economic value but also for their significance as foods formerly consumed almost exclusively by the mestizos (Orlove 1980b), and that some other foods, such as *isaño,* may be consumed less because they are seen as emblematic of an earlier, now discarded, way of life.

The analysis of consumption in general is complex and poorly developed. One can explain many aspects of consumption in the Andean highlands as necessary for survival and biological reproduction (diet is clearly a good example, as are housing and clothing). Othertypes of consumption may be seen as necessary for social reproduction; fiesta expenses would fall into this category, and certain culturally defined status items, such as rubber sandals, might as well. Still other items, such as transistor radios, T-shirts bearing the names of American football teams, and perhaps food items like ice cream cones, do not fit easily into either category. Without attempting to deny the importance of adaptation and political economy, it is worth recognizing that despite their relative remoteness and poverty, highland Andean peasants cannot simply be considered either as an isolated traditional people in balance with their local environment or as exploited peasants on the margin of survival. In his discussion of increasing sugar consumption in Europe and the United States, Mintz (1979) also considers this range of factors, including adaptation, political economy, and other sources of food preferences. He stresses the importance of a long-term diachronic perspective in the analysis of food consumption, paralleling the processual view in ecological anthropology (Orlove 1980a).

These complex arguments aside, the details of this paper may be readily summarized. A traditional diet emphasizing tubers, grains, and, to a lesser extent, meat and legumes provided Andean highland peasants with a generally adequate and balanced diet. The principal dietary problems were an insufficient quantity of vitamin A and the risk of insufficient caloric intake as a result of either disasters or low income. In recent decades highland peasants have begun to include more purchased foods in their diets because population growth and their increased need for cash have led to a greater participation in the money economy. The consequences of this shift depend both on the new income levels (including as income both subsistence production and cash earnings) and on the extent to which purchased foods have increased in proportion in their diet. Although higher income levels are associated with higher caloric intake and better nutritional status, declining subsistence ratios are tied to poorer nutrition. For the bulk of the highland peasants, it appears that the latter effect is the stronger one. It is also noted, however, that the shift away from

509

traditional diets is not irreversible. Unlike peasants in some other areas of the world, the rural peoples of the Andean highlands have the option of increasing the role of subsistence agriculture in their diet and budget, and in some cases they exercise this option.

Appendix

The ENCA Survey as a Source on Highland Andean Nutrition

The ENCA survey was conducted between August 1971 and August 1972 on a sample of 8,000 households chosen from the nine major geographic regions of Peru (north coast, central coast, south coast, northern highlands, central highlands, southern highlands, higher-elevation portions of the eastern slopes, lower-elevation portions of the eastern slopes and the Amazon basin, and greater Lima). It is fully described by Ferroni (1980:24–47). The sample represents 0.322 percent of all households in Peru, excluding the residents of military and religious institutions. The sample was independently chosen from three sorts of primary sampling units: urban areas whose population at the time of the 1961 census was over 50,000; towns and villages with populations between 2,000 and 50,000; and other areas. The first two were considered to be urban, an appropriate decision in Peru, where small settlements serve urban functions. ENCA divided these primary sampling units into secondary sampling units of city blocks in urban areas and segments of 80 to 200 houses in the rural areas; the actual households, the tertiary sampling units, were drawn from these.

ENCA collected data during a 12-month period in order to evaluate seasonal variation in diet. Each surveyed household was visited twice a day for a week by the same enumerator. (Each enumerator was assigned to 80 households in a year, since the year was divided into 40 periods of nine days each, in which seven days were spent interviewing two households and two days were dedicated to rest and travel.)

As Ferroni states, the ENCA survey

> merits attention from a methodological point of view because, unlike the usual household budget survey which records monetary expenditures, it was designed to monitor both dollar expenditures and physical quantities of food purchased and consumed. The substance of the enumerators' daily work with sampled households consisted of the rigorous weighing of all consumed food. The ingredients of the two main meals of the day were weighed in the raw state approximately at the times the meals were being prepared. The edible portions of foods were assessed by quantifying discarded parts such as peels and bones. The weight of plate wastes and left-overs was determined after meals, recorded, and subtracted from the initial weight of the edible portion of the ingredients. The quantitative composition of minor meals . . . was estimated on the basis of homemakers' recalls and sample weighings of representative quantities of the ingredients in question. (1980:31–32)

He also discusses the thorough training and supervision of enumerators and the return visits made to households where the initial survey results were judged inadequate.

Initial screening of the data indicated the need for editing because of errors in field recording and in coding and punching. The ENCA staff returned to the original questionnaires and checked for consistency of data, unusually high or low values, and invalid codes. Erroneous data that could not be corrected by inference were relabeled as missing. The cleaned data were then assembled into files to facilitate analysis. Ferroni devotes most of his attention to the files for the central and southern highlands. He lists the four main types of data in them: demographic, socioeconomic, and anthropometric data on each household member; the food consumed in the week (in turn divided into three sub-sets of data: the nutritional contribution of the food, the division between purchased and home-produced foods, and the construction of an index of weekly family presence at meals); the nutritional needs of the household, based on FAO/WHO requirements for calories, proteins, and other nutrients; and household expenditures on food and non-food items, taking into account subsistence production and current local retail prices.

Ferroni points out that these data are more complete than those available for virtually any other Third World country and that they are important for descriptive and analytical purposes, since they make it possible to describe dietary patterns in Peru and their variations on the basis of region and income. He indicates several weaknesses, though. In many studies, income is considered an independent variable that influences consumption; because of the importance of subsistence production in rural areas and which ENCA staff evaluated as income, however, these two variables are not independent. Collecting information on consumption was so time-intensive that it was difficult for enumerators to gather adequate data on income as well, including data on earnings from migratory wage labor, artisanal activities, and the like. The data are also too limited to permit detailed analysis of the effects of ecological variables. As Ferroni states:

> In the Andean Highlands environmental factors are particularly important determinants of the level of agricultural production, subsistence consumption, and sales of food. Interactive variation in altitude, topography and exposure creates a myriad of micro-ecological conditions in this region, without reference to which agricultural production and subsistence behavior cannot be understood. Since the ENCA sample is not based on an ecological stratification of the universe under study and does not contain production data that would permit inferences regarding the household's microclimatic situation it is not possible to dissociate the effect of ecology on consumption from that of socioeconomic characters and seasonality. Statistically speaking, the within strata variation cannot be distinguished from the variation between strata, because environmental effects transcend any classification of the data made on the basis of socioeconomic or seasonal criteria. (1980:44)

Despite these qualifications, the ENCA data remain an unusually rich source. They are particularly useful because they cover regions for which other surveys have been conducted at other times, thus allowing a further assessment of dietary change.

511

Acknowledgments

A number of people provided useful criticism on an earlier version of this paper. I particularly wish to thank Arnold Bauer, Libbett Crandon, Kathryn Dewey, Thomas Love, Enrique Mayer, Bonnie McCay, Ellen Messer, Scott Raymond, Mary Weismantel and other Wenner-Gren conference participants, for their comments. I would like to express my gratitude to John H. Rowe, who suggested in 1972 that I study meal patterns and dietary preferences in conjunction with other topics during my fieldwork.

References Cited

Allen, C.
    1981   To Be Quechua: The Symbolism of Coca Chewing in Highland Peru. *American Ethnologist* 8:157–71.

Antúnez de Mayolo, S.
    1981   *La Nutrición en el Antiguo Perú.* Lima: Banco Central de Reserva del Perú, Oficina Numismática.

Appleby, G.
    1976a   The Role of Urban Food Needs in Regional Development, Puno, Peru. In *Regional Analysis, vol. 1: Economic Systems,* C. A. Smith, ed., pp. 147–78. New York: Academic Press.
    1976b   Export Monoculture and the Regional Social Structure in Puno, Peru. In *Regional Analysis, vol. 2: Social Systems,* C. A. Smith, ed., pp. 291–307. New York: Academic Press.
    1978   Export and Its Aftermath: The Spatioeconomic Evolution of the Regional Marketing System in Highland Puno, Peru. Ph.D. dissertation, Stanford University.
    1979   Las Transformaciones del Sistema de Mercados en Puno: 1890–1960. *Análisis* (Lima) 8–9:55–71.
    1982   Price Policy and Peasant Production in Peru: Regional Disintegration During Inflation. Paper read at the annual meeting of the American Association for the Advancement of Science, Washington, D.C.

Barstow, J.
    1979   An Aymara Class Structure: Town and Community in Carabuco. Ph.D. dissertation, University of Chicago.

Brush, S. B.
    1977   *Mountain, Field and Family: The Economy and Human Ecology of an Andean Valley.* Philadelphia: University of Pennsylvania Press.

Burchard, R.
    1975   Coca Chewing: A New Perspective. In *Cannabis and Culture,* V. Rubin, ed., pp. 463–84. The Hague: Mouton.

Coaquira, C., and L. Huarachi
    1981   *Consumo de Alimentos e Implicancias en el Nivel Nutricional de la Com-*

unidad Campesina de Huancho. Puno: ORDEPUNO/Convenio Perú-Canadá.

Collins, J.
1981   Kinship and Seasonal Migration Among the Aymara of Southern Peru: Human Adaptation to Energy Scarcity. Ph.D. dissertation, University of Florida.

Custred, G.
1980   The place of ritual in Andean rural society. In *Land and power in Latin America: agrarian economies and social process in the Andes,* B. S. Orlove and G. Custred, eds., pp. 195–209. New York: Holmes and Meier.

Dewey, K.
1981   Nutritional Consequences of the Transformation from Subsistence to Commercial Agriculture in Tabasco, Mexico. *Human Ecology* 9:151–88.

Ferroni, M.
1980   The Urban Bias of Peruvian Food Policy: Consequences and Alternatives. Ph.D. dissertation, Cornell University.

Flores, J., ed.
1977   *Pastores de Puna, Uywamichiq punarunakuna.* Lima: Instituto de Estudios Peruanos.

Frisancho, R.
1976   Growth and Morphology at High Altitude. In *Man in the Andes: A Multidisciplinary Study of High-Altitude Quechua,* P. Baker and M. Little, eds., pp. 180–209. Stroudsburg, Pa.: Dowden, Hutchinson and Ross.

Gade, D. W.
1975   *Plants, Man and the Land in the Vilcanota Valley of Peru.* The Hague: D. W. Junk.

Goody, J.
1982   *Cooking, Cuisine and Class: A Study in Conparative Sociology* Cambridge: Cambridge University Press.

Gursky, M.
1969   A Dietary Survey of Three Peruvian Highland Communities. M.A. thesis, Pennsylvania State University.

Harris, O.
1981   Labour and Product in an Ethnic Economy, Northern Potosi, Bolivia. In *Ecology and Exchange in the Andes,* David Lehmann, ed., pp. 70–96. Cambridge: Cambridge University Press.

Hirschman, A. O.
1970.   *Exit, Voice, and Loyalty: Responses to Decline in Firms, Organizations, and States.* Cambridge: Harvard University Press.

La Barre, W.
1948   *The Aymara Indians of the Lake Titicaca Plateau, Bolivia.* Memoir no. 69. Washington, D.C.: American Anthropological Association.

Mazess, R. B., and P. Baker
1964   Diet of Quechua Indians Living at High Altitude: Nuñoa, Peru. *American Journal of Clinical Nutrition* 15:341–51.

513

Mintz, S. W.
  1979   Time, Sugar, and Sweetness. *Marxist Perspectives* 9:56–73.
Montoya, B.; F. Ccama; and S. Izquierdo
  1980   *La Cebada en la Economía de las Comunidades Campesinas de Puno.*
            Puno: ORDEPUNO/Convenio Perú-Canadá.
Murra, J.
  1960   Rite and Crop in the Inca State. In *Culture in History,* Stanley Diamond,
            ed., pp. 393–407. New York: Columbia University Press.
  1975   *Formaciones Económicas y Políticas del Mundo Andino.* Lima: Instituto
            de Estudios Peruanos.
Orlove, B. S.
  1974   Reciprocidad, Desigualdad y Dominación. In *Reciprocidad e intercambio
            en los Andes peruanos.* G. Alberti and E. Mayer, eds., pp. 290–321.
            Perú-Problema, no. 12. Lima: Instituto de Estudios Peruanos.
  1979   Recent Ethnographic and Ecological Research in Lake Titicaca. Paper
            read at the annual meeting of the American Anthropological Association,
            Cincinnati.
  1980a   Ecological Anthropology. *Annual Review of Anthropology* 9:235–73.
  1980b   Landlords and Officials: The Sources of Domination in Surimana and
            Quehue. In *Land and Power in Latin America: Agrarian Economies and
            Social Processes in the Andes,* B. S. Orlove and G. Custred, eds., pp.
            113–27. New York: Holmes and Meier.
  1982a   Evaluation of Two Development Projects in Bolivia (ARADO: La Paz,
            Cochabamba; ACLO: Chuquisaca, Potosí). Washington, D.C.: Inter-
            American Foundation.
  1982b   Las Técnicas Tradicionales de la Utilización de la Sal en la Sierra sur
            Peruana. In *Tecnologías agrícolas tradicionales en los Andes centrales.* S.
            Mutal, B. Orlove, and A. Hibon, eds., pp. 31–34. Lima: Corporación
            Financiera de Desarrollo y UNESCO.
  1984   *Tomar la Bandera:* Politics and Punch in Southern Peru. *Ethnos* (Stock-
            holm) 47:249–61.
Painter, M.
  1983   Agricultural Policy, Food Production, and Multinational Corporations in
            Peru. *Latin American Research Review* 18:201–18.
Picón-Reátegui, E.
  1976   Nutrition. In *Man in the Andes: A Mutlidisciplinary Study of High-Al-
            titude Quechua,* P. Baker and M. Little, eds., pp. 208–36. Stroudsburg,
            Pa.: Dowden, Hutchinson and Ross.
Platt, T.
  1981   The Role of the Andean *Ayllu* in the Reproduction of the Petty Com-
            modity Regime in Northern Potosí (Bolivia). In *Ecology and Exchange in
            the Andes,* D. Lehmann, ed., pp. 27–69. Cambridge: Cambridge Univer-
            sity Press.
  1983   *El Ayllu y el Estado Boliviano.* Lima: Instituto de Estudios Peruanos.

Tschopik, H.
   1946   The Aymara. In *Handbook of South American Indians,* vol. 2, Julian H. Steward, ed., pp. 501–74. Bureau of American Ethnology Bulletin 143. Washington, D.C.: Smithsonian Institution.

21

GRETEL H. PELTO

Social Class and Diet in Contemporary Mexico

IN CONTEMPORARY MEXICO THERE ARE SHARP CONTRASTS BE-tween the diets of the great masses of poor families and those of the (largely urban) middle and upper classes. The contrasts are demonstrable in data on "habitual diet," "amounts spent weekly on food," "degree of dependence on purchased foods," "variety of foods consumed," and "provenience of food items." Less obvious, but highly important, are the contrasts in "per capita nutrients consumed." Total energy costs, as well as other costs involved in the production and distribution of foods, also differ sharply when one compares the mass of low-income families with the more affluent sectors of the Mexican population. At yet another level of comparison, more fine-grained analysis would demonstrate important differences in bacterial and parasitic contamina-tion, which are in part the result of differing conditions of food conservation and preparation.

Many of the dietary contrasts between rich and poor are closely linked to rural-urban differences, and it is difficult to disentangle the effects of social class from rural-urban factors. Although the complex mosaic of food-use pat-terns in Mexico must be viewed in the light of long-term processes of cultural evolution, the velocity of these processes has increased greatly in the latter part of the 20th century. The difficulty of analyzing such changes, with their multiple effects on the diets of rich and poor alike, is compounded by the fact that cultural change in modern nations takes on different forms in rural, eco-nomically marginal regions and continually modernizing urban centers. The consequences of these differences can be examinet at the individual, communi-ty, and national levels, including the consequences for indivdiual health, for mortality and population structure, and for national resource utilization.

I will begin this discussion with a brief sketch of food use in two families in order to describe dietary differences in a qualitative fashion. I will then present

517

statistical data concerning differentials in dietary patterns and nutrient intakes, followed by analysis of the consequences of these patterns.

Dietary Patterns: Two Case Studies

Javier and Guadalupe Maria Lopez and their five children live in a small mountain village in the state of Mexico. They eke out a meager living through a combination of activities. They grow maize; Javier works occasionally as a day laborer; they sell foods such as squash blossoms, mushrooms, and maize fungus from their small fields; and periodically Javier travels to Mexico City to find temporary (unskilled) construction work.

Early morning in the Lopez household starts with coffee, laced with a couple of heaping tablespoons of sugar per mug. After several hours of work, Guadalupe Maria and the children gather for a mid-morning breakfast of tortillas and beans (cooked with onion, garlic, and salt), served with a sauce of coarsely chopped onion and chili. Javier's food is brought to him in the field during the agricultural season. His tortillas and beans are augmented by a liter of pulque, the moderately alcoholic beer made from the sap of the maguey plant (*Agave atrovirens*).

The main meal of the day (the *comida*), served after 3:00 P.M., when nine-year-old Danielo (the eldest son) returns from school, includes tortillas and a pasta (macaroni), prepared as a dry *sopa* with onion, garlic, salt, tomatoes, and a commercial soup concentrate for extra flavor. Sometimes rice replaces the macaroni, and sometimes beans are the main dish. The children drink water flavored with sugar and lime juice. Javier and Guadalupe Maria drink pulque— for Javier his third liter of the day.

In the early evening Guadalupe prepares tortillas, with "something" to put inside, wrapped to make a taco. In March and April that "something" is likely to be *nopales* (cactus leaves), chopped and fried with onion and chili. Fried potatoes, scrambled with an egg, beans, squash blossoms, or leftovers from the *comida* are likely alternatives. Sometimes the family has nothing available for the evening meal and goes to bed without eating.

Sunday is different. Sunday is market day in the nearby town. Often the family buys a little chicken, occasionally beef, to be prepared as a stew with squash, cabbage, or a few carrots. White bread rolls and sweet bread are also purchased. These are saved for breakfast and supper in the days following market day. Other special foods are purchased in the market to be eaten on the spot—frozen ices, smoked fish, and candy are favorites.

Young Danielo has his own resources for obtaining treats. Whenever he can acquire a few extra pesos, he buys gum, candy, factory-made "Gansitos," or other "Twinkies"-like cakes, filled with jelly or vegetable-based "creme" and sold by vendors near the school.

Special holidays—weddings, christenings, saints' days—provide a welcome departure from the usual fare at the Lopez household. The meals on such occasions are highly predictable: turkey in a sauce of chili and chocolate (*mole*), with rice, cake, or sweet bread; brandy or rum with Coca Cola for the adults, plus beer; and Coca Cola and other soft drinks for the children. Although the Lopez family is poor, they have relatives in several households and can count on being guests at several such special holiday feasts every year.

The town to which the Lopez family goes to market has a much wider repertory of foods than one finds in the Lopez house. In the weekly outdoor market, one sees the seasonal ebb and flow of tropical fruits from the (hot) lowlands— mounds of pineapples, papayas, mangoes, bananas, guayava, and others. Highland fruits and vegetagbles are also abundant. Cheese, fish, beef, pork, chicken, and a considerable array of canned goods can be purchased in the local stores. Commercial products, such as pancake mix and cornflakes, are readily available, but imported foods are only found in the city, where one also finds such speciality items as peanut butter, pizza, and whole wheat biscuits enriched with soy.

In Mexico City a great many foods practically uknown to the Lopez family find their way regularly to the table of the Villalba household. For Juan Villalba Mendez, many years of education and more than a modicum of good connections have brought a comfortable existence. Juan is trained as an electrical engineer and has a well-paid administrative position in the multinational computer corporation he joined some 10 years ago. Before her marriage, Carmen worked as a travel agent, and she expects to start her own travel firm in a few years, when her children are older.

On weekdays breakfast in the Villalba household is a simple affair: orange juice, toast, and coffee. Often the children have cereal and milk. Eggs are sometimes served on weekday mornings, and are nearly always prepared for weekend breakfasts, along with ham or bacon.

Mid-morning coffee, with a generous amount of sugar, sustains Juan until the 2:00 P.M. lunch break. This is his main meal of the day, taken in the company cafeteria or in one of the many restaurants in the vicinity of his office. Usually he has soup, salad, meat, chicken or fish, plus rice and bread. Juan wants to avoid the middle-aged paunch he associates with the onset of his father's diabetes, so he often forgoes the pie, custard, or ice cream offered with the midday *comida*.

Carmen is also concerned about dieting. She works hard to maintain a svelte figure, so she lunches at home on fruit and yoghurt, or salad and cheese. Once or twice a week she joins her friends for shopping or other activities, and that generally means a more substantial meal, similar to Juan's usual *comida*.

519

Evening meals in the Villalba household are quite variable. Sometimes Juan picks up a pizza, which is the children's favorite. Occasionally they have waffles or crepes, or perhaps an omelette. Frequently the evening meal parallels the afternoon *comida,* though it may be slightly less elaborate.

In the Villalba household there are always bowls of fresh fruit on the table (foods rarely seen in the Lopez family); but the children usually prefer to help themselves to potato chips, candied nuts, and other snack foods, along with the soft drinks that are practically always available in the refrigerator.

Sundays are also special in the Villalba family, but the weekend and weekday diets are not as noticeably different as they are in the Lopez household. Sunday meals are often no more elaborate than the meals of the rest of the week, and there is little difference in meat consumption. On the other hand, they may be different when the family goes out to picnic or enjoys an outing to the coun- tryside or to Chapultepec Park. On those occasions there will be more snacks, soft drinks, and perhaps a pizza, hamburgers, or a special "family meal" at Burger Boy, Shakey's, or Kentucky Fried Chicken. In addition to these "inter- national" versions of commerical meals, the Villalba family has a wide range of choices among the local specialties, sold by vendors of "typical" Mexican foods (tacos, sandwiches, ice cream, gelatins, corn on the cob, etc.), and roadside food stands. Often they purchase extra quantities of the special breads, can- dies, and fruits offered at roadside stands and shops to add to their weekday repasts.

The Villalba family frequently entertains guests and relatives and (unless they go out to a restaurant) their cook is asked to prepare an elegant even- ing meal. As gracious hosts, Juan and Carmen serve cocktails before din- ner, and a fine domestic wine from Baja California is offered with the main dish. Domestic wines are considered as nearly as good as imports these days, and the imports generally cost four times as much as the best domestic vintages.

The food pattern in our middle-class "sample case" resembles that of mid- dle-class North Americans and Europeans in many ways. In comparison with many Euro-American households, the Mexican middle-class family is perhaps somewhat less "international" in its home cooking in the sense that Chinese and other Asian cuisines, for example, are not represented. Certain aspects of "typical Mexican" cooking and eating are preserved in the middle-class style, though the tortillas sold in supermarkets are usually made from wheat rather than maize.

The Food and Diet of the Poor

The example of the Lopez family illustrates many features of the diet of rural, low-income populations in Mexico.[1] The basic diet, reflected in the vignette of the Lopez household, relies heavily on maize. In many rural families 60 to 80 percent of the caloric intake comes from maize (Ramirez et al. 1975:161). The maize kernels are usually ground into *masa* (a clay-like dough), after being soaked in water and calcium carbonate to loosen the tough outer husk. At present the grinding is usually done in local family-owned mills, for a small fee. The *masa* is usually made into the familiar tortillas. Other, less frequently utilized ways of preparing maize include a thin gruel called *atole,* and tamales, an elongated "package" of cornmeal dough filled with meat or some other stuffing and steamed in cornhusks or leaves.

In terms of their caloric contributions, the other important foods of the rural poor are beans, sugar, and fats (lard or vegetable oils). The beans are generally boiled, with fat added for extra flavor when financial resources permit. Fat is also used to reheat previously cooked beans and to saute the flavoring ingredients (including onions and garlic) in mixed dishes. Sugar is consumed in coffee and lime-flavored water and is occasionally added to fruit juice in families with somewhat better resources. These four foods–maize, beans, sugar, and fat— are the principal sources of calories in most areas of rural Mexico (Ramirez et al. 1977:161). Together they account for an average of 80 percent of the total calories in individuals' diets (Chavez, Madrigal, and Moreno 1980:22). Some exceptions to these patterns include the greater use of fruit in lowland warm areas.

Table 21.1 shows the contribution, by weight, of the main foods in the diet of the rural poor. The data are based on an extensive survey in one of the poorest rural regions in the state of Oaxaca.[2]

Maize is not only a critical source of calories; it is also the major source of protein, followed in importance by beans and animal products. About 80 percent of protein comes from vegetable products, and the other 20 percent from milk, eggs, and meat. The potential problem presented by the fact that maize is an "incomplete protein" is offset by the use of beans, which has a complementary amino acid pattern, providing a "complete protein" when the two foods are eaten together. Unfortunately, many families today are frequently substituting pasta and rice in increasing quantities in place of the relatively more costly beans. This practice, which reduces protein quality (utilizability), is probably not significant for adult nutrition, but recent studies suggest that protein quality does affect child growth (Torun, Young, and Rand 1981). Thus, the change from beans to pasta may compromise growth in poor children, particularly affecting the possibilities for "catch-up growth" following illness.

The consumption of vegetables and fruits is highly variable from one rural region to another, although it is generally quite low throughout the entire country. For a number of reasons, including changes in farming practices (especially the increased use of herbicides in the maize fields), there appears to be a sharp decline in the use of wild greens (Messer 1977). Regional differences in fruit and vegetable consumption among rural people reflect not only differences in

521

TABLE 21.1. Daily Food Consumption in
Rural Oaxaca (Grams per Person per Day)

Food	Per Capita (Adult)	Per Capita (Pre-School)
Maize	394	143
Bread	21	24
Pasta	6	3
Rice	8	3
Wheat	1	4
Beans	40	9
Potatoes	7	3
Green vegetables	14	6
Yellow vegetables	34	7
Bananas	23	18
Citrus fruit	13	9
Other fruit	11	11
Milk	7	13
Meat	26	12
Eggs	19	20
Sugar	29	13
Soft drinks	31	29
Fats	9	3

SOURCE: Adapted from Chavez et al. (1980:120).

the availability of particular products but also differences in poverty levels. Mexico is a large country with significant resource differentials from region to region. Differentials in food consumption in the various regions are dramatically apparent in comparisons of animal protein intake, as illustrated in Table 21.2.

Some of the regions with the lowest average food intakes are characterized by high dependence on subsistence farming; however, the 1979 national survey showed no rural regions in which the percentage of subsistence farmers (those capable of self-provisioning of staple foods) exceeded 60 percent. Moreover, in the entire national sample of rural households, only 37 percent of families were full-time *campesinos* (small farmers), while an additional 27 percent reported that they gained their livelihood from a combination of farming and working part-time as artisans or in other non-farm work. Thirty-six percent of the households in the national sample were landless, with the men working as day laborers in farm and non-farm activities. Thus, many poor families have to buy

TABLE 21.2. Animal Protein Intake in Various
Regions of Mexico (Grams per Person per Day)

Region	Milk	Meat	Eggs	Total
Texas border	215	73	54	342
Sonora	115	80	57	252
Guerrero	69	51	16	136
Chiapas	10	57	24	91
Oaxaca	4	26	19	49

SOURCE: Adapted from Chavez et al. (1980:44).

all or most of their food, which partially helps to explain their low levels of intake.

In situations of high dependence on subsistence farming, the relationship of food intake to food costs may be attenuated. However, contemporary rural Mexico is not, by any means, a subsistence-based economy, as the previous figures indicate. The relationship of food consumption to food costs is documented by an analysis of consumption in relation to family food expenditure. Table 21.3 shows the average per capita consumption (for a national rural sample) of selected foods in relation to the level of weekly expenditures for food. There is a positive linear relationship between food consumption and total food expenditure for all food categories, except for the staples—maize and beans. Maize consumption is negatively related to income, and beans show no relationship.

Despite the fact that total expenditures for food and level of income are both affected by family size (larger families earn more and spend more), there is a

TABLE 21.3. Food Consumption by Food Expenditure per Week
(Consumption in Grams per Person per Day)

Weekly Expenditure (Pesos)	Milk	Meat	Eggs	Sugar	Soft Drinks	Fat	Beans	Maize
Less than 250	46	32	18	34	43	19	35	373
250–500	106	58	28	40	82	28	36	326
500–1000	176	93	39	49	131	36	32	257
1000 plus	249	119	48	55	166	44	32	194

SOURCE: Adapted from Chavez et al. (1980:64–65).

very close correlation between per capita nutrient intake and these monetary measures. When food consumption patterns among rural families are analyzed for nutrients, the "nutritional meaning" of these diets begins to emerge. Table 21.4 presents the mean intakes (per capita) of a number of nutrients, by level of income.

Tables 21.3 and 21.4, which are based on surveys in rural regions of Mexico, document the direct effects of socioeconomic status on nutrition. The two top income categories may be regarded as compising the relatively more affluent sector of the rural population, though only a small fraction of these households could be regarded as "middle class." The more affluent rural families have taken on some urban patterns—for example, their shift from maize tortillas to wheat bread and the sharply increased use of milk in daily diets.

The casual traveler in rural Mexico, who sees large numbers of cattle, sheep, poultry, and other animals in all agricultural areas, might be surprised to learn that most of the families who own these meat animals have very low levels of meat and milk consumption, compared with urban people. In developing countries such as Mexico, meat and other animal products are too expensive for regular consumption. The meat, milk, and other products are better sold to urban dwellers for much-needed cash to buy less costly staples, including beans, pastas, and rice.

One of the most poignant ironies of life in the Third World is that the rural poor, living in the midst of food production resources, go hungry, while the inhabitants of poor urban communities appear to have somewhat better diets. This is not to say that malnutrition does not exist in urban slums, including the poverty-stricken slums of Mexican cities. But in comparison with the poorer rural regions, the low-income sectors in the cities appear to consume more food and to have a more varied diet, on average.

TABLE 21.4. Weekly Income and Nutrient Intake per Capita in Rural Mexico

Income (pesos)	Kcal.	Protein (grams)	Vitamin C (mg.)	Calcium (mg.)	Vitamin A (Retinol Equivalent)	Niacin (mg.)	Riboflavin (mg.)
Less than 250	1,604	42	25	639	230	13	0.7
250–500	1,813	49	35	494	259	15	0.8
500–1000	1,927	53	52	719	395	18	1.2
1000 plus	2,086	58	68	790	478	20	1.4

SOURCE: Adapted from Chavez et al. (1980).

TABLE 21.5. Food Consumption Among
Rural and Urban Poor in Sonora (Grams
per Person per Day)

Food	Urban Sample	Rural Sample
Milk	83	51
Eggs	29	14
Meat	37	38
Fats	40	8
Vegetables	49	44
Fresh fruit	37	4
Sugar/sweets	52	15
Tortillas/maize	37	41
Tortillas/wheat	246	252
Beans	74	92
Pasta/rice	17	15

SOURCE: Adapted from Arroyo et al. (1969:41).

A study carried out during the late 1960s in the border city of Agua Prieta and in a nearby rural community in the state of Sonora (one of the richest regions in the nation) provides detailed documentation of differences in food patterns and nutrient consumption between the urban and the rural poor. Table 21.5 presents data on differences in foods, while Table 21.6 shows the differences in nutrient intake.

As with the rural poor, we would expect the diets of urban poor people to vary from one part of the country to another, and the food patterns of the border town of Agua Prieta undoubtedly differ in many respects from those of towns in other parts of Mexico. The data from various urban low-income populations can also be expected to differ because of variations in the degree of poverty in specific neighborhoods and sub-communities.

Recent studies carried out by the Instituto National de Nutricíon in working-class and lower-class barrios of Mexico City provide a fuller picture of diet in the metropolis (Batrouni et al. 1981). The areas selected for data gathering in this study were *barrios populares,* all of which were considered to be "less than middle class" neighborhoods. Squatter settlements, or *"areas de miseria marginales,"* were not included. The neighborhoods were selected to represent three levels of income, the top category comprising working-class families. By North Amerian standards these are all very poor households. From the per-

TABLE 21.6. Nutrient Consumption Among Urban and Rural Poor in Sonora (per Person per Day)

Nutrient	Urban	Rural
Calories	2,098.0	1,726.0
Protein (grams)	59.0	57.0
Calcium (milligrams)	692.0	536.0
Iron (milligrams)	21.0	22.0
Vitamin A (Retinol equivalent)	500.0	287.0
Thiamine (milligrams)	1.6	1.8
Vitamin C (milligrams)	21.0	13.0

SOURCE: Adapted from Arroyo et al. (1969:44).

spective of most rural Mexican families, on the other hand, the "working poor" in Mexico City had substantial cash income in 1979–80.

From the dietary survey in the barrios, it appears that tortillas continue to be important items in the diet, although the urban dwellers often prefer wheat tortillas in place of the traditional maize (Table 21.7). However, they are consumed at about 60 percent of the rate reported for rural regions such as Oaxaca.

Compared with low-income rural people, city-dwelling working-class families eat more rice and beans and a great deal more bread and other baked goods. In most of these families the consumption of fruits and vegetables remains comparatively low, only slightly higher than that of their rural counterparts. Bananas, oranges, limes, mangos, tomatoes, onions, chilis, carrots, and peas are the most frequently consumed fruits and vegetables.

The sharpest dietary contrasts between the low-income city-dweller and the rural poor can be seen in the consumption of dairy products (milk and cheese), meat, and eggs. Even the lowest stratum of the Mexico City sample consumes more than twice as many eggs, twice as much meat, and fifty times as much milk as the rural poor in Oaxaca (see Table 21.2). Although the contrast with the diets in Sonora (see Table 21.5) is somewhat less striking, the time difference of more than 10 years is an important factor in this comparison.

When the diets of the low-income urban families are analyzed for nutrient content, one finds that most of the common deficiencies of rural populations have been eliminated, except in the poorest neighborhoods. Table 21.8 presents these data for the three urban strata.

TABLE 21.7. Food Consumption in a Working-Class Barrio Area of Mexico City, 1979 (Grams per Person per Day)

Food item	Neighborhood Income Level		
	High	Middle	Low
Bread/baked goods	67	83	87
Tortillas (maize/wheat)	198	224	243
Pasta	27	28	28
Beans	39	43	48
Milk	323	292	200
Meat	80	74	60
Eggs	57	51	50
Fruit	62	50	34
Vegetables	36	28	27
Soft drinks	235	201	220

SOURCE: Adapted from Batrouni et al. (1981:17).

TABLE 21.8. Average Percentage of Recommended Daily Allowances Consumed in Three Lower-Class Strata in Mexico City, 1979

Nutrients	Lower Socioeconomic Strata		
	High	Medium	Low
Calories	102	99	88
Protein	125	123	101
Calcium	172	178	137
Iron	144	142	123
Thiamin	149	152	124
Riboflavin	105	102	75
Niacin	117	177	90
Vitamin C	126	130	66
Vitamin A	68	69	46

SOURCE: Batrouni et al. (1981:20).

These data suggest that the urban poor also have low intake of some nutrients, especially vitamin A and vitamin C. In reading these statistics we must keep in mind that these are averages. If members of a population are, on average, meeting 100 percent of their caloric needs, it is quite possible that approximately half of the households in that population fall below the recommended daily allowances, while the other half exceed the 100 percent mark. Thus, it should be clear from Table 21.8 that there are considerable numbers of malnourished people in the low-income populations sampled in Mexico City.

The magnitudes of the differences between the urban and rural poor vary from region to region within Mexico, with the southernmost regions generally worse than the areas along the Texas border. Table 21.9 documents the observation that, nationally, urban working-class families are on average better off than rural families even in the most favored rural regions. However, the very poorest urban populations fall well below the average food consumption reported for rural families in areas of good resources, in part because such regions include modest numbers of affluent families, which serve to inflate the overall averages.

The National Nutrition Survey statistics, averaged across the regions, are also informative (Table 21.10). These data show that the threat of malnutrition is greater for rural schoolchildren than for urban children. To appreciate the significance of these figures, we need to remind ourselves that when the mean intake falls below recommended allowances, considerable numbers of individuals are experiencing severe deficits.

TABLE 21.9. Protein and Calorie Consumption by Region and Income

Regions/Populations	Total Calories	Total Protein (grams)	Total Animal Protein (grams)
Urban			
Working-class	2,380	86.1	45.8
Lower-class	2,320	67.1	23.5
Peripheral	2,030	59.0	14.3
Rural			
Areas of good nutrition	2,330	69.0	20.0
Areas of fair nutrition	2,120	60.0	15.1
Areas of poor nutrition	2,060	56.1	10.0
Areas of very poor nutrition	1,890	50.2	7.9

SOURCE: Adapted from Ramirez et al. (1975:163).

TABLE 21.10. Nutrient Intakes of
Rural and Urban Poor in Percentages
of Recommended Daily Allowances
(Combined Mean Values for All
Regions of Mexico)

Groups	Protein	Calories
Rural		
Family	94	92
Schoolchildren	62	68
Pre-schoolers	65	73
Urban		
Family	108	99
Schoolchildren	102	83
Pre-schoolers	83	93

SOURCE: Adapted from Ramirez et al. (1975:51).

The Food and Diet of the Middle and Upper Classes

Until very recently there has been little interest in the food-intake patterns of middle- and upper-class families in Mexico. To a large extent the lack of information reflects research priorities in a situation of limited resources and the pressing need to describe and understand the nature and consequences of undernutrition. At the same time, there has been a tendency among Mexican nutritionists, like professionals everywhere, to ignore diet and nutrition patterns in their own social class.

The dearth of data on middle- and upper-class diet in Mexico, and in many developing countries, is likely to be remedied in the next few years. There is growing concern about the "diet of affluence" and increasing recognition of the role of diet in the "diseases of civilization." Moreover, there is increasing sensitivity about the effects of middle- and upper-class dietary patterns on the overall availability of foods and the commercial production and distribution of agricultural products. These factors, as well as the need to develop more adequate national consumption data for forecasting future requirements, call for increased study of dietary patterns in the middle and upper socioeconomic sectors.

A recent study analyzing variation in garbage in Mexico City sheds light on the contrasts between upper- and lower-class diets (Restrepo and Phillips 1982). Based on careful examination of garbage samples from selected neighborhoods, the study by the National Consumers' Institute showed dramatic contrasts in the estimated frequencies of consumption of many foods (Table 21.11).

The relationships between consumption patterns and socioeconomic status are clearly evident in the differential utilization of major food products. Consumption of milk and milk products is approximately five times higher in the upper classes than in the lower socioeconomic strata (INN 1983). Fruit and vegetable consumption is three to four times higher; consumption of meat is more than three times higher, and the consumption of cereals (other than maize) is four times higher. Bean consumption drops slightly in the higher-income groups, whereas maize, the traditional mainstay of the diet of the poor, drops to less than 50 percent of the lower-class consumption level.

Historically, one of the most striking differences between the diets of the elite and those of the rest of the population has been the role of wheat bread. The Spaniards brought wheat to Mexico in the early 16th century. According to the historian Fernandez del Castillo, "by 1923 the sacred land of the Mexicans was covered with beautiful fields of wheat" (CulturaSep 1983). The Indians were forced to cultivate wheat on the lands confiscated by the Spanish crown, and milling and baking were also controlled by the Spaniards. Baking activities were concentrated in cities and towns, where, as in many parts of Europe, the price and weight of bread were carefully controlled. From its inception in Mex-

TABLE 21.11. Food Consumption Patterns in Lower- and Upper-Income Neighborhoods (Number of Days per Year Foods were Consumed)

Foods	Lower-Class	Upper-Class
Rice	28	183
Cheese	16	183
Fish	13	91
Shrimp, molluscs	17	36
Canned, dehydrated vegetables	30	183
Canned, dried fruit	15	91
Potatoes	41	122
Bacon	0	91
Baby foods, juices	0	122
"T.V. dinners"	0	122
Fruit, vegetable juices	17	61
Breakfast cereals	15	26

SOURCE: Adapted from Restrepo and Phillips (1982:99).

ico, wheat and wheat products have been controlled by the elite and have presented considerable opportunities for profit, particularly with the expansion of the Spanish population.

With the advent of industrialized baking in the early part of this century, followed later by the introduction of new "green revolution" wheat strains, the Mexican baking industry has expanded greatly. Government subsidies for wheat and the growth of cities, which facilitated distribution, contributed further to its profitability.

Not surprisingly in a situation in which a particular type of food becomes associated with the privileged class, bread was first incorporated into the diets of the poor as ceremonial food. In addition to its importance in the Catholic mass, the consumption of special breads is an integral part of both public and private ceremonials, including betrothals, weddings, and saints' days, of which All Saints Day (November 1) has the most elaborated bread and bread symbolism (CulturaSep 1983). As revealed in the dietary data summarized above, bread and other wheat products have become increasingly important in the diets of the poor, particularly the urban poor. Nonetheless, the differential consumption of wheat products by members of different social classes remains a noticeable feature of Mexican dietary patterns.

Consequences of Dietary Patterns for Health and Mortality

Having reviewed the major dimensions of dietary patterns, we will now turn to an examination of the implications of these patterns, first in relation to health and mortality, then in relation to national resource utilization.

The diet of Mexican farmers and unskilled, poor workers, derived from the centuries-old diet of pre-Hispanic times, is not without its strong points from a nutritional perspective. It is high in fiber, low in cholesterol, high in complex carbohydrates—all characteristics that are currently recommended to populations in the industrialized countries as preventive of heart disease, high blood pressure, diabetes, and some forms of cancer. People consuming the Mexican peasant diet should be at lower risk of experiencing these debilitating and life-threatening diseases.

However, most of the victims of cardiovascular disease, diabetes, and cancer are adults; thus, to be "at risk" for these diseases one had to live to adulthood. The major hazards of the dietary patterns of the poor in Mexico affect infants and young children. The low nutrient density of the diet (the ratio of other nutrients to calories) means that infants and children often cannot eat enough food to meet their nutrient needs. The result is retarded growth, in-

531

creased susceptibility to disease, and inadequate energy for activity. In an environment of poor sanitation, with high levels of exposure to pathogens, children (and adults) face recurrent illness, which causes further deterioration in nutritional status. If unchecked, the vicious cycle of disease and malnutrition leads to death; the synergistic relationship between them underlies the mortality statistics for Third World countries (see Mata 1978; Scrimshaw, Taylor, and Gordon 1966).

A low-fat, high-bulk diet also affects the health and well-being of the pregnant woman and her fetus. Food intake during pregnancy is one of the factors that affects pregnancy weight gain and infant birth weight. Like other poor women in Third World countries, Mexican rural women typically experience low pregnancy weight gains and often deliver babies whose weight at birth is well below birth weights in industrialized nations. Throughout the world birth weight is a primary factor associated with neonatal mortality (Habicht et al. 1973).

Inadequate caloric and nutrient consumption also affects a woman's ability to produce adequate breast milk over an extended period of time. Data from a careful longitudinal study in Tezonteopan, in the state of Puebla, demonstrated that poor rural women, consuming typical quantities of the basic rural diet, could not sustain a sufficient level of milk production to support their infants' growth, although there was considerable variability in the point at which milk production fell to seriously low levels (Chavez and Martinez 1979). Thus begins a pattern in which the undernourished infant, born at a low birth weight, cannot maintain an adequate growth trajectory. With increased disease experience as he or she grows older, malnutrition takes a progressively heavy toll. For some children this means death, but for many others it means low energy, poor physical development, and reduced opportunities to develop intellectually and emotionally (ibid.).

Although the link between malnutrition and mortality is most significant during infancy and early childhood, poor nutritional status affects the mortality risk during illness at all ages. Through its effects on mortality, nutrition affects population structure by two mechanisms: directly by eliminating individuals from the population, and indirectly by influencing fertility decision making.

In rural Mexico infant and young child mortality have declined in recent decades, partly as a function of improved access to medical care and modern drugs. However, mortality rates remain high compared with those of industrialized countries. Poor rural families can still expect to suffer the loss of children. For example, in the small town of Solis, in the state of Mexico (an area with greater resources than many other parts of the country), 39 percent of families interviewed in the early 1970s reported the death of at least one child (DeWalt, Bee, and Pelto 1972). In the Indian communities of the region, more than 60 percent of families had lost a child, and many had lost several.

The role of child loss in decision making about reprodutive behavior has received a good deal of attention in recent decades (see, for example, Salo and Valimaki 1981). The "child replacement hypothesis" postulates that parents are motivated to "replace" a child's death with a new birth for a complex of emotional and economic reasons. Although infant and child mortality is not necessarily the primary factor in decisions to use or reject contraception, when mortality is high it is probable that people will be less receptive to family planning services. Thus, malnutrition may have an indirect effect on population structure through its effect on contraceptive decision making.

Examining the health consequences of the peasant diet, it is important to remember that this diet is far from the one that sustained pre-Columbian Mexico. Refined sugar, consumed in coffee by both adults and children, as well as in soft drinks and candy, has taken a toll on the dental health of farmers and workers. Moreover, in the same communities in which one finds undernutrition, obesity is beginning to appear (Chavez and Diaz 1964). Ironically, poor people in Mexico are in danger of at least some of the diseases of affluence, at the same time that they are suffering from the consequences of a nutritionally inadequate diet.

The positive aspects of the middle-class diet, from the perspective of health and nutrition, are relatively obvious. Adequate protein and calorie intake during pregnancy and childhood promote growth, with energy left for various kinds of productive and leisure activities. People have adequate nutritional reserves to recover from illness and greater resistance to disease. Intake of vitamins and minerals is superior to that of the poor, thus further increasing the probability of good health.

On the other hand, the diet of the Mexican middle class, like that of middle-class people the world over, predisposes individuals to several of the major killer diseases. High saturated-fat intake, alhtough it has not definitively been shown to be a primary cause of cardiovascular disease, is widely regarded as a contributing factor. High protein intake is associated with problems of calcium retention and may be associated with the development of osteoporosis. Diets high in refined carbohydrate have been postulated to increase the risk of diabetes, while low-fiber diets have been associated with increased risk of intestinal cancer. Thus, to the extent that the diets of the Mexican middle class come to resemble diets in countries that have been industrialized for a longer period of time, one can expect that the morbidity and mortality patterns will also approximate those of the United States and Western Europe.

The health impact of commercially processed food, with its high levels of flavoring, stabilizing, and coloring agents, remains a controversial subject. It is probable that the Mexican middle and upper classes have higher exposure to such agents than do the rural poor. Again, to the extent that these products of modern industry affect health, we can expect that the health risk is currently greater for city-dwellers than for rural peoples, and for the middle-class than for poorer classes. On the other hand, the food preparation practices of middle-class families reduce the risk of exposure to bacterial contamination. Disinfecting agents, which are added to water and used to soak fresh fruits and vegetables, are now widely available in Mexico City supermarkets. The use of these products greatly reduces exposure to amoebas and other protozoa, as well as to bacteria.

In summary, the deficiencies in the diets of the most impoverished sectors of the Mexican population cause considerable suffering. Although the incidences of severe deficiency diseases are low compared with those in many other Third World countries, it is estimated that nutritional deficiencies still account directly for a quarter of the deaths of pre-school children (Chavez 1969). Mild and moderate levels of malnutrition take a heavy toll as well, not only on physical health, but also on growth, development, and personal well-being. Undernutrition, in conjunction with disease, poor sanitation, and limited access to health care, produces a social-physical environment in which children do not grow to their full potential: "Just as in war, malnutrition casualties should be counted not only by death, but also by the 'wounded' people, especially the permanently disabled" (Chavez et al. 1971).

At the other end of the economic spectrum, the diets of the affluent are not without their own risks. The maintenance of healthy eating patterns in the midst of plenty is apparently not easy in the modern world. The long-term health consequences of middle-class diets are not as obviously negative as the consequences of undernutrition, but they are not an unmixed blessing. Together with the other stresses of urban life, the high consumption of saturated fats, refined sugars and grains, and other products of modern, industrial food production pose significant health threats to the people who are affluent enough to maintain such diets.

Dietary Patterns and National Resource Utilization

Since the startling and disturbing revelations of the Club of Rome in its analysis of the limits of growth (Meadows et al. 1972), it has become increasingly clear that the industrialized countries use a grossly disproportionate share of the world's resources. This applies not only to raw materials and fossil fuels, but to food supplies as well. The widening gap in wealth and lifestyles between poor and affluent nations is increasingly reflected in the contrasts in resources, dietary patterns, and lifestyles between the poor and the affluent classes within the developing nations.

Consumption of Animal Products

As a basic comparison, we note the difference in caloric consumption between the poor and the affluent. The average differential of 400 to 500 calories per day is not insignificant when projected to a national level. However, this is but the tip of the iceberg. The energy costs of producing animal food products (which are disproportionately consumed by middle- and upper-income families) are very great compared with the costs of producing vegetable foods (Borgstrom 1972). When caloric intake is calculated in terms of "primary calories," which include the calories consumed by animals, the daily per capita caloric consumption by affluent people in the world exceeds 10,000 calories. The "gap" between recorded caloric intakes (averaging 2,500 to 3,000 kilocalories) and the actual caloric costs in food value is about 7,000. In contrast, according to Borgstrom's calculations, the estimated "calorie gap" for a peasant in India is only 1,000 kilocalories (Borgstrom 1972:31).

Taking this analysis a step further, Martinez and colleagues (1976) have calculated that a Mexican middle-class diet that includes 100 grams of animal protein per day costs 14,000 "agricultural calories" and a half million "industrial calories" (fuel, transport, equipment, etc.). On the other hand, they estimate that the diets of poor families, based mainly on maize, beans, and other vegetable foods, require only about 2,000 "agricultural calories" and 8,000 "industrial calories" per day (Martinez et al. 1976:245).

The inequities in food consumption are clear from dietary intake data, expressed as per capita consumption rates. When these are transposed to food dollar figures, as Gonzalez Casanova has done (1980), we see that the 15 percent of Mexicans with the most purchasing power purchase 50 percent of the total value of foods in the Mexican food system, while the poorest 30 percent in income purchase only 10 percent of the total (Gonzalez Casanova 1980:202). The calculations of Martinez and colleagues (1976) make it clear that the energy inequities are much greater than even the food consumption and food expenditure data demonstrate.

Much of the increased demand for animal products in Mexico is being met by increased domestic production. Table 21.12 shows the increase over the seven-year period from 1972 to 1979. It should be noted that the per capita consumption increases are less than the production increases, reflecting both the rapid increase in the Mexican population during the same period and the export of a portion of the animal food produced.

The demand for milk and other dairy products, although commendable from certain nutritional standpoints, also has important implications. Dairying is an energy-intensive industry and is becoming increasingly so with the adoption of modern dairying techniques. Processing, transportation, and preservation

TABLE 21.12. Increases in the
Production and Per Capita
Consumption of Animals in Mexico,
1972–79 (in Percentages)

	Production	Consumption
Beef	52	31
Pork	104	65
Chicken	70	35
Eggs	50	22
Milk	34	22

SOURCE: Adapted from DeWalt (1985).

costs are high, not only placing large-scale consumption of milk products out of the reach of the rural poor, but also demanding significant fossil fuel and other material resources for the manufacture and maintenance of equipment and transportation facilities.

Grains for Human Consumption and Animal Feed

Of great concern is the fact that during the recent period of increase in consumption of animal foods, the production of basic grains has dropped sharply (DeWalt 1985). In 1965 the annual per capita production of food grains was 280 kilograms. By 1979 it had dropped to 169 kilograms—60 percent of the 1965 figures. This decline is particularly dramatic when we consider that the "green revolution" was supposed to have saved the Mexican food grain situation in the 1960s. The decline in per capita grain production was not due primarily to population increases; rather, it resulted from government policies that encouraged the production of sorghum and discouraged basic grain production. Although sorghum is preferred for animal feeding, some of the basic grains (wheat, barley, and maize) have also been diverted to feed livestock.

The shift in the allocation of land from foods intended for direct human consumption to animal feed is not limited to large commercial farms. The small farmers have also converted a portion of their crops to fodder. For example, in the Solis Valley in central Mexico, it appears that many of the wheat and barley fields that can be seen among the fields of maize are planted to provide grains for animal consumption, "because it makes them grow faster." The majority of the meat animals fattened from these fields find their way to the tables of the middle and upper classes in Mexico City. Ramirez and associates (1975) estimate that nearly 50 percent of the increase in animal product production since 1960 is consumed in Mexico City. Thus, the consumption patterns of the affluent, which feature meat as a central component of the diet, have diverted scarce resources from food grain to livestock production—a far less efficient use of land and water resources.

The Hidden Costs of Contemporary Food Patterns

Other energy expenditures and environmental costs are associated with the dietary patterns of the middle and upper classes. The development of supermarkets, food-processing plants, and other components of the food industry not only increase the input of "agricultural" and "industrial" calories; they also increase the amount of solid waste (Restrepo and Phillips 1982:52). The containers—bags, boxes, cans, and bottles—that are used to transport and store foods contribute, perhaps, only a small portion to the total problem of solid waste, but the collective impacts of the new modes of obtaining and consuming food that characterize the more affluent sectors of the population not only contribute to the problem of "visual pollution," but carry other hidden costs in environmental degradation and the energy necessary for the management of waste disposal.

A number of years ago the Mexican anthropologist Rudolfo Stavenhagen used the term "internal colonialism" to refer to the relationship between marginal rural areas and the urban power centers (Stavenhagen 1967). The flow of food resources from the rural areas to the cities of Mexico, and beyond to other wealthy populations, can be seen as yet another manifestation of this process. Class differences in food patterns in contemporary Mexico go far beyond the dramatic differences in nutrient intakes. In addition to the hidden costs of malnutrition in the poorer sectors, the carnivorous appetites of affluence place an immense burden of energy costs on an already strained ecological system.

Acknowledgments

The reader scanning the bibliography will quickly note the frequency with which A. Chavez's name appears. As director of the Division of Community Nutrition of the National Institute of Nutrition, he has been responsible for a large share of the research projects that collectively provide a picture of nutrition in contemporary Mexico.

Beyond his prodigious efforts as a researcher and research administrator, his depth of understanding about the nature of malnutrition has influenced researchers all over the world. I am greatly indebted to him for whatever insights this paper may contain. I also want to thank Pertti J. Pelto and Lindsay H. Allen for their thoughtful and critical commentary.

Notes

1. The dietary patterns of the rural poor have been exceedingly well documented, primarily as a result of the massive efforts of the National Institute of Nutrition (INN) and other research groups. Available materials include large-scale surveys, which present statistical, descriptive data on food consumption and nutritional status (usually expressed as mean values for large population segments), and detailed longitudinal studies using small samples.

2. The reader unfamiliar with food weights might find it useful to note that an egg weighs 60 grams. In Table 21.1 the average per capita consumption of 26 grams of meat per day compares with an average North American consumption of 300 to 400 grams of meat per day.

References Cited

Arroya, P. A., et al.
  1969   *Alimentacion en una Region Fronteriza: Aqua Prieta y Esqueda, Sonora.* Publicacion L-15. Mexico City: Division de Nutricion, Instituto Nacional de la Nutricion.
Batrouni, L., et al.
  1981   *La Alimentacion y la Nutricion de los Barrios Populares de la Ciudad de Mexico.* Publicacion L-42. Mexico City: Division de Nutricion, Instituto Nacional de la Nutricion.
Borgstrom, Georg
  1972   *The Hungry Planet.* New York: Macmillan.
Chavez, A.
  1969   El Problema de la Nutricion Infantil. *Revista Technica de Alimentos Mexicanos* 4:22.
Chavez, A., and D. M. Diaz
  1964   Frequencia de Obesidad en Algunas Zonas de la Republica Mexicana. *Publicacion de la Sociedad Mexicàna de Endrocronologia* 5:119–29.
Chavez, A., et al.
  1971   Ecological Factors in the Nutrition and Development of Children in Poor Rural Areas. *Proceedings of the Western Hemisphere Nutrition Congress III.* 265–80.
Chavez, A.; H. Madrigal; and O. Moreno
  1980   *La Alimentacion en el Medio Rural.* Publicacion L-33. Mexico City: Division de Nutricion, Instituto Nacional de la Nutricion.

Chavez, A., and C. Martinez
1979   *Nutricion y Desarrollo Infantil.* Mexico City: Nueva Editorial Inter-
        americana.
CulturaSep
1983   *La Cosa Esta Del Cocol y Otros Panes Mexicanos.* Mexico City: Museo
        Nacinal de Culturas Populares.
DeWalt, B. R.
1985   Mexico's Second Green Revolution: Food for Feed. *Estudios Mexicanos*
        1:29–60.
DeWalt, B.; R. Bee; and P. J. Pelto
1972   *The People of Temascalcingo: A Regional Study of Modernization.* Mono-
        graph. Storrs, Conn.: Department of Anthropology, University of
        Connecticut.
Gonzalez Casanova, P.
1980   The Economic Development of Mexico. *Scientific American.*
        243(4):192–204.
Habicht, J.-P., et al.
1973   Relationships of Birthweight, Maternal Nutrition and Infant Mortality.
        Nutrition Reports International 7:533–46.
INN (Instituto Nacional de la Nutricion)
1983   Unpublished Data.
Martinez, C., et al.
1976   *La Estructura del Consumo de Alimentos en el Medio Rural Pobre.* Pub-
        licacion L-29. Mexico City: Division de Nutricion, Instituto Nacional de
        la Nutricion.
Mata, Leonardo
1978   *The Children of Santa Maria Cauque.* Cambridge, Mass.: MIT Press.
Meadows, D. H., et al.
1972   *The Limits to Growth.* New York: New American Library.
Messer, E.
1977   The Ecology of Vegetarian Diet in a Modernizing Mexican Community.
        In *Nutrition and Anthropology in Action,* T. K. Fitzgerald, ed., pp. 117–
        24. Amsterdam: Van Gorcum.
Ramirez Hernandez, J., et al.
1975   Problematica y Perspectivas de las Disponibilidades de Alimentos en
        Mexico. *Revista del Comercio External Mexicano* 25:559–66.
Restrepo, I., and D. Phillips
1982   *La Basura: Consumo y Desperdicio en Distrito Federal.* Mexico City:
        Instituto Nacional del Consumidor.
Salo, M., and H. Valimaki
1981   Infant Mortality, Birth Interval and Economic Development: An Exam-
        ple From Rural Finland. *Medical Anthropology* 5:507–22.
Scrimshaw, N.; C. Taylor; and J. Gordon
1966   *Interactions of Nutrition and Infection.* WHO Monograph Series, No.
        57. Geneva: World Health Organization.

Stavenhagen, R.
> 1967   Social Aspects of Agrarian Structure in Mexico. In *Agrarian Problems and Peasant Movements in Latin America,* R. Stavenhagen, ed. Garden City, N.Y.: Anchor Books.

Torun, B., V. R. Young, and W. Rand
> 1981   Protein-Energy Requirements of Developing Countries: Evaluation of New Data. *Food and Nutrition Bulletin Supplement.* No. 5. Tokyo: United Nations University.

MARK EDELMAN

From Costa Rican Pasture to North American Hamburger

SINCE THE MID-1950S, THE CENTRAL AMERICAN COUNTRIES HAVE experienced a new export boom based on the production of beef for the United States market. This paper first discusses the changes in U.S. beef production and consumption patterns that lie behind the expansion of export-oriented ranching in Central America. It then describes for one Central American country—Costa Rica—the roles played by international lending institutions, the national state, and the organized cattle lobby in bringing about this integration into the world beef market. Finally, it discusses the effects of export beef production on domestic beef consumption, land use, and Costa Rica's current economic crisis. It is suggested that "decisions" about who eats what cannot be understood apart from the unequal power relations that exist between rich and poor nations and between social classes in the underdeveloped countries.

The Changing Structure of the U.S. Beef Market

The incorporation of the Central American countries into the world beef market represents part of a relatively recent trend in which a few advanced capitalist nations, beset by a secular rise in beef prices, have attempted to maintain domestic consumption levels by relying on the output of underdeveloped countries where production costs are considerably lower. The price of a steer in Central America is generally about 40 percent lower than that of a comparable U.S. steer (Roux 1975:363). In the 1970s the United States, with 6 percent of the world's population and 9 percent of its cattle, accounted for 28 percent of global beef consumption (Solís 1981:62). The United States also accounts for almost one-third of world beef imports and, with respect to the Central American beef-exporting nations, exercises true monopsony power (USDA 1976:14).

Steers, of course, tend to have the finest meat, while cows sent to slaughter are usually quite tough from years of calving and are suitable primarily for industrial- or hamburger-quality meat. Traditionally in the United States, this industrial-grade meat was supplied largely by milk cows past the age of reproduction. In recent decades there has been a relative decline in the size of the dairy herd in relation to the beef cattle herd. Since the cows of the beef breeds are generally of greater longevity than dairy cows (Slutsky 1979:107), and since the consumption of hamburger and industrial-grade beef has been increasing, wholesalers were forced to look abroad for new sources of supply.

Production costs and beef prices in the United States have fluctuated in a 9- to 12-year "cattle cycle" for approximately the last four decades. The size of the commercial cattle slaughter in the United States is closely tied to herd size, which is in turn related to the cost of cattle feed. The steer-corn ratio—that is, the ratio of beef steer price to corn price—is the key measure of profitability in raising grain-fed cattle. In general, there is an inverse relationship between steer-corn ratio and herd size. A high steer-corn ratio is indicative of above-average profit opportunities and encourages ranchers to expand the herd by keeping more heifers for breeding purposes. Heifers usually calve at 27 to 33 months of age. These calves come to slaughter about 18 months later. It thus takes almost four years to produce a "finished" steer. The expansion phase of the cattle cycle is conditioned by this rate of increase and usually lasts six to eight years.

At the end of the expansion phase, when the quantity of beef produced can only be marketed at lower prices, ranchers and feed-lot operators are breeding and raising animals at a loss. They begin to sell cows and heifers, thus bringing about a contraction in herd size, lower prices, and a decreased capacity for herd increase. Cattle are brought into feed-lots at an older age and fed for a shorter time to a lower finished weight. The contraction phase generally lasts two to six years. When the cattle inventory is reduced enough to create high prices, those farmers who have not gone out of business begin to rebuild their herds.

Recently it has been demonstrated that the internationalization of the Latin American cattle complex has led to "the emergence of a world cattle cycle" (Sanderson 1982:14). There are several reasons why the U.S. cattle cycle has strong repercussions in the international beef market. Pressures brought by the U.S. livestock industry to limit imports are greatest during periods of low prices. Import quotas have—since 1980—been adjusted in order to dampen cyclical price fluctuations. Finally, the price paid for foreign grass-fed beef in the producing countries is directly tied to the price of cow meat in the Chicago market.

Until 1964 nations seeking to become exporters of beef to the United States had only to receive certification of their packing facilities by the U.S. Department of Agriculture (USDA). Certification was based on both the cleanliness of the particular packinghouse and the health of the national herd. The rapid rise in U.S. beef imports in the early 1960s led the cattle industry to press for protection. In 1964 the cattle cycle was nearing the end of its expansion phase, and ranchers and feed-lot operators began to hold back livestock from packing-houses in order to protest against low prices, which they charged were exacer-bated by imports (Wall Street Journal 1964). Low beef prices did not, of course, evoke any outcry from organized consumers or the fast-food lobby. The bal-ance of forces in Congress between consumer groups and the fast-food indus-try, on the one hand, and the cattle industry, on the other, was favorable to the latter.

Public Law 88-482, passed in 1964 and in effect through December 1979, established a basic import ceiling of 725 million pounds for fresh, chilled, and frozen beef, which was to be readjusted annually by the percentage of increase or decrease in domestic production in the current and the two preceding years. The quotas were ostensibly voluntary, because the State Department was con-cerned that mandatory quotas might violate the General Agreement on Tariffs and Trade. Nevertheless, if the secretary of agriculture determined that beef imports would exceed 110 percent of the base quotas during a given year, the president had either to make the quotas mandatory or to suspend them al-together. If an exporting nation violated the "voluntary" agreement, the presi-dent could halt the flow of its meat by invoking powers that pre-dated the 1964 law.

The import guidelines established under P.L. 88-482 tended to increase im-ports when production was rising and to decrease them when production was falling, thus exaggerating changes in supplies and prices. Because imports ex-ceeded the 110 percent "trigger level" in every year between 1970 and 1979, the contention between the livestock industry and the consumer and fast-food-chain groups focused largely on the president's ability to enforce or suspend quotas, with cattle ranchers pressuring for enforcement and the other groups for suspension.

In 1978 Congress passed a bill with a "countercyclical" quota formula strong-ly supported by the livestock industry, which had been suffering from the con-traction phase of the cattle cycle since 1974. The bill would have allowed small-er increases in imports than those which presidents had commonly allowed in times of tight supplies and rising prices. At the meeting of the Organization of American States Trade Council in October 1978, representatives of Guatema-la, El Salvador, Costa Rica, and the Dominican Republic lobbied U.S. officials for the veto of the proposed legislation (Quarterly Economic Report 1979:11). President Carter did veto the bill, charging that it was inflationary.

On December 31, 1979, however, the countercyclical legislation (P.L. 96-177) was approved. It curbed the president's power to allow beef imports and, after an initial increase to counter the effects of pre-1979 contraction, lowered import quotas toward the end of the expansion phase of the U.S. cattle cycle, until approximately 1986 or 1987. Then quotas would gradually increase to cushion consumers against the anticipated cyclical contraction. In the case of Costa Rica, it was estimated that after 1985 the U.S. market will no longer be able to absorb possible increases in exportable beef production (SEPSA 1980:21).

Beef prices in the United States, while influenced fundamentally by supply and demand, are set on a daily basis by the editors of the *National Provisioner Daily Market and News Service,* "a small group of men in a ramshackle old brownstone on Chicago's Near North Side" (Swanson 1979:433). The price statistics published in this industry market report, popularly known as the "Yellow Sheet," do not include highs or lows or volume traded, yet they are used to set prices for as much as 90 percent of all wholesale meat transactions and for a significant portion of futures contracts as well.

This system, which has been investigated by Congress and by Ralph Nader for possible price-fixing violations, is closely followed by packers and large ranchers in Central America, many of whom subscribe to the Yellow Sheet or receive the information it contains by telex. The price paid for steers in Central America's USDA-approved export packing plants is based directly on the Yellow Sheet's daily quotation for cow meat. The irony of this arrangement, in which Central America's best steer beef is sent abroad only to be classified as "cow meat," is not lost on the region's ranchers and consumers. In private, ranchers complain incessantly of this injustice, while their representatives maintain publicly that the U.S. market is by far the best, since alternatives in other countries, such as Venezuela or Israel, have proven to be less reliable in the long run. Central American consumers, as we shall see in more detail below, are forced to pay rapidly rising prices for low-quality meat on the domestic market because of the effects of higher export prices (and currency devaluations) on the availability and price of beef for national consumption.

In addition to the long-term fluctuations that accompany the cattle cycle, a secular increase in beef prices has been brought on in recent years by the high costs of energy-intensive grain cultivation, skyrocketing land values, rising populations, and rapidly eroding rangelands (Brown 1978a; Gardner and Nuckton 1979; Harris and Ross 1978; Ross 1980). The Department of Agriculture meat classification system, which assigns higher grades to fatty, "marbled" beef, has encouraged U.S. ranchers to specialize in producing steers for feed-lots, and has thus contributed to the reliance on imports for meeting much of the demand for industrial-grade beef. Whereas 63 percent of the meat produced in the United States in 1959 was classified by the Department of Agriculture as "supreme," "select," or "good," by 1972, 79 percent of U.S.-produced meat was placed in those categories (Solís 1981:63).

In spite of their preference for grain-fed beef, consumers in the United States have been decreasing the proportion of their beef consumption derived from steak and other choice cuts and increasing that based on grass-fed beef. The rapid growth of fast-food chains, which were able to provide meals at close to the cost of eating at home, has been a major force behind the shift to grass-fed beef. By 1977 nearly 40 percent of all beef used in the United States was consumed as ground beef (Fischer 1976). In 1976 an estimated 80 percent of the steak sold in U.S. restaurants was actually "fake steak" or "log steak," a product fabricated from tough grass-fed beef that is tenderized and then reconstituted using recently developed meat-processing technology (Forbes 1976).

This shift in production and consumption patterns in the United States and the relatively low prices of foreign, grass-fed steers are the major forces behind the importation of industrial-grade beef. Australia and New Zealand are by far the largest suppliers of beef to the United States. In recent years, however, tiny 51,000-square-kilometer Costa Rica has vied with Canada for the position of third-largest supplier of beef to the United States. Imported beef usually accounts for less than 10 percent of domestic production in the United States. It should be remembered, however, that what may seem of minor significance in the United States looks different when seen from Central America, where pasture is often the major land use and beef a key source of foreign exchange, and where fragile national economies are vulnerable to price fluctuations and politically motivated changes in import quotas.

The Rise of Export Beef Production in Costa Rica

The changing structure of demand for beef in the United States has had a particularly strong effect on new exporting countries in Central America, since the beef of traditional exporters, such as Argentina, was banned from the United States because of the presence of hoof and mouth disease in South America. The integration of Costa Rica into this new international market was facilitated by the policies of international lending organizations and the Costa Rican state, as well as by the pressures of the local cattle lobby.

International lending institutions have played a key role in the Central American cattle boom by financing road construction and related infrastructure, funding livestock improvement programs, providing production credit, and forcing national governments and banking systems to reorganize their operations to expedite the expansion of ranching (DeWitt 1977; León, Barboza, and Aguilar 1981: chap. 5; Williams, in press). Allocations by organizations like the World Bank and the Inter-American Development Bank (IDB) frequently constitute direct or indirect subsidies for private capital in particular sectors of agriculture in the underdeveloped countries (Feder 1980). The World Bank's 1975 sector policy paper on agricultural credit reported that "lending for livestock operations continues to be the single most important type of credit activity" (quoted in Payer 1982:214). World Bank loan contracts with Costa Rica *required* the creation by the country's Central Bank of a cattle technical extension division (León, Barboza, and Aguilar 1981:V-41).

Similarly, IDB loans to the Banco Nacional de Costa Rica specified that an animal husbandry and veterinary section had to be established in the Banco's branches in four of the country's principal cattle-raising zones (León, Barboza, and Aguilar 1981:V-41). In 1961–69, the IDB's first decade of operations, fully 21 percent of the loans made to Costa Rica from ordinary capital resources were for the cattle sector (IDB 1969:51). The bank's first loan to Costa Rica was $2.6 million for livestock improvement. It was channeled to 193 large ranchers through the Banco Nacional. As of 1977 the IDB had directed $15.7 million to livestock credit, more than one-third of its total loans to the agricultural sector (IDB 1980:8). Such lending agency decisions arose from and helped to create the growing international beef market. They continue to stimulate the flow of private capital to the cattle sector and help to ensure the profitability of what has long been one of the least lucrative of agricultural enterprises, the extensively operated livestock hacienda.

Although the expansion of export beef production has occurred throughout Latin America (Buxedas 1977; Da Veiga 1975; DeWalt 1982; Feder 1980; Nations and Nigh 1978; Parsons 1976; Partridge 1984; Rutsch 1980; Shane 1980; Slutsky 1979), the particular nature of the Costa Rican state in the post-1948 period has contributed to what is probably the most dramatic and thorough process of this kind anywhere on the continent. The social democrat–controlled junta that came to power in the wake of the 1948 civil war (Rojas 1979) drew much of its political support from ascendant middle sectors whose hopes of consolidating themselves as a new fraction of the bourgeoisie had been frustrated by the existing monopolies that dominated Costa Rica's banks, sugar mills, and coffee-processing industry. The traditional oligarchy lost much of its political power in the aftermath of the war, since the social democrats controlled the armed forces of the victorious side. In the 18 months of rule by decree that followed the war, the social democrats were able to lay the groundwork for a new model of economic development based on massive state support for import substitution industrialization and agricultural export diversification.

The junta's nationalization of the banking system allowed credit to be directed to areas of the country and to sectors of the economy that had previously been unable to obtain loans. The cattle sector, based in peripheral areas of the country not dominated by coffee and sugar and characterized by low start-up costs, was one of the few investment possibilities open to the junta's middle-class supporters (Solís 1981). Once beef exports started in the 1950s, bank branches were opened in many remote ranching areas, and the cattle sector absorbed a rapidly increasing share of national banking system credit.

With the help of the U.S. Agency for International Development (USAID) and the lending agencies, the Costa Rican state also made remarkably successful efforts to improve transport infrastructure in outlying areas. The completion of the Pan-American Highway and a large system of connecting roads proved crucial in linking distant ranches with export packing plants and in permitting refrigerator trailers to move rapidly from the plants to the ports. In addition to providing stimuli in the form of increased access to credit and improved transport, successive Costa Rican governments also established a significant network of institutions dedicated to livestock-related research, the extension of modern technology, and the training of technical personnel (León, Barboza, and Aguilar 1981). Although the effects of this effort, unparalleled in the other Central American countries, have been felt most directly on those large ranches dedicated to the breeding of stud bulls and exhibition animals, the Costa Rican herd as a whole has a higher proportion of brahmin blood than those of other countries in the region and is generally considered to compare favorably in terms of health, parturition rates, and other indices of technological advance (ibid.: chap. 3).

The rise of a powerful cattle lobby in the 1950s was another factor in the integration of Costa Rica into the international beef market. Founded first in the traditional ranching province of Guanacaste, the Cámaras de Ganaderos ("chambers of cattlemen") soon grew into a well-organized national federation whose members and supporters were strategically situated in the legislative assembly, the ministries, the banking system, and the major political parties. During its first year the Guanacaste Cámara succeeded in modifying the regulations governing loans for livestock production and, more importantly, secured legislative approval for a bill that permitted cattle exports (CGG 1954). In subsequent years the provincial Cámaras and the national federation proved to be one of the most effective lobbies in Costa Rica, not only bringing strong pressures to bear around issues of credit, pricing, and export policies, but also arguing against key aspects of the agrarian reform movement and for a more systematic repression of peasant squatters (CGG 1953–80).

The beginning of beef exports from Costa Rica followed successful efforts by the cattle lobby to pass legislation that permitted the sale abroad that were supposedly not needed to supply the domestic market. For nearly a century Costa Rica had imported substantial numbers of steers from Nicaragua. Only when this trade ended in 1950 was it considered feasible to begin exporting beef. The 1951 proclamation of national self-sufficiency in beef production was, however, as I have shown elsewhere in more detail (Edelman 1984), linked to a redefinition of the dietary needs of the population that was predicated on a sharply reduced level of beef consumption. This early willingness to employ political criteria in redefining dietary needs was later taken to its logical conclusion when beef exports began and national nutrition was explicitly sacrificed for foreign exchange.

The Effects of Beef Exports on Domestic Beef Consumption

At first, when exports began in 1953, live animals were shipped to Peru and the Caribbean. But in 1958, with the opening of the first modern, USDA-approved packing plant, exports increasingly took the form of chilled, deboned beef and went almost exclusively to the United States and Puerto Rico. As international lending institutions, government banks and extension agencies, and private investors poured resources into the livestock sector, the cattle herd grew rapidly. Beef exports expanded to become, after coffee and bananas, Costa Rica's third most important source of foreign exchange, although accounting in most years for less than 10 percent of total export earnings. Measured in head, close to one-half of the country's total slaughter has been exported since the 1960s (Table 22.1). The percentage of total beef weight extracted that is sent abroad has consistently been greater, however, since only steers—the largest animals—are processed for export.[1] Although herd growth has outstripped ppoulation growth and the per capita availability of beef has thus theoretically increased, the export of roughly one-half of the country's production has in fact brought about a trend toward lowered beef consumption that has only recently begun to level off (Table 22.2).

Figures on per capita beef consumption must be interpreted with some caution, since the methods used to calculate them vary considerably from country to country and from series to series. Before Costa Rica entered the international beef market, annual per capita beef consumption, based on estimates of slaughter weight, averaged 31.0 kilograms (DGEC 1949:189). Retail weight may be conservatively estimated at 51 percent of slaughter weight (SEPSA 1980:118), giving a 1949 annual per capita consumption figure of 15.8 kilograms. Per capita consumption was probably higher, however. Yields were almost certainly greater for the "creole" livestock that predominated before the export boom, since these animals did not have the heavy bones and hooves and cartilaginous hump characteristic of today's brahmin cattle.

Even if one accepts a baseline figure of 15.8 kilograms, however, the USDA data in Table 22.2, which are based on retail weight, bear out the critics' (Holden 1981; Parsons 1976; Spielman 1972) claims that local consumption has been sacrificed to meet foreign demand. A more recent work, which is probably the most careful compparative study of Central American beef consumption figures (Williams: in press), suggests that entrance into the export market was accompanied everywhere by drastic declines in beef consumption, which were only attenuated or reversed when herds expanded to meet export demand and increasing amounts of cow meat, offal, and contaminated or diseased steer meat unacceptable to U.S. inspectors were placed on local markets.

Meat contamination is, in fact, relatively common. Central American ranchers commonly clear their pastures with herbicides containing dioxin, and the excessive use of pesticides on cotton and rice crops in many ranching areas has become a scandal throughout the region (Romero 1976). Not surprisingly, most of the Central American countries suffer periodic closings of their export slaughterhouses when USDA inspectors detect chemical residues in their meat. Beef that local packinghouses know does not meet USDA standards is routinely channeled to domestic markets.

In Costa Rica, the allocation of animals between the domestic and export markets is the responsibility of the National Production Council (CNP), the principal public sector commodities agency. The CNP is charged with determining how much domestic demand for beef exists and how much surplus production is available for export. Each year it gathers declarations from all cattle producers about the number of animals they have and the number ready for slaughter. The CNP then calculates the "internal consumption quota" by multiplying 18.2 kilograms by the estimated population that year; what remains is placed in the "export quota."

Although an annual per capita consumption of 18.2 kilograms of beef would in most cases be adequate, providing that other proteins are also part of the diet, this amount is frequently not available on the domestic market because of the pressures of the cattle lobby and the artifices of individual ranchers. The export quota is allocated among different producers according to the number of steers declared by each rancher. The ranchers, however, routinely declare more steers than they actually have so that they can sell more animals at the higher price paid by the export packing plants. This practice also has the effect of inflating the CNP's estimate of the total herd and thus brings about frequent domestic shortages, since the internal consumption quota is calculated with exaggerated figures and beef that should have been placed on local markets is shipped to the United States.

The immediate cause of the decline in per capita beef consumption is the steep rise in beef prices brought about by the strength of export demand. Price ceilings for cattle and meat for domestic consumption are set by the government and fluctuate within relatively narrow margins. Nevertheless, export prices, which are tied to the Yellow Sheet's rate for cow meat and are always substantially higher than domestic prices, exert constant upward pressure on domestic prices. The greater the disparity between the two price levels, the

TABLE 22.1. Costa Rica: Beef Exports and Internal Consumption, 1969–81 (in Thousands of Head)

			Export		
				On Hoof (live)	
Year/Period	Total Slaughter	Total for Export	Steers Processed	Bulls	Females
1969	201.6	89.1	89.1	0	0
1970	216.6	98.0	98.0	0	0
1971	235.0	110.3	110.3	0	0
1972	275.0	148.9	126.2	1.0	21.7
1973	100.1	40.4	36.5	0.3	3.6
1974	276.3	161.9	136.6	0.3	25.1
1975	315.9	176.3	150.6	0.4	25.3
1976	309.9	173.5	170.5	0.6	2.5
1977	388.7	174.1	160.3	10.6	3.2
1978	410.2	189.3	186.3	1.8	1.2
1979	395.4	176.1	174.5	0.1	1.5
1980	348.0	137.8	137.8	0	0
1981	408.8	188.5	186.1	1.1	1.3

SOURCE: Departamento de Ganadería, Consejo Nacional de Producción, Guanacaste (1982).
NOTE: Before 1974, years refer to the 12 months from July to June of the following year; 1973 refers to the second half of 1973. After 1973, years are calendar years.

more the ranchers seek to elude CNP controls and divert steers to the export plants. With the appearance of domestic scarcities, a periodic occurrence, the government's regulatory bodies come under increasing pressure to grant price increases in order to ensure domestic supplies.

When external prices are especially high, ranchers seeking to free steers for export often slaughter young animals and females still able to bear young in order to supply the domestic market (OFIPLAN 1974:8). This practice, which has also been noted in Guatemala and other beef-exporting nations, limits the potential rate of increase of the national herd (ILPES 1967:II-45). Thus, the domestic beef price ceiling not only creates an incentive to evade quota rules and divert animals to the international market, but, in the absence of an effective inspection and enforcement apparatus, leads to short-sighted and destructive herd management policies.

This upward pressure on domestic prices places beef out of the reach of poor consumers, particularly in the rural areas. A 1978 study in Costa Rica found

	Internal Consumption			
Total for Internal Use	Bulls, Oxen, and Steers	Calves	Cows	% of Total Exported
112.6	46.9	2.3	63.3	44.2
118.6	42.7	4.3	71.5	45.2
124.7	41.5	5.1	78.0	46.9
126.2	34.4	4.4	87.3	54.1
59.7	16.1	1.3	42.3	40.4
114.4	43.9	2.2	68.3	58.6
139.7	47.1	2.7	89.8	55.8
136.5	21.2	4.5	110.7	56.0
214.6	34.1	6.2	174.3	44.8
220.9	43.7	4.1	173.1	46.1
219.3	44.5	2.1	172.8	44.5
210.2	67.2	1.0	142.0	39.6
220.3	58.1	2.0	160.2	46.1

that annual per capita beef consumption was 32.8 kilograms in urban areas, 17.1 kilograms in rural towns, and 10.6 kilograms in rural areas of dispersed population (*Encuesta Nacional de Nutrición,* cited in SEPSA 1980:26). Anthropometric data on one village in the livestock zone of Guanacaste indicate that the nutritional status of children diminished between 1966 and 1980 (Whiteford 1983).

Animal protein intake, however, varies not only with geography, but also with income level. In 1979 and 1981 a significant height disparity, thought to be due to nutritional differences, was found between public and private school children (Tristán et al. 1982). Overall, it was estimated in 1970 that the protein consumption of the lower-income half of the population was deficient by 30.1 percent, a serious enough deficit, but the lowest of any of the Central American countries (SIECA 1973:45). In Central America as a whole, it was estimated in 1970 that the average annual per capita beef consumption of the lower-income half of the population was 3.6 kilograms, whereas that of the upper 5

TABLE 22.2. Costa Rica and United States: Annual
Consumption of Beef and Red Meat, 1961–79
(in Kilograms per Capita)

	Costa Rica		United States	
Year	Beef/Veal	Total Red Meat	Beef/Veal	Total Red Meat
1961	11.4	15.1	42.8	79.1
1962	12.9	16.4	43.2	79.9
1963	11.9	15.3	45.4	82.6
1964	10.4	13.7	48.3	85.2
1965	13.4	17.0	48.3	81.0
1966	11.8	15.4	50.2	82.3
1967	10.2	13.3	51.0	85.8
1968	8.0	10.9	52.2	87.7
1969	10.0	13.0	52.0	83.0
1970	12.0	16.0	53.0	85.0
1971	13.0	17.0	52.0	87.0
1972	12.0	16.0	54.0	86.0
1973	10.0	14.0	51.0	80.0
1974	7.0	11.0	54.0	85.0
1975	10.2	13.4	56.6	83.1
1976	12.0	15.2	60.6	88.6
1977	16.9	20.1	58.8	87.7
1978	16.9	20.0	55.9	84.8
1979	16.5	19.8	49.8	82.7

SOURCE: USDA, *Foreign Agriculture Circulars,* FLM 2-77 (May 1977), FLM
5-78 (August 1978), and FLM 5-80 (August 1980).

percent of the population was 30.9 kilograms (Roux 1975:364). Furthermore, as Berg (1973) points out, meat in poor homes in the underdeveloped countries tends to be eaten by adults, usually the males, and is seldom included in the diets of the young.

Parsons (1976:125–26) has noted the paradox that increased beef exports may mean that larger supplies of low-priced viscera are available for poor consumers. This observation has been seized upon by officials of USAID, who, anxious to allay the critics' misgivings about declining protein consumption in beef-exporting countries, suggest that "edible offal and viscera [are] those parts of the animal's anatomy having the highest nutritive value" (quoted in Roux 1975:364–65).

It is unlikely, however, that the consumption of edible viscera is providing the poorest strata of Costa Rican society with adequate protein intake. The annual consumption requirement for all kinds of meat is estimated at 21.90 kilograms for children and 32.85 kilograms for adults, based on daily requirements of 60 grams for children and 90 grams for adults (SEPSA 1980:119). Nevertheless, as late as 1980 the average amount of *all* kinds of protein available was only 66 grams (Avilés and Mernies 1982:261). In 1978 the average annual per capita consumption of viscera for the country as a whole was estimated at 3.67 kilograms (SEPSA 1980:118). Those rural inhabitants whose average annual beef consumption is 10.6 kilograms would therefore have to eat roughly six times the amount of viscera eaten by the average Costa Rican in order to meet their minimum animal protein requirements of 32.85 kilograms. It is probable, therefore, that although viscera consumption has contributed to alleviating what would otherwise be serious protein malnutrition, it has not been sufficient to allow many poor Costa Ricans the recommended levels of meat in their diets. Moreover, it is precisely the fatty visceral tissues that are the principal collecting points in the animal's anatomy for the carcinogenic pesticide and herbicide residues that are frequently detected in Central American beef.

The "protein flight" (Dickinson 1973) from beef-exporting countries raises the issue of whether human protein needs are best met from animal sources. At times it is maintained (e.g., Lappé and Collins 1977:296) that grain-legume combinations are an adequate source of dietary protein and that agricultural and nutritional planning should concentrate on producing such combinations and making them available to nutritionally threatened sectors of the population. Recent work by Scrimshaw (1977) makes a strong case for the inclusion of more animal protein in the diets of the poor in the underdeveloped countries. Children, in particular, may have trouble obtaining their protein requirements from bulky grains and legumes. In addition, acute infections increase metabolic nitrogen loss, and gastrointestinal infections also lead to impaired nitrogen absorption. Episodes of acute infection bring about nitrogen depletion, which can only be corrected through consumption of "a margin above normal protein requirements" (Scrimshaw 1977:324). Since efficient protein utilization depends both on the quality of the protein itself and on an adequate caloric intake, calorie malnutrition exacerbates the effect of protein deficits. All of these considerations point to the need for a higher level of animal protein consumption among infection-prone and nutritionally threatened sectors of the population.

The Effects of Beef Exports on Ecology and Land Use

There is abundant evidence that the rapid herd growth that followed Central America's entrance into the world beef market occurred in large part because of the expansion of pastures rather than because of any significant intensification of production on existing grasslands. Although some intensification of production has resulted from improved breeding practices that permit faster growth, higher parturition, and higher rates of extraction of animals from the herd, the overall tendency of ranchers has been to minimize investments in order to continue turning out a low-priced product for the export market. This reluctance to invest, discussed in more detail below, has meant that the cattle boom has stimulated an unprecedented spread of grazing lands.

In Costa Rica, the area in pasture more than doubled between 1950 and 1973, from 622,402 hectares to 1,558,053 (DGEC 1950:57; DGEC 1973:13). In 1973 pasture constituted 76.1 percent of the total 2,048,512 hectares in agricultural and livestock uses; since many of the additional 283,571 hectares of brushlands counted by the census are also used for grazing cattle, as much as 89.9 percent of the country's productive land may be used primarily for livestock. This horizontal expansion of grassland has occurred at the cost of a dramatic destruction of Costa Rica's forests. In 1950, 72 percent of the country was covered with forests; 23 years later, only 49 percent of the country remained forested; and by 1978 the forest cover had been reduced to 34 percent of Costa Rica's territory (Sáenz 1981:26). This process of carving pasture out of the forest has been linked to a variety of ecological problems, including decreased rainfall, flooding, poor drainage, and soil erosion (Hagenauer 1980; Parsons 1976).

The spread of pasture has also occurred at the expense of subsistence crop production, particularly in traditional ranching areas, where cattle haciendas once tolerated peasant use of idle lands. In the traditional ranching province of Guanacaste, the area devoted to maize—the principal subsistence crop—declined from 14,711 to 12,045 hectares between 1950 and 1973. In the country as a whole, the picture was not much different: the area used for crop agriculture grew from 316,175 to 490,458 hectares, but this signified a decline from 33.4 to 23.9 in the percentage of utilized land under cultivation (DGEC 1950, 1973). Until special incentives were offered to rice-producers in the mid-1970s, the replacement of crop land by pasture meant that Costa Rica was forced to import large quantities of basic foods, making it one of the 14 countries worldwide pointed to by Brown (1978b:137) "as rapidly approaching primary dependence on imported foodstuffs."

Those smallholding peasants who produced the food crops were frequently led to abandon their plots to the expanding cattle ranches. The actual mechanisms through which this process occurred ranged from forced evictions and fraudulent titling to simple purchases by large landowners. Most importantly, however, the structure of the rural job market changed with expanding pastures, since livestock production absorbs very little labor. Whereas crop agriculture in Costa Rica employs an average of one worker per 2.9 hectares, in the livestock sector—including the more intensively exploited dairy farms—one worker attends an average of 47.6 hectares (SEPSA 1980:5). In the mid-1970s, when mechanized rice production began to expand in some of the ranching areas, it did little to alleviate the unemployment problem created by the growth of ranching. Sugar cane, the other major crop in the ranching areas, provides seasonal harvesting jobs but generally requires substantial investments that make it difficult for smallholding peasants to cultivate.

Not surprisingly, the major ranching zones are continually "exporting" people to other areas of the country. In Guanacaste, for example, in the 1968–73 period, it is estimated that the equivalent of over 50 percent of the province's natural population growth migrated elsewhere in search of employment (Fernández, Schmidt, and Basauri 1976:102–3). Some cantons within the province actually show zero growth or even declines in total population in recent years, something that is particularly striking in light of the fact that Costa Rica at this time had one of the highest birthrates in the world. It is important to emphasize that this expulsion of workers from the rural areas is taking place in a context where other sectors of the economy are not able to absorb them.

Another reason for the expulsion of population from the ranching regions involves the concentration of land ownership that is associated with beef cattle production. Grazing cattle is profitable only on a large scale and requires access to sizable properties, features that place it beyond reach for smallholding families. Land is needed not only for pasturing the animals—usually at densities of around one head per hectare—but also as collateral for the bank credit that is channeled disproportionately to medium- and large-size ranchers (Solís 1981). Census data on herd ownership indicate that 70 of the largest ranchers—the 0.1 percent of the total possessing estates of 2,500 or more hectares—own 9.7 percent of the cattle in the country; at the same time, the smallest 77 percent of the farm units with cattle—those under 50 hectares—own only 23 percent of the herd. Moreover, the fattening of cattle, which is the fastest, least risky, and most profitable stage of beef production and which requires access to substantial areas of pasture, is concentrated on the larger ranches. The small diversified farms that breed feeder calves for the large haciendas are less able to maintain inventories to cushion themselves from losses that may be incurred as a result of price fluctuations, seasonal drought, or other causes.

Beef Exports and the Costa Rican Economy

The beef cattle sector, while occupying three-quarters of the country's productive land, generates only about 10 percent of its foreign exchange and by far the lowest amount of value added per hectare of any agricultural activity. The dominance of this type of production presents serious problems in an economy beset by tendencies toward stagnation. Much of the expansion of pastures has occurred on lands that are suitable for cultivation and could generate greater income and employment if used for crops. Although pasture occupied an estimated 1,738,000 hectares in 1976, only 1,310,000 hectares in the country were considered suitable for that use. At the same time, of the 854,000 hectares considered suitable for either perennial or annual crops, only 527,200 hectares—61.7 percent—were actually cultivated (OPSA 1979:60); much of the remainder is in pasture, a use that would not be predicted from economic rules of optimal allocation of resources (CEPAL 1973:29; 1975:373).

The persistence of the seemingly irrational, extensively exploited livestock hacienda can only be explained by an examination of such factors as the massive flow of credit resources toward the cattle sector, the Costa Rican tax system, the way in which the country is integrated into the U.S. beef market, and the risks of agriculture in the key ranching zones. Once Costa Rica began to export beef, credit directed to the livestock sector grew almost three times as fast as that for crop cultivation, and much of it was in the form of long-term loans at low rates of interest (Solís 1981). Except in 1976–78, when the inflation rate was around 8 percent, this cattle credit has generally been granted at a negative real rate of interest. As might be expected under such circumstances, many of the loans are invested in savings certificates that bear higher interest or, particularly when inflation is high or currency devaluations are rumored, in purchasing more pasture lands. In either case, the low capitalization and low productivity of the traditional hacienda are maintained. Moreover, the fact that more highly capitalized farms pay higher taxes (Salas and Barahona 1980:74) further discourages the intensification of production.

The ranchers' fears of reductions in the U.S. beef quota, periods of low prices, and temporary market closings also have this effect. In this uncertain economic environment, land is seen as one of the few safe investments. Frequently land speculators will run cattle on their holdings primarily to prevent the agrarian reform agency from declaring the property unproductive, a step that would permit it to be expropriated. Finally, in areas such as Guanacaste that are characterized by widely varying annual precipitation, crop agriculture is often a high-risk undertaking (Hagenauer 1980). On mixed livestock and crop farms, cattle are often viewed as a kind of insurance against the losses that may result if too much rain falls on the cotton or too little on the rice.

The economic crisis of 1980—marked by worsened balance-of-payments difficulties, a currency devaluation of close to 500 percent, and inflation of around 100 percent (Edelman 1983)—must be understood at least in part as the result of a stagnant productive structure, the most conspicuous sector of which is constituted by the extensively operated livestock haciendas. As has been noted, the beef export economy has generated a host of problematic side effects, ranging from unemployment, unproductive investments, and irrational land use to malnutrition, ecological destruction, and concentration of wealth. The crisis of the early 1980s has exacerbated many of these problems. Ironcially, two developments in the United States—reduced beef consumption as a result of the recession and lower cattle-feeding costs as a result of recent massive grain harvests—had a further negative impact on Costa Rican beef exporters and on the Costa Rican economy as a whole. The quota reductions established by the U.S. anti-cyclical law for the rest of the 1980s portended further difficulties for the Central American beef industry. (However, in Costa Rica, because of massive U.S. economic aid the worse symptoms of crisis have been temporarily alleviated during the mid-1980s.)

Conclusion: Deciding Who Eats What

It is clear that beef production and consumption in Costa Rica are associated with significant historical and cultural "meanings," such as the prestige attached to being a cattle man or to eating fine cuts of meat. It would be difficult to argue, however, that these ideal determinants have played more than an auxiliary role in the new processes of capital accumulation that accompanied Costa Rica's entrance into the world beef market. The beef export economy in Costa Rica illustrates clearly how political and economic power, operating at various levels, determines not only who eats what, but who eats how much, and where. The beef export trade was established in Costa Rica as a result of market forces, pressures from international lending agencies, and the efforts of organized ranching interests. Policy-makers in underdeveloped countries have little ability or desire to resist such an onslaught, unless the class character and political priorities of the government permit the exploration of alternative models of development. For Costa Rica and Central America, the dietary, ecological, and economic effects of this forced decision making have been little short of disastrous.

Acknowledgments

Research for this article was supported by the Inter-American Foundation, the Social Science Research Council, the Institute for the Study of World Politics and the Sigma Xi Scientific Research Society. Responsibility for the content, however, belongs only to the author.

Note

1. A 1982 report by the agricultural attache of the U.S. embassy states that "traditionally, about 35 to 40 percent of Costa Rica's beef production is consumed domestically with the balance being exported, mainly to the U.S." (USDA 1982:6).

References Cited

Avilés, R., and J. Mernies
    1982   La Disponibilidad de Alimentos en Costa Rica: 1971–1980. *Revista Médica del Hospital Nacional de Niños* 17:255–64.
Berg, A.
    1973   *The Nutrition Factor: Its Role in National Development.* Washington, D.C.: Brookings Institution.
BID (Banco Interamericano de Desarrollo)
    1969   *Informe Anual.* Washington, D.C.: BID.
    1980   *El BID en Costa Rica.* Washington, D.C.: BID.
Brown, L.
    1978a   Why Meat Will Cost More and More and More . . . *Human Nature* 1(9):84–85.
    1978b   *The Twenty-Ninth Day.* New York: Norton.
Buxedas, M.
    1977   El Comercio Internacional de Carne Vacuna y las Exportaciones de los Paises Atrasados. *Comercio Exterior* (Mexico) 27:1494–1509.
CEPAL (Comisión Económica Para América Latina)
    1973   *Tenencia de la Tierra y Desarrollo Rural en Centroamérica.* San José: Editorial Universitaria Centroamericana.
CGG (Cámara de Ganaderos de Guanacaste)
    1954   *Informe Anual Período 1953–1954.* Liberia: CGG.
    1953–80   Minutes of meetings. Liberia: Archives of CGG.
Da Veiga, J. S.
    1975   A la Poursuite du Profit: Quand les Multinationales Font du "Ranching." *Le Monde Diplomatique,* September, pp. 12–13.
DeWalt, B.
    1982   The Big Macro Connection: Population, Grain and Cattle in Southern Honduras. *Culture and Agriculture* 14:1–12.
DeWitt, R. P.
    1977   *The Inter-American Development Bank and Political Influence with Special Reference to Costa Rica.* New York: Praeger.
DGEC (Dirección General de Estadística y Censos)
    1949   *Anuario Estadístico.* San José: DGEC.
    1950   *Censo Agropecuario.* San José: DGEC.
    1973   *Censo Agropecuario.* San José: DGEC.
Dickinson, J. C.
    1973   Protein Flight from Latin America: Some Social and Ecological Consid-

erations. *Latin American Development Issues,* David Hill, ed., *Proceedings of the Conference of Latin Americanist Geographers* 3:127–32.

Edelman, M.

1983   Recent Literature on Costa Rica's Economic Crisis. *Latin American Research Review* 18:166–80.

1985   Land and Labor in an Expanding Economy: Agrarian Capitalism and the Hacienda System in Guanacaste Province, Costa Rica, 1880–1982. Ph.D. dissertation, Columbia University.

Feder, E.

1980   The Odious Competition Between Man and Animal Over Agricultural Resources in the Underdeveloped Countries. *Review* 3:463–500.

Fernández, M. E.; A. Schmidt; and V. Basauri

1976   *La Población de Costa Rica.* San José: Editorial Universidad de Costa Rica.

Fischer, N. H.

1976   Ground Beef Consumption Hits Record as U.S. Becomes a "Hamburger Society." *Wall Street Journal,* October 18, p. 34.

Forbes

1976   Bum Steer? All that Sizzles These Days Is Not Necessarily Steak. *Forbes,* July 15, p. 47.

Gardner, B. D., and C. F. Nuckton

1979   Factors Affecting Agricultural Land Prices. *California Agriculture* 33(1):4–6.

Hagenauer, W.

1980   Análisis Agro-Metereológico en la Zona de Cañas y Bagaces (Guanacaste) en los Anos 1921 a 1979. *Informe Semestral* (Instituto Geográfico Nacional), July–December, pp. 45–59.

Harris, M., and E. B. Ross

1978   How Beef Became King. *Psychology Today* 12(5):88–94.

Holden, R. H.

1981   Central America Is Growing More Beef and Eating Less, as the Hamburger Connection Widens. *Multinational Monitor* 2(10):17–18.

IDB (Inter-American Development Bank)

1969   *Informe Anual.* Washington, D.C.: IDB.

1980   *El BID en Costa Rica.* Washington, D.C.: IDB.

Instituto Latinoamericano de Planificación Económica y Social (ILPES)

1967   *Centroamérica: Análisis del Sector Externo y de su Relación con el Desarrollo Económico.* Santiago, Chile: ILPES.

Lappé, F. M., and J. Collins

1977   *Food First!* New York: Houghton-Mifflin.

León, J. S.; C. Barboza V.; and J. Aguilar

1981   Desarrollo Tecnológico en la Ganadería de carne. Mimeographed. San José: Consejo Nacional de Investigaciones Científicas y Tecnológicas.

Nations, J. D., and R. B. Nigh

1978   Cattle, Cash, Food, and Forest: The Destruction of the American Tropics and the Lacandon Maya Alternative. *Culture and Agriculture* 6:1–5.

559

Oficina de Planificación Nacional (OFIPLAN)
    1974   *Estrategia y Plan Global: Versión Preliminar.* San José: OFIPLAN.
Oficina de Planificación del Sector Agropecuario (OPSA)
    1979   *Diagnostico del Sector Agropecuario de Costa Rica 1962–1976.* Mimeographed. San José: OPSA.
Parsons, J. J.
    1976   Forest to Pasture: Development or Destruction? *Revista de Biología Tropical* 24(suppl. 1):121–38.
Partridge, W. L.
    1984   The Humid Cattle Ranching Complex: Cases from Panama Reviewed. *Human Organization* 43(1):76–80.
Payer, C.
    1982   *The World Bank: A Critical Analysis.* New York: Monthly Review Press.
Quarterly Economic Report
    1979   *Quarterly Economic Report: Guatemala, El Salvador, Honduras.* no. 1. Economist Intelligence Unit. London: The Economist.
Rojas Bolaños, M.
    1979   *Lucha Social y Guerra Civil en Costa Rica.* San José: Editorial Porvenir.
Romero García, A.
    1976   Plaguicidas en los Agroecosistemas Tropicales: Evaluación del Conocimiento Actual del Problema. *Revista de Biología Tropical* 24(suppl. 1):69–77.
Ross, E. B.
    1980   Patterns of Diet and Forces of Production: An Economic and Ecological History of the Ascendancy of Beef in the United States Diet. In *Beyond the Myths of Culture: Essays in Cultural Materalism,* E. B. Ross, ed., pp. 181–225. New York: Academic Press.
Roux, B.
    1975   Expansion du Capitalisme et Développement du Sous Développement: L'integration de l'Amérique Centrale dans le Marché Mondial de la Viande Bovine. *Revue du Tiers Monde* 16:355–80.
Rutsch, M.
    1980   *La Cuestión Ganadera en México.* Mexico: Centro de Investigación Para la Integración Social.
Sáenz Maroto, A.
    1981   *Erosión, Deforestación y Control de Inundaciones en Costa Rica.* San José: Facultad de Agronomía, Universidad de Costa Rica.
Salas Marrero, O., and R. Barahona Israel
    1980   *Derecho Agrario.* 2d ed. San Jose: Oficina de Publicaciones de la Universidad de Costa Rica.
Sanderson, S. E.
    1982   The Emergence of the "World Steer": Internationalization and Foreign Domination in Latin American Cattle Production. Paper read at the International Congress of Americanists, University of Manchester.

Scrimshaw, N.

1977   Through a Glass Darkly: Discerning the Practical Implications of Human Dietary Protein-Energy Relationships. *Nutrition Reviews* 35:321–37.

SEPSA (Secretaría Ejecutiva de Planificación Sectorial Agropecuaria)

1980   *Características de la Ganadería de Carne y Lineamientos de Política.* San José: SEPSA.

Shane, D. R.

1980   *Hoofprints on the Forest: An Inquiry into the Beef Cattle Industry in the Tropical Forest Areas of Latin America.* Washington, D.C.: Office of Environmental Affairs, U.S. Department of State.

SIECA (Secretaría Permanente del Tratado General de Integración Económica Centroamericana)

1973   *El Desarrollo Integrado de Centroamérica en la Presente Década.* Buenos Aires: Instituto Para la Integración de América Latina.

Slutsky, D.

1979   La Agroindustria de la Carne en Honduras. *Estudios Sociales Centroamericanos* 22:101–205.

Solís Avendaño, M. A.

1981   La Ganadería de Carne en Costa Rica. M.A. thesis, University of Costa Rica.

Spielman, H. O.

1972   La Expansión Ganadera en Costa Rica: Problemas de Desarrollo Agropecuario. *Informe Semestral* (Instituto Geográfico Nacional), July–December, pp. 33–57.

Swanson, W.

1979   Playing for High Steaks: The Meat Price Tip Sheet. *Nation* 229: no. 14 (November 3):433–35.

Tristán, M., et al.

1982   Evolución de la Talla 1979–1981. *Revista Médica del Hospital Nacional de Niños* 17:285–96.

USDA (United States Department of Agriculture)

1976   *U.S. Foreign Agricultural Trade Statistical Report.* Washington, D.C.: USDA.

1982   Costa Rica: Agricultural Situation. USDA Attache Report CS2007. San Jose: U.S. Embassy.

Wall Street Journal

1964   Packers Idle Workers, Meat Prices Rise as Farmers' Group Holds Back Livestock. *Wall Street Journal,* August 24.

Whiteford, M. B.

1983   From *Gallo Pinto* to *Jack's Snacks:* Observations on Dietary Change in Rural Costa Rican Village. Paper read at the annual meeting of the American Anthropological Association, Chicago.

Williams, R. G.

(in press)   *Coffee, Cotton, Cattle and the Crisis in Central America.* Chapel Hill: University of North Carolina Press.

PART VI

Discussion and Conclusions

ANNA ROOSEVELT

The Evolution of Human Subsistence

WHY IS FOOD IMPORTANT IN THE LARGER SCHEME OF THINGS? from the first efforts to explain human biological and cultural evolution, subsistence has been causally implicated. The very origin of the species is thought to have been related to changes in primate subsistence, and some of the major epochs of our cultural history are based on significant changes in food getting: from the hunting and gathering stage to the agricultural "revolution." Many scholars feel that changes in subsistence changed the trajectory of our history, and it is certain at least that our history has changed our food patterns.

On an individual level, food is held in great importance by most humans. Good and adequate food gives energy, health, satisfaction, and pleasure, and the lack of it gives distress, illness, and, eventually, death. In most societies the food quest takes up a significant amount of people's daily activity, and the preparation and consumption of food are hedged about by many rules and ceremonies (Chapter 16; Farb and Armelagos 1980). It is an ethnographic truism that people value and try to preserve their traditional diet. On the other hand, archaeology and history show that traditional diets have changed repeatedly when new foods or methods of preparation became available or when economic and demographic contexts changed (see especially Chapters 1, 2, 10, 11, and 17). The conservation of traditional diets and the creation of new ones are contradictory phenomena that must ultimately be resolved in our explanations.

A human food system is made up of actual behavior stemming from people's conscious and unconscious decisions, and so the explanation of the history of food behavior must make sense in terms of individuals' attitudes and actions. It is ultimately through the aggregate behavior of individuals that the broad historical and regional patterns in food production and consumption come into being. These two aspects of food behavior—that of individuals at a point in time and that of groups over long periods—need to be integrated if we are to approach comprehensive explanations. Hence the explanatory utility for anthropology of a focus on food preferences and aversions. Most ethnologists automatically approach food behavior from this angle, probably because preferences and aversions are what people talk about, and these categories presumably reflect how people interpret their own food behavior. Analytically, food preferences and aversions are a useful vehicle for understanding the generation of food-related behavior because they articulate between behavior and belief (Chapter 1). The connection is exceedingly important for us, because it links individual behavior, one of the most important locuses of adaptation, with larger systems. To look at things primarily in terms of group adaptation or the welfare of the system is to say that the interests of the system are somehow more important or powerful than those of the individual. It is important, as Harris and Ross have urged, to look at the interrelatedness of individuals with the larger systems in which they operate.

As Johnson and Rozin point out, in order to understand how food behavior is selected, we need to understand how people come to make decisions about it. I see the possibility of building an integrated body of low-level theory about how food preferences and aversions relate individual behavior with other factors. Ultimately we should be able, as both Harris and Yesner have suggested, to generate characterizations and then explanations for the food ideology and behavior of people with different types of subsistence systems, but we have hardly approached this level of theory making so far. The likelihood that food behavior is interrelated with other factors means that its context needs to be considered in our explanations. The context consists of the presence of other individuals (in various demographic, social, and political relationships) and the relation between subsistence, technology, and the physical environment. It is unlikely that the various factors related to food behavior constitute a potpourri of equally weighted causes, and thus there may be a hierarchy of adaptations dependent upon an individual's ability to act.

The idea of different levels of causal relationships brings up the question of the "adaptiveness" of human behavior in relation to foodways. Cultural ecologists focus on the use of culture to adapt humans to their social, biological, and physical environments. It is sometimes assumed that, through time, cultural adaptation to ecological conditions leads to a closer articulation of populations to their environment and a progressively better buffering between people and the world (e.g., Hayden 1981). This assumption is the basis of optimization theory. However, the archaeological record (Cohen and Armelagos 1984) often contradicts this assumption, showing that subsistence evolution has sometimes led to diets of decreased adequacy for many people. This seems to have happened in some places because of the strong selective influence of human population growth upon food systems, repeatedly encouraging the intensification of food production per unit of land to support an increasing number of people (Cohen 1977; Harris 1977). In this process highly productive and caloric foods have sometimes increased in the diet at the expense of foods rich in protein, vitamins, and trace elements.

Sociobiology, represented in this work by Hawkes and Winterhalder (Chapter 13), has a somewhat different point of view from cultural ecology. The two approaches are not necessarily mutually exclusive, but in most sociobiological hypotheses the test of human adaptation in any instance is the maximization of reproductive fitness by natural selection. This is a narrower view than that of cultural ecology, which considers the enhancement of individual health and survival to be adaptive regardless of the relative representation of individual's genes in future generations. For sociobiologists, effective human subsistence adaptations are expected to enhance selectively the inclusive fitness of the individuals who carry them out.

Our history has produced from the beginning a pattern of unequal access to food resources in which only a portion of each group is able to satisfy its requirements well and reliably. In "egalitarian" societies there has apparently been systematic limitation in access to food for women and children. The evidence lies in patterns of paleopathology that show heightened nutritional stress for pregnant and lactating women and for infants and young children. In stratified societies, there has been in addition subsistence inequality between underclasses and elites, to judge from contrasts in nutritional pathology rates between these groups (Cohen and Armelagos 1984; Rathje and McGuire 1982). The question relevant to sociobiology is whether the advantaged have been able to increase their genes' representation in successive populations. If they have not, then natural selection turns out to be a poor predictor of past human subsistence adaptation. The subsistence discrimination in age-sex classes within egalitarian societies did not apparently result in unequal representation of men's and women's genes in following generations. What seems to have happened in stratified societies is that the disadvantaged majority had poorer health and longevity than the elite few but a higher reproductive rate, so that they bequeathed increasing numbers of their genes to following populations, in contrast to the elite.

The archaeological and ethnographic record may show that the development of human culture for biosocial adaptation has meant that non-genetic behavioral modes of adaptation have come to dominate the solution of problems of feeding, survival, and reproduction, as Winterhalder (Chapter 12) and Hamilton (Chapter 4) have pointed out. The problem of changing evolutionary modes is basic to anthropological theory, reaching to the very heart of the reasons for the origin of our species, the rise of culture, and the explanation of cultural change.

At the species level, subsistence evolution has indeed produced increases in the number of humans on the earth and has in the process eliminated many other living species. The survival of the progressively larger, denser human groups as biological populations seems to have been enhanced, although disease and mortality rates appear to have been much higher in large, dense prehistoric populations than in small, dispersed ones. Many prehistoric populations seem to have become extinct, although their cultures, especially the characteristic regional subsistence patterns, have usually survived in a transmissible form.

With the newly refined methods for studying biological distance in both living and prehistoric populations (e.g., Black 1980, 1983; Droessler 1981; Reichs 1975), there is no excuse for continuing to test sociogiological theories by measuring inclusive fitness indirectly. We need to see which populations, subgroups, and individuals have persisted and expanded and what their adaptive strategies have been. In its present state of analysis, the archaeological record tells more about the fate of cultures than of populations, the result of our emphasis on cultural rather than biological developments in ancient times. By most measures, human cultural evolution has favored the survival of larger stratified societies at the expense of small-scale egalitarian ones, enormously increasing the number, area, and population of such regimes. It also seems clear that the evolution of subsistence and society has often favored the most powerful people, the elites, whose health and individual survival seem universally to have been enhanced in the long run, although their genes may not have increased in following generations relative to those of the disadvantaged. However, the evolution of social stratification has apparently achieved an absolute improvement in health only for the elite. The great majority of people experienced a downturn in health and nutrition through the evolution of stratified society (Cohen and Armelagos 1984; Rathje and McGuire 1982). Thus, although human cultural evolution has multiplied the number of people on the earth, it has not necessarily improved the quality of life for the majority of them.

These evolutionary considerations bring up more questions about the adaptiveness of food patterns and the concept of optimization. For example, the question "Optimization of what, and for whom?" needs to be answered. In many cases we can see that an optimal subsistence adaptation is not open to an individual, family, or group because of its inability to avoid certain existing constraints. We have, I think, come to agree, in the course of our discussions, that in order to evaluate the "adaptiveness" of human food behavior, we always need to assess the ability of people to act in their best interests. To understand why optimization does not occur in certain cases, we need to study systematically the various possible constraints on human behavior. Several important areas of constraints are relevant to anthropological explanation: our genetic biogram, environmental contexts, demographic factors, and sociopolitical and socioeconomic processes. Many of us would agree that these groups of factors have significant interactions with human subsistence behavior, and so our research strategy must be to investigate them (Chapter 2).

Optimal foraging models are fascinating because they are systematic attempts to portray the interaction of variables in systems of human subsistence. Initially, many of these models have failed to predict actual human behavior. For example, the model described by Winterhalder (Chapter 12) attempts to create a subsistence economy, based on optimization principles for a Cree group. The fact that the modeled economy so little resembles the actual one suggests that some important contextual factors and analytical considerations have not been sufficiently considered. Several basic factors that help to shape traditional subsistence systems may need to be plugged into such models, such as the demographic situation of the group and its articulation with the local environment and with other human populations, through market and other interactions. In addition, for each case the likely subsistence limiting factors need to be identified; it is not enough simply to assume, as optimal foraging theorists do, that energy efficiency is the most important measure, for different economies and environments have different limiting factors. Thus, the failure of optimal foraging theory to predict ethnographic economies does not necessarily derive from problems in the general theory; rather, it may stem from a failure to factor crucial nutritional, environmental, technological, economic, sociopolitical, and demographic relationships into models (Chapter 1). Study of the reasons for the failures can lead to progressive improvements in the models. In terms of general anthropological research strategy, we need to follow the example of optimal foraging theorists and try to develop from our explanations explicit quantitative implications that can be compared in detail with the ethnographic and archaeological evidence. The kind of simulation exercises that these theorists use should be a basic tool for research on food behavior.

Our theories and data gathering also need to address the question of optimization by whom, of what, for what: for nutritional status, longevity, general health, inclusive fitness, maximum population growth and density, energy conservation, and so on. The archaeological and ethnographic record shows that there may be systematic interactions between different kinds of optimizations. For example, the optimization of energy costs is violated in protein capture by many American groups who subsist by cultivating starchy crops and by hunting and fishing (e.g., Chapters 15 and 16). Foraging secures the main protein component of their diets, and so its efficiency cannot be measured absolutely in terms of energy. Their horticultural energy procurement system is so efficient in terms of input/output ratio that it subsidizes the rather costly protein-getting system. Although consumed in rather small quantities, about 10 percent of calories, animal food is highly preferred and sought after because it is the main source of dietary protein for these people.

A prehistoric example of another kind of cost interaction is the apparent worldwide drop in subsistence labor costs during the mesolithic transition, when the development of abundant and starchy plant food sources improved the calorie productivity of subsistence labor and permitted people to fulfill their subsistence needs with greatly reduced costs in time and physical activity. The lessened effort of subsistence at this stage of development is documented by paleopathological evidence for the diminution of wear and tear on human bones and teeth (Cohen and Armelagos 1984).

Whether or not energy acquisition will be maximized in a particular subsistence activity will depend on the specific subsistence role of the activity, and that may be to provide energy, protein, minor nutrients, or some combination. Items that are limiting factors in subsistence may well be pursued with a greater investment of energy than other nutrients. It is important to recognize that the same substance is not the limiting factor at all times and places, although some scholars have emphasized either energy or protein to the exclusion of others. Which nutrient will be in shortest supply will vary depending on the population density, the environment, and subsistence technology. Under a hunting-gathering technology, grasslands may yield a calorie-poor, protein-rich diet through exploitation of herd animals by sparse, nomadic populations (Chapter 1), whereas a shift to agricultural production of cereals for direct consumption by a large, dense, sedentary population may lead to a diet rich in carbohydrates but low in high-quality protein. Thus, knowledge of demography, environment, and technology can help assess the adaptiveness and adequacy of a given diet.

In terms of constraints on the development of food systems, the authors of this book have rightly been interested in the nature of human nutritional needs: in calories, protein, fats, fiber, and micro-nutrients. We need this information for many reasons, but especially to further evaluate the "adaptiveness" of different human dietary systems—their adequacy for satisfying human needs for sustenance. We have learned some interesting things from our discussions about requirements. It turns out that male adults may not need large and well-balanced rations of amino acids. Nor does regular vitamin intake appear necessary for such people. We have not talked much about calorie requirements, but perhaps we all accept the need to maintain adequate calorie intake levels relative to activity, with the caveat that people on short rations of nutrients may become more efficient metabolically. Most interesting of all is the information that the amount and quality of protein and vitamins in the diet does indeed matter very much for pregnant and lactating women, infants, and young children. The requirements of these groups per unit weight are higher than those of adult men, but the ethnographic (e.g., Chapter 19) and archaeological (Cohen and Armelagos 1984) record seems to show that these groups generally get less of their requirements than do adult men, possibly because of their lesser ability to secure nutrients in a context of scarcity. This finding is of significance for ethnologists. It means that in order to assess the nutritional status of a population, we need to look at specific population sub-groups separately. Average per capita intakes and adult health status may obscure significant malnutrition. In addition, we need to recognize that if women and children are chronically in nutritional stress, then even though active stress will not be found among adult men, the majority of the population will have undergone significant nutritional stress during childhood and perhaps afterward. Such patterns of want may be responsible for the widespread low stature found in ethnographic populations, stunting by repeated growth arrests being a physiological response to inadequate nutrition during growth.

Another problem lies in the differences in per capita nutritional needs between healthy and sick people. We have agreed that sick people probably have greater requirements than healthy people. Pelto in discussion has suggested that existing nutritional standards may be inappropriate for most anthropological populations because they do not take into account the probability of an interaction between nutrition and disease. In order to know how well different diets fill the requirements of the populations subsisting on them, we need nutritional standards appropriate to the kinds of populations we study: populations with relatively high parasite and infection load, relatively small stature, high activity levels, large numbers of children, and pregnant or lactating women. Such considerations need to be taken into account when the "adaptiveness" of specific subsistence systems is evaluated.

Another major question about nutrition is: how people sense and regulate the intake level of nutrients, and how this process contributes to the evolution of diets. Rozin has pointed out that rats can detect the relative concentrations of certain nutrients in their food and can select different amounts of different foods to balance the diet, and it stands to reason that humans might be able to do this also. Our behavior in relation to food may to some degree reflect a response to this ability. The "taste" for bread and other forms of starchy food may be a response to physiological sensations of calorie needs, and many ethnologists have reported statements to the effect that people with starchy staple crops get "meat-hungry" when deprived of an adequate supplement of animal protein (Chapters 15 and 16). Sensations of hunger in humans seem to be partly nutrient-specific. If so, this important potential source of biological stimulus for food preferences and aversions should be investigated further.

Milton (Chapter 3) has shown how comparative study of our gastric apparatus can illuminate our nutritional biogram, illustrating our omnivore pattern and adaptation to concentrated high-nutrient food. This is interesting in view of the prevalance of high-bulk, low-nutrient cereal-legume diets among much of the world's peasantry (Chapters 18 and 19). Such diets seem to supply protein and calories in adequate amounts at the expense of digestibility, illustrating that almost all human diets have some adverse consequences for some groups in a population (Chapters 1 and 2). On the one hand, the almost exclusively vegetarian diet of many peasants may present problems for young children, whose smaller body size makes it difficult for them to consume enough high-bulk vegetable food to fill nutrient needs (Chapters 6 and 21). On the other hand, high-meat and -fat diets may have adverse effects on the circulatory and excretory systems of mature adults and the elderly (Chapter 9).

Human diets also vary in their ability to supply essential nutrients. Hunter-gatherer diets would seem to be high in most nutrients except calories, whereas horticultural diets may be abundant in calories but lack protein and micro-nutrients. Thus, different diet patterns would be expected to have different complexes of possible nutritional diseases and to elicit different food preferences and aversions. Moreover, the particular way that a traditional diet stresses its users can be expected to determine its effect on gene frequencies through natural selection (Chapters 4 and 9).

In addition to the problem of assessing the nutritional needs of the people that we study, we know little about the nutritional properties of the food that they eat. A little-documented area of particular importance is the interaction of foods and of foods and spices. Another area of concern is the effect of processing on the availability of nutrients. For example, temperature is known to alter the digestibility of food (Chapter 9) and preferences for eating certain foods at certain temperatures are part of both traditional food patterns and *haute cuisine*. Before we can explain the preferences, we need to know more about the biochemistry of subsistence procedures in relation to human taste and nutrition.

For practical purposes of integrating archaeological and ethnographic evidence about subsistence, it will be useful to know more about the levels of nutritional stress that produce skeletal pathologies. There is a vast potential corpus of data about prehistoric human nutritional pathology, but it is difficult to interpret because of the lack of information about pathologies in living populations of known physiological status. The only thing that seems indisputable is that bone pathologies generally result from appreciable physiological stress. Thus, the presence of nutrition-related bone pathology surely is evidence for significant nutritional inadequacy. Ethnologists can expand knowledge about the relationship of actual diets to specific types of nutritional disease and bone pathology by including medical anthropologists and nutritional anthropologists in their research projects. For example, evidence of the dental pathology of living people of known diet and health status could furnish valuable data for comparison with paleopathological data from prehistoric populations.

Several authors have stressed the explanatory importance of studying significant contextual factors. A basic prerequisite for understanding the adaptive or evolutionary role of diet is to know the relationship of diets to the physical environment. We have been neglectful in this, trying to explain why certain food systems developed and others did not without considering how well they might work in particular regions. Subsistence strategies need to be evaluated in terms of soil characteristics, topography, rain, temperature, the characteristics of crops, and technologies of transport and agriculture. Few of us would deny the significant influence of environmental variation on the productivity of subsistence systems, but few of the chapters here have explicitly related these factors to ethnographic and archaeological food patterns. The ability of a particular subsistence system to supply needed nutrients is affected by the environment and technology. For example, the tropical forest is often deficient in wild calorie and protein sources for humans, but abundant calories can be provided by the slash-and-burn cultivation of starchy agricultural crops. The animal food sources can then be employed more efficiently as dietary sources of protein. One possible way to understand why the Machiguenga, for example, do not live on a maize-beans diet (Chapter 15), is to evaluate the appropriateness of the soil and climate of their homeland for intensive seed crop cultivation. Their tropical rain-forest environment may limit the utility of seed crop economies in comparison with the existing economy of starchy crop horticulture and animal capture (Chapter 15; Roosevelt 1980).

Another basic parameter, as many have argued, is demography. Yet several chapters have dealt with subsistence change without providing information about population change, which could have been causally involved. The Siriono of Bolivia furnish an example of this process. These Amazonian Indians were classified as primeval hunter-gatherers until study of their history showed that their economy had turned away from agriculture during a period of population loss (Isaac 1977). In the case of the Machiguenga, even if the environment is no bar to a seed crop economy, population density may be so low at present as to make subsistence intensification at that level unnecessary (Chapter 15). Nutritional systems interact with levels of population and with labor availability, and so to understand a particular system we need to know the current state of population in relation to past states. We especially need a higher quality of documentation of synchronic patterns of age/sex distribution, mortality, and natality, as well as historic studies of population change. And we need to implement measures that can compare modern, historic, and prehistoric populations with each other. Perhaps comprehensive settlement pattern and demographic studies can achieve this by extending our demographic knowledge from prehistory through history to the present.

The other important area of constraints on human food patterns lies in the interaction of individuals and groups: the social, cultural, economic, and political organization of nutrition. Systematic answers to questions about why a certain group or subgroup is not acting "optimally" in terms of subsistence may depend on its sociopolitical and socioeconomic context. A people's sub-optimal diet or excessively labor-intensive cultivation system may stem from the expropriation of resources by more powerful or richer groups (e.g., the situation described in

Geertz 1963 and in Chapter 19). As discussed above, it seems clear from archaeology, ethnography, and studies of modern states that food and health are unequally distributed in most populations, whether egalitarian or stratified. It also seems clear that socioeconomic inequality is associated with differential distribution of food and of nutritional stress (Chapters 17, 19, and 21). We need to know much more about how and why this happens. It may be one of the most significant aspects of human social organization, but it seems the least studied. The biological consequences of human sociopolitical organization may help us to understand people's attitudes toward prestige and rank, as well as to food.

It is significant that the evidence seems to show that the nutritional inequalities are worse in larger and more stratified societies. Although women and children may be underprivileged nutritionally even in egalitarian societies, it is only in the more complex societies that relatively severe, chronic nutritional stress occurs to large numbers of people. This finding puts the rise of civilization and intensive agriculture in a rather unfavorable light. It makes it difficult to view it, as Renfrew (1972) has, as a general advance in the quality of life. For most people, it did not apparently improve subsistence. This information is relevant to decisions on how to "develop" the frontiers of modern Third World nations. Political leaders often see intensive, commercialized agriculture as the only "civilized" mode of exploitation, but less intensive methods may be more "adaptive" for the welfare of the general population. The highly intensive methods of production are historically related to expropriation and export by elites, not necessarily to the better support of the populace (Chapter 19).

Related to this subject is the theme of national and international integration. Wolf (1982) and a number of the authors in this book give examples of the impact of national and world systems on peasants and traditional people (see Chapters 1, 19, 21, and 22). In some cases it seems that the "traditional" ethnographic pattern may actually have been an artifact of the colonial interaction; in others, cultural patterns have been significantly altered by international relations. This means that ethnographers' explanations must always take into account their subjects' relationships with other people, especially with colonial groups and nation-states. For studies of hunter-gatherers, there are special problems in this area. Hutterer (1982) has pointed out that many states have created specialized hunter-gatherer groups at their borders to supply gathered and hunted products to urban and agricultural areas. Many of these people at the peripheries have given up horticultural subsistence in response to market demands for non-agricultural products. Thus, we cannot explain their hunting-gathering way of life as an adaptation to their physical environment alone, and we should not think of such people as relics of prehistoric lifeways (Chapter 4). They are something quite different in both origin and function. For example, the Aché "hunter-gatherer" subsistence-settlement system (see Chapter 13) may be an artifact of missionary interference and demographic reduction from introduced diseases. In order to evaluate the adaptive or evolutionary significance of a particular group's food patterns, it is very important to view them in historical, political, demographic, and socioeconomic contexts.

Much of the evidence for food patterns discussed in this book has been ethnographic, that is, traditional anthropological data. This accords with the traditional interests of anthropology in "primitive" people. Nevertheless, it is desirable for explanatory purposes to integrate the archaeological and prehistoric evidence with that of ethnology, history, and the industrial age. This was one of the purposes of the Wenner-Gren conference, whose participants included archaeologists, ethnologists, sociologists, historians, and physical anthropologists. We need, however, to go beyond interdisciplinary discussions to actual collaboration in planning and carrying out field research. Although the ethnographic material gives valuable insights into the ongoing processes of subsistence behavior, the non-ethnographic bodies of evidence are important primary data for the evolution of food patterns, for they document the earlier history of ethnographic peoples and relate them to the future.

Paleontology furnishes primary evidence about the nature of our biogram because this field controls the time during which our species was developing both biologically and culturally. Through paleontology we can address questions about the behavioral, ecological, and cultural contexts of this process. The paleontological record contains much potential evidence about subsistence behavior: micro-wear patterns on bones, teeth, and tools; plant and animal residues in fossils and tools; and actual plant and animal remains and artifacts. Recovery of needed information will require more meticulous field collection and conservation methods and better studies of the chemical and physical nature of finds. The archaeological record covers the important period when agricultural subsistence replaced foraging subsistence and when intensive subsistence systems and stratified social organization came into being. These data are primary evidence of the history of human subsistence, crucial for the testing of theories about human food preferences and aversions. With the capabilities of archaeological physical anthropology and bone chemistry (e.g. Huss-Ashmore, Goodman, and Armelagos 1982; Chapter 10), we have exciting new ways to track the subsistence behavior of individuals. We cannot usually get at actual food preferences and aversions, but we can trace dietary differences within populations at an individual level and can relate them to gender and to social, economic, and demographic status.

We have not talked much about this paleontological and archaeological record, but despite limitations in present knowledge, it could be a valuable source in the future. Zihlman (1983) believes that the major dietary shift undertaken by the early hominids was abandoning their emphasis on tree fruits in favor of a reliance on roots and seeds. The evidence suggests that both plants and meat were part of our earliest ancestors' food supply, though their quantitative proportions are not yet known. Possibly bone chemistry studies will help solve this problem in the future. The presence of hypoplasias in hominids indicates the existence of nutritional stress among the young. It would be useful to know more about the temporal and developmental patterning of early hominids' hypoplasias—chronic or periodic, infantile or weanling—so as to compare these populations with later humans. There may well have been a significant change in reproductive systems during the evolution of the human species (Fisher 1975, 1982; Lovejoy 1981), and there definitely were changes in population density and food-getting methods. We need to know much more about the nature and timing of such changes so that we can understand better their role in human subsistence history.

Early modern hunter-gatherers, who lived much more densely on the land than hominids, seem to have eaten substantial amounts of meat as a source of both calories and other nutrients (Chapter 10). Much has been made of the hunter-gatherer quest for animal protein, but our discussion has suggested the possibility that the focus was on highly caloric fatty foods rather than on meat protein per se. In carnivorous economies calories are more likely to become scarce than protein or vitamins. The health and stature of these early hunter-gatherers seem normal but are poorly documented. Most such populations seem to have experienced seasonal and periodic subsistence inadequacy, to judge from the presence of dental hypoplasias, but significant, widespread, chronic malnutrition seems to have been absent.

Later hunter-gatherers, even more numerous on the earth, show a significant development of plant staples, apparently increasing the caloric value of their diets over those of their predecessors (Chapter 10). These diets are similar to those of the earliest cultivators, who also derived substantial amounts of their calories from plants. In the transition between these two kinds of economies, there seems to have been a substantial increase in the efficiency of food production, in terms of both land area and labor. In addition to having less food available per hectare, the earlier hunter-gatherers seem, on the evidence of the size and ruggedness of their bones and teeth, to have had to work much harder for their daily food than the later ones. Thus, it seems that dietary evolution toward agriculture both increased the numbers of people who could be supported on the land and decreased the effort cost of subsistence. Although chronic nutritional stress was rare in these transitional populations, their pathology patterns suggest that most experienced periodic stress, indicative of continuing tension between population numbers and food resources.

The development of intensive agriculture in many regions of the world is associated with a rapid increase in population size, density, and sedentism. It also seems to give rise to numerous large, stratified social systems characterized by unequal access to food between socioeconomic classes. Although elites seem to have eaten a rich mixed diet containing significant quantities of animal protein, the majority of people in these large societies followed a high-plant, low-animal-food regime. To judge from the paleopathological record, this plant-rich diet was often consumed in inadequate quantities (Cohen and Armelagos 1984), a pattern that is still found among the populations of post-colonial Third World nations today. The fact that the process of socioeconomic stratification began long before the colonial expansion of modern nations confirms the relevance to each other of the modern and archaeological states with regard to the explanation of food preferences and aversions. It is not always recognized that modern state societies are based on socioeconomic differences that have an important impact on people's access to food.

From the start food behavior was involved in the development of our species and our culture. By investigating empirically the fit between human food behavior and the predictions of theories of human adaptation, we can generate important new data to test and refine the theories. From the ethnographic point of view, we can investigate how belief and behavior systems related to food arise, persist, and change. Studying what individuals do and say about food in ethnographic contexts in the light of long-term historic and prehistoric patterns of behavior will clarify the process of human subsistence adaptation and the process will be further elucidated through consideration of the changing social, political, and ecological contexts of human food preferences and aversions.

References Cited

Black, F.
 1980 HLA Antigens in South American Indians. *Tissue Antigens* 16:368–76.
 1983 Failure of Linguistic Relationships to Predict Genetic Distances Between the Waiapi and Other Tribes of Lower Amazonia. *American Journal of Physical Anthropology* 60:327–35.

Cohen, M.
 1977 *The Food Crisis in Prehistory.* New Haven: Yale University Press.

Cohen, M., and G. Armelagos
 1984 *Paleopathology and the Origins of Agriculture.* New York: Academic Press.

Droessler, J.
 1981 *Craniometry and Biological Distance: Biocultural Continuity and Change at the Late-Woodland-Mississippian Interface.* Evanston, Ill.: Center for American Archaeology, Northwestern University.

Farb, P., and G. Armelagos
 1980 *Consuming Passions: The Anthropology of Eating.* Boston: Houghton Mifflin.

Fisher, H.
    1975   The Loss of Estrous Periodicity in Hominid Evolution. Ann Arbor: University Microfilms.
    1982   *The Sex Contract: The Evolution of Human Behavior.* New York: William Morrow.

Geertz, C.
    1963   *Agricultural Involution: The Process of Ecological Change in Indonesia.* Berkeley: University of California Press for the Association of Asian Studies.

Harris, M.
    1977   *Cannibals and Kings: The Origins of Cultures.* New York: Random House.

Hayden, B.
    1981   Research and Development in the Stone Age: Technological Transitions Among Hunter-Gatherers. *Current Anthropology* 22:519–48.

Huss-Ashmore, R.; A. H. Goodman; and G. Armelagos
    1982   Nutritional Inference from Paleopathology. In *Advances in Archaeological Method and Theory,* vol. 5, M. B. Fisher, ed., pp. 395–474. New York: Academic Press.

Hutterer, K. L.
    1982   Interaction between Tropical Ecosystems and Human Foragers: Some General Considerations. Working paper, Environment and Policy Institute, East-West Center, Honolulu.

Isaac, B. L.
    1977   The Sirionó of Eastern Bolivia. *Human Ecology* 5:137–54.

Lovejoy, C. O.
    1981   The Origin of Man. *Science* 211:341–50.

Rathje, W. L., and R. H. McGuire
    1982   Rich Men . . . Poor Men. *American Behavioral Scientist* 25(6):705–15.

Reichs, K.
    1975   Biological Variability and the Hopewell Phenomenon: An Interregional Approach. Ph.D. dissertation, Northwestern University, Evanston, Illinois. [Ann Arbor: University Microfilms.]

Renfrew, C.
    1972   *The Emergence of Civilization: The Cyclades and the Aegean in the Third Millennium B.C.* London: Methuen.

Roosevelt, Anna
    1980   *Parmana: Prehistoric Maize and Manioc Subsistence along the Amazon and Orinoco.* New York: Academic Press.

Wolf, E. R.
    1982   Europe and the People Without History. Berkeley: University of California Press.

Zihlman, A.
    1983   Paper read at the Wenner-Gren Conference on Food Preferences and Avoidances. Cedar Key, Florida.

24

GEORGE ARMELAGOS

Biocultural Aspects of Food Choice

THE DETERMINATION OF FOOD CHOICE REMAINS ONE OF THE most perplexing anthropological problems. Traditional anthropological explanations have relied on cultural factors to interpret differences in food habits. Although some of the earlier functional explanations were framed in terms of the development of food procurement and preparation in response to a basic biological need—hunger—they tended to consider only the sociocultural aspects of the response. Recent attempts by physical anthropologists to explain dietary differences rely on an adaptive model that incorporates biological and cultural factors. The systematic application of this model has been called the "biocultural approach." A basic tenet of the adaptive model is that a food procurement system must meet the essential nutritional requirements necessary to maintain and reproduce the population (Chapter 9), although it would be possible for the group to maintain its size by recruiting new members from outside to replace those who do not survive.

The biocultural approach maintains that any positive adaptive feature of a food practice is a sufficient explanation for its existence. Many bizarre foods can be explained in such a manner. The eating of rotted wood garnished with honey, a food practice of the Vedda of Sri Lanka that is an enigma to many Westerners, may be adaptive, since B vitamins are produced by bacteria during the putrification process (Farb and Armelagos 1980:12). Similarly, clay eating (geophagy), a practice of some West African and black American groups, may, in fact, be a positive response to nutritional deficiency. Chemical analysis of the clay shows a mineral composition that compares favorably with the calcium, magnesium, potassium, copper, zinc, and iron content of a mineral supplement prescribed for pregnant women (Hunter 1973). The minerals may, however, be chemically bound in the clay and may not be biologically available.

The biocultural adaptive model has also been used to explain the food combinations that have developed in traditional cuisines. Among many American groups, the triad of maize, beans, and squash are used as central food items. This combination is interesting, since maize is deficient in the amino acid lysine and high in the amino acid methionine, whereas beans are low in methionine and high in lysine. The use of maize and beans in the same meal will provide a complementary source of the essential amino acids. Since the populations who initially domesticated these cultigens may not have realized the nutritional consequences of these combinations, how did these dietary practices develop? The adaptive model would argue that nutritional practices that provide the essential dietary requirements will be selected for in the Darwinian sense. Even if the food combinations developed fortuitously, the fact that they provide the essential nutrient will ensure the survival of the population biologically and the survival of the food practice culturally.

The adaptive approach is also relevant to methods of preparation (E. Rozin 1982). Katz and co-workers demonstrated the adaptiveness of the traditional Mexican method of maize processing (Katz, Hediger, and Valleroy 1974), which uses an alkali to make the protein in maize more bioavailable (P. Rozin 1982). The women who process the maize argue that the alkali makes a better tortilla and do not see the protein arguments as particularly relevant. The biocultural approach does not minimize the social importance of food but argues that if the cultural practice did not meet the biological needs of the group, the survival of the population would be in question.

Biology, Taste, and Food Choice

It would be worthwhile to consider the biological basis of food habits in *Homo sapiens*. Are there "natural" aspects of taste that can explain human food habits? As Rozin (Chapter 7) points out taste and taste aversions have two innate biological aspects. Humans and other mammals have a propensity for sweet substances. If these are introduced into the amniotic fluid, the fetus begins to suckle (De Snoo 1937, cited in Beidler 1982). Neurological analysis of mammalian fetuses suggests that taste nerves are functioning before birth in humans. The sweet preference in human babies is likely to be innate and involves the lower nervous centers of the brain (Beidler 1982:5). In other words, this preference is hard-wired into our neurobiology. The obvious adaptive value of this trait is that it programs a taste for sweetness, a good predictor of high energy sources and hence of nutritional value.

The abhorrence of bitter things is also a common trait in humans. The human tongue can detect bitterness at dilutions of one part in 2,000,000 (sweetness can be tasted at a dilution of one part in 200). The ability to taste bitter substances such as PTC (phenylthiocarbimide) at low concentration would be advantageous to hunter-gatherers (who really should be called gatherer-hunters) since bitter substances found in plants are often toxic.

The fact that we seem to have a craving for sweet substances or an abhorrence of bitter ones is not sufficient to explain our use of these substances. Our "sweet tooth" may explain the near-universal use of unrefined and refined sugars (Mintz 1982), but as Mintz (1985:xxix) notes, it is a social-political system that transforms these from a curiosity and a luxury into a necessity. Conversely, bitter substances such as quinine can be manipulated so that they become a desirable food item. The British made the anti-malarial agent quinine tolerable by adding gin to it. Gin and tonics are still enjoyed by many Americans who have never seen the mosquito that carries the parasite.

Some scientists believe that humans have an inborn biological wisdom about foods. The popular literature (e.g., Spock 1968:278) suggests that humans possess "instinctive knowledge" about their nutritional needs (Davis 1928, 1939). Over 50 years ago, rather crude experiments were conducted in which a small number of children were allowed to self-select food. Although the children showed a great deal of daily variation, they tended to select a healthful diet. The experimental design was poorly constructed, and the children were presented with an array of highly nutritious foods (eggs, milk, cereal, meat, fruits, and vegetables). If soft drinks, chocolate, cookies, and potato chips had been added to the more nutritious offerings, the results might have been different.

Arlin (1977), Fischer (1981:59–68), and Lytle (1977:23–27) have criticized the methodology of these early experiments. Epstein and Teitelbaum (1962), working with rats, have produced experimental data that support the concept of instinctive nutrition, but Young (1948) raises doubts about self-selection even among the rodents. Balagura (1973) has reviewed these studies and argues that self-selection is a result of both innate and learned behavior.

The Primate Legacy

Richard Wrangham (1985) of the University of Michigan has observed sick chimpanzees to methodically seek out and consume the leaves of an *aspilla* shrub, which contain a substance that is a potent anti-bacterial, anti-fungal, and anthelmintic agent. Do these observations have any relevance to our understanding of contemporary human food habits? Do they provide clues to the biological underpinnings of human food behavior? There is enough evidence to make it worthwhile to consider primate food patterns as a window into our biological past. Hamilton (Chapter 4) suggests that food patterns may be influenced by the dietary behavior of our past primate ancestors (near and remote) and that these primate features of diet remain incorporated in modern human eating patterns. Hamilton and Busse (1978) suggest that primates and humans have a "taste" for animal protein and fat and that this taste may have a genetic component. Harris (Chapter 2) states that the behavioral impact of predation and meat eating has special significance for chimpanzees. Furthermore, he argues that chimpanzees' meat-eating behavior expresses "instinctive recognition of that significance, elaborated and modified by social traditions and individual experience."

According to Hamilton, the use of primate models to interpret modern food patterns is also hampered by adaptive inertia. Adaptive inertia is the lag between what may be adaptive in contemporary society and what was adaptive in the past. The interpretation of the primate legacy and its influence on human food choices, according to Hamilton, is probably more art than science. Hamilton sees two features of our primate legacy reflected in the modern food pattern of overconsumption of meat and sugar. He concludes that culture is the culprit in the maladaptive use of these substances, since culture impedes evolutionary change in rapidly changing environments. An alternative interpretation is also possible. It may be that political and economic factors can rapidly change patterns of diet regardless of our primate legacy (Chapter 2).

Many zoologists accept optimality models of food selection, which predict that an animal will choose foods that provide an adequate diet at the least cost and risk (Orians 1980). Therefore, they reason, evolution should produce efficient systems that ensure a fit between the environment and food choices. When animals are found to have an inadequate diet, it is assumed that the environment is changing so rapidly that dietary changes cannot keep pace.

Even more basic aspects of human diet may be a reflection of our primate legacy. The omnivorous behavior of humans can surely be traced back to it (Chapter 4), for the use of vegetative parts of plants, fruits, seeds, and animal matter as food sources is a pattern found in primates. Recent studies indicate that food preferences exist among primates and that these choices are often constrained either environmentally or biologically. Even though primates may prefer insects and meat, these food sources may not always be available because of ecological factors or seasonal changes in the environment. Baboons may find meat desirable but may not have the physical ability to prey on the large carnivores that could provide an abundant source of flesh.

Although we assume that the jungle environment is an unlimited source of food for primates, it is in fact restricted by the toxins that plants have evolved for their own protection. Jolly (1985a:57) quotes Janzens (1978), who states that "the plant world is not colored green; it is colored morphine, caffeine, tannin, phenol, terpene, cavanine, latex, phytohaemagglutin, oxalic acid, saponin." The jungle demands taste discrimination, and as Jolly notes (1985a:57), primates "must choose carefully the items worth harvesting, or safe to harvest, in a limited world."

Primates have developed other adaptations to meet the challenge of the jungle food resources. They have evolved changes in the gut that make the processing of secondary compounds and fibrous plant materials possible. Milton has shown (Chapter 3) that transport time affects the absorption of plant protein. She suggests that the feeding repertoire of any animal is a combination of its behavior, morphology, and physiology. Humans, according to Milton, turn over food more rapidly than do the chimpanzees and orangutans. In humans, the small intestine is larger in volume and the colon smaller than those found in the great apes. This supports the contention that the human gut is well adapted to process high-quality dietary items that are concentrated and can be rapidly digested. Milton (1981) suggests that the ancestral lines leading to modern *Homo sapiens* may have depended on meat protein. Furthermore, hominids may have developed more efficient food search techniques to offset the costs of finding dispersed high-quality foods. If humans select plants that contain toxins or are high in non-digestible fiber, cultural processing (to remove the toxin and to break down the plant fibers) would be required to make these food items edible.

Glander (1982) and Milton (1979) report that primates are selective in their use of foods. Glander describes how the mantled howlers living in Costa Rica choose food items carefully and eat only a small portion of the leaf or fruit they select. In other words, they avoid the toxins by selecting those portions of the plant that are high in protein and have minimal amounts of the secondary compounds.

Foraging brings primates into contact with a wide range of foods, yet half of their diet comes from as few as 10 species of plants (Jolly 1985a). This observation supports the contention that the primates are optimizing their food search by selecting the items that provide their nutritional needs with the least effort. Within this framework, the animals do have distinct preferences and make choices.

Additional adaptations may be a part of our primate legacy. Primates do engage in active search for protein sources: many species stalk insects, and the "termiting" and "anting" of chimpanzees are well known. Meat eating by apes and baboons has been reported. While many of the meat-eating episodes of baboons are the result of scavenging, there is mounting evidence of actual hunting among chimpanzees (Harding 1973; Harding and Teleki 1981; Hausfater 1976; Strum 1976). Chimpanzees have been known to pass up carrion and stalk other primates. Some of these reports describe cooperative hunting, and the meat acquired in successful "hunts" is frequently shared. Furthermore, there appear to be sexual differences in some non-human primate subsistence activity. Male chimpanzees are more frequently the hunters, and females are more active in the search for termites.

The omnivorous feeding behavior of primates and other mammals creates a dilemma for the animal. The omnivore's dilemma (P. Rozin 1982:230; and Chapter 7) is the conflict between wanting new food sources but fearing that they may be toxic. The omnivores' "neophobia" has led to behavioral patterns in which they will taste small amounts of a novel item and develop an aversion to any that causes illness.

In summary, these studies provide evidence of a primate legacy that may have had some influence on the origin of hominid food patterns. Zihlman (1983) emphasizes the "generalist" nature of the primate dietary pattern. Sussman (1978) notes that primates, as omnivores, feed on a wider variety of foods than "specialists." This omnivorous behavior expands the primates' range and can accommodate seasonal variation from area to area (Zihlman 1983). Reliance on an omnivorous diet, a pattern of collecting with some predation, and the evidence of at least rudimentary sharing are features of the primate legacy that may have affected the dietary patterns of our hominid ancestors.

The Heritage of the Early Hominids

Much of our earlier speculation on hominid dietary behavior was based on the "man the hunter" model (Lee and DeVore 1968). This model has been criticized for overemphasizing limited aspects of early hominid behavior and subsistence patterns, and its focus on "hunting" as the major shaper of human behavior (Linton 1970; Zihlman and Tanner 1974, 1978). Following these criticisms, the role of gathering and its influence on behavior have been incorporated in more recent models. Studies show that among contemporary hunter-gatherers, women make a substantial contribution to the group's diet, collecting at least 60 percent of the dietary resources. Notwithstanding this reorientation, however, Jolly believes that the " 'hunting hypothesis' as a major selective trend in human evolution still stands, even though modified by the recent realization that gathering insects and seeds, with the necessary tool use and multiple-step attention, has a parallel role" (1985b:233–34).

Recent work by Isaac (1978, 1981, 1983) offers a more balanced perspective on social interactions during this phase in human evolution. Isaac's analysis of patterns of bones and stones suggests that early hominid society was characterized by a central-place foraging strategy and food sharing. Sharing and division of labor by sex ensured the selection of a wide variety of foods. Zihlman (1983) recognizes a suite of behaviors that allowed the early hominids to function in the mosaic environment of the savanna. The reliance on a generalist-omnivorous foraging strategy, tool use, food sharing, the ability to obtain unseen food, cognitive mapping behavior, and female mobility were adaptive features of early hominid subsistence. The dietary shift that characterized early hominid adaptation, according to Zihlman, involved a decreased reliance on fruits and fruit-bearing trees and greater reliance on plants protected by hard coverings and with their nutrients stored underground. In this scenario, bipedal locomotion would have aided the transport of food, tools, and water to and from the sources of food.

Lessons from Contemporary Hunter-Gatherers

Hawkes (Chapter 13) has applied the optimal diet model to the foraging strategy of hunter-gatherers. She argues that as members of a hunting-gathering group broaden their diet, they are forced to work harder to eat less. Hawkes tests this optimal diet model with data from the Aché and !Kung and reports that results were inconclusive. She argues, nevertheless, that any interpretation of diet must ultimately consider food habits in terms of the maximization of the fitness of the individual. Winterhalder (Chapter 12) offers a similar approach with his discussion of optimal foraging strategy at the group level. Optimal foraging strategy has been criticized for its limited approach to understanding diet. It assumes that we treat the cultural system as if it were an individual, thus obscuring individual variation in the analysis, and it fails to recognize that spatial differences in resources can be mitigated by sharing and temporal differences by storage (Martin Wobst, pers. comm.).

Lee's (1984) analysis of the dietary resources of the !Kung anticipated the models of optimal foraging strategy. Lee notes that in two hours of subsistence activity women collected 30 to 50 pounds of food, whereas men returned with 15 to 25 pounds. The women gathered food equivalent to 23,000 calories, which is enough to feed a person for 10 days, whereas men gathered enough food for a 5-day period (12,000 calories) (Lee 1984:36).

The !Kung have a variety of plants and animals from which to choose, recognizing 105 species of plants and 260 species of animals as edible. The 365 food items are selected from over 500 plants and animals identified in the environment by contemporary scientists. One source (the mogongo nut) is considered a primary food source; 13 plants are considered major food sources (they are widely available), and 19 species are considered minor foods (locally and seasonally available). The 14 items in the primary and major food categories make up 75 percent of the foods consumed by the !Kung (Lee 1979:159). A digging stick is required to recover about a quarter of the plants eaten. The other 72 plant species are considered supplementary, rare, or problematic food sources (Lee 1983:37). The !Kung are obviously selective in their food choices. Again, the preferences reflect the prediction made by optimal foraging theory: they maximize their efforts by collecting the fewest species of plants and animals

585

that can satisfy their biological needs. Lee states that meat is the most desired and the most scarce food item. Even with other desired plant foods, there may be variation with respect to individuals' efforts to recover these items. Younger men, for example, will travel longer distances for more desired food items, whereas older men are willing to eat the less desired foods that are nearer. Sharing of all of these foods is likely.

Speth and Speilmann (1983) provide an interesting example of the interaction of the biocultural model and optimal foraging strategy. During periods of marginal caloric intake, hunters and gatherers are likely to hunt large ungulates. Since these animals are also subsisting on declining resources, their reserves of body fat become depleted. Lean meat becomes a principal source of energy. The use of large quantities of lean meat has nutritional costs, including elevated metabolic rates, higher caloric requirements and deficiencies in essential fatty acids. Gatherers and hunters will subsequently develop subsistence strategies that increase carbohydrate and/or fat intake. Speth and Speilmann suggest that there are three strategies that can achieve these results: (1) an increase in the selection and procurement of smaller animals with high fat content; (2) storage of fat- and carbohydrate-rich foods; and (3) an exchange of these items with other groups. In most instances, the collecting strategy may be the most reasonable.

Eaton and Konner (1985) have reviewed paleolithic nutrition and claim that many of the diseases that plague modern humans (coronary heart disease, hypertension, diabetes, and many types of cancer) can be traced to the shifts in diet that have occurred over the last hundred years. In fact, they argue that the diet of our remote ancestors may be a reference standard for modern human nutrition—"a model for defense against certain 'diseases of civilization'" (Eaton and Konner 1985:288). Although I agree that the paleolithic diet offers some benefits, we should not overlook the fact that modern Western food systems have contributed in many nations to a life expectancy of over 70 years, far beyond the paleolithic average.

Biocultural Adaptation and Food Choices

I have mentioned a number of food practices that have received a biocultural interpretation. The eating of rotted wood, geophagy, the use of maize and beans, and the use of alakli in the preparation of maize have been explained in terms of their biocultural adaptiveness. Livingstone (1958) described the interaction of root crop agriculture and malaria in west Africa. Certain cultigens—yams and related plants—are well adapted to slash-and-burn agriculture (Wiesenfeld 1969). Groups engaged in this type of agriculture alter the environment to such an extent that the anopheline mosquito, which carries the malaria parasite, begins to feed on humans. Some members of the population exposed to the malaria develop a genetic response (sickle cell trait) that gives individuals who are heterozygous for the trait an immunity to severe malarial infection. The development of this genetic response will allow continued production of yams.

Katz (1982 and Chapter 5) has been one of the strongest proponents of the biocultural perspective. In his latest research, Katz explains the significance of the consumption of the fava bean (*Vicia faba*) by Mediterranean populations. Katz (Chapter 5) points out that the use of the fava bean is an enigma, since ingestion of the bean may produce severe hemolytic anemia in some individuals. The individuals at risk have glucose-6-phosphate dehydrogenase deficiency, an inherited disorder that protects them from malarial infection. Since these people cannot be identified until they have eaten the beans, the use of fava beans as a food is risky. However, for individuals without the G6PD deficiency, the ingestion of the fava bean may, according to Katz and his co-workers, itself provide protection from malaria. Hence the continued cultivation of fava beans.

The omnivore's—or generalist's—dilemma has implication for the food patterns of contemporary populations (Rozin prefers the latter term, since the wide variety of foods consumed may all come from plant sources). Paul Rozin (1982:229) suggests that this dilemma is manifest in humans as a preference for familiar foods combined with a desire for variety. Rolls, Rolls, and Rowe (1982:120) see this search for variety as an aid to ensuring a nutritionally balanced diet and suggest that there may be "built-in" mechanisms to ensure that we pursue some variety in our food search. Their studies show that when a person continues to eat a particular food for an extended period, that person loses his or her taste for it. The desire to eat other foods is not affected. We maintain palatability at a high level by eating a variety of foods. The Rozins (P. Rozin 1982; E. Rozin 1982) see the development of cuisine as a cultural attempt to mediate this biological conflict. For example, the use of certain principles of flavoring that identify the foods of a group may provide a reassuring familiarity that blunts the fear of new foods. Interestingly, these flavors can be manipulated to provide variety; for example, Indian curries can be combined in a number of ways to create, in the Rozins' terminology, themes and variations that help to solve the ominvore's dilemma (P. Rozin and E. Rozin 1981).

The discovery that diet can affect neural transmitters has implications for biocultural models. Diets high in carbohydrates produce a higher ratio of the amino acid tryptophan, which is a precursor for serotonin. The release of serotonin delivers signals to neurons that control mood, sleep, and appetite (Wurtman 1982). Interestingly, animals fed a high-protein diet have reduced tryptophan levels and consequently lower concentrations of serotonin in the brain. It seems that conversion of tryptophan to serotonin also depends on the amino acid ratios in the blood plasma. These other amino acids (tyrosine, leucine, isoleucine, valine, and phenylalanine) compete with the tryptophan, thus reducing the conversion. Wurtman reports that eating a carbohydrate-rich meal that is also poor in protein will increase serotonin synthesis, which will cause the animal to reduce its carbohydrate intake but not its protein intake.

P. Rozin (1982) relies on a biocultural model for the explanation of the use of chili pepper. Since the first taste of chili is usually painful and easily rejected, Rozin says that cultural pressures support continual use, which may allow a pleasurable response to develop. He hypothesizes that the pain associated with the ingestion of the chili may induce the release of endogenous opiates. This may be the factor that creates our liking of the chili.

Biocultural interpretations are not restricted to food choice. Eating patterns that are obviously influenced by the cultural system can also reflect aspects of human biology. Booth (1982) has analyzed appetite in humans, using computer simulation to model human physiology and activity and predict eating patterns. His findings suggest that there may be biocultural reasons for the pattern of three meals a day in a society that is well nourished and has a sedentary lifestyle.

Biocultural explanations have a certain appeal. They usually provide a reasonable interpretation of behavior that previously seemed puzzling. In addition, they integrate biological and cultural factors and make it possible to measure the adaptive aspect of the trait in Darwinian terms. If a practice is maladaptive, we should be able to see the biological evidence for this in increased morbidity or mortality.

There is, however, emerging evidence that suggests that sociocultural systems can persist for relatively long periods despite serious nutritional deficiencies. Prehistoric Sudanese Nubians show evidence that, for at least a thousand years, women and children were suffering from severe iron and calcium deficiencies. During the Meroitic (350 B.C.–A.D. 350), X-Group (A.D. 350–A.D. 550), and Christian (A.D. 550–A.D. 1400) periods, there is evidence for iron-deficiency anemia and problems with bone mineralization (Martin and Armelagos 1979). Women in the peak reproductive period (18–30 years) were resorbing calcium from the inner portions of their long bones, and although they were producing new cells on the outer surface, these cells were not mineralizing. The children in the same populations were also at risk. Although their long bones appear to have grown in length at near normal rates, the walls remained surprisingly thin. The cortex (wall of the bone) of 12-year-old children was only as thick as that of a 2-year-old. Buikstra (1983) discusses the health status of Illinois populations undergoing similar shifts to agriculture and Cohen (Chapter 10) argues that most archaeological populations that shift from hunting and gathering to agriculture experience a deterioration in their health.

Biocultural Adaptation and Cultural Materialism

Harris (Chapter 2) argues that the materialist strategy is based on the assumption that biopsychological, environmental, demographic, technological, and political-economic factors all influence food choice. A group's food choices will represent optimization of their efforts, and such choices are rational. Harris states this simply in his popular book *Good to Eat* when he writes: "Preferred foods (good to eat) are foods that have a more favorable balance of practical benefits over costs than foods that are avoided (bad to eat). . . . Nutritional costs and benefits form a fundamental part of the balance—preferred foods generally pack more energy, protein, vitamins, or minerals per serving than avoided foods" (1986:15).

Although Harris accepts the possibility of biocultural explanations, he argues that they must be interpreted in cultural materialist as well as biological materialist terms. For example, in his discussion of lactose intolerance, Harris (1985, 1986) agrees that the milk aversion of many groups, including the Chinese, is the result of a deficiency in the enzyme lactase that makes the digestion of milk difficult and can cause intestinal distress. Yet although this biocultural interpretation may explain the reluctance to use milk, it may also obscure a higher level of analysis, as Harris points out, by sidestepping the more important question of why the Chinese did not develop a dairying economy. Ecological, social, political, and economic factors may answer this question.

Social, political, and economic factors have a major influence on food patterns. Ross (Chapter 1), Edelman (Chapter 22), and Franke (Chapter 19) have demonstrated the importance of these factors in the American diet and the impact of capitalism on Third World diets.

The revival of a model from social psychology may help us interpret these influences. In 1943 Lewin developed the channel theory to explain how food flows through various channels to get to the table. The flow is governed by gatekeepers, who control the passage of each item (1943). Applying channel theory and the gatekeeper model to the wartime food habits of Americans, Lewin focused on the housewife as the key gatekeeper. He argued that changes in food patterns could be instituted by changing the attitudes of housewives. Unfortunately this model was applied in a limited fashion. He was concerned with the psychological state of the gatekeeper and neglected the economic factors that affect the flow of food through the channels. In addition, home economists, the primary users of the model, found it very difficult to change the gatekeepers' attitude (Lewin 1947).

The concept of gatekeeper may be worth reviving, since it provides a sys-

589

tematic method of analyzing how food choices are made and how food items flow through a social system. The application of the model will require a reorientation—a shift away from psychological factors to the social, political, and economic factors that regulate the channels and influence the gatekeepers.

Conclusions

The biocultural model of adaptation can provide insights into the food choices and aversions that characterize human dietary patterns. I have discussed a number of examples of food habits with a biological basis, including the taste for sweetness, the aversion to bitter substances, the omnivorous-generalist food patterns, and the importance of high-density foods. Many food practices may be understood through a biocultural adaptive model. The use of the fava bean, food combinations that provide complementary sources of amino acids, and lactose intolerance have been interpreted from this perspective. These explanations may not be sufficient; social, political, and economic factors can exert an influence and even override the biological basis of food choice. However, we should not neglect the potential value of the biocultural perspective in providing insights into human dietary choices and the interaction of these biocultural factors with economic and political systems.[1]

Note

1. I would like to dedicate this essay to Glynn Isaac, whose vision of human evolution has shaped our perception of our early ancestors and whose emphasis on the role of food in the origin and evolution of hominids has provided many insights into the history of our species.

References Cited

Arlin, M.
    1977   *The Science of Nutrition.* 2d ed. New York: Macmillan.
Balagura, S.
    1973   *Hunger: A Biopsychological Analysis.* New York: Basic Books.
Beidler, L. M.
    1982   Biological Basis of Food Selection. In *The Psychobiology of Human Food Selection,* L. M. Barker, ed., pp. 3–15. Westport, Conn.: AVI.

Booth, D. A.
    1982   How Nutritional Effects of Food Can Influence People's Dietary Choice.
            In *The Psychobiology of Human Food Selection,* L. M. Barker, ed., pp.
            67–84. Westport, Conn.: AVI.
Buikstra, J.
    1983   Paper read at the Wenner-Gren Foundation Conference on Food Prefer-
            ences and Avoidances, Cedar Key, Florida.
Davis, C. M.
    1928   Self-Selection of Diets by Newly Weaned Infants: An Experimental
            Study. *American Journal of Diseases of Children* 36:651–79.
    1939   Results of the Self-Selection of Diets by Young Children. *Canadian
            Medical Association Journal* 41:257–61.
De Snoo, K.
    1937   Sucking Behavior in the Human Fetus. *Monatsschrift Geburtshilfe*
            105:88–97.
Eaton, S. B., and M. Konner
    1985   Paleolithic Nutrition. *New England Journal of Medicine* 312:283–89.
Epstein, A., and P. Teitelbaum
    1962   Regulation of Food Intake in the Absence of Taste, Smell and Other
            Oropharingeal Sensations. *Journal of Comparative and Physiological
            Psychology* 55:753–759.
Farb, P., and G. Armelagos
    1980   *Consuming Passions: The Anthropology of Eating.* Boston: Houghton
            Mifflin.
Fischler, C.
    1981   Food Preferences, Nutritional Wisdom, and Sociocultural Evolution. In
            Food, Nutrition, and Evolution D. N. Walcher, ed., pp. 59–68. New
            York: Masson.
Glander, K.
    1982   The Impact of Secondary Compounds on Primate Feeding Behavior.
            Yearbook of Physical Anthropology 25:25–36.
Hamilton, W., and C. Busse
    1978   Primate Carnivory and Its Significance. *Bioscience* 28:761–66.
Harding, R. S. O.
    1973   Predation by a Troop of Olive Baboons (*Papio anubis*) *American Journal
            of Physical Anthropology* 38:587–92.
Harding, R. S. O., and G. Teleki
    1981   *Omnivorous Primates: Gathering and Hunting in Human Evolution.*
            New York: Columbia University Press.
Harris, M.
    1986   *Good to Eat: Riddles of Food and Culture.* New York: Simon and Schuster.
Hausfater, G.
    1976   Predatory Behavior of the Yellow Baboons. *Behavior* 56:44–68.
Hunter, J. M.
    1973   Geophagy in Africa and in the United States: A Cultural-Nutritional Hy-
            pothesis. *Geographical Review* 63:170–95.

591

Isaac, G.
1978   Food Sharing and Human Evolution: Archeological Evidence From the Plio-Pleistocene of East Africa. *Journal of Anthropological Research* 34:311–25.

1981   Archaeological Tests of Alternative Models of Early Hominid Behaviour: Excavations and Experiments. *Philosophical Transactions of the Royal Society, London* B 292:177–88.

1983   Aspects of Human Evolution. In *Evolution from Molecules to Men,* D. S. Bendall, ed., pp. 511–43. Cambridge: Cambridge University Press.

Janzen, D. H.
1978   Complications in Interpreting the Chemical Defenses of Trees Against Tropical Arboreal Plant-Eating Vertebrates. In *Ecology of the Arboreal Florivores,* G. G. Montgomery, ed., pp. 73–84. Washington, D.C.: Smithsonian Institution.

Jolly, A.
1985a   *The Evolution of Primate Behavior.* New York: Macmillan.

1985b   The Evolution of Primate Behavior. *American Scientist* 73:230–39.

Katz, S. H.
1982   Food, Behavior and Biocultural Evolution. In *The Psychobiology of Human Food Selection,* L. M. Barker, ed., pp. 171–88. Westport, Conn.: AVI.

Katz, S. H.; N. L. Hediger; and L. Valleroy
1974   Traditional Maize Processing Techniques in the New World. *Science* 184:765–773.

Katz, S. H., and J. Schall
1986   Favism and Malaria: A Model of Nutrition and Biocultural Evolution. In *Plants Used in Indigenous Medicine and Diet: Biobehavioral Approaches,* N. L. Etkin, ed., pp. 211–28. Bedford Hills, N.Y.: Redgrave.

Lee, R.
1979   *The !Kung San: Men, Women and Work in a Foraging Society.* Cambridge: Cambridge University Press.

1984   *The Dobe !Kung.* New York: Holt, Reinhart and Winston.

Lee, R., and I. DeVore
1968   *Man the Hunter.* Chicago: Aldine.

Lewin, K.
1943   Forces Behind Food Habits and Methods of Change. *Bulletin of the National Research Council* 108:35–65.

1947   Group Decision and Social Change. In *Readings in Social Psychology,* T. M. Newcomb and E. L. Hartley, eds., pp. 330–344. New York: Holt.

Linton, S.
1970   Woman the Gatherer: Male Bias in Anthropology. Paper read at the meeting of the American Anthropological Association, San Diego.

Livingstone, F. B.
1958   Anthropological Significance of Sickle Cell Distribution in West Africa. *American Anthropologist* 60:533–62.

Lytle, L.
  1977   Control of Eating Behavior. In *Nutrition and the Brain,* R. J. Wurtman
          and J. J. Wurtman, eds., pp. 1–145. New York: Raven Press.
Martin, D. L., and G. J. Armelagos
  1979   Morphometrics of Compact Bone: An Example from Sudanese Nubia.
          American Journal of Physical Anthropology 51:511–16.
Milton, K.
  1979   Factors Influencing Leaf Choice by Howler Monkey: A Test of Some
          Hypotheses of Leaf Selection by Generalist Herbivores. *American Nat-
          uralist* 114:362–78.
  1981   Food Choices and Digestive Strategies of Two Sympatric Primate Spe-
          cies. *American Naturalist* 117:476–95.
Mintz, S. W.
  1982   Choices and Occasion: Sweet Moments. In *The Psychobiology of Human
          Food Selection,* L. M. Barker, ed., pp. 157–69. Westport, Conn.: AVI.
  1985   *Sweetness and Power: The Place of Sugar in Modern History.* New York:
          Viking.
Orians, G. H.
  1980   Habitat Selection: General Theory and Application to Human Behavior.
          In *The Evolution of Human Social Behavior,* J. S. Lockard, ed., pp. 49–
          66. New York: Elsevier.
Rolls, B. J.; E. T. Rolls; and E. A. Rowe
  1982   The Influence of Variety on Human Food Selection and Intake. In *The
          Psychobiology of Human Food Selection,* L. M. Barker, ed., pp. 101–22.
          Westport, Conn.: AVI.
Rozin, E.
  1982   The Structure of Cuisine. In *The Psychobiology of Human Food Selec-
          tion,* L. M. Barker, ed., pp. 189–203. Westport, Conn.: AVI.
Rozin, P.
  1982   Human Food Selection: The Interaction of Biology, Culture and Indi-
          vidual Experience. In *The Psychobiology of Human Food Selection,* L. M.
          Barker, ed., pp. 225–54. Westport, Conn.: AVI.
Rozin, P., and E. Rozin
  1981   Culinary Themes and Variation. *Natural History* 90:6–14.
Speth, J., and K. A. Speilmann
  1983   Energy Source, Protein Metabolism, and Hunter Gatherer Subsistence
          Strategies. *Journal of Anthropological Archaeology* 2:1–31.
Spock, B.
  1968   *Baby and Child Care.* New York: Hawthorne.
Strum, S.
  1976   Primate Predation and Bioenergetics. *Science* 191:315–17.
Sussman, R.
  1978   Foraging Patterns of Nonhuman Primates and the Nature of Food Pref-
          erence in Man. *Federation Proceedings* 37:55–60.
Wiesenfeld, S. L.
  1969   Sickle-Cell Trait in Human Biological and Cultural Evolution. In *Environ-*

ment and Cultural Behavior, A. P. Vayda, ed., pp. 308–31. Garden City, N.Y.: Natural History Press.

Wrangham, Richard
　1985　　Ape Medicine? *Anthropology Quest* 33:7.

Wurtman, R. J.
　1982　　Nutrients That Modify Brain Function. *Scientific American.*

Young, P. T.
　1948　　Appetite, Palatability and Feeding Habits: Critical Review. *Psychological Bulletin* 45:289–320.

Zihlman, A.
　1983　　Paper read at the Wenner-Gren Conference on Food Preferences and Avoidances, Cedar Key, Florida.

Zihlman, A., and N. Tanner
　1974　　Becoming Human: Putting Women in Evolution. Paper read at the annual meeting of the American Anthropological Association, Mexico City.

Zihlman, A., and N. Tanner
　1978　　Gathering and the Hominid Adaptation. In *Female Hierarchies,* L. Tiger and H. Fowler, eds., pp. 163–94. Chicago: Beresford Book Service.

AFTERWORD

WITHOUT ATTEMPTING TO INDULGE IN TOO DETAILED OR COM-
prehensive a summary of all the varied themes and arguments contained in this
volume, it is appropriate to pick out several of the larger questions that have
been raised by its many papers.

First, there is inevitably the question whether this has been simply another
academic exercise. We think not. Although other circumstances might well
warrant a more succinct and polemical work, there is nothing inherently extravagant about the hope that we have entertained of compiling a volume to help
focus wider attention on the factors that shape the nature and quality of the
food we eat. While many of the authors give considered attention to beliefs
about food and the interactions between such beliefs and actual dietary behavior, none forgets that the study of diet is, above all, the study of a microcosm of
the cultural, economic, and political forces that constitute the energizing features of the social system in which human beings live. They have tended,
therefore, almost without exception, to view diet not as a static entity, but as a
process where biological or nutritional requirements, rooted in our evolutionary background, intersect with the social nature of human production.

It is this perspective that gives an underlying unity to this work, whether the
immediate subject is primate diet, neolithic foraging, or Third World consumption. To that extent, we regard this book as a particularly productive whole,
with the earlier papers helping to clarify the baseline of human metabolic needs
and later ones describing the varied ways in which different kinds of social and
economic formations have satisfied or denied them.

This intellectual reciprocity has broadened the perspective normally brought
to questions of diet in a number of ways, one of which is the realization by those
whose research has been confined largely to contemporary populations that,
despite facile arguments about human progress, millions of people today probably do not eat as well as their paleolithic ancestors. At the same time, work on
early human physical and cultural development has been informed by current
questions regarding the integration of social and biological processes in modern
dietary patterns. Bringing such an interdisciplinary perspective to bear on the
past and the present, we are impressed by the contribution that such efforts,
integrated by a shared evolutionary vision, can potentially make to a better
human future.

595

If nothing else, the papers in this volume have in common a conspicuous concern for the material realities of diet and a reluctance, despite an interest in foodway ideologies, to let belief systems obscure actual practice. In her summary essay, Roosevelt has properly emphasized one of the most important implications that emerged from this commitment—that unequal access to food resources has been a feature of human societies from early in our history, beginning with disparities between the sexes and age groups among foraging populations, and has extended perhaps even more dramatically into the present, where inequalities are based not only on age and gender, but on caste and class and the international division of labor. And as she has aptly observed, the constraints that underlie such disparities necessarily compromise the assumption that food practices are merely the outcome of some mechanical process of cultural optimization. In actual circumstances, social systems at any given point in time embody the intersecting and contradictory efforts of different individuals, categories of individuals, and social groups representing differing immediate interests; the outcomes are more likely to represent strategic compromises. Above all, there is not likely to be, or ever to have been, any resolution that is equitably apportioned among all sectors. It is recognition of this fact which places an important responsibility upon us to focus our attention on the variations in diet that reflect strategic differences in power and status within any given system, whether it be local, national, or international.

It remains to be said that the papers assembled here do not seem to us to give encouragement to those who argue that diet—or any other aspect of human behavior—is either the reflection of mysteriously encoded mental designs or the result of events so varied and complex that their origins are similarly beyond any comprehension. Both of these viewpoints would suggest that the character of human foodways is more or less impervious to scientific inquiry, but such a conclusion, while it may comfort those who wish to avoid direct confrontation with disquieting realities, finds little justification in the papers presented here.

If they demonstrate that dietary customs need not remain unalterably enigmatic, however, they specifically do not claim that these customs may be illuminated by easy formulas. Obviously, if that were possible, this would be a far shorter book. If anything, they suggest that a scientific view of dietary customs is decidedly *not* the easy option.

It is perhaps for that reason that there has been a reluctance to build grand models; nor is there any easy consensus here about how to construct a unified theory of food habits. Cohen (Chapter 10) exemplifies the more cautionary view, in this regard, when he contends that the level of "noise" in human cultural evolution is so high that "we cannot hope to explain the specifics of what people eat through any means other than the study of individual cultural histories." Yet, his paper cannot readily be construed as an argument to abandon a nomothetic research strategy. As much as any other paper in this volume, in fact, his demonstrates that one cannot hope to use the study of individual cultural histories to explain the specifics of what people eat without applying general principles that transcend individual cultures. As the book as a whole tends to show, through such principles we may begin to discriminate between "noise" and what is analytically salient; then, out of the seeming randomness of gastronomic behavior, plausible adaptationist theories may be proposed, tested, modified, or falsified.

We must emphasize that a commitment to an adaptationist strategy does not mean, however, that whatever is, is best. We have already made our position in this regard abundantly clear: that, as long as the costs and benefits of social customs and institutions are unequally distributed, it would be fatuous to regard the consequences of adaptive tendencies as anything but sub-optimal. Hence, we have no disagreement with Armelagos's (Chapter 24) observation that "sociocultural systems can persist for relatively long periods despite nutritional deficiencies." The fact that prehistoric Nubian Sudanic populations or others did so is in no sense a refutation of adaptationist research strategies. If anything, it is simply an invitation to explore more fully the specific biological, ecological, and political-economic conditions that were responsible for such deficiencies.

Yet, undoubtedly such apparently dissonant findings underlie the cautionary note sounded at the end of Cohen's thoroughly adaptationist paper, that "Cultural evolutionary theory can no more predict all of the features of cultural design than can the rules of biological evolution predict the design of specific organisms." While this is meant to be sobering, we are not particularly disheartened, for we know of no one who supposes that *all* the features of culture—whether of foodways or any other aspect of human social life—can be predicted or retrodicted.

Such an expectation would involve a fundamental misunderstanding of the nature of scientific enterprise, which deals in material probabilities and not in abstract certitudes. It is precisely for this reason that, while we believe this book presents substantial concrete evidence of the productivity of an adaptationist perspective on human diets, it does not aim to substitute absolute answers for intractable questions. It does seek to demonstrate, however, that, on the basis of such evidence, it is not unreasonable to expect that at least as much of the convergence and divergence in sociocultural systems as in biological systems may be brought within the explanatory purview of evolutionary theory.

M. H. and E. B. R.

About the Contributors

Glossary

Name Index

Subject Index

ABOUT THE CONTRIBUTORS

H. LEON ABRAMS, JR.
Abrams is associate professor of anthropology in the University System of Georgia at Swainsboro. He is also consulting anthropologist to the Price-Pottenger Nutrition Foundation and a member of the advisory board of the National Foundation for Nutritional Research. He has conducted field research among Mexican Indian groups. Among his published papers are "The Relevance of Paleolithic Diet in Determining Contemporary Nutritional Needs" (*Journal of Applied Nutrition* 1979) and "Vegetarianism: An Anthropological/Nutritional Evaluation" (*Journal of Applied Nutrition* 1980). His books include *Inquiry into Anthropology* (1976) and *The Mixtec People* (1977).

GEORGE ARMELAGOS
Armelagos is professor of anthropology at the University of Massachusetts at Amherst. His many articles include "Disease in Ancient Nubia" (*Science* 163) and "The Role of Diet, Disease and Physiology in the Origin of Porotic Hyperostosis" (*Human Biology* 49). He is also the author, with Peter Farb, of *Consuming Passions: The Anthropology of Eating* (1983).

MICHAEL BAKSH
Baksh is currently a researcher in the School of Public Health at the University of California at Los Angeles. He has done field research in the Peruvian Amazon and Kenya, principally in the areas of diet, nutrition, and health. He is author of "Faunal Food as a 'Limiting Factor' on Amazon Cultural Behavior: A Machiguenga Example" (*Research in Economic Anthropology* 1985) and, with Allen and Orna Johnson, of "Cognitive and Emotional Aspects of Machiguenga Color Terms" (*American Anthropologist,* in press).

MARK N. COHEN
Cohen is professor of anthropology at the State University of New York at Plattsburgh. An archaeologist with field experience in Peru and Chile, Kenya and Tanzania, his current research concerns patterns of health and genetic relationships in a colonial period Mayan population in Belize. Among his principal publications are *The Food Crisis in Prehistory* (1977) and *Paleopathology at the Origins of Agriculture* (1984), which he co-edited with George Armelagos.

MARC EDELMAN
Edelman is research director at the North American Congress on Latin America, an independent research institute in New York City. He has done fieldwork in Costa Rica,

Mexico, and the United States. Among his articles are "Agricultural Modernization in Smallholding Areas of Mexico: A Case Study in the Sierra Norte de Puebla" (*Latin American Perspectives* 1980) and "Human Behavior and Sociobiological Models of Natural Selection" (*The Philosophical Forum* 1981–82). He is an editor of *Costa Rica: Crisis in a Central American Democracy* (in press).

RICHARD W. FRANKE

Franke is professor of anthropology at Montclair State College in New Jersey and currently serves on the editorial board of the *Bulletin of Concerned Asian Scholars*. His fieldwork has included research in Indonesia, West Africa, Surinam, and Bougainville, and most recently involves questions of agricultural economy in the Indian state of Kerala. Among his articles are "Peanuts, Peasants, Profits, and Pastoralists—the Social and Economic Background to Ecological Deterioration in Niger and its Implications for Current Development Programs" (*Journal of Peasant Studies* 1979), "Mode of Production and Population Patterns—Policy Implications for West African Development," (*International Journal of Health Services* 1981), and "Miracle Seeds and Shattered Dreams in Java" (*Natural History* 1974). He is also co-author, with Barbara H. Chasin, of *Seeds of Famine: Ecological Destruction and the Development Dilemma in the West African Sahel* (1980).

KENNETH R. GOOD

Good received his M.A. from Pennsylvania State University and is currently an advanced graduate student at the University of Florida at Gainesville. For the last nine years he has been conducting research among the Yanomami Indians of Venezuela, among whom he currently resides.

WILLIAM J. HAMILTON III

Hamilton is professor in the Division of Environmental Studies at the University of California at Davis. He has studied various organisms, including desert insects, birds, and mice, but for the past 15 years has focused on relatively undisturbed naturally occurring baboon populations in the Namib Desert and in the Okavango Delta, Botswana. His published articles include "Primate Carnivory and its Significance to Human Diets" with C. D. Busse (*BioScience* 1978), "Omnivory and Utilization of Food Resources by Chacma Baboons, *Papio ursinus*" with R. E. and W. H. Buskirk (*BioScience* 1979), and "Social Dominance and Predatory Behavior of Chacma Baboons" with C. D. Busse (*Journal of Human Evolution* 1982).

DAVID R. HARRIS

Harris is professor of human environment at the Institute of Archaeology at the University of London. His research focuses on the ecology and evolution of agricultural and other subsistence systems, and he has carried out fieldwork in the Caribbean, South America, the Mediterranean region, Southwest Asia, tropical Australia, and Papua New Guinea. His main research commitment presently is to a comparative study of pre-European subsistence in the Torres Strait region of northeastern Queensland and southwestern Papua. He has authored numerous articles. His most recent major publication is *Human Ecology in Savanna Environments* (1980), which he edited.

MARVIN HARRIS
Harris is graduate research professor of anthropology at the University of Florida at Gainesville. He has conducted field research in Brazil, Mozambique, India, and Ecuador. Among his many articles are "The Cultural Ecology of India's Sacred Cattle" (*Current Anthropology* 1966) and "Animal Capture and Yanomamo Warfare: Retrospect and New Evidence" (*Journal of Anthropological Research* 1984). His books include *The Rise of Anthropological Theory* (1968), *Cultural Materialism* (1979), *Cannibals and Kings* (1977), and *Good to Eat* (1985).

KRISTEN HAWKES
Hawkes is associate professor in the Department of Anthropology at the University of Utah. Her field research includes work in Papua New Guinea and eastern Paraguay. Among articles are "Kin Selection and Culture" (*American Ethnologist* 1983), "Why Hunters Gather: Optimal Foraging and the Aché of Eastern Paraguay" with K. Hill and J. F. O'Connell (*American Ethnologist* 1982), and "Affluent Hunters? Some Comments in Light of the Alyawara Case" with J. F. O'Connell (*American Anthropologist* 1981).

ALLEN JOHNSON
Johnson is professor of anthropology at the University of California at Los Angeles. He has done fieldwork in northeast Brazil and the Peruvian Amazon. His published papers include "Time Allocation in a Machiguenga Community" (*Ethnology* 1975), "Reductionism in Cultural Anthropology" (*Current Anthropology* 1982), and "Nutritional Criteria in Machiguenga Food Production" with C. A. Behrens (*Human Ecology* 1982), and he is the author of *Sharecroppers of the Sertão* (1971) and *Quantification in Cultural Anthropology* (1978).

SOLOMON H. KATZ
Katz is professor of anthropology at the University of Pennsylvania and Director of the W. M. Krogman Center for Research in Child Growth and Development. His research has included the role of favism in protection against malaria, the ingestion of non-food materials to supplement diet, and the development of traditions of food preparation as a means of augmenting the nutrient quality of foods. He has published extensively in journals such as *Science, Medical Anthropology, Human Biology,* and the *Journal of Physical Anthropology.*

LESLIE SUE LIEBERMAN
Lieberman is associate professor of anthropology and pediatrics at the University of Florida at Gainesville. She has worked with native Americans and U.S. migrant groups, including Cubans and Haitians. Her research interests include nutritional anthropology, human growth and development and its biocultural correlates, and the behavioral and genetic epidemiology of diabetes, particularly among Amerindians and Black Americans. Among her publications are "Medico-nutritional Practices among a Group of Northeastern Urban Puerto Ricans" (*Social Science and Medicine* 1979), "Growth and Development, Nutrition and Activity among Diabetic Youngsters" (*Florida Scientist* 1980), and *Physical Anthropology: Laboratory Textbook* (1985), co-authored with Linda Wolfe.

603

SHIRLEY LINDENBAUM

Lindenbaum is associate professor of anthropology at the Graduate Faculty of the New School for Social Research in New York. She has investigated the social and medical dimensions of diarrheal diseases in Bangladesh and kuru (a disorder of the central nervous system) in Papua New Guinea. Her current research interests include the political economy of health, changing ideologies, and symbolism. Among her principal publications are "Implications for Women of Changing Marriage Transactions in Bangladesh" (*Studies in Family Planning* 1981) and *Kuru Sorcery: Disease and Danger in the New Guinea Highlands* (1979). She is presently editor of the *American Ethnologist*.

KATHARINE MILTON

Milton is professor of physical anthropology at the University of California at Berkeley. Her research focuses on the dietary ecology and digestive physiology of primates, both humans and non-humans, and has involved her in fieldwork with howler monkeys and Amerindian groups in the Brazilian Amazon. Her publications include the articles "Factors Influencing Leaf-Choice by Howler Monkeys: A Test of Some Hypotheses of Food Selection by Generalist Herbivores" (*American Naturalist* 1979), "Diversity of Plant Foods in Tropical Forests as a Stimulus to Mental Development in Primates" (*American Anthropologist* 1981), and "Protein and Carbohydrate Resources of the Maku Indians of Northwestern Amazonia" (*American Anthropologist* 1983), and the book *The Foraging Strategy of Howler Monkeys* (1980).

K. N. NAIR

Nair is an associate fellow of the Centre for Development Studies in Trivandrum, India. His major research interests are livestock, irrigation, commodity markets, and rural development. His publications include "Milk Production in Kerala: Trends and Prospects" (*Economic and Political Weekly* 1979), "To Butcher or Not to Butcher: Cattle Holdings and Milk and Meat Production in Kerala" (*Economic and Political Weekly* 1979), "Bovine Sex and Species Ratios in India" (with A. Vaidyanathan and M. Harris) (*Current Anthropology* 1982), and "Land Hunger and Deforestation: A Case Study of the Cardamom Hill in Kerala" (*Economic and Political Weekly: Review of Agriculture* 1986).

BENJAMIN S. ORLOVE

Orlove is associate professor of anthropology at the University of California at Davis. His field research has focused largely on the Peruvian Andes. Among his numerous articles are "Integration through Production: the Use of Zonation in Espinar" (*American Ethnologist* 1977), "Tomar la Bandera: Politics and Punch in Southern Peru" (*Ethnos* 1984), and "Ecological Anthropology" (*Annual Review of Anthropology* 1980). He is also the author of *Alpacas, Sheep and Men: The Wool Export Economy and Regional Society in Southern Peru* (1977) and co-editor, with Glynn Custred, of *Land and Power in Latin America: Agrarian Economics and Social Progress in the Andes* (1980).

P. L. PELLETT

Pellett is professor of nutrition at the University of Massachusetts at Amherst. He has published more than 130 research papers and reviews in the area of protein nutrition and, more recently, in the problems of nutrition in development. He has been a consultant to several national and international agencies and was a member of the 1980–85 Recommended Dietary Allowances Committee of the National Academy of Sciences.

GRETEL H. PELTO

Pelto is associate professor in the Department of Nutritional Sciences at the University of Connecticut at Storrs. Among her research interests are dietary modernization, biocultural interactions in maternal and infant–young child nutrition in developing countries, and nutritional planning. She has conducted fieldwork in Mexico, Finland, and the United States, and is currently engaged in an investigation in Mexico of the impact of marginal food intake on function. Among her publications are *Anthropological Research: The Structure of Inquiry,* co-authored with P. J. Pelto (1978), *The Evolution of Human Adaptations,* co-edited with J. Poggie and P. J. Pelto, 1976, and *Nutritional Anthropology* (1980), of which she was also co-editor.

ANNA ROOSEVELT

Roosevelt is currently on the staff of the American Museum of Natural History in New York City. Her archaeological research has concentrated on the South American tropical lowlands, particularly the middle Orinoco River and Marajo Island in the Amazon River delta. Among her publications are "Isotopic Evidence for Prehistoric Subsistence Change at Parmana, Venezuela" with N. van der Merwe and J. C. Vogel (*Nature* 1981) and *Parmana: Prehistoric Maize and Manioc Subsistence along the Amazon and Orinoco* (1980).

ERIC B. ROSS

Ross is currently adjunct assistant professor in the Department of Anthropology at the University of Florida at Gainesville. He has conducted research in Mexico, the Peruvian Amazon, Great Britain, and Ireland. Currently, his interests include fertility and development, the political ecology of diet and health, and the relationship between power and ideology in Western societies. Among his principal publications are the articles "Food Taboo, Diet, and Hunting Strategy: The Adaptation to Animals in Amazon Cultural Ecology" (*Current Anthropology* 1978), "The Evolution of the Amazon Peasantry" (*Journal of Latin American Studies* 1978), and "The Riddle of the Scottish Pig" (*BioScience* 1983). He is the editor of *Beyond the Myths of Culture: Essays in Cultural Materialism* (1980) and author, with M. Harris, of *Death, Sex, and Fertility: Population Regulation in Preindustrial and Developing Societies* (in press).

PAUL ROZIN

Rozin is professor of psychology at the University of Pennsylvania. His research interests have included specific hungers and poison avoidance in animals, pathologies of memory in humans, and the evolution of intelligence. Over the past 10 years he has focused on why humans eat the foods they do, the nature and origin of food preferences and avoidances, the emotion of disgust, and the psychobiological bases of culinary practices. Among his numerous articles are "The Nature and Acquisition of a Preference for Chili Pepper by Humans" with D. Schiller (*Motivation and Emotion* 1980), "Culinary Themes and Variations" with E. Rozin (*Natural History* 1981), "Family Resemblances in Attitudes to Foods" with A. E. Fallon and R. Mandell (*Developmental Psychology* 1984), and "Operation of the Laws of the Sympathetic Magic in Disgust and Other Domains" with L. Millman and C. Nemeroff (*Journal of Personality and Social Psychology* 1986).

BRUCE WINTERHALDER

Winterhalder is associate professor of anthropology and the curriculum in ecology at the University of North Carolina at Chapel Hill. His principal field research was among Cree-speaking foragers in northern Ontario, and he is presently adapting foraging models to encompass opportunity costs, risk and sharing, and the effects of prey depletion. He is currently directing a three-year project on agricultural production, storage, and exchange on the eastern Andean escarpment in southern Peru. His articles include "Opportunity Cost Foraging Models for Stationary and Mobile Predators" (*American Naturalist* 1983), "Environmental Analysis in Human Evolution and Adaptation Research" (*Human Ecology* 1980), and "Competitive Exclusion and Hominid Paleoecology: Limits to Similarity, Niche Differentiation and the Effects of Cultural Behavior" (*Yearbook of Physical Anthropology* 1981). He is also co-editor with E. A. Smith of *Hunter-Gatherer Foraging Strategies* (1981).

DAVID R. YESNER

Yesner teaches at the University of Southern Maine. His major research interests are prehistoric cultural ecology, paleonutrition, and the origins and development of coastal societies. His principal fieldwork has been in Alaska, coastal Maine, and most recently Argentine Tierra del Fuego. Among his publications are "Maritime Hunter-Gatherers: Ecology and Prehistory" (*Current Anthropology* 1980), "Population Pressure in Coastal Environments: An Archaeological Test" (*World Archaeology* 1974), and "The Structure and Function of Prehistoric Households in Northern New England" (*Man in the Northeast* 1984).

GLOSSARY

Amino acids, essential and non-essential. Among the organic compounds known as amino acids that are the principal constituents of proteins, the nine or ten that cannot be synthesized by humans from materials normally present in the diet, at a rate commensurate with normal metabolic needs, are termed essential. In contrast, a non-essential amino acid, while also required for protein synthesis, can normally be manufactured by the body at an adequate rate to meet all normal body needs.

Anadromous fish. Fish that spend most of their life cycle in salt water, but migrate upstream to spawn in fresh water. The opposite are catadromous fish.

Angiosperms. Flowering plants, characterized by seeds encapsulated in the ovary tissue of the parent plant.

Autochthonous. Indigenous, original inhabitants.

B.P. Before the present.

Basal energy needs (Basal metabolic rate). The minimum food energy needs compatible with life. In common usage, it approximates to resting energy expenditure: the energy expended by an individual in a normal life situation while at rest and under conditions of thermal neutrality.

Bovids (*Bovidae*). A family of ruminants, generally characterized by paired, unbranched horns; includes cattle, goats, and sheep.

Brahmin (Brahman) cattle. A number of highly disease- and parasite-resistant varieties of humped cattle that are the result of crosses between South Asian (zebu) breeds and North American animals.

C_4 metabolic pathway. A photosynthetic pathway common to tropical grasses and related plants.

Catadromous fish. Fish that spend most of their life cycle in fresh water but swim downstream to salt water to lay their eggs.

Cattle cycle. The fluctuation in the size of the U.S. beef cattle herd that occurs over nine- to twelve-year periods as a result of changes in production costs and market prices.

607

Central place foraging. Hunting-gathering strategies that involve the return of foods to a central base camp and sharing of harvest in that locale.

Cholesterol. A fat-soluble steroid, manufactured in several human organs (chiefly the liver) that is an essential precursor for the synthesis of Vitamin D, various adrenal and sex hormones, bile salts, etc.

Cribra orbitalia. A disease attributed to iron deficiency anemias, characterized by porosity and pitting of the skull.

Currency. The attribute(s) of a resource used to measure its value on some standardized scale. In foraging theory, often the metabolic energy content of the resource.

Diachronic. Through time, in a historical perspective.

Dicotyledonous. Pertaining to the largest subclass of angiosperms (*Dicotyledones*), distinguished by seeds with two leaves in the embryo.

Dietary breadth. The total number or range of resources eaten by a given population or a particular predator at any one point in time.

Diet-breadth model. A model chiefly applied to foraging species and human hunter-gatherers that attempts to predict which types of resources among those available are most likely to be pursued.

Eicosapentaenoic acid. A fatty acid found in relatively large concentrations in marine fish, sea-mammals, and shell-fish.

Electrolytes. Mineral compounds, often found in salts (such as those of calcium and sodium), that readily dissociate into positive and negative ions in solvents such as water or alcohol. As such, they can conduct an electrical current.

Emic. That which is deemed real, significant, or meaningful from the viewpoint of the participants of a particular culture.

Erythrocytic. Pertaining to erythrocytes, or red blood cells, producers of the respiratory pigment hemoglobin.

Etic. That which the scientific community of observers in a particular culture recognizes as real, significant, productive of theories that can be tested, and cross-culturally valid.

Felids (*Felidae*). Animals of the cat family of carnivores.

Folivore. A leaf-eating animal.

Glutathione. A tripeptide composed of the amino acids cysteine, glycine, and glutamic acid found in most living cells.

Green revolution. Programs of the 1960s and 1970s to improve world food output by introducing high-yielding seeds, fertilizers, pesticides, and more advanced irrigation, all extremely capital intensive, into selected Third World countries.

Harris lines. Radiometrically opaque lines found in the extremities of long bones, thought to be the result of disruption in growth due to shortages of calories and/or protein and of subsequent compensatory growth.

Hemolytic anemia. A subnormal concentration of hemoglobin in the blood caused by hemolysis, or destruction, of red blood cells.

Hominoidea. One of the three superfamilies in the suborder Anthropoidea, it is composed of all fossil and living apes and humans.

Hylobatids (*Hylobatidae*). One of the families of *Hominoidea* that includes gibbons and siamangs.

Hypoplasia. Defective or insufficient development of tissue, e.g., enamel hypoplasia, a defect in the deposition of dental enamel, probably related to acute deficiencies of minerals, vitamins, and/or calories.

Inclusive fitness. Reproduction of the genome or a part of it in successive generations. Traits that lead to a greater proportional representation in succeeding generations of one individual's genes compared to another's are said to have greater inclusive fitness.

L-DOPA (Levodihydroxyphenylalamine). Chemical precursor in the brain of dopamine, an important neurotransmitter.

Legacy hypothesis. The suggestion that phylogenetic traits may modify contemporary behavior, sometimes in maladaptive ways.

Marginal-value theorem. The foraging theory model that attempts to predict how long a forager will remain in a patch from which it is removing prey before moving on to another, undepleted patch.

Megafauna. Large mammals that became extinct at the end of the Pleistocene era.

Methemoglobin. A variant of hemoglobin in which the iron constituent is in the ferric rather than the ferrous state. Formed in certain cases of poisoning, methemoglobinaemia reduces the level of hemoglobin in the blood and leads to a diminution in respiratory capacity.

Monocotyledonous. Pertaining to the subclass of angiosperms characterized by one leaf in the embryo (*Monocotyledones*).

Nomothetic. Statements or viewpoints based on generalizations derived from the observation of the recurrence of similar events, relationships, or patterns under similar conditions.

Oligosaccharides. Carbohydrates containing from 2 to 10 simple sugars linked together.

Omnivore. An organism consuming a wide variety of food items from more than one trophic level—for example, leafy vegetation and animal matter.

Optimal foraging theory. A corollary of evolutionary theory that suggests that the likelihood of a resource being exploited is related to the "value" of that resource in terms of the efficiency with which it can be exploited.

Optimization. The assumption (basic to foraging models) that the choice of exploited resources is the best possible among a limited set of alternatives, according to some standardized measure.

Palynological. Pertaining to the scientific study of pollen.

Patchiness. Environmental heterogeneity, with numerous sub-units on which exploitation strategies may be focused.

Phospholipids. Fats (such as lecithin) containing phosphates and a nitrogenous substance in place of one of the fatty acids.

Polysaccharides. Macromolecular carbohydrate compounds including starch, glycogen, and cellulose.

Pongids (*Pongidae*). All contemporary and extinct varieties of apes, including orangutans, gorillas, and chimpanzees.

Prosimians. Family of primates that includes lemurs, tarsiers, and lorises and is regarded as morphologically simplest.

Prostaglandins. Compounds formed from fatty acids and having hormone-like functions in the human body, including regulation of smooth muscle activity and induction of fever and inflammation.

Red tide. A phenomenon caused by seasonal (usually early summer) blooms of certain protozoa, known as dinoflagellates, infesting shellfish and other marine invertebrates and often creating a reddened appearance in the tidal zone.

Ruminants. A division of even-toed ungulates whose stomachs have four separate cavities; includes deer, sheep, and cows.

Shared poverty. A concept offered by anthropologist Clifford Geertz in 1963 as a partial explanation for Javanese poverty and underdevelopment. Small farmers were said to share their meager wealth so that everyone got a little, but no one had a lot.

Species packing. Geographic aggregation of resources.

Stable isotope analysis. Analysis of the relative amounts of various non-radioactive (stable) isotopes of particular elements in the bones of different vertebrate species, including humans, that helps to indicate the diets of those whose bones are studied.

Steer-corn ratio. The ratio of the price of steers to that of corn used for cattle feed; an important measure of profits in raising grain-fed cattle.

Synchronic. In a given, fixed time period without reference to or ignoring historical antecedents or developments.

Time-minimizer/energy-maximizer. A dichotomous characterization of the trade-offs between energy and time faced by foragers. Given an increase in foraging efficiency (measured as a net acquisition rate), a time-minimizer elects to save time by foraging just long enough to get the same amount of energy as before. An energy-maximizer, on the other hand, elects to forage just as long as before in order to accumulate as much energy as possible.

Tooth micro-wear. Fine striations, grooves, chips, and other patterns of enamel wear, often visible only under high magnification, that vary according to the kind of food processed in the mouth.

Triglycerides. The major form in which fatty acids are found in the human diet.

Xerophthalmia. A serious advanced form of Vitamin A deficiency affecting the eye; the leading cause of preventable blindness in children.

NAME INDEX

Abrams, L., 79, 207, 216, 241, 242
Adair, L., 138, 139, 144
Aguilar, J., 545, 546, 547
Ahmad, N., 427, 428, 438
Ahmed, R., 438
Aigner, J. S., 293, 301
Alcantara, E. N., 240, 241
Alexander, J., 459
Alexander, P., 459
Alexander, R. D., 118, 120
Allen, C., 484
Allen, H., 290
Allen, L. M., 174
Allison, M., 268, 269, 270, 271, 274
Almroth, S., 474
Ambrose, S., 106
American Dietetic Association, 248
Ames, K., 297
Amphiaraus, 151
Anderson, B. M., 247
Anderson, J. W., 240
Andrew, E. M., 247
Andrews, A. C., 148, 150, 151, 152, 153
Angel, J. L., 265, 268, 269, 270, 271, 274, 275, 277
Angyal, A., 192, 193
Antúnez de Mayolo, S., 490
Appadurai, A., 193, 194
Appleby, G., 497, 500, 507
Araya, Hector, 43
Arie, T. H. D., 148, 151
Arimoto, K., 288, 289, 291
Aristotle, 151
Arlin, M., 581
Armelagos, G., 216, 264, 267, 268, 565, 566, 567, 568, 570, 575, 576, 577, 579, 588
Arroya, P. A., 525, 526
Aschmann, H., 290
Ascoli, W., 42
Asia Record, 467
Aviles, R., 553
Aylward, F., 141, 149, 153
Azim, Z. N., 439
Aziz, K. M. A., 439

Bailey, F. M., 362, 364
Bailey, K. V., 459, 460

Baker, G., 127
Baker, P., 500
Baksh, M., 73, 387, 388, 391, 397, 398
Balagura, S., 581
Baldus, H., 346
Balling, J. D., 118
Bangladesh Times, 436
Barahona Israel, R., 556
Barboza V., C., 545, 546, 547
Barer-Stein, T., 214
Barker, L. M., 181
Barstow, J., 505
Basauri, V., 555
Basedow, H., 209
Basso, E., 9, 210
Bates, M., 212
Batra, S. M., 450
Batrouni, L., 525, 527
Bayless, T. M., 71
Bayless-Smith, T., 468
Beauchamp, G. K., 182, 187
Beck, B., 103
Beckerman, S., 407, 420
Bee, R., 532
Beech, M. J., 440
Behrens, C., 16, 315, 394
Beidler, L. M., 580
Belsey, M. A., 138, 139, 144, 149
Bem, D., 189
Benfer, R., 268, 276
Benjamin, M., 470
Beresford, M., 472
Berg, A., 552
Bergan, J. G., 242, 247
Berk, G., 194
Berkes, F., 12
Berry, R. J. A., 100
Bertino, M., 182
Bettinger, R. L., 334
Beutler, E., 141, 146
Bhatia, B., 36
Bienzle, U., 138
Bigelow, R., 118
Binford, L., 76, 266, 286, 296, 299, 303
Birch, L. L., 189, 196
Birdsell, J. B., 208, 359

Black, F., 568
Bleek, D. F., 210
Blum, J., 28
Blurton Jones, N., 344, 345
Bodenheimer, F. S., 212
Bodzy, P. W., 247
Boesch, C., 105
Boesch, H., 105
Bolton, J., 21
Booth, D. A., 182, 187, 188, 588
Borgstrom, G., 291, 292, 295, 535
Botkin, S., 292
Bottini, E., 138, 146
Boucher, N. D., 298
Bourne, G. H., 209, 212
Bowdler, S., 290
Boyce, J., 430
Boyd, R., 120
Braidwood, R. J., 208
Braudel, F., 27, 28, 456, 457
Bray, G. A., 233
Briscoe, J., 436
Bristowe, W. S., 212
Broadley, H., 27
Bronowski, J., 208, 210
Bronson, B., 209
Brothwell, D., 212, 214, 276
Brothwell, P., 212, 214
Brown, D., 208
Brown, L., 544, 554
Brown, P. T., 242, 247
Brunser, O., 470
Brush, S. B., 486
Buechler, H. C., 211
Buechler, J. M., 211
Buikstra, J., 12, 120, 267, 268, 269, 270, 271, 273, 277, 588
Burbach, R., 41, 42, 43, 45 n.1, 464
Burchard, R., 484, 490
Bureau of Nutritional Sciences, 170
Burkitt, B. D., 240
Burkitt, D. P., 93, 101
Burton, B. T., 396
Buskirk, R. E., 103, 107, 123, 124, 125
Buskirk, W. H., 103, 107, 123, 124, 125
Busse, C., 79, 123, 124, 581
Butz, Earl, 40
Butzer, K., 18, 208
Buxedas, M., 546

Caldwell, J., 71
Cámara de Ganaderos de Guanacaste (CGG), 547
Campbell, B. G., 208, 209
Campbell, D., 279 n.1
Campbell, J. B., 357

Campbell, R. M., 101
Campbell, S., 207
Carbarino, M. S., 214
Carcassi, L. E. F., 146
Carlisle, A., 25
Carneiro, R., 9
Carpenter, Z. L., 396
Carroll, M., 75
Cassidy, C. M., 261, 268, 269, 270, 271, 272, 273, 277
Castro, Josué de, 460, 473
Cavanagh, J., 463
Ccama, F., 501
Celsus, 148
Centro Internacional de Mejoramiento de Maiz y Trigo (CIMMYT), 428, 429, 437
Chagnon, N., 14, 20, 21, 210, 407, 408
Chang, K. C., 76
Chard, P. S., 208
Charles-Dominique, P., 95, 96
Charnov, E. L., 124, 314, 315, 316, 317, 323, 332, 333, 344
Chasin, B. H., 462, 469
Chaudhury, R. H., 429
Chavez, A., 521, 522, 523, 524, 532, 533, 534
Chen, L., 168, 429
Chevion, M., 138, 141
Childe, V. G., 265, 266
Chisholm, B. S., 298
Chivers, D. J., 97, 99, 102, 103, 107
Christenson, A. L., 264
Cines, B., 186
Clairmonte, F., 463
Clarence-Smith, G., 461
Clark, G., 25, 290
Clastres, P., 9, 12, 346
Clay, E. J., 436
Cleaver, H., 466
Clemen, R., 40
Clemens, E. T., 99, 102
Clutton-Brock, J., 25
Clutton-Brock, T. H., 104
Coaquira, C., 501
Cody, M. L., 314
Cohen, G., 141, 335
Cohen, M., 76, 209, 262, 264, 265, 266, 267, 268, 296, 300, 302, 342, 566, 567, 568, 570, 576, 577
Collier, W., 468
Collins, J., 470, 485, 490, 507, 553
Comisión Económica Para América Latina (CEPAL), 556
Committee on Dietary Allowances, Food and Nutrition Board, 228, 230
Committee on Food Protection, Food and Nutrition Board, 249

Committee on Nutrition, American Academy of Pediatrics, 242
Connell, J. H., 313
Consulate-General of Uruguay, 34
Cook, D. C., 120, 267, 268, 269, 270, 271, 273, 277
Cook, R. A., 247
Coon, J., 249
Cooper, J. M., 209
Cowart, B. J., 182
Cowie, R. J., 315
Crader, D. C., 119
Crawford, W., 27
Cripps, A. W., 101
Crompton, E. W., 95
Crosby, W. H., 141
Crotty, R., 447
Cuatrecasas, P., 71
CulturaSep, 530, 531
Curran, C. H., 212
Custred, G., 491
Cybulski, J., 301

Dahlberg, F., 263
Dam, H. ten, 460
Darby, W., 60, 65
Darling, F., 26
Dart, R., 207
Da Veiga, J. S., 546
Davenport, H. W., 100
Davies, N. B., 129
Davis, A., 22
Davis, C. M., 581
Dawson, Jessie, 23
Deerr, N., 457
Deetz, J. J. F., 212
DeHavenon, A. L., 72
DeLuca, H. F., 164
Demment, M. W., 95, 101, 103, 104, 105
Denton, D., 82
Deshler, W. W., 64
De Snoo, K., 580
Desor, J. A., 196, 232
DeVore, I., 103, 207, 209, 341, 584
DeWalt, B., 532, 536, 546
DeWalt, K., 71
Dewey, K., 497
DeWitt, R., 42, 545
Diamond, J. M., 100
Diaz, D. M., 533
Dick, H., 467
Dickel, D., 268, 276
Dickinson, J. C., 553
Dinham, B., 466
Diogenes, 151

Dirección General de Estadística y Censos (DGEC), 548, 554
Dixon, R. M. W., 359, 372
Dodd, G., 32, 37
Doedhar, A. D., 164
Domhoff, G. W., 40, 44 n.3
Domning, D. P., 293
Douglas, M., 59, 60, 193
Downs, J. F., 212
Doyle, M., 247
Draper, H. H., 107, 232, 234
Draper, L. R., 100
Droessler, J., 568
Drummond, J., 22, 28, 36
Dublin Mansion House Relief Committee, 31
Dubos, R., 227, 232
Duby, G., 25
Duran, Fray D., 210
Durham, W. H., 120, 314
Dutt, R., 36
Dutton, H., 31
Dwyer, J. T., 247, 248

Earle, T., 264, 393
Eaton, J. W., 141, 143
Eaton, S. B., 586
Ebangit, M. L., 247
Ebert, I., 191
Eckman, J. R., 141, 143
Edelman, M., 547, 556
Edmundson, W., 467
Edozien, J. C., 107
Ehle, F. R., 102
Eibl-Eibesfeldt, I., 118
Eimerl, S., 207
Eisenberg, J. F., 94
Eisman, B., 472
Ellickson, J., 438
Ember, C., 18, 341
Engelman, K., 182
Eppright, M., 247
Epstein, A., 581
Erlandson, J., 291
Essig, E. O., 212
Etkin, N. L., 141
Evans-Pritchard, E. E., 211

Fagan, B., 262
Falk, J. H., 118
Fallon, A. E., 181, 183, 192, 193, 194, 196
Farb, P., 216, 565, 579
Farkas, C., 12
Faron, L. C., 212
Farwell, B., 37
Feder, E., 430, 546

Feinberg, E., 470
Feit, H., 12, 14
Felger, R., 291, 292
Fell, B. F., 101
Fernández, M. E., 555
Ferrell, R., 234, 239
Ferro-Luzzi, G. E., 67, 68, 185
Ferroni, M., 483, 485, 486, 487, 488, 489, 494, 495, 496, 497, 499, 501, 502, 504, 505, 507, 510, 511, 512
Findlater, C., 26
Finger, B., 40
Fischer, N. H., 545
Fischer, R., 196
Fischler, C., 93, 121, 581
Fisher, A. D., 212
Fisher, H., 576
Flannery, K., 75, 76, 209, 393
Flecker, H. G. B., 364
Flores, J., 486
Flynn, M., 237
Flynn, P., 41, 42, 43, 45 n.5, 464
Food and Agricultural Organization (FAO), 227, 230, 395
Food and Agriculture Organization/World Health Organization (FAO/WHO), 172, 229
Food and Agriculture Organization/World Health Organization/United Nations University (FAO/WHO/UNU), 171, 172
Forbes, 545
Forster, R., 25
Fossey, D., 97, 98
Foulks, E. F., 133
Fowler, S., 39
Franke, R. W., 460, 462, 466, 468, 469
Frayer, D. W., 265
Frazer, J. G., 192
Frazer, G., 237, 244
Freeland-Graves, J. H., 247
Freud, S., 193
Fribourg, M., 429
Friedman, J. M., 141, 143, 146
Friend, B., 42
Frisancho, R., 42, 489
Fuller, J., 188
Fuller, W. P., 436

Gabel, C., 212
Gade, D. W., 486
Galdikas-Brindamour, B., 207
Garb, J. L., 187
Gardner, B. D., 544
Garine, I. de, 65, 66, 73
Garn, S., 42
Garza, D., 172
Gaulin, S. J. C., 95, 96

Gause, G. F., 312
Geertz, C., 458, 459, 574
Gelfand, M., 212
Gentle, M. J., 100
Ghalioungui, P., 60, 65
Gibbs, J. L., Jr., 212
Gibson, K. R., 103, 105
Gibson, R. S., 247
Giles, E., 148
Gittins, S. P., 97, 98
Glander, K., 583
Glanz, W. E., 96
Glaser, G., 138
Glassow, M., 303
Gleibermann, L., 238
Glimpse, 432
Goldman, I., 15
Goldstein, A., 186
Golenser, J., 143
Gomez, F., 175
Gonzalez Casanova, P., 535
Good, K., 73, 74, 80, 420
Goodall, A. G., 97
Goodall, J., 79
Goodman, A., 268, 269, 270, 271, 273, 277, 575
Goody, J., 59, 76, 493, 496
Gorden, J. E., 165
Gorden, M. E., 301
Gordon, J., 532
Gould, S. J., 313, 314
Government of India, 448
Government of Pakistan, 431
Government of Vietnam, 471
Graham, S., 20
Grant, I., 26, 30
Greene, L., 196, 232, 250, 251
Greenfield Popular Union, 40, 41
Greenough, P. R., 427
Gregor, T., 210
Greiner, T., 474
Grieve, R., 30
Griffin, K., 468
Grim, C., 238
Grine, F. E., 105, 106
Grivetti, L., 60, 65, 209
Gross, D., 11, 12, 73, 74, 407, 464
Gross, J., 100, 101
Gruss, I., 194
Gursky, M., 500
Guthrie, H., 225, 226, 245, 246

Habicht, J.-P., 532
Hafid, A., 468
Hagenauer, W., 554, 556
Hague, D. C., 323, 330
Hakim, P., 470

Hall, R. L., 103, 195
Hallet, J., 212
Halloway, R. L., 106
Hames, R., 14, 15, 74, 265, 321, 395, 407, 408, 420
Hamilton, W. J., 79, 103, 107, 123, 124, 125, 129, 207, 581
Hanaoka, M., 100
Handley, J., 26
Hanis, C., 234, 239
Hanna, W. A., 456
Hansen, J. D. L., 341–42
Hanson, S., 33, 38
Harako, R., 342
Harcourt, A. H., 97, 98
Harding, R. S. O., 19, 93, 95, 103, 207, 209, 264, 583
Hardinger, M. G., 247
Harner, M., 210
Harris, D. R., 289, 292, 357, 373, 375
Harris, M., 8, 36, 61, 64, 65, 70, 72, 73, 75, 76, 77, 78, 80, 81, 197, 198, 231, 266, 276, 277, 342, 407, 449, 544, 566, 589
Harris, O., 490
Harris, R., 208, 212, 231
Harris, T. N., 100
Harrison, G., 72, 236
Harrison, P., 37
Harrison, R., 228
Hartmann, B., 430
Harvey, P. H., 104
Hasegawa, T., 80
Hassan, F., 18
Haughton, B., 439
Hausfater, G., 583
Hawes, G. A., 464
Hawkes, K., 9, 10, 11, 12, 14, 16, 74, 265, 287, 321, 326, 331, 342, 347, 348
Hayami, Y., 468
Hayden, B., 18, 60, 75, 107, 262, 265, 266, 287, 295, 566
Hayes, O. B., 237
Hediger, M. L., 146, 198, 243, 580
Heimann, L. S., 464
Heller, C. A., 288, 289, 291, 292
Henderson, R., 29
Henriquez, J., 471
Herodotus, 148, 152
Hershko, A., 138
Herskovits, M. J., 212
Hespenheide, H. A., 264
Heyden, D., 210
Hickerson, H., 212
Hill, K., 9, 10, 11, 12, 14, 16, 74, 265, 287, 321, 341, 342, 346, 347, 348, 352 n.1
Hill, W. C. O., 99, 100, 102
Hind, H., 189

Hines, C., 466
Hirschman, A. O., 496
Hitchcock, S. W., 212
Hladik, A., 96
Hladik, C. M., 95, 96, 98, 99, 100, 102, 103, 105, 107
Hodgson, H., 39
Hoffman, W. E., 212
Hoffmann, H., 16
Holden, R. H., 548
Holiday, 432
Hopkins, L., 39
Horn, L. van, 462
Hornabrook, R., 64
Horowitz, J. M., 164
Horsfall, N., 357, 383
Horton, D. R., 290
Horwitt, M. K., 164
House of Commons, 36, 37, 38
Howe, M., 36
Howell, N., 342
Hsu, F. L. K., 76
Hsu, V. Y. H., 76
Huarachi, L., 501
Hudson, B. J. F., 141, 149, 153
Hudson, C., 80
Hufford, D., 248
Huheey, J. E., 138, 139
Human Relations Area Files (HRAF), 211, 213, 214, 215
Hume, E. M., 163
Hunter, J. M., 579
Hurtado, A. M., 347, 348, 349
Huss-Ashmore, R., 267, 575
Hutchinson, G. E., 312
Hutterer, K. L., 574
Hyatt, K., 317, 323
Hylander, W. L., 123
Hytten, F., 70

Interfaith Center for Corporate Responsibility (ICCR), 463
Inden, R. B., 427
Indonesian Documentation and Information Center (INDOC), 467
Institute of Nutrition and Food Science (INFS), 427, 431
Instituto Latinoamericano de Planificación Económica y Social (ILPES), 550
Instituto Nacional de la Nutricion (INN), 530
Inter-American Development Bank (IDB), 546
International Development Research Center (IDRC), 469
Isaac, B., 350, 351, 573
Isaac, D. L., 119
Isaac, G., 93, 108, 584

Izaguirre, B., 15
Izquierdo, S., 501

Jackson, A., 228
Jackson, E., 42
Jackson, H. E., 302
Jackson, J., 15
Jacob, F., 314
Jamalian, J., 141, 149, 153
Janis, C., 104
Janzen, D. H., 582
Jay, R., 460
Jelliffe, D., 20, 427
Jenkins, D. J., 245, 246
Jennings, B., 466
Jennings, J. D., 212
Jewell, P., 24
Jochim, M., 315, 395, 396
Johanson, D. C., 207, 209
Johnson, A., 315, 387, 388, 392, 394
Johnsson, U., 164
Johnstone, R., 360
Jolly, A., 582, 583, 584
Jolly, C. J., 126
Jones, L. H. P., 127
Jones, R., 290
Journal of the Royal Agricultural Society of England (JRASE), 38
Jurmain, R. D., 301

Kaizer, S., 186
Kalat, J. W., 188
Kalb, V., 470
Kamminga, J., 263
Kaneda, T., 289
Kano, T., 97, 98
Kaplan, H., 347, 348
Karasov, W. H., 100
Karim, R., 431
Karmas, E., 231
Katona-Apte, J., 21, 432
Katz, S., 81, 133, 135, 136, 137, 138, 139, 141, 144, 146, 149, 150, 196, 197, 198, 243, 244, 250, 580, 587
Kay, R. F., 123
Keene, A., 13, 319
Kelley, P., 15
Kelly, R. L., 303
Keltie, J., 26
Kennedy, K. A. R., 265, 268, 270, 271, 272, 273, 274, 275
Kennel, K., 191
Kensinger, K. M., 61, 395
Kershaw, A. P., 357
Khan, N. S., 436
Kikuchi, M., 468

Kilbourn, G., 40
King, J., 247
King, T. F., 302
Kingsland, S., 311, 312, 313
Kirkman, H. N., 138
Kjekshus, H., 462
Klausen, A. M., 73
Klein, R. G., 208
Kliks, M., 104, 106
Kluckhohn, C., 212
Knobel, L., 210
Kolata, G., 82
Konda, S., 100
Konner, M., 95, 96, 586
Koong, L. J., 100
Kosower, E. M., 141
Kosower, N. S., 141
Kracke, W. B., 61
Krebs, H. A., 163
Krebs, J. R., 129, 315
Kretchmer, N., 119
Krey, S. H., 237, 248
Krondl, M., 183

La Barre, W., 492
Laertius, 151
Lancaster, J. B., 106, 108
Landry, S. O., 93
Langdon, S. W., 466, 474
Lange, F. W., 303
Lappé, F., 243, 431, 553
Larsen, C., 268, 269, 270, 271, 272, 274
Latham, M. C., 165, 474
Lathrap, D., 342, 350
Lau, D., 183
Laughlin, W. S., 293
Lea, K., 26
Leacock, E., 13, 14, 18, 22
Leakey, M. D., 208
Leakey, R., 342
Lee, R., 18, 74, 98, 107, 209, 210, 262, 297, 330, 331, 341, 342, 344, 345, 353 n.2, 584, 585
Leeds, A., 64
Leigh, R. W., 301
Leighton, D., 212
Leitner, K., 465
León, J. S., 545, 546, 547
Lepper, M. R., 189
Leutenegger, W., 106
Levander, O. A., 174
Levins, R., 314
Levinson, F. J., 431
Lévi-Strauss, C., 58, 59
Lewallen, J., 471
Lewin, K., 342, 589
Lewontin, R. C., 313, 314

Lieberman, L. S., 234, 238, 250
Liebman, B., 237, 241, 242
Liebowitz, J., 141
Liener, I., 235
Lin, J. Y., 141
Lindenbaum, S., 18, 71, 73, 431, 433, 439
Ling, K. H., 141
Linton, S., 584
Lischka, J. J., 290, 291, 294
Little, M., 20
Livingstone, F. B., 138, 139, 586
Lizot, J., 407, 420
Lloyd, L. E., 95
Lockwood, D. H., 71
Logue, A. W., 187
Long, N. V., 458
Loomis, F., 288, 293
Loosli, J. K., 99, 107
Los Angeles Times, 395, 396
Lourandos, H., 263
Lovati, M., 244
Lovejoy, C. O., 576
Loveland, F., 16
Lowie, R., 62, 63
Lowther, G., 129, 207
Lucas, A., T., 31
Luft, F., 238
Lumholtz, C., 360, 366, 367, 370, 371, 373, 374,
    375, 376, 377, 378, 379, 380, 381
Lumley, H. de, 208, 285
Lumsden, C. J., 120
Luzbetak, L., 64
Luzzatto, L., 139, 141
Lydus, 151
Lyon, P. J., 212
Lytle, L., 581

McArthur, M., 64
MacArthur, R. H., 316, 317, 319
McCabe, A., 36
McCarron, D., 235, 238, 239
McCarthy, F. D., 466
McCay, B., 322
McConnel, U. H., 359
McCracken, R. D., 236
McDonald, B. E., 95
McDonald, D. P., 77
McEwen, J., 35
McGrew, W. C., 105
McGuire, R. H., 567, 568
McHenry, H. M., 105, 106, 301
McKay, D., 125
MacKay, F., 28
MacKenzie, D., 26, 27
McLaren, D. S., 173
McLellan, D., 42

McNicholl, B., 119
Madrigal, H., 521
Maga, J. A., 190
Mager, J., 138
Maher, V., 21, 22, 73
Maini, J. S., 451
Maletnlema, T. N., 164
Maller, O., 196
Maloney, C., 439
Mandell, R., 192, 196
Manjon, M., 36
Marsh, A., 248
Marshall, J., 341
Marshall, L., 210, 341, 353 n.2
Martin, D. L., 138, 139, 268, 270, 588
Martin, Paul, 18
Martin, P. S., 209
Martin, R. D., 101, 102, 107
Martinez, C., 532, 535
Mata, Leonardo, 532
Mather, P., 188
May, J., 42
May, M. L., 105
Mayhew, H., 30
Maynard, L. A., 99, 107
Maynard Smith, J., 313, 344
Mayr, E., 326
Mazess, R. B., 500
Meadows, D. H., 534
Meehan, B., 291, 298
Meggitt, M., 64
Meighan, C., 288
Meigs, A. S., 193, 194, 195
Meiklejohn, C., 265, 268, 269, 270, 271, 272, 273,
    275, 277
Mernies, J., 553
Messer, E., 521
Meston, A., 360, 361, 364, 369, 371, 376, 380, 382
Metraux, A., 15, 210, 212, 346
Meyer-Rochow, V. B., 212
Miller, B., 73
Miller, L. G., 248
Miller, M. R., 100
Miller, O., 232
Millman, L., 192
Milton, K., 96, 97, 101, 103, 105, 106, 107, 108, 583
Mintz, S., 82, 197, 509, 581
Missen, G. J., 457
Mitchell, P. C., 97, 99, 100
Monsen, E. R. L., 174
Montellano, O. de, 61
Montgomery, G. G., 96
Montoya, B., 501
Moore, F., 211, 212
Moorsom, R., 461
Moreno, O., 521

Morgan, D., 430
Mori, J., 148, 151, 152
Morren, G., 20, 64
Morris, D. M., 470
Morris, J. G., 93, 94
Morton, A. L., 30, 38
Moseley, M., 303
Moser, M. B., 291, 292
Moskowitz, H. W., 232
Moss, R., 100
Motulsky, A. G., 138, 139, 146
Mountford, C. P., 209
Multiple Risk Factor Intervention Trial Research
    Group (MRFITRG), 237
Murchison, M. A., 272
Murdock, G. P., 209, 211, 212, 216, 298
Murphy, R., 9
Murra, J., 490, 491
Murray, D. M., 100
Mwangi, W. M., 466
Myers, N., 42, 212

Nair, K. N., 64, 72, 448, 450
National Academy of Sciences–National Research
    Council (NAS-NRC), 171, 172, 175, 396
National Center for Health Statistics (NCHS), 233,
    237, 238
National Livestock and Meat Board, 236, 237, 240,
    241
Nations, J. D., 546
Neel, J., 20, 239
Nelson, D. E., 298
Nelson, R. A., 107
Nemeroff, C., 192
Netting, R., 28, 31
New Nation, 429, 436
New York Times, 429
Nicholas, R. W., 427
Nietschmann, B., 17, 291
Nigh, R. B., 546
Nomoto, K., 100
Norr, L., 268, 269, 270, 275, 277
North, D., 39
Novak, T., 141
Nuckton, C. F., 544
Nutrition Search, Inc., 228, 229
Nuzum, C. T., 104
Nygaad, D., 172

Oakley, A., 44 n.2
Oasa, E. K., 466
O'Brian, E. M., 93
O'Connell, J. F., 11, 12, 14, 74, 265, 287, 321, 331,
    342, 347
Oddy, D., 28, 36
O'Dell, A., 26

O'Donovan, J., 30, 31
Oficina de Planificación del Sector Agropecuario
    (OPSA), 556
Oficina de Planificación Nacional (OFIPLAN), 550
Ogbeide, O., 21
O'Leary, T., 346
Oliver, D. L., 212
Oliver, T., 23, 36
Olson, D., 105
Olson, J. A., 175
Ophir, I., 187
Oppenheimer, J. R., 96, 103
Orians, G. H., 118, 317, 321, 323, 582
Orlove, B. S., 314, 488, 491, 503, 506, 507, 509
Ortner, S. B., 193
Osborn, A. J., 285, 286, 291, 293, 297, 300, 302,
    303
Ottenberg, P., 193, 212
Ottenberg, S., 212
Owen, R. C., 212

Page, L., 42
Painter, M., 503
Painter, N. S., 93, 101
Palkovich, A., 268, 270
Palmerston, C., 360, 364, 367, 369, 376, 379, 380,
    381
Paolisso, M., 73
Papavasiliou, P. S., 148, 154
Parker, S. T., 103, 105
Parra, R., 104
Parsons, J., 24, 25, 546, 548, 552
Partridge, W. L., 546
Payer, C., 431, 546
Payne, P. R., 230
Pearce, A., 468
Pearce, G. R., 102
Pearson, N. E., 321
Pelchat, M. L., 187
Pellet, P. L., 164, 168, 172
Pelto, G., 71
Pelto, P. J., 532
Perlman, S., 265, 290
Perry, R., 207
Perzigian, A. J., 268, 269, 270, 271, 272, 273, 274,
    277
Peters, C. R., 93
Peterson, F., 210
Peterson, N., 359
Philips, A., 37, 44 n.4
Phillips, D., 529, 530, 537
Phillips, R., 237, 241, 244, 246
Pianka, E. R., 316, 317, 319
Picón-Reátegui, E., 487, 500
Pinstup-Andersen, P., 169
Pire, N. W., 448

Platt, T., 491, 503
Pliner, P., 188, 189, 194, 196
Pliny, 151
Plutarch, 151
Popper, V., 302
Potts, R., 207
Pounds, N., 24, 27
Pulliam, R., 124, 314, 315, 316, 327, 344
Pyke, G., 124, 314, 315, 316, 344
Pyne, S. J., 212
Pythagorus, 151

Quain, B., 9
Quarterly Economic Report, 543
Quin, P. J., 212

Radcliffe-Brown, A. R., 210
Raemaekers, J. J., 97, 98
Rahman, S. H., 439
Rajalakshmi, R., 164
Rajalakshmi, S., 70
Ramakrishnan, C. V., 70, 164
Ramirez Hernandez, J., 521, 528, 529
Rand, W., 521
Ranum, O., 25
Rao, V. K. R. V., 452
Rappaport, R., 64
Rapport, D. J., 315
Rathbun, T., 268, 269, 270, 271, 272, 273, 274, 277
Rathje, W. L., 567, 568
Razin, A., 138
Read, J., 36
Read, M., 248
Reddy, S., 139, 141
Reed, P. B., 235, 245, 246
Regal, P. J., 94
Register, U. D., 247
Reichs, K., 568
Reidhead, V., 11, 319
Remington, C. L., 212
Renfrew, C., 574
Rennie, M., 228
Restrepo, I., 529, 530, 537
Rewell, R. E., 99, 100
Richerson, P. J., 314
Richter, C. P., 182
Rippy, J., 33
Ritchie, J., 25
Rivers, W. H. R., 211
Rizek, R., 42
Roberts, R., 22
Robertson, J., 26, 29
Robson, J. R. K., 233, 241, 252
Rodman, P. S., 97, 98, 104, 105
Rogers, Q., 93, 94

Rojas Bolaños, M., 546
Rolls, B. J., 587
Rolls, E. T., 587
Romero García, A., 549
Roosevelt, Anna, 573
Rosch, P., 237
Roscoe, J., 211
Rose, J., 268, 269, 270, 271, 272, 274, 275, 277
Rosenbaum, R., 232
Rosenberg, D. A., 468
Rosenberg, J. G., 468
Rosensweig, N., 71
Ross, E., 7, 8, 9, 11, 12, 14, 15, 24, 29, 33, 35, 36, 39, 40, 41, 61, 75, 77, 82, 321–22, 401, 544
Ross, J., 407
Roth, W. E., 360, 370, 371, 376
Rothschild, E., 431
Roulet, N., 193
Roux, B., 541, 552
Rowbotham, S., 22
Rowe, E. A., 587
Rowe, J. H., 210
Rowlett, R. M., 148, 151, 152
Rozin, E., 182, 197, 198, 232, 242, 580, 587
Rozin, P., 80, 82, 181, 182, 183, 186, 187, 188, 189, 190, 191, 192, 193, 194, 195, 196, 197, 198, 199, 232, 242, 580, 584, 587, 588
Rudd, J., 23, 37
Ruddle, K., 212
Russell, J. K., 96
Russell-Hunter, W. D., 292
Rutsch, M., 546

Sabry, J. H., 247
Sackett, R., 73
Saénz Maroto, A., 554
Sahagún, B. de, 210
Sahlins, M., 7, 61, 330, 331, 342
Salaman, R., 26, 31
Salas Marrero, O., 556
Salo, M., 533
Sanderson, S. E., 542
Sarker, P. C., 439
Sartori, E., 138, 141
Savory, C. J., 100
Schaefer, O. H., 232, 234
Schafer, E., 28
Schalk, R. F., 299, 302
Schall, J., 133, 135, 138, 139, 141, 144, 146, 149, 150, 243
Schaller, G., 129, 207
Scherer, P., 467
Schiller, D., 82, 190, 191
Schmidt, A., 555
Schneider, H., 64
Schoener, T. W., 124, 313, 320, 324

Schoeniger, M., 265
Schrire, C., 350, 351
Schull, J., 191
Schulz, P. D., 301
Schurch, B., 165
Schwartz, H. P., 298
Scott, E. M., 288, 289, 291, 292
Scott, M., 431, 470
Scott, S., 17
Scrimshaw, N., 71, 165, 172, 227, 246, 532, 553
Scrimshaw, S., 71
Secretaría Ejecutiva de Planificación Sectorial
    Agropecuaria (SEPSA), 544, 548, 551, 553, 555
Secretaría Permanente del Tratado General de Inte-
    gración Económica Centroamericana (SIECA), 551
Sen, A. K., 327
Senn, M. J. E., 193
Service, E. R., 209, 210, 211, 214
Sewell, J. R., 470
Shane, D. R., 546
Sharma, D., 19
Shawcross, W. F., 292
Sheets, P. D., 291
Sheine, W. S., 99
Shipman, P., 207
Shodell, M., 289
Shorter, E., 19
Sibly, R., 344, 345
Silberbauer, G., 210
Simms, S. R., 287
Simoons, F. J., 61, 81, 119, 196, 197, 236, 251, 290
Sims, L., 237, 248
Sinclair, J., 26
Singer, R., 285, 288
Siniscalco, M., 139
Sirtori, C., 244
Sivard, R. L., 463
Skelley, A., 37
Slutsky, D., 542, 546
Smith, D., 64
Smith, E. A., 8, 74, 262, 313, 314, 319, 320, 335
Smith, G. C., 396
Smith, J., 26
Smith, K. A., 101
Smith, P., 265, 268, 270, 271, 272, 274, 275, 276
Smith, R. R., 459
Smout, T., 26
Smurthwaite, D., 37
Snell, Betty, 402
Snowdon, D., 237, 241, 244, 246
Soekirman, 468
Soentoro, 468
Solecki, R. S., 209
Soler, J., 59
Solimano, G., 470

Solís Avendaño, M. A., 541, 544, 547, 555
Solnit, A. J., 193
Solomon, R. L., 191
Solomons, N. W., 174
Sonntag, C. F., 100
Sopher, D. E., 73, 78
Speckman, E. W., 240, 241
Spence, J., 76, 77
Spencer, I. R. G., 461
Spencer, R. F., 212
Speth, J., 12, 17, 74, 107, 232, 234, 235, 289, 315,
    586
Spielberg, S. P., 143
Spielmann, H. O., 548
Spielmann, K., 12, 107, 232, 234, 235, 289, 315,
    586
Spock, B., 581
Sponsel, L., 73
Srinivasan, D., 449
Stahl, A., 93
Stamp, D., 30
Stanogias, G., 102
Starin, E. D., 207
Stark, B. L., 292, 303
Stavenhagen, R., 537
Stearns, S. C., 327
Stefansson, V., 210, 214
Stein, M., 193
Stein, T., 247
Steiner, J., 80, 182
Stephens, D. W., 332, 333
Stephens, S., 364
Stephens, S. E., 364
Steven, H., 25
Steward, J., 15, 210, 212, 394
Stigler, G. J., 327
Stini, W., 231, 252
Stocks, A., 15
Stoler, A., 467
Stonier, A. W., 323, 330
Strauss, K. F., 187
Strum, S., 103, 108, 207, 583
Stuart, D. E., 299, 302
Stunkard, A., 187
Sunquist, M. E., 96
Sussdorf, D. H., 100
Sussman, R., 93, 96, 99, 584
Swadling, P., 292
Swanson, W., 544
Switzer, B. R., 107
Szalay, F. S., 126
Szymanski, A., 464, 465

Taber, L. A., 247
Tambiah, S. J., 192, 193

Tannahill, R., 214, 457
Tanner, A., 14
Tanner, N., 584
Tartaglia, L. J., 288
Taylor, C., 165, 532
Taylor, K. S., 457, 460, 465, 473
Taylor, R. L., 210, 212
Teitelbaum, P., 581
Teleki, G., 19, 79, 80, 98, 207, 209, 264, 583
Terborgh, J., 103
Theriot, L. H., 471
Thomas, D. C., 248
Thomas, E. M., 341
Thomas, G., 39
Thompson, A., 70
Thompson, E., 35
Thompson, R., 40
Thorp, J. P., 434, 438
Tindale, N. B., 358, 359
Tonkinson, R., 209
Torun, B., 521
Toyama, Y., 289
Trant, H., 21
Treistman, J. M., 208
Tristán, M., 551
Trowell, H., 93, 240
Truswell, A. S., 93, 341–42
Tschopik, H., 485
Tufts University Newsletter, 235, 237
Tulloch, N. M., 100
Turner, M. R., 83

Ubelaker, D., 268, 269, 270, 271, 273, 277
Ubell, R. N., 471
Underwood, B., 73, 464
United Nations, Department of International Economic and Social Affairs, 24, 25
Up de Graff, F. W., 16
Usanga, E., 139, 141
U.S. Congress, Office of Technology Assessment, 42
U.S. Department of Agriculture (USDA), 207, 429, 541, 555

Vaidyanathan, A., 64, 72, 211
Valdes-Brito, J., 471
Valente, F., 464
Valimaki, H., 533
Valleroy, L., 133, 198, 243, 580
Van Lawick–Goodall, J., 207
Van Soest, P. J., 94, 95, 99, 104
Vayda, A., 64
Vickers, W. T., 74, 265, 321
Viteri, F. E., 171

Volman, T. P., 285
Voorhies, B., 292, 303

Wadsworth, G. R., 233, 241, 252
Wagley, C., 73
Waksman, B. H., 100
Walker, A., 93, 101, 126, 127
Walker, P. L., 301
Wall Street Journal, 543
Walton, K., 26
Wang, Z., 100, 101
Wanmali, S., 468
Ward, K., 240
Wardrop, I. D., 127
Warner, W. L., 209
Washburn, S. L., 208
Waterlow, J. C., 230
Watson, J., 26
Webb, L. J., 380
Webster, D., 320
Weinberger, M., 238
Weismanzer, Mary, 496
Weiss, K., 234, 239
Welling, E., 21
Welsch, R., 59
Wertheim, W. F., 460
West, R., 237
Westoby, M., 107, 315
Weyer, E., Jr., 210
White, B., 459, 468
White, E., 208
White, L., 25
White, T. D., 207, 209
Whiteford, M. B., 551
Wiens, J., 313
Wiesenfeld, S. L., 586
Wilbert, J., 9
Wilbraham, A., 22, 28, 36
Williams, G., 343, 344
Williams, R. G., 545, 549
Williams, V. J., 101
Williston, S. W., 212
Wilmsen, E., 235, 342
Wilson, C., 28, 69, 70
Wilson, E. O., 120
Winter, W. H., 100
Winterhalder, B., 8, 10, 12, 14, 44 n.1, 74, 262, 264, 267, 313, 319, 320, 323, 335
Wiradi, G., 468
Wisner, B., 465
Wittfogel, K. A., 216
Wobst, M., 585
Wolf, E., 82, 456, 457, 574
Wolpoff, M., 265
Wong, S., 327

Wood, C., 67
Wood, G. D., 436
World Bank, 462, 465
Wrangham, R., 19, 97, 581
Wrick, K. L., 101
Wunder, B. A., 100, 101
Wurtman, J., 12
Wurtman, R., 12, 587, 588
Wymer, J., 285, 288

Yearbook of Agricultural Statistics of Bangladesh, 428
Yellen, J., 342, 345

Yesner, D. R., 285, 286, 290, 292, 293, 294, 295, 297, 299, 301
Yost, J., 15
Young, C., 34
Young, P. T., 581
Young, V. R., 172, 227, 246, 521

Zahorik, D., 188, 194
Zajonc, R. B., 188
Zellner, D. A., 188
Zihlman, A., 207, 575, 584
Zimmerman, S. I., 189
Zvelebil, M., 296, 302, 303
Zwanenberg, R. M. A. van, 460, 461, 473

SUBJECT INDEX

Acceptance/rejection of foods, 183–85, 232; motives in, 186; psychological categories of, 184–85(table). *See also* Food preferences and avoidances

Aché peoples: effect of modern missions on, 350–52; food preferences and avoidances among, 9–10; foraging and food quantities needed by, 341, 342, 346–49; hunting as source of calories for, 11–12; influence of the market economy on, 14; optimal foraging of, 321, 585

Achuara peoples: influence of market economy on, 14–15; meat distribution among, 20; sources of calories and dietary breadth among, 11

Adaman Islanders, 209

Adaptations, food. *See* Biocultural adaptive model

Adaptation to environment, 343–44

Adaptive inertia, 117–18, 121, 296, 581

Adrenarche, 146

Agribusiness, 455; and diet inequalities in the Third World, 463–66

Agricultural societies: animal protein/fat in, 211; health of, vs. hunter-gatherers, 269–75. *See also* Horticultural societies

Agricultural Trade Development Assistance Act, 430

Agriculture: and deforestation in Europe, 25–26; diet inequalities and the "green revolution" in, 466–69; intensive, 2–3, 576; modern, and profits, 40; shift from hunting-gathering to, 76, 263–79

Alaska, marine diet in, 285, 296

Aleut peoples, 234, 293

Amazonian peoples, 73, 573; food preferences and avoidances among, 9–10; and the market economy, 14–17. *See also* Machiguenga peoples; Yanomami peoples

Amerindians, North American, 12, 211–12, 214, 216, 299, 301

Amino acids, 163–64, 225, 226(table), 227, 588; complementary, 243–44, 580; human requirements of, 228(table); in marine foods, 291; and plant based diets, 243

Anadromous fish, 289, 294, 296, 299, 302

Andean highlands dietary patterns, 210, 481–83; changes in, 493–511; ENCA survey on, 493–502, 510–12; problems in study of, 483–84; traditional, 484–93

Anemia, 167, 169, 250, 270, 588. *See also* Favism; Hemolytic anemia; Iron

Angiosperms, 94

Animal protein and fat: in Australian aboriginal diet, 366–68, 378–79; biocultural consequences of diets high in, 231–41; commonly consumed, 215(table); consumption by Mexican poor, 523(table), 535; consumption in India, 21, 211, 445–47; contemporary cultures' use of, 214–15; with latter as preferred food element, 79, 207–23, 388, 395–97; insects as source of, 212–13; nutrients from, 232–35; preference for, 207–16; restrictions on, and Yanomami population growth, 407–20. *See also* Fats, dietary; Meat consumption; Protein

Anthropoids, 96, 98, 102

Appendix, 100

Aquatic food resources: and Australian rain forest aboriginal diet, 367–68; and dietary variety, 9–10, 16–17. *See also* Marine foods diet

Argentina, cattle industry in, 33, 545

Arginine, 291

Arthritis, 272–73

Australia, 63, 64, 545

Australian aborigines, 208, 209; annual settlement and subsistence cycle of, 376–82; cannibalism among, 368–73; population regulation of, 373–75; and tropical rain forest subsistence, 357–68

Australopithecines, 105–106; diet, 126–27, 207–208

Aymara peoples, 211

Aztec peoples, 76; and cannibalism, 61, 210

Baboon diet, 19, 103, 122, 123, 124(table), 125

Baganda peoples, 153

Bambala peoples, 63

Banco Nacional de Costa Rica, 546–47

Bangladesh, 427–28; food classification in, 432–39; rice and wheat in, 427–32

Bantu peoples, 63

Barotseland, 461

Basal energy needs, 95–96, 171–72, 233–35

Beef consumption: effect of beef exports on Costa Rican domestic, 548–53; taboo on, in India, 64–65, 77, 449, 450–52; in U.S., 61, 541–45; U.S.

Beef consumption *(cont.)*
  vs. Costa Rica, annual, 552(table). *See also* Cattle; Meat consumption
Beef prices, 543–44, 549–50
Bemba peoples, 22
Berber peoples, 21–22
Biocultural adaptive model: biology, taste and, 231–32, 580–81; and contemporary hunter-gatherers, 585–86; and cultural materialism, 589–90; and early hominids, 584–85; and food choice, 579–80, 586–88; and primates, 581–84
Biocultural evolution and food, 134–38
Biological dimension to biocultural evolution, 134(fig.), 135(fig.), 136
Biopsychological determinants of foodways, 79–82, 161–62, 589
Bitter taste avoidances, 182, 196, 580
Black Act, 25
Blindness and vision problems, 173, 440 n.4
Bone density and vegetarian diet, 248
Borboby, Australian aboriginal, 380–81
Bovids, 94
Brazil, 460, 464–65, 469, 471(table), 473 n.1
Broad-spectrum depression, 76
Broad-spectrum revolutions, 76, 263–67; and biological stress, 275–76
Buddhists, 450
Burmese peoples, 19, 63
Bushmen peoples, 210

C_3 plant foods, 95
C_4 plant foods, 95, 292
Calcium, 235, 236, 238, 488, 588
Calories: consumption of, among Mexican poor, 528(table), 529(table); labor productivity and efficiencies in, 389(table); sources of, among hunters, 11–13. *See also* Basal energy needs
Cámaras de Ganaderos, 547
Cameroon, 65, 66
Canada, 544
Cancers and diet, 239, 240–41
Canids, 102
Cannibalism: among Australian aboriginals, 368–73; among Aztecs, 61, 210
Capitalist societies, gender-related food distribution in, 22–23
Capitalist world system, 3, 15, 423. *See also* Market economy; Neocolonialism
Capuchin monkey, 96, 102, 103
Carbohydrate consumption, 245–46
CARE, 430
Caribbean colonies, English, 30
Carnivores, 94, 102
Cassava, 459–60
Catadromous fish, 289

Cattle: in Costa Rica, 42, 545–57; in Europe, 24, 25; in Ireland and Scotland, 29–34; in Latin America, 33–34, 541–57; taboos on killing, 63, 64, 449–50; in the U.S., 40, 541–45. *See also* Beef consumption
Cattle cycle, 542
Cecum, 99, 100
Celiac disease, 119, 251, 440 n.4
Central America, beef production in, 541–58
Chad, 66
Chickens, 63
Children, diet restrictions on, 22–23. *See also* Infants
Child replacement hypothesis, 533
Chile, 33, 470
Chile peppers, learning to like, 189–91, 588
Chimpanzee diet, 19, 79–80, 97, 105, 581, 583
China: meat consumption in, 27–28, 216; milk consumption in, 63, 64; optimization selection in, 76
Cholesterol, 233, 237, 244
Church World Service, 430
Class/caste and diet, 3, 34–38, 44 n.3, 78; in Mexican poor vs. middle and upper class, 517–38. *See also* Status
Clay eating, 579
Cocamilla peoples, 15–16
Coca plant, 484, 490, 508
Coffee, 186, 456, 464
Colonialism: effect of, on Third World diets, 455, 456–62; English, and meat consumption, 29–38; internal, 537. *See also* Neocolonialism
Competitive exclusion principle, 320
Compression hypothesis, 320
Consequences of eating certain foods, anticipated, 184
Consumption curve: indifference map and, 331(fig.); norms, 329(fig.); opportunity-cost model of forager's, 326(fig.)
Corn Laws, 35
Corporate management of food resources, 39–42. *See also* Transnational corporations
Costa Rica: beef export production in, 545–48; effect of beef exports on domestic consumption in, 548–53; effect of beef exports on ecology and land use in, 553–55; effect of beef exports on economy of, 555–57
Cree peoples, 14; optimal foraging of, 319–20
Cretinism, 251
Cribra orbitalia, 301
Cro-Magnon peoples, 208
Cuba, 470, 471(table)
Cubeo peoples, 15
Cultural evolution theory, 279 n.1
Culture, 7, 566; changes in, and dietary adaptation, 119–21; complexity of, and maritime populations,

302–304; as dimension in ecosystems approach to evolution, 134(fig.), 135(fig.). *See also* Biocultural adaptive model

Curare, 16

Currencies: optimization, 75; opportunity-cost, 325–28; simple and compound, 314–15

Cystine, 163, 291

Dahomean peoples, 211

Dangerous foods, 184(table); vs. distaste, 187

Deforestation in Europe, and swine production, 25–26

Demographic dimension to biocultural evolution, 134(fig.), 135

Diabetes, 239, 246

Dicotyledonous plant foods, 95

Dietary breadth, 44 n.1; and caloric needs, 11–13; model of, 316, 317(fig.), 322

Digestive tract: hominoid, 100–103; proportions for hominoids, 99(table); size of, and metabolic requirements of food, 95–96

Dingoes, 63, 64

Disease: and animal proteins/fats, 121, 235–41; in farmers vs. hunter-gatherers, 269–70; and nutritional inadequacies, 164–65, 166–69(table), 173–74, 270, 301–302, 531–32; of overconsumption, 42, 83, 236–37, 240, 533–34, 586

Disgust for certain foods, 184(table), 185; among Machiguenga, 402–403; "positive," 194–95; vs. inappropriateness, 191

Distasteful foods, 184(table); vs. dangerous foods, 187

Dogs, 63, 64, 491

Domesticated animals, ecological costs of, in Europe, 23–27

Dominican Republic, 463

Ecologies: costs to, of domesticated animals in Europe, 23–27; effect of Costa Rican beef exports on, 553–55; influences of, on wild foods in Machiguenga diet, 387–404; limiting influence of, on Yanomami diet, 407–20

Ecosystems approach to food and biocultural evolution, 134–38

Ecuador, 250

Eggs: as cholesterol source, 233; as reference protein, 229; taboos on, 78

Egypt: folklore about fava beans in, 152; malarial vectors and fava bean harvest in, 144(fig.)

Eclecticism and foodways, 62

Emic foodways, 5, 72; influence of, on wild food procurement among Machiguenga, 397–403; and post-partum taboos, 68–70

ENCA (Encuesta Nacional de Consumo de Alimentos) study, 483–84, 510–12

Energy. *See* Basal energy needs

Energy-maximizer opportunity-cost foraging model, 325(fig.)

England: colonialism in, 29–34, 460–61; folklore about fava beans in, 152; meat consumption in working class, 22–23, 27, 34–38; political economy of meat production for, 29–34

Environment: adaptations required by, 343–44, 572–73; as dimension in biocultural evolution, 134(fig.), 136. *See also* Ecologies

Eskimo peoples' diet, 107, 210, 211, 214, 233–34, 299

Ethnicity and food choice, 186, 508

Etic foodways, 5, 72; analysis of labor productivity and, 390–97; and post-partum taboos, 68–70

Eurethrocytes, effects of fava beans and malaria on, 140–45

Evolution: ecosystems approach to biocultural, 134–38; and human diet, 2–3, 565–77; and primate omnivorous diets, 117–30

Famine vulnerability, 457, 458, 462

Fast-food restaurants, 545

Fat, dietary: consequences of excessive, 42, 237, 240; from marine foods, 288–89, 300; nutritionally necessary, 395–96; preferences for animal, 79, 207–23, 388, 395–97. *See also* Animal protein and fat

Fava bean consumption, 2, 81, 133–34, 587; cultural information about, 146–50; and favism, 138–53; folklore about, 150–53; nutritional and agricultural potential of, 145; other biological effects of, 153; population genetics and, 145–46

Favism, 133–34, 138–53, 250; cultural information about, 146–50; distribution of, 138–39, 140(fig.); and malaria, 139–45, 587; population genetics and, 145–46

Felids, 94, 102

Fiber, dietary: in humans, 101, 163, 245; in primates, 95

Financial resources, and diet, 71, 165, 168, 169(fig.), 469–72; in Andean highlands, 504–508; in Costa Rica, 551–52; in Mexican middle and upper class, 529–31; in Mexican poor, 520–29

Fish consumption, 287, 289, 294, 296, 299, 302; in India, 73; and labor productivity among Machiguengas, 389(table), 392–97. *See also* Aquatic food resources; Marine foods diet

Fitness, 343–44, 351–52, 577–78; as currency, 326–28, 331(fig.)

Folklore and fava bean consumption, 150–53

Food(s): contamination of, 534, 549; dissemination of, during colonialism, 456–57; hard/soft, 434; hot/cold, 71, 433–34; meaning of, 59–61; mental/symbolic functions of, 58–59, 566; use, prefer-

Food(s) *(cont.)*
ence, and liking of, compared, 183; wet/dry, 433–34. *See also* Variation in diet
Food chain, human, 137(fig.)
Food choice. *See* Food preferences and avoidances
Food classifications, in Bangladesh, 432–39
Food combinations, 579–80
Food distribution: and age, 23–24, 165, 168; Costa Rican beef exports and, 548–53, 557; inequities between Mexican poor vs. middle and upper class, 517–38; meat, among Yanomami villages, 415, 419 n.5, n.6, n.7; and sex, 18–23, 165, 168; and status, 19–20. *See also* Colonialism; Neocolonialism
Food economies and diet, 261–62; evolution of, 565–78; health of hunter-gatherers vs. farmers, 269–75; skeletal pathology as indications of, 267–69; through time, 262–67
Food flavorings, 82, 587; psychological importance of, 197–98. *See also* Chile peppers
Food for Development, 430
Food for Peace, 430, 503
Food for Work, 430, 435
Food nutrients. *See* Nutrition, human
Food of London, The, 32
Food preferences and avoidances, 7; in Andean diet, 490–93, 504–506; biocultural aspects of, 579–90; biological and cultural constraints on, 196–97; bi-opsychological determinants of, 79–82; among early humans, 103–108; idealist approaches to, 57, 58–63; irrational and harmful, 62–72; in Machiguenga diet, 394–97, 400–403; and the market economy, 13–17; and nutritional status, 176; optimization and, 74–79; psychological determinants of, 181, 183–85; and social status, 72–74; theory of, 72; variances in, 195–96. *See also* Taboos on food; Taste preferences
Food preparation, 198–99, 253; in Andean highlands, 484–85, 488; fava bean, 149–50; maize, 133, 198, 243, 521, 580; manioc, 198, 250; nuts of Australian rain forest, 379–80, 383
Food preservation, 82
Food procurement: among Australian rain forest aborigines, 360–68; among early humans, 105–108; labor costs and benefits of Machiguenga, 387–88, 389(table), 390–97; labor costs and benefits, subjective evaluation of, 398–99. *See also* Foraging
Food quantity, needs of hunter-gatherer populations, 341–53
Food supply, reliability of, 294–98
Foragers. *See* Hunter-gatherer populations
Foraging: costs to early humans, 105–106, 108; models of, 315–19, 322–23, 585. *See also* Food procurement; Hunter-gatherer populations; Optimal foraging theory

France, 458
Fulani peoples, 66

G6PD genetic deficiency, 138–39, 140(fig.), 141–45, 250
Gallstones, 239
Ganda peoples, 211
Gender variation in diet, 18–23, 73, 165
Gene-culture coevolution, 2, 135(fig.); and fava beans, 81, 133, 138–53
General Agreement on Tariffs and Trade, 543
Genetic traits and foodways, 2, 79–82; fava bean consumption and, 81, 133, 138–53; lags in dietary adaptation, 119; and tastes, 196, 232
Geophagy. *See* Clay eating
Glutamic acid, 250
Goats, 63
Goiter, 167, 169, 249, 250–51
Goitrogens, 249, 250–51
Gorillas, 97, 104
Grains, 2; cereal, in primate diet, 95; for human consumption vs. animal feed, 39, 536–37; nutrient loss in refining, 230, 231(table). *See also* Rice; Wheat
Greece, 24; folklore about fava beans in, 151; malarial vectors and fava bean harvest in, 144(fig.)
Green revolution, 466–69
Guaraní peoples, 350–52
Guatemala, 42, 171
Gut. *See* Digestive tract

Hadza peoples, 20
Harris hypothesis, on adoption of agriculture, 276–78
Harris lines, 271–72, 276, 301
Heart disease, and diet, 236–37
Hemolytic anemia, 133, 138, 587. *See also* Favism
Herbivores, 94, 102, 104
Hinduism, and food preferences and avoidances, 21, 61, 64, 73, 78, 211, 433, 440 n.7, 449–50
Histidine, 163, 226, 228, 291
Hominoids, 2; biological heritage of, 584–85; diet of, 97, 98(table); gut volume proportions of, 99(table)
Homo erectus, 208
Homo habilis, 207
Homo sapiens, 2, 208, 583
Hookworm, 174, 271
Hopi peoples, 212, 216
Horses, 63, 491
Horticultural societies, animal fat/protein in, 210–11. *See also* Agricultural societies; Hunting-horticulturalist populations
Horticulture: decline in protein, and transition to, 12–13; labor productivity and, 389(table), 390–92; social responses to decline in protein in, 17–23.

See also Agriculture; Hunting-horticulturalist populations

Howler monkeys, 96, 401–402, 583

Humans: digestive tract, 101–102; food choices of early, 103–108; omnivorous diet in early, 126–27, 207–209

Hunger, causes of, and nutritional disorders, 166–69(table)

Hunter-gatherer populations: biocultural adaptation and, 585–86; effect of contemporary society on modern, 350–52, 574; health of, vs. farmers, 269–75; as models of omnivory, 127–29, 209–10, 576; optimal foraging models applied to, 312–13, 319–22; quantity of food needed by, 341–53

Hunting-horticulturalist populations: and dietary preference, 8–11; meat distribution among, 20; sources of calories, and dietary breadth, 11–13

Hunting populations: gender and food distribution among, 19–20; influence of the market economy on, 13–17; sources of calories, and dietary breadth, 11–13

Hu peoples, 195

Hylobatids, 97

Hypertension, 237–39

Hypoplasia, enamel, 271–72, 276, 300

Idealist approach to foodways, 5, 57, 58–63

Ideational factors, and food, 184–85

Inappropriate foods, 184(table), 185; vs. disgust, 191–94

Inca peoples, 483

Income level. *See* Financial resources, and diet

India, 193; animal protein consumption in, 21, 211, 445–53; diet and status in, 73–74; folklore about fava beans in, 153–54; optimization selection in, 76; taboo on killing/consuming cattle in, 64–65, 77, 449, 450–52; taboos related to pregnancy/childbirth, 67–70

Indifference map, idealized hunter-gatherer, 328–30

Indonesia, 466–68, 471(table)

Infanticide, 18, 20, 370

Infants: diarrhea in, 71; dietary restrictions on, 18–19; low birth weight and mortality, 167, 169, 532

Information, cultural, 135(fig.); and fava bean consumption, 139, 146–50

Insects as food: among humans, 126–27, 212–13; among primates, 96, 123, 125–26

Instituto Nacional de Nutricion, 525, 538 n.1

Inter-American Development Bank, 42, 545

The Interest of England in the Preservation of Ireland, 30

International lending institutions, and beef exports, 545–46

Inuit peoples, 233–34; optimal foraging of, 320–21

Iodine, 249

Iran: favism treatment in, 149; malarial vectors and fava bean harvest in, 144(fig.)

Ireland, effect of English industrialization and colonialism on, 29–32

Iron, nutritional, 174, 246–47, 264, 588

Isoleucine, 226, 228

Isouramil, 143

Israelite swine taboo, 59–60

Italy, malarial vectors and fava bean harvest in, 144(fig.)

Jaguar, 401

Jains, 450

Java, 459–60, 466–68

Jívaro peoples, 210

Kalapalo peoples, 9, 210

Kalinga peoples, 211

Karimojong peoples, 20

Kazak peoples, 211

Kenya, 460–61, 465–66, 469, 471(table), 474 n.4

!Kung peoples: foraging and food quantity needed, 341, 342, 344–45, 346–47(table), 585; and use/non-use of available foods, 74

Kwashiorkor, 166, 168

Labor migrations, 461

Labor productivity and diet: etic analysis of Machiguenga, 389(table), 390–97; Machiguenga, subjective evaluation of, 398–99

Lactase production, 64, 71–72, 80–81, 236

Landholding patterns, 458, 461, 464, 468, 472, 554–55

Lango peoples, 63

Language and food procurement, 106

Lapp peoples, 210

Lascaux caves, 209

Latin America: European economic interests in, 32–34; U.S. economic interests in, 41–42. *See also* Costa Rica

L-DOPA, 153

Lectins, 249

Legacy hypothesis, 117–19

Legumes, 145(fig.), 230(table), 249

Leucine, 226, 228

Liebig Extract of Meat, 34, 36

Life expectancy: in the Third World, 462; and transition from hunting-gathering to farming, 273–75

Likes/dislikes of foods, 186–89

Liking of foods, vs. use or preference, 183

Linoleic acid, 230, 233

Livestock management in India, 447–50

Logistic curve and equation, 311–13

Low-birth-weight infants, 167, 169, 532

Lysine, 226, 228, 291, 590

Machiguenga peoples, 387–90, 473; emic influences on diet, 397–403; etic analysis of labor productivity and diet, 390–97

Mae Enga peoples, 22

Maine, marine diets in, 285, 293, 294, 298

Maize, 28, 457; alkalai preparation of, 133, 198–99, 521, 580; cultivation by two Machiguenga communities, 392(table), 394, 397; Mexican poor's reliance on, 521

Malaria, and favism, 81, 139–40, 250, 586–87; biological and pharmacological factors of, 140–43; epidemiological data on, 143–45; geographical distribution of, 140(fig.); population genetics of, 145–46

Malaysian peoples, and post-partum food taboos, 68–70

Malnutrition, 164–65; factors causing, 169(fig.); in Mexico, 531–34; in the Third World, 463–69

Manioc, 407, 460; preparation, 198, 250

Marasmus, nutritional, 166, 168

Marginal-value theorem, 317, 318(fig.), 323

Marine foods diet, 285–86; consequences of adopting, 298–304; "garden of eden" vs. second-rate resource models of, 286–93; lower dependency ratio of, 293; maximum sustained yield, 292–93; nutrients in, 291–92; reliable resource model of, 294–98

Market economy: influence on hunting populations, 13–17; optimal foraging and, 322. See also Capitalist world system; Colonialism; Neocolonialism; Political economy

Massa peoples, and white sorghum taboo, 65–66

Materialist approach to foodways, 5–6, 58; and biocultural adaptation, 589–90; refutations of idealist approach, 63–65

Maya peoples, 303

Meat consumption, 2; declining, in underdeveloped countries, 42–43; excessive, and caloric needs among hunters, 11–12; excessive, in developed nations, 35–36, 42; excessive, linked to evolutionary past, 118, 121; gender-related restrictions on, 17–23; and health, 107, 121, 235–41; preferences for, 12–13, 79–80; in Western Europe, 27–29; Yanomami, 414–15, 419 n.5, n.6, n.7. See also Animal protein and fat; Beef consumption; Protein

Meat contamination, in Costa Rica, 549

Megafauna, 290

Mehinaku peoples, 210

Melanesian peoples, 63, 64

Mental functioning and vegetarianism, 248

Metabolic requirements from food, 171–72, 233–35; and digestive tract capacity, 95–96

Methemoglobin, 141

Methionine, 226, 228, 229(table), 243, 291, 580

Mexico, 71, 199, 210; diet and use of national resources in, 534–37; social class and diet in, 517–34

Military, English, and meat consumption, 37–38

Milk consumption, 2, 27; in China, 63, 64; in India, 446(table); and lactase production, 64, 71–72, 80–81, 236; in Mexico, 524, 526, 530

Minerals, nutritional, 163, 226; from marine foods, 292

Miskito peoples, influence of the market economy on, 16–17

Mobility of populations, and marine diets, 299–300

Monocotyledonous plant foods, 95

Monosodium glutamate, 249–50

Morocco, 21–22, 211

Mouth, as focus of food choice, 181–82

Muslims and food preferences, 73, 433, 437–48, 440 n.7

Mussey peoples, 65–66

Namibia, 461

Narcotics, 81, 82

National Food Consumption Survey of Peru. See ENCA study

National Health and Nutrition Examination Survey, 233, 238

National Provisioner Daily Market and News Service, 544

National resource utilization, and dietary patterns in Mexico, 534–37

Navaho peoples, 212

Neocolonialism, 455–56; Costa Rican beef exports to U.S. as, 541–58; effect of, on Third World diet, 462–69; strategies against, 469–72. See also Colonialism

New Guinea, 193, 195, 233

New Jersey fishermen, optimal foraging of, 322

New Zealand, 174, 544

Nicaragua, 547

Nicotinic acid, 164

Niger, 462

Nitrosamines, 240

Noise (non-systematic) fraction in food economies, 262

Nootka peoples, 75

Nubian peoples, 588

Nuer societies, 211

Nutmeg, 456

Nutrition, human, 161–62, 225–27, 570–72; and Andean diet, 486–90, 494, 495(table), 496–97; and animal proteins/fats, 232–35, 395–96; characteristics of major disorders in, 166–69(table); decline in Bangladesh of, 431–32; decline in the Third World, and agribusiness, 464–69; disease and, 164–69, 173–74, 270, 301–302, 531–34; es-

sential needs for, 226(table); in farmers, vs. hunter-gatherers, 270–71; information needed to assess, 171(table); intake among Mexican poor, 524(table), 526(table), 527(table), 529(table); major factors affecting, 169(table); and marine diets, 291–92, 300–301; nuts as source of, 365(table); plant foods and, 242–48; problems in assessing, 163–77; quantification of, 227–31; status of, and food preferences and avoidances, 176
Nuts, as Australian aboriginal food, 361, 362–63(table), 364(table), 365(table), 379–80, 383

Obesity, 239
Oleic acid, 233
Oligosaccharides, 153
Omnivore's dilemma. *See* Variation in diet
Omnivory, 93–94; biological basis of, in humans, 182, 582; in contemporary human diet, 121–22; in early humans, 126–27, 264; hunter-gatherers as models of, 127–29, 209–10; optimality models and, 129–30; in primates, 121–26. *See also* Meat consumption
Opportunity-cost models, 322–32; currency of, 325–28; for energy maximizer, 325(fig.); of foraging, 322–25; and hunter-gatherer indifference map, 328–30; risk-sensitive, 332–34; and satiety, 330–32; for time minimizer, 324(fig.)
Optimal foraging theory, 74, 313–18, 569–70; applied to hunter-gatherers, 313–14, 319–22, 585; applied to hunters/horticulturalists, 8–11; applied to marine vs. land food resources, 286–91; and food economies, 261–62, 264. *See also* Opportunity-cost models
Optimization-selection models of food use/non-use, 74–77, 569; biopsychological determinants and, 79–82; and omnivory, 129–30; and food taboos, 78–79; principles of, 313–14; short-term vs. long-term, 77
Orangutans, 104
Ovamboland, 461
Oxalates, 249
Oxygen, 163

Paleopathology, 267–69, 575
Pangu peoples, 63
Parkinson's disease, 153
Pastoral and nomadic herding societies, 211, 461
Patch-choice model, 319
Pellegra, 164
Peru, 33, 302, 303, 387. *See also* Andean highlands dietary patterns
Phenylalanine, 226, 228, 291
Philippines, 463
Physical Quality of Life Index (PQLI), 470, 471(table)

Phytates, 95, 249
Pigeons, 63
Plantain, 407
Plant foods, 94–97, 107, 136, 209; biocultural consequences of diets high in, 241–52; marine, 291–92. *See also* Vegetarianism
Political economy, 423–25; and Andean diet changes, 507; colonialism/neocolonialism and Third World diets, 455–74; of Costa Rican beef exports, 541–57; and mass preferences and aversions, 82–83; and meat production for imperial England, 29–34; and wheat consumption in Bangladesh, 428–32. *See also* Market economy
Pongids, 97, 104
Population density, 264, 573; among Australian aborigines, 373–75; and marine diets, 300–301
Portugal, 24
Potato: in Andean highlands diet, 484; in Bangladesh, 440 n.5; introduction of, into Western Europe, 28; in Ireland, 31
Preference of foods, vs. liking or use, 183. *See also* Food preferences and avoidances
Pregnancy, post-partum, and lactation foodways, 23, 67–70
Primaquine, 139
Primates: diet of, 94–96; digestive tract of, 97–100; human food choices and legacy of, 581–84; omnivorous diet of, linked to human diet, 121–22, 582; omnivory in, 122–26
Progress model of broad spectrum revolution, 265–66. *See also* Stress
Prosimians, 95, 99
Prostaglandins, 289
Protein: complementary plant, 243; consumption among Mexican poor, 521, 523(table), 528(table), 529(table); decline in available, and meat craving, 12–13; differences in needs for, 227–30; excessive consumption of, 42; human needs, 171, 172, 173, 174; marine vs. land sources of, 291–92; preference for animal, 207–23; quality of, from various food sources, 230(table); social responses to restricted, 17–23; Yanomami population growth and needs for, 407–20. *See also* Amino acids; Animal protein and fat; Meat consumption
Public Law 88-482, 543
Public Law 96-177, 543–44

Recommended dietary allowance (RDA), 70, 79; defining, 170–73, 227–31; intake by Mexican poor, 529(table). *See also* Nutrition, human
Red tide infestations, 300
Reproductive success, 2, 343–44, 567. *See also* Fitness
Respect, and food avoidance, 185
Revolution and diet improvements, 469–72

Rice cultivation in Bangladesh, 427–32
Rickets, 236
Risk-sensitive foraging models, 332–34
Rome, folklore about fava bean consumption in ancient, 151
Ruminants, 102
Rural vs. urban dietary differences, 467; and beef consumption in Costa Rica, 550–51; and meat consumption in India, 446(table), 447(table); in Mexico, 517–38
Rwala Bedouin peoples, 211

Sahel region, West Africa, 462, 469
Salt, 82; intake and health problems, 237–38
Satiety, and consumption, 330–32
Savannas as human habitat, 105, 118, 262, 584
Schistosomiasis, 174
Scotland: deforestation of, and swine production, 25–26; diet and social rank in, 35; effect of English industrialization on, 29, 30–31; rise of potatoes and swine decline in, 28–29
Sea birds as food, 287, 293, 294
Seafood. See Aquatic food resources; Marine foods diet
Sea mammals as food, 287, 288, 290, 291, 293
Sea-mink, 288, 293
Selenium, 163, 174
Senegal, 462
Sensory affective factors, and food, 183–84
Serotonin, 249, 587
Seventh-Day Adventists, 237, 241, 246
Sexual division of labor, 19–20, 437, 584. See also Women: labor of
Shared poverty, 462
Sheep, 24, 33, 63, 484
Shellfish, 287, 288, 289, 290, 291, 293, 294, 295, 298. See also Red tide infestations
Shipibo peoples, 16
Sickle cell anemia, 250
Siona-Secoya peoples, 321–22
Siriono peoples, 573
Skeletal remains, evidence of diets in, 265, 267–69
Snakes: as food, 378; as taboo food, 78, 400–401
Social controls, and consumption norms, 328
Sociobiology, 543–44, 567; applied to !Kung and Aché, 344–49, 351–52
Soybeans, 230(table), 243–44
Spain, 24, 25, 290
Spider monkeys, 96, 401
Sri Lanka, 579
Status: and food distribution, 6, 19–20; and food preference/avoidance, 61, 72–74. See also Class/caste and diet
Stimulants, ingestion of, 81, 82

Stochastic environments, and foraging, 332, 333(fig.), 334(fig.)
Stress: biological, and broad-spectrum revolution, 275–76; effects of, on health, 237; episodic, in farmers vs. hunter-gatherers, 271–72; model of broad-spectrum revolution, 265–66; physical, in farmers vs. hunter-gatherers, 272–73
Subsistence, and evolution, 565–77
Sugar, 245–46; colonialism and, 457, 460, 464; overconsumption of, 118, 122
Sweetness taste preferences, 80, 182, 580
Swine, 40, 63; digestive tract of, 102; ecological costs of, in Europe, 23–27; taboos on, 26–27, 59–60, 78
Switzerland, 28, 31
Systematic fraction in food economics, 262

Taboos on food, 5; (on beef) in India, 63, 64, 77, 449, 450–52; failure of optimal foraging theory to explain, 8–11; influence of market economy on, 16–17; among Machiguenga, 398–99; on Massa sorghum, 65–66; (on pork) in Scotland, 25–27, 59–60; in pregnancy, post-partum, and lactation, 23, 67–70; ruling-class-originated, in Brazil, 473 n.1; theory of, 78–79
Tamil Nadu peoples, 67–68
Tanaina Athapaskans, 296
Tapirapé peoples, 73
Tasmanians, 209, 290
Taste preferences, 80, 183–84, 196, 232, 580–81; beneficial substances and acquisition of, 187–89; role of fat in, 396
Tea, 457, 464
Technology, advances in, and food economies, 265–66
Third World: effects of colonialism on diets in, 455, 456–62; effects of neocolonialism on diets in, 462–69; as market for transnationals, 473 n.3; reform and revolution in, 469–72
Threonine, 226, 228
Time-minimizer opportunity-cost foraging model, 324(fig.)
Toads, 491
Tobacco, 82–83, 456–57
Toda peoples, 211
Tool use, 2
Tooth enamel, 106, 301; microwear and diet, in early man, 120, 126–27, 271–72, 276
Toxins in plant foods, 249–50
Transnational corporations: effect on Peruvian Andean diet, 502–504; as new colonialists, 463–66, 473 n.3; 474 n.4
Tropical forest environment, 573; hunter-gatherers in, 321–22, 357–82, 407–20. See also Aché peoples; Yanomami peoples

Trypsin, 243–44
Tryptophan, 226, 228, 240, 587
Tupuri peoples, 65–66
Tyrosine, 163, 164

United States, 174: beef consumption in, 61, 541–45; capitalist economy and dietary variety in, 38–43; food aid to Bangladesh, 428–32; optimization selection in, 76–77; typical diet in, 232–33
U.S. Agency for International Development, 547
U.S. Department of Agriculture meat certification program, 542–43, 544
Urban diet. *See* Rural vs. urban dietary differences
Uruguay, cattle rearing in, 33–34
Use of foods, vs. preference or liking, 183
Utility theory, 327, 331(fig.)

Valine, 228
Variation in diet, 44 n.4; historical overview of, 7–44; among Mexican poor vs. middle/upper classes, 517–34; omnivore's desire for, 182, 197–98, 587
Vegetarianism, 3, 241; health/disease and, 237, 249–52; in Indian females, 21; nutrition and, 242–48; in Western Europe, 27–29. *See also* Plant foods
Vietnam: effect of colonialism in, 458, 462; food re-distribution in, 471(table), 472
Vitamins, 226, 235–36; A, 163, 173, 175–76, 190, 395, 432, 482, 488; B$_2$, 246; B$_{12}$, 163, 246; C, 119, 164, 190; D, 81, 164, 236, 246, 395; E, 143, 289, 395; K, 395; marine food sources of, 292

Warao peoples, 9
Wheat consumption in Bangladesh, 427–32, 433, 435, 437–38, 439
Wild food, consumption of, in two Machiguenga groups, 392–95
Women: labor of, 19–20, 44 n.2, 341, 344–45, 348–49, 377, 436–37, 584; protein-restricted diets among, 18–23, 73; as victims of cannibalism, 371–72. *See also* Pregnancy, post-partum, and lactation foodways
Wood eating, 579
World Bank, 545, 546

Xerophthalmia, 167, 169, 173

Yahgan peoples, 209, 286, 299, 302
Yanoama peoples, 13, 20
Yanomami peoples, 407–21; hunting range of, 409(fig.), 412–13; meat consumption of, 414–15; meat distribution of, 415, 417(table) 419 n.5, n.6, n.7; residence patterns of, 410 n.11, 411–12, 413–14; subsistence patterns of, 408–11; village splits of, 416, 417(table)
Yanomamo peoples, 210, 321–22
Ye'Kwana peoples, 321–22
"Yellow Sheet," 544

Zambia, 461
Zulu peoples, 63
Zuni peoples, 212

Hale's
Medications & Mothers' Milk™
2019
A Manual of Lactational Pharmacology

Eighteenth Edition

Thomas W. Hale, R.Ph., Ph.D.

Professor

Department of Pediatrics

Texas Tech University

School of Medicine

Amarillo, Texas

SPRINGER PUBLISHING COMPANY

Springer Publishing Company, LLC
11 West 42nd Street
New York, NY 10036
www.springerpub.com

Acquisitions Editor: Elizabeth Nieginski
Compositor: Exeter Premedia Services Private Ltd.

The author gratefully acknowledges Lily Sophia, LLC, for the cover photograph

ISBN: 9780826135582
ebook ISBN: 9780826135629

18 19 20 21 22 / 5 4 3 2 1

The author and the publisher of this Work have made every effort to use sources believed to be reliable to provide information that is accurate and compatible with the standards generally accepted at the time of publication. Because medical science is continually advancing, our knowledge base continues to expand. Therefore, as new information becomes available, changes in procedures become necessary. We recommend that the reader always consult current research and specific institutional policies before performing any clinical procedure. The author and publisher shall not be liable for any special, consequential, or exemplary damages resulting, in whole or in part, from the readers' use of, or reliance on, the information contained in this book. The publisher has no responsibility for the persistence or accuracy of URLs for external or third-party Internet websites referred to in this publication and does not guarantee that any content on such websites is, or will remain, accurate or appropriate.

Contact us to receive discount rates on bulk purchases.
We can also customize our books to meet your needs.
For more information please contact: sales@springerpub.com

Printed in the United States of America.